The Media in the Movies

"The hand of God reaching down into a mine couldn't elevate one of them to the depths of degradation."
—Charles Winninger on reporters in *Nothing Sacred* (1937)

"I'll have the whole town so deep in tears that they'll be using canoes for taxi cabs."
—Reporter Lynn Bari in *Mr. Moto's Gamble* (1938)

"Holdups and murders are my meat. I'm Torchy Blane of the Star."
—Reporter Glenda Farrell in *Torchy Blane in Chinatown* (1939)

"An honest, fearless press is the public's first protection against gangsterism—local or international."
—Humphrey Bogart in *Deadline U.S.A.* (1952)

The Media in the Movies

A Catalog of American Journalism Films, 1900–1996

LARRY LANGMAN

McFarland & Company, Inc., Publishers
Jefferson, North Carolina and London

ALSO BY LARRY LANGMAN

Destination Hollywood: The Influence of Europeans on American Filmmaking (McFarland, 2000)

BY LARRY LANGMAN AND PAUL GOLD

Comedy Quotes from the Movies: Over 4,000 Bits of Humorous Dialogue from All Film Genres, Topically Arranged and Indexed (McFarland, 1994; paperback 2001)

The present work is a reprint of the library bound edition of The Media in the Movies: A Catalog of American Journalism Films, 1900–1996, *first published in 1998 by McFarland.*

LIBRARY OF CONGRESS CATALOGUING-IN-PUBLICATION DATA

Langman, Larry.
   The media in the movies : a catalog of American journalism films, 1900–1996 / by Larry Langman.
    p.   cm.
   Includes bibliographical references and index.

   ISBN 978-0-7864-4091-7
   softcover : 50# alkaline paper ∞

   1. Journalists in motion pictures. 2. Motion pictures—United States—Catalogs. I. Title.
PN1995.9.J6L35   2009
016.79143′652097—dc21   97-46949

British Library cataloguing data are available

©1998 Larry Langman. All rights reserved

No part of this book may be reproduced or transmitted in any form or by any means, electronic or mechanical, including photocopying or recording, or by any information storage and retrieval system, without permission in writing from the publisher.

Cover image ©2009 Shutterstock

Manufactured in the United States of America

McFarland & Company, Inc., Publishers
  Box 611, Jefferson, North Carolina 28640
    www.mcfarlandpub.com

Contents

Preface ix
Introduction 1
Abbreviations 15

THE FILMS 17

Appendix A: Newspaper Film Series 293
Appendix B: Newspaper Film Serials 294
Appendix C: Peripheral Newspaper Films 295
Bibliography 299
Index of Names 301

Preface

This reference work covers more than 1,000 features and serials released from 1900 through 1996, that are concerned with the different worlds of journalism—newspapers, periodicals, radio and television—and on characters portrayed as reporters, columnists, news photographers, camera operators, television newscasters, editors and publishers. It was decided to omit films dealing with the media only peripherally. However, for those interested in these works, their titles and release dates are listed in a separate appendix.

Several kinds of research goals can be achieved through the use of this filmography. Such questions can be answered as, How did these films depict the wide variety of topics that journalism deals with daily? How did the films depict journalists in their dealings with both news stories and the public? and How did matters change through the nine decades? This filmography shows just how realistically Hollywood portrayed people involved in the media and reveals the overall influence these largely newspaper films had on their audiences and our society.

Entries with the same title are arranged chronologically. The date of release and releasing company or distributor appear after the title. The director (Dir.), screenwriter (Sc.) and major cast credits follow, as in this example:

ASSIGNMENT PARIS (1952). Col.
 Dir. Robert Parrish; *Sc.* William Bowers; *Cast includes:* Dana Andrews, Marta Toren, George Sanders, Audrey Totter, Sandro Giglio, Donald Randolph.

Alternate titles, when they exist, are noted in the entries. Each alternate title is also in the main sequence of entries, cross-referenced to the main title under which the entry appears. Remakes are treated as individual entries, but are also listed within the entry of the original film. If the plot of a remake is similar to that of the original, the remake occasionally is given less space. Sometimes actors' names change in the screen credits from one film to another. Generally, we tried to adhere to the screen spellings, resulting in some players' names appearing in these pages with two different spellings.

Several people helped carry this book to its final stage. Special thanks must

Preface

go to Sharon Bonk, Chief Librarian, and Shoshana Kaufmann, Associate Librarian, both of Queens College, Flushing, New York, for the use of library materials; William Shelley for the invaluable use of his film resources; and New American Technology of Queens, New York, for keeping our computers functioning.

Larry Langman
Fall 1997

Introduction

The newspaper film was never as popular as the western, the gangster film, or other genres, but it contributed its share to the history and growth of the movies. Reaching its peak in the 1930s with a cycle of realistic, tough-talking entries, the newspaper film helped to enhance and broaden the uses of dialogue, especially in the years immediately following the silent era. Even after settling in to its comfortable set of clichés, the genre gained distinction for its several exceptional comedies—*His Girl Friday* (1940) was a notable one—and its influence upon other important dramas such as *Citizen Kane* (1941). The newspaper film was resurrected in the 1970s with such provocative works as *The Parallax View* (1974) and *All the President's Men* (1975) and is still with us today, largely by way of its new practitioners—the television newscasters.

The newspaper film blended comfortably with other genres, including comedies and musicals. Archie Mayo's *Oh! Sailor Behave* (1930), with American reporter Charles King stationed in Paris, was an early musical comedy drama, based on Elmer Rice's popular play *See Naples and Die*. One of the most influential dramas about reporters and the world of journalism, *The Front Page*, appeared the following year (1931) and dealt with gallows humor—sometimes literally. Frank Capra's *It Happened One Night* (1934), with Clark Gable and Claudette Colbert, gave us one of the earliest screwball comedies. William Wellman's *Nothing Sacred* (1937), with Carole Lombard and Fredric March, presented a cynical dark comedy.

The newspaper film even affected the western. As early as 1900, in *Horsewhipping an Editor*, perhaps the earliest entry in the newspaper genre, a tough cowboy enters an editorial office bent on punishing a local editor. And in 1916, William S. Hart directed and starred in *Truthful Tulliver*. He portrayed an editor who tames a wild frontier town. *Red Courage* (1921) starred Hoot Gibson as a good-natured cowboy who, in an effort to clean up a graft-ridden town, purchases the local newspaper. In *Grinning Guns* (1927), roving cowboy Jack Hoxie uses the power of the press (and his six-gun) to restore law and order to a frontier town. New York reporter Rex Bell in *The Diamond Trail* (1933) rounds up a gang of jewel thieves out West.

This trend of blending the western with the newspaper tale continued well into the sound era. Cowboy star Roy Rogers made several westerns dealing in part with the world of journalism, including *Bad Man of Deadwood* and *In Old Cheyenne*, both released in 1941, and *Don't Fence Me In* (1945) and *Home in Indiana* (1946), both with Dale Evans and George "Gabby" Hayes. Other popular cowboy heroes followed suit, including Bill Elliott, who portrayed Wild Bill Hickok in *Beyond the Sacramento* (1941). Charles Starrett foils a crooked newspaper publisher in *Down Rio Grande Way* (1942), Allan "Rocky" Lane in *Navajo Trail Raiders* (1949) exposes a crooked newspaper editor who is an outlaw leader, and Randolph Scott in *Carson City* (1952), who is hired to build a railroad, ends up avenging the death of a crusading newspaperman. Newspaper plots fitted smoothly into a variety of genres.

The News Hound

Several familiar characters dot the landscape of the newspaper world. Most important of all, obviously, is the peripatetic reporter. The experienced news hound who is often wise-cracking, fast-talking and cynical, and who can gain entrance to many inaccessible places, is friendly with law officers and law breakers alike, and is not above manipulating others to get the big scoop. The reporter can play the hero—and perhaps too often does. In *The Lost House* (1915), for instance, Wallace Reid rescues Lillian Gish, who has been committed to an asylum by her corrupt uncle. The news hound, like the lead in other films, can be very versatile. That same year also saw one of the earliest examples of an American reporter abroad in the adventure *Fire and Sword*. Again in 1915, in *The House of Tears*, star reporter Emily Stevens played a dual role, both as mother and long-lost daughter. The ploy was used again in *Double Adventure* (1921), with journalist Charles Hutchison involved in a dual role.

Films occasionally depict the journalist as a foreign correspondent, lured by the same spirit of exoticism, adventure or political involvement that attracts the main characters of other genres. These globe-trotting reporters have appeared in early silent comedies (*The Cub*, 1915), screwball comedies (*Affectionately Yours*, 1941), World War II dramas (*Berlin Correspondent*, 1942), biographical dramas (*Jack London*, 1943) and political dramas (*Under Fire*, 1983). The films may have been entertaining and exciting, and—because they showed the correspondent at work in foreign lands, interacting with diplomats and other officials—even educational at times. Perhaps of more importance, they often served as propaganda, suggesting the point of view of the screenwriter, director, studio or the country.

The news hound on rare occasions worked closely with government officials to bring down a pack of hoodlums, as in *Special Agent* (1935), with newsman George Brent being deputized as an undercover government agent to get the goods on racketeer Ricardo Cortez.

Reporters are followed (often literally) by cub reporters, youths who are yearning to prove their mettle to their idolized veteran journalists. One of the earliest appearances of a cub reporter occurred in 1914 in *A Prince of India*, which concerned the theft of a priceless diamond and included a climactic trolley wreck. That same year, a cub reporter in *The War Extra* urged his boss to let him cover war-torn Mexico. The cub reporter returned to his more familiar role of hero in *The Magic Cup* (1921), with Vincent Coleman rescuing hotel kitchen maid Constance Binney, and as a Douglas Fairbanks–type of athletic hero in *The Cub Reporter* (1922), with former stunt man Richard Talmadge. In *Extra! Extra!* (1922), cub reporter Johnnie Walker showed his ingenuity by posing as different characters to get his story.

The news hound himself often has a mentor, a more experienced old timer who either drinks too heavily or can no longer function at his peak—until he is motivated by his younger counterpart to bring in his last big scoop. For example, cub reporter Robert Young in *Paris Interlude* (1934) admires veteran journalist Otto Kruger. In *Behind the News* (1940), burned-out veteran reporter Lloyd Nolan, who has become a heavy drinker, is rehabilitated under the influence of neophyte newsman Frank Albertson. And as recently as 1994 in *I Love Trouble*, quick-witted cub reporter Julia Roberts admires rival veteran reporter-columnist Nick Nolte.

The Sob Sister

The woman reporter, often described as a "sob sister" or "news hen" by her peers and others, faced great odds because of a lack of cooperation or enthusiasm from her male counterparts, the police and the public, but she usually succeeded in returning with her story or unraveling a crime. She could exchange insults and wisecracks with the best of the news hounds or her editors. She appeared on screen as early as 1911 in *The Reform Candidate*, in which reporter Miriam Nesbitt foils an attempt by a railway financier to bribe a mayor. In 1914 the female journalist returned in two films. *The Adventures of a Girl Reporter* featured Ethel Grandin as the principal player in the title role, and *The Reporter on the Case* had Stella Razeto in the major role. In the years that followed, the woman reporter became a staple character in the genre with such films as *How Molly Malone Made Good* (1915), with Marguerite Gale, and *The Daring of Diana* (1916), with the lead player Anita Stewart as a star reporter helping her managing editor to preserve the integrity of his newspaper. Assisting a newspaperman seemed to emerge as part of a female journalist's job, at least according to such dramas as *What Love Can Do* (1916), in which Adele Farrington saves the life of a rich newspaperman. Again, in *Over the Hill* (1917), Gladys Hulette helps save her publisher's newspaper from losing advertisers because of its sensationalist policy.

It wasn't long before the sob sister was imitating the different complications that confronted her male counterpart in a variety of melodramatic plots.

In *Bondage* (1917), for example, young reporter Dorothy Phillips, newly arrived in New York City from a small town, falls into the Greenwich Village bohemian night life. Even more startling is the tale of reporter Elaine Hammerstein, who in *The Co-Respondent* (1917), is assigned to investigate a divorce case in which the co-respondent turns out to be the reporter. The sob sister was not always naive or on the receiving end of life's undulations. Sometimes they could just as mischievous and daring as the male city room pranksters, as the comedy *The Floor Below* (1918) clearly demonstrated. Mabel Normand portrays a "copy girl" who is fired for her antics, which included shooting dice with her fellow employees in the city room.

By the end of the decade the woman journalist was not only fulfilling the usual reporting tasks of her male counterparts but was covering and solving crimes. In *The Woman Under Cover* (1919), for instance, reporter Fritzi Brunette finds herself deeply entangled in a backstage murder. By 1920, a woman reporter is busy solving a murder in *The Fourth Face*.

Between melodramas and murders, the news hen occasionally faced personal problems when her professional career clashed with her marital duties. In *The Foolish Matrons* (1921), young reporter Mildred Manning spends more time shaping her career than attending to her husband, who, as a result of her neglect, finds his escape in alcohol. Another type of domestic dilemma involved members of her family, as in *Hold Your Breath* (1924), in which tenacious Dorothy Devore replaces her brother who has been fired from his job as reporter. Personal problems continued to plague the female reporter well into the following decades. In the drama *Another Time, Another Place* (1958), American correspondent Lana Turner, in London during World War II, is entangled in an affair with married Sean Connery, who is reported killed in action.

Big News (1929), with Carole Lombard, was the first sound film to feature a woman reporter. The sob sister even had her own series during the 1930s. Glenda Farrell usually played Torchy Blane, a spirited reporter who helped Barton MacLane, her police inspector pal, solve crimes. Perhaps she epitomizes the courage and self-assurance of the woman reporter, especially as exemplified in *Torchy Blane in Chinatown* (1939). These traits are apparent early in the film when a cop tries to stop Torchy from entering the scene of a crime. "You're wrong, boys," she snaps. "Holdups and murders are my meat. I'm Torchy Blane of the Star." Such traits were rarely found in female characters of other genres.

Sadly, the woman journalist as leading player fell onto hard times by the 1940s, a setback that continued for the next several decades. She often appeared only as an adjunct to the more clever, savvy and brave male reporter who got the scoop, solved the murder and helped to free the wrongly condemned. Sometimes the hero she helped was someone other than a newspaperman. In *Borrowed Hero* (1941), for instance, knowledgeable reporter Florence Rice assists young prosecutor Alan Baxter smash the city's widespread rackets. In *Big Town After Dark* (1947), police reporter Hillary Brooke gives crusading editor Phillip Reed a hand in smashing a gang of racketeers. Reporter Lucille Bremer in

Behind Locked Doors (1948) collaborates with private eye Richard Carlson, who poses as a patient in an insane asylum where he believes a crooked politician has taken refuge. In the dated cold war drama *Assignment Paris* (1952), American reporter Dana Andrews, stationed in Paris, tries to expose a plot by East Bloc countries against the West, with fellow reporter Marta Toren serving only as romantic interest for Andrews. At times, the newswoman may even sacrifice her career, as in the drama *Crime of Passion* (1957), in which San Francisco reporter Barbara Stanwyck gives up her career to marry Los Angeles cop Sterling Hayden.

The Crusaders

Crusading screen journalists usually come in two flavors, the publisher and the editor. The well-meaning or politically motivated publisher certainly has the financial means and the power to take on the influential and the mighty. The editor, on the other hand, simply has the backing of his or her employer. In addition, the editor is depicted as more conscience-driven. These idealists appeared as early as 1914 in, for instance, *The Truth Wagon*, in which fun-loving playboy Max Figman announces that he intends to buy a dying newspaper and wage a battle against corrupt local politicians. The crusader's wealth is often established early in the film, as in *The Gentleman from Indiana* (1915), in which college football star Dustin Farnum, upon graduation, buys a moribund newspaper which he intends to use to expose political corruption. And again in *The White Terror*, released in the same year, wealthy young Hobart Henley purchases a newspaper which he uses to expose the deplorable working conditions that exist in sweatshops and factories. Some dramas depict a formidable rite of passage for the youthful idealist. Young Carlyle Blackwell in *The Clarion* (1916) buys a newspaper to improve local social conditions and soon discovers that those closest to him are some of the worst offenders. Saving the world, or at least making a dent in the horrid social life of the poor, is the province not only of males. In *The Belle of the Season* (1919) pretty socialite Emmy Whalen takes control of the family business and, through her boyfriend's newspaper, introduces changes that benefit the downtrodden workers.

The path of a crusader was not exactly an easy one, for it could sometimes create roadblocks in family relationships. For instance, idealistic Raymond McKee, the son of a newspaper owner, accuses his father of sensationalizing the news and exploiting the poor in *The Little Wanderer* (1920). And at other times, the crusading newspaperman has to make a personal sacrifice, as in *Freedom of the Press* (1928). The son of a crusading newspaperman takes over the family paper after his father is brutally murdered and, following in his father's footsteps, battles to expose a corrupt politician.

The crusading spirit of newspaper films continued into the sound era. Richard Dix as Yancey Cravat, a compassionate newspaper publisher in *Cimarron*

(1931), based on the popular novel by Edna Ferber, fights against injustice, including the abuses inflicted upon the downtrodden Native Americans. But most of these dramas attacked the staple villains—corrupt politicians, gangsters and other lawbreakers. In *Night Alarm* (1934), for instance, ace reporter Bruce Cabot works for a crusading newspaper interested in going after local big boss H. B. Warner. And, as in some earlier films, the 1930s also had its share of crusaders who meet a tragic end. Warren Hull, as the son of a newspaper publisher who has been killed by the mob, determines to carry on the good fight against local corruption in *Star Reporter* (1939).

Films about crusaders reached their peak in the 1930s, although the screen occasionally returned to this device, touching upon various genres and subjects. For example, in the social drama *Jigsaw* (1949), crusading columnist Myron McCormick is killed trying to gain evidence against a fascist hate group residing in New York City. The venerable western showed up again, with *The Bushwackers* (1951), in which a newspaper editor gives his life to help establish law and order on the frontier. In the historical action drama *The San Francisco Story* (1952), set in the 1850s, crusading newspaper editor Onslow Stevens persuades wealthy miner Joel McCrea to join his vigilantes to battle the forces of corruption in San Francisco. In *Beyond a Reasonable Doubt* (1956), crusading newspaper editor Sidney Blackmer is determined to prove the dangers of circumstantial evidence to a skeptical district attorney. *The Tijuana Story* (1957) reenacts how Mexican journalist Rodolfo Acosta battled a crime syndicate; the film was inspired by actual incidents surrounding the newspaperman's assassination in Tijuana.

It was not until the 1970s that the major studios returned to making serious and timely topical films about crusading journalists. Two excellent examples are the highly successful *All the President's Men* (1976), with Robert Redford and Dustin Hoffman, and *The China Syndrome* (1979), with Jane Fonda and Michael Douglas.

The Rural Press

The year 1913 introduced the importance of rural newspapers with such crude films as *A Campaign Manageress*, featuring Muriel Ostriche, a popular film actress of the period. She takes over her sickly father's local newspaper and attacks the sheriff who is running for re-election and is supported by a political gang. Hollywood demonstrated to the rest of the country that rural America was not immune to crime in films like *The Black Circle* (1919), which featured criminals of every description, including swindlers, moonshiners and a crooked prosecutor. It took a young couple and their town newspaper to expose these elements. And in *Contraband* (1925), Lois Wilson, who inherits a small-town newspaper, discovers upon her arrival that bootleggers are operating a flourishing business. Finally, in *Jazzland* (1928), when a New England newspaperman tries to prevent a crooked nightclub from invading his community, he is murdered. These silent films soon gave way to sound features which gradually added subtlety and depth to their familiar plots.

In the 1934 comedy *The Quitters*, small-town newspaper owner Charles Grapewin leaves his wife to run the paper while he takes off to fulfill his wanderlust. In *Johnny Come Lately* (1943), former big-city reporter James Cagney, now down on his luck, helps determined middle-aged Grace George battle political corruption in her small town. Richard Conte, a small-town journalist, is duped by petty hoodlum Bruce Bennett in *The Big Tip-Off* (1955).

In more recent times when topics like the ecology make front-page news, Hollywood is not far behind—with two particularly fine entries. Small-town newspaper reporter Ed Harris in *A Flash of Green* (1984) breaks with his political cronies over a controversial environmental issue. In the fable-like comedy drama *The Milagro Beanfield War* (1988), dirt-poor Mexican farmer Chick Vennera decides to fight the powerful land developers seeking to exploit the local farmers—with the help of a local newspaper owner and others.

The small town, however, can also be a place of oppression, prejudice and bigotry, often inhabited by narrow-minded and mean-spirited citizens. The yellow journalism as practiced by a small-town newspaper in *The Famous Ferguson Case* (1932) has tragic consequences as the film exposes the sensational type of murder story that usually hits the front page. Boarding school runaway Ida Lupino in *Ready for Love* (1934) faces small-town bigotry when the town snobs treat her aunt, a former actress, with scorn, and then turn on Lupino. The townspeople hold a witchcraft-type trial which includes a ducking stool. In *The Lawless* (1950), newspaper editor Macdonald Carey battles intolerance against Mexicans in a California town bent on lynching a young Chicano.

Of more significance is the recurrent Hollywood theme which suggests that rural life, with its restorative powers, is superior to urban life, which is infested with crime, violence and corruption. This is evident in newspaper films with rural backgrounds, such as *The Jailbird* (1920). Escaped convict Douglas MacLean inherits a small-town newspaper and a small piece of property. Local incidents lead to his decision to reform and return to prison to serve out the remainder of his sentence. Again, in *The Man Under Cover* (1922), former thief Herbert Rawlinson returns to his home town determined to go straight. After buying a local newspaper, he saves the community from being swindled by some con men.

Rural America was celebrated again after World War II in such films as *Magic Town* (1947), a romantic comedy in which an ambitious and conniving James Stewart selects a small town to exploit, but he is eventually won over by its charm and its people. Newspaper films explored the wide variety of rural life, from interdependence to greed to anti-city attitudes. These communities, the films suggested, may be as complex as their larger urban cousins, but they affectionately remind us of an America that once was—a nation and a people ignited with spirit, pride and hope.

The Newspaper-Crime Drama

The newspaper film has a long and symbiotic connection to the crime drama, dating back to the early silent period. The major themes in these films deal with corruption, murder and other anti-social transgressions. Corruption and graft appeared in *The Big Boss* (1913), in which reporter Irving Cummings uses a Dictaphone to convict a crooked politician. Corruption was the dominant theme in the newspaper film *Living Lies* (1922), with incorruptible Edmund Lowe exposing a cabal of crooked financiers who try to bribe him. Directors and writers began to use the newspaper film to illustrate other types of crimes. The exposé became popular by 1915 with such films as *Buckshot John*, in which a young reporter helps to expose a phony spiritualist. The serial *A Hole in the Wall* (1921) covered the same topic. Reporter Tom Gallery goes under cover to expose the leader of a car theft ring in *The Heart of Twenty* (1920). *Million Dollar Mystery*, a 1914 serial, focused on spies and kidnapping.

By the 1930s, a decade which could well be called the golden age of the newspaper film, the two genres, newspaper and crime, were well intertwined. Even series like the Torchy Blane films were always newspaper-crime features. Film classics like *The Front Page* and *Five Star Final*, both released in 1931, contained crime elements, including corruption, death sentences and murder. *After Office Hours* (1935), about the lifestyles of the rich, included the murder of a wealthy married woman by her parasitic lover, with these events exploited by a voyeuristic press. Joan Blondell, an overly confident reporter in *Back in Circulation* (1937), helps in the arrest and conviction of a murder suspect, only to learn she has made a horrible mistake. The newspaper-crime film spilled over into the following decades as well. In *Chicago Deadline* (1949), hard-nosed Chicago reporter Alan Ladd investigates the unfortunate life of Donna Reed, a young woman of easy virtue whose sordid life was dominated by her associations with mobsters, gun molls, call girls and other underworld inhabitants.

The newspaper-crime drama was dominated by the minor studios and the low-budget products of the major studios, often portraying lesser known players in simplistic plots. Reporter Stuart Erwin in *Exclusive Story* (1936), for instance, joins with girlfriend Madge Evans in exposing a major numbers racket involving murder. In *The Cobra Strikes* (1948) newspaper columnist Richard Fraser solves several murders and a jewel heist.

The Newspaper Film as Social Drama

Social dramas appeared in movie theaters with the rise of films as a popular form of mass entertainment. Newspaper dramas soon began to incorporate social issues into their plots. *The Power of the Press* (1914), with a title stronger than its plot, depicted how a newspaper can turn public opinion around. *The Conspiracy* (1914), based on a 1912 play, explored the hot topic of white slavery.

The same subject dominated *Trapped in the Great Metropolis* (1914), with newspaperwoman Rose Austin posing as a slave buyer. In *The White Terror* (1915), another social conscience drama, wealthy Hobart Henley buys a newspaper to expose the horrific working conditions that exist in factories and sweatshops. *Deadline at Eleven* (1920) dealt with a woman reporter and a fellow alcoholic journalist, whom she saves from his affliction. *The Little Wanderer* (1920) attacked the sensational press and the exploitation of the poor. The social conscience comedy drama *The Tomboy* (1921), with reporter Eileen Percy, also attacks the problem of alcoholism.

Several films explored the dreaded scandal sheet which somehow attracted the perverse interests of many readers. One such film, *The Fear Market* (1920), showed the owner of such a publication blackmailing his victims. And in *Whispers* (1920), a scandal sheet almost ruins the reputation of an innocent young woman. The film anticipated such later and more powerful dramas as *Five Star Final* (1931), starring Edward G. Robinson. The subject reappeared years later in such exposés as *Scandal for Sale* (1932), *Scandal Sheet* (1940), *Scandal Sheet* (1952) and *Scandal Incorporated* (1956), most depicting unsavory publishers or editors willing to ruin careers to further their circulation or their pockets through blackmail.

Other films underscored the deleterious effects of drugs. In *The Lying Truth* (1922), for instance, a stepfather is driven to an early grave when he discovers that his only son is a drug addict. He then wills his newspaper to his stepson. In *Big News* (1929) reporter Robert Armstrong investigates a drug ring. A bright young newspaper reporter in *Assassin of Youth* (1937), posing as a soda fountain saleswoman, investigates the use of marijuana among teenagers. Other similar films include *The Pace That Kills* (1936), *Marihuana* (1937) and *The Burning Question* (also known as *Tell Your Children*) (1939). These early cautionary newspaper-oriented dramas were often more sensational or unintentionally funny than earnest explorations of a social problem.

The Newspaper Comedy Drama

The newspaper comedy drama sprouted up with *The Country Boy* (1915), with Marshall Neilan, and based on a 1910 play. These films ranged from major productions by the largest studios to the independents, with their numerous low-budget entries. Reporter Robert Kent in *Angel's Holiday* (1937) helps the young and impish Jane Withers, the niece of a local newspaper editor, rescue movie star Sally Blane. In *Cairo* (1942), MGM moved its singing star Jeanette MacDonald out of costume musicals and into an implausible comedy-drama (with several patriotic songs) set in World War II England and Egypt. Newspaper copyboy Leo Gorcey and his gang of East Side Kids in *Bowery Champs* (1944) turn reporters to help clear Evelyn Brent of a murder charge.

Crime occasionally took a back seat to comedy in these films. In *Exposed*

(1938), top photo magazine photographer Glenda Farrell helps the police to capture a gang of racketeers. Bumbling reporter Jack Haley, a former weak-willed chess player in *Scared Stiff* (1945), inadvertently stumbles across a murder and becomes the chief suspect. *The Corpse Came C.O.D.* (1947) has rival reporters George Brent and Joan Blondell determined to solve the mystery of why a corpse was shipped to movie actress Adele Jergens. *The Paper* (1994), a frenetic comedy drama about one day in the life of a New York tabloid newspaper, focused on two young African Americans who are falsely accused of killing two white men. The incident ends up as a rivalry between two editors, Michael Keaton and Glenn Close.

World War II did not stop the flow of newspaper comedy dramas. *The Lady Has Plans* (1942), a World War II comedy-drama concerning espionage in Lisbon, featured Ray Milland as an American war correspondent and Paulette Goddard as his assistant, both of whom help British intelligence to uncover a Nazi espionage ring. *Once Upon a Honeymoon*, also released in 1942 and starring Ginger Rogers as a burlesque entertainer and Cary Grant as an American reporter, somehow blended the devastation of Czechoslovakia, Poland and France with the frivolous desires and antics of young Rogers.

Rivalry was a frequent plot gimmick on which to focus these comedy dramas. Rival American news hounds Lee Tracy and Roger Pryor in *I'll Tell the World* (1934) end up in Europe to cover various royal personalities of a mythical kingdom. In *Front Page Woman* (1935), rival reporters for competing newspapers track murder suspects to their hideout and locate an incriminating weapon. In *The Daring Young Man*, released the same year, James Dunn and Mae Clarke, reporters on rival newspapers, often compete for the same story. And in *I Love Trouble* (1994), cub reporter Julia Roberts competes with rival veteran reporter-columnist Nick Nolte on a train-wreck story.

The Golden Age of the Newspaper Film

Newspaper films remained consistently in vogue during the 1930s. As proof of their success, journalism became the most popular occupation of screen heroes of the 1930s. Many of these films, like the popular gangster genre of the period, were concerned with crime and criminals. Writers always figured out a new twist involving reporters and hoodlums, reporters and police, or reporters and politicians. However, rarely were screen reporters at their desks writing a story. They tended to be more at home in nightclubs or snooping around crime scenes hoping for the big scoop, but often stepping into trouble.

The popular newspaper drama reached its peak in the 1930s, occasionally expanding the genre to include radio news reporters, magazine writers, columnists and newsreel cameramen. But such screen personalities as Lee Tracy, James Cagney and Pat O'Brien playing smart-alecky, fast-talking news hounds, and a host of actresses portraying tough sob sisters for big-city dailies dominated.

The world of journalism certainly had its dark side. David M. White and Richard Averson offered the following accurate description of the era in their 1972 study *The Celluloid Weapon*:

> The Thirties was a period of flamboyant, sensational, so-called yellow journalism, and a number of films had reporters who were not above trading their ethics for a byline.

Richard Barthelmess, as a reporter in *The Finger Points* (1931), goes on the take, suppressing stories unfavorable to the mob. In *Honor of the Press* (1932), aggressive reporter Edward Nugent discovers that a rival newspaper publisher heads a gang of crooks. *Behind Jury Doors* (1933) described how a young reporter investigating the murder of a nurse discovers that an editor has framed a juror. Lloyd Nolan, as a corrupt politician acquitted of graft charges in *Exclusive* (1937), buys a newspaper which he uses to blackmail local businessmen. In *Headline Crasher* (1937), criminal elements and an unscrupulous press combine forces to defeat an incumbent senator. And in *The Witness Vanishes* (1939), four corrupt London editors commit the newspaper owner to an asylum so that they can take over the daily. Some of these films strongly suggested that newspaper reporters came dangerously close to crossing the line between making the news and reporting the news.

The studios continued to churn out these comedies and dramas throughout the next several decades, again showing mostly cynical journalists—Hollywood style—exposing corruption, solving crimes, romancing pretty socialites and frequenting nightclubs—but rarely depicting them sitting at a typewriter transcribing their stories. More recent entries to the genre show cavernous newspaper offices with desktop computers, but the star journalists are more often away from these desks at more interesting locations. Also, the television newscaster has largely replaced the old-fashioned reporter who frequented the police precinct or the local bar—undoubtedly the result of a decline in the newspaper business.

Television had played a major role in journalism films as early as 1937 in such fast-paced action dramas as *Exiled in Shanghai*, in which fast-talking newsreel cameraman Wallace Ford hits upon the idea of using television to transmit news events. However, the new media quickly became male dominated, and the genre had to wait patiently until the 1970s before Hollywood recognized television news and its women reporters in earnest. The gutsy newspaperwoman was suddenly transformed into a daring television newscaster, often in a leading role. The tense thriller *The China Syndrome* (1979) starred Jane Fonda as a television news reporter who, while covering a nuclear power plant, experiences a potentially disastrous malfunction with global implications. That same year saw television newscaster Cathy Lee Crosby in *The Dark* become involved in a series of gruesome murders.

This trend continued to flourish for the next two decades, with 1981 alone offering three such releases. In *Eyewitness*, television newscaster Sigourney Weaver is drawn into a web of intrigue by her admirer William Hurt. Two horror films of 1981, *The Howling* and *The Seduction*, concerned television news reporters. In the first, Dee Wallace visits a California psychiatric retreat for her own sexual trauma, and in the second, Morgan Fairchild is pursued by peeping-tom photographer Andrew Stevens. In 1988, *The Front Page* was revived once again, this time titled *Switching Channels*, with Kathleen Turner as a television newscaster who will go anywhere for a story; she works for managing editor Burt Reynolds, her ex-husband. The next decade offered a variety of genres, from politics to comedy to horror, featuring women telecasters. *A Show of Force* (1990), for instance, was a political drama set in Puerto Rico with television news reporter Amy Irving investigating the suspicious deaths of two activists who were found badly beaten and murdered. In the romantic comedy *He Said, She Said* (1991), rivals Kevin Bacon, an obituary writer, and Elizabeth Perkins, a reporter, end up married and hosting a television talk show. In the satirical comedy *Hero* (1992), which pokes fun at the media's penchant for its exaggeration of heroism, television news reporter Geena Davis searches for the unidentified hero who rescued passengers from a wrecked airliner. Terry Farrell portrays a television newswoman in a low-grade horror film titled *Hellraiser III: Hell on Earth*, also released in 1992. Like the female journalists of the 1930s, the contemporary reporters display a persistent sense of purpose, a strong character, and a fierce independence that occasionally seems to threaten their male counterparts.

The genre leaves in its wake several disturbing shortcomings. After almost a century of newspaper dramas and comedies, few films have depicted minorities working as journalists; indeed, several portrayed African Americans and other minorities in derisive roles. Few have discussed subjects about the nature of journalism, such as the influence of the press, the potential for corruption, the manipulation of the masses, the never-ending search for objectivity. Many films unrealistically portrayed the daily work of a journalist. Others showed members of the press as stereotypes. "Public journalism" has emerged as a recent topic that raises the questions of the newspaper's responsibility in helping to improve communities. And several recent dramas cast television reporters and news anchors as characters in such dramas as *Independence Day* (the McLaughlin Group), *The Net* (Daniel Schorr) and *The Paper* (Chuck Scarborough). Some critics believe this practice of mixing fact and fiction may affect the journalist's credibility with the public.

However, one can make a strong case in favor of these films about the world of journalism, with their focus upon contemporary and American settings. The films, like those of other genres, were basically designed as escapist fare, yet they often tackled important themes. They painted the sensational press and the scandal sheets as profound social evils. At times, they attacked corruption in politics, business and law enforcement. They occasionally exposed the prejudice and bigotry within our own borders. They raised the image of women, presenting them as educated, intelligent and self-sufficient—during decades that relegated them chiefly to the role of blonde bimbo, romantic playmate or sex object. In other words, they held up a mirror for us to see ourselves and our society, reminding us of our strengths and our shortcomings. Perhaps unintentionally, these films have repeatedly hinted at the importance of an independent and free press. They often reminded us of the legions of men and women who "got the news, got it out and got it published." Indeed, these films have had a profound, and generally positive, impact on us as a nation and as a people.

Abbreviations

AA	Allied Artists
AE	Associated Exhibitors
AI	American-International
AP	Associated Producers
ARC	American Releasing Corporation
BV	Buena Vista
Che.	Chesterfield
EL	Eagle-Lion
FBO	Film Booking Offices of America
FC	Film Classics
FN	First National
GN	Grand National
MGM	Metro-Goldwyn-Mayer
Mon.	Monogram
Par.	Paramount
PRC	Producers Releasing Corporation
Rep.	Republic
RKO	Rand-Keith-Orpheum
TCF	Twentieth Century–Fox
U	Universal
UA	United Artists
UI	Universal-International
WB	Warner Bros.
Dir.	Director
Sc.	Screenplay
St.	Story

The Films

1 ABANDONED (1949), U.

Dir. Joseph Newman; *Sc.* Irwin Gielgud; *Cast includes:* Dennis O'Keefe, Gale Storm, Jeff Chandler, Meg Randall, Raymond Burr, Marjorie Rambeau.

Reporter Dennis O'Keefe, while helping Gale Storm find her missing sister, uncovers a baby-stealing ring in this stark, semi-documentary drama. After Storm's sister turns up in a morgue, O'Keefe continues to investigate her death until he learns that she was murdered while trying to recover her illegitimate baby. Those responsible for her demise include Marjorie Rambeau, head of the vicious gang, and unscrupulous private sleuth Raymond Burr. The film was based on news stories about a similar Los Angeles illegal operation dealing in black market babies. News hound O'Keefe undergoes more shootouts and fights than reporting in this action-packed film noir.

2 ABOVE THE CLOUDS (1934), Col.

Dir. Roy William Neill; *Sc.* Albert DeMond; *Cast includes:* Robert Armstrong, Richard Cromwell, Dorothy Wilson, Edmund Breese, Morgan Wallace, Dorothy Revier.

Newsreel cameraman Robert Armstrong's drinking problem results in his assistant, Richard Cromwell, losing his job in this routine action drama. Armstrong is considered a crack cameraman who not only gets his pictures but brings back spectacular shots. Of course, no one really knows that it is his assistant that is responsible for much of the excellent camera work. Although he has been dismissed, Cromwell is given another chance and proves his worth. But this annoys Armstrong, whose incompetency includes losing lenses and ruining several assignments. Finally recognized for his skills, Cromwell gets his superior's job and the young woman he loves, Dorothy Wilson.

3 ABSENCE OF MALICE (1981), Col.

Dir. Sydney Pollack; *Sc.* Kuer Luedtke; *Cast includes:* Paul Newman, Sally Field, Bob Balaban, Melinda Dillon, Luther Adler, Barry Primus.

Ambitious newspaper reporter Sally Field, who is duped into writing suggestive articles about honest businessman Paul Newman, finds herself reprimanded by a Washington investigator in this absorbing and powerful drama. The film underscores the potential harm that may result from reckless reporting. Bob Balaban, heading a federal task force on racketeering, targets alleged mobster Luther Adler. To help him get information on Adler, Balaban also targets Newman, Adler's nephew. He leaves a folder on his desk for the reporter to read, hoping she will publish something about Newman, who will then talk about his uncle's criminal activities. Field violates the ethics of a reporter by printing her stories without confirming them with another source. Following several complications, including the suicide of an innocent young woman named by

Field, Newman decides to frame those who have been spreading the allegations which have resulted in the suicide. This leads to no-nonsense Washington investigator Wilford Brimley gathering all parties to a meeting and his condemnation of the representatives of the press. "You can't have people goin' around leaking stuff for no reason," he announces to Field and her superiors. "It ain't legal. And worse than that, by God, it ain't right." The paper is forced to confess its inaccuracies, and Brimley asks for Balaban's resignation.

4   ACE IN THE HOLE (1951), Par.

Dir. Billy Wilder; *Sc.* Billy Wilder, Lesser Samuels, Walter Newman; *Cast includes:* Kirk Douglas, Robert Arthur, Richard Benedict, Jan Sterling, Porter Hall, Frank Cady.

Kirk Douglas portrays a broken-down big-city reporter who, while searching for a job in New Mexico, comes across a potentially big story in this realistic and suspenseful drama. When the cynical Douglas learns that Richard Benedict is trapped in a mine, the reporter plans to exploit the incident into a national front-page event in the hopes of making a comeback. "He crawled into a hole for a story," Douglas recalls a fellow newsman, "and crawled out with a Pulitzer Prize." He inundates newspapers with human interest stories about the victim's progress while surreptitiously preventing an early rescue. Curious crowds arrive to gawk and a singing cowboy warbles a song about the victim's predicament as Douglas crawls into the mine to comfort and interview Benedict. The ruthless reporter even charms the trapped victim who enjoys the publicity. "My picture in the paper?" Benedict remarks. "No kidding?" In the end, it is too late to rescue Benedict. Director Wilder underscores the harrowing experience while presenting a scathing indictment of man's greed. The incident stems from a 1925 national story about Floyd Collins, a man who was similarly trapped in a mine shaft—while all America anxiously awaited the outcome. The film, which may have been too depressing for its audiences, failed at the box office. It often appears on television under its alternate title, *The Big Carnival.*

5   ACTION IN ARABIA (1944), RKO.

Dir. Leonide Moguy; *Sc.* Philip MacDonald, Herbert Biberman; *Cast includes:* George Sanders, Virginia Bruce, Lenore Aubert, Gene Lockhart, Robert Armstrong, Michael Ansara.

Nazi agents try to stir up an Arab revolt and plan to destroy the Suez Canal in this World War II action drama. George Sanders, as a savvy American reporter in 1941 Damascus, manages to foil the villainous plot while romancing Virginia Bruce, a secret agent. The routine story opens with Sanders attempting to solve the murder of a fellow journalist. The implausible plot then has Sanders, a dashing, sophisticated pre-James Bond hero, frequenting gambling casinos and charming worldly women in one sequence and, in another, stealing a German airplane, which frustrates the efforts of Nazi agents Gene Lockhart and Alan Napier.

6   THE ACTIVE LIFE OF DOLLY OF THE DAILIES (1914) serial, Edison.

Dir. Walter Edwin; *Cast includes:* Mary Fuller, Yale Boss, Charles Ogle, Harry Beaumont, Gladys Hulette, William West.

Mary Fuller portrays the title character in this 12-chapter silent serial concerning the trials and tribulations of a woman reporter. After being attacked for her satirical newspaper articles about a local ladies' league, Dolly decides not to meet the league's demand that she apologize. Instead, she leaves her small town for the big city. Following several other incidents, including writing stories for which another reporter gets the credit and accidentally walking out of a store with a dress she hasn't purchased, a publisher who learns about her work hires her to write a column for his paper. The remaining chapters follow her progress through

Broken-down big-city reporter Kirk Douglas has a few choice words for Jan Sterling in Billy Wilder's cynical drama, *Ace in the Hole* (1951).

various adventures—including several in which she gets a chance to play detective—until she ends up marrying her boss. The serial was considered one of the best of the period.

7 ADVENTURE IN MANHATTAN (1936), Col.

Dir. Edward Ludwig; *Sc.* Sidney Buchman, Harry Sauber, Jack Kirkland; *Cast includes:* Joel McCrea, Jean Arthur, Reginald Owen, Thomas Mitchell, Herman Bing, Victor Kilian.

Thomas Mitchell, managing editor of a big-city newspaper, hires criminologist Joel McCrea to track down an elusive burglar who specializes in stealing art treasures in this romantic mystery based loosely on the novel *Purple and Fine Linen* by May Edington. Fortunately for McCrea, his taste in art happens to be quite similar to that of master thief Reginald Owen, allowing the former to anticipate Owen's next move. The art thief's final caper is quite ingenious. Establishing himself as a legitimate theatrical producer, he buys a theater next to a bank containing a valuable diamond. He then rehearses and stages a full-fledged World War I drama whose war scenes include loud cannon firings. The noise is designed to cover the blasting into the bank by Owen's henchmen. Jean Arthur portrays an actress who provides the romantic interest for the criminologist-hero.

8 ADVENTURE IN WASHINGTON (1941), Col.

Dir. Alfred E. Green; *Sc.* Lewis R. Foster, Arthur Caesar; *Cast includes:* Herbert Marshall, Virginia Bruce, Gene Reynolds, Samuel S. Hinds, Ralph Morgan, Dickie Jones.

Radio gossip reporter Virginia Bruce, as the result of a feud with her beau, U.S. senator Herbert Marshall, becomes involved in a scandal among senate pages in this farfetched political drama. Young page Gene Reynolds, it seems, has been selling senatorial secrets to a stock manipulator who is profiting from the inside tips. His fellow pages eventually conduct a mock trial in the hallowed halls where Reynolds admits his guilt.

9 THE ADVENTURES OF A GIRL REPORTER (1914), Imp.

Cast includes: Ethel Grandin, Ed Mortimer.

An early silent newspaper film, this two-reeler features Ethel Grandin in the title role.

10 ADVENTURES OF JANE ARDEN (1939), WB.

Dir. Terry Moore; *Sc.* Vincent Sherman, Lawrence Kimble, Charles Curran; *Cast includes:* Rosella Towne, William Gargan, James Stephenson, Benny Rubin, Dennie Moore, Peggy Shannon.

Rosella Towne portrays the title character, an investigative reporter and part-time heroine detective, in this mildly interesting low-budget drama. Towne soon clashes with James Stephenson, as head of a gang of gem smugglers and murderers. He and his henchmen use women for their illegal activities and then kill them when the latter learn the truth. Maris Wrixon, as one of their victims, is gunned down by members of the gang. William Gargan portrays Towne's managing editor of a Manhattan newspaper. Lovelorn columnist Dennie Moore and boyfriend Benny Rubin provide the comic relief. The characters, who also appeared on radio at the time of the film's release, were based on the comic strip characters created by Monte Barrett and Russell E. Ross.

11 THE ADVENTUROUS BLONDE (1937), WB.

Dir. Frank McDonald; *Sc.* Robertson White, David Diamond; *Cast includes:* Glenda Farrell, Barton MacLane, Anne Nagel, Tom Kennedy, George E. Stone, Natalie Moorhead.

Feisty newspaper reporter Torchy Blane (Glenda Farrell) once again outsmarts Steve McBride, her detective boyfriend (Barton MacLane), and other policemen by solving a murder in this third entry in the Torchy Blane series. The opening sequences have Blane about to marry McBride. But she is tricked into answering a false police alarm in which an actor plays dead. The ploy, conceived to fool the reporter, backfires when the actor is found murdered. Blane begins to investigate and soon comes up with the guilty party whom she presents to the dumbfounded police. Farrell played Blane in seven of the nine entries, including the initial *Smart Blonde* (1936). Other actors who played the peppery reporter were Lola Lane and Jane Wyman, the latter appearing in the final entry, *Torchy Plays With Dynamite*.

12 ADVICE TO THE LOVELORN (1933), UA.

Dir. Alfred Werker; *Sc.* Leonard Praskins; *Cast includes:* Lee Tracy, Sally Blane, Sterling Holloway, Jean Adair, Paul Harvey, Matt Briggs.

Newspaper reporter Lee Tracy is relegated to handle the agony column of his paper in this sometimes gushy drama loosely based on the novel *Miss Lonely Hearts* by Nathanael West. This portion of the plot anticipates *Hi, Nellie!* (1934), a comedy drama featuring Paul Muni and Glenda Farrell. Tracy's new position, accredited to his heavy drinking and his botching up a major earthquake story, has unexpected results. He proves so popular that a local mobster forces him to include coded instructions to gang members in his columns. Tracy finally rids himself of this and other problems, including his involvement in the lives of some of his readers. But the film digresses from the original source by having the columnist work towards exposing cut-rate drug stores that deal in counterfeit brands of drugs. Perhaps the most rewarding element of the production is Tracy's fast-talking characterization—one he would repeat in several more newspaper films. West's incisive novel was adapted once again for the screen in 1958 and titled *Lonelyhearts*, a cynical and depressing drama featuring Montgomery Clift, Myrna Loy and Robert Ryan.

13 AFFAIRS OF JIMMY VALENTINE (1942), Rep.

Dir. Bernard Vorhaus; *Sc.* Olive Cooper, Robert Tasker; *Cast includes:* Dennis O'Keefe, Ruth Terry, George E. Stone, Roman Bohnen.

Several murders occur when a reward of $100,000 is offered to anyone who can locate the legendary Jimmy Valentine in this drama based on O. Henry's fictional reformed safecracker. Advertising employee Dennis O'Keefe, seeking to boost the ratings of a radio show titled "Jimmy Valentine," makes the offer, unaware of the consequences. The former convict turns out to be a middle-aged newspaper editor, played by character actor Roman Bohnen. The film (later retitled *Unforgotten Crime* and edited for television) is a much improved remake of *Return of Jimmy Valentine* (1936), which featured Roger Pryor and Charlotte Henry.

14 AFFECTIONATELY YOURS (1941), WB.

Dir. Lloyd Bacon; *Sc.* Edward Kaufman; *Cast includes:* Dennis Morgan, Merle Oberon, Rita Hayworth, Ralph Bellamy, George Tobias, James Gleason.

Crack reporter Dennis Morgan struggles to win back his ex-wife Merle Oberon in this dull screwball comedy. Tired of her peripatetic correspondent husband, she journeys to Reno and obtains a divorce. Morgan, on an overseas assignment, hears the bad news and is determined to reconcile their differences. Back in the States, he learns she is engaged to Ralph Bellamy, a rival suitor. Meanwhile, attractive Rita Hayworth, a fellow reporter who is in love with Morgan, makes her play. Like the numerous similar films of this genre, Oberon and Morgan finally rekindle their former love.

15 AFTER OFFICE HOURS (1935), MGM.

Dir. Robert Z. Leonard; *Sc.* Herman J. Mankiewicz; *Cast includes:* Constance Bennett, Clark Gable, Stuart Erwin, Billie Burke, Harvey Stephens, Katharine Alexander.

The plot of this fast-paced society-newspaper-crime drama concerns the lifestyles of the rich, including the murder of a wealthy married woman by her parasitic lover. These events are exploited by a voyeuristic press. Clark Gable, as a hardworking, demanding managing editor, at first fires Constance Bennett, an outspoken, controversial music critic, but rehires her when he learns that her socialite background and contacts make her a valuable source for society news. Angered at his publisher's request to suppress a society scandal involving the free-loading Tommy Bannister (Harvey Stephens), Gable uses Bennett to learn more about the affair. Bennett soon becomes involved with Bannister, who murders an unfaithful wife. Gable suspects him and returns to Bannister's quarters in time to rescue Bennett from the killer's clutches. Screenwriter Herman J. Mankiewicz, like many of his fellow contemporary writers of newspaper films, was an experienced journalist. He had worked for the Hearst press and later wrote the classic *Citizen Kane* (1941).

16 ALIAS MARY SMITH (1932), Mayfair.

Dir. E. Mason Hopper; *Sc.* Edward T. Lowe; *Cast includes:* John Darrow, Gwen Lee, Raymond Hatton, Henry B. Walthall, Blanche Mehaffey, Myrtle Stedman.

John Darrow and Gwen Lee are major players in this interesting murder mystery. They portray reporters who help to unravel the killing by finding several important fingerprints which the police originally thought were missing.

17 ALL THE KING'S MEN (1949), Col.

Dir. Robert Rossen; *Sc.* Robert Rossen;

Cast includes: Broderick Crawford, Joanne Dru, John Ireland, John Derek, Mercedes McCambridge, Sheppard Strudwick.

Newspaper reporter John Ireland witnesses the rise and fall of a powerful Southern politician in this award-winning drama based on the Pulitzer Prize–winning novel by Robert Penn Warren which in turn was allegedly inspired by the life of Huey Long, the former governor of Louisiana. Broderick Crawford portrays Willie Stark, a crafty, brutal and hypocritical aspiring politician who rises from the backwoods of a Southern state to governor. When Ireland asks his editor what's so special about Stark, his superior replies, "They say he's an honest man." Stark cleverly exploits the gullibility of the populace after his early defeat as an idealistic candidate for a minor office. Newsman Ireland, following Stark's political career from the beginning, falls for his charm and charisma. When his editor is instructed to quash further stories about Stark, Ireland quits and, after he is hired by Stark, introduces him to influential members of society. Some remain skeptical about Stark's promises and methods. The politician's cynical secretary-mistress Mercedes McCambridge, at first spellbound by Stark, eventually grows disillusioned with the politician, as does Ireland. "There's something on everybody," Stark maintains. "Man is conceived in sin and born in corruption." He is finally slain on the steps of the state capitol at the height of his triumph by Sheppard Strudwick, a sensitive doctor, who is then gunned down by Stark's bodyguard. To Strudwick, whose sister the politician had seduced, Stark was a corrupting and dangerous force who had to be stopped. One of the most scathing indictments of political demagogues, the film won Academy Awards for best picture, best actor (Crawford) and best supporting actress (McCambridge).

18 ALL THE PRESIDENT'S MEN (1976), WB.

Dir. Alan J. Pakula; Sc. William Golding; Cast includes: Dustin Hoffman, Robert Redford, Jack Warden, Martin Balsam, Hal Holbrook, Jason Robards.

Based on the popular book by Carl Bernstein and Bob Woodward, this fascinating drama captures the mystery and intrigue of the Watergate cover-up that dominated the nation during President Nixon's last years in office. Dustin Hoffman and Robert Redford portray the two Washington Post investigative reporters respectively. The mysterious Deep Throat (filmed always in the shadows) helps the news hounds ferret out the essential facts. "The list is longer than anyone can imagine," the voice warns. "It leads everywhere ... Follow the money." Jason Robards, portraying Washington Post editor Ben Bradlee, cautiously supports his two reporters, continually warning them to confirm their stories with other sources. It is fun to watch the two persevering journalists conduct their interviews, asking questions, then following up on the answers, and eliciting even more information from their interviewees. The film won Oscars for Best Screenwriting (William Golding) and Best Supporting Actor (Jason Robards).

19 AN AMERICAN DREAM (1966), WB.

Dir. Robert Gist; Sc. Mann Rubin; Cast includes: Stuart Whitman, Janet Leigh, Eleanor Parker, Barry Sullivan, Lloyd Nolan, Murray Hamilton.

Television talk show commentator Stuart Whitman, who inadvertently causes his unfaithful wife's death, is suspected of murder by the police in this mediocre drama about present-day crime and punishment based on the novel by Norman Mailer. During an argument, Whitman accidentally pushes his obnoxious wife, Eleanor Parker, from her penthouse apartment thirty floors to her death. To protect himself, he tells policemen Barry Sullivan and Murray Hamilton that his wife committed suicide. But his problems soon multiply. It seems his wife landed on a gangster's limousine that was stalled in traffic, and the occupants are seeking revenge. In addition, Lloyd Nolan, Parker's wealthy Catholic father, cannot get the Church to bury his daughter because of Whitman's claim that she had taken her own life. Finally, his ex-mistress Janet Leigh returns to him but in the end betrays him to the police.

20 ANGEL'S HOLIDAY (1937), TCF.

Dir. James Tinling; *Sc.* Frank Fenton, Lynn Root; *Cast includes:* Jane Withers, Robert Kent, Joan Davis, Sally Blane, Harold Huber, Frank Jenks.

Reporter Robert Kent helps the young and impish Jane Withers, the niece of a local newspaper editor, rescue movie star Sally Blane in this mildly entertaining comedy drama. Withers habitually meddles in other people's affairs, often creating chaos. She decides to intervene in the romantic life of Kent, a former boyfriend of the actress, by rekindling the romance. Meanwhile Blane, who has returned to her home town for a visit, is part of a publicity scheme concerning her disappearance. But the plan backfires when the gang of racketeers who have kidnapped her demand a ransom. Withers manages to garner the police and fire departments in her efforts to capture the culprits.

21 ANGELS IN THE OUTFIELD (1951), MGM.

Dir. Clarence Brown; *Sc.* Dorothy Kingsley, George Wells; *Cast includes:* Paul Douglas, Janet Leigh, Keenan Wynn, Donna Corcoran, Lewis Stone, Spring Byington, Bruce Bennett.

Pittsburgh newspaper reporter Janet Leigh, assigned to cover baseball "from the woman's angle," experiences a strange phenomenon in this fantasy comedy about America's national pastime. Blasphemous baseball manager Paul Douglas, who has been having a disastrous season, is suddenly helped by angels. This seems to be the result of prayers from small orphan Donna Corcoran. As long as Douglas stops his swearing and bullying, his team keeps winning. Leigh interviews the little girl, and the story brings forth an investigation of Douglas's sanity, since he, too, admits to seeing angels. Meanwhile, vindictive sports writer Keenan Wynn, desiring Douglas's job, tries to discredit the beleaguered manager. But all ends happily for the reformed manager, the inquisitive reporter and the imaginative orphan. A remake appeared in 1994 featuring Danny Glover and Tony Danza.

22 THE ANGRY HILLS (1959), MGM.

Dir. Robert Aldrich; *Sc.* A. I. Bezzerides; *Cast includes:* Robert Mitchum, Elisabeth Mueller, Stanley Baker, Gia Scala, Theodore Bikel, Sebastian Cabot.

American war correspondent Robert Mitchum, carrying vital information about members of the Greek underground, attempts to escape from Greece where he is pursued by the Gestapo in this World War II drama set in 1941 on the eve of Nazi occupation. Mitchum, who agrees to help the Greek resistance by delivering a list of Greek agents to British intelligence, becomes the target of the Nazis who want the list of names while anti-Nazi forces try to assist him in his escape. Elisabeth Mueller portrays an undercover Greek agent and mistress to a Gestapo chief. Gia Scala, a poor villager, nurses Mitchum back to health, helps him make contact with the Greek underground and falls in love with him. Theodore Bikel, a vicious and cowardly Greek collaborator, offers his pretty half-sister to German officials as a means of furthering his own career. The clever dialogue and finely etched characterizations are a notch above the average espionage drama in this work based on Leon Uris's novel. "You journalists," Donald Wolfit, as an intellectual, anti-Fascist Greek patriot, muses to Mitchum, "I envy you. The world's in flames, and you stand apart as if you were gods. The folly of man is no more to you than a news item." Marius Goring, as a hypochondriac German officer, ponders cynically about his nation's military successes. "The Fuhrer leads us from victory to victory," he says to Gestapo chief Stanley Baker.

"And each victory leads us further away from home. A few more such victories and we may never return." Baker gives a sympathetic and humane portrayal of the Gestapo chief who abhors violence—an interpretation often employed by Hollywood in World War II dramas produced after the conflict.

23 ANOTHER TIME, ANOTHER PLACE (1958), Par.

Dir. Lewis Allen; *Sc.* Stanley Mann; *Cast includes:* Lana Turner, Sean Connery, Glynis Johns, Barry Sullivan, Terence Longdon, Sidney James.

American correspondent Lana Turner, in London during World War II, finds herself entangled in a love affair with married Sean Connery in this slow-paced, lackluster drama filmed in England. She only learns that he is married and has a child as he leaves to cover a story. The ill-fated affair ends when Connery is reported killed in action. Turner then has a nervous breakdown over the news. However, she is so obsessed with Connery that she visits his widow and child. Glynis Johns portrays the long-suffering widow, and Barry Sullivan appears as Turner's fiancé. The film was released to exploit Turner's involvement in a sensational murder trial.

24 ANY MAN'S DEATH (1990), INI.

Dir. Tom Clegg; *Sc.* Iain Roy, Chris Kelly; *Cast includes:* John Savage, William Hickey, Mia Sara, Ernest Borgnine, Michael Lerner, James Ryan.

Burnt-out reporter John Savage, who is sent to Namibia to investigate some strange photographs, instead uncovers a nest of Nazi war criminals in this rather shallow and sometimes overly talky drama. William Hickey portrays a Jewish survivor who participated as a victim in Nazi concentration camp experiments. Ernest Borgnine, as a major Nazi war criminal, is captured by the Israelis and made to stand trial. Reporter Savage, who is chiefly non-committal throughout the film, eventually turns moral.

25 ANYBODY'S BLONDE (1931), Action Pictures.

Dir. Frank Strayer; *Sc.* Betty Burbridge; *Cast includes:* Dorothy Revier, Reed Howes, Lloyd Whitlock, Edna Murphy, Nita Marian, Gene Morgan.

Newspaper reporter Dorothy Revier is determined to find the murderer of her prizefighter brother in this undistinguished minor drama. To accomplish this, she poses as a dancer and gets a job in a nightclub owned by Lloyd Whitlock, whom she suspects as her brother's killer. Revier hopes to play up to Whitlock and perhaps trap him into a confession. Meanwhile Edna Murphy, another revue entertainer, grows jealous when Whitlock, her lover, begins to take more than a passing interest in the reporter. In addition, Revier's boyfriend, Reed Howes, thinks he is being two-timed when he discovers she is romantically involved with Whitlock. Following these and other complications, Revier finally avenges her brother's untimely death when she brings about the nightclub owner's downfall.

26 ANYTHING FOR A THRILL (1937), Conn Pictures.

Dir. Lee Goodwins; *Sc.* Joseph O'Donnell, Stanley Lowenstein; *Cast includes:* Frankie Darro, Kane Richmond, June Johnson, Ann Evers, Johnstone White, Horace Murphy.

Newsreel cameraman Kane Richmond and his brother and young assistant Frankie Darro capture a gang of kidnappers in this farfetched action drama. Earlier in the film Richmond is fired for botching an assignment in which he is supposed to film camera-shy heiress Ann Evers, but Darro and his girlfriend June Johnson, who want to be newsreel photographers, extricate him from his predicament by getting the coveted pictures. Evers, angry over the incident, buys the newsreel firm. When Richmond and his kid brother help to capture the gang planning to kidnap the heiress, Evers forgets the past intrusions upon her privacy and falls in love with Richmond. Popular young actor Darro and Richmond made several similar action dramas during this period.

27   ANZIO (1968), Col.

Dir. Edward Dmytryk; *Sc.* Harry A. L. Craig; *Cast includes:* Robert Mitchum, Peter Falk, Earl Holliman, Robert Ryan, Mark Damon, Reni Santoni.

One of the more important European campaigns of World War II is trivialized in this weak drama. Robert Mitchum, as a cynical newspaper correspondent, belittles the top military brass who progress from one blunder to the next. Robert Ryan portrays an American general more interested in making the front pages than in fighting the war efficiently. Arthur Kennedy, another general, is overcautious, losing strategic opportunities against the enemy. Action sequences include the Anzio invasion, but the remainder of the film is rather slow.

28   THE APE MAN (1943), Mon.

Dir. William Beaudine; *Sc.* Barney Sarecky; *Cast includes:* Bela Lugosi, Wallace Ford, Louise Currie, Minerva Urecal, Henry Hall, Ralph Littlefield, J. Farrell MacDonald.

Newspaper reporters Wallace Ford and Louise Currie, each yearning for a scoop, investigate a suspicious scientist in this unintentionally funny horrorless drama. Bela Lugosi, the ambitious man of science, finds a way to transform an ape to human form. However, his experiments require human spinal fluid. He acquires the precious liquid by having his pet gorilla strangle innocent victims. During their investigation, the two journalists themselves almost fall victim to the crazed scientist but are rescued by the police.

29   APPOINTMENT WITH A SHADOW (1958), U.

Dir. Richard Carlson; *Sc.* Alec Coppel, Norman Jolley; *Cast includes:* George Nader, Joanna Moore, Brian Keith, Virginia Field, Frank de Kova, Stephen Chase.

Alcoholic reporter George Nader, who witnesses a killing, tries unsuccessfully to convince others that the victim is not a notorious gangster but an impostor in this weak drama based on a magazine story by Hugh Pentecost. Because of his reputation as a drunk, no one believes Nader's story. He insists that the real mobster is still alive and had planned the killing of his double. The plot is similar to that in *His Kind of Woman* (1951), with gang leader Raymond Burr planning to kill Robert Mitchum and substitute his body for the gangster's.

30   ARE YOU LISTENING? (1932), MGM.

Dir. Harry Beaumont; *Sc.* Dwight Taylor; *Cast includes:* William Haines, Madge Evans, Anita Page, Karen Morley, Neil Hamilton, Wallace Ford.

William Haines portrays an unhappily married radio writer who is eventually convicted of manslaughter in this dreary drama based on a story by J. P. McEvoy. Haines, who is married to shrewish Karen Morley, takes up with Madge Evans, whose two sisters, Anita Page and Joan Marsh, arouse the romantic interests of others. Jean Hersholt desires the former, while Neil Hamilton tries to bed the latter. Meanwhile, unscrupulous tabloid editor John Miljan double-crosses Haines by obtaining an alleged confession by means of a radio-telephone connection in which the radio writer admits to the accidental killing of his wife.

31   THE ARGYLE SECRETS (1948), Film Classics.

Dir. Cyril Endfield; *Sc.* Cyril Endfield; *Cast includes:* William Gargan, Marjorie Lord, Ralph Byrd, Jack Reitzen, John Banner, Barbara Billingsley.

A collection of documents that contain evidence of treason by well-known Americans during World War II becomes the focus of a reporter and various blackmailers in this drama set in postwar America. William Gargan, the journalist, wants the papers so that he can expose the traitors who collaborated with the Nazi regime. Meanwhile, assorted agents representing different extortion rings, are also interested in getting the documents. Several murders are committed before the intrigue is unraveled. Marjorie Lord portrays one of the blackmailers. Ralph Byrd, better known for his portrayals of Dick Tracy in serials and feature films, plays the local police detective.

32 ARISE, MY LOVE (1940), Par.

Dir. Mitchell Leisen; *Sc.* Charles Brackett, Billy Wilder; *Cast includes:* Claudette Colbert, Ray Milland, Dennis O'Keefe, Walter Abel, Dick Purcell.

A romantic drama with strife-torn Europe as its background, the film stars Claudette Colbert as an ambitious American reporter and Ray Milland as a young idealistic flier willing to fight for any underdog against oppression. Sent to France on the eve of World War II to report on the latest women's fashions, Colbert is quickly bored with this assignment. She journeys to fascist Spain where she finds Milland, a fellow American, about to be executed for flying for the Republic. She poses as his wife and effects his release. But the couple are pursued by soldiers. They steal an airplane and narrowly escape their pursuers across the border to France. As a reward for this front-page story, her editor sends her to Berlin. Following a slight holiday with Milland, they decide to sail for home. But the ship they are on is torpedoed by a Nazi submarine. The disaster brings the couple to the realization that their romantic bliss must be postponed while the world is in flames. Colbert sends in the story to alert the world of the ruthless sinking while Milland enlists in the Royal Air Force. The title comes from "The Song of Solomon"—"Arise, my love, my fair one, come away"—which Milland is fond of quoting and which Colbert paraphrases in the last scene as an anti-Nazi call to all Americans to rise up and defend themselves against the encroaching tyrannical forces. Director Mitchell Leisen combines a romantic, often humorous, story (which won an Oscar) with serious world events. One of Milland's two buddies, who fought with him in Spain against the Fascists, reminds him why they are so far from home: "Because you said a lot of big guys were kicking the tar out of some little guys, and you said it wasn't fair, and you said it was up to us to come over to even things out."

33 THE ARKANSAS TRAVELER (1938), Par.

Dir. Alfred Santell; *Sc.* Viola Brothers Shore, George Sessions Perry; *Cast includes:* Bob Burns, Fay Bainter, John Beal, Jean Parker, Lyle Talbot, Irvin S. Cobb.

Itinerant printer Bob Burns comes upon a small rural community where he helps the widow and daughter of an old friend save their family newspaper in this entertaining drama. It seems that Lyle Talbot, an unscrupulous politician, is bent on seeing the paper go under. Using his homespun philosophy and charm, Burns plays Cupid to a pair of lovebirds (John Beal and Jean Parker) while assisting widow Fay Bainter to keep her presses rolling. Humorist and author Irvin S. Cobb provides much of the humor portraying the town constable.

34 ARM OF THE LAW (1932), Mon.

Dir. Louis King; *Sc.* Leon Lee; *Cast includes:* Rex Bell, Marceline Day, Lina Basquette, Bryant Washburn, Robert E. O'Connor, Dorothy Revier.

Sleuthing reporter Rex Bell solves a double murder in this conventional drama based on the story "The Butterfly Mystery" by Arthur Hoerl. A nightclub star who has just undergone a divorce scandal is found poisoned along with her married lover. Both remaining mates, a dancer and a lawyer, are considered suspects by detective Robert Emmett O'Connor, until the resolute news hound proves otherwise.

35 ARSON GANG BUSTERS (1938), Rep.

Dir. Joe Kane; *Sc.* Alex Gottlieb, Norman Burnstine; *Cast includes:* Robert Livingston, Rosalind Keith, Jackie Moran, Warren Hymer, Jack LaRue, Clay Clement.

A gang of arsonists cashing in on a series of fires becomes the target of an investigation by the fire department in this routine action drama aimed chiefly at juvenile audiences. The department reassigns firefighter Robert Livingston to go under cover in an effort to find the arsonists. He soon unmasks those responsible, especially screen villain Jack LaRue, who receives orders from Clay Clement, the leader of the gang. Clement is a member of the board of insurance underwriters. On the scene to hamper the investigation and antagonize the beleaguered authorities is Rosalind Keith, a reporter for a local scandal sheet. Jackie Moran, the firehouse mascot, is adopted by the men following the death of the boy's firefighting father who was killed in action fighting a blaze. Warren Hymer, a dimwit firefighter, provides some comedy relief. The film is sometimes listed under an alternate title, *Arson Racket Squad.*

36 ASSASSIN OF YOUTH (1937), Leo J. McCarthy.

Dir. Elmer Clifton; *Sc.* Elmer Clifton, Charles A. Brown; *Cast includes:* Luana Walters, Dorothy Short, Fern Emmett, Arthur Gardner, Earl Dwire.

A bright young newspaper reporter, posing as a soda fountain saleswoman, investigates the use of marijuana among teens in this dated exposé of drug use among the nation's youth. The plot focuses on two sisters, one fairly temperate and the other rather rambunctious, both of whom fall victim to the drug habit. Several films of the period, including *The Pace That Kills* (1936), *Marihuana* (1937) and *The Burning Question* (also known as *Tell Your Children*) (1939), touched upon the controversial topic. Like the others, the current drama (which was "condemned" by the Catholic Legion of Decency at the time) was more inane and sensational than cautionary.

37 ASSIGNMENT PARIS (1952). Col.

Dir. Robert Parrish; *Sc.* William Bowers; *Cast includes:* Dana Andrews, Marta Toren, George Sanders, Audrey Totter, Sandro Giglio, Donald Randolph.

American reporter Dana Andrews, stationed in Paris, tries to expose a plot by East Bloc countries against the West in this dated cold war drama. Andrews is sent to Budapest to investigate a link between the Hungarian dictator and Tito. He obtains a picture as proof of the plot and smuggles it out of the country. But he is caught and made to confess that he is a spy. He then escapes to safety. Marta Toren plays a fellow reporter with whom Andrews falls in love. George Sanders, a journalist in charge of the Paris office, is also in love with Toren. The film, based on "Trial by Terror," a story by Pauline and Paul Gallico, gives a fair depiction of the difficulties of newspaper work under the censorship procedures in Communist countries.

38 ATLANTIC ADVENTURE (1935), Col.

Dir. Albert Rogell; *Sc.* John T. Neville, Nat Dorfman; *Cast includes:* Lloyd Nolan, Nancy Carroll, Harry Langdon, Arthur Hohl, Robert Middlemass, E. E. Clive.

Lloyd Nolan portrays a reporter who, although fired from his job, proves his worth in this pedestrian drama set chiefly aboard a luxury liner. After being dismissed for allegedly paying too much attention to his fiancée Nancy Carroll—resulting in his leaving the scene of an important story to take Carroll to dinner—Nolan sets out to capture the killer of a local district attorney. Tipped off by an informant that the killer intends to flee aboard a liner, Nolan takes his photographer, Harry Langdon, and Carroll with him on the voyage. He not only accomplishes this but helps to round up a gang of jewel thieves. Former silent film comic Langdon adds some humor to the waterlogged plot.

39 ATOM MAN VS. SUPERMAN (1950) serial, Col.

Dir. Spencer G. Bennet, Derwin Abrahams; *Cast includes:* Kirk Alyn, Noel Neill, Lyle Talbot, Tommy Bond, Pierre Watkin, Jack Ingram.

In this fifteen-chapter sequel to the 1948 serial *Superman*, the Man of Steel (Kirk Alyn) battles his arch enemy, the villainous Luthor (Lyle Talbot), who is on the verge of completing a disintegration machine capable of destroying entire cities by sound vibration. Noel Neill returns as Clark Kent's fellow reporter and romantic interest.

40 ATTA BOY (1926), Pathé.

Dir. Edward H. Griffith; *Sc.* Charles Horan; *Cast includes:* Monty Banks, Virginia Bradford, Ernie Wood, Fred Kelsey, Virginia Pearson, Henry A. Barrows.

Although newspaper copy boy Monty Banks serves as the butt of a prank, he proves to be a formidable news hound in this fast-paced comedy. Star reporter Ernie Wood, after antagonizing the father of a kidnapped baby, sends Banks to interview the man, saying that Banks has just been moved up in rank to reporter. Confronted by several problems, Banks finds a ransom note left behind and follows the kidnapper to a private gambling house. He then poses as a waiter so that he can infiltrate the establishment. He locates the baby and rushes back to his office with the infant while the gambling club is raided by the police. The happy father then presents Banks with a reward.

41 THE AVERAGE WOMAN (1924), Burr.

Dir. William Christy Cabanne; *Sc.* Raymond S. Harris; *Cast includes:* Pauline Garon, David Powell, Harrison Ford, Burr McIntosh, William Tooker, Russell Griffin.

Reporter Harrison Ford, researching material for a story describing "The Average Woman," meets Pauline Garon, the daughter of a judge, in this romantic drama based on the short story by Dorothy De Jagers. She finally agrees to meet with Ford once a week for the purpose of helping him with his research. Meanwhile, the reporter has a rival in David Powell, a silent partner in an iniquitous roadhouse. Powell tries to blackmail Garon into marrying him by showing her incriminating letters allegedly written by her mother. However, Garon refuses to be forced into marriage and instead turns to Ford, who proposes to her.

42 BABIES FOR SALE (1940), Col.

Dir. Charles Barton; *Sc.* Robert D. Andrews; *Cast includes:* Glenn Ford, Rochelle Hudson, Miles Mander, Joseph Stefani, Isabel Jewell, Georgia Caine.

Persistent newspaper reporter Glenn Ford investigates a crooked maternity-home physician in this minor exposé drama. Miles Mander, as the corrupt doctor, persuades mothers to give up their babies for adoption—which he then sells to waiting couples for a large sum. Rochelle Hudson, as an abused wife, enters Mander's charity-subsidized home where she intends to give birth. Mander's entire seedy racket is finally brought down by the introduction of babies' footprints as an identifying feature. This was one of several quasi-exploitation dramas the studio turned out during this period, including, among others, *Missing Daughters* (1939), *Girls of the Road* (1940) and *Girls Under 21* (1940), all of which revealed their plots in their titles.

43 BACK IN CIRCULATION (1937), WB.

Dir. Ray Enright; *Sc.* Warren Duff; *Cast includes:* Pat O'Brien, Joan Blondell, Margaret Lindsay, John Litel, Ben Welden, Eddie Acuff.

Joan Blondell, an overly confident reporter, helps in the arrest and conviction of a murder suspect only to learn she has made a horrible mistake in this newspaper-crime drama that takes a swipe at the sensational press. Margaret Lindsay portrays a former showgirl whose husband has been poisoned. Pat O'Brien, a city editor hungry for every dirty detail in the accused's life, assigns his staff to hound Lindsay, who is virtually convicted in the emotionally charged stories written about her. Hard-nosed Blondell, once she realizes her mistake, defies her boss, O'Brien, and gathers enough evidence to exonerate the railroaded widow from the death house. Lindsay, at times, has a few choice words for those members of the press who seek out the sordid and sensational at the expense of the innocent and vulnerable.

44 BAD MAN OF DEADWOOD (1941), Rep.

Dir. Joseph Kane; *Sc.* James R. Webb; *Cast includes:* Roy Rogers, George "Gabby" Hayes, Carol Adams, Henry Brandon, Herbert Rawlinson, Sally Payne.

Local newspaper publisher Henry Brandon secretly heads a group of citizens who control all the lucrative businesses in town in this routine entry in the "Roy Rogers" series of B westerns. Otherwise known as a reformer and respected civic leader, Brandon, to protect his oligopoly, sends out his henchmen to prevent others from opening any rival establishments. Rogers and his pal George "Gabby" Hayes, who runs a medicine show, unite the frustrated honest businessmen and together they put the culprits out of action. Rogers starred in several westerns dealing in part with the world of journalism, including *In Old Cheyenne*, also released in 1941, *Don't Fence Me In* (1945) and *Home in Indiana* (1946), both with Dale Evans and Hayes.

45 BADGE OF HONOR (1934), Mayfair.

Dir. Spencer Gordon Bennet; *Sc.* George Morgan; *Cast includes:* Buster Crabbe, Ruth Hall, Ralph Lewis, Betty Blythe, John Trent.

Ace reporter Buster Crabbe can manage any assignment in this farfetched action drama. The son of a wealthy society family, Crabbe poses as a reporter for the excitement and adventure. His background allows him to enter some of the swankest and restricted places. Between his fancy automobile driving and his fighting in saloons, it's surprising he has time and energy left to pound out his stories. "Well," he explains to a young woman he rescues during another escapade, "a newspaperman can do a little of everything." Director Bennet and screenwriter Morgan were soon to work on numerous action serials through the next couple of decades. Crabbe, an Olympic swimming champion, gained greater fame for his Flash Gordon serials than for his countless B westerns and action dramas.

46 BANNERLINE (1951), MGM.

Dir. Don Weis; *Sc.* Charles Schnee; *Cast includes:* Keefe Brasselle, Sally Forrest, Lionel Barrymore, Lewis Stone, J. Carrol Naish, Spring Byington.

Cub reporter Keefe Brasselle's impulsive decision to print a phony front page filled with civic reforms leads to surprising results in this fair newspaper-crime drama. The young news hound is inspired by dying professor Lionel Barrymore's detailed civic reforms. Although the general public treats the reforms with complacency, the criminal elements are sufficiently stirred up, especially chief racketeer J. Carrol Naish. Some of his henchmen beat up the reporter, an act that arouses a grand jury. By the last reel, the community witnesses the installation of all the once-fictitious reforms. Veteran character actor Lewis Stone portrays an old-time newspaperman who is now in charge of the daily's morgue. The film indicts a complacent citizenry that allows its community to be infested by vice, crime and political corruption.

47 BAREE, SON OF KAZAN (1918), Vitagraph.

Dir. David Smith; *Cast includes:* Nell Shipman, Alfred Whitman, Al Garcia, Joe Rickson.

The son of a murdered newspaper owner avenges his father's death and escapes into Canada where he is confronted with other problems in this northwest drama. Alfred Whitman portrays Jim Carvel, who seeks refuge in Canada's Northwest. He soon becomes infatuated with Nepeese, a trapper's daughter. A villainous trading-post owner kills her father and places the blame on Jim, who is pursued by Indians. Meanwhile, the murderer kidnaps Nepeese, but Baree, her dog, tracks them down and overpowers the killer. Jim, rescued by his Indian friend, is reunited with Nepeese and they start a new life together. The film was adapted from the 1917 novel by James Oliver Curwood.

48 BARRICADE (1939), TCF.

Dir. Gregory Ratoff; *Sc.* Granville Walker; *Cast includes:* Alice Faye, Warner Baxter, Charles Winninger, Arthur Treacher, Keye Luke, Willie Fong.

Chinese bandits threaten the lives of several Americans, including dance-hall entertainer Alice Faye, foreign correspondent Warner Baxter, and U.S. consul Charles Winninger, in this feeble action drama set in the East. Bewildered American citizens seek safety in a consulate compound when native outlaws rise up in strife-torn China. Faye, who is on the run from the law, and Baxter had met earlier on a train which had been attacked by native bandits. The couple eventually fall in love. The besieged group are later rescued by the Chinese army after Baxter and Faye elude the attackers and telegraph for help.

49 BASKET CASE 2 (1990), Shapiro Glickenhaus.

Dir. Frank Henenlotter; *Sc.* Frank Henenlotter; *Cast includes:* Kevin Van Hentenryck, Annie Ross, Kathryn Meisle, Judy Grafe, Heather Rattray, Chad Brown.

Newspaper reporter Jason Evers tracks fugitive Kevin Van Hentenryck and his terribly deformed twin brother to a house of freaks where the pair have sought refuge. This awful low-budget horror tale is a sequel to a much better 1982 film turned out by the same director. The sequel was followed by *Basket Case 3* in 1992, a slight improvement over the present feature.

50 THE BASKETBALL FIX (1951), Realart.

Dir. Felix Feist; *Sc.* Peter R. Brooke, Charles K. Peck Jr.; *Cast includes:* John Ireland, Marshall Thompson, Vanessa Brown, William Bishop, Hazel Brooks, John Sands.

Talented basketball player Marshall Thompson, finding himself embroiled in gambling debts, is forced to agree to shave points in a major game in this earnest drama narrated by John Ireland, who portrays a sports columnist. Ireland had scouted Thompson and helped to get the promising young player a college scholarship. Thompson lives up to the sports writer's expectations. Gambler William Bishop then exerts the right amount of pressure to corrupt the up-and-coming star. However, the alert gaming commission spots the scheme and cracks down hard on Thompson, who ends up banished from the sport.

51 BATTLEGROUND (1949), MGM.

Dir. William A. Wellman; *Sc.* Robert Pirosh; *Cast includes:* Van Johnson, John Hodiak, Ricardo Montalban, George Murphy, Marshall Thompson.

This World War II drama pays tribute to the men who stopped the Nazis at Bastogne in the famous Battle of the Bulge.

Known affectionately as the "battling bastards of Bastogne," these stalwart G.I.s figured the war would be over by Christmas of 1944. Instead, they found themselves surrounded by the enemy. But they held their ground against overwhelming odds and stopped the German advance. As in most war films of this type, the fictional part of the battle focuses on a group of weary infantrymen from all walks of life who gripe, chase French women and muse about their postwar plans. Van Johnson, an easygoing, likable soldier, takes time out to woo Denise Darcel. George Murphy, as an old-timer who is discharged, finds himself a civilian in the midst of the German counterattack. John Hodiak, as a cynical newspaperman, enlisted after reading and believing his own columns. James Whitmore's portrayal of a seasoned sergeant won him critical acclaim. It was during this encounter that General McAuliffe's famous reply, "Nuts," was given to the German commander who requested the surrender of the American troops. The drama, shot entirely within a studio, has been singled out for introducing a "new realism" in war films and as partially responsible for reviving the popularity of the war drama. Robert Pirosh won an Oscar for his screenplay.

52 BEAUTY ON PARADE (1950), Col.

Dir. Lew Landers; *Sc.* Arthur E. Orloff, George Bricker; *Cast includes:* Ruth Warrick, Lola Albright, Robert Hutton, John Ridgely, Hillary Brooke, Wally Vernon.

Reporter Robert Hutton witnesses former beauty queen Ruth Warrick come to terms with the importance of a career in her life in this fair drama. Hutton is engaged to Lola Albright, whose mother (Warrick), out of frustration at her own curtailed career, prods her daughter to succeed as Miss U.S.A., almost at the sacrifice of the daughter's romance. Warrick had given up her career for marriage. But Albright chooses to surrender her beauty throne, accepting Hutton and marriage in its place. Her mother then resigns herself to the same role, realizing that putting one's career before marriage is not for everyone. John Ridgely plays Albright's father.

53 THE BEDFORD INCIDENT (1965), Col.

Dir. James B. Harris; *Sc.* James Poe; *Cast includes:* Richard Widmark, Sidney Poitier, Martin Balsam, James MacArthur, Eric Portman, Wally Cox.

Richard Widmark, the hard-nosed captain of the destroyer U.S.S. *Bedford,* clashes with wise-guy magazine journalist Sidney Poitier in this tense but flawed drama about the tracking of a Soviet submarine during the cold war. Widmark, part of the new peacetime navy and worshiped by his loyal crew, is obsessed with going after the sub regardless of the risks. Poitier tries to remind him of his larger obligation. Reserve medic Martin Balsam, a relic of World War II who has been recalled to duty, contrasts sharply with the authoritarian Widmark, and cannot understand the motivations of the new sailors. Also on board is Eric Portman, a NATO consultant and former Nazi U-Boat commander. Portman symbolizes the confusing alliances in which yesterday's enemies are today's allies, etc. Poitier, who earlier had been featured as an African-American protagonist in dramas about race relations, here simply played a journalist, a role in which race was not a factor. He made other similar films, including *Paris Blues* (1961), *Lilies of the Field* (1963) and *A Patch of Blue* (1965), all attesting to his popularity and talent.

54 BEHIND GREEN LIGHTS (1946), TCF.

Dir. Otto Brower; *Sc.* W. Scott Darling; *Cast includes:* Carole Landis, William Gargan, Richard Crane, Mary Anderson, John Ireland, Charles Russell.

Cub reporter Richard Crane inadvertently solves a murder in this diverting but slow-placed drama set chiefly during one night in a police station. Much of the film is set in the precinct's press room. The plot at first focuses on tough policeman

William Gargan, who ponders over choosing between his duty to uphold the law and succumbing to political corruption. Gargan's life becomes complicated because of his romantic involvement with Carole Landis, who falls under suspicion during a political-murder case. With the help of the reporter, Gargan finally exonerates her by proving that medical examiner William Forrest Jr. is a conspirator in the murder and corruption scheme.

55 BEHIND JURY DOORS (1933), Mayfair.

Dir. Breezy Eason; *Sc.* J. T. Neville; *Cast includes:* Helen Chandler, William Collier Jr., Blanche Frederici, Franklin Parker, John Davidson, Walter Miller.

In this highly implausible melodrama, a young reporter investigates the murder of a nurse. A doctor has been convicted of the crime, but William Collier Jr., the curious reporter who is interested in the physician's daughter (Helen Chandler), turns up enough evidence to have the case reopened. It seems that the doctor's jealous wife shot the nurse while an editor framed a juror so that he could win a $25,000 bet. Thus, Collier helps to exonerate Chandler's father who has been convicted by a corrupt district attorney. After learning that his editor was the one who did the framing, Collier takes his story to a rival newspaper.

56 BEHIND LOCKED DOORS (1948), EL.

Dir. Budd Boetticher; *Sc.* Malvin Wald, Eugene Ling; *Cast includes:* Lucille Bremer, Richard Carlson, Douglas Fowley, Tom Browne Henry, Herbert Heyes, Ralf Harolde.

Reporter Lucille Bremer collaborates with private eye Richard Carlson, who poses as a patient in an insane asylum where he believes a crooked politician has taken refuge, in this suspenseful drama. Those in charge begin to suspect Carlson, who almost cracks under the strain before breaking the case and winning a $10,000 reward for the capture of the fugitive—a reward he shares with the reporter, his outside contact who has been posing as his wife.

57 BEHIND THE EVIDENCE (1934), Col.

Dir. Lambert Hillyer; *Sc.* Harold Shumate; *Cast includes:* Norman Foster, Donald Cook, Sheila Mannors, Geneva Mitchell, Samuel S. Hinds, Frank Darien.

A familiar dramatic plot seen on screen numerous times, this film features a brash reporter who captures a notorious mobster. Norman Foster, as an ex-playboy turned journalist, finds time to woo Sheila Mannors between assignments. Donald Cook, as the villain brought down by Foster, does not make a terribly menacing gangster—perhaps because of his obsession with entering the world of high society.

58 BEHIND THE HEADLINES (1937), RKO.

Dir. Richard Rosson; *Sc.* Edmund L. Hartmann, J. Robert Bren; *Cast includes:* Lee Tracy, Diana Gibson, Donald Meek, Paul Guilfoyle, Frank M. Thomas, Philip Huston.

Aggressive radio reporter Lee Tracy competes for scoops with his girlfriend Diana Gibson, a journalist for a rival newspaper, in this fast-paced action drama. The basic plot revolves around a gang of thieves who steal a shipment of gold headed for the newly constructed U.S. depository at Fort Knox. They then kidnap Gibson, who is about to inform her boss about the scheme, and hold her as hostage in the hills near Fort Knox. Reporter Gibson, who earlier had resented some of Tracy's tactics in getting his stories, uses a radio transmitter to help federal agents find the gang's hideout and the stolen gold. She then forgives Tracy after she is rescued. The delightful pixie-like character actor, Donald Meek, so aptly named in his numerous roles in lighter films, here plays the obsessed and demented leader of the gold thieves who would rather die holding on to the bullion than surrender to the authorities.

59 BEHIND THE MASK (1946), Mon.

Dir. Phil Karlson; *Sc.* George Callahan; *Cast includes:* Kane Richmond, Barbara Reed, Tom Dugan, Joseph Crehan, George Chandler, Pierre Watkin.

Journalists are not always heroes in Hollywood dramas, as in this feeble entry in the Shadow mystery series. Sometimes they are victims or perpetrators or both. A murder interferes with the wedding of Kane Richmond, alias "The Shadow." About to marry Margot Lane (Barbara Reed), Richmond learns that Robert Shayne, a ruthless blackmailing columnist, has been killed by someone disguised as the Shadow. To protect his crime-fighter alter ego, Richmond investigates the murder. One trail leads to a disreputable nightclub whose only function is to fleece its patrons. Following several other incidents, he smashes a bookie operation and eventually unravels the murder. The final trail takes him to a newspaper office where he exposes the city editor as the head of a blackmailing scam. The characters were based on "The Shadow," a famous long-running weekly radio drama of the period.

60 BEHIND THE NEWS (1940), Rep.

Dir. Joseph Santley; *Sc.* Isabel Dawn, Boyce De Gaw; *Cast includes:* Lloyd Nolan, Doris Davenport, Frank Albertson, Robert Armstrong, Paul Harvey, Charles Halton.

Burned-out veteran reporter Lloyd Nolan, who has become a heavy drinker, is rehabilitated under the influence of neophyte newsman Frank Albertson in this drama. Together, they expose a major crime syndicate whose chief villain is none other than the city's district attorney. A predictable newspaper-crime tale, the film has many elements of this sub-genre, including the kibitzing of the cub reporter by his more experienced peers, a host of cynical journalists led by Nolan, and the devoted girlfriend of the drunken reporter. A routine remake appeared in 1955 titled *Headline Hunters*.

61 BEHIND THE RISING SUN (1943), RKO.

Dir. Edward Dmytryk; *Sc.* Emmett Lavery; *Cast includes:* Margo, Tom Neal, J. Carrol Naish, Robert Ryan, Gloria Holden.

This World War II drama, set chiefly in Japan, focuses on a Japanese family before and after the attack on Pearl Harbor. J. Carrol Naish, a newspaper publisher with important ties to government officials, rises to minister of propaganda. He believes in his country's aspirations of world conquest. His U.S.-educated son (Tom Neal), on the other hand, has many American friends and defends the American way of life. But in time he is indoctrinated with Japan's imperialistic ideas. He returns from the war against China as a strong supporter of his country while his father suspects Japan will be defeated by the U.S. Neal, reassigned as a pilot, goes to his death defending Japan against American planes during a raid over Tokyo. His father, disillusioned with Japan's political and military aims, takes his own life. Of his son's death, he writes: "To have died without reason is to have lived without reason." Of his own misguided life, he concludes: "One cannot build honor upon dishonor." The film describes a host of Japanese atrocities. Chinese civilians are brutalized, and their children forced into slave labor. Captured American civilians and pilots receive similar treatment. Many of the incidents depicted on the screen were based on a factual book written by James R. Young, a foreign correspondent for the International News Service and stationed in prewar Tokyo. One of the more interesting aspects of this wartime drama is its depiction of some Japanese, represented by Neal's enlightened newspaper-publishing father and Neal's ex-fiancée (Margo), who are opposed to their country's goals of conquest.

62 THE BELLE OF THE SEASON (1919), Metro.

Dir. S. Rankin Drew; *Sc.* S. Rankin Drew; *Cast includes:* Emmy Whalen, S.

Rankin Drew, Walter Hitchcock, John Macklin, Louis Wolheim.

Pretty socialite Emmy Whalen, as the title character, takes control of the family business and introduces changes that benefit the downtrodden workers in this social drama based on a poem by Ela Wheeler Wilcox. The former executors, she learns, had been exploiting the workers. She meets and falls in love with the young idealistic S. Rankin Drew, whose wealthy father owns a newspaper. He rescues her from bully Louis Wolheim, who later incites striking laborers to attack Whalen's executor. But Drew again comes to the rescue. Against his father's wishes, Drew donates $10,000 toward a much-needed settlement house in one of the poorest districts of the city. He suddenly disappears from sight when he reads a newspaper story about Whalen, but he later reconciles his differences with her and the couple are married.

63 BERLIN CORRESPONDENT (1942), TCF.

Dir. Eugene Forde; *Sc.* Steve Fisher, Jack Andrews; *Cast includes:* Virginia Gilmore, Dana Andrews, Mona Maris, Martin Kosleck, Sig Rumann, Kurt Katch.

This World War II drama takes place in Berlin prior to America's entry into the war. Dana Andrews, an American radio correspondent, comes into possession of highly secret Nazi war information. Constantly under guard by Nazis, especially while he is broadcasting, he has a difficult time getting the information out of the country. However, he manages this feat by smuggling the story past the Nazis in the form of a presumably harmless news story. Eventually he steals a plane and, taking with him a converted Nazi sympathizer (Virginia Gilmore), escapes to England. Martin Kosleck, who virtually made a career of impersonating Germans, portrays a high-ranking Nazi official who suspects Andrews.

64 BETWEEN THE LINES (1977), Midwest Film Production.

Dir. Joan Micklin Silver; *Sc.* Fred Barron; *Cast includes:* John Heard, Lindsay Crouse, Jeff Goldblum, Jill Eikenberry, Marilu Henner, Stephen Collins.

A publishing empire is about to buy a successful underground Boston newspaper in this disappointing superficial comedy drama. Meanwhile, staff members John Heard, Lindsay Crouse and others worry about the fate of their counter-culture tabloid and their own future. The film explores the private and professional lives of some of workers, including their interrelationships. Heard, a crack investigative reporter, and Crouse, the staff photographer, are romantically involved. Stephen Collins, a reporter in the midst of authoring a book, is romantically tied to Gwen Welles, another member of the staff. Conscientious Jeff Goldblum portrays a rock music reviewer who is underpaid. "It's not that I'm unhappy here," he admits to his publisher. "I'm fucking broke."

65 BEWARE OF LADIES (1937), Rep.

Dir. Irving Pichel; *Sc.* L. C. Dublin; *Cast includes:* Donald Cook, Judith Allen, George Meeker, Goodee Montgomery, Russell Hopton, William Newell.

Newspaper reporter Judith Allen, estranged from her useless husband, covers candidate Donald Cook, who is running for the office of district attorney, in this mildly entertaining comedy drama. She soon begins to fall in love with the candidate. Meanwhile, the rivalry between the two office seekers grows vicious. Cook's adversary uses a compromising photograph of the couple to discredit Cook. In addition, the opposing party stirs up Allen's weak husband to sue her for alienation of affections. Following these incidents, both Allen and Cook become entangled with racketeers and are finally rescued, with Cook ending up the winner of the election. Some of the awkward action sequences near the end of the film tend to invoke laughter rather than their intended suspense.

66 BEYOND A REASONABLE DOUBT (1956), RKO.

Dir. Fritz Lang; *Sc.* Douglas Morrow; *Cast includes:* Dana Andrews, Joan Fontaine, Sidney Blackmer, Barbara Nichols, Shepperd Strudwick, Arthur Franz.

Dana Andrews portrays a mystery writer who sets out to expose a flaw in the judicial system concerning circumstantial evidence in this dark, nerve-wracking drama. He permits himself to be falsely accused of murder. Crusading newspaper editor Sidney Blackmer, his future father-in-law and associate in the scheme, is the only other person who can prove his innocence. Blackmer is determined to prove the dangers of circumstantial evidence to the present district attorney who has virtually built his career on it. Unfortunately, the editor dies in a car accident, creating a life-threatening dilemma for the writer. Joan Fontaine, Andrews's fiancée, tries to save him and when that fails, she tries to get him pardoned—until, in a disarming and twist ending, she and others learn that he indeed had committed the murder. Several earlier films dealt with a similar theme, including, among others, *Circumstantial Evidence* (1935) and *The Man Who Dared* (1946).

67 BEYOND THE SACRAMENTO (1941), Col.

Dir. Lambert Hillyer; *Sc.* Luci Ward; *Cast includes:* Bill Elliott, Evelyn Keyes, Dub Taylor, John Dilson, Bradley Page, Frank LaRue.

Bill Elliott, portraying Wild Bill Hickok, exposes a pair of swindlers in this routine western, part of a series starring popular cowboy star Elliott. Saloon owner Bradley Page and newspaper publisher Frank LaRue, both inhabitants of the town of Lodestone, try to fleece its citizens by selling them questionable bonds. Dub Taylor suspects the pair and calls in his pal, Elliott, to investigate. Elliott sneaks into LaRue's printing office one night, sets up a front page exposing both men and their phony bonds and distributes the paper to all. This puts an end to the scheme. When asked how he knows so much about the newspaper field, Elliott replies, "My first job was as a printer's devil."

68 BIG BAD MAMA II (1987), Concorde.

Dir. Jim Wynorski; *Sc.* R. J. Robinson, Jim Wynorski; *Cast includes:* Angie Dickinson, Robert Culp, Danielle Brisebois, Julie McCullogh, Bruce Glover, Jeff Yahger.

Philadelphia reporter Robert Culp joins Angie Dickinson, as the tough title character, on her kidnapping escapade in this meaningless action drama set during the Great Depression. Dickinson, in her attempt to hurt Bruce Glover, who is running for Governor of Texas, kidnaps Jeff Yahger, his son. Culp is interested in wooing Dickinson while exploiting the story of her trail of crime. To give the senseless film some sort of "social significance," the plot has Dickinson siding with a group of striking miners and a community of homeless unemployed. Car chases, some machine-gunning and a few nude sequences are included in this hodge-podge of exploitation.

69 THE BIG BOSS (1913), Reliance.

Dir. Frederick Sullivan; *Sc.* Lu Senarens; *Cast includes:* George Siegmann, Irving Cummings, Muriel Ostriche, A. Balfour, E. P. Sullivan.

"Big Boss" politician George Siegmann offers to award an aqueduct contract to financially desperate A. Balfour—only if his daughter, Muriel Ostriche, agrees to marry Siegmann in this early drama about political graft. Ostriche, however, is promised to reporter Irving Cummings, who has been assigned to expose the prevalence of corruption that has gripped the city. The young couple use a Dictaphone to gain evidence of Siegmann's duplicity. But the crooked politician discovers the device and pummels the reporter. Balfour comes to Cummings's rescue and persuades Siegmann to reform and allow the contract to go to the lowest bidder.

70 THE BIG BOSS (1941), Col.

Dir. Charles Barton; *Sc.* Howard J. Green; *Cast includes:* Otto Kruger, John Litel, Gloria Dickson, Don Beddoe, Robert Fiske, George Lessey.

Gloria Dickson and Don Beddoe portray reporters in this familiar drama in which Otto Kruger and John Litel are orphan brothers who have been separated early in life. They meet years later, each on opposite sides of the law and politics. Kruger emerges as a corrupt politician while Litel has risen to the position of a reform governor. The inevitable confrontations occur between the two leads, with law and order prevailing. Cynical news hound Beddoe early suspects the crooked motives of Kruger and helps to bring him down.

71 BIG BROWN EYES (1936), Par.

Dir. Raoul Walsh; *Sc.* Bert Hanlon, Raoul Walsh; *Cast includes:* Joan Bennett, Cary Grant, Walter Pidgeon, Lloyd Nolan, Isabel Jewell, Douglas Fowley.

Joan Bennett, as a manicurist-turned-reporter, joins police officer Cary Grant in smashing a gang of jewel thieves and murderers in this minor drama. When Bennett loses her job in a barber shop, she is somehow hired instantaneously as a reporter and helps her boyfriend Grant in his investigation of gang leader Walter Pidgeon and murderer Lloyd Nolan. Comedy relief is handled by Douglas Fowley, one of Pidgeon's underlings, and society woman Marjorie Gateson. Bennett contributes substantially to the comedy with her own wisecracking—a side of her that makes detective Grant rather uneasy.

72 THE BIG CARNIVAL (1951) *see* Ace in the Hole (1951).

73 THE BIG CLOCK (1948), Par.

Dir. John Farrow; *Sc.* Jonathan Latimer; *Cast includes:* Ray Milland, Charles Laughton, Maureen O'Sullivan, George Macready, Rita Johnson, Elsa Lanchester.

Ray Milland, talented crime magazine editor with a penchant for unmasking killers, tries to solve a murder in which all the clues point to him in this clever, convoluted and highly suspenseful murder mystery stylishly directed and based on the novel by Kenneth Fearing. Charles Laughton, Milland's pompous publisher who is obsessed with time and clocks, is the actual killer. He tries to pin the crime on Milland, who finally confronts his boss with the truth. At this point Laughton intends to make his assistant, the calculating George Macready, the fall guy. When Macready objects, Laughton shoots him and, while attempting to escape, plunges to his death down an elevator shaft. The film offers a fascinating look into how crime reporters track down clues, suspects and other pieces of information to help them solve a case. A remake titled *No Way Out* appeared in 1987, starring Kevin Costner and Gene Hackman.

74 BIG NEWS (1929), Pathé.

Dir. Gregory La Cava; *Sc.* Walter De Leon; *Cast includes:* Robert Armstrong, Carole Lombard, Tom Kennedy, Warner Richmond, Wade Boteler, Sam Hardy.

Reporter Robert Armstrong is falsely accused of killing a newspaper owner in this pedestrian drama. He investigates a drug ring he believes is headed by Sam Hardy, a local speakeasy owner who is responsible for Armstrong's being fired. The intrepid reporter, however, returns with a confession incriminating Hardy in a gangland murder. When the speakeasy owner overhears Armstrong's conversation, he kills newspaper editor Charles Sellon and

Crime reporter Ray Milland (2nd from r.) is suspected of murder while his employer Charles Laughton (2nd from l.) listens to George Macready's suspicions in John Farrow's drama, *The Big Clock* (1948).

frames Armstrong by leaving the reporter's knife behind. But a Dictaphone in the dead man's office exonerates the reporter and condemns the murderer. Carole Lombard, Armstrong's wife and rival reporter for another paper, struggles to keep her husband away from his excessive drinking. This was the first sound feature to portray a woman reporter. The film, noted by contemporary reviewers for its realistic newspaper settings, was released in both a silent and sound version. This was one of several dramas that embraced the latest popular scientific and mechanical gadgets of the period. For example, the Dictaphone device was also used in *Back to Liberty* (1928).

75 THE BIG NIGHT (1951), UA.

Dir. Joseph Losey; *Sc.* Joseph Losey, Stanley Ellin; *Cast includes:* John Barrymore Jr., Preston Foster, Howard St. John, Howard Chamberlain, Joan Lorring, Dorothy Comingore.

When sports columnist Howard St. John beats up Preston Foster, the father of John Barrymore Jr., the son, seeking vengeance, searches for the writer in this gloomy drama based on the novel *Dreadful Summit* by Stanley Ellis. Foster, a widow and former boxer, put up no resistance. Young Barrymore's journey takes him into a seedy world of sleazy hotels and watering holes where he finally confronts St. John. The columnist then reluctantly reveals the dark side of the young man's father—a side he had never known.

76 THE BIG NOISE (1928), FN.

Dir. Allan Dwan; *Sc.* Tom Geraghty; *Cast includes:* Chester Conklin, Alice White, Bodil Rosing, Sam Hardy, Jack Egan, Ned Sparks.

Innocent subway guard Chester Conklin

becomes the victim of a sensational press in this entertaining satirical comedy based on a story by Ben Hecht. Involved in a subway accident and hospitalized, Conklin is exploited by both reporters and politicians. For instance, when the news hounds and photographers arrive at Conklin's living quarters and learn that he has only one grown daughter, they round up some tenement urchins and photograph them with Conklin's wife for added human interest. When he awakens in the hospital and sees the picture, the bemused Conklin turns to the nurse and asks: "How long have I been here?" He later goes to the campaign headquarters of the candidate promoted by the newspaper and learns that both have exploited him. Meanwhile, his daughter marries the son of a dairy farmer. The couple then invite Conklin to help manage the farm.

77 THE BIG SHOT (1937), RKO.

Dir. Edward Killy; *Sc.* Arthur T. Horman, Bert Granet; *Cast includes:* Guy Kibbee, Cora Witherspoon, Dorothy Moore, Gordon Jones, Russell Hicks, Frank M. Thomas.

Guy Kibbee plays a small-town veterinarian who inherits a fortune and business interests, including an organization which controls various city rackets in this comedy. The rackets are run by Russell Hicks, who wants the naive Kibbee to sign everything over to him, including millions of dollars. Kibbee, meanwhile, trying to perform a social service to please his nagging wife, gives financial backing to a newspaper about to expose the crooked organization. When Kibbee congratulates one of his bookkeepers at his proficiency, the man responds, "I picked it up while I was doin' a stretch in Atlanta." The corrupt Hicks immediately informs Kibbee that "the best bookkeepers come from the South." The broad comedy works well in the film which also takes a swing at public indifference. A crusading newspaper publisher exclaims: "A city of 5,000 worms are bullied by 500 rats!"

78 THE BIG TIP OFF (1955), AA.

Dir. Frank McDonald; *Sc.* Steve Fisher; *Cast includes:* Richard Conte, Constance Smith, Bruce Bennett, Cathy Downs, James Millican, Dick Bennett.

Richard Conte, a small-town journalist, is duped by smalltime hoodlum Bruce Bennett in this murky drama whose flashbacks only add to the confusion of the plot. Con artist Bennett poses as a respectable citizen who organizes telethons and ends up scooping large portions of the take for his own use. Conte witnesses Bennett murder his secretary who is about to expose her crooked employer. The con artist then frames Conte for the crime. The writer finally extricates himself from his dilemma while Bennett ends up paying for his crimes.

79 BIG TOWN (1932), Invincible.

Dir. Arthur Hoerl; *Sc.* Arthur Hoerl; *Cast includes:* Lester Vail, Frances Dade, John Miltern, Geoffrey Bryant, Edith Broder, Alan Brooks.

A crusading newspaper editor exposes corrupt members of a vice committee in this unexciting drama that blends the newspaper genre with that of the crime film. The crooked members extend their villainy from extortion to murder, killing those who refuse to pay tribute. The large cast includes several veteran performers of the silent era. Despite its title, the film is not part of the Big Town newspaper series released by Paramount in the 1940s.

80 BIG TOWN (1947), Par.

Dir. William C. Thomas; *Sc.* Geoffrey Homes; *Cast includes:* Philip Reed, Hillary Brooke, Robert Lowery, Byron Barr, Veda Ann Borg, Nana Bryant.

Crusading newspaper editor Philip Reed uses a series of articles to ensnare a murderer who is terrorizing the town in this disappointing drama based on the popular radio program of the period. Reed plays editor Steve Wilson who has earlier been accused of practicing yellow journalism.

This was the first entry in a short-lived series drawn from the "Big Town" radio show.

81 BIG TOWN AFTER DARK (1947), Par.

Dir. William C. Thomas; *Sc.* Whitman Chambers; *Cast includes:* Philip Reed, Hillary Brooke, Richard Travis, Anne Gillis, Vince Barnett, Joe Sawyer.

Fighting newspaper editor Philip Reed exposes the town's crime ring which engages in kidnapping and other wrongdoings in this minor drama based on the popular contemporary radio show "Big Town." Reed's publisher is kidnapped while Anne Gillis's uncle is being blackmailed by the mob. Police reporter Hillary Brooke assists the crusading editor in smashing the gang's activities, which also include running crooked poker clubs.

82 BIG TOWN CZAR (1939), U.

Dir. Arthur Lubin; *Sc.* Edmund L. Hartmann; *Cast includes:* Ed Sullivan, Barton MacLane, Tom Brown, Esther Dale, Eve Arden, Jack LaRue.

A condemned man goes to the electric chair regretting his past activities in this minor cautionary drama based on a story by newspaper columnist Ed Sullivan, who appears as himself in the film. Barton MacLane portrays the title character, a racketeer who fought his way up from the tenements to become a powerful gang boss. Tom Brown, as his kid brother, drops out of college and, although MacLane protests, joins the gang. The boy is killed by a rival mob, and MacLane, after a gun battle, is arrested and convicted of murder. Columnist Sullivan provides a "crime-does-not-pay" epilogue to this timeworn tale.

83 BIG TOWN GIRL (1937), TCF.

Dir. Alfred Werker; *Sc.* Lou Breslow, John Patrick, Robert Ellis, Helen Logan; *Cast includes:* Claire Trevor, Donald Woods, Alan Dinehart, Alan Baxter, Murray Alper, Spencer Charters.

Claire Trevor portrays the title character, a nightclub singer who is on the run from her husband, an escaped convict, in this fair drama. She masquerades as a French countess as a means of eluding him. Later, she rises to radio stardom, but curious reporter Donald Woods discovers her secret and falls in love with her. Alan Dinehart, her manager, provides comic relief as he tries to protect her identity from Woods. Alan Baxter portrays the menacing husband.

84 BIG TOWN SCANDAL (1948), Par.

Dir. William C. Thomas; *Sc.* Milton Raison; *Cast includes:* Philip Reed, Hillary Brooke, Stanley Clements, Darryl Hickman, Carl "Alfalfa" Switzer, Roland Dupree.

Battling newspaper editor Philip Reed helps to reform paroled youths while exposing a professional gambling racket in this familiar drama based on the popular radio show "Big Town." Reed sets up a youth center to help rehabilitate a group of young offenders, but one of them, Stanley Clements, is influential in corrupting several of the others. In the process, the boys end up reforming Clements, who finally exposes a gang of crooks who have killed one of the teens.

85 THE BLACK CIRCLE (1919), World.

Dir. Frank Reicher; *Sc.* Giles R. Warren; *Cast includes:* Creighton Hale, Virginia Valli, Jack Drumier, Walter Horton, Clarette Clare, Edwin Denison, John Davison.

A small-town newspaper is the focus of this drama which features a variety of characters, including swindlers, moonshiners, a crooked prosecutor, and a railroaded sheriff. To expose these elements, Lucy Baird, portrayed by Virginia Valli, and Andrew Ferguson, played by Creighton Hale, take over the town paper. They receive a note emblazoned with a black circle as a death threat, but they are undeterred. After a number of thrilling action sequences, a gang of crooks is rounded up, the prosecutor is exposed and the innocent sheriff is exonerated.

86 BLACK DIAMONDS (1940), U.

Dir. Christy Cabanne; *Sc.* Sam Robins, Clarence Upson Young; *Cast includes:* Richard Arlen, Andy Devine, Kathryn Adams, Mary Treen, Paul Fix, Pat Flaherty.

Inquisitive newspaper reporter Richard Arlen exposes a crooked inspector responsible for hazardous working conditions in a local coal mine in this routine drama. Arlen's curiosity is aroused about a possible scam when he returns to his home town and learns that his father has been hurt in a mine blast. Kathryn Adams provides the love interest for the reporter. The film is a loose remake of a British production released in 1932.

87 BLACK LIKE ME (1964), Continental.

Dir. Carl Lerner; *Sc.* Carl Lerner, Gerda Lerner; *Cast includes:* James Whitmore, Sorel Brooks, Robert Gerringer, Al Freeman Jr., Roscoe Lee Browne, Clifton James.

James Whitmore portrays a white writer who poses as an African American for a series of magazine articles on race relations in America in this flawed drama based on the book by John Howard Griffin. As a black man, Whitmore, with his self-applied dark skin stain, hitchhikes across several states confronting various Americans who often question him about the sexual activities of his (black) race. This obvious exploitation angle is just one of the weaknesses of the film. Another is Whitmore's northern accent—although he is supposed to be from the South. Perhaps the most glaring weakness is his continuous use of his real name during his research. Meanwhile, his articles using his name for the byline are being published nationally with his pictures as both a white and an African American. Yet no one he meets ever suspects him. The film was one of many released during the 1960s to deal with racial prejudice, including, among others, the western *Sergeant Rutledge* (1960), the psychological drama *Pressure Point* (1962), the Southern rural drama *To Kill a Mockingbird* (1962) and the racially charged *In the Heat of the Night* (1967).

88 BLACKWELL'S ISLAND (1939), WB.

Dir. William McGann; *Sc.* Crane Wilbur; *Cast includes:* John Garfield, Rosemary Lane, Dick Purcell, Victor Jory, Stanley Fields, Morgan Conway.

This prison exposé is based on conditions found on New York's Welfare Island in 1934 by the New York Commissioner of Corrections. The drama depicts the corruption and abuses of a few officials who turned the penal institution into a virtual country club controlled by gangsters and murderers. Stanley Fields portrays a gang leader who orders the brutal killing of a policeman and a barge owner. Crusading reporter John Garfield's stories help to put Fields and his gang behind bars. To help prove Fields directed the murders, Garfield volunteers to go under cover to the same prison. His efforts result in a raid on the prison which ends the corrupt conditions. In addition, the ruthless Fields gets his come-uppance.

89 BLESSED EVENT (1932), WB.

Dir. Roy Del Ruth; *Sc.* Howard Green; *Cast includes:* Lee Tracy, Mary Brian, Allen Jenkins, Ruth Donnelly, Ned Sparks, Dick Powell.

Unscrupulous New York gossip columnist Lee Tracy double-crosses Mary Brian, a young nightclub singer, in this fast-paced, absorbing comedy based on the play by Manuel Seff and Forrest Wilson. Tracy, portraying a Walter Winchell-type columnist who was popular at the time, is drunk with his own power. Ruth Donnelly plays Tracy's comical, world-weary and wisecracking secretary; Ned Sparks an irascible veteran reporter; and Dick Powell a young, repugnant crooner. Some film historians consider this otherwise obscure newspaper comedy, with its satirical barbs aimed at radio, newscasters and minorities, one of the best of the genre. Tracy became one of the most popular portrayers of the fast-talking, wisecracking big-city reporter during the 1930s. He starred or was featured in a variety of films, including among others *Born Reckless* (1930), *Doctor X* (1932), *Advice to the Lovelorn* (1933) and *I'll Tell the World* (1934). Another landmark in this film is Emma Dunn's line: "Well, I'll be damned." The remark, with its "shocking" use of the word "damn," predates Clark Gable's famous last line in *Gone With the Wind* (1939), in which he says to Vivien Leigh, "Frankly my dear, I don't give a damn."

90 BLONDE FOR A DAY (1946), PRC.

Dir. Sam Newfield; *Sc.* Fred Myton; *Cast includes:* Hugh Beaumont, Kathryn Adams, Cy Kendall, Marjorie Hoshelle, Richard Fraser, Sonia Sorel.

Hugh Beaumont, as private eye Michael Shayne, becomes embroiled with several dangerous women while investigating the strange shooting of a reporter friend in this drama based on the story "Mike Shayne, Detective" by Brett Halliday. The investigation soon entails multiple murders in a neighboring apartment house. The sleuth ends up rescuing the reporter from being bumped off by a gang of hoodlums. The news hound had been pursuing the gang's connection to the series of killings. Kathryn Adams portrays Shayne's secretary.

91 BLONDE ICE (1948), FC.

Dir. Jack Bernhard; *Sc.* Kenneth Gamet; *Cast includes:* Leslie Brooks, Robert Paige, Walter Sande, John Holland, James Griffith, Russ Vincent.

This is another example of a journalist who is definitely not a credit to the profession. Demented society editor Leslie Brooks, who seems to delight in scandal and notoriety, engages in killing her lovers and husbands over a span of years in this offbeat drama. Psychologist David Leonard eventually induces the high-strung Brooks to confess to her deadly affairs. However, she accidentally goes to her death trying to escape from the police. The film is an early example of a cycle of dramas featuring deadly females that were popular throughout the 1940s and 1950s.

92 BLONDES AT WORK (1938), WB.

Dir. Frank McDonald; *Sc.* Albert DeMond; *Cast includes:* Glenda Farrell, Barton MacLane, Tom Kennedy, Rosella Towne, Donald Briggs, John Ridgely.

Glenda Farrell returns as the wisecracking reporter who continually outsmarts the police department in the Torchy Blane crime comedy series. This average entry has her getting tips from her bemused boyfriend, police lieutenant McBride (Barton MacLane), in a rather indirect way. It seems Tom Kennedy, his slow-witted chauffeur, keeps a very up-to-date diary about the present investigation which Torchy gains access to in her quest to unravel the murder of a department store owner. The film offers plenty of laughs.

93 BLOOD ON THE SUN (1945), UA.

Dir. Frank Lloyd; *Sc.* Lester Cole; *Cast includes:* James Cagney, Sylvia Sidney, Rosemary De Camp, Wallace Ford, Robert Armstrong, John Emery.

James Cagney portrays a tough American newspaper editor in pre-World War II Japan who discovers a Japanese plot for world conquest in this tense drama of intrigue. The Japanese police try to retrieve the controversial plan before it is made public. Finally, it is up to Cagney to smuggle the important document out of the country. Sylvia Sidney, a double agent, is employed by Japanese officials to recover the plans from Cagney. In reality, she is working for the Chinese who want to expose the Japanese militarists. In the final moments Cagney must run a gauntlet of

Japanese secret police waiting to stop him from entering the American embassy. A bullet wounds him, but an American official comes out of the embassy in time to save the editor's life. Embarrassed by his failure, the head of the Japanese secret police tries to smooth over the awkward incident. The self-righteous embassy official declares: "The United States Government doesn't settle for a deal." Colonel Tojo (Robert Armstrong), another Japanese official who had tried to kill Cagney, offers his hand in friendship. "You have saying, 'Forgive your enemies.' I am willing," he says. "Sure, forgive your enemies," Cagney replies defiantly, "but first get even." Released during the last months of World War II, the drama joins the long list of anti-Japanese propaganda films of that period. The infamous Tanaka Plan, or Tanaka Memorial, was an actual document stolen in 1927. Exposed in the international press, it included detailed maps and other information revealing Japan's secret plans about a future war with China, Korea and the U.S. It even told of Japan's plot to bomb America's naval base at Pearl Harbor. The plan was so outlandish at the time that no one treated it seriously.

94 THE BLUE GARDENIA (1953), WB.

Dir. Fritz Lang; *Sc.* Charles Hoffman; *Cast includes:* Anne Baxter, Richard Conte, Ann Sothern, Raymond Burr, Jeff Donnell, Richard Erdman.

After columnist Richard Conte cajoles Anne Baxter into confessing to a murder, he begins to have doubts about her guilt in this familiar drama based on a story by Vera Caspary. Baxter explains to him that during a blind date with Raymond Burr, she was forced to protect herself by striking him with a poker when he tried to rape her. She then fled from his apartment. Conte later tracks down another woman who has just attempted suicide and who confesses to killing Burr after telling him that she is carrying his child. The journalist and Baxter then continue their romance. The title refers to a Hollywood restaurant where the couple meet.

95 BOMBAY CLIPPER (1942), U.

Dir. John Rawlins; *Sc.* Roy Chanslor, Stanley Rubin; *Cast includes:* William Gargan, Irene Hervey, Charles Lang, Maria Montez, Lloyd Corrigan, Mary Gordon.

Millions of dollars' worth of industrial diamonds, necessary for England's war effort, becomes the focal point of this drama set during World War II. American foreign correspondent William Gargan and his wife Irene Hervey, as passengers aboard a plane traveling from Bombay to San Francisco, find themselves entangled in a hijacking. Truman Bradley, the leader of a group of international spies, forcibly takes over control of the clipper. His target is the large supply of diamonds that are aboard. They are India's gift to embattled Britain. Gargan soon springs into action and disarms the master spy, thereby rescuing the other innocent passengers and the vital cargo.

96 BONDAGE (1917), Bluebird.

Dir. Ida May Park; *Sc.* Ida May Park; *Cast includes:* Dorothy Phillips, Gretchen Lederer, Gertrude Astor, William Stowell, J. G. McLaughlin, Jean Porter.

Young reporter Dorothy Phillips, recently arriving in New York City from a small town, becomes a victim of the Greenwich Village bohemian night life in this undistinguished silent drama based on a story by Edna Kenton. She meets lawyer William Stowell, who lambastes her lifestyle. She then turns to a magazine editor who falls in love with her after she writes a satire about the attorney's prudish morality. They plan to marry, but the editor suddenly elopes with someone else. The despondent Phillips, now faint from hunger, meets Stowell, who helps to restore her back to health. They marry, but after only one year she begins to miss her former night life in the Village. She returns to her old haunts where she sees the editor who is now a widower. Although she finds him abhorrent, she agrees to stay with him. Again Stowell finds her wandering in the streets and again he takes her back. He then starts out to pummel the editor for maltreating Phillips.

97 BORN FOR TROUBLE
(1945) *see* Murder in the Big House (1942).

98 BORN RECKLESS
(1930), Fox.

Dir. John Ford; *Sc.* Dudley Nichols; *Cast includes:* Edmund Lowe, Catherine Dale Owen, Lee Tracy, Marguerite Churchill, William Harrigan, Warren Hymer.

An Italian-American gangster turns war hero in this drama based on the novel *Louis Beretti* by Donald Henderson Clarke. Edmund Lowe, as Louis Beretti, a thief caught in the act, is offered a prison sentence or a hitch in the army during World War I. This was the result of a newspaper crusade kicked off by tough reporter Lee Tracy. Beretti opts for the latter and returns a hero. He abandons his former criminal life after meeting and falling in love with socialite Catherine Dale Owen. When his vindictive rival, Warren Hymer, kidnaps Owen's little daughter, Lowe rescues the child and kills Hymer. Impressive underworld settings enhanced this film about rival gangs and rehabilitation which was remade with Brian Donlevy in 1937.

99 BORN YESTERDAY
(1950), Col.

Dir. George Cukor; *Sc.* Albert Mannheimer; *Cast includes:* Judy Holliday, Broderick Crawford, William Holden, Howard St. John.

Boorish millionaire junk dealer Broderick Crawford hires suave newspaperman William Holden to instill some culture into Judy Holliday, Crawford's mistress, in this bright comedy based on the play by Garson Kanin. Set in Washington, D.C., the spicy dialogue and humorous situations blend well with the satirical allusions to honesty, integrity and democratic principles. Holliday, as the quintessential dumb blonde, soars over her two leading men, a performance which won her the Best Actress Oscar for the year. She is thrown off base by the cultivated demeanor of her handsome tutor. "Let me ask you something," she says to Holden, getting right down to basics. "Are you one of these talkers or would you be interested in a little action?" Holliday, dominated by Crawford, finally stands up to him. "This country and its institutions," she proudly announces, "belong to the people who inhibit it." She even goes so far as to criticize his personal habits. "You eat terrible," she rails at him, "you got no manners! That's another thing—picking your teeth. You're just not couth!" At one point, a U.S. Congressman and his wife visit Crawford and the untutored Holliday in their Washington hotel suite. "Too bad the Supreme Court is not in session," the Congressman's wife says in an effort to strike up a conversation with Judy. "You'd love that." "So what is it?" Judy innocently asks. A fair remake appeared in 1993, with Melanie Griffith, John Goodman and Don Johnson.

100 BORN YESTERDAY
(1993), Hollywood Pictures.

Dir. Luis Mandoki; *Sc.* Douglas McGrath; *Cast includes:* Melanie Griffith, John Goodman, Don Johnson, Edward Herrmann, Max Perlich, Michael Ensign.

Playwright Garson Kanin's comedy about a crude tycoon and his blonde mistress turns out to be a fairly entertaining remake of the 1950 original film. Wealthy John Goodman hires sophisticated reporter Don Johnson to help cultivate Melanie Griffith, and he enlightens her in matters of social graces and government. But his pupil proves to be not so dumb a blonde as Goodman and Johnson had originally thought. In fact, she educates both men in some areas. Johnson eventually wins Griffith's love, with gruff Goodman, the loser. Goodman is portrayed more of a canny businessman and less of a predator, as painted by Broderick Crawford in the original film. The updating of this remake may be reflected in such lines as the following in which Griffith responds to news of the collapse of the Eastern Bloc. "When the block collapsed," she asks, "were people hurt, or was it just property damage?"

101 BORROWED HERO (1941), Mon.

Dir. Lewis Collins; *Sc.* Earle Snell; *Cast includes:* Alan Baxter, Florence Rice, John Hamilton, Stanley Andrews, Constance Worth, Wilma Francis.

Knowledgeable newspaper reporter Florence Rice assists young prosecutor Alan Baxter smash the city's widespread rackets in this familiar drama. Baxter, who has been suddenly drafted into the assignment, finally destroys the main syndicate, but only after learning that the chief crime czar in reality is John Hamilton, who has been posing as the social leader of a reform movement. Ironically, Hamilton has been publicly needling Baxter for not ridding the city of its criminal element.

102 BOWERY CHAMPS (1944), Mon.

Dir. William Beaudine; *Sc.* Earle Snell; *Cast includes:* Leo Gorcey, Huntz Hall, Billy Benedict, Jimmy Strand, Bobby Jordan, Anne Sterling.

Newspaper copyboy Leo Gorcey and his gang of East Side Kids turn reporters to help clear Evelyn Brent of a murder charge in this comedy drama, an above-average entry in the popular East Side comedy series. The boys hide Brent, the former wife of the murdered man, until they establish that the real killers are Ian Keith and Thelma White. Jimmy Strand portrays a police reporter in love with Anne Sterling. Gorcey and Huntz Hall, as usual, handle most of the comedy and slapstick.

103 BRENDA STARR (1990), New World.

Dir. Robert Ellis Miller; *Sc.* Noreen Stone, James David Buchanan, Della Ephron; *Cast includes:* Brooke Shields, Timothy Dalton, Tony Peck, Diana Scarwid, Nestor Serrano, Jeffrey Tambor.

Brooke Shields portrays the title character, a hard-working, tireless reporter based on the comic strip by Dale Messick, in this confusing adventure fantasy. The inane plot has Shields involved in pursuing Diana Scarwid, a Nazi scientist hiding in the jungles of South America. Scarwid has developed a new fuel. During her pursuit, Shields clashes with two Russian spies and meets the handsome Timothy Dalton, a mysterious hero who rescues her on several occasions. Major confusion arises when artist Tony Peck enters the plot to persuade his reporter character to return to his comic strip. Like other failed films based on comic strips (*Popeye, Captain America*), *Starr* falls short as a result of weaknesses in its plot, humor and characters.

104 BRENDA STARR, REPORTER (1945) serial, Col.

Dir. Wallace Fox; *Cast includes:* Joan Woodbury, Kane Richmond, Douglas Fowley, Syd Saylor, Joe Devlin, George Meeker.

Joan Woodbury portrays the title character, a determined, intrepid newspaper journalist in this thirteen-chapter serial based on the popular comic strip created by Dale Messick. As she rushes to get her scoop and bring down big-city gangsters and other villains, she weekly finds herself in a life-threatening dilemma. However, she is often rescued by her equally intrepid friend, Kane Richmond. Character player Syd Saylor provides the comedy relief. The serial probably benefited from the background of director Wallace Fox, a former newspaper editor.

105 BRIDE OF THE MONSTER (1955), Banner.

Dir. Ed Wood Jr.; *Sc.* Alex Gordon, Ed Wood Jr.; *Cast includes:* Bela Lugosi, Tor Johnson, Tony McCoy, Loretta King.

Overly curious newspaper reporter Loretta King investigates the demented Dr. Varnoff in this ineffectual, very low budget horror film. Bela Lugosi, as the scientist, has captured twelve victims on whom he wants to experiment. Using atomic energy, he intends to transform his captives into supermen. "Home. I have no home," he rationalizes his behavior at one point. "Hunted, despised, living like an animal. The jungle is my home. For twenty years I have lived in this jungle hell. I was classed as a madman, a charlatan. Outlawed in the world of science, which had previously hailed me as a genius. Now here in this jungle hell, I have proved that I was right." Lugosi also threatens the life of the reporter in his swamp-bound mansion. Director Ed Wood Jr., who became known for his schlock films, was the subject of the award-winning feature *Ed Wood*, with Johnny Depp as the title character and Martin Landau portraying the pathetic drug-addicted character actor Lugosi.

106 THE BRIDE WORE CRUTCHES (1941), TCF.

Dir. Shepard Traube; *Sc.* Ed Verdier; *Cast includes:* Lynn Roberts, Ted North, Edgar Kennedy, Robert Armstrong, Lionel Stander, Richard Lane.

Ted North, a hard-working young newspaperman, witnesses a bank hold-up in this fast-paced hackneyed action drama. The not-too-bright reporter, influenced by fellow journalist Lynn Roberts, decides to track down the bank robbers. North works himself into the confidence of the gang and eventually turns them over to the authorities. Roberts, who originally urged him to pursue the gang, is thoroughly impressed. Several otherwise fine comic character actors, including Edgar Kennedy as the stereotypical dumb cop, fail to raise the entertainment value of the film.

107 BRILLIANT MARRIAGE (1936), Invincible.

Dir. Phil Rosen; *Sc.* Paul Perez; *Cast includes:* Joan Marsh, Ray Walker, Inez Courtney, John Marlowe, Doris Lloyd, Ann Codee.

Scheming newspaper reporter Ray Walker almost succeeds in ruining the life of socialite Joan Marsh in this colorless drama based on the novel by Ursula Parrott. When an exposé of her parents' past comes to light, Marsh seeks escape, comfort and affection in Walker, who ends up double-crossing her. Ann Codee, an ex-convict with blackmail on her mind, is responsible for exposing the dark past of Marsh's parents. Meanwhile, John Marlowe, a wealthy friend who loves Marsh, remains faithful while others have turned against her. He rescues Marsh just as she is about to make the mistake of running off with the globe-trotting and treacherous Walker. Marlowe then marries Marsh.

108 BROADCAST NEWS (1987), TCF.

Dir. James L. Brooks; *Sc.* James L. Brooks; *Cast includes:* William Hurt, Albert Brooks, Holly Hunter, Robert Prosky, Lois Chiles, Joan Cusack.

William Hurt, Albert Brooks and Holly Hunter portray different kinds of television reporters in this entertaining and informative character study about some of the people engaged in TV broadcasting. Hurt is a canny ex-sportscaster who uses his charm and instincts to capture an audience while sometimes manipulating the facts. Hunter, who loves Hurt but questions his methods, is a brilliant reporter often working on the edge. The idealistic Brooks, who also doesn't think much of Hurt's methods or depth of reporting, comments on Hurt's negative influence. "What do you think the devil is going to look like if he's around?" he remarks to Hunter. "He'll be attractive and he'll be nice and helpful and he'll get a job where he influences a great God-fearing nation...." Brooks yearns for a shot at being an anchorman instead of just writing for someone else. But when he gets the chance (in a funny and sad scene), he blows it by showing his nervousness and lack of presence before the TV cameras. "Wouldn't this be a great world," he wonders out loud to Hunter, "if insecurity and desperation made us more attractive?"

109 BROADWAY BIG SHOT (1942), PRC.

Dir. William Beaudine; *Sc.* Martin Mooney; *Cast includes:* Ralph Byrd, Virginia Vale, William Halligan, Dick Rush, Herbert Rawlinson, Cecile Weston.

Reporter Ralph Byrd, stepping out of his more popular role as Dick Tracy, goes under cover as a convict to get a big story in this familiar low-budget comedy drama. Sentenced on a false charge, he is easily accepted by fellow prison inmates and succeeds in his mission, along with winning the love of Virginia Vale, the warden's daughter. In a failed comedy attempt, Byrd takes charge of the prison football team—a sequence better handled and with more hilarious results in such films as *M*A*S*H* (1970), with Elliott Gould and Donald Sutherland, and *The Longest Yard* (1974), starring Burt Reynolds.

110 BROADWAY MELODY OF 1936 (1935), MGM.

Dir. Roy Del Ruth; *Sc.* Jack McGowan, Sid Silvers; *Cast includes:* Jack Benny, Eleanor Powell, Robert Taylor, Una Merkel, Sid Silvers, Buddy Ebsen.

Jack Benny portrays a Walter Winchell-type columnist who tries to frame show producer Robert Taylor by using dancer Eleanor Powell in this musical comedy whose music and comedy add up to more than the thin plot. While Powell demonstrates her exceptional tap dancing, the laughs are largely supplied by publicity agent Sid Silvers. "I can speak French," Silvers boasts to columnist Benny, and proceeds to utter: "Si, si, señor." "That's Spanish," Benny corrects him. "Gee," the astonished Silvers utters, "I can speak Spanish, too." At another point, the columnist comments to Silvers that when a rich socialite and a Broadway producer flirt with each other, "one of them's got something the other one wants." "Same as in The Bronx," Silvers quips. In another scene, a man determined to get on the Broadway stage approaches Silvers. "What do you do?" Silvers inquires. "I snore." "Oh, you're part of the audience," Silvers quips.

111 BROKEN BARRIERS (1928), Excellent Pictures.

Dir. Burton King; *Sc.* Isadore Bernstein; *Cast includes:* Helene Costello, Gaston Glass, Joseph Girard, Frank Beal, Carl Stockdale, Frank Hagney.

Star newspaper reporter Gaston Glass discloses a cover-up of a dead mayoral candidate, but the story is never printed in this offbeat drama. A cowardly mayoral candidate, faced with exposure, opts not to run. But political boss Joseph Girard threatens the timid soul at the point of a gun. The candidate suddenly dies of a heart attack, and Girard is forced to make it seem that the man died as the result of a car accident. Glass discovers the deception, but his editor quashes the story as a present to the reporter who is about to marry Helene Costello, the daughter of the political boss.

112 THE BROKEN COIN (1915) serial, U.

Dir. Francis Ford; *Sc.* Grace Cunard; *Cast includes:* Francis Ford, Grace Cunard, Harry Mann, Eddie Polo, John Ford, Mina Cunard.

Two parts of a coin which when put together hold the secret of a vast fortune are coveted by various characters seeking either fame or fortune in this 22-episode serial. Grace Cunard, as a reporter, sees a good story in solving the mystery while others dream of the wealth the coin can bring. The problem is that each half is worthless without the other. Director Francis Ford portrays a Count who also desires the coin. His brother, John Ford, has a small role in the serial.

113 BUCKSHOT JOHN (1915), Par.

Dir. Hobart Bosworth; *Sc.* Hetty Grey;

Cast includes: Hobart Bosworth, Courtenay Foote, Carl von Schiller, Helen Wolcott, Herbert Standing, Marshall Stedman.

A young reporter exposes a phony spiritualist who tricks convict Buckshot John into revealing the hiding place of a large cache of stolen money in this exciting silent drama based on the novelette *The Message to Buckshot John* by Charles E. Van Loan. Gang member Hobart Bosworth, imprisoned for thirty years for taking part in a robbery and refusing to reveal the hiding place of the gang's cache, eventually decides to reform. Seeking an honest man in whom he can confide, he finds seemingly kindly spiritualist Courtenay Foote and divulges the whereabouts of the gang's $200,000, which he wishes to be restored to the rightful owners. But Bosworth is unaware that Foote intends to keep the money for himself. When the reporter informs Bosworth of the truth, the convict escapes, finds Foote and retrieves the stolen money. He then returns it to the company which suffered the loss. The convict then returns to prison where he is pardoned.

114 BULLDOG EDITION (1936), Rep.

Dir. Charles Lamont; *Sc.* Richard English; *Cast includes:* Ray Walker, Evalyn Knapp, Regis Toomey, Cy Kendall, Billy Newell, Oscar Apfel.

A local racketeer uses his gang of hoodlums to strong-arm a newspaper into selling out to him in another drama that combines the newspaper world with that of the underworld. While mobster Cy Kendall intimidates news dealers and peddlers, circulation manager Ray Walker and managing editor Regis Toomey, both of a rival paper, compete for the affections of reporter Evalyn Knapp. Toomey succumbs to the racketeer's offer to take over the rival paper. Following several complications, Walker and Knapp are kidnapped by the gang who plan to kill them. However, things turn out successfully for the couple and badly for the villains. Several supporting players were once major stars in silent films, including Robert Warwick, who plays a newspaper owner, and Betty Compson, as Kendall's girlfriend who likes her liquor. The film was adapted from the story "Back in Circulation" by Danny Ahearn.

115 BURNDOWN (1990), Virgin.

Dir. James Allen; *Sc.* Anthony Barwick, Colin Stewart; *Cast includes:* Peter Firth, Cathy Moriarty, Hal Orlandini, Michael McCabe, Hugh Rouse, Victor Melleney.

Reporter Cathy Moriarty and sheriff Peter Firth join forces to expose a cover-up at a nuclear plant site responsible for a series of murders in this anti-nuclear drama. After a series of strange rapes and murders terrorize a community near the plant, its designer, Hal Orlandini, guards against any investigation. When the reporter learns from the sheriff that the deaths are linked to radiation sex crimes, she exposes the story in her paper. It seems the killer is a radioactive mutant. Orlandini becomes even more secretive after the story is printed. Firth is assigned somewhere else, and Moriarty's editor suppresses her second story. The persistent journalist finally locates a witness who can prove the plant has had a series of accidents which were never reported. The reporter and the sheriff find themselves trapped in the plant after they are caught snooping around, but they escape in time before some infected employees blow up the structure.

116 THE BUSHWHACKERS (1951), Realart.

Dir. Rod Amateau; *Sc.* Rod Amateau, Thomas Gries; *Cast includes:* John Ireland, Wayne Morris, Lawrence Tierney, Dorothy Malone, Lon Chaney, Myrna Dell.

Another crusading newspaper editor gives his life to help establish law and order to the frontier in this well-paced western drama. Civil War veteran John Ireland, after experiencing the horrors of the conflict between the states, vows never to pick up a weapon against another person as he heads west. In Missouri he witnesses settlers suffering under the heel of brutal land baron Lon Chaney. The veteran joins forces with school teacher Dorothy Malone and her father, newspaper editor Frank Marlowe, to fight against the oppressors. When Marlowe is shot to death, Ireland reluctantly returns to his gun and organizes the settlers to fight for their rights. Together, they wipe out Chaney and his gang of outlaws. When the smoke of battle clears, Ireland settles down with Malone.

117 CAFÉ SOCIETY (1939), Par.

Dir. Edward H. Griffith; *Sc.* Virginia Van Upp; *Cast includes:* Madeleine Carroll, Fred MacMurray, Shirley Ross, Jessie Ralph, Claude Gillingwater, Allyn Joslyn.

Society news reporter Fred MacMurray, after marrying glamorous heiress Madeleine Carroll, learns that she has used him to get into the society columns in this fairly entertaining comedy. The reporter meets the globe-trotting socialite while taking photos of her upon her return to the States where she desperately wants to be acknowledged by noted society columnist Allyn Joslyn. "Café society," grouses Shirley Ross, MacMurray's friend. "I'd rather read about the zoo." Upset with his bride's initial deception, the ego-bruised groom decides to teach her a lesson—with a nod toward *The Taming of the Shrew.* Following a string of complications, including a slight affair between MacMurray and café entertainer Ross, the married couple resolve their differences. They receive a helping hand from quirky Claude Gillingwater, Carroll's millionaire uncle, who at one point apologizes for his own permissiveness toward Carroll. "If I had started smacking her earlier," he confides to MacMurray, "maybe it wouldn't have been necessary for you to do it now." Earlier, Gillingwater criticizes her lifestyle. "You never had an idea in your life," he charges. "You've done nothing all your life except give parties, each one sillier than the rest."

118 CAIRO (1942), MGM.

Dir. W. S. Van Dyke II; *Sc.* John McLain; *Cast includes:* Jeanette MacDonald, Robert Young, Ethel Waters, Reginald Owen, Grant Mitchell.

MGM moved its singing star Jeanette MacDonald out of costume musicals and into an implausible comedy-drama (with several patriotic songs) set in World War II England and Egypt—with mixed results. MacDonald portrays an American movie actress residing in England who hires Robert Young as her butler. Young, a Yankee reporter assigned to cover the war in North Africa, suspects MacDonald of being a Nazi agent and accepts the position to keep an eye on her. He engages in virtually every pratfall that can be attributed to a bumbling butler. The plot ultimately takes the couple to Cairo. Young follows a group of spies to their hidden desert lair where they have surreptitiously assembled an airplane. MacDonald manages to open a secret pyramid by reaching the musical note of high C. Ethel Waters, MacDonald's maid, sings several songs and adds to the comedy. Mona Barrie portrays a Nazi spy. The film added little to the careers of the two leading players.

119 CALL NORTHSIDE 777 (1948), TCF.

Dir. Henry Hathaway; *Sc.* Jerome Cady, Jay Dratler; *Cast includes:* James Stewart, Richard Conte, Lee J. Cobb, Helen Walker, Betty Garde, Moroni Olsen.

Cynical reporter James Stewart is convinced that convict Richard Conte, who has served eleven years for killing a policeman, is innocent. Stewart is first introduced to the case by his editor Lee J. Cobb, who saw an ad placed by Conte's mother. The elderly woman has scrubbed floors for a decade to raise enough money toward a reward for evidence to free her son. The reporter reluctantly investigates the case, including a visit to the state prison. "Up here," the warden says to Stewart, "every man claims to be innocent." He then informs the reporter that the convicts all believe in Conte's inno-

Reporter James Stewart tries to free an innocent man from prison while his employer Lee J. Cobb looks on in *Call Northside 777* (1948).

cence. After finding a police cover-up and other suspicious anomalies pertaining to the case, Stewart eventually convinces the parole board of Conte's innocence. His best piece of evidence comes from the date of a newspaper in a photograph. "It's a big thing when a sovereign state admits an error," he says to the exonerated Conte. "And remember this, there aren't many governments in the world that would do it." "Yes," the former convict replies, "it's a good world—outside." The semi-documentary drama, filmed on location in Chicago, was based on the actual case of Joe Majczek and subsequent newspaper articles written by James P. McGuire.

120 THE CAMERAMAN (1928), MGM.

Dir. Edward Sedgwick; *Sc.* Richard Schayer; *Cast includes:* Buster Keaton, Marceline Day, Harry Gribbon, Harold Goodwin, Sidney Bracy.

Still photographer Buster Keaton, enamored of Marceline Day, a secretary with a newsreel company, strives to work for that firm in this hilarious comedy. With Day's help, he gets a chance to show his abilities as a cameraman—but with disastrous results. She then informs Keaton of a looming tong war in Chinatown, and he rushes to cover the event. He learns too late that he has no film in the camera. The next day he busies himself at filming a regatta at which Day's life is in danger when a cowardly fellow cameraman abandons her in the water to save himself. Keaton immediately swims toward the woman he loves and rescues her.

121 A CAMPAIGN MANAGERESS (1913), Thanhouser.

Dir. Carl Gregory; *Sc.* Lloyd Lonergan, Carl Gregory; *Cast includes:* Muriel Ostriche, Marie Eline, Boyd Marshall.

When illness strikes Muriel Ostriche's father, a small-town newspaper owner, she decides to run the paper in this little comedy drama. Earlier, her father had refused

Buster Keaton tries to figure out how to work his movie camera in Edward Sedgwick's classic silent comedy, *The Cameraman* (1928).

to use his press to support Boyd Marshall, his daughter's boyfriend, who is running for town sheriff as a political reform candidate. The publisher believed it wasn't ethical to favor his daughter's beau. But Ostriche, now in control, writes glowing endorsements of Marshall while assailing his rival, the choice of a local political ring. The infuriated opponent storms into the newspaper office with a whip in one hand and a revolver in his pocket. The neophyte journalist, using her feminine charm, cajoles him into surrendering his weapons to her and walks him outside. Meanwhile an angry crowd, concluding that he had tried to attack her, hurls epithets and stones at him. After her boyfriend wins the sheriff's post, Ostriche rationalizes her double-dealing actions. "All is fair in politics," she states, "especially for a campaign manageress who loves her candidate."

122 CAPRICORN ONE (1978), WB.

Dir. Peter Hyams; *Sc.* Peter Hyams; *Cast includes:* Elliott Gould, James Brolin, Brenda Vaccaro, Sam Waterston, O. J. Simpson, Hal Holbrook.

This thriller about America's first manned space flight to Mars that turns out to be a hoax offers an interesting premise. However, the drama soon deteriorates into a series of implausible incidents as curious reporter Elliott Gould becomes enmeshed in the conspiracy. Head of the space agency Hal Holbrook is forced to cancel the flight because of some defective equipment. To protect the space program, he sets up a mock landing, replete with cameras, sound equipment and a realistic background, to fool the President, politicians and public. He persuades the three astronauts (James Brolin, Sam Waterston, O. J. Simpson) to go along with the scheme. "We are not your enemy," he explains when they voice their opposition to the scam. "We're all working for the same thing." Brolin, the chief astronaut, has strong reservations at first, as do his fellow spacemen. "If the only way to keep something alive is to become everything I hate," he states, "I don't know if it's worth keeping alive." Finally, Holbrook is forced to reveal that a covert organization representing business and other interests has threatened the lives of the astronauts' families if they do not cooperate. He explains that he has lost control of the program—that more powerful forces have taken charge. The hoax goes off smoothly during the next several months until problems arise during the reentry of the capsule. Holbrook is forced to announce that the astronauts died when the capsule burned up. Consumed by his ambitious scheme which he tries to keep alive, he orders the astronauts, who have been kept hidden all these months, to be killed. They escape, but only Brolin manages to stay alive in the desert wastes following a relentless pursuit by Holbrook's agents. Meanwhile Gould investigates the project after his friend, who had been working on the flight, disappears. Gould himself becomes the target of several assassination attempts but eventually rescues Brolin. They make a dramatic appearance at a funeral tribute to the lost astronauts, exposing Holbrook and his entire conspiracy.

123 THE CAPTIVE CITY (1952), UA.

Dir. Robert Wise; *Sc.* Karl Kamb, Alvin M. Josephy Jr.; *Cast includes:* John Forsythe, Joan Camden, Harold J. Kennedy, Ray Teal, Marjorie Crossland, Victor Sutherland.

Newspaper publisher John Forsythe investigates large-scale corruption in his community in this tense drama which sought to benefit from the Kefauver hearings of the period. Forsythe learns that chief crime boss Victor Sutherland controls the town, including police chief Ray Teal and his men. Threatened by the gang and criticized by local businessmen, Forsythe and his wife flee to the state capital to testify before Senator Estes Kefauver's committee investigating organized crime in America. Although Forsythe is promised a small fortune by the crime syndicate not to testify, he turns down the offer. Senator Kefauver appears at the end of the film to caution the public about the rise of organized crime—a ploy which adds authenticity to the drama. "There is no such thing as a little harmless local vice," he warns. "Multiply a little organized crime by a thousand and you have a vicious, powerful nationwide criminal syndicate." Exposing organized crime was a major theme in several films of the 1950s, including, among others, *The Racket* (1951), *Hoodlum Empire* (1952), *Kansas City Confidential* (1952), *The Miami Story* (1954) and *The Phenix City Story* (1955).

124 CAPTURED IN CHINATOWN (1935), Superior Pictures.

Dir. Elmer Clifton; *Sc.* Elmer Clifton, Arthur Durlam; *Cast includes:* Marion Shilling, Charles Delaney, Philo McCullough, Robert Ellis, Robert Walker.

Newspaper reporters Marion Shilling and Charles Delaney, assigned to Chinatown to cover a story about a wedding between two hostile families, find themselves embroiled in danger and a possible tong war in this routine low-budget drama. The marriage is designed to end the enmity between two factions. But when a $50,000 diamond necklace that the groom presented to his bride is stolen, the young man's family assumes a member of the rival clan stole it. Actually Philo McCullough, a notorious jewel thief, is the culprit. Believing the reporter knows too much, he holds Shilling prisoner. But her police dog, Tarzan, finds her and returns to Delaney to get help. Later, the dog attacks McCullough and discovers the hiding place of the necklace. The police round up the gang, and the tong war is prevented as the two families once again make peace. Although the plot and characters are conventional if not simply trite, the leased sets add a note of authenticity to the otherwise economical production.

125 CARSON CITY (1952), WB.

Dir. Andre De Toth; *Sc.* Sloan Nibley, Winston Miller; *Cast includes:* Randolph Scott, Lucille Norman, Don Beddoe, Raymond Massey, Richard Webb, James Millican.

Newspaperman Don Beddoe is murdered after discovering that a suspicious mine is not being developed but is being used as a front for the activities of a gang of outlaws, in this fair western drama. When construction engineer Randolph Scott is hired to build a railroad between Carson City and Virginia City, outlaw leader Raymond Massey plots to stop him. Massey finds the original stagecoach line more lucrative as a source for his holdups. Meanwhile Scott is falsely accused of killing Beddoe. Following several complications, Scott gets to finish the railroad, but Massey plans the theft of a gold shipment on the first train out. A final fight between the two ends in Scott's victory and his winning the love of Lucille Norman, Beddoe's daughter. Both major and minor westerns occasionally included a plot which involved a local newspaper.

126 A CASE AT LAW (1917), Triangle.

Dir. Arthur Rosson; *St.* William Dudley Pelly; *Cast includes:* Riley Hatch, Pauline Curley, Dick Rosson, Jack Dillon, Ed Sturgis.

Dick Rosson portrays a young alcoholic reporter in this pre-Prohibition anti-liquor drama. An Easterner with a weakness for booze, Rosson journeys to a small town in the West with Pauline Curley, his fiancée, both hoping he will recover there from his problem. But during his first day on the job, he celebrates with his fellow reporters and staggers home drunk. His wife calls upon Riley Hatch, the local doctor, a staunch enemy of alcohol, who takes the young man to his home to cure him. After recovering sufficiently, Rosson is assigned to interview local saloon keeper Jack Dillon about the national drinking problem. Dillon, an enemy of the doctor, decides to take his revenge out on the reporter, who again returns drunk. The irate Hatch storms into the saloon and shoots up the place, an act that results in his wounding Dillon in the arms and legs. At his trial, the jury acquits the doctor, dismissing the shooting as "justifiable self-defense."

127 THE CASE OF THE BLACK PARROT (1941), WB.

Dir. Noel M. Smith; *Sc.* Robert E. Kent; *Cast includes:* William Lundigan, Maris Wrixon, Eddie Foy Jr., Paul Cavanagh, Luli Deste, Charles Waldron.

News hound William Lundigan and photographer Eddie Foy Jr. investigate a theft and two murders in this routine drama based on the play *In the Next Room* by Eleanor Belmont and Harriet Ford and the novel *Mystery of the Boule Cabinet* by Burton E. Stevenson. The film is set chiefly aboard a ship, with the theft occurring during a submarine alert. Lundigan, who suspects that the notorious international thief known as the Black Parrot is behind the crime, eventually unmasks the culprit.

128 CASE OF THE MISSING MAN (1935), Col.

Dir. D. Ross Lederman; *Sc.* Lee Loeb,

Harold Buchman; *Cast includes:* Roger Pryor, Joan Perry, Arthur Hohl, Thurston Hall, George McKay, Tommy Dugan.

Reporter-photographer Roger Pryor becomes the target of a criminal when he accidentally photographs a jewel thief exiting from a store he has just robbed in this suspenseful drama. Arthur Hohl, as the thief, desperately wants to retrieve and destroy the incriminating film. Meanwhile Pryor, aware of the potential evidence and a possible scoop, tries to prevent Hohl and his gang of crooks from getting their hands on the coveted negative and print. The thieves had committed a murder in the course of their store robbery. George McKay and Tommy Dugan provide sufficient comedy relief.

129 THE CAT CREEPS (1946), U.

Dir. Erle C. Kenton; *Sc.* Edward Dein, Jerry Warner; *Cast includes:* Noah Beery Jr., Lois Collier, Paul Kelly, Douglass Dumbrille, Fred Brady, Rose Hobart.

Reporter Fred Brady and photographer Noah Beery Jr. combine their talents to locate missing funds belonging to a newspaper and solve an old mystery in this offbeat and highly entertaining drama. Spooky elements dot the production, including a black cat that helps in the solution of several murders and possesses the soul of a dead woman. The film ends with Brady's solving a fifteen-year-old suicide — in reality, a murder — that has led to a string of additional killings. Meanwhile a local newspaper tries to pin a murder on Jonathan Hale, a political candidate, whose daughter is in love with the reporter.

130 CATSPAW MURDER MYSTERY (1942) *see Scattergood Survives a Murder* (1942).

131 CAVE OF OUTLAWS (1951), U.

Dir. William Castle; *Sc.* Elizabeth Wilson; *Cast includes:* Macdonald Carey, Alexis Smith, Edgar Buchanan, Victor Jory, Hugh O'Brian, Charles Horvath.

Ex-convict Macdonald Carey, imprisoned for ten years for taking part in a bank robbery, returns to search for the stolen money in this interesting western filmed in and around Carlsbad Caverns. Meanwhile, Wells Fargo lawman Edgar Buchanan is busy tracking Carey, seeking to retrieve the loot for the company. Carey pauses in town and meets widow Alexis Smith with whom he begins to fall in love. Together, they revive her husband's newspaper. Following some complications, Buchanan rescues Carey in the cave where he is about to be killed by the villainous Victor Jory. Carey returns the gold to Buchanan and settles down with Smith for a new life.

132 A CERTAIN RICH MAN (1921), Hodkinson.

Dir. Howard Hickman; *Cast includes:* Carl Gantvoort, Claire Adams, Robert McKim, Jean Hersholt, Joseph J. Dowling, Lydia Knott.

A small-town newspaper provides part of the background for this sprawling silent drama based on the 1909 novel by William Allen White. Jean Hersholt arrives in town to start a newspaper and unknowingly places his money in a bank whose owner is short of funds. Hersholt falls in love with Claire Adams, but when she rejects him, he decides to leave town. Robert McKim, a wheat dealer in financial trouble, threatens Adams, who loves Carl Gantvoort, the banker's son. He tells her that many in town will suffer if she does not marry Hersholt, who will take his funds with him when he leaves. She then reluctantly agrees to the marriage. Twenty years later Hersholt becomes an alcoholic, leaving his wife to run the paper, now owned by her former boyfriend. The angry Hersholt shoots Gantvoort and bolts from the town. When they learn about her husband's eventual death, Adams and Gantvoort rekindle their love and marry.

133 CHAIN GANG (1950), Col.

Dir. Lew Landers; *Sc.* Howard J. Green; *Cast includes:* Douglas Kennedy, Marjorie Lord, Emory Parnell, William Phillips, Thurston Hall, Harry Cheshire.

Newspaper reporter Douglas Kennedy goes under cover to expose the brutality and exploitation of prisoners of a chain gang in this humdrum action drama that combines the newspaper-crime format with the prison genre. For all his noble efforts, Kennedy is almost gunned down by a hail of bullets when his real identity is discovered by the corrupt camp authorities. Another dilemma the reporter is forced to confront, one which was a plot cliché many years before the release of this film, is the fact that the father of his girl friend Marjorie Lord is the chief villain.

134 CHARLIE CHAN AT TREASURE ISLAND (1939), TCF.

Dir. Norman Foster; *Sc.* John Larkin; *Cast includes:* Sidney Toler, Cesar Romero, Pauline Moore, Victor Sen Yung, Douglas Fowley, June Gale.

When a sinister psychic blackmails his victims and then forces them to commit suicide, Charlie Chan (Sidney Toler) steps in to bring the culprit to justice. The suicide of a friend whets the sleuth's curiosity and desire for justice, leading him to a fraudulent mystic known as "Zodiac," who blackmails his clients. The detective joins forces with stage magician Cesar Romero and together they unmask the fraud. Douglas Fowley plays a reporter interested in exposing the phony spirituals and astrologers. As in virtually all the Chan entries, the sleuth offers some choice aphorisms for one of his sons. "Confidence," he says to Sen Yung, "is like courage of small boy at dentist—most evident after tooth extracted." Some critics single out this entry, which includes stock footage of the San Francisco Fair, as the best entry in the studio's Charlie Chan series.

135 CHARLIE CHAN ON BROADWAY (1937), TCF.

Dir. Eugene Forde; *Sc.* Charles Belden, Jerry Cady; *Cast includes:* Warner Oland, Keye Luke, J. Edward Bromberg, Leon Ames, Joan Marsh, Douglas Fowley.

A banquet in the title character's honor is interrupted as the famous Chinese detective, played by Warner Oland, solves a murder in this mystery set chiefly in New York. Before arriving in the city, a young woman hides her diary, which contains politically sensitive information. She manages to conceal her diary in Charlie Chan's trunk aboard an ocean liner before she is killed in a Manhattan nightclub. Chan samples some of the city's night life as he goes about uncovering the murderer—the least suspicious suspect—ambitious scandal columnist Donald Woods. Elements of comedy relief run through the production. For example, when police inspector Harold Huber greets Chan at the dock, he says, "The bigwigs expect you to tear a duck apart with them tonight." "So sorry," Chan replies. "Come again, please?" "You'll have to excuse the inspector's broken English, Mr. Chan," Woods interjects. "He's a Brooklyn immigrant." Chan offers one of his famous aphorisms to Hawaiian-born number one son Key Luke, who wants to taste the Big Apple at night. "New York like mouth of great river," Chan explains; "many reefs in channel to wreck small boat from Honolulu."

136 THE CHASE (1994), TCF.

Dir. Adam Rifkin; *Sc.* Adam Rifkin; *Cast includes:* Charlie Sheen, Kristy Swanson, Ray Wise, Henry Rollins, Josh Mostel.

This mixed-up concoction of drama, thrills and comedy pokes fun at several institutions, including the news media. Car thief Charlie Sheen uses well-dressed Kristy Swanson as a hostage and shield when the police confront him in a convenience store. He uses a Butterfinger candy bar pressed into her back for a gun as he makes his getaway. The remainder of this quirky film concerns the chase between the law and Sheen in which the media, chiefly through television coverage, sensationalizes the wild pursuit. TV announcers and reporters headline and exaggerate the crime, the getaway and Sheen in such terms as "Terror on the Freeway." They compete with each other by jockeying for position, either dangling from a helicopter or hanging from the side of a panel truck to video the young couple being pursued. Some pursuing police are portrayed as self-serving and self-pitying. "We're standard issue street soldiers," one tells a TV reporter. At first, Sheen's pretty captive attacks him with the automobile cigarette lighter, but Swanson soon falls in love with Sheen, who turns out to be caring and sensitive, unlike Ray Wise, her compassionless millionaire-industrialist father, who seeks to exploit the kidnapping to his political advantage as he plans to run for governor. Many of the chase sequences are derivative of those in films like *Convoy* and the *Smokey and the Bandit* series. The entire work entertains most when it is parodying the media.

137   CHASING DANGER (1939), TCF.

Dir. Ricardo Cortez; *Sc.* Robert Ellis, Helen Logan; *Cast includes:* Preston Foster, Lynn Bari, Wally Vernon, Henry Wilcoxon, Joan Woodbury, Harold Huber.

Star newsreel cameraman Preston Foster, stationed in Paris, is assigned to cover an Arab rebellion in Morocco in this routine comedy action adventure hampered by an unrealistic script. Following several complications in which Foster and his assistant Wally Vernon are forced to talk their way out of danger, Foster eventually uncovers the identity of the chief culprit of a spy ring dealing with illegal arms shipments to the dissident tribes. It seems a jewel thief who has been considered dead is the instigator of the present desert warfare against French authority. Virtually the only realistic segment of this film is the aerial bombing of a desert fort.

138   CHASING THROUGH EUROPE (1929), Fox.

Dir. David Butler, Alfred L. Werker; *St.* Andrew Bennison, John Stone; *Cast includes:* Sue Carol, Nick Stuart, Gustav von Seyffertitz, Gavin Gordon, E. Alyn Warren.

Freelance newsreel cameraman Nick Stuart takes Sue Carol on one of his world tours of filming famous sites and persons in this offbeat action drama. Carol was about to be placed in an asylum by her guardian after she refused to marry his nephew when Stuart came to her rescue. Together they visit France, Italy and other places, and film such international personalities as Mussolini and the Prince of Wales. But their idyllic journey is interrupted by the villainous Gustav von Seyffertitz and his henchmen who covet Carol and her inheritance. They try to kidnap her while Stuart is out filming a landmark, but he returns in time to effect the arrest of their pursuers. The couple then return to the U.S. where they plan their wedding. Director Butler and Stuart had worked on a similar film the previous year, titled *The News Parade*, which evidently proved popular enough to inspire a sort of sequel.

139   CHEATING BLONDES (1933), Equitable.

Dir. Joseph Levering; *Sc.* Lewis B. Foster; *Cast includes:* Thelma Todd, Ralf Harolde, Inez Courtney, Milton Wallis, Mae Busch, Dorothy Gulliver.

Thelma Todd plays a dual role in this murder mystery. The plot concerns twin sisters, one a murder suspect and the other a nightclub singer. Ralf Harolde, as an aggressive and curious reporter, is not fooled when the sisters switch roles—the fugitive twin playing the entertainer while the other sister leaves town to have her baby. Earlier in the film, the reporter is rebuffed by entertainer Todd, which leads him to try to pin the murder on her.

140   CHEERS OF THE CROWD (1936), Mon.

Dir. Vin Moore; *Sc.* George Waggner;

Cast includes: Russell Hopton, Irene Ware, Bradley Page, Harry Holman, Betty Blythe, Wade Boteler.

Newspaper reporter Irene Ware joins forces with public relations wizard Russell Hopton as they solve a mystery involving a string of chain-letter murders in this mediocre drama. Hopton, like the more popular Lee Tracy, seemed to specialize in reporter and sleuthing roles during the 1930s, except that the former worked chiefly in low-budget productions.

141 CHICAGO DEADLINE (1949), Par.

Dir. Lewis Allen; *Sc.* Warren Duff; *Cast includes:* Alan Ladd, Donna Reed, June Havoc, Irene Hervey, Arthur Kennedy, Berry Kroeger.

Hard-nosed Chicago reporter Alan Ladd investigates the unfortunate life of Donna Reed, a young woman of easy virtue whom he finds dead of tuberculosis in this minor newspaper-crime drama based on the 1933 novel *One Woman* by Tiffany Thayer. Told chiefly in flashbacks, this film noir recounts Reed's associations with mobsters, gun molls, call girls and other characters who inhabit the noir underworld. Her story involves murders and blackmail. Reed's friend, call girl June Havoc, helps Ladd assemble the puzzle of the dead woman's life, and he concludes that a big-time gangster caused Reed's downfall. To protect her privacy, Ladd, who attends her funeral, burns her private address book.

142 CHINA GIRL (1942), TCF.

Dir. Henry Hathaway; *Sc.* Ben Hecht; *Cast includes:* Gene Tierney, George Montgomery, Lynn Bari, Victor McLaglen, Alan Baxter.

Japanese agents plot the destruction of China in this World War II drama set in Mandalay and China during the Sino-Japanese War, prior to Japan's attack on Pearl Harbor. George Montgomery, an American newsreel cameraman, falls in love with Gene Tierney, a young Chinese woman educated in the U.S. Meanwhile, Japanese planes bomb China's cities. When Tierney is killed during one of the raids, Montgomery lays aside his professional objectivity and wreaks revenge upon the Japanese planes by firing at them with a machine gun. Lynn Bari and Victor McLaglen portray spies, with Bari falling for Montgomery. Several exciting war scenes enhance an otherwise routine tale. Produced during a period in which Hollywood eschewed interracial relationships, the film solved the problem the old-fashioned way—by simply killing off one of the lovers.

143 THE CHINA SYNDROME (1979), Col.

Dir. James Bridges; *Sc.* Mike Gray, T. S. Cook, James Bridges; *Cast includes:* Jane Fonda, Jack Lemmon, Michael Douglas, Scott Brady, James Hampton, Peter Donat.

Television news reporter Jane Fonda and photographer Michael Douglas, both covering a nuclear power plant, experience a potentially disastrous malfunction with global implications in this tense thriller. At first, they are told the problem is "a routine turbine trip." But they soon learn that the "problem" could result in a meltdown, or a "China Syndrome," which could bring about the destruction of the planet. Jack Lemmon, as supervisor of the plant, remains dedicated to his company—until he realizes the potential catastrophe of the plant. After his life is threatened during a harrowing car chase by unknown assailants, he returns to the plant determined to shut it down. He locks himself in the control room in defiance of his superiors and alerts the media of the inherent danger to everyone if the plant continues to operate. Douglas's filming of the crisis forces a confrontation between antinuclear forces and those in control of the plant who are determined to cover up what is occurring. Douglas surrenders his professional objectivity when he sides with the former group. In its effort to turn out a socially conscious drama, the film paints the latter too heavily as villains.

144 THE CHINESE RING (1947), Mon.

Dir. William Beaudine; Sc. W. Scott Darling; Cast includes: Roland Winters, Mantan Moreland, Victor Sen Yung, Warren Douglas, Louise Currie, Philip Ahn.

A Chinese princess who has recently arrived in the U.S. is murdered in detective Charlie Chan's quarters in this routine mystery. The victim, carrying one million dollars, had intended to smuggle airplanes to China. Meanwhile, intrusive newspaper reporter Louise Currie unintentionally interferes with the sleuth's progress. Chan, however, eventually proves that the killing and two other deaths are the work of a crooked bank manager who wanted a large chunk of the princess' money. Espousing persistence, the sleuth offers one of his famous aphorisms. "Man who ride on merry-go-round all the time," he declares, "sooner or later must catch brass ring." This was Roland Winters's debut as the Chinese sleuth, replacing Sidney Toler who had died after appearing in twenty-two entries in the popular series.

145 CHRISTMAS IN CONNECTICUT (1945), WB.

Dir. Peter Godfrey; Sc. Lionel Houser, Adele Commandini; Cast includes: Barbara Stanwyck, Dennis Morgan, Sydney Greenstreet, Reginald Gardiner, S. Z. Sakall, Una O'Connor.

Barbara Stanwyck portrays a magazine columnist, supposedly knowledgeable in homemaking, in this trifling but delightful comedy. But in reality her writings are all fictitious. Believed to be married and a mother, she is assigned by Sydney Greenstreet, her housekeeping magazine publisher, to prepare a dinner at her home for war hero Dennis Morgan. Greenstreet is unaware that she does not even know how to cook. The hectic Stanwyck, to protect her job, searches desperately to find a husband, a baby, a farm and an expert cook to rescue her. She manages to acquire suitor Reginald Gardiner's farm. Following several frenetic incidents, the forgiving publisher learns the truth about his columnist, and Stanwyck and Morgan fall in love. *Man's Favorite Sport?* (1964) offered a similar plot, with Rock Hudson as a fishing expert who has never fished.

146 CIMARRON (1931), Par.

Dir. Wesley Ruggles; Sc. Howard Estabrook; Cast includes: Richard Dix, Irene Dunne, Edna May Oliver, Estelle Taylor, Nance O'Neil, William Collier Jr.

Based on the popular novel by Edna Ferber, this historical epic, set in Oklahoma during the 1889 great land rush, stars Richard Dix as Yancey Cravat, a crusading newspaper publisher, and Irene Dunne as his long-suffering wife. Dix fights against a series of injustices, including the abuses inflicted upon the downtrodden Native Americans. But his restless wandering nature takes him away from his paper and family, leaving his faithful wife to carry on the work of fighting the good cause alone while also enduring the ingratitude of her children. Highlights of the drama include a recreation of the famous Oklahoma land rush and the depiction of the oil boom of the 1920s—two events that helped spell the death of the frontier. Dix's ardor and Dunne's strength and resolve symbolize those qualities that helped to build America. The film, which won an Oscar for Best Picture, was remade in 1960 with Glenn Ford and Maria Schell.

147 CIRCUMSTANTIAL EVIDENCE (1935), Che.

Dir. Charles Lamont; Sc. Ewart Adamson; Cast includes: Chick Chandler, Shirley Grey, Arthur Vinton, Claude King, Dorothy Revier, Lee Moran.

Newspaper reporter Chick Chandler, determined to prove his theory about circumstantial evidence, falsifies a murder in this rather unique drama. Horrified when a defendant at a murder trial is condemned to death on circumstantial evidence, Chandler is determined to expose these unjust trials as uncivilized. After winning the approval of his fiancée Shirley Grey and his publisher Claude King, he plans to have accomplice Arthur Vinton, a wealthy columnist on his paper, hide until he, Chandler, is convicted on circumstantial evidence of killing Vinton. They arrange a brawl between them and other incidents intended to "prove" that the reporter had a motive to kill Vinton. They then set a fire in which a skeleton would represent the victim. Chandler is arrested, tried and sentenced to death. However, the assistant fails to reveal himself. Unknown to Chandler, Vinton, a jealous womanizer, hates the reporter and secretly loves Grey. Intending to let the reporter hang for murder, the columnist books passage for Europe. Meanwhile, Chandler's publisher helps the reporter to escape. Following several more complications, the police trace the fugitive to King's penthouse where Chandler tries to flee. When King tries to stop the officers from shooting, he is struck by the bullets. The mortally wounded publisher confesses that he killed Vinton, who had earlier abused King's wife. Chandler is released, proving his case against circumstantial evidence — but paying an almost terrible price. The drama was timely since the infamous Lindbergh kidnapping involved the controversial conviction of Bruno Hauptmann on circumstantial evidence. The convicted kidnapper was executed in April 1936.

148 CITIZEN KANE (1941), RKO.

Dir. Orson Welles; *Sc.* Orson Welles, Herman J. Mankiewicz; *Cast includes:* Orson Welles, Joseph Cotten, Dorothy Comingore, Everett Sloane, Ray Collins, George Colouris.

This remarkable drama was the first film directed by the youthful and iconoclastic Orson Welles, who had achieved earlier successes on the stage and in radio. But no one expected this "boy wonder" to have turned out such a significant and controversial production. The film was important for its striking and clever use of numerous visual and sound techniques, including deep focus photography, uncommon camera angles, odd lighting, Bernard Herrmann's ominous music, striking sound effects, and overlapping dialogue from one sequence to the next. The controversy arose from the basic plot — the notorious private and public life of American newspaper publisher Charles Foster Kane — which suggested many incidents in the life of William Randolph Hearst. Both Kane and Hearst used the power of press to influence public opinion. Kane even paraphrases Hearst when, in one scene, he utters: "You provide the pictures, and I'll provide the war!" As a result, the Hearst chain of papers banned any mention of the audacious film and several movie chains refused to distribute or exhibit it. Welles's scathing exposé of America's potentially fruitless obsession with power and materialism is exemplified by the ultimately empty and lonely life of Kane. Joseph Cotten portrays Jed Leland, Kane's life-long friend whom Kane eventually fires when Leland turns in a negative review of the operatic performance of Dorothy Comingore, the publisher's mistress. "He was disappointed in the world," Leland says during an interview, "so he built one of his own." Everett Sloane, as Kane's longtime bookkeeper, remained faithful over the years but realized his employer's shortcomings. After Kane's death, a group of reporters gawk at the vast number of packing cases, containing only some of the treasures he accumulated during his lifetime. "Mr. Kane," concludes one reporter, "was a man who got everything he wanted, then lost it."

149 CITY LIMITS (1934), Mon.

Dir. William Nigh; *Sc.* George Waggner; *Cast includes:* Frank Craven, Sally Blane, Ray Walker, Claude Gillingwater.

Aggressive reporter Ray Walker poses as a doctor's assistant to gain access to an ill railroad magnate in this comedy based on the novel by Jack Woodford. Meanwhile, the railroad president, Frank Craven, disappears and befriends a couple of oddball hoboes. Following a string of humorous incidents, Walker ends up with Craven's daughter and a scoop, thanks to

Craven, who also saves the railroad in the nick of time.

150 CITY OF CHANCE (1940), TCF.

Dir. Ricardo Cortez; *Sc.* John Larkin, Barry Trivers; *Cast includes:* Lynn Bari, C. Aubrey Smith, Donald Woods, Amanda Duff, June Gale, Richard Lane.

Inquisitive reporter Lynn Bari investigates a gambling casino and ends up finding romance in this well-mounted drama that explores several facets of the gambling racket. Bari meets her former Texas boyfriend Donald Woods, who owns the casino, and they both fall in love. While she tries to extricate Woods from the gambling racket, one of his enemies plans to kill him. Woods barely escapes with his life. Fortunately for the couple, he finally sells the casino moments before the police raid the joint. Venerable English actor C. Aubrey Smith portrays a veteran gambler known as "the judge." The film, whose plot, many varied characters and limited setting, is somewhat reminiscent of *Grand Hotel* (1930).

151 CITY OF MISSING GIRLS (1941), Select.

Dir. Elmer Clifton; *Sc.* Oliver Drake, George Rosener; *Cast includes:* H. B. Warner, Astrid Allwyn, John Archer, Sarah Padden, Philip Van Zandt, George Rosener.

A fraudulent art school serves as a supplier of young women for a nightclub where several "recruits" are found murdered in this weak newspaper-crime mystery. Reporter Astrid Allwyn relentlessly complains in her articles that John Archer, the assistant district attorney, is not doing enough to solve the killings—until she learns that Philip Van Zandt, her own theatrical-agent father, runs the scam and is responsible for the deaths.

152 THE CITY THAT NEVER SLEEPS (1924), Par.

Dir. James Cruze; *Sc.* Walter Woods, Anthony Coldeway; *Cast includes:* Louise Dresser, Ricardo Cortez, Kathlyn Williams, Virginia Lee Corbin, Pierre Gendron, James Farley.

Reporter Pierre Gendron helps widowed Louise Dresser expose an unsavory suitor interested in Dresser's daughter in this silent drama set chiefly along New York's Bowery. Dresser had earlier placed her child in the home of a respectable society woman and struggled to convert her Bowery saloon to a cabaret. Kathlyn Williams, her daughter, has grown into a self-centered young flapper who has fallen under the influence of Ricardo Cortez, a known hoodlum. After Gendron, Williams's childhood sweetheart, enlightens her about Cortez, she realizes the reporter is her true love. The film is based on the 1924 story "Mother O'Day" by Leroy Scott.

153 THE CLARION (1916), World.

Dir. James Durkin; *Cast includes:* Carlyle Blackwell, Howard Hall, Marion Dentler, Charles Mason, George Spencer, Rosemary Dean.

Young and idealistic Carlyle Blackwell buys a newspaper to improve local social conditions and soon discovers that those closest to him are some of the worst offenders in this social drama based on the novel by Samuel Hopkins Adams. When he learns that his own father is profiting from the manufacture and sale of a quack drug, the crusading publisher refuses to accept the latter's advertising. Next, Blackwell discovers that the father of Marion Dentler, his girlfriend, owns property in the worst slum section of the city—an area whose vile living conditions he is exposing in his paper. His intimacy with Dentler does not prevent him from continuing his attacks. After anarchists destroy the newspaper, Blackwell's father acknowledges his shortcomings and reforms, and Dentler is reunited with the man she loves.

154 THE CLEAN-UP (1929), Excellent.

Dir. Bernard F. McEveety; *Sc.* Carmelita Sweeney; *Cast includes:* Charles

Delaney, Betty Blake, Bruce Gordon, Lewis Sargent, Harry Myers, J. P. McGowan.

A crusading newspaper editor and a determined police captain battle their city's gangsters in this low-budget melodrama. The officer is killed by the gang, while Charles Delaney, the editor, and Betty Blake, the captain's daughter, continue the fight, eventually bringing the gang leader to justice.

155 CLEAR ALL WIRES (1933), MGM.

Dir. George Hill; *Sc.* Bella Spewack, Samuel Spewack; *Cast includes:* Lee Tracy, Benita Hume, Una Merkel, James Gleason, Alan Edwards, C. Henry Gordon.

This drama offers a rare glimpse into a different type of foreign correspondent than the one audiences are familiar with—a journalist who is double-crossing and self-serving. This is in sharp contrast to the more typically cynical but honorable reporter. Lee Tracy portrays the former, a quick-witted, slick Moscow correspondent, while Alan Edwards plays an ethical journalist from the *Times* and Benita Hume a hard-working and dedicated correspondent. The plot emphasizes the contrast in the two styles of reporting.

156 CLOSE-UP (1948), EL.

Dir. Jack Donohue; *Sc.* John Bright, Max Wilk; *Cast includes:* Alan Baxter, Virginia Gilmore, Richard Kollmar, Loring Smith, Phil Huston, Russell Collins.

Ex-Nazis operating undercover in New York try to destroy newsreel clips which contain damaging evidence against one of their members in this slow-paced drama. Alan Baxter, the cameraman who took the pictures and can prove that the former Nazi is currently in the city, becomes the target of some of the gang members. Virginia Gilmore, an associate of the gang, helps to effect Baxter's capture. However, the culprits soon learn that all Baxter possesses is a copy of the newsreel; the original eventually reaches the local police. Richard Kollmar, the chief villain, plots to have the negatives and the original destroyed to protect his cover. The drama was shot in New York City for authenticity and was one of the earliest of many post-World War II films to use location shooting there.

157 THE CLUTCHING HAND (1936) serial, Stage & Screen Productions.

Dir. Albert Herman; *Sc.* Leon D'Usseau, Dallas Fitzgerald; *Cast includes:* Jack Mulhall, Ruth Mix, Marion Shilling, William Farnum, Yakima Canutt, Rex Lease.

The mysterious villain of the title turns out to be the inventor of a hoax in this 15-chapter serial based on a novel by Arthur Reeve and featuring the famous scientific detective Craig Kennedy, played by Jack Mulhall. The inventor supposedly has a formula for making synthetic gold, but the formula, which is phony, leads to a general cover-up. When the directors of a research foundation assemble to witness a demonstration of doctor Robert Frazer's experiment, they discover that he has been kidnapped by the Clutching Hand. Newspaper reporter Rex Lease, the fiancé of Marion Shilling, the doctor's daughter, calls upon Mulhall to investigate the kidnapping. There follows a chain of perilous escapades thrust upon either the detective, the reporter and/or the inventor's daughter—all precipitated by the Clutching Hand and his henchmen. Finally, in the last chapter titled "The Lone Hand," the detective assembles the directors and discloses that the doctor is the chief villain. In addition, he explains that the Clutching Hand is not Shilling's real father but her guardian, and he has been stealing large sums of money from her estate. He fabricated the gold formula and the fiendish villain to throw off suspicion of his misappropriations. The doctor then escapes to his laboratory where he takes his own life.

158 THE COBRA STRIKES (1948), EL.

Dir. Charles F. Reisner; *Sc.* Eugene

Conrad; *Cast includes:* Sheila Ryan, Richard Fraser, Leslie Brooks, Herbert Heyes, James Seay, Richard Loo.

Newspaper columnist Richard Fraser solves several murders and a jewel heist in this weak newspaper-crime drama. Scientist Herbert Heyes, who has invented an instrument that can be either a boon or curse to mankind, becomes the target of an assassination. After he is shot, his invention is stolen and a string of murders stumps the police. Fraser tracks down a jewel thief who happens to be the murderer. Offering little in the way of mystery or suspense, this cobra remains toothless.

159 COLLEGE CONFIDENTIAL (1960), U.

Dir. Albert Zugsmith; *Sc.* Irvin Shulman; *Cast includes:* Steve Allen, Jayne Meadows, Mamie Van Doren, Rocky Marciano, Cathy Crosby, Herbert Marshall.

College professor Steve Allen, who is conducting a survey of college students and their sexual habits, is charged with indecency in this inane exposé which offers more exploitation than insight. Perhaps the only interesting aspect of this weak drama are the appearances of actual contemporary journalists present at Allen's trial. They include, among others, Walter Winchell, Sheilah Graham, Earl Wilson and Louis Sobel. The strange casting also takes in famous prizefighter Rocky Marciano, who portrays a local sheriff.

160 COLONEL EFFINGHAM'S RAID (1945), TCF.

Dir. Irving Pichel; *Sc.* Kathryn Scola; *Cast includes:* Charles Coburn, Joan Bennett, William Eythe, Allyn Joslyn, Elizabeth Patterson, Donald Meek.

Charles Coburn portrays the title character, a retired army officer who tries to bring political reform to his small town in this charming comedy drama based on the novel by Barry Fleming. Coburn intends to accomplish this through a series of columns he writes for a local newspaper. Although his writings originally focused on his military expertise, he has recently directed his barbs at local politicians, including Thurston Hall, the mayor. William Eythe, an idealistic young reporter, is inspired by the old-timer's literary attacks. Meanwhile, the corrupt City Hall boys go after Coburn and almost succeed in stifling him. But young Eythe rises to his mentor's defense with patriotic zeal and defeats the crooked politicians.

161 COME FILL THE CUP (1951), WB.

Dir. Gordon Douglas; *Sc.* Ivan Goff, Ben Roberts; *Cast includes:* James Cagney, Phyllis Thaxter, Raymond Massey, Gig Young, Selena Royle, Larry Keating.

James Cagney portrays a newspaper reporter who, after being fired from his job, struggles to conquer his drinking problem in this dour drama. Ex-alcoholic James Gleason befriends the troubled Cagney, who has deteriorated to skid row status and ended up in a ward for alcoholics. Meanwhile, he loses Phyllis Thaxter, his girlfriend, to Gig Young, publisher Raymond Massey's nephew. He overcomes his problem, returns to his profession and advances to city editor. He then undertakes the responsibility to help Young battle a similar drinking problem. The reformed drunk then takes on some gangsters, including Sheldon Leonard, in a typical Cagney fistfight which brings the film to a happy ending. "When it comes to newspapermen," Cagney informs fellow reporter Larry Keating, "give me a reformed lush every time. Your solid citizen writes the facts and watches the clock. The ex-dipso lets himself go. Work takes the place of liquor. He's dedicated."

162 COMPANY OF KILLERS (1970), U.

Dir. Jerry Thorpe; *Sc.* E. J. Neuman; *Cast includes:* Van Johnson, Ray Milland, John Saxon, Brian Kelly, Fritz Weaver, Clu Gulager, Susan Oliver.

Obnoxious New York reporter Clu Gulager nettles police detective Van Johnson in this routine murder mystery filmed on location in the Big Apple. Johnson is on the trail of seriously wounded hit man John Saxon, who has been hired by crime boss Fritz Weaver. When Saxon kills a policeman while escaping from his most recent "job," the cold-blooded Weaver orders his execution as well.

163 THE COMPANY SHE KEEPS (1950), RKO.

Dir. John Cromwell; *Sc.* Ketti Frings; *Cast includes:* Lizabeth Scott, Jane Greer, Dennis O'Keefe, Fay Baker, John Hoyt, James Bell.

Newspaper columnist Dennis O'Keefe drops parole officer Lizabeth Scott for allegedly dishonest parolee Jane Greer in this contrived and trite drama about some of the problems women parolees face on the road back. At first, Scott suspects that Greer, because of her background (passing bad checks, reform schools, iniquitous lifestyle), is incapable of reform. Greer, who hungers for a man, flirts with and wins O'Keefe, who has been going with Scott. But when Greer tries to help a fellow ex-convict who has gone wrong, she is arrested. Scott, however, rescues Greer from returning to the slammer.

164 COMRADE X (1940), MGM.

Dir. King Vidor; *Sc.* Ben Hecht, Charles Lederer; *Cast includes:* Clark Gable, Hedy Lamarr, Felix Bressart, Eve Arden, Oscar Homolka, Sig Ruman.

American reporter Clark Gable while in Russia meets streetcar conductor Hedy Lamarr and a weird love affair blossoms in this frenetic comedy set in Moscow during the late 1930s and which tried to capture the flavor of *Ninotchka*, an earlier success. Avowed anti-Communist Felix Bressart wants Gable to marry his daughter, Lamarr, and take her to the States. Anxious to spread the Marxist doctrine, icy Lamarr agrees to marry Gable. On their wedding night she espouses the antithesis of the ideal American match. "It is like going into partnership with somebody," she says flatly. "It's like opening a store. If business is bad, you close the store." The witty dialogue is arguably the best part of this satirical comedy aimed at the Soviet Union. Ruthless Communist police chief Oscar Homolka, for example, explains to foreign reporters in Moscow why they cannot speak with the official press spokesman: "The former head of the press department was a victim last night of a traffic accident. He apparently, shall we say, did not watch his step." In Moscow, Gable is prepared to share his former hotel room, but its present occupant, stern German correspondent Sig Ruman demands it all. "That's a fine way to talk," Gable responds. "I get the room, I fix it up, I pay for it in advance, and I live in it. And you march in and try to throw me out. Now is that a nice way for a Nazi to act—I ask you?" Bressart escapes from Russia and joins his daughter and Gable in the U.S. They take him to his first baseball game where he is awakened suddenly by a cheering crowd. "What happened?" he asks. "The Dodgers are murdering the Reds!" Lamarr shouts with joy. "Aha!" proclaims Bressart. "The counter-revolution!" Like *Ninotchka* (1939) and *He Stayed for Breakfast* (1940), the film uses the plot device of exposing a devoted communist to the world of capitalism by underscoring the joys of romance and materialism.

165 CONFIRM OR DENY (1941), TCF.

Dir. Archie Mayo; *Sc.* Jo Swerling; *Cast includes:* Don Ameche, Joan Bennett, Roddy McDowall, John Loder, Raymond Walburn, Arthur Shields.

London during World War II and the influence of a government teletype operator turn American news bureau chief Don Ameche into a more responsible newscaster in this wartime drama. Ameche, an aggressive foreign correspondent with a swell head, meets English teletype operator Joan Bennett during a blackout. She has been assigned by her government to check his news items before they are sent abroad. The major conflict facing Ameche, who has received highly secret information about Hitler's invasion plans, is whether to publicly announce his scoop and bring down the wrath of the British upon him or suppress the information. Aside from these melodramatics, the film depicts realistically the devastation of parts of London caused by Nazi air raids. Several American films released during the war years were burdened with an inherent structural dichotomy as exemplified in this film—an implausible story carried by highly romanticized characters placed in realistic surroundings. *Arise, My Love* (1940) also exemplifies this type of drama.

166 CONFLICT (1936), U.

Dir. David Howard; *Sc.* Charles Logue, Walter Weems; *Cast includes:* John Wayne, Jean Rogers, Tommy Bupp, Eddie Borden, Frank Sheridan, Ward Bond.

Feisty newspaper reporter Jean Rogers, while working under cover as a social worker, meets fighter John Wayne in this disappointing drama based on the story "The Abysmal Brute" by Jack London. Set in the 1890s, the plot explores the crooked fight racket of the period. Wayne, a dishonest boxer, reforms under the influence of orphan boy Tommy Bupp, whom he had saved from drowning, and Rogers, with whom he has fallen in love. The film, although well produced, focuses more on Hollywood melodrama than on the author's intent.

167 CONSOLATION MARRIAGE (1931), RKO.

Dir. Paul Sloane; *Sc.* Humphrey Pearson, J. Roy Hunt; *Cast includes:* Irene Dunne, Pat O'Brien, John Halliday, Matt Moore, Leslie Vail, Myrna Loy.

Reporter-sports writer Pat O'Brien receives help with his marital problems from his hard-nosed editor John Halliday in this comedy drama. O'Brien, while on assignment, met Irene Dunne in a speakeasy and immediately they fell in love. Later, their marriage is held together by a loving child. However, a conflict arises when the reporter renews his relationship with Myrna Loy, a former girlfriend. Dunne handles the problem quietly as she goes about seeking a separation. But Halliday intercedes in bringing the couple together after O'Brien admits to straying and repents.

168 THE CONSPIRACY (1914), Par.

Dir. Allan Dwan; *Cast includes:* John Emerson, Lois Meredith, Harold Lockwood, Iva Shepherd, Francis Byrne, Hal Clarendon.

Cub reporter Harold Lockwood finds himself embroiled in a murder and a gang of white slavers in this mystery based on the 1912 play by Robert B. Baker and John Emerson. Lois Meredith, the sister of the district attorney, had been kidnapped by a white slavery gang. She escapes and, while looking for proof to convict the ring, she is caught by the gang leader whom she is forced to kill in self-defense. Mystery writer John Emerson brings down the gang and exonerates Meredith, who falls in love with Lockwood.

169 CONSPIRACY (1930), Radio.

Dir. Christy Cabanne; *Sc.* Beulah Marie Dix; *Cast includes:* Bessie Love, Hugh Trevor, Ned Sparks, Ivan Lebedeff, Rita La Roy, Gertrude Howard.

Bessie Love and her brother Bert Moorehouse resolve to smash a drug ring which caused their father's death in this remake of the 1916 silent drama *The Conspiracy*, both based on the play by Robert Baker and John Emerson. Love wins the confidence (and affection) of newspaper reporter Hugh Trevor and, together with mystery author Ned Sparks, playing a senile old-timer, they capture the gang. "We've got to get Marco's gang," someone remarks passionately in this anti-drug tract. "Because it's narcotics they peddle. I've seen the workings of that gang with my own eyes. I've seen all the girls drugged in those filthy joints. Boys who beat their own mothers to buy the stuff. And men and women who do things—oh, even savages couldn't do. Things I couldn't speak of. Things I don't want to remember."

170 THE CONTENDER (1944), PRC.

Dir. Sam Newfield; *Sc.* George Sayre, Jay Dolen, Raymond Schrock; *Cast includes:* Buster Crabbe, Arline Judge, Julie Gibson, Donald Maye, Glenn Strange, Milton Kibbee.

Sports columnist Arline Judge, who has encouraged former truck driver-turned fighter Buster Crabbe to continue in the fight game, soon finds herself with a rival in this mundane drama. Crabbe has taken up prizefighting to pay his son's bills at a military academy. But when he meets the mercenary blonde Julie Gibson, who introduces him into the fast night life, he severs all ties with his pals and Judge. As a result of these actions, the promising fighter's career founders. However, the same friends he has abandoned rescue him from Skid Row and, with the help of the sports writer, whom he really loves, and his son, he snaps out of his sense of failure and despair. His son informs him he would like to leave the military academy and become a reporter. One-time Olympic athlete Crabbe had a varied Hollywood career, which included playing comic strip spacemen Flash Gordon and Buck Rogers in several serials, appearing in numerous B westerns and other action features, and finally portraying an officer in the French Foreign Legion in a television series.

171 CONTINENTAL DIVIDE (1981), U.

Dir. Michael Apted; *Sc.* Lawrence Kasdan; *Cast includes:* John Belushi, Blair Brown, Allen Goorwitz, Carlin Glynn, Toni Ganlos, Val Avery.

John Belushi portrays a popular, streetwise *Chicago Sun Times* columnist who is sent out of harm's way of a corrupt politician he has been attacking in his articles in this farfetched romantic comedy. His new assignment is to interview Blair Brown, a reporter-hating bird lover, somewhere in the Rocky Mountains. When he reaches her mountain retreat, Brown learns that he cannot leave until his guide returns. He stays and they fall in love. When he returns to Chicago and exposes the politician, he discovers that his love for Brown still lingers on. They meet again, but they realize they are each bound to their own surroundings. Belushi, the crusading columnist, meets many admirers as he walks the streets of his beloved Chicago. "That was a great piece!" a prostitute calls out to him, referring to his latest column. "It's about time you said that about me!" he returns. This is exactly the lifestyle he cannot give up, even for Brown.

172 CONTRABAND (1925), Par.

Dir. Alan Crosland; *Sc.* Jack Cunningham; *Cast includes:* Lois Wilson, Noah Beery, Raymond Hatton, Raymond McKee, Charles Ogle, Luke Cosgrave.

Lois Wilson plays an impoverished young woman who inherits a small-town newspaper in this drama based on the 1923 novel by Clarence B. Kelland. When she arrives in town she discovers a gang of bootleggers operating a flourishing business. Raymond McKee, a local professor who has recently been dismissed as a superintendent of schools, helps Wilson to capture the gang who, in the course of its operations, has killed the local sheriff. Her series of articles helps to put public pressure on the gang of bootleggers. She then exposes their leader.

173 CONVICTED (1931), Artclass.

Dir. Christy Cabanne; *Sc.* Jo Van Ronkel; *Cast includes:* Richard Tucker, Wilfred Lucas, Niles Welch, John Vosburg, Aileen Pringle, Harry Myers.

A curious reporter foils a thief and killer while exonerating an innocent actress in this generally routine mystery. Theatrical producer Richard Tucker boards a ship with thousands of dollars he has stolen from his show and is soon murdered. Aileen Pringle, an actress in his last show, is suspected of the crime until the reporter sorts out a string of other suspects and finds the guilty party—a ship's officer who was after the stolen money.

174 CONVICTED WOMAN (1940), Col.

Dir. Nick Grinde; *Sc.* Joseph Carole; *Cast includes:* Rochelle Hudson, Frieda Inescort, June Lang, Lola Lane, Glenn Ford, Iris Meredith.

Fighting newspaper reporter Glenn Ford is determined to expose the brutality imposed on female inmates in this familiar prison reform drama. This entry deals with a women's reformatory in which the inmates are permitted to set up their own self-government following the uncovering of a series of the usual abuses carried out by those in charge. Frieda Inescort portrays a reform-minded lawyer who institutes radical changes in the institution. Rochelle Hudson plays a young woman who, while out of work, is wrongfully convicted of a crime and sentenced to a stretch in the reformatory.

175 THE CO-RESPONDENT (1917), Jewel.

Dir. Ralph W. Ince; *Cast includes:* Elaine Hammerstein, Wilfred Lucas, George Anderson, Winifred Harris, Richard Neill, Charles Smith.

Reporter Elaine Hammerstein is assigned by her boyfriend, editor Wilfred Lucas, to investigate a divorce case—with unexpected results—in this domestic drama based on the 1916 play by Alice Leal Pollock and Rita Weiman. The divorce involves an unnamed co-respondent who turns out to be the reporter. Hammerstein had earlier had an affair with the woman's husband before she met Lucas. She tells Lucas the truth and he refuses to print the article. However, to help him retain his credibility for always publishing the truth, she writes the story. Lucas then beats up her former lover and forces him to apologize to the reporter, after which the editor proposes to her.

176 THE CORPSE CAME C.O.D. (1947), Col.

Dir. Henry Levin; *Sc.* George Bricker, Dwight Babcock; *Cast includes:* George Brent, Joan Blondell, Adele Jergens, Jim Bannon, John Berks, Fred Sears.

Rival reporters George Brent and Joan Blondell are determined to solve the mystery of why a corpse was shipped to movie actress Adele Jergens in this fast-paced comedy drama based on the novel by Jimmy Starr. Set chiefly in Hollywood, the film covers three murders and a chase sequence before the culprit, a crooked police detective, is unmasked. It seems the corpse was connected to a ring of jewel thieves.

177 THE CORPSE VANISHES (1942), Mon.

Dir. Wallace Fox; *Sc.* Harvey Gates; *Cast includes:* Bela Lugosi, Luana Walters, Tristram Coffin, Elizabeth Russell, Minerva Urecal, Vince Barnett.

Curious newspaper reporter Luana Walters investigates the strange disappearance of seven brides in this cliché-ridden, unexciting mystery. Crazed scientist Bela Lugosi, she later learns, has been using the blood of the kidnapped victims to keep Elizabeth Russell, his eighty-year-old wife, forever youthful. The reporter sets up a scheme that eventually brings an end to Lugosi, who sleeps in a coffin, and his inhuman and pernicious experiments.

178 THE COSTELLO CASE (1930), Educational.

Dir. James Cruze; *Sc.* F. McGrew Willis; *Cast includes:* Tom Moore, Lola Lane, Wheeler Oakman, Roscoe Karns.

Roscoe Karns, as a fast-talking reporter—a character soon to become a film cliché—provides some comedy relief to this confusing and inept drama. Tom Moore portrays the stereotyped kind-hearted Irish police officer who is forced to deal with an incomprehensible plot. The inane incidents involve a mysterious young woman (Lola Lane), a gangster (Wheeler Oakman) and a burglar.

179 COUNSEL FOR THE DEFENSE (1925), AE.

Dir. Burton King; *Sc.* Arthur Hoerl; *Cast includes:* Jay Hunt, Betty Compson, House Peters, Rockliffe Fellowes, Emmett King, Bernard Randall.

Newspaper editor House Peters helps the fledgling lawyer-daughter of a typhoid specialist extricate her father of criminal charges in this drama based on the 1912 novel by Leroy Scott. The doctor, falsely accused of taking a bribe, has been framed by Rockliffe Fellowes, a prominent town lawyer and banker, who wants a municipal water works placed in private hands. The distraught daughter, Betty Compson, as a neophyte attorney recently out of law school, takes the case after other local lawyers refuse to help. But, overwhelmed by a mass of circumstantial evidence, she loses and her father is sent to prison. Fellowes then hires someone to sabotage the plant, leading to an outcry that it be taken over by private interests. This leads to an outbreak of typhoid epidemic. Compson joins forces with editor Peters who uncover the conspiracy and prove that the lawyer-banker framed her father to gain control of the water works.

180 THE COUNTRY BOY (1915), Par.

Dir. Frederick Thompson; *Cast includes:* Marshall Neilan, Florence Dagmar, Dorothy Green, Loyola O'Connor, Horace B. Carpenter, Edward Lewis.

Journalist Horace B. Carpenter persuades despondent Marshall Neilan to start a newspaper in Neilan's home town in this comedy drama based on the 1910 play by Edgar Selwyn. Neilan, the title character, had come to the big city to make his fortune after his sweetheart's father objected to the young couple's marriage. Following complications with chorus girl Dorothy Green, he loses his true girlfriend Florence Dagmar and his job. He then agrees to join Carpenter in the newspaper venture. After its success, Neilan and Dagmar reconcile their differences, and her father approves of their marriage plans.

181 CRIME, INC. (1941) *see Gangs, Inc.* (1941).

182 CRIME, INC. (1945), PRC.

Dir. Lew Landers; *Sc.* Ray Schrock; *Cast includes:* Leo Carrillo, Tom Neal, Martha Tilton, Lionel Atwill, Grant Mitchell, Sheldon Leonard.

Aggressive reporter Tom Neal goes after a gang of hoodlums in this disappointing minor drama based on the book by Martin Mooney. The gangsters carry out several murders before Neal exposes the entire operation. The syndicate leader, under the guise of a respectable citizen, is foreman of the grand jury in this predictable tale set during Prohibition era. Neal plays a role not unlike that of real-life author Mooney, a former crime reporter whose refusal to reveal information almost led to a prison term.

183 CRIME OF PASSION (1957), UA.

Dir. Gerd Oswald; *Sc.* Jo Eisinger; *Cast includes:* Barbara Stanwyck, Sterling Hayden, Raymond Burr, Fay Wray, Royal Dano, Virginia Grey.

San Francisco reporter Barbara Stanwyck, who gives up her career to marry Los Angeles cop Sterling Hayden, connives to advance her husband's career—with tragic results—in this action drama. Willing to do virtually anything to help her decent husband, the ambitious Stanwyck gives herself to his superior, inspector Raymond Burr. She hopes that Burr, about to retire, will name Hayden as his successor. But when Burr chooses duty over desire, she kills him. Hayden, investigating the killing, is then reluctantly forced to arrest his wife.

184 CRIME OF THE CENTURY (1933), Par.

Dir. William Beaudine; *Sc.* Florence Ryerson, Brian Marlow; *Cast includes:* Jean Hersholt, Wynne Gibson, Stuart Erwin, Frances Dee, David Landau, Gordon Westcott.

Jean Hersholt portrays a doctor of mental suggestion who admits to a crime that has not yet occurred in this highly original mystery based on the play *The Grootman Case* by Walter Espe. Burdened with an unfaithful younger wife, Hersholt tells a detective that he has hypnotized a bank official to steal a large sum of money. He then has second thoughts and pledges to prevent the crime. Meanwhile his wife and her lover plan to abscond with the money. When both the bank agent and the wife are killed, Hersholt becomes the prime suspect. But aggressive reporter Stuart Erwin unmasks the real murderer—the detective handling the case. The unique ending shows a clock on the screen which ticks off the seconds for a complete minute, giving the audience one last chance to figure out who the killer might be.

185 CRIME OF THE CENTURY (1946), Rep.

Dir. Philip Ford; *Sc.* O'leta Rhinehart, William Hagens, Gertrude Walker; *Cast includes:* Stephanie Bachelor, Michael Browne, Martin Kosleck, Betty Shaw, Paul Stanton, Mary Currier.

Michael Browne investigates the disappearance of his reporter brother in this minor mystery about an industrialist who tries to suppress the news of his associate's death. When the reporter learns the truth, the industrialist has him kidnapped. The dead man's daughter helps Browne unravel the mystery when she leads him to her father's corpse. An interesting title is wasted on a routine drama.

186 CRIME RING (1938), RKO.

Dir. Leslie Goodwins; *Sc.* J. Robert Bren, Gladys Atwater; *Cast includes:* Allan Lane, Frances Mercer, Clara Blandick, Inez Courtney, Bradley Page, Ben Welden.

Newspaper reporter Allan Lane and unemployed actress Frances Mercer team up to expose fake fortune tellers and stock swindlers in this action drama. The crooked psychics, with their pseudo knowledge of the spiritual world, persuade their victims to invest their money in wild speculations. Lane, with the help of a crusading district attorney, persuades Mercer to pose as a fortune teller. She infiltrates the ring which is running a protection racket involving all the mystics. Following two murders, a kidnapping and other various acts of mayhem, the ringleaders are brought to justice. The fighting district attorney was not unlike New York's famous prosecutor of the period, Thomas A. Dewey, in many respects (the actor sports a similar mustache and is named Thomas Redwine). Hollywood released several other films loosely based on Dewey's exploits, including, among others, *Missing Witnesses* (1937), *The Last Express* (1938), and *Smashing the Rackets* (1938).

187 CRIMINAL CARGO (1939), Col.

Dir. Lewis D. Collins; *Sc.* Albert DeMond; *Cast includes:* Jack Holt, Eduardo Ciannelli, Dick Purcell, Irene Ware, Donald Briggs, Harry Carey.

Determined G-Man Jack Holt investigates the flow of counterfeit money emanating from a posh gambling ship in this routine action drama. Reporters Irene Ware and Donald Briggs lend Holt a helping hand. Posing as a crew member, Holt suspects ship owner Eduardo Ciannelli as the leader of the operation. After Dick Purcell, as Holt's partner, is murdered, the federal agent cracks down and smashes the counterfeiting ring. That same year the studio released *Behind Prison Gates*, another action drama in which the hero goes under cover to trap the villains.

188 CRIMINALS OF THE AIR (1937), Col.

Dir. C. C. Coleman; *Sc.* Owen Francis;

Cast includes: Charles Quigley, Rosalind Keith, Rita Hayworth, John Gallaudet, Marc Lawrence, Patricia Farr.

Police officer Charles Quigley poses as a pilot in his efforts to smash an alien-smuggling ring operating in a town on the Mexican-American border in this action drama. Rosalind Keith portrays an ambitious reporter who travels to the town, expecting to get a sensational story of the gang's illegal activities. Gang leader Russell Hicks owns a café across the border which he and his cronies use as their base of operations. Young Rita Hayworth, a dancer at the joint, makes a play for Quigley, but the stalwart lawman rejects her.

189 CRIMINALS WITHIN (1941), PRC.

Dir. Joseph Lewis; *Sc.* Arthur Hoerl; *Cast includes:* Eric Linden, Ann Doran, Constance Worth, Donald Curtis, Weldon Heyburn, Ben Alexander.

Enemy aliens seek to steal a secret formula known only to five chemists in this inept and muddled drama set before America's entry into World War II. The spies slay one of the scientists, hoping to obtain the list of his assistants. Eric Linden, an army draftee, becomes embroiled in the intrigue and, together with snooping reporter Ann Doran, soon discovers a nest of spies in his own company. The young couple soon become romantically involved. Constance Worth portrays one of the enemy agents.

190 CROOKS CAN'T WIN (1928), FBO.

Dir. George M. Arthur; *Sc.* Enid Hibbard; *Cast includes:* Ralph Lewis, Thelma Hill, Sam Nelson, Joe E. Brown, Eugene Strong, Charles Hall.

Newsman Joe E. Brown helps to clear a young policeman, who at first is hailed as a hero, but is later dismissed from the force for leaving his post, in this routine police drama. Ralph Lewis, the adopted son of a police family whose father is a proud, retired member of the force, captures a bank robber on his first day on the job. But later, when he refuses to explain that he had been called away to help his brother, he is dismissed from the force for abandoning his duty. Working as a truck driver, he arranges with Brown and other news reporters to have the police raid a gang of silk thieves, thereby regaining his reputation and job on the force.

191 THE CRUSADER (1932), Majestic.

Dir. Frank Strayer; *Sc.* Edward T. Lowe; *Cast includes:* Evelyn Brent, H. B. Warner, Lew Cody, Ned Sparks, Walter Byron, Marceline Day.

Hard-nosed newspaper reporter Ned Sparks and other typical Hollywood-style news hounds and managing editors focus their claws upon the reforming district attorney H. B. Warner in this trite drama based on a play by Wilson Collison. Warner is occupied with trying to get his wife, accused of a shooting, acquitted. Sparks, ironically, becomes entangled in the seedy affair when he learns that his sister is somehow involved in the shooting. Meanwhile, the world of journalism has a field day exploiting the incident.

192 THE CUB (1915), World.

Dir. Maurice Tourneur; *Cast includes:* John Hines, Martha Hedman, Robert Cummings, Jessie Lewis, Bert Starkey, Dorothy Farnum.

Cub reporter John Hines is assigned to cover a feud in the hills of Virginia in this diverting silent comedy drama based on the 1910 play by Thompson Buchanan. Hines is sent only because the major reporter is sick and only the cub is available. Attired as though he were a war correspondent, Hines arrives in the midst of the feud between the Renlows and the Whites which flared up when the former's pig was seen chewing up the latter's turnips. The cub, despite attempts to remain neutral, soon becomes embroiled in a chain of misadventures, including innocently kissing a mountaineer's daughter at a local dance. He is unaware that his action would lead to his being considered engaged to the young woman—although he happens to love the daughter of the opposing clan. He is captured and held prisoner, but luckily he was able to send an encoded message to his paper. A cavalry troop arrives in time to rescue him.

193 THE CUB REPORTER (1909), Lubin.

No other detailed information is available at the present time concerning this early one-reel film.

194 THE CUB REPORTER (1922), Goldstone.

Dir. Jack Dillon; *Sc.* George Elwood Jenks; *Cast includes:* Richard Talmadge, Edwin B. Tilton, Jean Calhoun, Ethel Hallor, Wilson Hummell, Lewis Mason.

Richard Talmadge plays the title character, an energetic young man in the manner of Douglas Fairbanks, who rescues the heroine from the clutches of some villainous Chinese in this routine action drama. Bent on getting back a jewel stolen from the eye of a Chinese idol, they kidnap young Jean Calhoun, who is the daughter of a San Francisco collector of Oriental jewels. This otherwise undistinguished film was designed chiefly to showcase the athletic antics of its star, a former stunt man for Fairbanks. Talmadge plunges head first through a skylight into the sanctum of the villains and undergoes the perils of the underground passages of the underworld before he rescues the pretty captive.

195 CURTAIN AT EIGHT (1934), Majestic.

Dir. E. Mason Hopper; *Sc.* Edward T. Lowe; *Cast includes:* Dorothy Mackaill, C. Aubrey Smith, Paul Cavanagh, Marion Shilling, Russell Hopton, Sam Hardy.

Overly familiar incidents and too many stereotyped characters contribute to the failure of this backstage murder mystery. Sam Hardy, the proverbial inept policeman, and Russell Hopton, the familiar tiresome wisecracking reporter, go through their usual paces until the murderess, an actress who has suffered from unrequited love, is finally revealed.

196 THE CZAR OF BROADWAY (1930), U.

Dir. William James Craft; *Sc.* Gene Towne; *Cast includes:* John Wray, Betty Compson, John Harron, Claude Allister, Wilbur Mack.

John Harron portrays a reporter who values friendship above his profession in this drama which criticizes the world of journalism. Harron is hired by a managing editor to expose underworld czar John Wray, who controls a large portion of the city's night activities as well as much of the press. Harron, posing as a naive country boy, befriends Wray, who eventually learns Harron's identity. Wray assigns one of his men to kill Harron, but the czar and his henchman are gunned down by a rival gang before the order can be carried out. Because of their friendship, Harron refuses to print an exposé of the gangster and resigns his position. At one point, nightclub hostess Betty Compson questions Harron's choice of occupation. "Why did you have to pick such a rotten racket?" she asks. "If you have to be a reporter, why can't you work on the society columns?"

197 DANCE, FOOLS, DANCE (1931), MGM.

Dir. Harry Beaumont; *Sc.* Richard Schayer; *Cast includes:* Joan Crawford, Lester Vail, Cliff Edwards, William Bakewell, William Holden, Clark Gable.

Socialite Joan Crawford turns reporter after her father loses his money in the stock market in this seedy romantic drama. When her own funds run out and her rich society friends turn against her, Crawford finds employment as a reporter to earn a living. William Bakewell, her brother, is entangled with hoodlum Clark Gable and a gangland shooting—similar to the infamous St. Valentine's Day Massacre—which Gable has arranged. After fellow reporter Cliff Edwards, who has been investigating the massacre, is killed by her brother, Crawford goes undercover to solve the murders. She meets Gable, who then discovers her real motive and orders her to be killed. Bakewell intervenes and in a fight with Gable both men are killed. A rich friend then realizes the strength of Crawford's character and can't help falling in love with her. Gable, in one of his earliest roles, establishes his tough-guy image here, in spite of such hackneyed dialogue as the following: "Now listen close because I don't repeat myself," he utters to one of his minions. "You got us into this jam and you're going to get us out. You're going to meet this bird at the subway entrance and you're going to let him have it!" This incident was based on the real-life slaying of Jack Lingle, a Chicago newspaperman who was closely associated with members of the underworld. *The Finger Points*, another film based on Lingle's newspaper career, was released the same year, with Richard Barthelmess portraying the ill-fated reporter.

198 DANCING CO-ED (1939), MGM.

Dir. S. Sylvan Simon; *Sc.* Albert Mannheimer; *Cast includes:* Lana Turner, Richard Carlson, Artie Shaw, Ann Rutherford, Lee Bowman, Thurston Hall.

College reporter Richard Carlson, while trying to expose a "plant" placed in his college by a publicity agent, falls in love with entertainer Lana Turner in this entertaining comedy drama. When a film producer learns that a member of a dancing team scheduled for his new production is pregnant, he desperately looks around for a replacement. Press agent Roscoe Karns suggests a national contest to find a dancing co-ed for the movie role. Meanwhile, the breezy agent surreptitiously places Turner in college where she will end up winning the contest. She is accompanied by Ann Rutherford, Karns's secretary. Carlson uncovers the plot but falls for the attractive dancer. Following several complications, fellow student Rutherford ends up winning the contest and the film contract for the leading role.

199 DANGER STREET (1947), Par.

Dir. Lew Landers; *Sc.* Maxwell Shane, Winston Miller, Kae Salkow; *Cast includes:* Jane Withers, Robert Lowery, Bill Edwards, Elaine Riley, Audrey Young, Lyle Talbot.

Two young people face a variety of problems while running a photo magazine, including the unraveling of a murder, in this mystery. In need of more money, young Jane Withers and Robert Lowery, who have purchased the magazine they had been working for, sell a controversial photo of Charles Quigley, the fiancé of wealthy Elaine Riley, to a rival magazine. When the buyer is killed, the young couple turn to sleuthing. Following another murder, Withers tricks the killer into confessing. Quigley, she learns, had been plotting to marry the young woman for her money.

200 A DANGEROUS AFFAIR (1931), Col.

Dir. Edward Sedgwick; *Sc.* Howard J. Green; *Cast includes:* Jack Holt, Ralph Graves, Sally Blane, Susan Fleming, Blanche Frederici, Edward Brophy.

Police lieutenant Jack Holt and newspaper reporter Ralph Graves, as friendly rivals, investigate the murder of a lawyer in this slow-moving drama. The tale is set in a normally quiet, outlying district police precinct where the two pals proceed in solving the killing.

201 DANGEROUS TRAFFIC (1926), Goodwill.

Dir. Ben Cohen; *Sc.* Ben Cohen; *Cast includes:* Francis X. Bushman, Jack Perrin, Mildred Harris, Tom London, Ethan Laidlaw, Hal Walters.

Newspaper reporter Francis X. Bushman, on the staff of the *Seaside Record,* investigates the activities of a gang of smugglers in this familiar drama. The gang had already exacted its toll upon revenue agent Jack Perrin, who was wounded in a gunfight with one of the smugglers. Working undercover by joining the gang, Bushman finally gets enough evidence to convict its members. The hero meets and falls in love with Mildred Harris. She is working as a cigarette girl at a local seaside inn where she is trying to gather proof concerning the death of her brother at the hands of the smugglers.

202 THE DARING OF DIANA (1916), V-L-S-E.

Dir. S. Rankin Drew; *St.* Charles L. Gaskill; *Cast includes:* Anita Stewart, Charles Wellesley, Francis Morgan, Anders Randolf, Julia Swayne Gordon, Joseph Donohue.

Star reporter Anita Stewart helps out hard-working Charles Wellesley, managing editor of his father's New York newspaper, in this farfetched silent drama. The editor refuses to deal with crooked politicians seeking special favors. While Wellesley rejects any form of compromise, Francis Morgan, his father, who resides in Paris and whom he has never seen, wires that he is coming home. Actually, Morgan has been retained in Europe by his business manager who plans to impersonate him in New York and come to terms with the politicians. Fortunately, Stewart, Wellesley's girlfriend, exposes the scheme and saves the integrity of the paper. One interesting sequence concerns a factory fire in the Bronx which shows young female workers leaping from the windows of the burning structure. The incident is reminiscent of the tragic 1911 Triangle Fire in New York in which 146 young women died as a result of poor sweatshop conditions. *The Still Alarm* (1911), *The Crime of Carelessness* (1912), *The Locked Door* (1914) and *The High Road* (1915) were other silent dramas based on the tragic fire.

203 THE DARING YOUNG MAN (1935), TCF.

Dir. William A. Seiter; *Sc.* William Hurlbut; *Cast includes:* James Dunn, Mae Clarke, Neil Hamilton, Sidney Toler, Warren Hymer.

James Dunn and Mae Clarke, reporters on rival newspapers, often compete for the same story in this familiar but good-natured minor comedy drama. At one point, Dunn is assigned to write about prison life at New York's Welfare Island. He soon detects criminal Warren Hymer, who had earlier robbed the United States Treasury, hiding out behind bars! Meanwhile, Clarke is left behind at the church waiting for the groom to show up. The incident involving the criminal was similar to one which had actually occurred and was reported in the press. Dunn occasionally appeared in other newspaper films. Sidney Toler, who played a minor role, later gained fame portraying Earl Derr Biggers's fictional Hawaiian detective Charlie Chan in a popular series of films. Clarke had the dubious distinction of being the recipient of James Cagney's grapefruit, which he perversely squashed in her face, in the gangster classic *The Public Enemy* (1931).

204 THE DARK (1979), Film Ventures.

Dir. John Cardos; *Sc.* Stanford Whitmore; *Cast includes:* William Devane, Cathy Lee Crosby, Richard Jaeckel, Keenan Wynn, Jacquelyn Hyde, Biff Elliot.

Writer William Devane and television newscaster Cathy Lee Crosby become involved in a series of gruesome murders in this well-produced but familiar science fiction thriller set in a California town. It seems that an alien invader has taken it upon itself to engage in a killing spree. Victims are either decapitated or disintegrated by the creature's laser-like eyes. The film gets bogged down in a chain of repetitive sequences showing the stalking and killing of victims. Ironically, the creature appears as a werewolf in jeans! The ending depicts both Devane and Crosby, who have been tracking the killer, trapped in the dark by the alien. But for no earthly reason, the alien suddenly self-destructs—perhaps planning a triumphal return in a sequel. The film is sometimes listed under its alternate title: *The Mutilator*.

205 THE DAY OF FAITH (1923), Goldwyn.

Dir. Tod Browning; *Sc.* June Mathis, Katharine Cavanaugh; *Cast includes:* Eleanor Boardman, Tyrone Power, Raymond Griffith, Wallace MacDonald, Ford Sterling, Charles Conklin.

Reporter Raymond Griffith, hired by millionaire Tyrone Power to discredit the work of missionary Eleanor Boardman, decides instead to join her in this social drama based on the 1921 novel by Arthur Somers Roche. The greedy millionaire disapproves of his son, Wallace MacDonald, who has fallen in love with Boardman, and hopes to end the romance with her failure. However, when the reporter witnesses her sincerity and the importance of her work in the faces of the needy, he volunteers his services at the mission. Meanwhile an angry mob, resentful of the millionaire's many injustices, attacks his son who is beaten to death. After the loss of young MacDonald, the despondent father contrasts his own greed and selfishness to the benevolent work of Boardman and decides to reform.

206 DEAD MEN DON'T DIE (1991), Waymar.

Dir. Malcom Marmorstein; *Sc.* Malcolm Marmorstein; *Cast includes:* Elliott Gould, Melissa Anderson, Mark Moses, Mabel King, Philip Bruns, Jack Betts.

Television anchorman Elliott Gould, who is killed while targeting suspected criminals, returns as a zombie in this deadly horror comedy. He then goes about solving his own murder. Meanwhile, the film conjures up a number of clichés, including the dumb police officer, the even dumber criminals, the not-too-bright blonde, voodoo-practicing blacks, and greedy television executives. Mabel King, as the Jamaican cleaning woman with voodoo skills, resurrects Gould for her own ulterior motives. The plot ends with Gould's killers being turned into zombies along with their victim. The dialogue of this pointless film never reaches above the level of the following line issued by a news manager to a co-anchorwoman: "Let's have some open blouses. More cleavage around here!"

207 DEADLINE AT ELEVEN (1920), Vitagraph.

Dir. George Fawcett; *Sc.* Lucien Hubbard; *Cast includes:* Corinne Griffith, Maurice Costello, Frank Thomas, Dodson Mitchell, Webster Campbell, Alice Calhoun.

Independent-minded socialite Corinne Griffith, who walks out on her family after refusing to marry someone she does not love, succeeds as a columnist in this romantic drama. She gets a job on a big city paper where she meets experienced reporter Frank Thomas, whom she soon influences to give up his heavy drinking. Thomas is later found at the scene of a murder where he is arrested and wrongly accused of the crime. Although promoted as editor of the lovelorn column, Griffith takes it upon herself to track down the real killer. Her efforts exonerate the man she loves, and she gets a front-page story in by the eleven o'clock deadline. The film is noteworthy for its realistic portrayal of the workings of a typical newspaper, particularly its settings, including that of the city room.

208 DEADLINE FOR MURDER (1946), TCF.

Dir. James Tinling; *Sc.* Irving Cummings; *Cast includes:* Paul Kelly, Kent Taylor, Sheila Ryan, Jerome Cowan, Renee Carson, Joan Blair.

Good-natured big-shot gambler Kent Taylor finds himself in a web of theft and murder while trying to help a friend, Joan Blair, in this routine drama of intrigue. Taylor joins forces with police detective Paul Kelly to prevent thieves Jerome Cowan and Renee Carson from stealing a government paper regarding foreign oil deposits. However, both Taylor and Kelly are often hindered in their efforts by overly conscientious reporter Sheila Ryan. Kelly arrives in time to arrest Cowan for killing those who have previously possessed the coveted document.

209 DEADLINE U.S.A. (1952), TCF.

Dir. Richard Brooks; *Sc.* Richard Brooks; *Cast includes:* Humphrey Bogart, Ethel Barrymore, Kim Hunter, Ed Begley, Paul Stewart, Martin Gabel.

One of the better newspaper films to come out of Hollywood, this drama focuses on the demise of a respected daily while underscoring the importance of a free and fair press. Humphrey Bogart, as its idealistic and dauntless managing editor, struggles unsuccessfully to keep it from being sold by its uncaring heirs to a rival company. "An honest, fearless press," he pleads, "is the public's first protection against gangsterism—local or international." Meanwhile, his reporters are on the verge of breaking a story about the murder of a young woman who might have been involved with Rienzi, the city's number one mobster (Martin Gabel). Questioned at a senate crime commission hearing about how he could possibly have accumulated so much wealth and property on his lowly income, the arrogant Rienzi replies glibly, "Sometimes I wonder myself, Senator." When his thugs brutally beat up one of Bogart's reporters who is investigating the murder, Bogart concentrates one of the last editions of the paper on exposing Rienzi and his related rackets. After the hoodlums kill the murdered woman's brother who is willing to implicate Rienzi, the mother of the two victims, a loyal reader of the moribund paper, enters the newspaper office and hands Bogart a shoe box filled with enough evidence to convict the gangster.

210 DEATH FROM A DISTANCE (1935), Che.

Dir. Frank R. Strayer; *Sc.* John W. Krafft; *Cast includes:* Russell Hopton, Lola Lane, George Marion Sr., John St. Polis, Lee Kohlmar, Lew Kelly.

A planetarium serves as setting for an otherwise routine murder mystery. While Lee Kohlmar, an eccentric professor at the Trowbridge Planetarium is presenting a lecture, a gunshot rings out in the dark, resulting in the death of a wealthy drug manufacturer. Detective Russell Hopton is assigned to investigate the cleverly executed murder by an unknown killer. Several astronomers immediately fall under suspicion, all of whom disagree about the direction of the shot. Newspaper reporter Lola Lane, who provides some humor as she parries insults with Hopton and his slow-witted assistant Lew Kelly, arrives to cover the story. When she tries to leave to report her scoop, Hopton refuses to give her permission. She slips past the guard and calls in her story, which includes a rebuke aimed at the lieutenant and his incompetent assistants. Her articles continue to attack Hopton, who nevertheless has made progress in the case. Finally, Lane acknowledges the officer's skills and joins forces with him. They soon discover that the fatal bullet was fired through a device affixed to the planetarium apparatus. The pair set a trap for the killer who then reveals himself and confesses. The title provides a hint as to how George Marion Sr., as the murderer, did away with his victim. The comic interplay between Hopton and Lane adds human interest to this fairly suspenseful whodunit.

211 DEATH ON THE DIAMOND (1934), MGM.

Dir. Edward Sedgwick; *Sc.* Harvey Thew, Joseph Sherman, Ralph Spence; *Cast includes:* Robert Young, Madge Evans, Nat Pendleton, Ted Healy, C. Henry Gordon, Paul Kelly.

This murder mystery with a baseball background, based on the novel by Cortland Fitzsimmons, struck out with most contemporary critics who complained about the lack of human interest in the characters. Three players of the St. Louis Cardinals are murdered before a grounds laborer is targeted as the killer. The plot offers other likely suspects, including C. Henry Gordon as a villainous gambler and Paul Kelly portraying an officious traveling reporter. The best part of the film is the comic rivalry between Nat Pendleton, as a catcher, and Ted Healy, playing a pitcher.

212 DECEPTIONS II: EDGE OF DECEPTION (1995), Libra.

Dir. George Mihalka; *Sc.* Simon Abbott, Miguel Tejada-Flores; *Cast includes:* Mariel Hemingway, Stephen Shellen, Jennifer Rubin, Wally Dalton, Vladimir Kulich, Zachary Throne.

Crime reporter Mariel Hemingway becomes deeply involved in the private life and affairs of Stephen Shellen, a police lieutenant living on the edge, in this sleazy film noir hindered by a convoluted and farfetched plot. Taken off duty for drunkenness and general neglect of his job, Shellen finds himself enchanted by Jennifer Rubin, a sexy wife who has moved across the street from his apartment. He soon discovers she is being physically abused by her husband, Vladimir Kulich, whom the detective kills when the husband threatens his wife with a gun. Shellen is suspended from the force for his suspicious involvement in the shooting, but continues his love affair with the widow. Meanwhile, reporter Hemingway presses him for an interview about romantic relations between policemen and victims. Following a string of improbable complications, Shellen learns that Hemingway and Rubin had been roommates in college and they have both conspired to spin a web of murder which has ensnared him. Finally, Shellen is forced to kill Hemingway in self-defense and arrest Rubin for conspiracy.

213 DELIVERANCE (1928), Stanley Advertising.

Dir. B. K. Blake; *Sc.* Duncan Underhill.

A reporter is assigned by his employer, a newspaper owner and state senator, to undertake a survey about the effects of Prohibition in this social drama based on the books *Prohibition at Its Worst* (1926) and *Prohibition Still at Its Worst* (1928), both by Irving Fisher. The owner had almost been killed by a drunk driver, his own managing editor, earlier. Lobbyists, learning of the reporter's survey, join forces with the managing editor, a major bootlegger, and try to bribe the reporter. But the journalist, in preparation of the illicit offer, has hidden a Dictaphone in his office and records the bribery deal. As a result, the owner dismisses the editor, and the reporter marries his employer's daughter.

214 THE DEMON SHADOW (1919) *see Zudora (The Twenty Million Dollar Mystery)* (1914).

215 DESIGN FOR SCANDAL (1941), MGM.

Dir. Norman Taurog; *Sc.* Lionel Houser; *Cast includes:* Rosalind Russell, Walter Pidgeon, Edward Arnold, Lee Bowman, Jean Rogers, Mary Beth Hughes.

When newspaper publisher Edward Arnold is hit with an alimony suit, he assigns his crack newspaper reporter, Walter Pidgeon, to discredit judge Rosalind Russell in this fairly entertaining comedy burdened with a familiar plot. Pidgeon trails Russell to Cape Cod where he begins to woo her. Of course, he ends up falling in love with the judge. Russell detects his original motive and drags him and his employer into court, charging them with conspiracy. All is forgiven, however, when under cross-examination, Pidgeon reveals he truly loves her.

216 DESIGNING WOMAN (1957), MGM.

Dir. Vincente Minnelli; *Sc.* George Wells; *Cast includes:* Gregory Peck, Lauren Bacall, Dolores Gray, Sam Levene, Tom Helmore, Jesse White.

Crusading sports writer Gregory Peck marries fashion designer Lauren Bacall, but their disparate worlds soon collide in this winning comedy reminiscent of the Spencer Tracy-Katharine Hepburn romps of the past. One major conflict arises from their differences in choice of friends. Hers stem from the world of society while his pals spring from arenas and gyms. In addition, Peck's ex-flame, Dolores Gray, adds to the couple's problems. Meanwhile, Peck becomes the target of hoodlums resulting from his exposés of the fight game. Comic situations are enhanced by the bright dialogue. During a fight between the couple, for example, Bacall accidentally draws blood when she opens a wound on Peck's nose. Noticing her lack of emotion at the incident, Peck acidly asks, "How is it that you can't stand the sight of blood on anyone except me?" In another scene Bacall comments upon her stormy marriage. "We never argue anymore," she explains. "And when we do, it never lasts for more than a week or two. We're happily married." Screenwriter George Wells won an Academy Award for Best Story and Screenplay.

217 THE DEVIL'S CARGO (1925), Par.

Dir. Victor Fleming; *Sc.* A. P. Younger; *Cast includes:* Wallace Beery, Pauline Starke, Claire Adams, William Collier Jr., Raymond Hatton, George Cooper.

Newspaper editor William Collier Jr. strives to reform the citizens of Sacramento during the Gold Rush of 1849 in this drama. He mistakes Pauline Starke for a minister's daughter, but when he discovers that her father is a notorious gambler and she entertains at the local casino, he condemns her. Later, when vigilantes find Collier in Starke's room, they wrongly imagine the worst and label him a hypocrite. The aroused citizens then gather up all the gamblers and sinners, including Collier and Starke, and place them aboard a cargo ship. Following several complications aboard the vessel, Collier rescues Claire Adams, his sister, from the clutches of lascivious Wallace Beery. Another ship rescues them and Collier is reunited with Starke, preferring to spend the rest of his life with her than as a crusader.

218 DEVIL'S MATE (1933), Mon.

Dir. Phil Rosen; *Sc.* Leonard Fields, David Silverstein; *Cast includes:* Peggy Shannon, Preston Foster, Ray Walker, Hobart Cavanaugh, Paul Porcasi, Barbara Barondess.

Newspaper reporter Peggy Shannon and police inspector Preston Foster join forces to help unravel a mystery in this routine drama with an offbeat opening. Paul Fix, a young criminal convicted of murder, is being escorted to his execution in the electric chair. Realizing all chances for a reprieve are gone, he is about to name a major crime lord who had arranged and ordered the murder when a poisoned dart suddenly silences his lips. The only suspects are members of the press and other official witnesses to the scheduled execution, all of whom are held for questioning by inspector Foster. Shannon's brusque manner almost costs her her life as she stumbles about in search of clues. Foster eventually arrests Harry Holman, a politician and pal of the deceased. Holman cannot explain why he, a nonsmoker, has a cigarette case in his possession. Shannon, meanwhile, who is looking for fellow reporter Ray Walker, is not convinced that Foster has the right man. Following a series of complications, including another suspect held for the murder and another killing again involving poison, Shannon discovers enough evidence that leads the inspector to arrest Hobart Cavanaugh, a local philanthropist and candidate for the Prison Board.

219 THE DIAMOND TRAIL (1933), Mon.

Dir. Harry Fraser; *Sc.* Sherman Lowe; *Cast includes:* Rex Bell, Frances Rich, Lloyd Whitlock, Bud Osborne, Norman Foster, Jerry Storm.

Courageous New York reporter Rex Bell wins the confidence of the leader of a gang of jewel thieves in this overly familiar western action feature. Having once helped out the leader, he is trusted by the gang whose members head west to meet their contact man. Bell has been functioning as their liaison. As expected, the gang members discover the reporter's real identity and a fist fight ensues. The culprits eventually are rounded up and the reporter wins the affection of Frances Rich, the young heroine who has had little to do while waiting to be wooed by the Manhattan news hound.

220 DISCARDED LOVERS (1932), Tower.

Dir. Fred Newmeyer; *Sc.* Edward T. Lowe; *Cast includes:* Natalie Moorhead, J. Farrell MacDonald, Sharon Lynn, Russell Hopton, Jason Robards, Robert Frazer.

When actress Irma Gladden (Natalie Moorhead) is found dead, several of her former lovers and husbands and other assorted characters become suspects in this mystery set at times in a movie studio. New York reporter Russell Hopton, adept at solving murders, is called in by the local police. Film rushes of an opening scene, shown in the screening room, prove that the scenario writer, who was jealous of the victim's many affairs, committed the murder. The film studio background proved the most interesting aspect of the humdrum plot.

221 DISHONORED LADY (1947), UA.

Dir. Robert Stevenson; *Sc.* Edmund H. North; *Cast includes:* Hedy Lamarr, Dennis O'Keefe, John Loder, William Lundigan, Morris Carnovsky, Paul Cavanagh.

Psychologically troubled magazine publisher Hedy Lamarr is wrongly accused of murdering John Loder, her former lover, in this fairly absorbing, sometimes heavy-handed, drama based on the play by Edward Sheldon and Margaret Ayer Barnes. Earlier, a failed attempt at suicide leads Lamarr to seek psychiatric help from doctor Morris Carnovsky. She meets young doctor Loder, falls in love with him, and they break up. She then meets Dennis O'Keefe and they fall in love. Eventually, she is exonerated in this depiction of her rather promiscuous lifestyle.

222 DOCTOR X (1932), WB.

Dir. Michael Curtiz; *Sc.* Robert Tasker, Earl Baldwin; *Cast includes:* Lionel Atwill, Lee Tracy, Fay Wray, Preston Foster, Arthur Edmund Carewe, John Wray.

Lee Tracy portrays an inquisitive reporter who investigates strange goings-on at a laboratory in this part-horror and part-murder mystery based on the play by Howard W. Comstock and Allen C. Miller. A series of gruesome murders puzzle the police and the medical staff of a surgical research laboratory, headed by doctor Lionel Atwill. Tracy undergoes confinement to a closet filled with skeletons, suffers an attack of gas fumes and barely escapes with his life from a struggle with a monster. He eventually rescues Fay Wray, Atwill's daughter, from laboratory assistant Preston Foster, the crazed murderer, who earlier does not fall under any suspicion because of a missing left hand. But it seems Foster, in the dark of night, carried out his macabre strangulations and dismemberments by using a synthetic hand. At one point, Atwill shows sympathy for his deranged assistant. "You're not feeling well? Atwill inquires. "Your arm is troubling you? Well, it's foolish to sit there in discomfort." Foster then yanks off his artificial arm. One of the earliest sound dramas to be produced in Technicolor, the film uses the process judicially.

223 DON'T FENCE ME IN (1945), Rep.

Dir. John English; *Sc.* Dorrell McGowan, Stuart E. McGowan; *Cast includes:* Roy Rogers, George "Gabby" Hayes, Dale Evans, Robert Livingston, Moroni Olsen, Marc Lawrence.

New York magazine photographer-reporter Dale Evans is assigned to investigate the history of a once-famous western outlaw in this better-than-average B western. Evans journeys to a dude ranch where she meets entertainer Roy Rogers and old-timer George "Gabby" Hayes, who says he had known the outlaw years earlier. The overly inquisitive Evans searches the old-timer's room and discovers that Hayes is Wildcat Kelly, the infamous outlaw. It seems a former crooked lawman, now dead, had buried another in the outlaw's grave to claim the reward. Moroni Olsen, the lawman's partner, wants Hayes dead to prevent any further investigation and sends one of his gangsters to kill him. Hayes is wounded and Rogers and his singing group track down the culprits. This part-satirical entry in the Roy Rogers western series has its lighter moments. Wildcat's epitaph reads: "For Wildcat Kelly life held no terror; forgetting to duck was his only error." Even Rogers offers a couple of one-liners. When a matronly ranch guest remarks that "the West is so big," he retorts, "Yes, it runs all the way to the East." The cowboy star, Evans and the "Sons of the Pioneers" sing several popular ballads, including "Along the Navajo Trail" and the title song. The following year the three leads appeared in another entertaining western about the world of journalism titled *Home in Oklahoma.*

224 DON'T GO NEAR THE WATER (1957), MGM.

Dir. Charles Walters; *Sc.* Dorothy Kingsley, George Wells; *Cast includes:* Glenn Ford, Gia Scala, Earl Holliman, Anne Francis, Keenan Wynn, Fred Clark.

Set on a Pacific island during World War II, this delightful comedy, adapted from the novel by William Brinkley, relates the adventures of U.S. Navy public relations officers. These land-locked navy men, who have never seen active duty and have never even been aboard a ship, spend the war catering to visiting stateside politicians and satisfying reporters' requests for human interest stories for the folks back home. Mickey Shaughnessy is hilarious as a foul-mouthed sailor whose every other word is blanked out on the sound track by a raucous honk. The clever dialogue adds to the comedy. A sailor on the island cannot find proper substitutes for loin cloths for the natives. "You'd be surprised at the variance in loins," he says in earnest to Glenn Ford. "Well," Ford quips, "live and loin, man." Later, when an attractive woman asks Ford to introduce her to an admiral, he says he can't. "Why not?" she asks. "You're both in the same war." In another scene a sailor takes his date for an evening walk on the beach. "During this time of the year," he explains, "these slippery little creatures come up on the beach, stop, spawn, and then go out to sea again." "Sounds like some naval officers I know," his date wisecracks.

225 DON'T NEGLECT YOUR WIFE (1921), Goldwyn.

Dir. Wallace Worsley; *Sc.* Louis Sherwin; *Cast includes:* Mabel Julienne Scott, Lewis Stone, Charles Clary, Kate Lester, Arthur Hoyt, Josephine Crowell.

Neglected wife Mabel Julienne Scott selects bright newspaper reporter Lewis Stone for her companion—with almost tragic results—in this domestic drama set chiefly in 1876 San Francisco. After several meetings, the lovers decide to end the affair to avoid further pain to both parties and her husband. But a scandal ensues in spite of their good intentions, and the husband, Charles Clary, requests that Stone leave the city. The reporter quits his job and ends up on New York's tough Bowery as an alcoholic. Scott, meanwhile, divorces her husband and searches for Stone. She then helps to regenerate him to his former status. This is another in a long line of plots associating journalists with a drinking problem—a practice that will continue unabated for the next couple of decades.

226 DOUBLE ADVENTURE (1921) serial, Pathé.

Dir. W. S. Van Dyke; *Cast includes:* Charles Hutchison, Josie Sedgwick, Ruth Langston, Carl Stockdale, S. E. Jennings, Louis D'Or.

Charles Hutchison plays a dual role in

this fifteen-chapter serial from a story by Jack Cunningham. He portrays a young reporter who helps to rescue the grand-niece of a murdered millionaire as well as the reporter's look-alike, the dead man's son. In the role of journalist, he prevents the heroine, Josie Sedgwick, from being kidnapped by Carl Stockdale, the dead man's crooked business manager, who had committed the murder. The victim had learned that Stockdale had embezzled the young woman's fortune.

227 DOUBLE ALIBI (1940), U.

Dir. Philip Rosen; *Sc.* Harold Buchman, Roy Chanslor, Charles Grayson; *Cast includes:* Wayne Morris, Margaret Lindsay, William Gargan, Roscoe Karns, Robert Emmett Keane, James Burke.

Estranged husband Wayne Morris is accused of killing his wife and two other persons in this suspenseful mystery. Reporter Margaret Lindsay, who at first believes Morris is guilty, helps the wounded fugitive by removing a bullet from his arm. Following several complications, Morris is exonerated when the real murderer, a police captain played by James Burke, is unmasked. News cameraman Roscoe Karns and fellow reporter Robert E. Keane handle the comedy relief in this diverting drama.

228 DOUBLE EXPOSURE (1944), Par.

Dir. William Berke; *Sc.* Winston Miller, Maxwell Shane; *Cast includes:* Chester Morris, Nancy Kelly, Phillip Terry, Jane Farrar, Richard Gaines.

Nancy Kelly, as a news photographer working for weekly photo magazine editor Chester Morris, finds herself embroiled as a suspect in a murder in this fast-paced low-budget drama. Morris had recently hired Kelly from the Midwest, thinking he was employing a man. However, he soon began falling in love with her, especially when she proved to be effective at her work. When the police suspect her in a murder case and arrest her, Morris, unable to free her, sets out to unmask the real killer. He accomplishes this through trick photography, which forces the culprit to confess. Morris, an underrated actor, was better known for his role as Boston Blackie in a popular comedy drama series released throughout the 1940s.

229 THE DOUBLE ROOM MYSTERY (1917), U.

Dir. Hobart Henley; *Sc.* E. J. Clawson; *Cast includes:* Gertrude Selby, Hayward Mack, Edward Brady, Edward Hearn, Ernest Shields.

Reporter Hayward Mack captures an escaped convict and murderer while rescuing boardinghouse maid Gertrude Selby in this routine silent crime drama. Edward Hearn, the convict, has returned to kill Edward Brady, his crooked lawyer. Brady has lured the innocent maid to his room when Hearn suddenly appears. The convict shoots Brady, and Mack, residing in the next apartment and who has heard the noise, enters and captures Hearn. He flees to his office to write up his story and learns that the maid, Selby, has been charged with the killing. The reporter then presents the real murderer to the police.

230 DOWN AMONG THE SHELTERING PALMS (1953), TCF.

Dir. Edmund Goulding; *Sc.* Claude Binyon, Albert Lewin, Burt Styler; *Cast includes:* William Lundigan, Jane Greer, Mitzi Gaynor, David Wayne, Gloria De Haven, Gene Lockhart.

Spurned journalist Gloria De Haven creates problems for U.S. Army officer William Lundigan in this mild World War II service comedy. While American troops are occupying a South Pacific island during the war, Lundigan is forced to set the tone among his men concerning non-fraternization between them and the native women. Although he has fallen in love with Jane Greer, the daughter of missionary Gene Lockhart, he restrains himself. Following complications involving the journalist, whom Lundigan shuns, she writes negative reports about conditions on the island. An investigation is held and Lundigan is eventually cleared of any charges. The non-fraternizing restriction is finally dropped, and nature proceeds to take its course among the soldiers and the islanders. Songs like the title tune and "I'm a Ruler of a South Sea Island," along with native dances and costumes and the use of Technicolor, capture the atmosphere of a romantic tropical paradise.

231 DOWN RIO GRANDE WAY (1942), Col.

Dir. William Berke; *Sc.* Paul Franklin; *Cast includes:* Charles Starrett, Russell Hayden, Britt Wood, Rose Anne Stevens, Norman Willis, Davidson Clark.

Davison Clark, a newspaper publisher in a small Texas town who is busily engaged in fermenting trouble, is in collusion with anti-Texas factions in Washington in this minor western yarn set during the stormy early days in the history of the state. Texas Ranger Charles Starrett is assigned to put a stop to the turbulence in certain regions before a congressional committee arrives to observe the stability of these counties. Following several fights with Clark's henchmen, Starrett ferrets out the publisher as the chief villain. Rancher Russell Hayden, who is looking forward to statehood, assists the Ranger.

232 DRAG (1929), FN.

Dir. Frank Lloyd; *Sc.* Bradley King; *Cast includes:* Richard Barthelmess, Lucien Littlefield, Katherine Parker, Alice Day, Tom Dugan, Margaret Fielding.

Young Richard Barthelmess has a difficult time making up his mind about which of two women he loves in this romantic comedy drama based on the novel by William Dudley Pelley. After taking over publication of a Vermont newspaper, he marries Alice Day, the overly devoted daughter of parents who own a boarding house. Day remains inseparable from her family. Barthelmess had earlier liked Lila Lee, a local young woman who seemed too sophisticated for the town. He goes to New York to sell a play he has finished and meets Lee, now a prominent costume designer. She helps him sell his musical and, upon learning that he intends to remain married, she then leaves for Paris. Although he discovers he loves her, he decides to stay with his wife whom he sends for. When Day and her entire family arrive, Barthelmess realizes he no longer cares for her and leaves to join the woman he truly loves.

233 DRIFTING (1932), Powers.

Dir. Morris R. Schlank; *Sc.* Douglas Doty, Norman Houston; *Cast includes:* Shirley Grey, Theodore von Eltz, Raymond Hatton, Edmund Breese.

Raymond Hatton, a tough, cynical newspaper reporter, rescues a wealthy victim from a scam involving a drunk driving charge in this mediocre drama. Framed for running down a pedestrian while driving under the influence, the dupe is offered a proposition that for $5,000 a woman will testify that she was with him elsewhere at the time of the accident. The witness claims she needs the money for her father's operation. Hatton investigates the scheme and exposes it, thereby freeing the victim from the false allegations.

234 DUKE OF CHICAGO (1949), Rep.

Dir. George Blair; *Sc.* Albert DeMond; *Cast includes:* Tom Brown, Audrey Long, Grant Withers, Paul Harvey, Skeets Gallagher, Lois Hall.

Newspaper reporter Audrey Long helps her beau, prizefighter Tom Brown, overcome a nest of greedy gamblers in this timeworn action drama based on a novel by Lucien Cary. Brown, a former fighter presently in the book-publishing business, is compelled to return to the ring to bail out his financially pressed firm. Gamblers who think he can't win the big fight then intervene and want him to take a dive, but he refuses. Although suffering a broken hand, he goes on to win the bout. The police then arrive in time to rescue the champ from gambler Grant Withers and his minions, who want to kill Brown for not throwing the fight.

235 DUTY'S REWARD (1927), Ellbee.

Dir. Bertram Bracken; *Sc.* A. B. Barringer; *Cast includes:* Allan Roscoe, Eva Novak, Lou Archer, Edward Brownell, George Fawcett.

Newspaper reporter Lou Archer is determined to expose the man responsible for the collapse of a large building in this familiar silent drama. The structure was built with inferior material and with the full knowledge of Allan Roscoe, the chief conspirator. Another plot involves a brave motorcycle cop who rescues heroine Eva Novak. The most startling and disturbing sequence in an otherwise routine film is the early segment in which the large building collapses.

236 DYNAMITE SMITH (1924), Pathé.

Dir. Ralph Ince; *Sc.* C. Gardner Sullivan; *Cast includes:* Charles Ray, Jacqueline Logan, Bessie Love, Wallace Beery, Lydia Knott, S. D. Wilcox.

Newspaper reporter Charles Ray, usually demure by nature, runs off to Alaska with Bessie Love, the wife of a killer, in this sprawling drama. Assigned to cover a San Francisco murder case, he meets the despondent wife and, sympathizing with her, decides to protect her from further abuse by settling down with her in a remote place. But Wallace Beery, her surly and degenerate husband, manages to find the couple. Ray flees with Love's baby and meets Jacqueline Logan, a restaurant worker. Later, Beery shows up again, but this time Ray sets a bear trap for him and Beery, who is caught in the snare, finally perishes in an explosion.

237 EACH DAWN I DIE (1939), WB.

Dir. William Keighley; *Sc.* Norman Reilly Raine, Warren Duff, Charles Perry; *Cast includes:* James Cagney, George Raft, George Bancroft, Jane Bryan, Maxie Rosenbloom, Stanley Ridges.

Newspaper reporter James Cagney is framed on a manslaughter charge by crooked politicians and ends up in prison in this highly exciting drama based on the novel by Jerome Odlum. After gathering enough evidence to convict influential politicians, Cagney is kidnapped before he is able to print his scoop. He is knocked unconscious, soaked with liquor and placed at the wheel of a car which kills a pedestrian. In prison he befriends racketeer George Raft, who had earlier met reporter Cagney. "Write a piece about me," Raft jokingly requests of the newsman. "I like my name in the paper." Later, Cagney helps the gangster to escape. Cagney, although embittered about his frame-up and failure to win a parole, does not participate in a jail break. "I'll get out," he utters at one point, "if I have to kill every screw in the hole!" Meanwhile Raft, mortally wounded, repays his debt to Cagney. He wrests a confession, overheard by the warden, from a prisoner involved in Cagney's incarceration. The reporter is finally exonerated and released.

238 EASY TO WED (1946), MGM.

Dir. Edward Buzzell; *Sc.* Dorothy Kingsley; *Cast includes:* Van Johnson, Esther Williams, Lucille Ball, Keenan Wynn, Cecil Kellaway, Ben Blue.

A metropolitan newspaper in the midst of a libel suit by wealthy socialite Esther Williams hires ladies' man Van Johnson to romance Williams, thereby weakening her case, in this entertaining musical comedy. Comic character actor Keenan Wynn, the paper's manager, contrives the scheme to rescue the paper. To win Williams's affection—in a very comical sequence—Johnson joins her and her father Cecil Kellaway during a duck hunt in which a canine steals the show. Of course, the couple finally fall in love and the socialite drops her suit. The film is a remake of *Libeled Lady*, released earlier in 1936, with Myrna Loy and William Powell as the leads.

239 THE ELECTRIC HORSEMAN (1979), Col.

Dir. Sydney Pollack; *Sc.* Robert Garland, Paul Gaer; *Cast includes:* Robert Redford, Jane Fonda, John Saxon, Alan Arbus, Wilford Brimley, Willie Nelson.

Ambitious reporter Jane Fonda tracks down five-time rodeo champion Robert Redford, who has disappeared into the desert with a $12-million show horse, in this fairly entertaining, slow-paced comedy which is hampered by its verbose script. Redford, a pitchman for a breakfast cereal corporation, is bored with his degrading personal appearances at commercial establishments. In addition, he equates Rising Star, the continually tranquilized horse, with the equally unflappable consuming public. He frees the horse and returns a hero. Ironically, the cereal sales rise to new heights. Fonda and Redford soon fall in love. John Saxon symbolizes the greedy corporate executives. The film is similar in theme to *Lonely Are the Brave* 1962), with Kirk Douglas.

240 ELENI (1985), WB.

Dir. Peter Yates; *Sc.* Steve Tesich; *Cast includes:* Kate Nelligan, John Malkovich, Linda Hunt, Ronald Pickup, Oliver Cotton, Rosalie Critchley.

An investigative reporter for the *New York Times,* Nicholas Gage decides to track down those who were responsible for his mother's 1948 execution during the Greek Civil War in this flawed drama based on Gage's 1983 memoir. John Malkovich portrays the reporter, and Kate Nelligan plays Eleni, his mother, whom we meet through the son's vivid memories and in shattering flashbacks. He learns that his mother, an apolitical woman only concerned about the safety of her family, has been tortured and killed by Greek Communists. When he finally confronts an elderly villager, his mother's chief enemy, the son loses his desire for revenge. His thoughts of Eleni's moral strength and commitment to life contrast sharply with his own lack of conviction in following through in killing this pathetic old man before him. The reporter, a colorless person detached from his wife and children because of his obsession with his own early childhood, has met the demons of his past and has failed to come to terms with them.

241 EMERGENCY SQUAD (1940), Par.

Dir. Edward Dmytryk; *Sc.* Stuart Palmer, Garnett Weston; *Cast includes:* Louise Campbell, William Henry, Richard Denning, Robert Paige, John Marston, Anthony Quinn.

Cheeky reporter Louise Campbell investigates a gang of crooks and finds herself in a serious dilemma in this minor action drama. At first unable to find work as a reporter, she is finally given a chance by a tough editor who tells her if she brings back a scoop, she will be hired. She does and is. Later, trapped in a cave-in, she is finally rescued in the nick of time. She then charges the gang with sabotage.

242 THE EMPTY CAB (1918), Bluebird.

Dir. Douglas Gerrard; *Sc.* F. McGrew Willis; *Cast includes:* Franklyn Farnum, Eileen Percy, Harry De More, Frank Brownlee, Harry Lindsey, Fred Kelsey.

Cub reporter Franklyn Farnum rescues a kidnapped young woman and smashes a counterfeiting ring in this familiar silent drama. Assigned to locate the gang of counterfeiters, he is distracted by a strange scene. He observes Eileen Percy, a young woman whom he had earlier seen passing a phony bill, being forced into a taxi. He follows the cab but later discovers it is empty. In a club known to be inhabited by the gang, he learns that Percy is being held against her will. He rescues her and rushes back to his office to write his story. But the next day the story is not printed in the paper. He then finds out the entire incident was a hoax concocted by his superiors to evaluate his prospects as a full-fledged reporter.

243 THE ESCAPE (1939), TCF.

Dir. Ricardo Cortez; *Sc.* Robert Ellis, Helen Logan; *Cast includes:* Kane Richmond, Amanda Duff, June Gale, Edward Norris, Henry Armetta, Frank Reicher.

Smalltime hoodlum Edward Norris escapes from prison and sacrifices his life to save that of his kidnapped child in this complicated drama told chiefly through a series of flashbacks to newspaper reporter Jack Carson. While Norris is behind bars, members of his gang kidnap the district attorney's adopted daughter as a ploy to keep the father from arresting and convicting them. The child happens to be Norris's daughter that he and his wife, June Gale, had given up for adoption. Police officer Kane Richmond, a friend of the family, arranges for the convict's escape so that Norris can rescue the little hostage. Norris is eventually killed in a shootout during the otherwise successful rescue. An elderly doctor relates the entire story to reporter Carson, who has rushed into the apartment of June Gale, the secret wife of gangster Edward Norris, who has just been slain.

244 ESPIONAGE (1937), MGM.

Dir. Kurt Neumann; *Sc.* Manuel Seff, Leonard Lee, Ainsworth Morgan; *Cast includes:* Edmund Lowe, Madge Evans, Paul Lukas, Leonid Kinsky, Ketti Gallian, Skeets Gallagher.

The business activities of sophisticated international munitions magnate Paul Lukas attract reporters as well as assassins in this pre-World War II drama. Foreign correspondents Edmund Lowe and Madge Evans board the same European train as Lukas to get a scoop. Also tracking the arms manufacturer is an American Communist assassin in the employ of Russia. Lukas, however, surprises his pursuers when they learn that the object of his mysterious rail journey is to quietly marry his true love and retire from the munitions business. Added to the spying element are satirical barbs aimed at capitalism and Communism in this adaptation of Walter Hackett's stage play.

245 ETERNITY (1990), Atlas.

Dir. Steven Paul; *Sc.* Dorothy Koster Paul, Steven Paul, Jon Voight; *Cast includes:* Jon Voight, Armand Assante, Eileen Davidson, Wilford Brimley, Kaye Ballard, Lainie Kazan.

Idealistic television reporter and documentarian Jon Voight damages his professional credibility when he becomes romantically involved with a suspect in this action drama with a strong supernatural motif. The young woman seems to be involved in a corrupt operation run by right-wing industrialist Armand Assante that the reporter is investigating. Voight and Assante, who have been belligerent brothers in an earlier life, personify respectively the unending struggle between good and evil.

246 EVE KNEW HER APPLES (1945), Col.

Dir. Will Jason; *Sc.* E. Edwin Moran; *Cast includes:* Ann Miller, William Wright, Robert Williams, Ray Walker, Charles D. Brown, John Eldredge.

Radio singer Ann Miller, to escape the pressures of her manager and press agent, takes a vacation in this pale musical remake of the classic screwball comedy *It Happened One Night* (1934). Between her four songs, including "Someone to Love," Miller meets and falls in love with newspaper reporter William Wright. A third version of the 1934 film appeared in 1956 titled *You Can't Run Away From It*, starring Jack Lemmon as the journalist and June Allyson as the runaway heiress.

247 EVERYTHING HAPPENS AT NIGHT (1939), TCF.

Dir. Irving Cummings; *Sc.* Art Arthur, Robert Harari; *Cast includes:* Sonja Henie, Ray Milland, Robert Cummings, Maurice Moscovich, Leonid Kinsky, Alan Dinehart.

British journalist Ray Milland vies with Robert Cummings, his American counterpart, for a scoop and the love of Sonja Henie, in this romantic drama set chiefly in Switzerland. Both reporters discover that the international political commentator Maurice Moscovich, reported slain, is alive and well and living with his daughter Henie. The two newspapermen begin to compete with each other for the story. Other complications arise when both fall in love with Henie. They resolve their differences by allowing Milland to get the big story and Cummings to win the daughter's love. A skating champion in real life, Henie shows some of her expertise on ice by performing solo in several scenes.

248 EXCLUSIVE (1937), Par.

Dir. Alexander Hall; *Sc.* John C. Moffitt, Sidney Salkow, Rian James; *Cast includes:* Fred MacMurray, Frances Farmer, Charlie Ruggles, Lloyd Nolan, Fay Holden, Ralph Morgan.

Competition between an honest newspaper run by Charlie Ruggles and its sleazy, sensational rival owned by Lloyd Nolan serves as background for this disappointing newspaper-crime drama that lacks credibility in plot and character. Idealistic assistant city editor Fred MacMurray helps to expose the crooked publisher of the rival daily. Nolan, as a corrupt politician acquitted of graft charges, buys a newspaper which he uses to blackmail local businessmen. When the owner of a department store refuses to go along, Nolan has his henchmen sabotage the store elevator, creating an accident—an incident Nolan predicts in his paper. (At least one critic commented on the spectacular crash in the elevator scene.) MacMurray is determined to bring down Nolan. After editor Ruggles is murdered by Nolan's henchmen, the angry citizens, who have learned the truth about the mobster, destroy his plant and almost lynch Nolan. But the police arrive in time to rescue him. Ruggles had gone to Nolan's office to persuade his daughter, Frances Farmer, who has joined the staff of Nolan's scandal sheet, to quit. She finally returns to her true love, MacMurray, the new city editor. In an early sequence MacMurray and Ruggles engage in some comical drinking antics, including one in which they are brought home in a police ambulance. "Newspaper people!" an infuriated neighbor declares. "A disgrace to the street." The newspaper backgrounds of several persons associated with the film, including screenwriters Moffitt and James, contributed to its realistic atmosphere.

249 EXCLUSIVE STORY (1936), MGM.

Dir. George B. Seitz; *Sc.* Michael Fessier; *Cast includes:* Franchot Tone, Madge Evans, Stuart Erwin, Joseph Calleia, Robert Barrat, J. Farrell MacDonald.

Reporter Stuart Erwin joins with girlfriend Madge Evans in exposing a major numbers racket involving murder in this conventional newspaper-crime drama. Evans, as the daughter of a grocer who is forced to take part in the numbers racket, finds the body of a rival gangster. She phones Erwin, who now gets involved in investigating the syndicate and its illegal activities. Joseph Calleia and Robert Barrat portray the major gangsters in the plot. Opening scenes effectively show how organized crime took the relatively minor numbers racket away from the African-American community and transformed it into a major, syndicated policy industry.

250 EXILE EXPRESS (1939), GN.

Dir. Otis Garrett; *Sc.* Edwin Justus Mayer, Ethel LaBlanche; *Cast includes:* Anna Sten, Alan Marshal, Jerome Cowan, Jed Prouty, Walter Catlett.

Alan Marshal, a sympathetic reporter, comes to the aid of Anna Sten, a young refugee seeking American citizenship, in this World War II drama. About to be deported, she escapes from the train journeying from the West Coast to the East. Foreign spies, who need her assistance in deciphering a secret formula, pursue her.

Marshal and Sten soon become romantically involved. Comic relief is supplied by Jed Prouty, Walter Catlett and, as a local deputy sheriff, Vince Barnett.

251 EXILED TO SHANGHAI (1937), Rep.

Dir. Nick Grinde; *Sc.* Wellyn Totman; *Cast includes:* Wallace Ford, June Travis, Dean Jagger, William Bakewell, Arthur Lake, Jonathan Hale.

Fast-talking newsreel cameraman Wallace Ford hits upon the idea of using television to transmit news events in this otherwise dull drama whose only memorable feature is its misnomer of a title. Ford, following the typical complications, finally ends up revolutionizing the field of news dissemination. Dean Jagger portrays the visionary cameraman's easily upset managing editor in one of the worst examples of stereotyping.

252 EXPOSED (1938), U.

Dir. Harold Schuster; *Sc.* Charles Kaufman, Franklin Coen; *Cast includes:* Glenda Farrell, Otto Kruger, Herbert Mundin, David Oliver, Lorraine Krueger, Charles D. Brown.

Top photo magazine photographer Glenda Farrell helps the police to capture a gang of racketeers in this action drama which is suspiciously similar to the Torchy Blane series of comedy dramas. Farrell, who often played Blane, a pert newspaper reporter, decides in the current film to help former district attorney Otto Kruger, now a gin-soaked resident of a flop house. He had earlier sent a defendant to his death. Spurred by feelings of remorse, he seeks atonement at the bottom of the proverbial bottle. Farrell clashes with a mobster while searching for the victim's daughter so that Kruger can offer some help. After assisting the determined photographer expose the mobster and his gang, Kruger gives up his depraved life on skid row.

253 EXTORTION (1938), Col.

Dir. Lambert Hillyer; *Sc.* Earl Felton; *Cast includes:* Thurston Hall, Mary Russell, Scott Colton, J. Farrell MacDonald, Frank C. Wilson, Arthur Loft, Gene Morgan.

The murder of an unpopular college proctor brings forth a stream of suspects in this feeble comedy drama. Thurston Hall, a physics professor, is one of the suspects. Mary Russell plays his daughter. Scott Colton, as the editor of the college paper, unravels the mystery. It seems the victim was blackmailing several persons on the campus, including the murderer—an honor student who had been stealing examination papers in advance of the tests. By getting suspect Hall off the hook, Colton wins the affection of the professor's daughter. The honor student is played by Albert Van Dekker, who later changed his name simply to Albert Dekker.

254 EXTRA! EXTRA! (1922), Fox.

Dir. William K. Howard; *Sc.* Arthur J. Zellner; *Cast includes:* Edna Murphy, Johnnie Walker, Herschel Mayall, Wilson Hummell, John Steppling, Gloria Woodthorpe.

Cub reporter Johnnie Walker poses as a victim who is almost drowned and later as a butler to get a story about a business merger in this minor silent drama. Sent as an assistant to veteran reporter Wilson Hummell to help the latter cover the story of an impending merger, Walker is forced to feign drowning when Hummell fails to show up and is able to fulfill the assignment. Hummell is fired and Walker is then assigned for a further interview with Theodore von Eltz, a businessman who abhors newsmen. So the cub reporter masquerades as a butler and finds himself entangled in a plot to steal several important papers concerning the merger. The film ends with Hummell getting his job back and Walker getting a promotion.

255 EYES OF THE UNDERWORLD (1929), U.

Dir. Leigh Jason, Ray Taylor; *Sc.* Leigh Jason, Carl Krusada; *Cast includes:* Bill

Cody, Sally Blane, Arthur Lubin, Harry Tenbrook, Charles Clary, Monty Montague.

A wealthy sportsman rescues his girlfriend and helps to bring a gang of murderers to justice in this action drama. Bill Cody, as the athletic hero, visits Sally Blane, the daughter of a crusading newspaper publisher who has been murdered by a gang of thieves. The wealthy publisher had planned to expose a gang of criminals with the incriminating evidence he had been gathering before they killed him. The killers decide to break into the publisher's home and destroy the damaging evidence. Cody foils their attempt to steal the papers from the victim's home, follows them to their hideout, is captured, escapes and manages to round up the culprits. His reward: the love of the grieving daughter.

256 EYEWITNESS (1981), TCF.

Dir. Peter Yates; *Sc.* Steve Tesich; *Cast includes:* William Hurt, Sigourney Weaver, Christopher Plummer, James Woods, Irene Worth, Kenneth McMillan.

William Hurt, an office-building janitor, discovers the body of a murdered Asian jeweler during his night shift and weaves himself and television newscaster Sigourney Weaver into a web of intrigue in this engrossing mystery. Hurt has been watching Weaver's broadcasts for some time and has fallen in love with her. To get closer to her, he leads her into thinking he knows more about the murder than he really does. He agrees to allow himself to be a target for the killers. The romantic relationship that develops between the reporter and the janitor seems farfetched. Meanwhile her boyfriend, Christopher Plummer, an Israeli secretly and politically involved in the crime, manipulates newscaster Weaver into setting up Hurt for elimination. Instead, she reports to the police, a move that ends in Plummer's death and in Weaver's falling in love with Hurt. "I'll tell you right now," overconfident Hurt informs Weaver as they get into bed, "It's going to be wonderful."

257 A FACE IN THE FOG (1936), Victory.

Dir. Bob Hill; *Sc.* Al Martin; *Cast includes:* June Collyer, Lloyd Hughes, Lawrence Gray, Al St. John, Jack Mulhall, Jack Cowell.

Drama editor June Collyer and news hound Lloyd Hughes help to solve a series of murders in this low-budget mystery based on the novel *The Great Mono Miracle* by Peter B. Kyne. Collyer, in an effort to draw a suspect out, unwisely writes that she can identify "The Fiend," a crazed hunchback whose assaults on cast members of the play *Satan's Bride* strikes fear in the remaining players. Reporter Hughes rescues her from one attempt upon her life by The Fiend. The pair then set out to expose the assailant to whom the police have attributed several murders. The victims, the couple learn, have been poisoned by an unidentified substance. An actor then invites them to the theater, but this is only a ploy. The place is darkened and the actor is slain. Lawrence Gray, as a playwright with some expertise in crime, is also investigating the strange goings-on. Following these horrendous killings and other complications, Hughes learns that Gray is the murderer. Just as Gray is about to claim the captured Hughes as another of his victims, Al St. John, the reporters' goofy photographer, arrives with the police. They shoot the playwright just as he is about to fire his gun at the helpless reporter. Despite its tight budget, the film offers attractive sets, suspenseful moments and a surprise ending.

258 THE FALCON STRIKES BACK (1943), RKO.

Dir. Edward Dmytryk; *Sc.* Edward Dein, Gerald Geraghty; *Cast includes:* Tom Conway, Harriet Hilliard, Jane Randolph, Edgar Kennedy, Cliff Edwards, Rita Corday.

Reporter Jane Randolph, the girlfriend of the title character played by Tom Conway, assists the amateur sleuth in uncovering a nest of vipers in this routine entry in the popular detective series based on characters created by Michael Arlen. Conway at one point is a suspect in a war bond theft, a charge that leads him to a mountain lodge where a murder is committed. Together with his assistant Cliff Edwards and reporter Randolph, Conway must study a group of suspects and find the guilty party or parties before he can absolve himself. He finally ferrets out Wynne Gibson as the head of the bond theft gang. Often in this type of drama, the reporter's role, especially when relegated to that of a girlfriend, is sublimated in favor of the main detective.

259 THE FALCON TAKES OVER (1942), RKO.

Dir. Irving Reis; *Sc.* Frank Fenton, Lynn Root; *Cast includes:* George Sanders, Lynn Bari, James Gleason, Helen Gilbert, Allen Jenkins, Ward Bond.

Brutish hoodlum Ward Bond persuades George Sanders, also known as the title character, to search for his missing girlfriend in this murder mystery based on Raymond Chandler's 1940 novel *Farewell, My Lovely*. Lynn Bari portrays a reporter who helps the adventurer-sleuth on the case. The series usually abounded in comedy, sometimes even repeating lines from one entry to another. For example, when reporters ask Sanders if he is going to work on a particular murder case, he says that the police will now be on their own. "What a break for crime!" quips his chauffeur Allen Jenkins—who had used the same line just one year earlier in *A Date With the Falcon*. Chandler's work was rewritten for the "Falcon character." It was later remade into a superior whodunit titled *Murder, My Sweet* (1944), with Dick Powell as Chandler's private detective Philip Marlowe.

260 THE FALCON'S BROTHER (1942), RKO.

Dir. Stanley Logan; *Sc.* Stuart Palmer, Craig Rice; *Cast includes:* George Sanders, Tom Conway, Jane Randolph, Don Barclay, Amanda Varela, George Lewis.

Tom Conway, who is the real-life brother of George Sanders, portraying the title character, helps him smash a spy ring in this standard spy drama. Conway tracks down a fashion magazine editor whose periodical covers are being used as a conduit for Nazi agents to send their messages across the nation. Decoding the latest magazine cover as a clue, he and plucky reporter Jane Randolph visit a small community where the spies have entrenched themselves in preparation for an assassination. Conway and his female companion are captured, brought into an abandoned church and tied up while the plane carrying the important statesman lands. The visitor is escorted through a gate as the assassins take aim. Although bound, Conway manages to pull a nearby rope which rings the church bells. Sanders hears the signal and pushes the foreign emissary out of harm's way as a concealed rifle cracks and kills the private detective instead of its intended target. Police officers round up the gang of spies following a brief gun battle. The first half of this spy drama goes nowhere and can be summed up by heroine Jane Randolph's unintentionally funny remark: "I wish I knew what this is all about." George Sanders, who portrayed the adventurer in three earlier entries, tired of the role, so Conway, his brother, took over as the adventurous private sleuth.

261 THE FAMOUS FERGUSON CASE (1932), WB.

Dir. Lloyd Bacon; *Sc.* Courteney Terrett, Harvey Thew; *Cast includes:* Joan Blondell, Tom Brown, Adrienne Dore, Vivienne Osborne, Walter Miller, Leslie Fenton.

The yellow journalism as practiced by a newspaper has tragic consequences in this drama based on the story "Circulation" by Granville Moore. The film exposes the sensational type of murder story that usually hits the front page. When banker George Ferguson is murdered in a small town, yellow journalists, especially hard-hearted reporter Kenneth Thomson, are quick to point their fingers at Mrs. Ferguson and her alleged lover as the killers. But the real slayers are soon caught somewhere in Boston. The damage done by the sensational press, however, cannot be reversed. The arrest of the lover leads to his wife's death. Joan Blondell, who appeared in numerous newspaper films during the decade, appears as a reporter. Several reviews of the drama point out the similarity between the plot and the real-life Hall-Mills and Albert Snyder cases of the period. *Five Star Final* (1931) was another contemporary newspaper drama in which sensational journalism led to tragic results.

262 THE FATAL FORTUNE (1919) serial, SLK.

Dir. Donald MacKenzie; *Cast includes:* Helen Holmes, Jack Levering, Leslie King, Bill Black, Frank Wunderlee, Floyd Buckley.

Determined newspaper reporter Helen Holmes smells a story about a buried treasure on Devil's Isle, located in the South Seas, in this 15-episode serial. She soon learns that the old recluse who hid the coveted fortune was her father. After finding a map that he had left behind, she loses it to a villain known only as "The Faceless Terror." Lieutenant Jack Levering, a pilot, assists her in finding the treasure and unmasking the chief villain.

263 THE FATAL HOUR (1940), Mon.

Dir. William Nigh; *Sc.* Scott Darling; *Cast includes:* Boris Karloff, Grant Withers, Marjorie Reynolds, Charles Trowbridge, John Hamilton, Craig Reynolds.

Newspaper reporter Marjorie Reynolds trails along with boyfriend police inspector Grant Withers and private sleuth Boris Karloff in this routine entry in the "Mr. Wong" detective series. Karloff, portraying the intelligent and clever Chinese detective, helps Withers solve an otherwise difficult case for the ordinary police. Reynolds helps somewhat. The three leads appeared in several entries in the generally mediocre mystery series.

264 THE FATAL MISTAKE (1924), Perfection.

Dir. Scott Dunlap; *Cast includes:* William Fairbanks, Eva Novak, Wilfred Lucas, Dot Farley, Bruce Gordon, Harry McCoy.

William Fairbanks portrays a cub reporter whose paper, *The Star,* is at war with *The Herald,* in this action comedy drama. When his editor refuses to allow the novice the opportunity of photographing a famous socialite, Fairbanks strikes out on his own. He secretly snaps a picture of the wealthy young woman trying on a wedding dress. The photo appears in the paper, but when his supervisor learns the subject was only a maid who was trying on the gown, he fires the cub reporter. Fairbanks meets the maid, who also has been dismissed as the result of the picture, and she turns out to be his long lost girlfriend from his home town. Following several complications, he ends up a hero by rescuing the kidnapped maid and capturing a jewel thief. He returns to his newspaper, secures a raise from his editor and borrows a few dollars he needs for a marriage license. He then leaves, promising to telephone the entire story of the crime to the paper, thereby scooping its competitor.

265 THE FATAL 30 (1921), Pacific Film Co.

Dir. John J. Hayes; *Cast includes:* John J. Hayes, Fritzi Ridgeway, Lillian West, Carl Stockdale, Al Fremont.

Newspaper reporter John J. Hayes and his girlfriend, Fritzi Ridgeway, become involved with a cult of religious sun worshipers in this offbeat adventure drama. It seems the group believes in making human sacrifices to the sun. Later, the couple find themselves visiting a string of underworld dives in their quest to locate a lost chart which can lead to great wealth. Hayes and Ridgeway eventually succeed in their unusual search.

266 THE FEAR MARKET (1920), Realart.

Dir. Kenneth Webb; *Sc.* Clara Beranger; *Cast includes:* Alice Brady, Frank Losee, Harry Mortimer, Richard Hatteras, Edith Stockton, Bradley Parker.

A scandal sheet, owned covertly by Frank Losee and which thrives on blackmailing its victims, leads to the suicide of a young woman in this familiar drama. The victim had been a friend of Alice Brady, who also has been caught in a scandal. However, unlike her more unfortunate friend, Brady vows to expose the owner. But she is unaware that the paper's owner is her father. She joins forces with newspaper editor Harry Mortimer, who loves her, and the couple eventually uncover the identity of the scandal sheet's owner. The daughter confronts her father who then promises to close down his publication.

267 FEEL MY PULSE (1928), Par.

Dir. Gregory La Cava; *Sc.* Keene Thompson, Nick Barrows; *Cast includes:* Bebe Daniels, Melbourne MacDowell, George Irving, Charles Sellon, William Powell, Richard Arlen.

Innocent Bebe Daniels visits a family-owned island sanitarium, unaware that it has been taken over by a gang of rum runners, in this entertaining comedy. Daniels has been raised since childhood to believe she is ailing. Meanwhile the spineless caretaker has allowed the hoodlums access to the place, while Daniels believes they are patients. One of the gang, Richard Arlen, is actually an undercover reporter who is seeking to expose the entire operation. He tries to warn the young visitor to leave because of the danger. When gang members see him talking to her, they attack him, thinking he is betraying them. However, Daniels beats them off with chloroform and other medical implements. She then realizes she is not as sickly as her family had made her out to be. When one of her uncles arrives, he is surprised to discover that his niece has captured the entire gang.

268 FEMALE JUNGLE (1956), ARC.

Dir. Bruno Ve Sota; *Sc.* Burt Kaiser; *Cast includes:* Lawrence Tierney, John Carradine, Jayne Mansfield, Burt Kaiser, Kathleen Crowley, James Kodl.

Police detective Lawrence Tierney, to improve his relations with his superiors, is determined to bring in the killer of a blonde movie star in this inane drama. Following a string of interrogations, mostly with buxom women, he narrows down the suspects to newspaper columnist John Carradine, the slain woman's mentor, and caricaturist Burt Kaiser. The latter, a demented individual, proves to be the murderer. He is finally gunned down after strangling Jayne Mansfield, his second victim.

269 A FEMALE REPORTER (1909), Essanay.

No other details are known about this early short silent film other than its length of half a reel, with the other half consisting of *An Amateur Hold-up.*

270 FEVER PITCH (1985), MGM/UA.

Dir. Richard Brooks; *Sc.* Richard Brooks; *Cast includes:* Ryan O'Neal, Catherine Hicks, Giancarlo Giannini, Bridgette Andersen, Chad Everett, John Saxon.

Sports writer Ryan O'Neal, while researching the mysterious lure of gambling, falls under its spell in this bad bet of a mediocre drama, set chiefly in Las Vegas. The film revolves around the desperate and tragic world of the addicted gambler, but the real interest is in the gambling sessions rather than in the characters. O'Neal's obsession can be blamed for the death of his wife who is killed in a car accident rushing to bring him more money. Famed Italian actor Giancarlo Giannini portrays a big-time gambler who befriends O'Neal before the latter is beaten up for bad debts. O'Neal's editor back at the *Los Angeles Herald Examiner* is played by John Saxon.

271   THE FIGHTING CUB (1925), Truart.

Dir. Paul Hurst; *Sc.* Adele Buffington; *Cast includes:* Wesley Barry, Mildred Harris, Pat O'Malley, Mary Carr, George Fawcett, Stuart Holmes.

An ambitious copy boy fulfills his dream of becoming a reporter after he discovers the secret lair of a gang of thieves in this little drama. Popular contemporary juvenile screen personality Wesley Barry plays the copy boy who relentlessly pesters the city editor for a chance at reporting. His superior finally promises him a promotion if he can coax an interview out of a close-mouthed philanthropist who avidly avoids members of the press. Barry persuades Mildred Harris, the man's daughter, to help him. He wins his promotion to a cub reporter and coincidentally discovers the hideout of a gang of crooks. A fellow reporter who is in collusion with the thieves overhears the cub telling his editor the location and secretly informs the police. Barry goes to the address and is surprised to learn that the gang leader is the philanthropist. When the police arrive to round up the band, Barry rescues him by explaining the leader has reformed. Barry then suppresses the story to protect the father and his daughter.

272   THE FIGHTING MARINE (1926), Pathé.

Dir. Spencer Gordon Bennet; *Sc.* Frank Leon Smith; *Cast includes:* Gene Tunney, Marjorie Gay, Walter Miller, Virginia Vance, Sherman Ross, Mike Donlin.

Stalwart newspaper reporter Gene Tunney volunteers to protect Englishwoman Marjorie Gay and her inheritance in this action drama. He gets this assignment after replying to an newspaper advertisement. According to an eccentric relative's will, Lady Chatfield, the young woman, is set to inherit large mining properties only on the condition that she remain on the property for six months. If she leaves the property, the land falls under control of the mining superintendent and the workers. Determined to gain possession of the mine, Walter Miller, the unscrupulous superintendent, plots against the unwary new owner. Following a string of complications, Tunney manages to foil each attempt designed to dissuade the heiress from completing the terms of the will. The obligatory romance develops between Tunney and Gay. Gene Tunney, a famous prizefighter at the time, made a handful of popular action films.

273   THE FINAL CLOSE-UP (1919), Par.

Dir. Walter Edwards; *Sc.* Julia Crawford Ivers; *Cast includes:* Shirley Mason, Francis McDonald, James Gordon, Betty Bouton, Eugene Burr, Mary Warren.

Good-natured reporter Francis McDonald helps shop girl Shirley Mason, who has fainted from the heat of a particularly hot summer day, in this far-fetched romantic comedy based on the 1918 short story by Royal Brown. Out on the prowl for a good news story about how citizens are coping with the heat, McDonald, the son of a millionaire, meets young Mason, finds out her address and borrows 200 dollars from his father to send her on a vacation. She ends up at the same seaside hotel where McDonald, who has been fired from his paper, is pitching for his baseball team. Following several complications including a hotel theft in which Mason is suspected, she traps the thief. Her heroic actions win her the love of McDonald and the approval of his wealthy father.

274   THE FINAL EDITION (1932), Col.

Dir. Howard Higgin; *Sc.* Dorothy Howell; *Cast includes:* Pat O'Brien, Mae Clarke, Mary Doran, Bradley Page, Morgan Wallace, James Donlan.

Mae Clarke, as a cheeky, aggressive reporter, brings down a master criminal and his gang in this drama that blends the newspaper genre with the gangster film. Morgan Wallace, as the gang leader, orders the death of a new crime commissioner who is hot on Wallace's trail and has gathered sufficient evidence to convict him. Clarke seduces Wallace's second in command, gets the proof to convict the entire gang, and scoops the other papers. But first, her editor Pat O'Brien had to rescue her after she was entrapped by Wallace. The film depicts the typical distorted Hollywood concept of a harried big-city newspaper office—a surprising element, since Roy Chanslor, who wrote the story, had been an experienced newspaperman and should have known better. He contributed several newspaper stories to Hollywood, including, among others, *Hi, Nellie!* (1934), *Front Page Woman* (1935) and *The Girl on the Front Page* (1936). Pat O'Brien, who portrays the usual volatile city editor, began his film career playing wisecracking newsmen, including the famous role of Hildy Johnson in the first screen version of *The Front Page* (1931).

275 THE FINAL EXTRA
(1927), Lumas.

Dir. James Hogan; *Sc.* Herbert C. Clark; *Cast includes:* Marguerite De La Motte, Grant Withers, John Miljan, Frank Beal, Joseph Girard, Leon Holmes.

Aggressive young newspaper columnist Grant Withers, to avenge the murder of a fellow journalist, vows to expose a bootlegging operation in this action drama. Withers, often assigned to less meaningful stories such as covering a musical revue, hopes someday to cover the more exciting stories Frank Beal, the deceased reporter, had been given. The columnist meets chorus girl Marguerite De La Motte, the victim's sister, and promises to expose Beal's killer. Taking over Beal's assignment, Withers arrives in time at a party where he rescues De La Motte from the clutches of John Miljan, a famous impresario. The columnist is captured by Miljan's henchmen after a fight but escapes in time to prove the impresario is the leader of the bootlegging gang and the murderer the police have been searching for. Miljan remained a popular player throughout the 1930s, often portraying villains in such dramas as *Are You Listening?* (1932) and *Torchy Runs for Mayor* (1939).

276 FIND THE WITNESS
(1937), Col.

Dir. David Selman; *Sc.* Grace Neville, Fred Niblo Jr.; *Cast includes:* Charles Quigley, Henry Mollison, Rosalind Keith, Rita La Roy, Wade Boteler, James Conlin.

Charles Quigley, as an inexperienced reporter, scoops the police in solving a murder in this newspaper-crime drama set chiefly at a resort. The main suspect is a magician, played by Henry Mollison, who is performing at the hotel. He claims he is innocent of the charge of killing his wife since he was confined in a sealed box at the bottom of the sea at the time of the murder. Quigley proves that the husband received help from a deep sea diver who transported Mollison and his box to shore where the magician could exit and commit the murder. Quigley again played a reporter in *Girls Can Play*, a thriller released the same year.

277 THE FINGER POINTS
(1931), FN.

Dir. John F. Dillon; *Sc.* W. R. Burnett, John Monk Saunders, Robert Lord; *Cast includes:* Richard Barthelmess, Fay Wray, Regis Toomey, Clark Gable, Robert Elliott, Noel Madison.

Richard Barthelmess, as a reporter from the South, learns quickly about big city journalism, the underworld and corruption in this drama based loosely on the murder of Jake Lingle, a reporter for the *Chicago Tribune*. Barthelmess goes on the take, suppressing stories unfavorable to the mob, and at one point receiving $100,000 for quashing a story. At one point, Gable threatens the reporter. "You're not talking to a chump," Barthelmess points out. "You're talking to a representative of the press. Quite a few people believe in it." The newsman erroneously believes Gable would not have a reporter killed. He is finally gunned down by a hail of machine-gun bullets when a gang leader points him out as a target. At the reporter's funeral, a colleague ironically comments, "He was one fellow money couldn't touch." Fay Wray, as the romantic interest, fails to persuade Gable to reform. The film was adapted from a story by John Monk Saunders, who often wrote air adventures and war tales. Lingle had been a reporter on the *Chicago Tribune* and an acquaintance of hoodlums. He was gunned down in a crowded subway. Another film that touched upon Lingle's life was *Dance, Fools, Dance*, also released in 1931.

278 FIRE AND SWORD (1914), State Rights.

Dir. T. Hayes Hunter; *Cast includes:* Tom McEvoy, Isabel Rea.

American newspaper reporter Tom McEvoy rescues a fellow citizen, the daughter of a rich industrialist, in this far-fetched adventure. Isabel Rea, a young woman who is visiting Tangiers, is abducted by the Grand Vizier. In the desert with his valet, McEvoy is captured by a bandit chief who discovers that the reporter and he belong to the same secret society. The chieftain then permits the Americans to continue on their journey. McEvoy, who is later caught and tortured by those who have abducted Rea, manages to escape and rescue the young woman. They then return to the States where they make plans to marry.

279 FIT FOR A KING (1937), RKO.

Dir. Edward Sedgwick; *Sc.* Richard Flournoy; *Cast includes:* Joe E. Brown, Helen Mack, Harry Davenport, Paul Kelly, Halliwell Hobbes, John Qualen.

Joe E. Brown, portraying a copy boy on his uncle's newspaper, desperately wants to become a full-fledged reporter in this fairly entertaining comedy. He is finally given an opportunity when he is assigned to cover a story about archduke Harry Davenport, who is pursued by assassins. Brown stows away aboard the same vessel as the archduke's to get the full story. Also present is Brown's rival, the more experienced news hound Paul Kelly, who continually scoops the cub. In the course of his assignment, Brown falls in love with princess Helen Mack, who is traveling incognito. Suddenly discovering a plot to kill the princess, who has become a queen, Brown foils the villains. Motorcycles, cars and other means of transportation all play a role in the climactic chase sequence.

280 FIVE OF A KIND (1938), TCF.

Dir. Herbert I. Leeds; *Sc.* Lou Breslow, John Patrick; *Cast includes:* Jean Hersholt, Claire Trevor, Cesar Romero, Slim Summerville, Henry Wilcoxon, Inez Courtney.

Rival journalists and radio news broadcasters Claire Trevor and Cesar Romero double-cross each other as they try to monopolize the world-famous story about the Dionne Quintuplets in this frivolous, cutesy tale. The two reporters journey to Canada where the four-year-old quints live and where Trevor sets up a remote radio broadcast featuring the children. She then arranges for a sponsor to pay for a series of programs. Romero, desperate to get his share of the exploitation, inadvertently ruins a chance for the quintuplets to appear for a charitable cause in New York. He then changes his attitude and organizes a television appearance for the children at the same benefit. Jean Hersholt, who portrayed the kindly doctor in the first two films about the famous five, returns in the present entry, as do Slim Summerville and John Qualen.

281 FIVE STAR FINAL (1931), FN.

Dir. Mervyn LeRoy; *Sc.* Byron Morgan; *Cast includes:* Edward G. Robinson, Marian Marsh, H. B. Warner, Anthony Bushell, George E. Stone, Frances Starr.

A stark drama attacking the sensational aspects of the tabloids, the film was based on the stage play by Louis Weitzenkorn. The plot tells how the executives of a New York newspaper, determined to increase their circulation, callously wreck the lives of several innocent people. Edward G. Robinson, the *Gazette*'s basically decent managing editor, nevertheless yields to the pressures of his superiors and goes along with them and several others in resurrecting a twenty-year-old story about a pregnant young woman who had shot her lover when he refused to marry her. Exonerated of the crime, she married H. B. Warner and the couple raised the love child in relative obscurity. Marian Marsh, the daughter, is about to marry Anthony Bushell when the *Gazette* resurrects the details of the forgotten sordid affair as part of their new series. The couple, unable to cope with the public exposure or get the paper to cancel further stories, commit suicide. Aline McMahon, Robinson's cynical but loyal secretary, earlier comments, "You can always get people interested in the crucifixion of a woman." She hints to him that he is compromising his principles by printing this sleazy series. "If we lost our jobs," she says, "we'd feel like a pair of pants that have been disinfected." Robinson, who hopes to save enough money for his old age, justifies his actions. "Ideals," he retorts, "won't put a patch on your pants." Marsh, the distraught daughter, storms into the *Gazette* office and exclaims, "Why did you kill my mother?" The nervous publisher replies unfeelingly, "Newspapers are only great mirrors that reflect the world." Robinson, fed up with the new policy, smashes the publisher's office window and resigns. A remake titled *Two Against the World* appeared in 1936. *Five Star Final*, unlike *The Front Page*, another classic newspaper drama released the same year, was unrelenting in unfolding its dark, spare tragic plot while the latter film focused chiefly on dark humor. Both, however, were spiced with sufficient doses of cynicism.

282 FIVE WEEKS IN A BALLOON (1962), TCF.

Dir. Irwin Allen; *Sc.* Charles Bennett, Irwin Allen, Albert Gail; *Cast includes:* Red Buttons, Fabian, Barbara Eden, Cedric Hardwicke, Peter Lorre, Richard Haydn.

Flaky young reporter Red Buttons accompanies a British expedition determined to journey cross Africa by balloon in this unexciting adventure laced with humor and based on the novel by Jules Verne. Cedric Hardwicke leads the group whose purpose is to anchor the English flag on unclaimed territory before international slave traders arrive there. In one scene Barbara Eden condemns the slave trade. "Trafficking in human lives is everyone's concern," she proclaims. "Either you're for it or against it." "Well," Peter Lorre replies, "I'm for it." The group faces a series of obstacles, including several initiated by the bumbling Buttons. The film provides something for all age groups, ranging from a tongue-in-cheek approach for adults to stock animal footage for the youngest audiences. Two romances soon develop, one which pairs Fabian with Barbara Luna and the second pairing Buttons with Barbara Eden. Lorre, Billy Gilbert and Richard Haydn handle most of the comedy.

283 THE FLAMING CRISIS (1924), Mesco.

Cast includes: Calvin Nicholson, Dorothy Dunbar.

One of a handful of rare films about blacks in the West, this western drama tells about an African-American newspaperman falsely accused of murder who finds a new life on the frontier. Calvin Nicholson portrays the journalist who escapes from prison and travels to the Southwest where he meets and falls in love with pretty cowgirl Tex Miller. After successfully battling a gang of outlaws, Nicholson surrenders to the local sheriff. He then learns he is no longer wanted by the law since the real killer has confessed. Basking in his new-found freedom, he returns to Tex with plans to settle down to a quiet life in the West.

284 THE FLASH (1923), Russell.

Dir. William J. Craft; *St.* George Hively; *Cast includes:* George Larkin, Ruth Stonehouse.

Reporter George Larkin rescues the innocent daughter of a police chief in this routine silent drama. When the chief of police of a large city begins his unrelenting drive against crime, he provokes the wrath of corrupt local elements, including a gambling syndicate. The crooks frame Ruth Stonehouse, the lawman's daughter, in an effort to stop his campaign. The newsman intervenes and rescues the young woman who is abandoned in a rowboat drifting perilously toward some rapids. The criminal activities are eventually smashed. The usual auto chases add to the suspense and action.

285 A FLASH OF GREEN (1984), Spectrafilm.

Dir. Victor Nunez; *Sc.* John D. MacDonald, Victor Nunez; *Cast includes:* Ed Harris, Blair Brown, Richard Jordan, George Coe, Joan Goodfellow, Jean De Baer.

Tough small-town newspaper reporter Ed Harris breaks with his political cronies over a controversial environmental issue in this well-meaning drama set in Florida and based on the 1962 novel by John D. MacDonald. Burdened by his dying, brain-damaged wife, Harris at first agrees to work for Richard Jordan, the corrupt and greedy county commissioner. The journalist's job is to find material that can be used to blackmail members of a conservationist group. Jordan hopes to make millions by developing a public bay area for a housing development. "The world needs folks like me," Jordan boasts, "people with a raw need for power." Following several complications, Harris eventually allies himself with the conservationists. Jordan then escalates the conflict by stirring up a right-wing group against the environmentalists. Harris, with the help of George Coe, another journalist, finally succeeds in stopping Jordan and his development project. The title refers to a local Gulf Coast phenomenon in which the sky momentarily flashes green before turning into night. The film anticipates other similar dramas such as *The Milagro Beanfield War*, released in 1988.

286 FLESH AND FURY (1952), U.

Dir. Joseph Pevney; *Sc.* Bernard Gordon; *Cast includes:* Tony Curtis, Jan Sterling, Mona Freeman, Wallace Ford, Connie Gilchrist, Harry Shannon.

Newspaper feature writer Mona Freeman falls in love with deaf-mute prizefighter Tony Curtis but faces competition from sexy Jan Sterling in this fairly absorbing romantic drama which says little about the world of journalism or the fight game. Curtis is torn between the two women—until he regains his hearing following an operation. After another setback, he realizes Freeman is the woman for him.

287 FLETCH (1985), U.

Dir. Michael Ritchie; *Sc.* Andrew Bergman; *Cast includes:* Chevy Chase, Dana Wheeler-Nicholson, Tim Matheson, Joe Don Baker, Richard Libertini, Geena Davis.

Chevy Chase portrays the title character, a newspaper columnist hunting down the infamous con man Tim Matheson in this very entertaining comedy mystery based on the novel by Gregory MacDonald. The plot deals with corruption, but it takes a back seat to the laughs which stem from Chase's glibness and his numerous antics. In one particular scene, for example, Chase is trying to uncover vice in a city administration. "What's your occupation?" suspicious police chief Joe Don Baker snaps at him. "I'm a shepherd," Chase promptly replies. Later, when Baker threatens the reporter's life, Chase invokes the law. "I don't know anything about the law," he insists, "but I think this is a violation of my civil liberties." His life is again threatened by Tim Matheson. "You know," Fletch warns him, "if you shoot me, you'll lose all those humanitarian awards." Other humorous incidents involve several of Chase's disguises, including that of a surgeon at an autopsy and that of a legionnaire among a convention of members of the Veterans of Foreign Wars. A sequel appeared in 1989.

288 FLETCH LIVES (1989), U.

Dir. Michael Ritchie; *Sc.* Leon Capetanos; *Cast includes:* Chevy Chase, Hal Holbrook, Julianne Phillips, Cleavon Little, R. Lee Ermey, Richard Libertini.

Chevy Chase returns to portray the title character, a Los Angeles reporter who inherits his aunt's Louisiana estate in this inane comedy, a sequel to *Fletch*, released in 1985. When he arrives at the estate, he finds a run-down property and a dead real-estate broker. Chase is arrested and falsely accused of the crime. "You feel like making a statement?" a suspicious sheriff asks him. "A statement?" Chase repeats. "'Ask not what your country can do for you; ask what you can do for your country.'" Other one-liners help to salvage an otherwise completely frivolous film. For example, when Chase lands on a gangster's limousine, the hoodlum instructs the driver: "If it's a cop, kill him, if it's a reporter, cripple him." An attorney informs Chase that he owes $4,387 in back alimony and, if he doesn't pay, he will end up in jail. "You're right," Chase quips. "I've been foolishly squandering my salary on food and heat." "Are you religious?" acquaintance Cleavon Little later asks Chase, who has been investigating a big-time television evangelist. "I believe in a God that doesn't need heavy financing," the reporter returns. Chase's journalistic background has him snooping around until he discovers the murderer and those who want his newly acquired property.

289 FLIGHT TO MARS (1951), Mon.

Dir. Lesley Selander; *Sc.* Arthur Strawn; *Cast includes:* Marguerite Chapman, Cameron Mitchell, Arthur Franz, Virginia Huston, John Litel, Richard Gaines.

Newspaper reporter Cameron Mitchell accompanies four scientists on a flight to Mars where they meet that planet's inhabitants in this disappointing space drama. The Martians, because of their hostile atmosphere, are forced to live underground. But they enjoy a life of luxury below ground. The Martians permit the visitors, who have crash-landed, to rebuild their space ship. But surreptitiously, they intend to duplicate the ship and invade Earth with a fleet of their own. A trio of amiable Martians help the earthlings, who then escape with two Martians aboard. Reporter Mitchell and scientist Virginia Huston fall in love during their strange adventure, and Arthur Franz, a fellow scientist, falls for Martian Marguerite Chapman.

290 THE FLOOR BELOW (1918), Goldwyn.

Dir. Clarence C. Badger; *Sc.* Elaine Sterne; *Cast includes:* Mabel Normand, Tom Moore, Helen Dahl, Wallace McCutcheon, Lincoln Plumer, Charlotte Granville.

Mabel Normand portrays a "copy girl" on a local newspaper who is eventually fired for her antics in this farfetched drama. During business hours, Normand shoots dice with her fellow employees in the city room, plays a harmonica and engages in sundry pranks that lead to her dismissal. When a reporter suggests that she investigate a series of robberies, she agrees and soon meets wealthy Tom Moore, a missionary worker who thinks she is a burglar. He takes her home where he and his mother try to rehabilitate her. Several complications follow, including one in which Moore's jealous fiancée steals a money box and accuses Normand of the theft. She is finally exonerated by Moore, who has fallen in love with her. This occurs when he discovers that his unfaithful fiancée is the actual thief.

291 FLORIDA SPECIAL (1936), Par.

Dir. Ralph Murphy; *Sc.* David Boehm,

Marguerite Roberts, Laura Perelman, S. J. Perelman; *Cast includes:* Jack Oakie, Sally Eilers, Kent Taylor, Frances Drake, J. Farrell MacDonald, Claude Gillingwater.

Romance, comedy and music pervade this mystery set aboard a Florida-bound train and based on the story "Recreation Car" by Clarence Budington Kelland. One of the passengers, meddlesome reporter Jack Oakie, ends up helping to rescue Sally Eilers. Claude Gilllingwater, as an eccentric millionaire carrying a million dollars in diamonds, hires vacationing policeman J. Farrell MacDonald as his bodyguard. Meanwhile, a gang of crooks and a solo jewel thief are on board making plans to steal the diamonds. Other passengers include drunken playboy Kent Taylor and hostess Eilers. Following several complications, including the disappearance of the diamonds and their owner, Gillingwater turns up posing as an invalid with an ice bag on his head. The real diamonds were hidden in the bag while the counterfeit ones were stolen. Oakie handles much of the wisecracking comedy. For instance, when a porter remarks that a gentleman handed him a note in Newark, Oakie quips: "What's a gentleman doing in Newark?"

292   THE FLOWER OF DOOM (1917), U.

Dir. Rex Ingram; *Sc.* Rex Ingram; *Cast includes:* Wedgewood Nowell, Yvette Mitchell, Nicholas Dunaew, M. K. Wilson, Gypsy Hart, Tommy Morrissey.

Reporter M. K. Wilson, while on a date with cabaret dancer Gypsy Hart, finds himself in the middle of a Tong war in this suspenseful silent drama. During their walk, he pins a flower on her lapel, unaware that it represents one of the Tong factions. Hart is kidnapped and the police fail to locate her. Wilson turns for help to a Chinese friend whose life he had once saved. The two men go to an opium den and kidnap Yvette Mitchell, who belongs to the faction holding Hart. Later, Wilson arranges to exchange his prisoner for the missing cabaret dancer.

293   FLY-AWAY BABY (1937), WB.

Dir. Frank McDonald; *Sc.* Don Ryan, Kenneth Gamet; *Cast includes:* Glenda Farrell, Barton MacLane, Gordon Oliver, Hugh O'Connell, Marcia Ralston, Tom Kennedy.

A mysterious murder involving stolen gems brings spirited reporter Torchy Blane, played by Glenda Farrell, onto the scene in this newspaper-crime drama. In an effort to help her police lieutenant fiancé Barton MacLane and to prove her talents for solving crimes, the flippant Blane volunteers to join two other reporters on an airplane trip around the world. She suspects that one of the journalists was involved in the murder. Following some slow-paced sequences concerning the journey, Blane proves that reporter Gordon Oliver is the killer. This was the second Torchy Blane entry. The first, *Smart Blonde*, was released in 1936.

294   THE FLYING SERPENT (1946), PRC.

Dir. Sherman Scott; *Sc.* John T. Neville; *Cast includes:* George Zucco, Ralph Lewis, Hope Kramer, Eddie Acuff, Wheaton Chambers, James Metcalf.

As early as the 1930s, radio newscasters began to compete with newspapermen in Hollywood melodramas. In this inept horror film, featuring George Zucco as a mad archaeologist, young radio news reporter Ralph Lewis, assigned to cover a series of strange murders, solves the crimes. Zucco, to protect his discovery of a priceless Aztec treasure somewhere in New Mexico, releases a winged serpent trained to kill those who seem to be getting close to his secret. Before unraveling the mystery, Lewis meets Hope Kramer, Zucco's stepdaughter, and a romance blossoms amid the gruesome killings. The young woman is also targeted for destruction but she escapes.

295   FOG OVER FRISCO (1934), WB.

Dir. William Dieterle; *Sc.* Robert N.

Lee, Eugene Solow; *Cast includes:* Bette Davis, Donald Woods, Margaret Lindsay, Lyle Talbot, Hugh Herbert, Arthur Byron.

Bette Davis portrays a millionaire's wanton daughter who finds herself in the center of a stolen-securities ring in this standard drama. Davis shows pathological traits as she willingly engages in dangerous operations with the gang members who soon extend their activities to murder. Donald Woods plays a snooping reporter upbraided by Margaret Lindsay, Davis's half-sister, for associating Davis with unsavory nightclub owner Irving Pichel and other members of the underworld. Davis, encouraged by her boyfriend Lyle Talbot to quit the rackets, does so and nearly loses her life when she is captured by Pichel and his gang who think she knows too much about their operations. Reporter Woods, after finding Talbot murdered, tracks Davis to the gang's hideout where a gunfight breaks out between the police and the gang. Davis is finally rescued. A loose remake titled *Spy Ship* appeared in 1942.

296 THE FOOD GAMBLERS (1917), Triangle.

Dir. Albert Parker; *St.* Robert Shirley; *Cast includes:* Wilfred Lucas, Elda Millar, Mac Barnes, Russell Simpson, Jack Snyder, Eduardo Ciannelli.

Reporter Elda Millar, assigned to write a story about the high price of food, ends up reforming the leader of a gang of food speculators in this simplistic early social drama. Millar visits a tenement neighborhood where women are on the verge of rioting because of exorbitant food prices. She interviews Wilfred Lucas, who is the leader of those who are manipulating the prices. At first he tries to buy her off but soon finds himself falling in love with the idealistic journalist. In a preachy sequence, she finally convinces him of the terrible results of his greed. Unable to resist her sermon, he decides to join her in bringing about new legislation designed to break the food trust.

297 FORBIDDEN (1932), Col.

Dir. Frank Capra; *Sc.* Jo Swerling; *Cast includes:* Barbara Stanwyck, Adolphe Menjou, Ralph Bellamy, Dorothy Peterson, Thomas Jefferson, Charlotte Henry.

Here is a sordid drama about an unscrupulous journalist, for a change — although the morality of the other characters leaves much to be desired. Newspaper reporter Ralph Bellamy, who is in love with Barbara Stanwyck, harasses her lover, Adolphe Menjou, a lawyer turned politician. Stanwyck, an attractive rural librarian, has agreed to become the discreet mistress of Menjou, whose wife has been crippled in a car accident, the result of Menjou's driving. It is not until she tells Menjou that she is pregnant that he admits that he is married. Still believing in their illicit affair, the overly romantic Stanwyck asks her lover, "It's never going to strike twelve for us, is it?" To protect the lawyer's career, Stanwyck reluctantly marries Bellamy, although she does not love him. When the reporter threatens to expose Menjou's sordid past, Stanwyck kills him and is sentenced to prison. Early in the film, Stanwyck establishes her tough character as she exchanges wisecracks with Menjou. "I'm the census taker," he announces. "Oh," she replies, I lost my senses long ago."

298 FOREIGN CORRESPONDENT (1940), UA.

Dir. Alfred Hitchcock; *Sc.* Charles Bennett, Joan Harrison; *Cast includes:* Joel McCrea, Laraine Day, Herbert Marshall, George Sanders, Albert Basserman, Robert Benchley.

Hitchcock's highly suspenseful and exciting drama of political intrigue on the eve of World War II was his second American film. Joel McCrea, an American reporter sent to Europe in August of 1939 to uncover the truth about the threat of war, becomes entangled in an international spy ring whose members are posing as part of a peace organization. He witnesses the kidnapping of a famous Dutch diplomat and the assassination of the diplomat's double. Several attempts are made on his own life as he tries to expose the leaders of the ring. George Sanders, a fellow reporter, aids him in the search. Herbert Marshall portrays the mastermind behind the plot. His daughter, Laraine Day, unaware of her father's ties to Nazi Germany, falls in love with McCrea. The director has loaded the film with his usual inventive devices and witty style. McCrea's pursuit of an assassin through a crowd of umbrella-carrying onlookers is cleverly executed, as is the climactic plane crash of a transatlantic clipper. There is probably more of Hitchcock's humor in this film than in any of his other works. Robert Benchley, another correspondent, spends half his day rewriting government press releases and the other half drinking. There is the running gag of McCrea's losing a variety of hats. Much of the dialogue is witty. When McCrea is about to be arrested by Dutch authorities, he says: "I hope the chief of police speaks English." "We all speak English," the officer replies. "That's more than I could say for my country," McCrea quips. Once war breaks out near the end of the film, the dialogue—much of it written by James Hilton and Robert Benchley—turns serious and patriotic. "This is London," a radio announcer says at the beginning of a worldwide broadcast. "We have as a guest tonight one of the soldiers of the press—one of the little army of historians who are writing history from beside the cannon's mouth." McCrea, about to go on the air, is interrupted by an air raid and the lights go out. As bombs rain down on London, he addresses America from the darkened radio studio: "The lights are all out everywhere—except in America. Keep those lights burning. Cover them with steel. Ring them with guns. Build a canopy of battleships and bombing planes around them. Hello, America. Hang on to your lights. They're the only lights left in the world." Few Americans who saw the film realized at the time that the British government had asked the director to stay in Hollywood and continue to turn out propaganda dramas arousing anti-Nazi sentiments. Britain also hoped that such films would prod the U.S. to enter the war.

299 FORGOTTEN GIRLS
(1940), Rep.

Dir. Phil Rosen; *Sc.* Joseph March, F. Hugh Herbert; *Cast includes:* Louise Platt, Donald Woods, Wynne Gibson, Robert Armstrong, Eduardo Ciannelli, Jack LaRue.

Innocent Louise Platt becomes the target of her unscrupulous aunt, Wynne Gibson, in this teary drama. Gibson, in collusion with mobster acquaintances, frames Platt for a murder which Gibson committed, and the niece is sent to prison. Reporter Donald Woods, who has fallen in love with Platt during her trial, tries to help her. He undertakes to force the aunt into confessing. Only after Gibson is thrown from a speeding car and on her deathbed does she confess to the murder.

300 FORGOTTEN WOMEN
(1932), Mon.

Dir. Richard Thorpe; *Sc.* Adele Buffington; *Cast includes:* Marion Shilling, Rex Bell, Beryl Mercer, Virginia Lee Corbin, Carmelita Geraghty, Edna Murphy.

Rex Bell, recently promoted from reporter to city editor, helps to expose a film producer who is in collusion with a local mob in this conventional romantic drama set in and around Hollywood. Bell's new title has resulted from his bringing in a scoop about the capture of a major gang of thieves. Bell is romantically involved with Marion Shilling, a publisher's daughter, and Virginia Lee Corbin, an aspiring screen actress. He settles for Shilling at one point. Later, the journalist is forced to choose between following a car with gangsters or one holding Corbin. The film ends in an exciting chase and rescue as he opts for the latter, rekindling his love for the actress. One of the more interesting elements of the film is its look inside the world of movie-making.

301 FORT WORTH (1951), WB.

Dir. Edwin L. Marin; *Sc.* John Twist; *Cast includes:* Randolph Scott, David Brian, Phyllis Thaxter, Helena Carter, Dick Jones, Ray Teal.

Another western with a newspaper background, this average actioner stars Randolph Scott as an ex-gunslinger who settles down in Fort Worth as a crusading newspaper editor. Two friends influence his decision to rid the community of lawbreakers—David Brian and Phyllis Thaxter, Brian's fiancée. In reality, Brian is trying to control town property, anticipating the railroad's arrival to ship the cattle. Following the usual conflicts, the two pals clash with the inevitable results—Scott temporarily giving up his printer's ink for his six-gun. He rids the town of Brian and his followers and wins Thaxter.

302 THE FOUNTAINHEAD (1949), WB.

Dir. King Vidor; *Sc.* Ayn Rand; *Cast includes:* Gary Cooper, Patricia Neal, Raymond Massey, Kent Smith, Robert Douglas, Henry Hull, Ray Collins.

Opportunistic newspaper columnist Robert Douglas plays a significant role in ruining the blossoming career of an idealistic architect in this disappointing drama based on the popular novel by Ayn Rand. Gary Cooper portrays Howard Roark, the strong-willed architect who believes a person's individual integrity takes precedence over the law. "Every new idea in the world," his dying mentor, architect Henry Hull, had once told him, "comes from the mind of some one man." Although his work and ideas are generously promoted by newspaper publisher Raymond Massey, the support crumbles with Massey's financial decline. "We have no choice but to submit or rule," he asserts to his date, Patricia Neal. Later, although now married to Massey, she tries to seduce Cooper. "If it gives you pleasure to know you are breaking me down," she confesses, "I'll give you greater satisfaction—I love you." Douglas, a vindictive columnist and critic, relentlessly attacks the architect's work. Always the individualist, Roark ends up dynamiting a charity project after the builders modify his original architectural design. He then applies the author's philosophy in his defense during his trial. "The world is perishing in an orgy of self-sacrifice," Cooper warns. Made during a period in which the House Un-American Activities Committee was charging Hollywood with producing leftist films, the current drama sharply promoted right-wing ideology. True freedom, Roark suggests, exists only with the individual's right to carry out his own will, without restricting the individual to bend to the collective will.

303 FOUR'S A CROWD (1938), WB.

Dir. Michael Curtiz; *Sc.* Casey Robinson, Sig Herzig; *Cast includes:* Errol Flynn, Olivia de Havilland, Rosalind Russell, Patric Knowles, Walter Connolly, Hugh Herbert.

Publicity agent Errol Flynn reverts to his old role of newspaper editor to help promote the image of his latest client, Walter Connolly, in this fair screwball comedy based on the novel *All Rights Reserved* by Wallace Sullivan. Mean-spirited Connolly presents a difficult case for Flynn to promote. "Posterity?" the tycoon rails at suggestions to emulate other philanthropists. "What's posterity ever done for me? Why should I do anything for posterity?" Flynn is interested in romancing the tight-fisted millionaire's daughter, Olivia de Havilland, while at the same time wooing reporter Rosalind Russell. Following the usual complications, Flynn marries Russell, and his boss, Patric Knowles, ends up with de Havilland.

304 THE FOURTH ESTATE (1916), Fox.

Dir. Frank Powell; *Sc.* Frank Powell; *Cast includes:* Clifford Bruce, Ruth Blair, Victor Benoit, Alfred Hickman, Samuel Ryan, Aline Bartlett.

Innocent and dedicated labor leader

Clifford Bruce, who is forced to leave town following threats from corrupt businessmen and their henchmen, eventually returns to exonerate himself in this absorbing silent drama based on the 1909 play by Joseph M. Paterson and Harriet Ford. When reporter Victor Benoit learns that judge Alfred Hickman had ordered the leader's arrest, the judge has the newspaperman fired. Two years later Bruce, having accumulated some wealth in Canada, returns to the States, buys a newspaper and hires Benoit as his managing editor. They soon discover a murder the judge had committed, and their exposé leads to his arrest.

305 THE FOURTH FACE (1920), State Rights.

St. Marjorie Van Beuran.

A young woman reporter helps to solve a murder in a deserted mansion in this obscure mystery drama that takes place in Greenwich Village. Of the four suspects in the case, the reporter proves that the killer is a jealous woman. Very little is known about this film which is sometimes listed as *The Mystery of Washington Square*.

306 FRAMED (1940), U.

Dir. Harold Schuster; *Sc.* Roy Chanslor; *Cast includes:* Frank Albertson, Constance Moore, Jerome Cowan, Robert Armstrong, Sidney Blackmer, Judith Allen.

Hotshot reporter Frank Albertson finds himself framed for murder in this predictable newspaper-crime drama that ends only in reminding audiences that they have seen this plot before. Albertson manages to outwit the police by trapping the killer and solving the murder. In addition, he gets a scoop for his newspaper. Jerome Cowan portrays the chief culprit, with Robert Armstrong serving as Albertson's city editor.

307 FRAMING FRAMERS (1917), Triangle.

Dir. Ferris Hartman, Philip J. Hurn; *Sc.* Philip J. Hurn; *Cast includes:* Chadlee Gunn, Edwin Jobson, George Pierce, Laura Sears, Edward Martin, Lee Phelps.

Star reporter Chadlee Gunn finds himself in the middle of a political rivalry in which one party owns the newspaper he works for in this weak comedy drama. While trying to cover a social event, the news hound is knocked unconscious. Now mistaken for a derelict, he is selected as part of a wager to prove whether or not "clothes make the man." Gunn is attired fashionably and accepted into society where one rival faction tries to use him to slander the other by causing social ruin to the family. Here he meets Laura Sears, the daughter of one of the political bosses whom he is to embarrass. However, Gunn turns the tables on both sides by winning the election and becoming mayor. He then marries Sears.

308 FRANCIS COVERS THE BIG TOWN (1953), U.

Dir. Arthur Lubin; *Sc.* Oscar Brodney; *Cast includes:* Donald O'Connor, Yvette Dugay, Nancy Guild, Gene Lockhart, Larry Gates.

Francis, a talking mule, helps Donald O'Connor, who works for a New York newspaper in this weak entry in the popular comedy series. "Let's see," O'Connor, arriving down-and-out in New York, ponders, "what would I be good at? I think the newspaper business." He is hired as a copy boy and supplies several scoops to experienced news hounds based on tips from his talking mule. However, O'Connor soon finds himself suspected of murder. But Francis testifies in his behalf and he is acquitted. Venerable character actor Gene Lockhart portrays an editor, and Chill Wills provides the voice for Francis.

309 FREEDOM OF THE PRESS (1928), U.

Dir. George Melford; *Sc.* J. Grubb Alexander; *Cast includes:* Lewis Stone, Malcolm McGregor, Henry B. Walthall,

Marceline Day, Robert E. O'Connor, Hayden Stevenson.

The son of a crusading newspaperman takes over the family paper after his father is brutally murdered in this mystery drama. Malcolm McGregor, as the idealistic son following in his father's footsteps, battles to expose corrupt politician Lewis Stone, who intends to run for mayor. The fighting journalist succeeds in bringing to justice the politico who also happens to be the leader of the local underworld. The plot is based on the real-life murder of Canton, Ohio, newspaper publisher Don Mellett. The film was originally released for review under the title *Graft*, which is not related to a 1931 sound drama with the same title.

310 FRIENDS OF MR. SWEENEY (1934), WB.

Dir. Edward Ludwig; *Sc.* Warren Duff, Sidney Sutherland; *Cast includes:* Charles Ruggles, Ann Dvorak, Eugene Pallette, Dorothy Burgess, Dorothy Tree, Robert Barrat.

Charles Ruggles, a timid, hack editorial writer for a conservative periodical during Prohibition experiences a sudden change in his life in this good-natured comedy based on the novel by Elmer Davis. This transformation is brought about by Eugene Pallette, an old college crony, who awakens the sleeping lion in the currently meek lamb. Early in the film, Ruggles displays resentment of his own persona of a cowering dupe for Berton Churchill, his sanctimonious boss. The writer, after a night of carousing with his friend Pallette, springs into his new personality—resulting in plenty of comical situations as he exposes in print a host of thugs, along with William Davidson, a crooked politician he had earlier eulogized on orders from his boss.

311 THE FRINGE OF SOCIETY (1917), State Rights.

Dir. Robert Ellis; *Sc.* Pierre V. R. Key; *Cast includes:* Ruth Roland, Milton Sills, Leah Baird, J. Herbert Frank, George Larkin, Tammany Young.

Aggressive reporter George Larkin exposes a crooked politician and rescues his own publisher in this drama which deals peripherally with Prohibition. Publisher Milton Sills, who has a drinking problem, supports the idea of Prohibition. When he finds his wife, Ruth Roland, with powerful politician J. Herbert Frank, he thinks she has been unfaithful. Sills is then kidnapped to prevent him from exposing Frank's activities. Larkin, the reporter, rescues his boss and publishes the story about Frank and his liquor interests. The publisher's wife then explains to her husband that Frank forced himself upon her, and the couple are reunited.

312 FROM HELL TO HEAVEN (1933), Par.

Dir. Erle Kenton; *Sc.* Sidney Buchman, Percy Heath; *Cast includes:* Jack Oakie, Carole Lombard, Sidney Blackmer, Bradley Page, Shirley Grey, Adrienne Ames.

Jack Oakie portrays a radio announcer who comments on activities at a race track and a nearby fashionable hotel in this aimless, *Grand Hotel*-like drama based on the play by Lawrence Hazard. Carole Lombard, a young woman desperately in need of money, bets her virtue. Lecherous Sidney Blackmer, a local bookie, takes her wager. However, when she loses and agrees to pay her debt, Blackmer suddenly turns honorable and cancels her debt. Meanwhile, a couple at the track try to retrieve $5,000 the husband has illegally appropriated from his company. Like MGM's popular and more successful *Grand Hotel* (1932), the film ends with Oakie's final comment: "People come and go, but nothing ever happens," a repetition of Lewis Stone's words at the end of the 1932 drama.

313 THE FRONT PAGE (1931), UA.

Dir. Lewis Milestone; *Sc.* Bartlett Cormack, Charles Lederer; *Cast includes:*

Adolphe Menjou, Pat O'Brien, Mae Clarke, George E. Stone, Edward Everett Horton, Frank McHugh.

Part dark comedy and part satire, this film adaptation of the highly successful play by Charles MacArthur and Ben Hecht became the forerunner for numerous newspaper films featuring wise-cracking dialogue by a host of cynical reporters. The film, set chiefly in the press room of a criminal courts building, concerns a group of newsmen covering the hanging of an anarchist who has killed a policeman. Adolphe Menjou portrays Walter Burns, a callous, scheming editor. Pat O'Brien, as crack reporter Hildy Johnson, can't seem to break away from his boss to marry Mary Brian and quit the newspaper racket. "It's peeking through keyholes," he cries, denigrating his profession. "It's running after fire engines, waking up people in the middle of the night... It's stealing pictures off little old ladies after their daughters get attacked...." George E. Stone, as the condemned man, escapes and is hidden by O'Brien, who has the proverbial printer's ink for blood and who sees a scoop in Stone's escape. The reporter expertly maneuvers his editor, the fugitive and his fiancée as the police, sheriff and others frantically search for Stone. With O'Brien locking up the story and Menjou getting it for his paper, the latter wishes the couple well and gives his own watch as a present to his favorite reporter. When the lovebirds leave, Menjou telephones the police to report that his watch has been stolen. The dialogue is filled with wit and humor. In an early scene, reporter Frank McHugh telephones a woman from the city hall press room as other newspapermen listen in. "Is it true, madam," McHugh inquires, "that you are the victim of a peeping Tom?" "Ask her if she's worth peeping at," one colleague quips. "Tell her to come over here," suggests another. "We'd like to reenact the crime." Later, the ominous sound of a gallows trap door can be heard below. "What was that?" asks an edgy Mary Brian, the condemned man's girlfriend. "They're fixing up a pain in the neck for your boyfriend," a reporter cracks. When O'Brien's sweetheart enters the press room, she demands to know what's going on. "Tell her nothing!" exclaims hardboiled Burns, who then adds, "She's a woman, you fool!" Several remakes of the film, which satirizes both political corruption and journalistic ethics, include *His Girl Friday* (1940) with Cary Grant, Rosalind Russell and Ralph Bellamy; *The Front Page* (1974) with Jack Lemmon, Walter Matthau and Carol Burnett; and *Switching Channels* (1988) with Kathleen Turner, Burt Reynolds and Christopher Reeve.

314   THE FRONT PAGE (1976), U.

Dir. Billy Wilder; *Sc.* Billy Wilder, I. A. L. Diamond; *Cast includes:* Jack Lemmon, Walter Matthau, Carol Burnett, Susan Sarandon, Vincent Gardenia, David Wayne.

Based on the popular play by Ben Hecht and Charles MacArthur, this third film version is disappointing, considering the talents of its director, writers and cast. Jack Lemmon stars as Hildy Johnson, star reporter on the verge of marrying Carol Burnett and quitting his job. Walter Matthau, as the conniving managing editor Walter Burns, uses a bag of dirty tricks to keep Johnson around. Set in a Chicago police press room of the 1920s, the plot revolves around a politically motivated execution of an alleged radical who killed a policeman during a struggle. The condemned man's jailbreak sets off a chain of events leading to Johnson's getting a scoop. The fugitive is captured but is spared from hanging. Burns, meanwhile, pulls another stunt to prevent Johnson from leaving with his bride-to-be. One major change from the original is the liberal use of expletives. This screen version, to its credit, retains the famous last line of the play: "The son of a bitch stole my watch!" Burns exclaims, referring to Johnson.

315   A FRONT PAGE STORY (1922), Vitagraph.

Dir. Jesse Robins; *Sc.* F. W. Beebe; *Cast*

includes: Edward Everett Horton, Lloyd Ingraham, James Corrigan, Edith Roberts, W. E. Lawrence, Buddy Messenger.

Edward Everett Horton portrays a reporter who brings together two rivals, newspaper owner James Corrigan and local mayor Lloyd Ingraham, in this light comedy based on a story by Arthur Goodrich. The two men, actually friendly enemies, have been battling for years. Horton, after bluffing his way onto the staff of Corrigan's paper, writes scathing articles about the mayor, much to the regret of Corrigan. Because of the reporter's excessive attacks, the two adversaries realize they have been behaving foolishly over the years and decide to reconcile their differences. Meanwhile Horton, who later went on to play character roles in major sound features, falls in love with Edith Roberts, his employer's daughter.

316 FRONT PAGE WOMAN (1935), WB.

Dir. Michael Curtiz; *Sc.* Laird Doyle; *Cast includes:* Bette Davis, George Brent, Roscoe Karns, Winifred Shaw, Walter Walker, J. Carrol Naish.

Rival reporters for competing newspapers track murder suspects to their hideout and locate the incriminating weapon in this action comedy drama which at least one contemporary critic called "farfetched." Bette Davis and George Brent are the aggressive competitors who, besides engaging in a battle of the sexes, would do virtually anything for a scoop. In one sequence, for example, the less ethical Brent drills a hole in the wall to a jury room and listens to the jurors debate a case. "Hold the four-star for a stop-press!" he calls in, reporting the blow-by-blow description to his paper. Later, his quip that "Women make rotten newspapermen" infuriates Davis and goads her to prove her mettle. When she insists she is a reporter, Brent berates her. "No, you're not," he replies. "You're just a sweet little kid whose family let her read too many newspaper novels." The frenetic film ends up as just another entry in the newspaper-crime genre. One of the more outrageous sequences includes the rival reporters discovering a murder, identifying the corpse, following the suspects, locating the appropriate weapon and explaining the details to the nonplused police. In another sequence, Davis reports a false story to her paper about the results of a trial. The paper prints it and later fires her from its staff. However, one hour later she is rehired and covering another front page story. Again, while Davis and Brent are eating in a restaurant, they respond quickly to a fire alarm without any knowledge of the location of the blaze. Jury tampering reappeared in *Grand Jury Secrets* (1939), when ambitious reporter John Howard surreptitiously places a shortwave transmitter in a jury room.

317 FUGITIVE IN THE SKY (1936), WB.

Dir. Nick Grinde; *Sc.* George Bricker; *Cast includes:* Jean Muir, Warren Hull, Gordon Oliver, Carlyle Moore Jr., Howard Phillips, Winifred Shaw.

Crime and mayhem take to the skies in this mediocre action drama involving government agents, murderers and reporters. The convoluted plot unfolds both during the flight with a struggle aboard the plane, and after a forced landing in the middle of a dust storm. Warren Hull went on to play leading roles in serials.

318 FUTUREWORLD (1976), AI.

Dir. Richard T. Heffron; *Sc.* Mayo Simon, George Schenck; *Cast includes:* Peter Fonda, Blythe Danner, Arthur Hill, Yul Brynner, Jim Antonio, John Ryan.

Investigative reporters Peter Fonda and Blythe Danner are hired to help publicize the special theme park of the title in this action drama, a fairly exciting sequel to *Westworld* (1973). The pair soon uncover a sinister plot concocted by the owners of this pleasure dome. The latter want to use their robot technology to dominate the world. The climax of the film includes an exciting chase sequence involving robot duplicates intended to replace political and financial figures.

319 G.I. WAR BRIDES (1946), Rep.

Dir. George Blair; *Sc.* John K. Butler; *Cast includes:* Anna Lee, James Ellison, Harry Davenport, William Henry, Stephanie Bachelor, Robert Armstrong.

Newspaper reporter Robert Armstrong, aboard a ship transporting World War II English war brides to the U.S., witnesses one young woman switching places with another in this minor comedy drama. By assuming the identity of a young bride no longer in love with her husband, Anna Lee plans to slip by immigration authorities to join her American boyfriend. But she soon learns he no longer is interested in her. Faced with deportation, Lee is rescued by the reporter who brings her together with her original, alleged husband.

320 GAILY, GAILY (1969), UA.

Dir. Norman Jewison; *Sc.* Abram S. Ginnes; *Cast includes:* Beau Bridges, Melina Bercouri, Brian Keith, George Kennedy, Hume Cronyn, Margot Kidder.

Beau Bridges portrays a naive cub reporter in 1910 Chicago in this lavishly produced, but excessively broad comedy based on the novel by Ben Hecht. The young reporter often acts more foolishly than innocently. An inexperienced farm boy recently introduced to some of the gamier sides of city life, he awakens in a brothel. He finds his woman-of-the-night next to him and, with a contrite heart, laments: "I've ruined you!" Bridges stumbles through the bustling city's teeming streets, the train depot and traffic jams on assignments handed out by his city editor Brian Keith. "There's a sex maniac loose in the city," Keith reminds the aspiring young reporter. "Do you know what a sex maniac does?" "I think so," Bridges replies hesitatingly. "I'll tell you what a sex maniac does!" the editor blares out. "A sex maniac sells newspapers!" One basic plot incident revolves around Keith's efforts to restore to life an executed wife-murderer with the help of a quack doctor.

321 GAMBLING ON THE HIGH SEAS (1940), WB.

Dir. George Amy; *Sc.* Robert E. Kent; *Cast includes:* Wayne Morris, Jane Wyman, Gilbert Roland, William Pawley, Murray Alper, Frank Wilcox.

Inquisitive reporter Wayne Morris is determined to get the goods on mobster and murder suspect Gilbert Roland, who owns a gambling ship, in this predictable but very trim little newspaper-crime drama. During his investigation, Morris finds time to fall in love with Jane Wyman, Roland's secretary, who helps Morris trap her boss for district attorney John Litel. Morris appeared as a reporter in several newspaper films, including *The Return of Dr. X* (1939) and *The House Across the Street* (1949).

322 GANGS, INC. (1941), PRC.

Dir. Phil Rosen; *Sc.* Martin Mooney; *Cast includes:* Joan Woodbury, Jack LaRue, Linda Ware, John Archer, Vince Barnett, Alan Ladd.

Alan Ladd has a minor role as an undercover newspaper reporter in this fast-paced crime drama of revenge. Innocent Joan Woodbury takes the rap for her wealthy boyfriend who is involved in a hit-and-run driving accident. But when she learns the playboy and his father have tricked her, she vows vengeance. She demands a cut in the payoffs upon discovering that the father, an alleged political reformer, is in reality involved in the rackets. The film ends with both Woodbury and the father going to prison. The original title, *Paper Bullets*, was changed to *Crime, Inc.*, and several years later to *Gangs, Inc.*, when it was re-released to take advantage of Ladd's growing popularity.

323 GANGS OF SONORA (1941), Rep.

Dir. John English; *Sc.* Albert Desmond, Doris Schroeder; *Cast includes:* Robert Livingston, Bob Steele, Rufe Davis, June

Johnson, Ward McTaggart, William Farnum.

Wyoming's struggle to gain entrance into the Union results in violence and bloodshed in this routine entry in the Three Mesquiteers western series. Crusading newspaper editor William Farnum and his assistant are gunned down by those elements who don't want statehood before the heroic trio, Robert Livingston, Bob Steele and Rufe Davis, begin to battle the lawbreakers and bring back law and order to the community. Elderly newsperwoman Helen MacKeller, meanwhile, bravely carries on the late editor's work in denouncing the villains and advocating statehood.

324 GATEWAY (1938), TCF.

Dir. Alfred Werker; *Sc.* Lamar Trotti; *Cast includes:* Don Ameche, Arleen Whelan, Gregory Ratoff, Binnie Barnes, Gilbert Roland, Raymond Walburn.

Foreign correspondent Don Ameche, returning from the Spanish Civil War, meets Irish immigrant Arleen Whelan aboard an ocean liner bound for New York in this fair drama about immigration. The innocent young woman who is on her way to meet her fiancé in New York is molested by Raymond Walburn, a lascivious, middle-aged, small-town mayor. In the struggle he is injured. The incident later results in her detention by immigration officials when the vessel reaches Ellis Island. But the correspondent intervenes in Whelan's behalf, and following some turmoil on the island, she is finally exonerated. The film describes a variety of passengers seeking entry to the U.S., including Gregory Ratoff as a counterfeit Russian aristocrat, Eddie Conrad as a communist bent on inciting revolution, and Gilbert Roland as a gangster trying to sneak back into the States.

325 GENTLE JULIA (1936), TCF.

Dir. John Blystone; *Sc.* Lamar Trotti; *Cast includes:* Jane Withers, Tom Brown, Marsha Hunt, Jackie Searl, Francis Ford, George Meeker.

Young newspaperman Tom Brown is in love with Marsha Hunt, the title character, but the couple suffer from the antics of Jane Withers, Julia's younger sister, in this homespun rural comedy loosely based on the novel by Booth Tarkington. The bashful reporter is on the verge of losing his girlfriend to George Meeker, a slick scoundrel who has recently arrived in town, until the younger sister takes a hand in the matter. Young Withers saves the romance but manages to foul up other situations from which she eventually extricates herself and those involved to the satisfaction of all by the time the film ends. The emphasis of the author's original plot has shifted from the title character to her impish sister in this screen adaptation, chiefly to take advantage of Withers's rising popularity with young audiences.

326 THE GENTLEMAN FROM INDIANA (1915), Par.

Dir. Frank Lloyd; *Cast includes:* Dustin Farnum, Winifred Kingston, Herbert Standing, Page Peters, Howard Davies, Joe Ray.

College football star Dustin Farnum, upon graduation, buys a moribund newspaper which he intends to use to expose political corruption and other illegalities in this drama based on the 1899 novel by Booth Tarkington. After exposing a corrupt gambling mob, he is beaten up and left for dead. A vigilante committee forms to punish the gang that the committee believes is controlled by a local politician and rival of Farnum, who is running for the same Congressional office. Meanwhile Winifred Kingston, his girlfriend, takes over the newspaper and contrives to have Farnum win the election.

327 GENTLEMAN'S AGREEMENT (1947), TCF.

Dir. Elia Kazan; *Sc.* Moss Hart; *Cast includes:* Gregory Peck, Dorothy McGuire, John Garfield, Celeste Holm, Anne Revere, June Havoc.

Magazine writer Gregory Peck takes on an assignment to explore the subject of anti-Semitism in America—with some surprising results—in this hard-hitting social problem drama based on the novel by Laura Z. Hobson. Posing as a Jew, he encounters daily hostilities and prejudice, both direct and subtle, from fellow employees, hotel clerks, doctors and others close to him. Checking in at a New England hotel for which he has reservations, he inquires if the place is "restricted." The surprised hotel clerk gets into a confrontation with Peck and calls the manager who diplomatically states that there is no vacancy—that Peck's reservation was a mistake. A similar incident occurs with a local New York doctor who discourages Peck from using a Jewish physician to examine his mother. Peck even clashes with Dorothy McGuire, his girlfriend and the daughter of his publisher, who considers herself free of bigotry. At a party Peck meets Sam Jaffe, a world-famous physicist who claims he follows no religion but insists he is a Jew. "I remain a Jew because the world makes it an advantage not to be one," Jaffe quips. "So, for many of us, it becomes a matter of pride to call ourselves Jews." Shot chiefly in New York, the film won several Oscars, including best direction, best picture and best supporting actress (Celeste Holm). Postwar Hollywood began to turn out several well-produced and highly acclaimed dramas attacking bigotry and prejudice, including, among others, *Crossfire* (1947), another film about anti-Semitism, and *Pinky* (1949), about a young black woman passing for white.

328   GENTLEMEN OF THE PRESS (1929), Par.

Dir. Millard Webb; *Sc.* Bartlett Cormack; *Cast includes:* Walter Huston, Katherine Francis, Charles Ruggles, Betty Lawford, Norman Foster, Duncan Penwarden.

When crack reporter Walter Huston learns that his daughter has just married, he changes his lifestyle in this domestic drama based on a play by Ward Morehouse. Devoted only to his beloved journalism and an occasional drinking binge, Huston now decides to quit and go into the more lucrative public relations field to help the young marrieds. His daughter, Betty Lawford, has married struggling cub reporter Norman Foster. Following several complications, Huston returns to his old job as reporter. His daughter gives birth, but because of her critical condition she remains hospitalized. Huston is about to visit her when he is assigned to cover a big story. He remains at the office to help put out an extra edition. When he finally arrives at the hospital, he learns that his daughter is dead. The author, Morehouse, like many other writers who turned out newspaper plays and films, had experience in the world of journalism.

329   THE GHOST AND MR. CHICKEN (1966), U.

Dir. Alan Rafkin; *Sc.* James Fritzell, Everett Greenbaum; *Cast includes:* Don Knotts, Joan Staley, Liam Redmond, Dick Sargent, Skip Homeier, Reta Shaw.

Inept newspaper typesetter Don Knotts, always aspiring to be a great reporter, becomes embroiled in a libel suit and a haunted house in this hackneyed comedy drama. How he ends up as a hero is depicted in a series of sometimes funny but more often stale incidents. Joan Staley portrays reporter Skip Homieier's girlfriend who eventually falls for modest hero Knotts. Publisher Dick Sargent gets after Knotts, who claims to have seen ghosts in the haunted house, to prove his statements. The film includes other eccentric characters, such as janitor Liam Redmond, banker's wife Reta Shaw who is obsessed by seances, and elevator operator Eddie Quillan.

330   GIFT OF GAB (1934), U.

Dir. Karl Freund; *Sc.* Rian James, Lou Breslow; *Cast includes:* Edmund Lowe, Gloria Stuart, Ruth Etting, Phil Baker, Ethel Waters, Alice White.

Radio announcer Edmund Lowe, after being fired, makes a strong comeback with the help of Gloria Stuart, his girlfriend, in this minor musical. She helps him get a major scoop, after which he locates a downed airplane that has been reported missing. One clever segment depicts Lowe broadcasting his story as he parachutes to the site. Boris Karloff and Bela Lugosi appear in ludicrous roles, the former in a top hat and the latter as an Apache dancer! Perhaps some will consider them the highlight of this otherwise bland film.

331   THE GILDED LILY
(1935), Par.

Dir. Wesley Ruggles; *Sc.* Claude Binyon; *Cast includes:* Claudette Colbert, Fred MacMurray, Ray Milland, C. Aubrey Smith, Luis Alberni, Edward Craven.

Reporter Fred MacMurray, in love with typist Claudette Colbert, finds stiff competition in Ray Milland, the roguish son of an English duke, in this frothy romantic comedy set in New York City. The romantic Colbert falls in love with hardworking MacMurray, but is later swayed by the charming Englishman. However, she finally returns to the reporter, selecting him as her mate for life. "I'm going home to sit on a bench and eat popcorn," she remarks after her disappointing fling with Milland. She then turns to her reporter-love and says, "You old mug, take off your shoes and kiss me." MacMurray and Colbert appeared together in several romantic comedies, with the former as a newspaperman in such films as *Exclusive* (1937), *Café Society* (1939) and *The Oregon Trail* (1959). Colbert appeared in several newspaper comedies and dramas, including *I Cover the Waterfront* (1933), *It Happened One Night* (1934), *Arise, My Love* (1940) and *Texas Lady* (1955).

332   THE GIRL FROM GAY PAREE (1927), Tiffany.

Dir. Phil Stone; *Sc.* Violet Clark; *Cast includes:* Lowell Sherman, Barbara Bedford, Malcolm McGregor, Betty Blythe, Walter Hiers, Margaret Livingston.

Impoverished Barbara Bedford, who steals a meal from a restaurant and is pursued by police, accidentally meets newspaper reporter Malcolm McGregor in this light comedy. To avoid the law, she ducks into a café where she finds herself on line waiting for an interview. She is hired to impersonate a French star who has not shown up. McGregor is assigned to interview the star and meets Bedford instead. Later, an acquaintance of the real French star sees a picture of Bedford and decides to visit her. When he begins to make advances toward her, she resists, thinking she has killed him in the ensuing struggle. Suddenly the real star shows up. Following a string of complications, the reporter extricates Bedford from her dilemma and the couple fall in love.

333   GIRL FROM RIO
(1939), Mon.

Dir. Lambert Hillyer; *Sc.* Milton Raison, John T. Neville; *Cast includes:* Movita, Warren Hull, Alan Baldwin, Kay Linaker, Clay Clement, Adele Pearce.

Movita portrays the sister of a young man who is accused of arson and murder in this slow-paced drama that exploits the star's singing talents. Arriving in New York from South America to help exonerate her brother, she and her boyfriend, newspaper reporter Warren Hull, set about to find the real culprits. She gets a job singing at a nightclub run by Clay Clement, who is suspected of fraud by insurance investigators. He has collected heavily following the loss of several of his other night spots that have been destroyed by fire. At one point, Movita is trapped in Clement's office and identified as the accused's sister, but she is rescued by Hull and others. Finally, evidence is uncovered to prove Clement used tracer bullets to set the previous fires.

334   GIRL OF THE OZARKS
(1936), Par.

Dir. William Shea; *Sc.* Stuart Anthony, Michael Simmons; *Cast includes:* Virginia Weidler, Leif Erikson, Elizabeth

Russell, Henrietta Crosman, Janet Young, Russell Simpson.

Kindly small-town editor Leif Erikson adopts the young, spirited Virginia Weidler after her mother dies, in this time-worn and tear-invoking drama. Romance is furnished by Erikson who, needing a mother for his new charge, chooses Elizabeth Russell, his fiancée. Comedy is plentiful in the antics of the brattish but good-natured Weidler, who seems to continually foul up one situation after another. She is living in a county orphan asylum at the time of her mother's death. By the last reel, of course, the threesome find a kind of happiness together in their Ozark community that boasts its own newspaper and a grandmother (Henrietta Crosman) who packs a double-barreled shotgun and smokes a pipe.

335 THE GIRL ON THE FRONT PAGE (1936), U.

Dir. Harry Beaumont; *Sc.* Austin Parker, Alice D. G. Miller, Albert Perkins; *Cast includes:* Gloria Stuart, Edmund Lowe, Reginald Owen, David Oliver, Spring Byington, Gilbert Emery.

Tough, cynical newspaper editor Edmund Lowe clashes with socialite Gloria Stuart, who has inherited the paper, in this mediocre comedy. At first, Stuart poses as a recently hired reporter. But trouble brews between the two adversaries once he discovers her true identity. Following a subplot involving a blackmail scheme precipitated by crooked butler Reginald Owen, the battling couple resolve their differences in this overly familiar plot. However, much of the witty dialogue and comic situations provoke a fair amount of laughter, especially the sequence in which Owen is being forced to confess. Roy Chanslor, who co-wrote the original story with Marjorie Chanslor, had been a reporter and contributed several stories to Hollywood studios about newspaper people, including, among others, *Final Edition* (1932), *Hi, Nellie!* (1934) and *Front Page Woman* (1935).

336 THE GIRL ON THE SPOT (1946), U.

Dir. William Beaudine; *Sc.* Dorcas Cochran, Jerry Warner; *Cast includes:* Lois Collier, Richard Lane, Edward Brophy, Billy Newell, Jess Barker, Fuzzy Knight.

Crack crime photographer Jess Barker finds himself embroiled with innocent singer Lois Collier and a murdered nightclub owner in this routine little drama. Hoodlums Richard Lane, Edward Brophy and Billy Newell bump off the owner and try to frame Collier, who has arrived for an audition. She meets Barker, who helps her out of her dilemma while they fall in love with each other. The real killers are soon caught, and the couple continue their romance.

337 THE GIRL REPORTER (1910), Motion Picture Distributors.

No other detailed information is available about this one-reel silent film produced by the once-popular Thanhouser Film Company.

338 A GIRL WITH IDEAS (1937), U.

Dir. S. Sylvan Simon; *Sc.* Bruce Manning, Robert T. Shannon; *Cast includes:* Wendy Barrie, Walter Pidgeon, Kent Taylor, George Barbier, Dorothea Kent, Ted Osborn.

When wealthy Wendy Barrie buys a newspaper that had once maligned her, Walter Pidgeon, its former owner, is humiliated enough to seek some sort of revenge in this fast-paced romantic comedy. The farfetched world of journalism depicted in this film might make reporters and editors cringe. Once in control of the paper, Barrie, now managing editor, begins to write and print about what is really happening around town—thanks to her society pals who provide the lowdown on politics, finance and personal affairs. To the surprise of many, the circulation of the paper soars. Pidgeon, in retaliation and in hopes of retaining the paper if and when Barrie fails, sets up a feigned kidnapping of George Barbier, her father. He then hands the story to Barrie's competitor in an effort to discredit her. Barbier goes along with the scheme for laughs. All ends well as the two rivals reconcile their differences.

339 GIRLS CAN PLAY (1937), Col.

Dir. Lambert Hillyer; *Sc.* Lambert Hillyer; *Cast includes:* Jacqueline Wells, Rita Hayworth, Charles Quigley, John Gallaudet, George McKay, Gene Morgan.

Murder, journalism and a women's softball team combine uneasily in this weak mystery drama that anticipates *A League of Their Own* (1992), about another early female baseball team. Ex-convict John Gallaudet, who sells weak liquor with phony labels out of his drug store, organizes a women's softball team to advertise his sleazy business. When his friend shows up and is murdered, the police and a reporter arrive to investigate. Guinn Williams portrays a dumb police lieutenant, and Charles Quigley a slow-witted reporter who is in love with pitcher Jacqueline Wells. Rita Hayworth, as the girlfriend of the crooked Gallaudet, is the team's catcher who meets with an early death in the film. Quigley played a cub reporter in *Find the Witness*, another crime drama released the same year.

340 THE GLASS ALIBI (1946), Rep.

Dir. W. Lee Wilder; *Sc.* Mindret Lord; *Cast includes:* Paul Kelly, Douglas Fowley, Anne Gwynne, Maris Wrixon, Jack Conrad, Selmer Jackson.

Unscrupulous reporter Douglas Fowley persuades wealthy Maris Wrixon, who is suffering from a heart ailment, to marry him in this drama about greed and murder. The impatient Fowley, encouraged by his girlfriend Anne Gwynne, decides to speed matters up by shooting his wife. However, he is unaware that she has already expired from heart failure. Although homicide detective Paul Kelly knows that Wrixon was already dead when Fowley decided to shoot her, he remains silent as Fowley is convicted of murder.

341 GO AND GET IT (1920), FN.

Dir. Marshall Neilan; *Sc.* Marion Fairfax; *Cast includes:* Pat O'Malley, Wesley Barry, Agnes Ayres, J. Barney Sherry, Noah Beery, Bull Montana.

Newspaper publisher J. Barney Sherry conspires with another of a rival paper to ruin Sherry's paper so that Sherry can gain control of it in this comedy drama. Meanwhile, reporter Pat O'Malley is assigned to get the scoop on a crazed scientist who places the brain of a murderer into a huge ape. O'Malley, the athletic hero, undergoes a series of thrilling adventures, including an airplane pursuit. Bull Montana portrays the terrifying creature, and Agnes Ayres a wealthy heroine. Ayres owns the paper the deceitful publisher is trying to control. The reporter scoops the other dailies, saves Ayres's paper and marries the owner. The focus of the multilayered plot on action sequences suggests a satirical nod toward the popular Douglas Fairbanks films of the period.

342 GOING WILD (1931), FN.

Dir. William A. Seiter; *Sc.* Humphrey Pearson, Henry Moriarty; *Cast includes:* Joe E. Brown, Lawrence Gray, Laura Lee, Walter Pidgeon, Ona Munson, Frank McHugh.

Failed newspaper reporter Joe E. Brown journeys south by train and ends up at a lush resort where he is mistaken for an expert pilot in this inept comedy. Two young women coax the simpleminded and good-natured Brown into entering a flying derby although he has no experience. The remainder of the film consists of a series of supposedly comical schemes against him and incidents occurring in the air, with Brown displaying fear as his uncontrollable plane encounters near catastrophes.

He is forced into the airplane to evade an attempt on his life.

343 THE GOLDEN ARROW (1936), WB.

Dir. Alfred E. Green; *Sc.* Charles Kenyon; *Cast includes:* Bette Davis, George Brent, Eugene Pallette, Dick Foran, Ivan Lebedeff, Earle Foxe.

Newspaper reporter George Brent becomes the dupe of Bette Davis, who tricks him into a marriage of convenience, in this inconsequential comedy based on the unproduced play by Michael Arlen. Cafeteria cashier Davis, hired by a cosmetic company's publicity agent to pose as a wealthy heiress and promote the firm's facial cream, marries Brent to ward off annoying and revulsive foreign fortune hunters. Brent, financially strapped but proud, rejects the world of polo playing and yachting to which Davis introduces him. Not until he learns the truth about her masquerade from rival socialite Carol Hughes does he reveal his love for his wife. Veteran character actor Eugene Pallette, as Hughes's wealthy oil magnate father, adds some comedy relief.

344 THE GOLDEN IDIOT (1917), K-E-S-E.

Dir. Arthur Berthelet; *Sc.* H. Tipton Steck; *Cast includes:* Bryant Washburn, Virginia Valli, Arthur Metcalfe.

Impoverished reporter Bryant Washburn struggles to accumulate enough money to be the recipient of his eccentric millionaire uncle's will in this comedy drama. The uncle had promised that either Washburn or another nephew, a successful stock broker, will receive his fortune, depending which one can raise the most money. Following a series of setbacks, Washburn, although virtually penniless, wins his uncle's fortune when his rival, the broker, finds himself in debt for half a million dollars.

345 GOOD TO GO (1986), Island.

Dir. Blaine Novak; *Sc.* Blaine Novak; *Cast includes:* Art Garfunkel, Robert DoQui, Harris Yulin, Reginald Daughtry, Richard Brooks, Paula Davis.

Relegated to covering crime stories, reporter Art Garfunkel receives a scoop from the police about the latest crime wave caused by go-go music in this obscure drama originally attacked for its negative depiction of the Washington, D.C. African-American community. After he submits his story, he discovers the police have used him to discredit the music which he does not find offensive. He then witnesses detective Harris Yulin brutally beat to death a gang member. The reporter is able to quell ghetto tensions, an act that raises him to something of a hero in the community.

346 GOODNIGHT, SWEETHEART (1944), Rep.

Dir. Joseph Santley; *Sc.* Isabel Dawn, Jack Townley; *Cast includes:* Robert Livingston, Ruth Terry, Henry Hull, Grant Withers, Thurston Hall, Lloyd Corrigan.

Smart-alecky city newspaperman Robert Livingston arrives in a small town to take control of his half interest in a local paper and soon learns a lesson in humility in this farfetched newspaper tale. To gain a larger circulation over a rival paper, he specializes in exposé stories, especially concerning his competitor's mayoral candidate. But his attacks boomerang when Ruth Terry, the niece of the candidate, double-crosses Livingston, teaching him a lesson. He soon retaliates against her. Following several complications between these two rivals, they finally reconcile their differences as they fall in love.

347 GRAFT (1931), U.

Dir. Christy Cabanne; *Sc.* Barry Barringer; *Cast includes:* Dorothy Revier, Regis Toomey, Boris Karloff, William Davidson, Harold Goodwin, George Irving.

Frustrated cub reporter Regis Toomey witnesses the murder of a local district attorney in this highly implausible action drama. Hoping to advance in the journalism field, the not-too-bright neophyte pursues the killer. During the wild chase he manages to woo Dorothy Revier. Regis Toomey appeared in numerous action and newspaper dramas, usually low-budget productions, including *The Finger Points*, (1931), *Great God Gold* (1935) and *Bulldog Edition* (1936).

348 GRAND JURY (1936), RKO.

Dir. Albert Rogell; *Sc.* Philip Epstein, Joseph A. Fields; *Cast includes:* Fred Stone, Louise Latimer, Owen Davis Jr., Moroni Olsen, Frank M. Thomas, Guinn Williams.

A prominent social figure is unmasked as the head of a gang of racketeers and as a killer in this inane comedy drama that touches upon the topic of citizen apathy. Owen Davis Jr., a cub reporter in love with young Louise Latimer, joins forces with Fred Stone, her eccentric grandfather, to expose the leader and the racketeers. Stone, as a law-abiding and outraged citizen, is fed up with hoodlums escaping the law by way of legal loopholes. Together, the pair manage to help round up the culprits. The Grand Jury of the title appears only in some of the opening scenes in which an indictment of murderer Guinn Williams is dropped. A distraught father of the victim condemns the jury, shoots Williams in the shoulder, and is arrested. The film earlier points out how average citizens would rather not serve as jurors. When Stone's son, a worried businessman, complains that he has been called as a juror, Stone berates him. "You can be an important force for good," he reminds him. "You can justify your existence as a citizen." But his son rejects those sentiments. "I believe in letting well enough alone," the younger man argues, adding, "and in minding my own business."

349 GRAND JURY SECRETS (1939), Par.

Dir. James Hogan; *Sc.* Irving Reis, Robert Yost; *Cast includes:* John Howard, Gail Patrick, William Frawley, Harvey Stephens, Jane Darwell, Porter Hall.

An overly ambitious reporter scores a scoop by eavesdropping on a Grand Jury room and later helps to solve a case involving fraud in this absorbing drama. John Howard, as the aggressive news hound, plants a shortwave transmitter in the jury room. Meanwhile his brother, district attorney Harvey Stephens, who disapproves of Howard's methods, is trying to gather evidence against a gang of investment crooks. Porter Hall and Morgan Conway portray the villains. Gail Patrick, as Stephens's secretary, provides the romance. Jury tampering appeared in an earlier newspaper drama, *Front Page Woman* (1935), in which aggressive reporter George Brent drills a hole in the wall of a jury room so that he can listen in.

350 THE GRAND PASSION (1918), U.

Dir. Ida May Park; *Sc.* Ida May Park; *Cast includes:* Dorothy Phillips, Jack Mulhall, William Stowell, Lon Chaney, Bert Appling, Evelyn Selbie, Alfred Allen.

The corrupt boss of an untamed munitions town in the West redeems himself in this silent western drama. William Stowell, the crooked power behind Powdertown, asks his pal Jack Mulhall to start up a newspaper. Although Stowell wants the paper to promote his self-interests, Mulhall convinces him that it should work for reform and help clean up the town's evils. When Dorothy Phillips, a young woman the two friends love, is abducted by the villainous Bert Appling and taken to a brothel, both men rescue her. They return to the newspaper office while the town is aflame. Stowell encourages his two friends to escape. But Phillips, who loves him, stays as he dies in her arms. The film was adapted from Thomas Addison's 1916 story "The Boss of Powderville."

351 GREAT GOD GOLD (1935), Mon.

Dir. Arthur Lubin; *Sc.* Norman Houston; *Cast includes:* Sidney Blackmer,

Martha Sleeper, Regis Toomey, Gloria Shea, Edwin Maxwell, Ralf Harolde.

Newspaper reporter Regis Toomey helps Martha Sleeper, whose father was a victim of a financial swindle, expose the receivership racket practiced by crooked lawyers in this fairly absorbing drama. Sleeper targets Sidney Blackmer, a formerly honest financier whose weaknesses for money, power and women have led to his moral degeneration. Blackmer has allowed himself to serve as the front for a couple of corrupt lawyers. Blackmer's collusion results in the ruin of innocent men and women who have placed their savings in his care. Sleeper's father was one such client. To gain evidence concerning his shady dealings, she poses as a young woman romantically interested in Blackmer. He lets his guard down and, with the newspaperman helping her, Blackmer falls into her web.

352 THE GREAT MAN (1957), U.

Dir. Jose Ferrer; *Sc.* Jose Ferrer, Al Morgan; *Cast includes:* Jose Ferrer, Dean Jagger, Keenan Wynn, Ed Wynn, Julie London, Jim Backus.

Radio reporter Jose Ferrer is assigned by network executive Dean Jagger to do a story on the legendary Herb Fuller, the title character, a popular radio personality who turns out to be an unscrupulous reprobate in this absorbing, incisive character study based on the novel by Al Morgan. Promising the reporter a promotion after the broadcast, Jagger declares, "We'll sell you the way we sell soap." After much research and many interviews, Ferrer learns the scathing truth about Fuller, who beat his mistress, engaged in bribes and payoffs, and lied and cheated his way to the top. Ed Wynn portrays an eccentric owner of a small radio station who gave Fuller his first break. He asks Ferrer why he is not telling the truth about the corrupt "great man." "It's a job," Ferrer admits. The reporter, upon completion of his study, begins his broadcast with a conventional eulogy, but suddenly places his script aside and announces he will reveal the "real, true" story of Herb Fuller. The film satirizes the radio and television industry, its hucksters and its hero-worshiping public.

353 THE GREAT MR. NOBODY (1941), WB.

Dir. Ben Stoloff; *Sc.* Ben Markson, Kenneth Gamet; *Cast includes:* Eddie Albert, Joan Leslie, Alan Hale, John Litel, William Lundigan, Dickie Moore.

Accident-prone newspaper reporter Eddie Albert suffers through a life marked by a series of catastrophes in this entertaining romantic comedy. One of his problems is his perpetual kindness to those down on their luck. This brings the bewildering newsman into conflict with his paper, as in the case of his filching want ads to help his unemployed friends. Another problem is his blind trust. He exhibits good, creative ideas, but he tells them to co-worker John Litel, who steals them from him and gets all the praise and recognition. After many such exasperating incidents he finally gets wise, much to the delight of his girlfriend Joan Leslie.

354 THE GREAT RACE (1965), WB.

Dir. Blake Edwards; *Sc.* Arthur Ross; *Cast includes:* Jack Lemmon, Tony Curtis, Natalie Wood, Peter Falk, Keenan Wynn, Arthur O'Connell.

Aspiring reporter Natalie Wood, in an effort to persuade a newspaper to hire her, joins a well-publicized 1908 auto race from New York to Paris in this broad, lavishly produced comedy. The New York publisher permits Wood to join the race and cover it for his paper. But her Stanley Steamer putters out on the prairie, forcing her to get a lift from Tony Curtis, attired in white, who is the arch rival of the treacherous Jack Lemmon, dressed in black and another crack driver determined to win the contest at all costs. She then manages to ride with Lemmon. As she flips back and forth between the two rivals, she submits her exclusive stories to her paper by carrier pigeon. For comedy, director Edwards resorts to a pie-throwing scene, a blizzard in which a polar bear seeks refuge in Lemmon's vehicle, and a sequence reminiscent of *The Prisoner of Zenda*, with Lemmon playing dual roles.

355 THE GREEN BERETS (1968), WB.

Dir. John Wayne, Ray Kellogg; *Sc.* James Lee Barrett; *Cast includes:* John Wayne, David Janssen, Jim Hutton, Aldo Ray, Raymond St. Jacques, Bruce Cabot.

David Janssen portrays a newspaper reporter who, although early voicing objections against the Vietnam War, slowly changes his views, following the horrors he witnesses, in this hackneyed propaganda action drama based on the novel by Robin Moore. John Wayne, who produced and directed the film, portrays a tough, likable colonel. At one point in the film, the reporter complains to Wayne about the torturing of Viet Cong prisoners. "There is still such a thing as due process," Janssen reminds the colonel. "Out here," Wayne snaps back, "due process is a bullet." When reporter Janssen converts, he confesses to Wayne the problem he has with his liberal publication. "If I write what I want to say," he admits, "I may not have a job." The plot is filled with the familiar stereotyped characters of earlier war movies. We meet the farm boy who is killed in action (Luke Askew), the sentient medic (Raymond St. Jacques), the lovable, dependable sergeant (Aldo Ray), the grunt who takes a host of enemies with him before he dies (Mike Henry), and the young manipulator who can "appropriate" all sorts of supplies (Jim Hutton). The battle sequences and general action are more reminiscent of World War II than of the Vietnam War. The obligatory orphan shows up to milk audience sentimentality and to allow Wayne to finally say, "You are what this war is all about." He states this while looking across the Pacific toward the United States as they both watch the sun set in the East! Hollywood at this time stayed away from the controversial Vietnam War, fearing any film would alienate half the audience. Wayne, on the other hand, believed he could produce a successful major film about the war—and proved it.

356 THE GREEN HORNET (1939) serial, U.

Dir. Ford Beebe, Ray Taylor; *Cast includes:* Gordon Jones, Keye Luke, Anne Nagel, Wade Boteler, Philip Trent, Walter McGrail.

Gordon Jones portrays a crusading newspaper publisher who, as the masked title character, secretly fights criminals like the villainous gang leader Cy Kendall. The Green Hornet operated in a contemporary setting, using a specially high-powered car marked with the symbol of a hornet. This twelve-chapter serial was based on the popular radio adventures of the hero and Cato, his Asian assistant. A sequel titled *The Green Hornet Strikes Again* was released the following year in 1940, with Warren Hull replacing Jones as the title character. Keye Luke returned as Cato, along with Anne Nagel as the heroine.

357 GRIEF STREET (1931), Che.

Dir. Richard Thorpe; *Sc.* Arthur Hoerl; *Cast includes:* Barbara Kent, John Holland, Dorothy Christy, Crauford Kent, Lillian Rich, James Burtis.

John Holland portrays a reporter who solves a backstage murder in this mystery that blends the world of the theater with that of journalism. The film opens following the last scene of a stage play. An actor has been strangled in his dressing room. After a shooting and the wounding of his girlfriend, Holland turns over the guilty party to a stereotyped dumb police officer. The title, not mentioned in the overly talky script, evidently refers to Broadway.

358 THE GRIM GAME (1919), Par.

Dir. Irvin Willat; *Sc.* Walter Woods; *Cast includes:* Harry Houdini, Thomas

Jefferson, Ann Forrest, Augustus Phillips, Tully Marshall, Arthur Hoyt, Mae Busch.

The famous escape artist Harry Houdini portrays a reporter who is framed for murdering his penny-pinching uncle in this routine drama designed to exploit the star's talents. Foolishly, he agrees to a scheme involving the fake murder of his uncle in which he will be the chief suspect. His uncle is then murdered and Houdini is charged with the crime. Following a series of complications and familiar stunts involving Houdini, the reporter eventually succeeds in proving his innocence by exposing the real culprits. Perhaps the highlight of the film is a startling smash-up of two airplanes—a scene not part of the original script. Fortunately, no one was hurt during the accident. The director decided to include the incident in the final cutting, adding the only realistic note to an otherwise unimpressive film.

359 GRINNING GUNS (1927), U.

Dir. Albert Rogell; *Sc.* Grover Jones; *Cast includes:* Jack Hoxie, Ena Gregory, Robert Milasch, Arthur Morrison.

A roving cowboy known as "Grinner" Martin uses the power of the press (and his six-gun) to restore law and order to a frontier town in this above-average western drama. Jack Hoxie, as the deceptively cheerful stranger, rides into a town looking for George French, an author he has grown to admire. He finds his man running a newspaper with Ena Gregory, his pretty daughter, and struggling to expose some of the criminal elements of the community. Hoxie, together with his sidekick, Robert Milasch, intimidates each local tough at the point of a gun to take a subscription to the paper which weekly warns another lawbreaker to leave town or else. After the town and its surroundings are made safe, our hero wins the love of the editor's daughter who gladly accepts Hoxie's affections.

360 GUEST WIFE (1944), UA.

Dir. Sam Wood; *Sc.* Bruce Manning, John Klorer; *Cast includes:* Claudette Colbert, Don Ameche, Dick Foran, Charles Dingle, Grant Mitchell, Wilma Francis.

Famous foreign correspondent Don Ameche, whose employer Charles Dingle requires his workers to be married, is forced to pose as a husband in this fluffy comedy. To meet this demand, he gets Claudette Colbert, who is married to Dick Foran, Ameche's pal, to pose as his wife. This leads to several farcical results, including Colbert's being accused of living with a married man (her own husband) and Foran's jealousy of Ameche, who is accused of taking advantage of the circumstances. The generally trite story succeeds only because of the talents of the three leads.

361 GUILTY AS HELL (1932), Par.

Dir. Erle Kenton; *Sc.* Arthur Kober, Frank Partos; *Cast includes:* Victor McLaglen, Edmund Lowe, Richard Arlen, Henry Stephenson, Adrienne Ames, Noel Francis.

A doctor strangles his unfaithful wife and hopes to commit a perfect murder in this drama based on the play *Riddle Me This* by Daniel Rubin. Henry Stephenson, as the betrayed husband, plans an almost foolproof scheme to get rid of his wife, establish an alibi and frame his wife's lover. Victor McLaglen, portraying a police captain, and Edmund Lowe, a wisecracking reporter, combine their talents—when they are not bickering—to solve the crime and rescue innocent Richard Arlen from the electric chair. The film was remade with John Barrymore in 1937 and retitled *Night Club Scandal*. The Lowe-McLaglen team first appeared on screen in the 1926 silent comedy drama *What Price Glory*.

362 GUILTY OF TREASON (1950), EL.

Dir. Felix Feist; *Sc.* Emmet Lavery; *Cast includes:* Charles Bickford, Paul Kelly, Bonita Granville, Richard Derr, Roland Winters.

This cold war drama reenacts the 1949 trial of Josef Cardinal Mindszenty in Communist Hungary. Charles Bickford portrays the cardinal who resists the Communist state's intrusion into the Catholic church's schools. After several conflicts with the totalitarian regime, he is arrested, accused of being an "enemy of the people," and put on trial. A secret meeting of state bureaucrats, controlled by a Soviet commissar, suggests that Mindszenty's eventual confession was the result of the state's use of hypnosis, psychological torture and drugs. Paul Kelly, an American correspondent who serves as guide throughout the drama, arrives in Budapest to report the entire story of the verbal attacks upon the cardinal and his eventual arrest and trial. Earlier, Kelly visits the cardinal at his remote farm where the cardinal confides to the American that he is resigned to his fate at the hands of the Communists. "Is there no chance for some compromise?" Kelly asks. "What chance is there of an agreement between Christ and the anti-Christ?" the religious leader replies. This mood of pessimism and frustration pervades much of the dialogue and attitudes of ordinary Hungarians. A romantic subplot involving young Hungarian Bonita Granville and Russian colonel Richard Derr parallels the main story, with Granville, physically tortured by Communist guards, goes to her death rather than confess to false charges concerning the cardinal. As with other cold war propaganda films of the period, this entry displays similar shortcomings. It fails to convince because of its stereotyped one-dimensional characters, its didactic speeches, and other heavy-handed propaganda elements. The film is based partially on *As We See Russia*, a compilation of writings produced by the Overseas Press Club.

363 A GUY COULD CHANGE (1946), Rep.

Dir. William K. Howard; *Sc.* Al Martin; *Cast includes:* Allan Lane, Jane Frazee, Twinkle Watts, Bobby Blake, Wallace Ford, Adele Mara.

Sometimes a newspaper drama delves into a reporter's personal life, as in this weakly scripted film about journalist Allan Lane, whose wife dies during childbirth. Lane then rejects his child, but Jane Frazee, whom he intends to marry, criticizes him for this neglect. As he prepares to change his attitude toward his child, convict Gerald Mohr escapes from prison. The vindictive fugitive stalks Frazee, who had earlier testified against him. As he is about to strike at her, Lane rushes to her rescue and a battle ensues, with the inevitable outcome.

364 HALF A ROGUE (1916), U.

Dir. Henry Otto; *Sc.* Henry Otto; *Cast includes:* King Baggot, Lettie Ford, Clara Beyers, Joseph Castellanos, Mathilde Brundage, Edna Hunter.

A newspaper opposed to a popular Mayoral candidate tries to involve him in a scandal in this early political drama based on the 1906 novel by Harold McGrath. New York playwright King Baggot, upon returning to his home town, is nominated as mayor. The opposing party, desperate to discredit the popular Baggot, discovers that an actress had spent the night in the playwright's apartment. In reality, she had fainted and Baggot had given her shelter. A newspaper favoring his opponent exaggerates the incident in its columns. After he explains the situation to the husband of the actress, Baggot pummels the person who printed the story.

365 HALF ANGEL (1936), TCF.

Dir. Sidney Lanfield; *Sc.* Bess Meredyth, Gene Fowler, Allen Rivkin; *Cast includes:* Frances Dee, Brian Donlevy, Charles Butterworth, Helen Westley, Henry Stephenson, Sara Haden.

Young Frances Dee is falsely accused of poisoning two people in this bland mystery. At first, she is acquitted of poisoning her father; then she is accused of being responsible for the death of Helen Westley, one of her benefactors, when the police discover the deceased has been poisoned. Enterprising reporter Brian Donlevy falls in love with Dee and believes she is innocent. He is fired from his job but continues to investigate until he turns up evidence to prove she has been framed in both cases. The only surprise in this drama comes at the end with the discovery that one of the more charming characters is in reality the guilty party.

366 THE HARDER THEY FALL (1956), Col.

Dir. Mark Robson; *Sc.* Philip Yordan; *Cast includes:* Humphrey Bogart, Rod Steiger, Jan Sterling, Mike Lane, Max Baer, Jersey Joe Walcott.

Humphrey Bogart portrays an ambitious sports writer who grows disillusioned with the corruption of the fight racket in this realistic and hard-hitting drama based on the novel by Budd Schulberg. Corrupt boxing promoter Rod Steiger, in collusion with Bogart, publicizes his new white hope, Mike Lane, a giant-like fighter from South America, whose intimidating exterior belies his inability in the ring. Steiger sets up a few phony fights for Lane, who soon believes his own publicity. He thinks he can beat Max Baer, the champ, whom Steiger has arranged for him to fight. The big event proves a disaster for Lane, who suffers a brutal beating. Lane is then sent back to South America with only $49, his share after all expenses. At this point, Bogart shows his revulsion to what has transpired, holding those who promote the racket responsible for "every bum who ever got his brains knocked loose in the ring." When he threatens to write a series of articles exposing the fight game, corrupt Steiger replies, "Who reads? Who cares?" Steiger, like his fellow promoter Edward Andrews, believes that "fighters ain't human." But Bogart is resolute in his condemnation. "Professional boxing should be banned," he maintains, "even if it takes an act of Congress to do it."

367 HASHIMURA TOGO (1917), Par.

Dir. William C. De Mille; *Sc.* Marion Fairfax; *Cast includes:* Sessue Hayakawa, Florence Vidor, Mabel Van Buren, Walter Long, Tom Forman, Raymond Hatton.

A persistent reporter saves the honor and life of wrongly disgraced Japanese servant Sessue Hayakawa in this romantic comedy drama based on the novel by Wallace Irwin. Noble Hayakawa, after accepting the blame for his dissolute brother's loss of an important government document, leaves Japan for the U.S. He is employed as a butler for an American family, and particularly adores Florence Vidor, their young daughter who is in love with doctor Tom Forman. In the States, Hayakawa discovers that Vidor has personal trouble, so he writes to a local newspaper, addressing his letter to George Washington, whom he believes is still living. Not only is he fired from his job, but his father, who has arrived in the country and is embarrassed by the incident, orders his son to commit hari-kiri. However, the reporter arrives in the nick of time to prove that Vidor's crooked trustee has forged some of her estate documents, which he is using to force her into marrying him. Hayakawa and the reporter rush to the church and halt the wedding. Vidor and her doctor are reunited, and Hayakawa is forgiven for his awkward letter.

368 THE HATER OF MEN (1917), Triangle.

Dir. Charles Miller; *Sc.* C. Gardner Sullivan; *Cast includes:* Bessie Barriscale, Charles K. French, Jack Gilbert.

Newspaper reporter Bessie Barriscale, strongly affected by a highly charged divorce trial she is assigned to cover, decides to break off her engagement to a fellow journalist in this simplistically resolved comedy drama. Believing that all men will eventually behave in the detestable manner as demonstrated by the husband in the case, she decides to return her fiancé's ring and live a happy and singular life.

Her freedom brings her a host of men who fill her apartment, drink heavily and eventually begin to tell off-color stories in her presence. As she begins to tire of this bohemian life, an old confidant persuades her to return to the young man she loves. He arranges a meeting between the lovers, and the couple are reconciled.

369 THE HAUNTED BEDROOM (1919), Par.

Dir. Fred Niblo; *Sc.* C. Gardner Sullivan; *Cast includes:* Enid Bennett, Dorcas Matthews, Jack Nelson, Lloyd Hughes, William Conklin, Harry Archer.

Reporter Enid Bennett is assigned the task of learning what or who is haunting a Virginia mansion in this "old dark house" comedy mystery. Also on her agenda is investigating the mysterious disappearance of Jack Nelson, the owner's brother. Bennett poses as a maid to gain entrance and soon tangles with a detective who suspects Lloyd Hughes, the son of a local doctor. The reporter decides to clear the suspect with whom Bennett has fallen in love. After several complications involving a disappearing ghost, she discovers a secret passage which leads to the ghost who turns out to be the missing Nelson. The crazed man happens to be an international forger. Bennett opts to stay in Virginia with Hughes.

370 THE HAUNTED HOUSE (1940), Mon.

Dir. Robert McGowan; *Sc.* Dorothy Reid; *Cast includes:* Jackie Moran, Marcia Mae Jones, George Cleveland, Henry Hall, John St. Polis, Jessie Arnold.

Teenagers Jackie Moran and Marcia Mae Jones try to help a friend who has been accused of murder in this little mystery aimed at juvenile audiences. Moran, a newspaper office boy, is joined by publisher's niece Jones as they seek out and finally expose the real murderer. This was one of a series of juvenile films released by the studio and one of three featuring the two young leads.

371 HE SAID, SHE SAID (1991), Par.

Dir. Marisa Silver, Ken Kwapis; *Sc.* Brian Hohlfeld; *Cast includes:* Elizabeth Perkins, Kevin Bacon, Sharon Stone, Nathan Lane, Anthony LaPaglia, Stanley Anderson.

Ladies' man Kevin Bacon, who is an obituary writer on a Baltimore newspaper, and rival social news reporter Elizabeth Perkins compete for the same column in this disappointing romantic comedy filmed on location, with the *Baltimore Sun*'s newsroom serving as one of the sets. "There are no small jobs here," Bacon informs Perkins early in the film. "A newspaper is a daily miracle." Both hold down equally lackluster jobs. Bacon meanwhile fears any permanent commitment to the opposite sex, and Perkins seeks only a husband. Their editor runs their first articles alongside of each other and decides, because of the positive response, to make their opposing columns a permanent feature. The writers soon find themselves falling in love, with Bacon bogged down with jealous Sharon Stone, another girlfriend, and Perkins focused upon marriage. Their columns are successful and bring them a talk show on television titled "He Said, She Said." The plot opens at this point, with the film engaging in several flashbacks. During one television show, Perkins throws a coffee mug at Bacon, hitting him in the head, and storms out of the studio. The first flashback begins as Bacon recalls their first meeting. "A newspaper is a daily miracle," he says glibly to fellow reporter Perkins, "and we're all part of it." Clashes concerning their private and professional lives mount until the final scene in which they reconcile their petty differences.

372 HEADIN' FOR GOD'S COUNTRY (1943), Rep.

Dir. William Morgan; *Sc.* Elizabeth Meehan, Houston Branch; *Cast includes:* William Lundigan, Virginia Dale, Harry Davenport, Harry Shannon, Addison Richards, Eddie Acuff.

An enemy agent leads a Japanese assault on a small Alaskan village in this low-budget World War II drama that takes place immediately following Japan's attack on Pearl Harbor. William Lundigan, a stranger in the community who has been mistreated as a vagrant, is befriended only by Virginia Dale, the local radio operator who eventually falls in love with him, and Harry Davenport, the local newspaper publisher. When the straitlaced citizens jail Lundigan for vagrancy, he later retaliates by printing a false story in Davenport's paper about the U.S. being at war. Harry Shannon, the enemy agent working with the Japanese, steals a tube from the only radio receiver in the community, contacts the small force of Japanese, and guides them into the village. Lundigan then organizes the defense of the isolated village and leads its inhabitants against the raiding party which is eventually annihilated.

373 THE HEADLEYS AT HOME (1939), Standard Pictures.

Dir. Chris Beute; *Sc.* Carrington North, Nicholas Bela; *Cast includes:* Evelyn Venable, Grant Mitchell, Robert Whitney, Betty Roadman, Vince Barnett, Benny Rubin.

The Headleys, an average family living in a small, peaceful town, find themselves involved with a bank robber in this dull, low-budget comedy drama. Betty Roadman, as a socially ambitious wife, urges her mild-mannered husband, Ernest Headley, played by Grant Mitchell, to invite an important visiting New York banker for dinner. Robert Whitney, a local reporter who is in love with Evelyn Venable, their daughter, volunteers to substitute another in place of the banker—whom Headley does not even know. It turns out the substitute guest is a bank robber. Following the usual complications, including the capture of the thief, the Headleys return to the peace and quiet of their small town. Veteran character players Vince Barnett and Benny Rubin, portraying a pair of bickering doctors, add some comedy to an otherwise commonplace film.

374 HEADLINE CRASHER (1937), Conn Pictures.

Dir. Les Goodwins; *Sc.* Harry O. Hoyt; *Cast includes:* Frankie Darro, Kane Richmond, Muriel Evans, John Merton, Richard Tucker, Edward Earle.

Criminal elements and an unscrupulous press combine forces in a scheme to defeat a veteran senator in this weak and meaningless action drama. Frankie Darro, as the politician's son, undergoes several close calls at the hands of his father's enemies who want to either capture or kill him. Honest reporter Kane Richmond, inspired by his love for Muriel Evans, the senator's secretary, gives up his position at a sleazy tabloid and exposes how the newspaper has framed the senator's son in an effort to ruin the father's career. John Merton, a recently paroled gangster, directs his hoodlums in the unwarranted attack upon the senator.

375 HEADLINE HUNTERS (1955), Rep.

Dir. William Witney; *Sc.* Frederick Louis Fox, John K. Butler; *Cast includes:* Rod Cameron, Julie Bishop, Ben Cooper, Raymond Greenleaf, Chubby Johnson, John Warburton.

When a dedicated cub reporter determines to carry out his assignments with an abundance of enthusiasm, it leads to problems for him in this routine crime drama. This occurs when he decides to expose a local gang of racketeers ripping off the city. The film is a remake of *Behind the News*, released in 1940.

376 HEADLINE SHOOTER (1933), RKO.

Dir. Otto Brower; *Sc.* Agnes Christian Johnston, Allen Rivkin; *Cast includes:* William Gargan, Frances Dee, Ralph Bellamy, Robert Benchley, Jack LaRue, Gregory Ratoff.

Audacious newsreel cameraman William Gargan, showing more devotion to his work than to Frances Dee, his wife, almost loses both in this fast-paced action drama loosely based on the story "Muddy Waters" by Wallace West. The neglected and hopelessly romantic wife, a fellow journalist, begins to take an interest in compassionate and debonair Ralph Bellamy. But following several complications, including a perilous confrontation with mobsters, the couple are reunited. The film contains newsreel inserts of an earthquake, a bathing beauty contest, a large fire, and a flood. Co-screenwriter Allen Rivkin, like many Hollywood writers, was a former reporter; he turned out several newspaper films, including *Is My Face Red?* (1932), *Picture Snatcher* (1933) and *Behind the News* (1940). Poor Ralph Bellamy had a long movie career often playing the other man, or the one who never gets the young woman.

377 THE HEADLINE WOMAN (1935), Mascot.

Dir. William Nigh; Sc. John Natteford, Claire Church; Cast includes: Heather Angel, Roger Pryor, Jack LaRue, Ford Sterling, Conway Tearle, Franklin Pangborn.

A rivalry between a city editor and an upper-crust police commissioner compels crack newsman Roger Pryor to find other means of gaining information in this often incredulous cliché-ridden drama. When a war between gambling syndicates erupts, Conway Tearle, the commissioner, stops all reporters from accessing any information. Pryor, however, helps cop Ford Sterling solve several crimes so that he is promoted to detective lieutenant. Sterling in return becomes Pryor's private source for his scoops. At one point, Heather Angel, the publisher's daughter, is involved in the killing of one of the gamblers. Pryor rescues her and keeps her under wraps for his own exclusive story. But when he discovers her real identity, he hushes up the story and prevents his rivals from exposing her. Character player Ward Bond in a minor role portrays the stereotyped alcoholic reporter—a character too often found in earlier newspaper dramas and one whom many writers virtually abandoned by 1935.

378 HEADLINES (1925), AE.

Dir. E. H. Griffith; Sc. Peter Milne, Arthur Hoerl; Cast includes: Alice Joyce, Malcolm McGregor, Virginia Lee Corbin, Harry T. Morey, Ruby Blaine, Elliott Nugent.

Newspaper feature writer Alice Joyce has problems with her rebellious eighteen-year-old daughter, whose existence the mother has kept secret for years, in this domestic drama. Virginia Lee Corbin, as the daughter, is expelled from a high-class boarding school because of her extravagant behavior and returns home, posing as her mother's sister. She soon becomes involved in a couple of romances, including one with Malcolm McGregor, her mother's boyfriend. When she becomes embroiled in a scandal, her mother poses as the guilty party to protect her daughter. Corbin then realizes she has acted irresponsibly and decides to reform through the help of Elliott Nugent, a modest young editor. Mother and daughter reconcile their differences as do McGregor and Joyce.

379 THE HEART OF TWENTY (1920), Robertson-Cole.

Dir. Henry Kolker; St. Sarah Y. Mason; Cast includes: ZaSu Pitts, Jack Pratt, Percy Challenger, Hugh Saxon, Tom Gallery, Aileen Manning.

Working under cover, newspaper reporter Tom Gallery eventually gains enough evidence to expose the leader of a car theft ring in this comedy drama. At first, Gallery rescues despondent ZaSu Pitts from a suicide attempt in a village pond. Next, he obtains a job in the local auto plant where he later learns that manager Jack Pratt is the actual ringleader of the gang. Following this exposure, he identifies himself and is rewarded with the love of the young woman he had earlier rescued. Several westerns and newspaper-crime dramas borrowed from the gangster genre in having the hero infiltrate a gang under suspicion. What is surprising is that the studios that continually ground out these films never seemed to tire of this plot device. Judging by the sheer number of these dramas, neither did audiences seem to have enough of them.

380 HEARTACHES (1947), PRC.

Dir. Basil Wrangell; *Sc.* George Bricker; *Cast includes:* Sheila Ryan, Edward Norris, Chill Wills, Ken Farrell, James Seay, Frank Orth.

A movie singer's life is threatened in this minor mystery set in Hollywood. Ken Farrell portrays the targeted crooner. After a talent agent is killed and Farrell's own agent is shot, the police and reporter Edward Norris take the threats more seriously. Eventually the killer is caught, and Norris gains the affection of Sheila Ryan.

381 HELL BENT FOR 'FRISCO (1931), Sono-Art.

Dir. Stuart Paton; *Sc.* Arthur Hoerl; *Cast includes:* Charles Delaney, Vera Reynolds, Carroll Nye, Wesley Barry, William Desmond.

Charles Delaney is featured as the hero-reporter and Vera Reynolds the heroine in this cliché-ridden drama about deadlines, scoops and demanding city editors. Delaney investigates a local murder and figures out who killed Reynolds's brother.

382 THE HELL CAT (1934), Col.

Dir. Al Rogell; *Sc.* Fred Niblo Jr.; *Cast includes:* Ann Sothern, Robert Armstrong, Benny Baker, Minna Gombell, Purnell Pratt, Charles Wilson, J. Carrol Naish.

Another hackneyed entry in the newspaper-crime genre, this film features Ann Sothern as a young socialite posing as a journalist and Robert Armstrong as the stereotyped hard-boiled reporter. They put aside their bickering long enough to expose a gang of racketeers who have commandeered her father's yacht as a base for their illegal operations. The gang had been engaged in smuggling Chinese into the U.S. Armstrong comes to Sothern's assistance and grudgingly accepts her as a full-fledged sob sister following their recent harrowing experience.

383 HELL ON DEVIL'S ISLAND (1957), TCF.

Dir. Christian Nyby; *Sc.* Steven Ritch; *Cast includes:* Helmut Dantine, William Talman, Donna Martell, Jean Willes, Rex Ingram, Jay Adler.

Former newspaperman Helmut Dantine, after serving an eight-year sentence on Devil's Island, helps to expose the miserable conditions of the infamous French penal colony in this overly familiar drama. Dantine helps the new governor who is determined to close down the institution. Dantine learns that convicts work on a local plantation whose owners are in collusion with William Talman, the prison's overseer. The plantation conceals a gold mine from which they illegally ship out the diggings. The former journalist exposes the entire operation. Donna Martell, the governor's daughter, provides the romance in this plot that was popular in the 1930s.

384 HELLRAISER III: HELL ON EARTH (1992), Dimension Pictures.

Dir. Anthony Hickox; *Sc.* Peter Atkins; *Cast includes:* Terry Farrell, Paula Marshall, Ken Carpenter, Doug Bradley, Kevin Bernhardt, Ashley Laurence.

Television newswoman Terry Farrell clashes with Doug Bradley, who portrays Pinhead, the star of the inane horror series, in this gross entry based on characters created by Clive Barker. An arrogant nightclub owner buys a large sculpture, which in reality contains an evil cube that wreaks havoc at the club. Journalist Farrell investigates the strange events and, following a series of even stranger incidents, the evil Pinhead is banished to Hell. Pinhead's grotesque skull has pins protruding from the intersections where it has been sliced and diced. Protagonist and antagonist come together in a supernatural world following an unnecessary trail of slaughter. This unfunny film abounds in its many inept qualities, including its tastelessness.

385 HENRY ALDRICH, EDITOR (1942), Par.

Dir. Hugh Bennett; *Sc.* Muriel Roy Bolton, Val Burton; *Cast includes:* Jimmy Lydon, Charles Smith, Rita Quigley, John Litel, Olive Blakeney, Charles Halton.

Jimmy Lydon portrays the title character, a trouble-prone high-school student who, as editor of his school paper, gets into further difficulties in this inept entry in the comedy series based on a popular contemporary radio show. His new journalistic endeavors have him covering local fires, the result of which has the police suspect him of arson. Charles Smith portrays his pal Dizzy, Rita Quigley his girlfriend, and John Litel his distraught father. Paramount intended the series to compete with more and better-produced Andy Hardy comedies starring Mickey Rooney.

386 HER FATHER'S GOLD (1916), Mutual.

Dir. W. Eugene Moore; *St.* Crittenden Mariott; *Cast includes:* Harris Gordon, Barbara Gilroy, William Burt, Louise Emerald Bates.

An innocent reporter becomes entangled with part of a treasure map, stolen gold and the daughter of a mine owner in this farfetched early drama. Sent to investigate both the shooting of a gang member who had absconded with a gold cache and rumors about a man-eating alligator, reporter Harris Gordon finds half of a map the thief had hidden behind a picture. The map had been found earlier by Louise Emerald Bates, a member of the gang whom the victim had betrayed, but in her haste, she left with only half. The map holds the location of the stolen gold taken from a mine in Mexico. The reporter meets Barbara Gilroy, the owner's daughter, and Bates, from whom he obtains the other half of the coveted map. He and Gilroy find the gold, but the last remaining gang member, who has taken the couple by boat to an island off the coast of Florida, now holds them at gunpoint and gives them two minutes to say their prayers. Suddenly a man-eating alligator snatches the gangster off the boat and devours him. The fortunate couple are then rescued by friends.

387 HER KIND OF MAN (1946), WB.

Dir. Frederick de Cordova; *Sc.* Gordon Kahn, Leopold Atlas; *Cast includes:* Dane Clark, Janis Paige, Zachary Scott, Faye Emerson, George Tobias, Howard Smith.

This mediocre cops-and-robbers drama about the rise of a gambler is set during the Roaring Twenties and told in flashback. Zachary Scott portrays the gambler and former bootlegger who loves singer Janis Paige. She in turn has fallen in love with newspaper columnist Dane Clark. Although Clark tries to remove Scott by way of his columns, the gambler is rubbed out instead by bullets. The film was adapted from the story "Melancholy" by Charles Hoffman.

388 HER REPUTATION (1923), FN.

Dir. John Griffith Wray; *Sc.* Bradley King; *Cast includes:* May McAvoy, Lloyd Hughes, Casson Ferguson, Eric Mayne, Winter Hall, James Corrigan.

Irresponsible reporter Brinsley Shaw, using very little evidence, almost destroys the reputation of an innocent young woman in this drama based on the 1923 novel by Talbot Mundy and Bradley King. Following a shooting in which a rejected suitor kills a Louisiana plantation owner, Shaw slants his story so that the blame falls on the latter's ward, May McAvoy. In reality, the owner, knowing he had but a short time to live, marries his ward so that she will inherit his estate. McAvoy, his ward, had completely rejected the deranged suitor. The reporter implies that she had been having an affair with the despondent killer. She flees and joins a troupe of dancers. Later, Lloyd Hughes, the newspaper owner's son, falls in love with her and exonerates her from any responsibility after Shaw discovers her whereabouts.

389 HERE COMES CARTER (1936), WB.

Dir. William Clemens; *Sc.* Roy Chanslor; *Cast includes:* Ross Alexander, Glenda Farrell, Anne Nagel, Craig Reynolds, George E. Stone, Hobart Cavanaugh.

Radio columnist Ross Alexander, after being fired as a press agent, turns vindictive as he seeks to discredit those responsible for his dismissal in this often unrealistic drama set chiefly in Hollywood. His main barbs are thrust at film star Craig Reynolds, who precipitated Alexander's ouster. When the columnist prints a story revealing that Reynolds's brother is a gangster, the actor's career takes a dive. Eventually, Alexander's love for Anne Nagel tempers his revenge, and he promises to no longer disparage the actor or anyone else. The otherwise interesting premise is hampered by its thin plot.

390 HERE COMES THE GROOM (1951), Par.

Dir. Frank Capra; *Sc.* Virginia Van Upp, Myles Connolly; *Cast includes:* Bing Crosby, Jane Wyman, Franchot Tone, Alexis Smith, James Barton, Robert Keith.

Bing Crosby portrays a happy-go-lucky, singing reporter who must find a wife in a hurry if he is to adopt two war orphans in this delightful comedy. He discovered the children while on assignment in Paris. However, complications set in for him when he returns to Boston and learns that Jane Wyman, his ex-fiancée whom he has chosen to wed, is about to marry wealthy Franchot Tone. "You have to work fast, son," warns Wyman's father, James Barton. "They're hauling her in this Saturday—in a a forty-million-dollar net." Bing heeds Barton's advice and manages to whisk her away from Tone, although Wyman finds the change not too disagreeable. She easily succumbs to Crosby's charms as well as those of the orphans.

391 HERE COMES TROUBLE (1948), UA.

Dir. Fred Guiol; *Sc.* George Carleton Brown, Edward E. Seabrook; *Cast includes:* William Tracy, Joe Sawyer, Emory Parnell, Betty Compson, Paul Stanton, Beverly Lloyd.

Moon-faced William Tracy portrays an ex-serviceman-turned-cub reporter who happens to have a photographic memory in this inane comedy that depends too heavily on slapstick. The bungling Tracy, who works for pompous publisher Emory Parnell, is assigned to cover a tough police beat where he is subjected to exploding cigars and other indignities. Joe Sawyer, his former army buddy, is now a police officer. One may well wonder why this silly sophomoric material, which ends in a conventional chase set in a theater, was produced in Cinecolor (an inferior process compared to the more advanced and popular Technicolor of the period).

392 HERE'S FLASH CASEY (1937), GN.

Dir. Lynn Shores; *Sc.* John Krafft; *Cast includes:* Eric Linden, Boots Mallory, Cully Richards, Holmes Herbert, Joseph Crehan, Howard Lang.

Eric Linden portrays the title character, a newspaper photographer with large dreams for his future, and Boots Mallory plays a woman reporter in this innocuous little drama. After winning a photo award while in school, Linden allows himself two years before he owns the largest photo news agency.

393 HERO (1992), Col.

Dir. Stephen Frears; *Sc.* David Webb Peoples; *Cast includes:* Dustin Hoffman, Geena Davis, Andy Garcia, Joan Cusack, Kevin J. O'Connor, Maury Chaykin.

Aggressive television news reporter

Geena Davis searches for the unidentified hero who rescued passengers from a wrecked airliner in this sharp comedy that pokes fun at the media's penchant for exaggerating heroism. Homeless Andy Garcia, sensing a chance to exploit the situation, steps forward and takes credit for the noble gesture. Actually, petty thief and ne'er-do-well Dustin Hoffman was responsible for the rescues while he was in the process of stripping the unconscious or dead passengers of their valuables. Garcia receives accolades from the public and the media while Hoffman gladly remains chiefly in the shadows—until Davis discovers his role and plans to exploit him. The characters and incidents are, in some ways, reminiscent of Frank Capra's classic *Meet John Doe* (1941).

394 HI, MOM (1970), Sigma III.

Dir. Brian De Palma; *Sc.* Brian De Palma; *Cast includes:* Robert De Niro, Charles Durnham, Allen Garfield, Abraham Goren, Lara Parker, Jennifer Salt.

Semi-professional film maker Robert De Niro turns out sex films for the New York City peep shows in this quirky, offbeat comedy drama with a confused ending. After renting a run-down apartment on the Lower East Side across from a newly erected high-rise cooperative, De Niro witnesses an urban guerrilla assault on the apartment building. The African Americans are gunned down in the co-op's hallway by a white family with a machine gun. The film maker then poses as an insurance salesman, goes to the laundry room and plants dynamite there which levels the structure. The next scene pictures De Niro attired as a Vietnam veteran being interviewed on television about the bombing.

395 HI, NELLIE! (1934), WB.

Dir. Mervyn LeRoy; *Sc.* Abem Finkel, Sidney Sutherland; *Cast includes:* Paul Muni, Glenda Farrell, Douglass Dumbrille, Robert Barrat, Ned Sparks, Hobart Cavanaugh.

Insubordinate managing editor Paul Muni, relegated to the demeaning role of heart-throb columnist, redeems himself by solving a murder in this well-produced comedy drama reminiscent of *Advice to the Lovelorn*, a drama released one year earlier with Lee Tracy in the main role. Earlier in the film, Muni had treated Glenda Farrell, a blonde reporter who had fouled up a big story, in the same manner. He assigned her to handle the "Advice to the Lovelorn" column. Now Berton Churchill, Muni's superior, turns the column over to Muni, who is mockingly greeted by his colleagues with "Hi, Nellie!" He temporarily resorts to drinking heavily to forget his dilemma—a recurrent motif in many newspaper dramas—until Farrell helps him to regain his confidence. Determined to win back his former title, he makes the column the most successful feature of the paper and unravels the murder of a prestigious banker. His coup proves he was right all the time. Muni, in addition to a continuing battle-of-the-sexes with Farrell, at times portrays a tough newsman, as reflected in such lines as: "You tell His Honor I'll rip him apart on Page One tomorrow." Despite its failure at the box office, three remakes followed: *Love Is on the Air* (1937), *You Can't Escape Forever* (1942) and *House Across the Street* (1949).

396 THE HIDDEN ENEMY (1940), Mon.

Dir. Howard Bretherton; *Sc.* C. B. Williams, Marian Orth; *Cast includes:* Warren Hull, Kay Linaker, William von Brinken, George Cleveland, William Castello, Fern Emmett.

A World War II drama, the film concerns an experimental metal that is three times lighter than aluminum and at the same time much stronger than steel. International spies as well as others would like to obtain the secret of this valuable formula. George Cleveland portrays the American inventor, and Warren Hull plays his son, a newspaper reporter who soon finds himself entangled in the plot to steal his father's discovery. The "hidden enemy" of the title seems to suggest Russian and Italian agents although these countries are never mentioned directly.

397 THE HIDDEN MENACE (1925), Steiner.

Dir. Charles Hutchison; Sc. John F. Natteford; Cast includes: Charles Hutchison. Newspaper reporter Charles Hutchison rescues a young woman from a crazed sculptor in this minor low-budget action drama. At first, Hutchison rescues the young woman from an impending accident and begins to fall in love with her. He wins her love later when he foils the attempts of the mad sculptor who plans to turn her into a human sacrifice. He kidnaps her, planning to use her as a model for his intended masterpiece. When he is about to sacrifice her, Hutchison arrives in the nick of time.

398 THE HIGGINS FAMILY (1938), Rep.

Dir. Gus Meins; Sc. Paul Gerard Smith, Jack Townley; Cast includes: James Gleason, Lucille Gleason, Russell Gleason, Lynn Roberts, Harry Davenport, William Bakewell.

James Gleason, the harassed patriarch of the Higgins family of the title, goes through a variety of comical mishaps involving his ambitious wife, their eccentric son, their romantically inclined daughter, and robust Grandpa, in this fairly entertaining domestic comedy. But it is Lucille Gleason, his wife, who causes most problems when, as a radio commentator, she acts as spokesperson for a league of housewives over the airwaves. Once on the radio, she denounces several fraudulent products sold to unwary housewives. This allows the film to take a few satirical swipes at the world of advertising. Following a rather comical courtroom sequence in which the couple sue for divorce in front of a bored judge, husband and wife resolve their differences and the family is ready for a second entry in this comedy series. James Gleason and his real-life wife Lucille and their actual son Russell helped to make the series a success. Harry Davenport portrays Grandpa.

399 HIGH GEAR (1933), Goldsmith.

Dir. Leigh Jason; Sc. Rex Taylor, Leigh Jason, Charles Saxon; Cast includes: James Murray, Joan Marsh, Jackie Searl, Eddie Lambert, Theodore von Eltz, Ann Brody.

Newspaper reporter Joan Marsh falls in love with auto racing driver James Murray, who temporarily loses his nerve, in this weak, overly sentimental drama. The couple meet when Marsh, desperate for an interview, invades Murray's bathroom. Jackie Searl elicits an abundance of tears from the audience as a young boy who is orphaned when his father is killed in a race. Eventually Murray regains his confidence, thanks to Marsh's encouragement and the boy's faith in him, and goes on to win the next race.

400 HIGH SOCIETY (1956), MGM.

Dir. Charles Walters; Sc. John Patrick; Cast includes: Bing Crosby, Grace Kelly, Frank Sinatra, Celeste Holm, John Lund, Louis Calhern.

Picture magazine writer Frank Sinatra and his assistant, photographer Celeste Holm, are assigned to cover the upcoming wedding of socialite Grace Kelly in this entertaining musical based on the play *The Philadelphia Story* by Philip Barry. Meanwhile, Bing Crosby, Kelly's ex-husband, arrives to stir up the old romance. Kelly intends to marry stodgy John Lund, a pillar of New England society. Wisecracking Holm adds her quips to the zany events when Sinatra begins to make a play for Kelly. "When the cat's away," she paraphrases, "why should the mouse act like a rat?" Following the usual love-triangle complications (this time, even adding a fourth component in the form of Sinatra, who also begins to fall in love with the bride-to-be), Crosby and his ex-wife reconcile their differences. "If my wonderful, beautiful, marvelous virtue is still intact," she announces to Crosby and Lund, "it is no thanks to me, I assure you." The plush production is rich in color and music, but it lacks the bite of the 1940 film version which kept the title of the play and starred Cary Grant, Katherine Hepburn and James Stewart.

401 HIGH STEPPERS (1926), FN.

Dir. Edwin Carewe; *Sc.* Lois Leeson; *Cast includes:* Lloyd Hughes, Mary Astor, Dolores Del Rio, Rita Carewe, John T. Murray, Edwards Davis.

Expelled from Oxford University because of his unacceptable behavior, young Lloyd Hughes returns home to face other problems in this social drama set in England and based on the 1923 *Heirs Apparent: a Novel* by Philip Hamilton Gibbs. He discovers his mother and sister are both leading frivolous lives while his father is editor of a weekly scandal sheet. Hughes meets Mary Astor, a bright fellow student who has also been expelled, and joins her as a reporter. Now reformed under the influence of Astor, Hughes exposes Edwards Davis, the publisher of his father's weekly, for stealing charity money. After an angry mob kills Davis, his equally unsavory son, who has been misleading Hughes's sister, flees the country. Hughes then marries Astor.

402 HIGH TENSION (1936), TCF.

Dir. Allan Dwan; *Sc.* Lou Breslow, Edward Eliscu; *Cast includes:* Brian Donlevy, Glenda Farrell, Norman Foster, Helen Wood, Robert McWade, Theodore von Eltz.

Sea-diving engineer Brian Donlevy, who has always thought of himself as a strong-willed ladies' man, meets his counterpart in Glenda Farrell in this fast-paced comedy. Farrell, a successful magazine writer, exploits Donlevy's expertise for background material for her stories. As their relationship develops, they find themselves clashing over who is controlling the courtship. Eventually, romance strikes the fast-talking engineer as well as the clever writer. Lively dialogue, humorous situations and a cast of competent character players, including Robert McWade and Hattie McDaniel, contribute to this highly entertaining film.

403 HIGH TIDE (1947), Mon.

Dir. John Reinhardt; *Sc.* Robert Presnell; *Cast includes:* Lee Tracy, Don Castle, Julie Bishop, Anabel Shaw, Regis Toomey, Douglas Walton.

Private detective Don Castle is called upon by newspaper editor Lee Tracy to protect him from alleged threats in this lively newspaper-crime mystery. Unknown to the sleuth, Tracy has murdered his publisher in an effort to take control of the paper. Castle competes with police inspector Regis Toomey in solving the murder. Toomey, who often played law officers, occasionally portrayed reporters as well throughout the 1930s.

404 HIS GIRL FRIDAY (1940), Col.

Dir. Howard Hawks; *Sc.* Charles Lederer; *Cast includes:* Cary Grant, Rosalind Russell, Ralph Bellamy, John Qualen, Gene Lockhart, Helen Mack.

A frenetic remake of *The Front Page* (1931), this dark comedy, based on the original play by Ben Hecht and Charles MacArthur, switched the role of Hildy Johnson from male to female, with Rosalind Russell portraying the reporter and ex-wife of hard-boiled managing editor Walter Burns (Cary Grant). When she resigns from the paper to marry stodgy insurance man Ralph Bellamy, Grant tries to persuade her otherwise. "You can't quit," he insists, "you're a newspaperman!" "That's why I'm getting out," she replies. "I want to go some place where I can be a woman." He then tricks her into covering one last big story while diverting Bellamy. She reluctantly sets out to cover demented radical John Qualen, who is about to be hanged for murder. He escapes to the courthouse press room where Russell hides him from the police. Following a rash of complications, she gets her scoop, including a reconciliation with her ex-husband. The dialogue is as clever and funny as the situations. In one scene, for example, smalltime hoodlum Abner Biberman, working for Grant, accidentally crashes his car into a police patrol wagon. "Imagine bumping into a load of cops!" he exclaims. "They come rolling out like oranges." And when Russell, questioning him about her future mother-in-law, asks: "What did you pull on Mrs. Baldwin this time—you and that albino of yours?" "You talkin' about Angelina," Biberman protests. "She ain't no albino. She was born in this country." When Bellamy says naively he thinks Grant has a lot of charm, Russell replies, "He comes by it naturally. His grandfather was a snake." Other film versions of the play include *The Front Page* (1974) with Jack Lemmon and Walter Matthau and *Switching Channels* (1988) with Kathleen Turner, Burt Reynolds and Christopher Reeve.

405 HIS OWN HOME TOWN (1918), Par.

Dir. Victor Schertzinger; *Sc.* Larry Evans; *Cast includes:* Charles Ray, Katherine MacDonald, Charles French, Otto Hoffman, Andrew Arbuckle, Carl Forms.

Young Charles Ray, rather than appearing as a hypocrite, disagrees with his minister father's way of life and leaves home in this early silent drama. Following several complications, Ray finally establishes himself as a playwright. Meanwhile, Katherine MacDonald, the daughter of the town's honest newspaper owner, also leaves home and joins a burlesque show and eventually stars in one of Ray's Broadway plays. Ray learns that her father, upon his death, has left him the paper as a means of battling the local corruption. Ray returns and carries out the owner's vision and wins the affection of his benefactor's daughter.

406 HOLD THAT GIRL (1934), Fox.

Dir. Hamilton McFadden; *Sc.* Dudley Nichols, Lamar Trotti; *Cast includes:* James Dunn, Claire Trevor, Alan Edwards, Gertrude Michael, John Davidson, Robert McWade.

Claire Trevor portrays an aggressive newspaper reporter who is involved in a love-hate relationship with detective James Dunn in this highly entertaining romantic comedy. In one particular comical sequence, Trevor, masquerading as one of several fan dancers, is caught in a police raid and hauled into court with the entire troupe. Dunn, also in the courtroom, spots the reporter and contrives with the magistrate to compel Trevor to demonstrate her talents at fan dancing—much to her humiliation. Later, the plot throws in a crime element involving a gang of jewel thieves. Trevor eventually has to be rescued from the gang by Dunn. Robert McWade plays Trevor's hard-boiled city editor.

407 HOLD THE PRESS (1933), Col.

Dir. Phil Rosen; *Sc.* Horace McCoy; *Cast includes:* Tim McCoy, Shirley Grey, Henry Wadsworth, Oscar Apfel, Wheeler Oakman, Samuel Hinds.

Cowboy star Tim McCoy puts aside his western accouterments for urban paraphernalia in this farfetched action drama about a snooping reporter who gets his scoop and wins the love of the heroine. As a streetwise reporter well known in both local dives and precinct houses, McCoy turns to the keys of a typewriter instead of the trigger of the six-gun to lasso the culprits. He cajoles a judge to give him a slight prison sentence to help him gather from a convict the evidence he needs to solve a murder. McCoy, like his fellow western star Tom Mix and others, occasionally ventured into different landscapes for a change of pace. He starred as an officer of the law in another non-western action drama, *Police Car 17*, released earlier the same year.

408 HOLD YOUR BREATH (1924), Hodkinson.

Dir. Scott Sidney; *St.* Frank Roland

Conklin; *Cast includes:* Dorothy Devore, Walter Hiers, Tully Marshall, Jimmie Adams, Priscilla Bonner, Jimmy Harrison.

Tenacious Dorothy Devore replaces her brother as reporter in this delightful comedy. He has been fired from his job. After she herself has lost her job in a beauty parlor, Devore is determined to succeed. But she has problems with her early newspaper assignments, at which she fails miserably. Finally, she maneuvers an interview with a kooky jewelry collector. When he permits her to observe an almost priceless bracelet, a monkey suddenly snatches it from an open window. Devore pursues the creature up the side of a skyscraper until she retrieves the valuable stolen bracelet.

409 THE HOLE IN THE WALL (1921), Metro.

Dir. Maxwell Karger; *Sc.* June Mathis; *Cast includes:* Alice Lake, Allan Forrest, Frank Brownlee, Charles Clary, William De Vaull, Kate Lester.

The crooked world of mediums is explored in this tale of mystery and suspense based on the play by Fred Jackson. When the notorious medium Madame Mysteria learns where her clients hide their valuables, she proceeds to notify members of her gang who then rob the victims. Young and innocent Alice Lake is forced to replace Madame Mysteria, who has been killed in an accident. Meanwhile, hero Allan Forrest, a reporter-detective, is hot on the trail of the gang. One major point which weakens the already shaky credibility of the film deals with Lake's ability to actually communicate with the "other" world. Paramount released a sound version of Jackson's play in 1929, featuring Claudette Colbert and Edward G. Robinson. Other films in which journalists expose the crooked world of mystics include *Sucker Money* (1933) and *Mystic Circle Murder* (1939).

410 THE HOLLYWOOD REPORTER (1926), Hercules.

Dir. Bruce Mitchell; *Sc.* Grover Jones; *Cast includes:* Frank Merrill, Charles K. French, Peggy Montgomery, William Hayes, Jack Richardson, Violet Schram.

Hollywood reporter Frank Merrill gets his editor out of a tight spot in this routine action drama. Merrill is in love with Peggy Montgomery, editor Charles K. French's daughter. Shady political boss Jack Richardson, seeking the mayor's job, threatens to blackmail French, who had earlier served a prison term. Richardson wants French to help him win the election. Merrill agrees to help French by trying to find something on the politician. When he discovers that Richardson is running a gambling concession from his home, the Hollywood reporter floods the front page with the story and accompanies it with an incriminating photograph of the establishment taken by his assistant. Meanwhile, his editor proves that his own earlier conviction was a frame-up, leading to a full exoneration of any criminal charges.

411 HOLLYWOOD SPEAKS (1932), Col.

Dir. Eddie Buzzell; *Sc.* Norman Krasna, Jo Swerling; *Cast includes:* Pat O'Brien, Genevieve Tobin, Lucien Prival, Rita Le Roy, Leni Stengel, Ralf Harolde.

Gossip columnist Pat O'Brien prevents aspiring actress Genevieve Tobin from committing suicide and decides to take her under his wing in this routine behind-the-scenes exposé of Hollywood. Promising to make her a star, he first changes her name to Greta Swan, teaches her some of the right moves to attract producers, and introduces her to the appropriate movie people. But all his efforts are in vain when a local hoodlum creates a scandal involving Tobin. As a sort of consolation prize, O'Brien marries her. O'Brien, who made his screen debut playing Hildy Johnson in *The Front Page* (1931), followed in the steps of fellow actor Lee Tracy in two respects. First, Tracy originated the Johnson role on Broadway, and, second, he quickly became popular in films portraying glib, fast-talking reporters. O'Brien, too, began playing cynical, urban newsmen in several films, including *The Final Edition* (1932), in which he appeared as a tough, fast-talking editor.

412 HOLLYWOOD STADIUM MYSTERY (1938), Rep.

Dir. David Howard; *Sc.* Stuart Palmer, Dorrell McGowan, Stuart McGowan; *Cast includes:* Neil Hamilton, Evelyn Venable, Jimmy Wallington, Barbara Pepper, Lucien Littlefield, Lynn Roberts.

Sports commentator Jimmy Wallington surprises everyone when he turns out to be the guilty party who committed the ringside murder of a fighter in this clumsily plotted low-budget mystery. The crime occurs in a packed stadium in full view of the spectators just before the victim is to challenge the champion. On the case are Evelyn Venable, who is a noted crime writer, and Neil Hamilton, the local district attorney, both of whom are confronted with the usual suspects. While Hollywood dredged up a notable share of corrupt reporters and editors, only a handful of questionable sports writers or commentators made their way to the screen, including James Dunn in *The Payoff* (1935), David Bruce in *Joe Palooka in the Big Fight* (1949) and Keenan Wynn in *Angels in the Outfield* (1951).

413 HOME IN OKLAHOMA (1946), Rep.

Dir. William Witney; *Sc.* Gerald Geraghty; *Cast includes:* Roy Rogers, George "Gabby" Hayes, Dale Evans, Carol Hughes, George Meeker, Lanny Rees.

Small-town newspaper editor Roy Rogers investigates the murder of a cattle rancher in this better-than-average B western, part of the cowboy star's western action series for Republic studio. Following the customary battles with the culprits and a handful of songs by Rogers, he rounds up the killers. The climactic battle on a rolling freight car adds the proper suspense and excitement to the film. Veteran comic character player George "Gabby" Hayes portrays Rogers's ranch foreman.

Dale Evans appears as a city reporter who assists Rogers in his hunt for the villains. The three leads also appeared in *Don't Fence Me In* (1945), another western which likewise dealt partly with the world of journalism.

414 HOME TOWN STORY (1951), MGM.

Dir. Arthur Pierson; *Sc.* Arthur Pierson; *Cast includes:* Jeffrey Lynn, Donald Crisp, Nelson Leigh, Melinda Plowman, Alan Hale, Marjorie Reynolds.

Newspaper editor Jeffrey Lynn learns about the benefits of big business when his sister is buried in a cave-in in this heavy-handed drama. Embittered after his defeat in state politics, Lynn returns to his home town to take over his uncle's newspaper. He uses the paper to attack local industrialist Donald Crisp and big business interests in general, believing they helped to defeat him, and rails against large profits. But when Melinda Plowman, his little sister, is trapped in a cave-in and rescued by Crisp's machinery and is flown to a hospital in Crisp's private plane, Lynn changes his opinion and realizes the worth of large companies. Alan Hale Jr. is a reporter on Lynn's paper, and Marjorie Reynolds provides the romance for the editor. The film was financed by General Motors to show consumers how they, too, benefit from the large profits earned by business. *Ace in the Hole*, a more realistic drama about a cave-in and the press, was released the same year.

415 HONOR OF THE PRESS (1932), Mayfair.

Dir. Breezy Eason; *Sc.* John T. Neville; *Cast includes:* Edward Nugent, Rita La Roy, Dorothy Gulliver, Russell Simpson, John Ince, Franklyn Farnum.

Aggressive reporter Edward Nugent discovers that a rival newspaper publisher heads a gang of crooks in this improbable drama. Each time Nugent phones in his story, it seems another newsman has scooped him. Rita La Roy, his girlfriend, helps him solve the mystery by unintentionally giving him several clues. For some inexplicable reason, the writers have placed the two "big city" rival papers in East Orange, New Jersey. Newspaper rivalry was a commonplace plot device in this sub-genre, as witnessed in such films as *Big News* (1929), *Bulldog Edition* (1936), *Behind the Headlines* (1937) and *Five of a Kind* (1938), although these competing dailies were not all set in East Orange.

416 HORSEWHIPPING AN EDITOR (1900), Biograph.

A tough cowboy enters an editorial office bent on punishing a local editor in this early burlesque of western tales. Instead, he is met with a copy boy brandishing a sling shot and a cleaning woman swinging a lethal mop at the intruder who is summarily subdued.

417 HOT NEWS (1928), Par.

Dir. Clarence Badger; *Sc.* Florence Ryerson; *Cast includes:* Bebe Daniels, Neil Hamilton, Paul Lukas, Alfred Allen, "Spec" O'Donnell, Ben Hall.

A talented young woman with a camera competes with a rival photographer in this battle-of-the-sexes action drama. Bebe Daniels portrays the brave daughter of a newspaper publisher who hires his daughter. Neil Hamilton, her adversary, is a star cameraman. When his boss tells him to break in Daniels, his daughter, as a photographer, the sexist Hamilton refuses, quits and goes to work for a rival paper. The cheeky Daniels, who overhears Hamilton's arrogant remarks, decides to go it alone. Both become entangled with a jewel thief whom Daniels exposes. The pair are then held captive on the villain's yacht until they are rescued in the nick of time by the Coast Guard.

418 HOT NEWS (1953), AA.

Dir. Edward Bernds; *Sc.* Charles R. Marion, Elwood Ullman; *Cast includes:* Stanley Clements, Gloria Henry, Ted de Corsia, Veda Ann Borg, Scotty Beckett, Mario Siletti.

Former fighter-turned-sports columnist Stanley Clements is determined to expose a gambling syndicate controlled by Ted de Corsia in this routine newspaper-crime drama. The columnist's crusade increases after his pal Myron Healey is killed as the result of a mismatched fight. His probing almost ends in his own death at the hands of the racketeers, but the columnist manages to bring de Corsia and his henchmen to justice.

419 HOT SUMMER NIGHT (1957), MGM.

Dir. David Friedkin; *Sc.* Morton Fine, David Friedkin; *Cast includes:* Leslie Nielsen, James Best, Colleen Miller, Edward Andrews, Jay C. Flippen, Marjorie Hellen.

Unemployed reporter Leslie Nielsen seeks to interview the head of a gang of thieves as a stepping stone to furthering his foundering career in this minor offbeat drama. The gang's latest caper consisted of robbing a bank and killing a worker. Instead of winning an exclusive interview with gang boss Robert Wilke, complications arise and Nielsen is kidnapped. By the time the reporter is rescued by his nervous bride Colleen Miller and the police, several more killings have occurred, including the death of Wilke and the near death of Nielsen himself.

420 HOT WATER (1937), TCF.

Dir. Frank R. Strayer; *Sc.* Robert Chapin, Karen De Wolf; *Cast includes:* Jed Prouty, Shirley Deane, Spring Byington, Russell Gleason, Kenneth Howell, George Ernest.

Young George Ernest, a mayoral candidate's son, creates a problem for the boy's family in this comedy, a typical entry in the Jones Family series. Ernest prints a clandestine newspaper in which he attacks his father's political opponent. Jed Prouty, father of the Jones clan, is quoted quite liberally in the underground press. As a result, he soon finds his other son, Kenneth Howell, falsely charged with a scandal by his opponent. But Ernest, the younger boy, continues to publish the maverick paper. He exposes the frame-up, resulting in his father winning the election in their small town.

421 THE HOUSE ACROSS THE STREET (1949), WB.

Dir. Richard Bare; *Sc.* Russell Hughes; *Cast includes:* Wayne Morris, Janis Paige, Alan Hale, James Mitchell, Barbara Bates, Bruce Bennett.

Crusading newspaper editor Wayne Morris is determined to pin a murder on a notorious racketeer in this overly familiar newspaper-crime drama, a remake of a couple of earlier films, *Hi, Nellie* (1934) and *Gambling on the High Seas* (1940). The editor's publisher is forced to relegate Morris to the lovelorn column when the racketeer, Bruce Bennett, whom the editor is after, puts pressure on the paper. But Morris, in possession of new clues, accomplishes his sleuthing task with the help of reporter Janis Paige.

422 THE HOUSE OF HORROR (1929), FN.

Dir. Benjamin Christensen; *Sc.* Richard Bee; *Cast includes:* Louise Fazenda, Chester Conklin, Thelma Todd, William V. Mong, Dale Fuller, Tenen Holtz.

Louise Fazenda and Chester Conklin, as the owners of a country store, soon become entangled with a gang of diamond smugglers in this weak part-silent part-sound mystery comedy. The film relies heavily on the trappings of the conventional "old dark house" genre for its laughs and thrills, including the usual sliding panels, mysteriously falling items, and dizzying chases. Thelma Todd poses as one of the crooks until she reveals her true identity—that of a reporter trying to unravel the diamond riddle before the police solve the case. The film, a sequel to *The Haunted House*, released one year earlier, featured the same director and screenwriter and included several of the original players.

423 THE HOUSE OF TEARS (1915), Metro.

Dir. Edwin Carewe; *Sc.* Frank Dazey; *Cast includes:* Emily Stevens, Henri Bergman, Walter Hitchcock, Madge Tyrone, George Brennan, Bernard Randall.

Young star reporter Emily Stevens is assigned to interview popular Walter Hitchcock, a recent millionaire who in reality had been the lover of the reporter's mother, in this domestic drama. Many years earlier, Stevens's mother had run off with Hitchcock, abandoning her Wall Street husband and baby daughter. But her lover eventually left her and later struck it lucky at gambling. Further investments made him a very wealthy man and public figure. When Hitchcock observes that the reporter closely resembles his former love, he dates her and they are soon engaged. Meanwhile, Stevens's mother sees the announcement in the press, arrives in town and learns that the reporter is her daughter. Both lay a trap for Hitchcock, who thinks he has seen a ghost when the mother enters the room. He flees from the scene and is killed in a car accident. The mother and daughter, now happily reunited, embrace each other with deep affection. Stevens plays a dual role as both mother and daughter in the film.

424 THE HOUSEKEEPER'S DAUGHTER (1939), UA.

Dir. Hal Roach; *Sc.* Rian James, Gordon Douglas; *Cast includes:* Joan Bennett, Adolphe Menjou, John Hubbard, William Gargan, George E. Stone, Peggy Wood.

Cub reporter and millionaire's son John Hubbard is on the trail of a murderer in this frenetic comedy based on the novel by Donald Henderson Clarke. The road leads uncomfortably close to gangster Marc Lawrence, who has his minions threaten the journalist, but to no avail. Each time they try to attack him, they fail. Meanwhile Joan Bennett, one of the gang, returns to visit Peggy Wood, her mother, who is a housekeeper. Soon, others become involved in the crime, including crack reporter Adolphe Menjou and photographer William Gargan, both of whom devote more interest to Bennett than to their assignment. Following a string of hectic and hilarious misadventures, the film climaxes with a fireworks battle on a roof.

425 HOW MOLLY MALONE MADE GOOD (1915), Kulee.

Dir. Lawrence B. McGill; *Sc.* Burns Mantle; *Cast includes:* Marguerite Gale, Helen Hilton, John Reedy, William H. Tooker, W. A. Williams, Armand Cortes.

The title character, an Irish immigrant determined to find her missing reporter brother, succeeds as a determined journalist in this early silent drama. At first, Molly, played by Marguerite Gale, takes on a newspaper assignment to interview a popular opera singer. The editor, astonished at her superior work, assigns her to interview ten stage actors in three days. Despite several complications caused by a dismissed cameraman and a disgruntled reporter, Molly comes through in the true tradition of a star reporter. The persons she interviews were actual stage personalities of the period and included, among others, German opera singer Madame Fjorde, May Robson, Henry Kolker, Cyril Scott, Julien Eltinge, Robert Edeson and Henrietta Crosman.

426 THE HOWLING (1981), Avco-Embassy.

Dir. Joe Dante; *Sc.* John Sayles, Terrence H. Winkless; *Cast includes:* Dee Wallace, Patrick Macnee, Dennis Dugan, John Carradine, Christopher Stone, Belinda Balaski.

Television news reporter Dee Wallace, visiting a California psychiatric retreat for her own sexual trauma, discovers the encounter-group community is crawling with werewolves in this very effective horror tale based on a novel by Gary Brandner. Many elements found in standard horror films are present. For example, although Christopher Stone, her husband, accompanies her to the retreat, Wallace goes out alone into the gentle night with only a flashlight to investigate eerie sounds. Meanwhile, reporters Belinda Balaski and Dennis Dugan at the television station have been working on a story involving werewolves. "Silver bullets or fire," occult bookstore owner Dick Miller recommends as methods of getting rid of werewolves. "They're worse than cockroaches." The clues direct the two reporters to the retreat where they join Wallace. Psychologist Patrick Macnee offers some pop advice to his patients. "Repression is the father of neurosis," he expounds. "We should never try to deny the beast, the animal in us." Sprinkled among thrills and solid special effects are in-jokes which refer to B-movie directors and others. Several sequels followed.

427 HUMAN CARGO (1936), TCF.

Dir. Allan Dwan; *Sc.* Jefferson Parker, Doris Malloy; *Cast includes:* Claire Trevor, Brian Donlevy, Alan Dinehart, Ralph Morgan, Helen Troy, Rita Cansino (Rita Hayworth).

The transportation of illegal aliens into the U.S. and the subsequent blackmail of these foreigners form the plot of this routine drama. The cold-blooded smugglers have no qualms about hurling their human cargo overboard to dispose of any incriminating evidence whenever the U.S. Coast Guard comes too close. Claire Trevor, as a free-spirited socialite who aspires to a career in journalism, and rival reporter Brian Donlevy investigate the suspected smugglers by boarding their vessel. However, they are soon discovered by the gang but manage to escape and expose the lucrative racket. Rita Cansino portrays a dancer who allows herself to become involved with the smugglers—a decision that results in her death. (The following year she changed her name to Rita Hayworth.) Several newspaper yarns during the 1930s dealt with the smuggling of illegal aliens, including *Secrets of Wu Sin* (1932) with Lois Wilson and Grant Withers, *I Cover the Waterfront* (1933) with

Ben Lyon and Claudette Colbert and *Yellow Cargo* (1936), with Conrad Nagel and Eleanor Hunt.

428 THE HUMMING BIRD (1924), Par.

Dir. Sidney Olcott; *Sc.* Forrest Halsey; *Cast includes:* Gloria Swanson, Edward Burns, William Ricciardi, Cesare Gravina, Mario Majeroni, Adrienne D'Ambricourt.

Gloria Swanson, as the leader of a Parisian gang of thieves, reforms under the influence of love and patriotism in this drama based on the 1923 play by Maude Fulton. American reporter Edward Burns meets Swanson and they soon fall in love. When the Great War erupts, Burns enlists and Swanson encourages her gang to do likewise and fight for their country. She is then imprisoned for theft, although she has turned over all her loot to the Church. Burns returns wounded, and Swanson escapes to be with him. Later, she is awarded the War Cross for helping to recruit heroic soldiers.

429 HUTCH OF THE U.S.A. (1924), Sterling.

Dir. James Chapin; *Sc.* J. F. Natteford; *Cast includes:* Charles Hutchison, Edith Thornton, Frank Leigh, Ernest Adams.

Charles Hutchison stars as the familiar American hero who becomes entangled in a South American revolution in this minor action drama. Hutch, a journalist, is sent to investigate events in mythical Guadala where he falls in love with the ward of General Moreno. The general is planning to overthrow the president and make himself dictator. Hutch decides to join the revolution which ultimately fails. But Hutch gets the girl. Several battles occur with plenty of fighting on Hutch's part as he straightens matters out almost single-handedly. There is some comic relief from Ernest Adams. The continuous instability of countries south of the border gave impetus to a series of adventure dramas and satires during the 1910s and 1920s concerning revolution and general unrest, but only a handful involved reporters.

430 I COVER BIG TOWN (1947), Par.

Dir. William Thomas; *Sc.* Whitman Chambers; *Cast includes:* Philip Reed, Hillary Brooke, Robert Lowery, Robert Shayne, Louis Jean Heydt, Mona Barrie.

Newspaperwoman Hillary Brooke demonstrates her expertise as a crack crime reporter by unmasking a killer in this newspaper-crime drama, the second entry in the series based on the popular radio show of the period. In addition, Brooke rescues a suspect who has been framed for murder and exposes a scam designed to bankrupt a company. Paramount released four entries to the Big Town series during the 1940s, all featuring Philip Reed as the crusading newspaper editor.

431 I COVER THE WAR (1937), U.

Dir. Arthur Lubin; *Sc.* George Waggner; *Cast includes:* John Wayne, Gwen Gaze, Don Barclay, Pat Somerset, Arthur Aylesworth, Jack Mack.

Newsreel cameraman John Wayne helps to foil an Arab revolt, uncover the villainous leader and rescue a company of lancers, in this romantic adventure. While on assignment in Mesopotamia, he and his assistant Don Barclay become embroiled in a native uprising stirred up by revolutionary leader Charles Brokaw. Wayne finds time to woo and win the niece of a British commandant, whose troop of lancers is threatened with annihilation by the hostile Arab rebels. The film is a low-budget affair but provides Wayne with a rare opportunity to temporarily step out of a western series he had starred in for Lone Star Productions, a poverty-row studio. Iraq had a sporadic history of domestic disturbances during the 1920s and 1930s. Universal, it seemed, used this collective background of desert turmoil as a loose pretext for the film, which is set during the Iraqi Rebellion of 1935.

432 I COVER THE WATERFRONT (1933), UA.

Dir. James Cruze; *Sc.* Wells Root, Jack

Jevne; *Cast includes:* Ben Lyon, Claudette Colbert, Ernest Torrence, Hobart Cavanaugh, Purnell Pratt, Wilfred Lucas.

Ben Lyon, a wise-cracking, cynical reporter, is bent on exposing Ernest Torrence's smuggling racket in this gritty drama based on the book of memoirs by Max Miller. The only problem Lyon has is that he has fallen in love with Claudette Colbert, Torrence's pretty daughter, whom he had planned to use to get to the father. Torrence's unsavory ways range from snuffing out someone's cigarette by spitting on it to tossing an illegal alien overboard to protect himself from the Coast Guard. Lyon then drops such a corpse onto his editor's desk as proof of the captain's illegal activities. Finally, the reporter brings the law down on the smuggler. Aside from the rough and witty dialogue, the film provides a realistic atmosphere of a Pacific waterfront replete with its ratty inhabitants and sleazy dives.

433   I LIVE ON DANGER (1942), Par.

Dir. Sam White; *Sc.* Lewis Foster, Richard Murphy, Maxwell Shane; *Cast includes:* Chester Morris, Jean Parker, Elisabeth Risdon, Roger Pryor, Dick Purcell, Douglas Fowley.

Special events radio reporter Chester Morris unexpectedly discovers a murder while searching for a worthwhile story in this minor drama. He decides to help Edward Norris, Jean Parker's brother, who has been accused of the murder. Morris eventually scrapes up enough proof to clear the brother.

434   I LOVE TROUBLE (1994), Buena Vista.

Dir. Charles Shyer; *Sc.* Nancy Meyers, Charles Shyer; *Cast includes:* Julia Roberts, Nick Nolte, Saul Rubinek, Robert Loggia, James Rebhorn, Charles Martin Smith.

Cub reporter Julia Roberts competes with rival veteran reporter-columnist Nick Nolte on a train-wreck story in this romantic comedy drama set in Chicago. In the tradition of Rosalind Russell, Myrna Loy and other early actors who had to contend with inflated male egos, Roberts not only holds her own against cocky womanizer Nolte but often bests him at his own game. "Don't you worry," she assures her anxious editor, "I own this story. Besides, a little competition is healthy." Working for the *Globe,* she unearths information about the wreck that suggests foul play. Prodded by her scoops, experienced *Chronicle* news hound Nolte begins to delve deeper into the story and uncovers his own evidence. They meet, clash, join forces, betray each other and eventually fall in love. When frustrated Nolte suggests they collaborate, the independent and suspicious Roberts replies, "I'm your competition, not your girl Friday." Meanwhile, they expose a plot by a chemical company to promote a genetically engineered hormone for dairy cows that has the potential for generating profits of a billion dollars a year. The only problem is that the hormone also causes cancer. Unscrupulous officers of the company resort to murder to suppress this fact. The film captures the fun of the thirties newspaper films in which news hounds clashed with sob sisters. Even the title recalls such entries as *I Live on Danger* (1942), *I Cover the Waterfront* (1933) and *I Cover Big Town* (1947).

435   I RING DOORBELLS (1946), PRC.

Dir. Frank Strayer; *Sc.* Dick Irving Hyland; *Cast includes:* Anne Gwynne, Robert Shayne, Roscoe Karns, Pierre Watkin, Harry Shannon, John Eldredge.

Robert Shayne, after failing to establish himself as a playwright, returns to his job as a newspaper reporter and cracks a murder case in this conventional low-budget newspaper-crime drama based on the book by Russell Birdwell. Shayne's publisher, whose son has fallen under the spell of a mercenary blonde, wants the reporter to gather enough evidence to discredit the woman's reputation. To help him accomplish this task, Shayne begins to woo the blonde's maid. Following a series of complications, the blonde seductress is murdered. The star reporter then proves that his own paper's drama critic is the murderer. Feature writer Anne Gwynne provides the romantic interest for Shayne, and news photographer Roscoe Karns offers some comedy relief.

436 I WANT TO LIVE! (1958), UA.

Dir. Robert Wise; *Sc.* Nelson Gidding, Don Mankiewicz; *Cast includes:* Susan Hayward, Simon Oakland, Virginia Vincent, Theodore Bikel, Wesley Lau, Philip Coolidge.

Based on the harrowing events in the life of hooker-thief Barbara Graham, this tense drama contends that Graham, who died in the gas chamber, was framed on a murder charge. Director Robert Wise's intelligent depiction of Graham's hedonistic life and its tragic consequences helped Susan Hayward win an Academy Award for her gritty performance. She plays the subject as hard and cynical. When one of her "Johns" remarks, "Ain't life a funny thing?" she replies: "Compared to what?" Following a string of convictions including prostitution and perjury, she is charged with and convicted of murder. Although she insists upon her innocence, she is finally sentenced to death after numerous postponements. Simon Oakland portrays reporter Ed Montgomery, whose articles became the basis of the screenplay. Early in the film Montgomery insensitively describes her as the "tiger woman," but later, believing that she has been railroaded, he unsuccessfully campaigns for her pardon.

437 I WAS FRAMED (1942), WB.

Dir. D. Ross Lederman; *Sc.* Robert E. Kent; *Cast includes:* Michael Ames, Julie Bishop, Regis Toomey, Aldrich Bowker, Sam McDaniel, Joan Winfield.

Reporter Michael Ames's snooping into politics results in his being framed and jailed in this pedestrian drama, virtually a remake of *Each Dawn I Die* (1939), starring James Cagney. After escaping from jail, Ames exonerates himself and brings to justice those responsible for framing him. Ames played a death row convict who is murdered before going to his execution in another crime film, *Murder in the Big House*, released the same year.

438 I'LL GET HIM YET (1919), Par.

Dir. Elmer Clifton; *St.* Harry Carr; *Cast includes:* Dorothy Gish, George Fawcett, Richard Barthelmess, Ralph Graves, Edward Peil, Porter Strong.

Innocent reporter Richard Barthelmess becomes the target of millionairess Dorothy Gish, who is determined to have him as her husband, in this fast-paced comedy. Although he has vowed never to marry a wealthy young woman after her father evicted him, Gish is nevertheless persistent and persuades the reporter to agree to marriage after she promises to live only on his salary. But he is soon fired. Following a series of complications involving her former suitors, the couple are reunited and Barthelmess decides to manage his wife's railroad.

439 I'LL TELL THE WORLD (1934), U.

Dir. Edward Sedgwick; *Sc.* Dale Van Every, Ralph Spence; *Cast includes:* Lee Tracy, Gloria Stuart, Roger Pryor, Onslow Stevens, Alec Francis, Lawrence Grant.

Rival American news hounds Lee Tracy and Roger Pryor end up in Europe to cover various royal personalities of a mythical kingdom in this inept comedy drama. Tracy during a date is assigned by a United Press editor to cover visiting royalty. He reluctantly agrees and follows his targets across the Atlantic. To elude his competitor Pryor, he disguises himself and meets princess Gloria Stuart. Following several unrealistic and wild complications, including the meddling of the two American reporters in foreign intrigue and their disconnecting telephones to prevent each from scooping the other, Tracy saves the kingdom from a turgid plot and wins the heart of the future queen. Tracy soon

Fast-talking news hound Lee Tracy dominates more than the newspaper media in Edward Sedgwick's drama, *I'll Tell the World* **(1934).**

emerged as the quintessential wisecracking reporter of the thirties. The film was remade in 1945.

440 IN OLD CHEYENNE
(1941), Rep.

Dir. Joseph Kane; *Sc.* Olive Cooper; *Cast includes:* Roy Rogers, George "Gabby" Hayes, Joan Woodbury, J. Farrell MacDonald, Sally Payne, George Rosener.

Newspaper reporter Roy Rogers journeys to Cheyenne to track down notorious outlaw George "Gabby" Hayes in this routine western. But it seems Hayes has been framed by the villainous George Rosener, a local big shot. Rogers joins forces with J. Farrell MacDonald, the town's crusading newspaper editor, and old-timer Hayes to find the varmints. The reporter, after a series of fistfights, gun battles and hard riding, rounds up the outlaws. Rogers and the studio made a handful of better-than-average westerns dealing with reporters several years later, including *Don't Fence Me In* (1945) and *Home in Indiana* (1946), both with Dale Evans.

441 IN THE HEADLINES
(1929), WB.

Dir. John Adolfi; *Sc.* Joseph Jackson; *Cast includes:* Grant Withers, Marion Nixon, Clyde Cook, Edmund Breese, Pauline Garon, Frank Campeau.

When reporter Grant Withers, investigating a double murder in this newspaper-crime drama, fails to come up with a story, his editor sends journalism school graduate Marion Nixon to help him. Together, they face several harrowing situations in the course of their escapades. Withers suspects that the two victims, both brokers, either shot each other or were killed over a woman. When Withers refuses to take his assistant out of town—a request made by Alice Adair, his half-sister—the fledgling reporter is kidnapped. Withers tracks down the victims' office manager and Adair in their apartment where he arrives in time to rescue Nixon, who is about to be drugged. She then explains that one broker killed his partner and the manager killed the other. The killer and Adair are then arrested, and the two reporters celebrate with their honeymoon.

442 IN THE NEXT ROOM (1930), FN.

Dir. Eddie Cline; *Sc.* Harvey Gates, James A. Starr; *Cast includes:* Jane Winton, Crauford Kent, Edward Earle, Jack Mulhall, Robert O'Connor, Alice Day.

This vacuous mystery begins in the 1880s and is set in an old mansion where an angry husband secretly eliminates his wife's lover. Three decades later, flippant reporter Jack Mulhall becomes romantically involved with Alice Day, the daughter of the new inhabitant of the mansion— now the scene of several strange murders. Robert O'Connor, the detective investigating the crimes, adds some comedy relief to the somber events of this film based on a play by Eleanor Robson Belmont and Harriet Ford.

443 INHERIT THE WIND (1960), UA.

Dir. Stanley Kramer; *Sc.* Nathan E. Douglas; Harold Jacob Smith; *Cast includes:* Spencer Tracy, Fredric March, Gene Kelly, Dick York, Harry Morgan, Claude Akins.

Noted Chicago lawyer Clarence Darrow clashes with silver-tongued orator William Jennings Bryan in Jerome Lawrence and Robert E. Lee's thinly disguised play about the famous Scopes Monkey Trial of the mid-1920s. Spencer Tracy portrays Henry Drummond (Darrow), an admitted agnostic who defends a Southern teacher on trial for teaching Darwin's theory of evolution—a violation of the law in Tennessee. "I came here," the brilliant attorney says, "to defend the right to be different." Fredric March, as the bombastic prosecuting attorney Matthew Harrison Brady (Bryan), considers the teaching of evolution as a threat to the fundamentalist belief in the *Bible* as being perpetrated by big-city intellectuals and "agnostic scientists." Gene Kelly portrays the cynical and caustic reporter E. K. Hornbeck, loosely based on the real-life Baltimore journalist H. L. Mencken. He rarely misses an opportunity to sneer at and mock the townspeople and Brady for their religious beliefs. When an elderly lady ask him if he would like a nice clean place to stay, he retorts, "I had a nice clean place to stay, and I left it to come here." During the trial Drummond and Brady engage in a battle of wits over personal and religious issues, with the former expanding the issues to a person's right to think and ending with an attack on fanaticism, bigotry and ignorance. Brady insists that the people need their idea of faith, a sort of "golden chalice of hope." Both sides suggest a metaphorical struggle between the present and progress. Although Brady wins the support of the local crowds, Drummond wins a moral victory in the courtroom, with his teacher-client simply fined a nominal one hundred dollars. Brady, disappointed, collapses. When the courtroom empties, the reporter insults Brady. "A giant once lived in that body!" Drummond reminds the reporter. He then packs both a copy of the *Bible* and Darwin's work in his brief case. The astonished journalist calls Drummond a hypocrite who still believes in religion. Drummond, in turn, berates the reporter, claiming he leads a barren and lonely existence.

444 INSIDE STORY (1938), TCF.

Dir. Ricardo Cortez; *Sc.* Jerry Cady; *Cast includes:* Michael Whalen, Jean Rogers, Chick Chandler, Douglas Fowley, John King, Jane Darwell.

Another entry in the Roving Reporter series, this drama again features Michael Whalen as Barney Callahan, the ace newsman. In his latest venture for a good human-interest story, he searches for the loneliest young woman in New York so that he can offer her a traditional

Local citizens protest the teaching of evolution in their high school while supporting the Bible-preaching Matthew Harrison Brady in Stanley Kramer's drama, *Inherit the Wind* (1960).

Christmas holiday on a farm. Jean Rogers, a tough nightclub hostess, poses as a stenographer, hoping to get chosen. She ends up helping Whalen, who has a gift for unraveling crimes, gain evidence against a killer. Comedy relief is handled ably by regular Chick Chandler and the sister team of Jan Duggan and Louise Carter.

445 INTERNATIONAL CRIME (1938), GN.

Dir. Charles Lamont; *Sc.* Jack Natteford; *Cast includes:* Rod LaRocque, Astrid Allwyn, Thomas Jackson, Oscar O'Shea, William von Brinken, William Frawley.

Foreign agents try to foil the underwriting of a large bond transaction in this somewhat suspenseful drama based on "The Fox Hound," a story by Maxwell Grant. Rod LaRocque, as Lamont Cranston, a nationally famous radio and newspaper crime reporter, suspects foul play and eventually exposes the underhanded manipulations after a financier is murdered. Astrid Allwyn, as Phoebe Lane, a fellow reporter who at times frustrates LaRocque's sleuthing, provides the romantic element. William von Brinken heads the foreign cartel. Former convict William Frawley and local cabby Lew Hearn supply some comedy relief. Another entry in The Shadow series, the story retains very little of the original fictional character created by Walter B. Gibson. There is no black costume or other paraphernalia to mark the famous crime fighter. Instead, Cranston, alias The Shadow, is now a crime reporter and radio personality busily engaged as an amateur sleuth in exposing foreign agents and fifth columnists.

446 INTRIGUE (1947), UA.

Dir. Edwin L. Marin; *Sc.* Barry Trivers, George Slavin; *Cast includes:* George Raft, June Havoc, Helena Carter, Tom Tully, Marvin Miller, Dan Seymour.

Former army pilot and smuggler George Raft turns against his own gang members when he learns they are keeping food from Chinese orphans in this hackneyed drama set in post-World War II Shanghai. Embittered after his dismissal from the service, Raft joins the black marketeers. Newspaperman Tom Tully, who is trying to expose the gang, pleads unsuccessfully with Raft not to become involved with them. As Tully gets closer to the truth about the identity of the gang leader, he is suddenly murdered. The gang has managed to control the price of food, creating havoc among the starving masses. The latest revelation and death of his reporter pal turn Raft around. "There's no price tag on my principles," Raft explains, as he goes after the gang leader. June Havoc portrays a sultry dragon lady known as Madame Baranoff, the White Russian boss of the crooked operation.

447 INVASION USA (1952), Col.

Dir. Alfred E. Green; *Sc.* Robert Smith; *Cast includes:* Gerald Mohr, Peggie Castle, Dan O'Herlihy, Robert Brice, Erik Blythe, Wade Crosby.

Television reporter Gerald Mohr covers a mock invasion of the U.S., as witnessed by patrons of a New York bar, in this propagandistic but effective cautionary drama. What the customers see via television is an atomic attack on the nation by an unnamed but suspected Soviet foe. The war spreads from Alaska to Washington, D.C. and New York as the nation's industries are overrun by enemy troops. However, the entire scenario turns out to be the fabrication of a TV channel, with mass hypnotist Dan O'Herlihy mesmerizing his malleable subjects. The film suggests that Americans had better be prepared for such a possible event. For authenticity, the production used stock footage provided by the Atomic Energy Commission. The power of television upon the public was explored earlier in the offbeat drama *S.O.S. Tidal Wave* (1939).

448 INVASION U.S.A. (1985), Cannon.

Dir. Joseph Zito; *Sc.* James Bruner, Chuck Norris; *Cast includes:* Chuck Norris, Richard Lynch, Melissa Prophet, Alexander Zale, Alex Colon, Eddie Jones.

Melissa Prophet portrays a courageous reporter who questions the violent methods of former U.S. agent Chuck Norris in this action drama filled with repetitious slaughter, wrecked cars and demolished real estate. A crazed Russian agent leads a small military force in an assault on Florida. Rostov, the Soviet spy (Richard Lynch), fears only one man who may interfere with the success of his invasion—Norris, a U.S. intelligence super agent. So he assigns some of his top underlings to annihilate Norris, who is currently retired and living with his wife in Florida's Everglades. His former chief asks Norris to return to duty, suggesting that Rostov, his old nemesis, is somewhere in the U.S. plotting subversive activities. But the contented Norris rejects the request. When Rostov's henchmen blow up his house and murder an old Indian friend, Norris swings into action. Following a series of confrontations and a trap which Norris sets for Rostov, the two adversaries confront each other in an abandoned building and engage in a fight to the death. At the same time, U.S. Army troops wipe out Rostov's army of terrorists.

449 THE INVISIBLE ENEMY (1916), State Rights.

Dir. William Stormer; *Sc.* Emma K. Oswald; *Cast includes:* Marceau Moore, Lucille Young, Leon Kent, Frederick Vroom, Jack Cummings, William Parsons.

A newspaper, upon learning that the governor has renounced his own son for marrying a tubercular young woman of the tenements, exposes the horrid slum conditions in this social drama. Following the public's outrage resulting from the devastating series of articles, Frederick Vroom, the governor, begins to advocate slum reform. Emma K. Oswald, Vroom's daughter, emulates her courageous and nonconformist brother by marrying Leon Kent, a doctor who is fighting the ravages of tuberculosis.

450 THE INVISIBLE KILLER (1940), PDC.

Dir. Sherman Scott; *Sc.* Joseph O'Donnell; *Cast includes:* Grace Bradley, Roland Drew, William Newell, Alex Callam, Frank Coletti, Sydney Grayler.

Newspaper reporter Grace Bradley and policeman Roland Drew help to smash a gambling syndicate and end a series of vicious murders in this fast-moving mystery. The title refers to the diabolical method the killers use to do away with their victims. They release poison gas from telephone receivers.

451 IS MY FACE RED? (1932), RKO.

Dir. William Seiter; *Sc.* Ben Markson, Casey Robinson; *Cast includes:* Ricardo Cortez, Helen Twelvetrees, Jill Esmond, Robert Armstrong, Arline Judge, ZaSu Pitts.

The arrogant and clever newspaper columnist Ricardo Cortez is more interested in scandal than in hard news in this generally realistic and entertaining drama based on a play by Ben Markson and Allen Rivkin. Unscrupulous and egocentric, Cortez sees no difference between the two types of stories. The Walter Winchell-type news hound gets himself into trouble on several occasions, with girlfriend Helen Twelvetrees present to soothe his troubles. His vanity leads him into one particularly perilous dilemma when he decides to print in his column a story about a murder before the police release it. At another point, an adversary even sends him a bomb which he quickly gets rid of in the nick of time. Robert Armstrong, who would gain fame for his role as movie producer Carl Denham in the classic *King Kong* the following year, portrays Cortez's rival newspaperman. Although Cortez appeared in numerous melodramas during the 1930s, he was not known for his journalistic roles as was Lee Tracy and Pat O'Brien during the same period. Playwright Rivkin, a former journalist, wrote other newspaper films, either alone or with others, including *Picture Snatcher* (1933), *Headline Shooter* (1933) and *Behind the News* (1940).

452 IS THAT NICE? (1926), F.B.O.

Dir. Del Andrews; *Sc.* Paul Gangelin; *Cast includes:* George O'Hara, Doris Hill, Stanton Heck, Charles Thurston, Roy Laidlaw, Babe London.

Exuberant cub reporter George O'Hara gains possession of important incriminating papers from a corrupt politician's safe in this mild silent comedy drama. At first, the owner of the newspaper and his managing editor are delighted—until they learn that O'Hara has no proof of the suspect's acts of corruption. His story, it seems, borders chiefly on being libelous. Following several complications, the neophyte newspaperman, with the help of girlfriend Doris Hill, collects the evidence needed to bring down the politician. Laughs depend chiefly on disguises, thrill sequences such as those outside skyscraper windows, car chases and clever title cards.

453 IS THERE JUSTICE? (1931), Sono-Art.

Dir. Stuart Paton; *Sc.* Betty Burbridge; *Cast includes:* Rex Lease, Blanche Mehaffey, Henry B. Walthall, Robert Ellis, Joseph Girard.

A tough district attorney learns a bitter lesson about mercy in this minor drama. Henry B. Walthall, as the district attorney, sends a thief and his innocent wife to prison. When the latter dies behind bars, her husband vows vengeance upon Walthall. Later, Walthall's daughter is caught in a nightclub raid while she is dancing in shorts. The ex-convict, having a photograph of the scene, blackmails Walthall, but he is conveniently killed by a longtime enemy. When Rex Lease, the daughter's innocent reporter-boyfriend, is imprisoned for murder, Walthall, imbued with a sense of redemption, maneuvers to rescue him.

454 THE ISLAND (1980), U.

Dir. Michael Ritchie; *Sc.* Peter Benchley; *Cast includes:* Michael Caine, David Warner, Angela Punch McGregor, Frank Middlemass, Don Henderson, Jeffrey Frank.

British reporter Michael Caine persuades his editor to let him investigate a series of ship disappearances during recent years in this farfetched and violent drama based on the novel by Peter Benchley. Forced to take along his son, Jeffrey Fran, Caine charters a plane in Miami and crash-lands on a remote island inhabited by a band of pirates who have been inbreeding for hundreds of years. They have been preying on pleasure ships, gathering sustenance and supplies. David Warner, the tribal leader, wants Caine's son for a successor and brainwashes the boy. Following several bloody and gross incidents, Caine manages to machine-gun the entire band of cutthroats and escape with his son.

455 THE ISLAND OF DESIRE (1917), Fox.

Dir. Otis Turner; *Sc.* Otis Turner; *Cast includes:* George Walsh, Margaret Gibson, Anna Luther, Herschel Mayall, William Burress, William Clifford.

Newspaper editor George Walsh joins an Australian dance-hall owner and a Chinese gambler in a search for pearls on a remote South Sea island in this early adventure drama. The trio learn that the captain of a trading schooner and his daughter have discovered an island where pearls seem to be plentiful. Walsh eventually falls in love with the daughter, Margaret Gibson, and begins to reform. He sides with her after the death of her father. Following several confrontations with his unscrupulous partners, Walsh and Gibson leave the island with their cache of valuable pearls. This is one of the earliest island films in which pearls play a large role.

456 IT CAN'T LAST FOREVER (1937), Col.

Dir. Hamilton McFadden; *Sc.* Lee Loeb, Harry Buchman; *Cast includes:* Ralph Bellamy, Betty Furness, Raymond Walburn, Robert Armstrong, Thurston Hall, Ed Pawley.

Theatrical producer Ralph Bellamy and newspaper reporter Betty Furness become enmeshed with a gang of thieves in this slow-paced drama. Bellamy schemes to exploit a phony stock situation by exposing it as a fraud, but racketeers muscle in on him in the convoluted plot. However, he ends up getting the girl while the police capture the villain. This is a rare moment for Bellamy, who, in a string of comedies, such as *His Girl Friday* (1940) and *Affectionately Yours* (1941), portrayed the chump who never wins the leading lady. In the first he loses out to Cary Grant, and in the second, to Dennis Morgan.

457 IT HAPPENED ONE NIGHT (1934), Col.

Dir. Frank Capra; *Sc.* Robert Riskin; *Cast includes:* Clark Gable, Claudette Colbert, Walter Connolly, Jameson Thomas, Roscoe Karns, Alan Hale.

Frustrated reporter Clark Gable, recently fired from his newspaper for drunkenness, discovers that sitting next to him on a New York-bound bus is runaway socialite Claudette Colbert in this classic screwball comedy based on the story "Night Bus" by Samuel Hopkins Adams. When Walter Connolly, her millionaire father, disapproved of the man she was to marry, she fled from home. Connolly has offered a $10,000 reward for her return. Gable smells two benefits: the exorbitant reward and a terrific scoop. Soon a romance blossoms between the couple. Following a series of comical incidents and complications, the lovebirds are reunited—but not before Colbert complains about Gable. "He despises me," she confides to her father. "He despises everything about me. He says that I'm spoiled and selfish and pampered and thoroughly insincere. He doesn't think so much of you either. And he blames you for everything that's wrong with me. He says that you raised me stupidly. Oh, he's marvelous!" Among the memorable moments in this five-Academy-Award winner are the singing scene in the bus, the "walls of Jericho" sequence, and the one in which Colbert shows up the boasting Gable on how to thumb a ride. After several cars speed by and ignoring Gable's various attempts, Colbert extends her shapely leg sideways onto the road and brings the next car to a screeching halt. "I proved once and for all," she asserts to Gable, "the limb is mightier than the thumb." The film, along with other similar comedies such as *Hands Across the Table* (1935) and *My Man Godfrey* (1936), promoted the myth of the period that even if you are poor, you can always marry a rich mate, and fostered the American fantasy that love is more powerful than class distinctions.

458 IT HAPPENED TOMORROW (1944), UA.

Dir. Rene Clair; *Sc.* Rene Clair, Dudley Nichols; *Cast includes:* Dick Powell, Linda Darnell, Jack Oakie, Edgar Kennedy, Ed Brophy, George Cleveland.

Reporter Dick Powell meets mysterious, elderly John Philliber, a newspaper librarian who gives the reporter the next day's newspaper in this entertaining comedy fantasy. "News is what happens," Philliber explains. "Time is only an illusion." The unusual newspaper predicts events in advance, such as race track winners. Powell, who has advanced from obituary writer to cub reporter, is ecstatic—until he reads in one edition a report of his own death! Following a series of nerve-wracking and suspenseful moments for the anxious reporter, he is relieved to discover that his wallet was found upon a corpse that was incorrectly identified as the reporter. Powell, who starred chiefly in light musicals during the 1930s, moved successfully into dramas and westerns during the next two decades.

459 IT HAPPENS EVERY THURSDAY (1953), U.

Dir. Joseph Pevney; *Sc.* Dane Lussier; *Cast includes:* Loretta Young, John Forsythe, Edgar Buchanan, Jimmy Conlin, Frank McHugh, Palmer Lee.

Big-city newspaperman John Forsythe and his wife Loretta Young take over a small-town dying newspaper in this absorbing drama based on a novel by Jane S. McIlvain. The couple's economic struggles to keep their paper from going under are finally resolved when Forsythe decides to hire a rainmaker for the rain-starved California farm community. At first the inhabitants frown upon the idea, but when the rains come, all are ecstatic. Veteran character players Edgar Buchanan and Jimmy Conlin enhance matters with their warmth and humor as two old-time, loyal employees of the paper.

460 IT SHOULDN'T HAPPEN TO A DOG (1946), TCF.

Dir. Herbert I. Leeds; *Sc.* Eugene Ling, Frank Gabrielson; *Cast includes:* Carole Landis, Allyn Joslyn, Margo Woods, Henry Morgan, Reed Hadley, Jean Wallace.

Reporter Allyn Joslyn, in trouble with his editor, teams up with dizzy female cop Carole Landis and her dog in this zany comedy mystery. Landis, on the trail of a gangster engaged in black market activities, finally captures him with the help of Joslyn and her Doberman pincher. Gag lines as well as hilarious incidents enliven the film. Interested in meeting Landis, who is walking her dog, Joslyn tries an indirect approach. "Does he do tricks—retrieve, things like that?" he asks. "Yes," Landis answers politely, "but he doesn't pick up." In another scene, Joslyn, searching for a witness, asks the missing woman's landlady for a description of the fugitive. "She's thin, she's got red hair and I think she's a Republican," the woman replies.

461 JACK LONDON (1943), UA.

Dir. Alfred Santell; *Sc.* Ernest Pascal; *Cast includes:* Michael O'Shea, Susan Hayward, Osa Massen, Harry Davenport, Frank Craven, Virginia Mayo.

Michael O'Shea gives a vivid portrayal of the popular author and correspondent who led a lusty and adventurous life in this highly fictional biographical drama. Since the film was made during World War II, the screenplay emphasizes the Russo-Japanese War and graphically depicts the Japanese penchant for ruthlessness and desire for world conquest. London, as a reporter and guest of the ambitious Captain Tanaka, learns of Japan's plans for the proposed takeover of England and the U.S. "The rising sun has a destiny," the captain confides to the writer, "her expansion is inevitable. The taking of Korea is only the first step—the first act of the drama. But the play is on, the curtain is up and it will ring down upon a Japanese world." London, as a correspondent during that conflict, witnesses Russian prisoners senselessly slaughtered by Japanese machine-gun fire. When he scoops more experienced correspondents on the Russo-Japanese War, they at first resent his actions. Then one suggests that they commend him with a toast from one of his own books. "Here's to the man on the trail at night," a reporter quotes. "May his grub hold out; may his matches never misfire." (This scene resembles the ending of *Lost Horizon* (1937), in which club members toast adventurer Ronald Colman and his quest for Shangri-La.) According to the script, London tries to warn the U.S. of Japan's potential for treachery, but the country, at peace with Japan and doing billions of dollars of business with the empire at the time, views his theories as too provocative. "Those sawed-off little runts in their papier-mache island," his editor scoffs, "why, we could lick them with one hand tied behind our back." The film rarely touches upon London's early idealistic writing which conveys the author's interest in social and economic reform. The script is based upon *The Book of Jack London*, written by his wife, Charmian London, who is portrayed on screen by Susan Hayward.

462 JAIL BUSTERS (1955), AA.

Dir. William Beaudine; Sc. Edward Bernds, Elwood Ullman; Cast includes: Leo Gorcey, Huntz Hall, Bennie Bartlett, David Condon, Bernard Gorcey, Percy Helton.

Leo Gorcey and Huntz Hall help out a reporter pal who has been hurt while investigating a prison story in this average entry in the Bowery Boys comedy series. They persuade the friend's editor, Lyle Talbot, to go along with a fake jewelry theft so they can gain entrance to the prison where they can carry out their own investigation. Once behind bars, Gorcey and Hall discover that Talbot is the guilty party. Before they are released, they expose a bit of corruption going on within the walls between inmates and guards.

463 THE JAILBIRD (1920), Par.

Dir. Lloyd Ingraham; Sc. Julien Josephson; Cast includes: Douglas MacLean, Doris May, Lew Morrison, William Courtright, Wilbur Higby, Otto Hoffman.

Convict Douglas MacLean, who escapes from prison, inherits a small-town newspaper and a small piece of property in this comedy of reformation set in Kansas. At first he and his pal Lew Morrison, a fellow jailbird, promote a crooked oil scam, but to their surprise, the deal ends up profitable when the bogus well on his property strikes oil. The two pals decide to reform, with MacLean returning to prison to serve out the remainder of his sentence. Doris May provides the romantic interest for MacLean.

464 JAILBREAK (1936), WB.

Dir. Nick Grinde; Sc. Robert Andrews, Joseph Hoffman; Cast includes: June Travis, Craig Reynolds, Barton MacLane, Richard Purcell, Addison Richards, George E. Stone.

A routine prison drama with a banal plot, the film features Richard Purcell as a convict falsely accused of killing fellow prisoner and rival Joseph King. In reality, another inmate did the killing in an effort to gain access to King's alleged fortune stashed away on the outside. Reporter

Craig Reynolds temporarily dons prison stripes and, with the help of police detective Barton MacLane, clears Purcell of the charge. June Travis, who works for the prison, falls in love with the reporter and they eventually get married. The film, based on the story "Murder in Sing Sing" by Jonathan Finn, was remade in 1939 as *Smashing the Money Ring* and featured Ronald Reagan. Several newspaper dramas used prison backgrounds, including *Missing Girls*, released the same year, with Roger Pryor as an intrepid reporter who, while serving time for contempt of court, unravels a plot to assassinate a senator.

465 THE JAZZ GIRL (1926), Motion Picture Guild.

Dir. Howard Mitchell; *Cast includes:* Gaston Glass, Edith Roberts, Howard Truesdale, Murdock MacQuarrie, Coit Albertson, Ernie Adams.

Pretty socialite Edith Roberts, bored with her lifestyle, turns amateur sleuth in this minor silent action drama about bootleggers. While trying to track down the bootleggers, she meets reporter Gaston Glass, who is assigned to the same task that has enticed Roberts. But she is not aware of his profession. Each suspects the other of being in cahoots with a gang of rum runners. When both hero and heroine finally learn the truth about each other, Glass and Roberts team up to help expose the chief villain and his gang.

466 JAZZLAND (1928), Quality.

Dir. Dallas Fitzgerald; *Sc.* Ada McQuillan; *Cast includes:* Vera Reynolds, Bryant Washburn, Carroll Nye, Forrest Stanley, Virginia Lee Corbin, Violet Bird.

A New England newspaperman trying to prevent a crooked nightclub from invading his community is murdered in this drama. As the plot unfolds, the human-interest element of the tale involves two sisters, one the product of the big-city tempo while the other, who has stayed at home, personifies the qualities of small-town life. Meanwhile, the leader of the town's most important citizens falls under suspicion of being in collusion with the lawbreakers. The plot was reportedly inspired by the real-life murder of Canton, Ohio, newspaper publisher Don Mellett. Another film, *Freedom of the Press*, released one year earlier, dealt with a similar theme.

467 JAZZMANIA (1923), Metro.

Dir. Robert Z. Leonard; *Sc.* Edmund Goulding; *Cast includes:* Mae Murray, Rod LaRocque, Robert Frazer, Edward Burns, Jean Hersholt, Lionel Belmore.

American correspondent Edward Burns finds himself steeped in foreign intrigue in this slight drama. He persuades Mae Murray, the queen of mythical Jazzmania, to abdicate and flee her country which is in the midst of a revolution. The trouble arises after the queen rejects Prince Otto who has been chosen for her husband. In return, Otto incites the revolution. Once in Monte Carlo, Murray meets Rod LaRocque, another American. She eventually returns to her restive native land to quash the turmoil and establish a republic. With calm restored to the land, she is ready to marry LaRocque.

468 A JEWEL IN PAWN (1917), Bluebird.

Dir. Jack Conway; *Sc.* Maie B. Havey; *Cast includes:* Ella Hall, Antrim Short, Walter Belasco, Jack Connolly, George Pearce, Marshall Mackaye.

A local reporter learns about Ella Hall, who had been an abandoned child left at a pawn shop by a widowed mother in this little drama set in a slum district. The reporter senses an appealing human interest story. It seems many years ago an impoverished widow left her little daughter with elderly Jewish pawnbroker Walter Belasco in exchange for enough funds to travel to her wealthy father. But during the journey she dies before she can reveal the fate of her daughter. Belasco raises the child as his own until the story is printed. The girl's grandfather comes to the rescue and sends Hall to a fine private school and plans to have her marry into wealth. But Hall returns to her boyfriend in the slums whom she marries in the old pawn shop amid her childhood friends and neighbors.

469 JIGSAW (1949), UA.

Dir. Fletcher Markle; Sc. Fletcher Markle, Vincent O'Conor; Cast includes: Franchot Tone, Myron McCormick, Winifred Lenihan, Jean Wallace, Marc Lawrence, Betty Harper.

Filmed chiefly in New York City, this offbeat drama with an anti-racist theme features assistant district attorney Franchot Tone's search for a gang of fascist racketeers who have murdered a journalist. After crusading columnist Myron McCormick is killed trying to gather evidence against the fascists, Tone persuades socialite Winifred Lenihan to infiltrate the hate group. A showdown occurs in an art gallery where Tone learns the identity of the leader who turns out to be one of the most respected women in society. Several popular stars of the period, including John Garfield, Henry Fonda, Burgess Meredith and Marlene Dietrich, make unbilled guest appearances in the film.

470 JIM HANVEY, DETECTIVE (1937), Rep.

Dir. Phil Rosen; Sc. Joseph Krumgold, Olive Cooper; Cast includes: Guy Kibbee, Tom Brown, Lucie Kaye, Catherine Doucet, Ed Brophy, Ed Gargan.

Cub reporter Tom Brown, an aspiring writer who is seeking material for his novel, discovers that his writing has innocently embroiled him in a jewel theft in this inept minor comedy drama. Character actor Guy Kibbee portrays the title character made famous in a series of magazine stories by Octavus Roy Cohen. He reluctantly helps an insurance company by investigating a case involving the missing jewels. The sleuth quickly determines the theft was a hoax perpetrated by young Brown as part of his research. However, complications arise when crooks Ed Brophy, Ed Gargan and Theodore von Eltz take an interest in the jewels. Kibbee then unmasks the real thief—an officer in the insurance firm.

471 JOE BUTTERFLY (1957), U.

Dir. Jesse Hibbs; Sc. Sy Gomberg, Jack Sher, Marion Hargrove; Cast includes: Audie Murphy, Burgess Meredith, George Nader, Keenan Wynn, Fred Clark, John Agar.

Former Japanese house boy Burgess Meredith applies his wily ways on American G.I.s and journalists in this strained comedy set in post-World War II Japan. Brazen photographer Audie Murphy and civilian correspondent Keenan Wynn are only two of Meredith's victims who must pay to avoid bureaucratic red tape. Distraught and frantic reporters who have to meet deadlines, especially in preparation for the first waves of occupying troops, depend heavily on Meredith. The film, suspiciously similar to *The Teahouse of the August Moon* (1956), depicts in part the ingenuity the G.I.s are forced to use to circumvent official army protocol.

472 JOE PALOOKA IN THE BIG FIGHT (1949), Mon.

Dir. Cyril Endfield; Sc. Stanley Prager; Cast includes: Leon Errol, Joe Kirkwood, Lina Romay, David Bruce, George O'Hanlon, Virginia Welles.

Corrupt sports columnist David Bruce makes plenty of trouble for Joe Kirkwood, who portrays the title character, an honest and courageous prizefighter, in this routine entry in the popular series based on the comic strip characters created by Ham Fisher. Large-scale gambling and murder almost engulf the champion who is framed on the night of his big fight. Accused of drunkenness and then murder, Palooka begins his own investigation and uncovers the gang of gamblers and Bruce, their crooked leader. Bruce, in the course of seeking to take over the boxing game, is responsible for the murder of Lina Romay, an entertainer who was about to spill all to the champ. Leon Errol, as Knobby Walsh, Palooka's manager, provides some comedy relief in this murder mystery.

473 JOHN D. AND THE REPORTER (1907), Lubin.

When a newspaper offers a $10,000 reward to anyone who can serve a court summons on John D., an ambitious reporter accepts the challenge in this early silent satirical comedy on the controversial oil millionaire. But John D. flees before the reporter can find him, so the journalist begins to track him down. Following John D.'s escape by airship, which crashes into an oil tank, its occupant falls into the tank belonging to the Rancid Oil Company and is rescued by a workman. As John D. emerges, he sees the reporter waiting for him with the summons. An officer of the court suddenly appears with a check for John D. amounting to $29 million, a sum gotten from the consumers. The ecstatic John D., known for his penny-pinching, welcomes the check. This little film has its acerbic moments.

474 JOHNNY COME LATELY (1943), TCF.

Dir. William K. Howard; *Sc.* John Van Druten; *Cast includes:* James Cagney, Grace George, Marjorie Main, Hattie McDaniel, Margaret Hamilton, George Cleveland.

Former reporter James Cagney, now down on his luck, helps crusading middle-aged Grace George battle political corruption in this satisfactory drama based on the novel *McLeod's Folly* by Louis Bromfield. George, who owns a small-town newspaper, saves Cagney from a jail sentence when he is charged with vagrancy. She then hires him to work on her paper and help her clean up local politics and foil political leader Ed McNamara. After he succeeds, Cagney moves on, much to the regret of those new friends he has made. This was stage actress Grace George's only screen appearance.

475 JUNE BRIDE (1948), WB.

Dir. Britaigne Windust; *Sc.* Ranald MacDougall; *Cast includes:* Bette Davis, Robert Montgomery, Barbara Bates, Raymond Roe, Fay Bainter, Tom Tully.

Bette Davis portrays a forceful magazine editor intent on devoting the June issue to a June wedding in this sparkling satirical comedy about human nature and domestic magazines.

Her crack reporter happens to be Robert Montgomery, her former lover and a foreign correspondent who treats her subject matter glibly. "Even when I was making love to you," Montgomery recalls, "I had the feeling that you were wondering what time it was." Problems arise for Davis when she discovers the Indiana couple who are to be married are each in love with someone else. She decides to bring the young couple back together although her own love life concerning Montgomery undergoes the same on-again off-again chaos. Meanwhile her staff redecorates the Indiana home so that it looks more like what her magazine readers are accustomed to.

476 JUNGLE BRIDE (1933), Mon.

Dir. Harry O. Hoyt, Albert Kelly; *Sc.* Leah Baird; *Cast includes:* Anita Page, Charles Starrett, Kenneth Thompson, Eddie Borden, Clarence Geldert.

Reporter Kenneth Thompson is deputized to bring in fugitive Charles Starrett, wanted for murder, in this routine drama set at first aboard a ship and later on an island. Accompanying Thompson aboard the vessel is Anita Page, his fiancée, whose brother is in jail and charged with the crime attributed to Starrett. A shipwreck casts the principals upon an island. Following a series of complications involving perilous lions and other creatures, Starrett and Page fall in love. The couple later learn that her brother has confessed to the crime and died, thereby freeing Starrett of any further charges.

477 THE JURY'S SECRET (1938), U.

Dir. Ted Sloman; *Sc.* Lester Cole, Norman Levy; *Cast includes:* Kent Taylor, Larry Blake, Fay Wray, Samuel S. Hinds, Nan Grey, Halliwell Hobbes.

In this taut drama, a juror at a murder trial must judge a defendant he knows is innocent because he, the juror, has committed the crime. Writer Kent Taylor is the juror tossed into this ironic set of circumstances in which Larry Blake, as a stevedore, is accused of killing publisher Samuel S. Hinds. Blake, a vocal resident opposed to the publisher's resistance to flood control regulations, is found near the body and charged with the crime. Taylor finally heeds his conscience and confesses that he was the one who plunged a knife into Hinds. Judge Granville Bates spends most of his time on the bench perusing a catalog of trout flies. Fay Wray, a reporter and former flame of Taylor's, suspects him of the murder.

478 JUST OFF BROADWAY (1942), TCF.

Dir. Herbert I. Leeds; *Sc.* Arnaud D'Usseau; *Cast includes:* Lloyd Nolan, Marjorie Weaver, Janis Carter, Phil Silvers, Richard Derr, Joan Valerie.

Private eye Michael Shayne, serving as a juror, disappears from this responsibility to solve the case of a witness who is murdered while giving testimony during a trial in this offbeat drama. The detective, played by Lloyd Nolan, is assisted by reporter Marjorie Weaver, both of whom finally gather enough evidence to prove defense attorney Richard Derr is the double murderer. Ironically, Nolan is rewarded for his brilliance with a sixty-day jail sentence for violating courtroom procedures. This was the sixth entry in the detective series based on the fictional character created by Brett Halliday. Comedian Phil Silvers provides the comedy relief.

479 KATHY O' (1958), U.

Dir. Jack Sher; *Sc.* Jack Sher, Sy Gomberg; *Cast includes:* Patty McCormack, Dan Duryea, Jan Sterling, Mary Fickett, Sam Levene, Ainslie Pryor.

Patty McCormack portrays the title character, a famous child star "loved by millions" but a spoiled brat to those who are forced to work with her, in this entertaining comedy based on a magazine story by director-screenwriter Jack Sher. Flustered studio publicity agent Dan Duryea practically has to bribe her to behave for her interview with his ex-wife, columnist Jan Sterling. Surprisingly, the youngster gets along quite well with the writer. Following some minor complications, including a fear that the child has been kidnapped, the film ends with McCormack's emergence from a temperamental star to a well-adjusted and likable youngster.

480 KEEPER OF THE FLAME (1942), MGM.

Dir. George Cukor; *Sc.* Donald Ogden Stewart; *Cast includes:* Spencer Tracy, Katharine Hepburn, Richard Whorf, Margaret Wycherly, Forrest Tucker, Frank Craven.

Newspaper reporter Spencer Tracy, while probing a mysterious car accident, stumbles across a fascist plot designed to take control of the country in this turgid drama based on the novel by I. A. R. Wylie. A war correspondent returning home from an assignment in Europe, Tracy decides to attend the funeral of a famous American World War I hero. He then gains access to the family estate where he meets other members of the family, including the man's widow, Katharine Hepburn, with whom Tracy soon falls in love. As the reporter pieces together more about her husband's life, he discovers the dead man was setting himself up as the leader of an emerging powerful fascist organization. Hepburn dies, leaving the journalist to expose the entire story of one of the nation's so-called heroes, a seemingly loyal American, who all along had been plotting a political coup. The earlier *Meet John Doe* (1941) was another film which warned about the dangers of fascism threatening the nation—this time

Investigative reporter Spencer Tracy (left) relaxing before coming across a fascist plot designed to take control of the country in George Cukor's turgid drama, *Keeper of the Flame* (1942).

in the guise of unscrupulous American industrialist Edward Arnold.

481 THE KID (1916), V-L-S-E.

Dir. Wilfrid North; *Sc.* Wilfrid North; *Cast includes:* Lillian Walker, Ned Finley, Eulalie Jensen, Robert Gaillard.

Lillian Walker portrays the title character, an illegitimate child raised by reporter Robert Gaillard, in this gushy drama. The unfortunate daughter of a naive, wronged woman and her deceitful lover, Walker vows to expose all of the city's political scandals. She succeeds in obtaining a position on the same paper as Gaillard and is assigned to investigate the rising price of meat. Several complications follow, including a murder, an attempted prison escape and her discovery that Ned Finley, the man she is hunting down, is her real father. Finley, who had abandoned her even before her mother's death, entreats her forgiveness. Although she had pleaded with the authorities to let him go, she acknowledges that Gaillard, the man who has raised her, is her only true father.

482 THE KID FROM CLEVELAND (1949), Rep.

Dir. Herbert Kline; *Sc.* John Bright; *Cast includes:* George Brent, Lynn Bari, Rusty Tamblyn, Tommy Cook, Ann Doran, Louis Jean Heydt.

Sympathetic radio sports reporter George Brent takes twelve-year-old street urchin Rusty Tamblyn under his wing in this sentimental baseball drama. The boy, tottering toward delinquency, is unable to get along with his stepfather but is mesmerized by the Cleveland Indians baseball team. Brent develops a relationship with the young hoodlum and, to the boy's joy, introduces him to the actual players on the team. In fact, all the members of the team sort of adopt him, and they become "thirty godfathers" to the boy. The ballplayers and Brent help to rehabilitate the lad who then returns home.

483 KILLER AT LARGE (1947), PRC.

Dir. William Beaudine; *Sc.* Fenton Earnshaw, Tom Blackburn; *Cast includes:* Robert Lowery, Anabel Shaw, Charles Evans, Frank Ferguson, George Lynn, Dick Rich.

Crusading reporter Robert Lowery goes after a racketeer whose gang preys upon World War II veterans who need housing in this familiar newspaper-crime drama. But before he can expose the head of the illegal ring, he has to resolve another dilemma. It just so happens that the chief villain's daughter, Anabel Shaw, works for the same paper, and Lowery has fallen in love with her. He now must choose between love and duty. All is resolved by the last reel.

484 KING OF GAMBLERS (1937), Par.

Dir. Robert Florey; *Sc.* Doris Anderson; *Cast includes:* Akim Tamiroff, Lloyd Nolan, Claire Trevor, Evelyn Brent, Harvey Stephens, Buster Crabbe.

Investigative reporter Lloyd Nolan joins forces with nightclub warbler Claire Trevor to bring an end to the shady career of gambling king Akim Tamiroff in this routine drama. Tamiroff is at the peak of his gambling empire and known as the czar of slot machines. When Helen Burgess, Trevor's roommate, is murdered by the ruthless Tamiroff, Trevor decides to help bring down the gambler's world. The plot is suspiciously similar to that of Warner's *Marked Woman*, starring Bette Davis, released the same year.

485 KNICKERBOCKER HOLIDAY (1944), UA.

Dir. Harry Joe Brown; *Sc.* David Boehm, Rowland Leigh, Harold Goldman; *Cast includes:* Nelson Eddy, Charles Coburn, Constance Dowling, Ernest Cossart, Shelley Winters, Percy Kilbride.

Idealistic newspaper publisher Nelson Eddy fights for freedom in the new world in this disappointing musical comedy based on the play by Maxwell Anderson and Kurt Weill and set in Peter Stuyvesant's old New Amsterdam colony. The dishonest council members at first want to hang Eddy, but settle for putting him into the stocks for his attacks on their underhanded business practices. Eddy considers the council head a conniving scoundrel. Unfortunately, the young publisher of the *Weekly Gazette* is in love with his daughter, Constance Dowling, who wants him to give up his paper's attacks on the council. "This is a new country," Eddy explains. "The making of it is in our hands. We came to a place where everybody can enjoy the right to freedom without oppression." Meanwhile Peter Stuyvesant (Charles Coburn) arrives to take over as governor of New Amsterdam. Portrayed broadly as the consummate politician, the pompous Coburn orders Eddy's release, fearing the council will make a hero of him. "When you make a martyr out of a nuisance, he becomes a hero," he says to the council. Coburn follows this with an insincere speech to the crowd, then whispering to his aide that "they always get most enthusiastic when they haven't the faintest idea what you're talking about." Coburn then sends Eddy away as his emissary while plotting to steal his girlfriend. Eddy returns in time to stop Coburn from forcing Dowling into marrying him. Several songs and dances lace the stagy production, including Coburn's rendition of "September Song."

486 LADIES CRAVE EXCITEMENT (1935), Mascot.

Dir. Nick Grinde; *Sc.* Wellyn Totman; *Cast includes:* Norman Foster, Evalyn Knapp, Esther Ralston, Eric Linden, Purnell Pratt, Gilbert Emery.

A rivalry between two newsreel companies brings together crack cameraman Norman Foster and Evalyn Knapp, whose father owns the competing firm, in this generally unconvincing action drama. Their first meeting is an unpleasant one, but the couple eventually fall in love. At one point, Foster films a pair of villains drugging a racehorse owned by Knapp's father. Developing an interest in newsreel camera work, Knapp decides to join forces with Foster to produce a "March of Events" documentary. Complications arise for the couple when an escaped prisoner commandeers Knapp and her car for his getaway. Foster and his assistant, Eric Linden, follow and are overwhelmed by the convict. But the fugitive is no match for Knapp, who knocks him unconscious with the heel of her shoe. The film gives an unrealistic picture of newsreel cameramen.

487 LADIES LOVE DANGER (1935), Fox.

Dir. H. Bruce Humberstone; Sc. Samson Raphaelson; Cast includes: Mona Barrie, Gilbert Roland, Donald Cook, Adrienne Ames, Hardie Albright, Herbert Mundin.

Playwright and amateur detective Gilbert Roland and newspaper reporter Mona Barrie become involved in a triple murder in this undistinguished backstage mystery. The pair eventually solve the murders of a rich play backer, a leading lady and a theater manager. Comic character actor Herbert Mundin provides some humor as Roland's eccentric butler. Several newspaper-crime films during the 1930s used theatrical backgrounds, including *Grief Street* (1931), *Curtain at Eight* (1934) and *Phantom of 42nd Street* (1945).

488 LADY FROM NOWHERE (1936), Col.

Dir. Gordon Wiles; Sc. Fred Niblo Jr., Arthur Strawn, Joseph Krumgold; Cast includes: Mary Astor, Charles Quigley, Thurston Hall, Victor Kilian, Spencer Charters, Norman Willis.

Manicurist Mary Astor, who witnesses a gangland killing, tries to escape from both the gangsters and the police in this minor drama. The film makes a biting commentary about human greed. Astor ends up in a small Connecticut town and poses as a runaway heiress. Charles Quigley, a local reporter, believes her story and soon falls in love with her. When the gangsters finally track her down and try to kidnap her, local citizens in an exciting car chase block all exits out of the town to prevent her leaving. These modern "minute men," however, are more interested in getting the reward for the alleged heiress than in fighting crime. Other crime films have used the ploy of a fugitive witness, including *Woman on the Run* (1950), with Ross Elliott seeing a gangland murder, and *Dangerous Mission* (1954), with detective Victor Mature trying to locate murder witness Piper Laurie.

489 THE LADY HAS PLANS (1942), Par.

Dir. Sidney Lanfield; Sc. Harry Tugend; Cast includes: Paulette Goddard, Ray Milland, Roland Young, Albert Dekker, Margaret Hayes, Cecil Kellaway.

A World War II comedy-drama concerning espionage in Lisbon, the film features Ray Milland as an American war correspondent and Paulette Goddard as his assistant. Together, they help British intelligence by uncovering a Nazi espionage ring led by Albert Dekker at a nearby seaport. The plot hinges on Goddard's being mistaken for a spy who has been temporarily tattooed with secret plans. Nazi and British agents attempt to undress her in an effort to pry upon the supposed plans. Milland and Goddard supply some good-natured humor as well as romance in this implausible but entertaining tale. The clever use of the tattoo appeared in an earlier film, *The Hidden Code* (1920), about a scientist who tattoos a portion of a secret formula on his daughter's shoulder.

490 LADY LUCK (1936), Che.

Dir. Charles Lamont; Sc. John Krafft; Cast includes: Patricia Farr, William Bakewell, Duncan Renaldo, Iris Adrian, Lulu McConnell, Jameson Thomas.

The winning of a sweepstakes leads to unexpected results, including murder, for an innocent young couple in this unimpressive romantic drama. When Patricia Farr, as manicurist Mamie Murphy, is announced as the lottery winner, she attracts a stream of fortune hunters, much to the annoyance of William Bakewell, a local screen reporter romantically interested in her. Bakewell is further separated from Farr when she is swarmed by offers for testimonials and a lucrative stage contract. Suddenly another Mamie Murphy, played by Lulu McConnell, shows up and proves she is the actual winner. However, she wants only the money and is content to leave the oppressive notoriety to Farr. Nightclub owner Duncan Renaldo is willing to commit murder to gain possession of the coveted winning ticket.

491 THE LAND UNKNOWN
(1957), U.

Dir. Virgil Vogel; *Sc.* Laszlo Gorog; *Cast includes:* Jock Mahoney, Shawn Smith, Warren Reynolds, Henry Brandon, Douglas R. Kennedy, Phil Harvey.

Reporter Shawn Smith accompanies U.S. Navy scientist Jock Mahoney and helicopter pilot Warren Reynolds on a mission which is forced down by a storm somewhere in the South Pole in this science fiction adventure. The strange area, untouched by the Ice Age, is inhabited by prehistoric monsters. At one point the survivors, including mechanic Phil Harvey, are rescued by Douglas R. Kennedy, another scientist who had crashed here a decade earlier. Following a series of harrowing adventures and other complications, they join together to repair their helicopter with parts from Kennedy's downed plane and escape from this hostile land to safety. The film is weak on characterization but strong on special effects.

492 LARCENY ON THE AIR
(1937), Rep.

Dir. Irving Pichel; *Sc.* Andre Bohem, Richard English; *Cast includes:* Robert Livingston, Grace Bradley, Willard Robertson, Pierre Watkin, Granville Bates, William Newell.

A crusading doctor turns radio reporter in his efforts to expose sellers of phony medicinal cures in this well-paced routine drama. Robert Livingston, as the idealistic physician, uses his radio broadcasts to debunk the charlatans and their fraudulent products. When the doctor discovers that Granville Bates, the father of Grace Bradley, his girlfriend, is a slick mobster who is extorting protection money from his victims, Livingston ostensibly joins the mob. He tracks down the leader's base of operations and smashes the entire patent medicine racket. His future father-in-law then promises his daughter and Livingston that he will go straight.

493 THE LAST EDITION
(1925), F.B.O.

Dir. Emory Johnson; *Sc.* Emilie Johnson; *Cast includes:* Ralph Lewis, Lila Leslie, Ray Hallor, Frances Teague, Rex Lease, Lou Payne.

Star news hound Rex Lease proves the innocence of an elderly assistant foreman of a San Francisco printing press crew who has been accused of causing a building cave-in in this occasionally unrealistic drama. The foreman, Ralph Lewis, learns from an edition going to press that his son, working in the district attorney's office, has been framed and sent to jail. He tries to stop the edition from being printed, but the publisher refuses the father's request. When an explosion in the boiler room results in the collapse of the skyscraper, the foreman is held responsible and arrested. But reporter Lease proves that a big-shot politician plotted the devastation and sent his henchmen to the boiler room to get the workers drunk. Earlier, the politician, in collusion with a crooked assistant district attorney, had framed Lewis's son to divert attention from their corruption. Lewis is then promoted, and the reporter marries Lila Leslie, the foreman's daughter.

494 THE LAST GANGSTER (1937), MGM.

Dir. Edward Ludwig; *Sc.* John Lee Mahin; *Cast includes:* Edward G. Robinson, James Stewart, Rose Stradner, Lionel Stander, Douglas Scott, John Carradine.

The lives of former big-time mobster Edward G. Robinson and newspaper reporter James Stewart are intertwined in this fairly entertaining underworld drama. Robinson, as the title character, is sent to prison for ten years where he grows obsessed with thoughts of his son whom he has never seen. The gangster had married his foreign wife (Rose Stradner) just to have a son and heir to his underworld empire. His wife discovers Robinson is just a common thug and divorces him to protect the child's future. She then marries sympathetic and kindly newsman Stewart, who adopts the gangster's child. After serving his sentence in Alcatraz, Robinson, burdened with a Napoleonic complex, searches for his son and seeks revenge upon his ex-wife and her husband. However, members of his former gang intervene and try to force him to reveal where he has hidden a large sum of money. When he refuses, they kidnap his son and threaten to harm the boy. Robinson reluctantly gives them the information they want. Alone with his son, he realizes the boy will never accept him as his father. He returns the child to his parents and, realizing the warm and stable environment the boy has, leaves. Inadvertently he meets an old enemy, resulting in the two veteran gangsters killing each other in a gun battle. One contemporary critic cited two bloopers in the film. Robinson is charged with income tax evasion in 1927, a legal ploy not used by the government until 1934. Also, he is sent to Alcatraz in 1927, a prison not opened as a federal penitentiary until 1934. The drama, which marked the beginning of the demise of the gangster genre, paralleled the decline of the newspaper film, both types reaching their peaks in the 1930s.

495 LAST PLANE OUT (1983), Jack Cox Productions.

Dir. David Nelson; *Sc.* Ernest Tidyman; *Cast includes:* Jan-Michael Vincent, Julie Carmen, Mary Crosby, David Huffman.

An American journalist takes the audience through the final days of Nicaragua's Somoza regime in this inept semi-documentary drama. Jan-Michael Vincent portrays Jack Cox, a long-time reporter of Latin-American activities, who manages to interview spokespersons from both sides of the revolution. However, the rebel forces think he is a C.I.A. agent and warn him to leave strife-torn Nicaragua. The remainder of the film deals with melodramatic events as Cox, whose life is on the line, tries to escape while carrying on an affair with rebel leader Julie Carmen. In the chaotic background, the government of Anastasio Somoza (Lloyd Battista) is collapsing. Carmen, Cox's romantic interest, has to choose between the rebel cause and her love for the journalist in this low-budget film.

496 THE LAST RIDE (1932), U.

Dir. Duke Worne; *Sc.* Arthur Hoerl; *Cast includes:* Virginia Brown Faire, Frank Mayo, Tom Santschi, Francis Ford, Bobby Dunn, Charles Morton.

Bootleggers and hijackers battle it out in this old-fashioned action drama produced near the end of the Prohibition era. Reporter Charles Morton, whose brother, Tom Santschi, heads the hijacking gang, vows revenge when Santschi is "taken for a ride" by his rival. He joins his dead brother's gang for a chance to get the chief of the bootleggers, but almost meets with the same fate as that of his brother. However, heroine Virginia Brown Faire rescues him.

497 THE LAST TRAIN FROM MADRID (1937), Par.

Dir. James Hogan; *Sc.* Robert Wyler,

Louis Stevens; *Cast includes:* Dorothy Lamour, Lew Ayres, Gilbert Roland, Karen Morley, Anthony Quinn.

Lew Ayres portrays an American reporter in this drama which combines the *Grand Hotel* format of bringing together a variety of characters in a tense situation with the Spanish Civil War as background. However, little of the conflict comes through either in the dialogue or the action, except for some street fighting. The conflict serves as a frame for an assortment of principals who board a Madrid train bound for the safety of Valencia. Helen Mack portrays a prostitute and Anthony Quinn a Spanish captain. The studio decided to take a neutral stand on the issues of the war in this inept drama. This was the first Hollywood film to use the Spanish Civil War as backdrop for its drama. *Blockade*, starring Henry Fonda and Madeleine Carroll, appeared the following year. Again, an overcautious studio emphasized the romantic element and avoided any specific political or social issues concerning the war. Despite its heedful approach, the innocuous film was attacked by both factions of the political spectrum.

498 LAUGHING AT TROUBLE (1937), TCF.

Dir. Frank R. Strayer; *Sc.* Robert Ellis, Helen Logan; *Cast includes:* Jane Darwell, Sara Haden, Lois Wilson, Margaret Hamilton, Delma Byron, Allan Lane.

Matronly Jane Darwell, a small-town newspaper publisher, helps fugitive Allan Lane, who has been wrongly accused of murder, in this minor comedy drama. Lane, who is engaged to Delma Byron, Darwell's niece, escapes from the law and hides out in the publisher's home. Darwell is aware of the real murderer's identity and springs a trap in which he confesses, thereby freeing Lane. Adding to the romantic entanglements is James Burke, the romantically inclined, middle-aged local sheriff, who holds more than a little affection for the strong-willed Darwell.

499 LAURA (1944), TCF.

Dir. Otto Preminger; *Sc.* Jay Dratler, Samuel Hoffenstein, Betty Reinhardt; *Cast includes:* Gene Tierney, Dana Andrews, Clifton Webb, Vincent Price, Judith Anderson, Dorothy Adams.

Police detective Dana Andrews is assigned to investigate the murder of Gene Tierney in this stylish murder mystery based on the novel by Vera Caspary. Alone in the dead woman's apartment, Andrews feels himself becoming involved in her life as he examines her portrait and belongings. When the door suddenly opens, he is astonished to see Tierney enter. The woman in the portrait has come alive, at least in the detective's eyes. The killer, it seems, mistaking an acquaintance who had been using Tierney's apartment for the owner, killed the guest instead. Arrogant art critic and intellectual columnist Clifton Webb, who could not bear to share Tierney with others, turns out to be the murderer. He also has the best lines in the film. When Andrews unceremoniously enters Tierney's apartment, Webb snaps, "Haven't you heard of science's newest triumph—the doorbell?" In another scene Webb boasts, "In my case, self-absorption is completely justified. I have never discovered any other subject quite so worthy of my attention." "It's lavish," he later comments about his own luxurious apartment, "but I call it home."

500 LAVENDER AND OLD LACE (1921), Hodkinson.

Dir. Lloyd Ingraham; *Cast includes:* Marguerite Snow, Seena Owen, Louis Bennison, Victor Potel, Zella Ingraham, Lillian Elliott.

Louis Bennison plays a dual role in this silent romantic drama based on the 1902 novel by Myrtle Reed about love and devotion. As a Boston reporter passing through a village, he has trouble with his eyes and is taken by Seena Owen to the home of matronly Marguerite Snow. The older woman has been waiting thirty years for a captain to return to marry her. She suddenly sees a striking resemblance in

Police detective Dana Andrews (right) questions columnist Clifton Webb about the murder of a young woman in Otto Preminger's atmospheric mystery, *Laura* (1944).

young Bennison. When he reveals he is the son of the captain who had died years earlier, the woman swoons. As she slowly loses consciousness, she reveals that the captain was her boyfriend. The reporter and Owen, who have fallen in love with each other, learn from the dead woman the meaning of true love and devotion.

501 THE LAWLESS (1950), Par.

Dir. Joseph Losey; *Sc.* Geoffrey Homes; *Cast includes:* Macdonald Carey, Gail Russell, John Sands, Lee Patrick, John Hoyt, Lalo Rios.

Newspaper editor Macdonald Carey champions the cause of racial tolerance between Mexicans and Americans in a California town in this strong contemporary social conscience drama. Mexican migrants who work the fruit orchards of this California community, eking out a meager living, become the target of young white bigots, especially at a dance that ends in a riot. During the fray, a young Mexican hits a cop, resulting in an angry white mob's pursuit of the offender. Editor Carey, who at first tries to remain neutral, changes his views after meeting Gail Russell, a young Mexican woman. He then takes sides against the forces of intolerance—representing the conscience of any trace of decency remaining in the town. In return, the bigots advocate lynching the fugitive and smash Carey's newspaper office. The persecution of this one youngster symbolizes the larger hostility toward all the community's Mexican Americans. Other films dealing with bigotry toward Mexican Americans include, among others, *Right Cross* (1950), *My Man and I* (1952) and *Trial* (1954).

502 THE LAWLESS NINETIES (1936), Rep.

Dir. Joseph Kane; *Sc.* Joseph Poland; *Cast includes:* John Wayne, Ann Rutherford, Harry Woods, George Hayes, Al Bridge, Lane Chandler.

The U.S. government assigns John Wayne to stop the lawless element threatening the homesteaders in the territory of Wyoming in this routine western. Local newspaper editor George Hayes champions the forces of law and order, but his stubbornness in not submitting to the outlaws' threats leads to his murder. Wayne, who liked the old-timer, has a double reason to clean up the criminal element. Ann Rutherford, the editor's daughter, takes over her father's crusading paper while providing the romantic interest for Wayne. The film continued the tactless Hollywood policy of the period of giving degrading names to African-American comic character actors—in this case, the screen credits state that the character Mose is played by "Snowflake."

503 THE LAWLESS WOMAN (1931), Che.

Dir. Richard Thorpe; *St.* Barney Gerard; *Cast includes:* Carroll Nye, Vera Reynolds, Thomas Jackson, Wheeler Oakman, James Burtis, Gwen Lee.

Cub reporter James Burtis proves to his superiors that he is as capable as the more experienced newsmen in this cliché-ridden action drama marked by its low production values. During one of his assignments Burtis meets and falls in love with gang affiliate Vera Reynolds, whom he soon persuades to reform. He eventually rescues her from the clutches of the gang leader and his henchmen whom the cub outsmarts. In addition, Burtis solves two murders which have been baffling the police.

504 LEAP TO FAME (1918), World.

Dir. Carlyle Blackwell; *Sc.* Raymond Schrock; *Cast includes:* Carlyle Blackwell, Evelyn Greeley, Muriel Ostriche, Alec B. Francis, Frank Beamish.

German secret agents try to steal the plans of an important secret weapon in this World War I drama. Carlyle Blackwell portrays a New York cub reporter who ultimately foils the spies' plot to appropriate the invention which the American military is depending upon to help win the war. Earlier in the story Blackwell's father had cast him off for wasting his time in college. After he rescues the valuable documents and the scientist's pretty daughter, his father forgives him.

505 LEGALLY DEAD (1923), U.

Dir. William Parke; *Sc.* Harvey Gates; *Cast includes:* Milton Sills, Margaret Campbell, Claire Adams, Edwin Sturgis, Faye O'Neill, Charles Stevenson.

A reporter who believes that most victims of capital punishment are wrongfully sentenced to death is himself executed for murder in this strange drama. Milton Sills, as the journalist, witnesses the murder of a detective. He picks up the gun and pursues the killer who escapes. Sills is arrested, tried and convicted of the crime. After he is executed, a doctor brings him back to life by using adrenaline. The film is saved from the commonplace by introducing elements of science fiction and a concern for victims of capital punishment. Other silent dramas, but not necessarily newspaper films, explored the latter theme, including *The Wheel of the Law* (1916), *Hate* (1922), *Capital Punishment* (1925) and *Ladies of the Mob* (1928). Of course, capital punishment occasionally became the subject of such sound films as *Wolf of New York* (1940).

506 THE LEGEND OF BLOOD MOUNTAIN (1965), Craddock.

Dir. Massey Cramer; *Sc.* Massey Cramer, Don Hadley, Bob Corley; *Cast includes:* George Ellis, Zenas Sears, Glenda Brunson, Erin Fleming, Sheila Stringer.

Small-town newspaper reporter George Ellis's investigations reveal strange happenings in this weak horror tale. When he is not busily engaged in his professional task of getting a scoop about a local monster terrorizing the community, Ellis finds himself romancing several young women.

507 LET 'ER GO GAL-LEGHER (1928), Pathé.

Dir. Elmer Clifton; *Sc.* Elliott Clawson; *Cast includes:* Junior Coghlan, Harrison Ford, Elinor Fair, Wade Boteler, E. H. Calvert, Ivan Lebedeff.

Harrison Ford, a cocky, abrasive cub reporter who is fired for neglecting his assignments, decides to regain his reputation by capturing a local criminal in this drama. He is aided by the title character, an impoverished newsboy portrayed by Junior Coghlan. The boy had earlier given his pal a scoop after witnessing a shooting. The youngster, after following the killer into the woods, contacts the reporter once again. Ford and a detective arrive in the nick of time to rescue the brave lad who has been captured by the criminal. The film was adapted from the 1890 story "Gallegher: A Newspaper Story" by Richard Harding Davis.

508 LET FREEDOM RING (1939), MGM.

Dir. Jack Conway; *Sc.* Ben Hecht; *Cast includes:* Nelson Eddy, Virginia Bruce, Victor McLaglen, Lionel Barrymore, Edward Arnold, Guy Kibbee.

Recent Harvard graduate Nelson Eddy returns home to his father's ranch where he witnesses a railroad baron exploiting his workers and threatening the ranchers in this patriotic drama set in the late 1860s. He immediately takes up the cause of the railroad workers, who represent immigrants from many foreign lands, and the ranchers. This leads him into conflict with both railroad magnate Edward Arnold and Lionel Barrymore, his own physically handicapped father, who disowns him for going against his social class. Eddy takes over a newspaper and publishes articles attacking Arnold's browbeating tactics. Following a physical struggle with brawny foreman Victor McLaglen and other complications, Eddy and his 200 workers win their demands and break Arnold's hold on the community. The film ends with Eddy leading his followers in singing an inspiring rendition of "America." The film was one of several patriotic features Hollywood turned out as war clouds hovered over Europe and Asia in the late 1930s.

509 LIBELED LADY (1936), MGM.

Dir. Jack Conway; *Sc.* Maurine Watkins, Howard Emmett Rogers, George Oppenheimer; *Cast includes:* Jean Harlow, William Powell, Myrna Loy, Spencer Tracy, Walter Connolly, Charley Grapewin.

Managing editor Spencer Tracy assigns suave troubleshooter William Powell to prevent angry socialite Myrna Loy from pressing libel charges against his newspaper in this scintillating screwball comedy. Slapstick situations and witty dialogue predominate as Powell tries to disparage Loy's reputation, thereby forcing her to drop her suit. In one of several hilarious sequences, he resorts to masquerading as an expert angler so that he can join Loy and her father on a fishing trip. He eventually falls in love with her, much to the displeasure of Jean Harlow, his patient, long-suffering girlfriend. Earlier, the manipulative Tracy appeals to Loy's sense of social responsibility. "If you go through with this case," he pleads, "it's going to throw 500 people out of employment. Men and women—jobless—walking the streets—women like yourself, tired, cold and hungry, driven to drink, ruined." "You write the editorials, don't you?" the rich socialite replies. In another scene, Tracy, intending to use a phony story planted in his paper as a ploy, hands the bogus page to copy boy Billy Benedict. "Tell Douglas to print up one copy of the evening edition," Tracy orders. "One copy?" Benedict questions. "That's what I said." "Gosh," the bewildered copy boy mumbles, "our circulation is certainly falling off." The film was remade as a musical comedy in 1946 under the title *Easy to Wed*, with Van Johnson and Esther Williams as the romantic leads.

510 LIFE BEGINS AT 40 (1935), TCF.

Dir. George Marshall; *Sc.* Lamar Trotti; *Cast includes:* Will Rogers, Rochelle Hudson, Richard Cromwell, George Barbier, Jane Darwell, Slim Summerville.

Humorist Will Rogers, portraying a small-town newspaper editor, helps young Richard Cromwell, wrongly accused of embezzling bank funds, in this homespun yarn suggested by the book by Walter H. Pitkin. Believing the lad is innocent, Rogers says so in his paper, but this raises the ire of banker and mayoral candidate George Barbier, who forecloses on the editor. In return, Rogers encourages the town derelict to run in the mayoral election against Barbier. Following several further complications, Rogers uncovers the real thief (the banker's son), thereby exonerating Cromwell. The banker and the editor reconcile their differences and Rogers withdraws his candidate. The plot may be familiar, but Rogers's charm is contagious and his witty lines are fresh and funny.

511 THE LIFE OF JIMMY DOLAN (1933), WB.

Dir. Archie Mayo; *Sc.* David Boehm, Erwin Gelsey; *Cast includes:* Douglas Fairbanks Jr., Aline MacMahon, Loretta Young, Guy Kibbee, Lyle Talbot, Shirley Grey.

Douglas Fairbanks Jr. portrays the title character, a prizefighter who flees after accidentally killing a reporter at a party, in this drama based on a play by Bertram Millhauser and Beulah Marie Dix. He quickly redeems himself by helping to finance a health farm for invalid children. In the process, he falls in love with Loretta Young. John Garfield appeared as the prizefighter in the 1939 remake titled *They Made Me a Criminal.*

512 LIGHTNING REPORTER (1926), Ellbee.

Dir. Jack Noble; *Sc.* Jack Noble; *Cast includes:* Johnny Walker, Sylvia Breamer, Burr McIntosh, Lou Archer, Nelson McDowell, Joseph Girard.

Cub reporter Johnny Walker becomes embroiled in a rival business venture in this familiar minor drama, released near the end of the silent period. He finds himself helping the president of a railroad outmaneuver a competitor on Wall Street. As a result, the cub reporter wins the love of Sylvia Breamer, the railroad magnate's pretty daughter.

513 LIGHTNING SPEED (1928), FBO.

Dir. Robert North Bradbury; *Sc.* Robert North Bradbury; *Cast includes:* Bob Steele, Mary Mabery, Perry Murdock, Barney Furey, William Welsh.

Newspaper reporter Bob Steele, in love with Mary Mabery, the governor's daughter, rescues her from kidnappers in this timeworn action drama. Steele discovers a plot hatched by hoodlum Barney Furey to kidnap Mabery so that he can blackmail the governor into pardoning Furey's brother. Steele fails to warn his girlfriend in time and Furey succeeds in his scheme. Later, the reporter tracks down the notorious criminal and rescues Mabery before she can be taken away in an air balloon. Furey is killed during his getaway when the balloon crashes. Director Robert Bradbury and his son, Bob Steele, were more successful turning out B westerns during the thirties than in making straight action dramas.

514 THE LION MAN (1919) serial, U.

Dir. Albert Russell, Jack Wells; *Cast includes:* Kathleen O'Connor, Jack Perrin, Mack Wright, J. Barney Sherry, Gertrude Astor, Henry Barrows.

Newspaper reporter Kathleen O'Connor starts out to cover a private circus sponsored by a millionaire and ends up uncovering a plot to assassinate its sponsor in this eighteen-chapter serial based on the novel *The Strange Case of Cavendish* by Randall Parrish. A disgruntled nephew conspires with an unscrupulous lawyer to kill the millionaire (J. Barney Sherry) and destroy his latest will. A strange intruder, known only as the Lion Man, assists in keeping the plotters from succeeding.

515 LITTLE ACCIDENT
(1939), U.

Dir. Charles Lamont; *Sc.* Paul Yawitz, Eve Green; *Cast includes:* Hugh Herbert, Florence Rice, Richard Carlson, Joy Hodges, Edgar Kennedy, Sandra Lee Henville.

Newspaper advice columnist Hugh Herbert, who writes under a female pseudonym, undergoes the mixed blessing of finding an abandoned baby in this minor comedy loosely based on the play by Floyd Dell and Thomas Mitchell. Ernest Truex, the actual father, deliberately leaves the baby on Herbert's desk. To avoid an unsavory reputation, the columnist claims it is his grandchild. Further complications arise when he turns the infant over to his unmarried daughter. An old-fashioned chase to retrieve a laundry bag containing the baby provides a suitable ending for this remake of a 1930 version of the play.

516 LITTLE BOY LOST
(1953), Par.

Dir. George Seaton; *Sc.* George Seaton; *Cast includes:* Bing Crosby, Claude Dauphin, Nicole Maurey, Gabrielle Dorziat, Peter Baldwin, Christian Fourcade.

Bing Crosby portrays an American reporter who returns to France after World War II to find his long-lost son in this tearjerking yarn. The child had been lost during an air raid that killed Crosby's wife. Although he has never seen the boy, he is directed to an orphanage where he thinks he sees the missing child. He grows fond of the boy, even after learning the orphan is not his son. He adopts the child anyway and brings him back to the States. Crosby had appeared as a reporter interested in orphans in an earlier film, *Here Comes the Groom* (1951), a comedy with Jane Wyman.

517 THE LITTLE LIAR
(1916), Triangle.

Dir. Lloyd Ingraham; *Sc.* Anita Loos; *Cast includes:* Mae Marsh, Robert Harron, Olga Gray, Carl Stockdale, Jenny Lee, Ruth Handforth.

Reporter Robert Harron tries to help free Mae Marsh, whose compulsive lying has landed her in jail, in this little drama. Although she is innocent of a charge of shoplifting, the real crooks have done a good job of framing her. Since she has a history of lying, she is sent to jail. Meanwhile, Harron struggles desperately to find evidence which can free Marsh, whose only escape from her life of poverty in the slums is her fertile imagination. The judge, who has received Marsh's personal journal, realizes she has the potential to become a great writer. Harron then arrives with the necessary proof to free her and both men rush to the prison to bring her the good news. But they are too late. They learn that she has taken her own life.

518 LITTLE TOKYO, U.S.A.
(1942), TCF.

Dir. Otto Brower; *Sc.* George Bricker; *Cast includes:* Preston Foster, Brenda Joyce, Harold Huber, Don Douglas, June Duprez, George E. Stone.

The Japanese-American quarter of Los Angeles known as "Little Tokyo" provides the background of this drama set just prior to the Japanese attack on Pearl Harbor. Radio news reporter Brenda Joyce helps Preston Foster, a police officer on duty in this section, to uncover an espionage network. The Japanese-American citizens had enough problems resulting from their evacuation to internment camps during the war and a general national hostility toward them as a minority group without this low-budget film attributing fictitious acts of betrayal to these otherwise loyal Americans. According to the F.B.I. and other government sources, not one act of espionage or sabotage was ever committed during the war by any Japanese-American.

519 THE LITTLE WANDERER (1920), Fox.

Dir. Howard M. Mitchell; *Sc.* Denison Clift; *Cast includes:* Shirley Mason, Raymond McKee, Cecil Vanauker, Alice Wilson, Jack Pratt.

Idealistic Raymond McKee, the son of a newspaper owner, accuses his father of sensationalizing the news and exploiting the poor in this comedy drama. To prove he is right, the son sets out to reform a slum inhabitant. He targets street waif Shirley Mason, whom he helps by getting her a job as a waitress. McKee soon falls in love with her, but when his father sees her, he recognizes her as the daughter of his former partner who had cheated him. Mason's father, however, appears and proves the newspaper owner was the real swindler. McKee's father finally acknowledges the truth, and the son is allowed to take over the paper and apply his own editorial policies.

520 THE LITTLE WHITE SAVAGE (1919), Bluebird.

Dir. Paul Powell; *Sc.* Waldemar Young; *Cast includes:* Carmel Myers, Harry Hilliard, William Dyer, Richard Cummings, John Cook.

A reporter who is refused permission to interview a sideshow act known as "The Savage," is invited by two carnival men to hear the entire story. They tell how they found Carmel Myers, the woman in question, on a remote island in the South Atlantic and how she fell in love with one of the men after thinking he was a god. Later, when she is taken back to civilization, she shocks a church congregation by appearing scantily clad. Following the regaling of this tale, the reporter questions Myers, only to discover the previous story was false.

521 LIVIN' LARGE! (1991), Goldwyn.

Dir. Michael Schultz; *Sc.* William M. Payne; *Cast includes:* Terrence Carson, Lisa Arrindell, Blanche Baker, Nathaniel Hall, Julia Campbell, Bernie McInerney.

Terrence Carson, an African-American hipster and dry-cleaning clerk, inadvertently finds fame and fortune as a popular television news reporter in this Faustian comedy spoof of the media and of fame. However, there are moments when the film takes on the mantle of a racist comedy. Carson, who is a graduate of a questionable school of broadcasting, chances upon a hostage situation and fills in for a TV reporter who has been killed. Television executive Blanche Baker, desperate for higher ratings, hires Carson for the series "Homeboy About Town." To entice him further, she provides him with money, a car and a young woman. After selling his soul to the Devil white man, Carson loses his girlfriend as his star rises. The ugly message of this comedy, which is filled with smarmy sight gags, seems to be to reject completely anything associated with white culture.

522 LIVING IT UP (1954), Par.

Dir. Norman Taurog; *Sc.* Jack Rose, Melville Shavelson; *Cast includes:* Dean Martin, Jerry Lewis, Janet Leigh, Edward Arnold, Fred Clark, Sheree North.

Jerry Lewis, a railway station master at a remote western junction who allegedly has radiation poisoning, is exploited by big-city reporter Janet Leigh in this fairly entertaining comedy, a remake of *Nothing Sacred*, released in 1937. Leigh, envisioning a long-running human-interest series about the obscure railroad clerk, tries to interest her New York editor Fred Clark in the story. "'The *Morning Chronicle* Pays Its Debt to Humanity!'" she suggests as a headline. "It wouldn't hurt circulation either," Clark adds. "I knew your better instincts would triumph," she says sarcastically. Although he agrees to the series, Clark harbors at least one major drawback. "What if this kid doesn't die in three weeks?" he asks Leigh. But Leigh finally convinces her boss. "Think of the headlines," she says enticingly. "'Humanitarian Editor Saves Hero's Life'. . .

There's always politics. Think what it means to be a senator. Your mail goes free." They give poor soul Lewis the red carpet treatment in the Big Apple. But Lewis, who is accompanied by Dean Martin, his doctor, discovers by this time that he is well, and has a difficult time keeping the news from Leigh. The original film, with Carole Lombard as the sickly guest and Fredric March as the reporter, was more cynical about the press. It later appeared on stage as a musical titled *Hazel Flagg*.

523   LIVING LIES (1922), Clark-Cornelius.

Dir. Emile Chautard; *Cast includes:* Edmund Lowe, Mona Kingsley, Kenneth Hill.

News reporter Edmund Lowe is assigned by his suspicious editor to investigate several financiers suspected of illegal activities in this minor drama based on the 1917 story "A Scrap of Paper" by Arthur Somers Roche. Lowe accidentally finds a signed paper that has blown out of a window. He is startled to learn it contains proof of a conspiracy between a corrupt syndicate and others involving an illegal traction deal. At first, the syndicate head tries to bribe the journalist to return the incriminating paper, but when this fails Lowe and Mona Kingsley, his girlfriend, are captured and held prisoner. Lowe is then tortured into revealing the hiding place of the paper. However, the couple eventually effect their escape, retrieve the evidence and expose the crooked scheme in the next edition of the paper.

524   LONE STAR (1951), MGM.

Dir. Vincent Sherman; *Sc.* Borden Chase; *Cast includes:* Clark Gable, Ava Gardner, Broderick Crawford, Lionel Barrymore, Beulah Bondi, Ed Begley.

Texas rancher Clark Gable seeks to convince Sam Houston that Texas should become a state in this sprawling western set in 1845. However, he is opposed by Broderick Crawford, who secretly wants to head his own republic. Joining Crawford is Austin newspaper publisher Ava Gardner, who mistakenly thinks Houston opposes statehood. Forget about historical accuracy and any semblance of realism (Gardner sings "Lovers Are Meant to Cry" in the midst of the political and social turmoil). Instead, enjoy the old-fashioned gun-fighting and fist-throwing as Gable wins Gardner away from Crawford.

525   THE LONE WOLF AND HIS LADY (1949), Col.

Dir. John Hoffman; *Sc.* Michael Boylan; *Cast includes:* Ron Randell, June Vincent, Alan Mowbray, William Frawley, Collette Lyons, Douglas Dumbrille.

The Lone Wolf is forced to solve the theft of the world's third largest diamond after he is falsely accused of the crime in this last entry in the mystery series. Ron Randell plays Joseph Louis Vance's fictional character, Michael Lanyard, alias the Lone Wolf, who first appeared in silent films as early as 1917. In this entry, he accepts an assignment as a reporter covering an exhibit of the famous diamond. When the gem disappears, he tracks down the real culprits. Nine different actors portrayed the dashing, reformed fictional jewel thief in the series.

526   LONELYHEARTS (1958), UA.

Dir. Vincent J. Donahue; *Sc.* Dore Schary; *Cast includes:* Montgomery Clift, Robert Ryan, Myrna Loy, Maureen Stapleton, Dolores Hart, Jackie Coogan.

Newspaper editor Robert Ryan hires idealistic young writer Montgomery Clift to run the advice-to-the-lovelorn column in this glum drama based on the 1933 novel *Miss Lonelyhearts* by Nathanael West. Clift soon finds himself so enmeshed in the depressing and pathetic lives of those who write to him that in one case, he allows himself to be seduced by a middle-aged housewife. The embittered editor, burdened with his own marital problems, had warned him that the letters were written by "fakes, like the rest of the human race." "What kind of crazy world is this," Clift muses, "that where if you try to help somebody, you're considered an oddball?" The affair almost ends in tragedy for Clift when the husband shows up at the newspaper office threatening to shoot the columnist. Instead, the man breaks down in tears in the presence of both Clift and Ryan. The columnist and the editor come to understand, through the desperation of the husband, this crucial need everyone has for love. Clift leaves with Dolores Hart, his girlfriend, a little richer for his experience, and Ryan brings some flowers to his wife whom he has continually mocked.

527 LOOKING FOR TROUBLE (1926), U.

Dir. Robert N. Bradbury; *Sc.* George Hively; *Cast includes:* Jack Hoxie, Marceline Day, J. Gordon Russell, Clark Comstock, Edmund Cobb, Bud Osborne, Peggy Montgomery.

Jack Hoxie stars as Don Quickshot, the fast-riding and hard-fighting hero of this western drama in which he rescues the proverbial heroine. About the only digression from the routine plot involves a scurrilous local newspaper editor who uses the paper for sensational stories. Having written falsehoods about the heroine Marceline Day, the editor is forced by our hero, who loves the libeled gal, to print a retraction and apology. The cast is made up of many veterans of screen westerns. Perhaps the most familiar name is that of Edmund Cobb, who earlier appeared as leading or supporting player in dozens of western shorts and features.

528 LOST ANGEL (1943), MGM.

Dir. Roy Rowland; *Sc.* Isobel Lennart; *Cast includes:* Margaret O'Brien, James Craig, Marsha Hunt, Philip Merivale, Henry O'Neill, Donald Meek.

Police reporter James Craig, assigned to check out a story about a little girl prodigy, finds young Margaret O'Brien being raised by a group of scientists in this delightful comedy drama. The child, an orphan taken in by the scientists, is bright but lacks a normal childhood. Craig takes her to live with him. He and his girlfriend, Marsha Hunt, help to rehabilitate her so that she recovers her lost childhood.

529 THE LOST HOUSE (1915), Mutual.

Dir. William Christy Cabanne; *Cast includes:* Lillian Gish, Wallace Reid, F. A. Turner, Elmer Clifton, A. D. Sears.

Reporter Wallace Reid rescues Lillian Gish, who has been placed in an insane asylum by her crooked uncle, in this early silent drama based on the 1911 short story by Richard Harding Davis. F. A. Turner, the uncle, has spent all of his ward's money and seeks, with a corrupt doctor, to kill her. But first they place her in the doctor's asylum where she manages to drop a message to Reid. He poses as a madman to gain entrance, but the suspicious doctor locks him into the same room with Gish. Meanwhile, Reid has notified his friend that if he does not return at a certain time, his friend is to notify the police. The two reprobates are killed in a fierce battle with the law, and the heroic reporter wins the love of the young woman he has rescued.

530 THE LOST PRINCESS (1919), Fox.

Dir. Scott Dunlap; *Sc.* J. Anthony Roach; *Cast includes:* Albert Ray, Elinor Fair, George Hernandez, Maggie Halloway Fisher, Edward Cecil, Burt Wesner.

Sympathetic reporter Elinor Fair helps country boy Albert Ray get a job on her newspaper in this little comedy drama. Ray, fresh off his father's farm where his dreams of becoming a reporter conflicted with his daily chores, finds the big city a generally heartless place—until he meets Fair. She encourages him to write a story about a lost princess who is hiding in the States. An archduke arrives, looking for the princess—who turns out to be Elinor Fair. Ray rescues Fair, who is being forced to return to her homeland. He wakes up to discover that the entire story was a dream. But he is encouraged to write another story which is successful, and then proposes marriage to the young woman he loves.

531 THE LOST WORLD (1925), FN.

Dir. Harry O. Hoyt; Sc. Marion Fairfax; Cast includes: Bessie Love, Lloyd Hughes, Lewis Stone, Wallace Beery, Arthur Hoyt, Margaret McWade.

Lloyd Hughes portrays Ed Malone, a budding reporter who helps Professor Challenger (Wallace Beery) prove that dinosaurs are alive and well and living in the Amazon in this intriguing fantasy based on the novel by Sir Arthur Conan Doyle. The managing editor of a London newspaper threatened with a lawsuit by the professor, assigns the awkward reporter to cover Challenger's lecture that same evening. "I believe Professor Challenger is insane," the editor remarks to a colleague. "He nearly killed three reporters I sent to interview him today." He turns to Malone and, referring to the lecture hall, warns: "Reporters are barred—but get in." Following two confrontations with the easily excitable professor, Malone is finally accepted as a member of the expedition, especially after promising to get his paper to sponsor a rescue mission to find the father of Paula White (Bessie Love). The famous explorer Sir John Boxton (Lewis Stone), who has befriended Malone, also volunteers for the journey. Scientists mock Challenger's belief that dinosaurs still exist and consider him a fraud. The remainder of the film is a tribute to the special effects persons who have created a world that may have existed millions of years ago—a strange place where ferocious creatures prowl the terrain and struggle to survive. Members of the small expedition undergo a series of dangers, witnessing a dinosaur, pterodactyl and brontosaurus, before they return to London. They bring with them a brontosaurus they had captured. But the great creature breaks loose from its confinement and, in several remarkably filmed scenes, wreaks havoc upon the city and its terrified inhabitants. Finally, it smashes through London Bridge and disappears down the Thames River to the open sea. The film anticipates the classic adventure film *King Kong* (1933). Willis O'Brien created the animals and sets for both films.

532 THE LOST WORLD (1960), TCF.

Dir. Irwin Allen; Sc. Charles Bennett, Irwin Allen; Cast includes: Michael Rennie, Jill St. John, David Hedison, Claude Rains, Fernando Lamas, Richard Haydn.

A remake of the superior 1925 silent version of Arthur Conan Doyle's tale, this adaptation adds color, more special effects and a romantic triangle as an expedition journeys into remote territory of the Amazon in search of prehistoric creatures. David Hedison portrays a reporter with whom Jill St. John falls in love. She started on the trek as the girlfriend of sportsman Michael Rennie. Several members perish on the expedition led by scientist Claude Rains. He theorizes that somewhere in the Amazon life has not changed since prehistoric times. His beliefs are soon realized beyond his expectations.

533 LOVE AND HISSES (1937), TCF.

Dir. Sidney Lanfield; Sc. Curtis Kenyon, Art Arthur; Cast includes: Walter Winchell, Ben Bernie, Simone Simon, Bert Lahr, Joan Davis, Dick Baldwin.

Famed newspaper columnist Walter Winchell and popular band leader Ben Bernie clash over attractive singer Simone Simon in this light comedy. The two leads play themselves as they go about trying to better each other. Unaware that the singer is under contract to Bernie, Winchell builds up Simon in his column when Bernie complains that she is a failure as an entertainer. Finally realizing he has been tricked by his rival, the columnist arranges for the band leader's kidnapping and has him delivered to his own club. At

534 THE LOVE GOD? (1969), U.

Dir. Nat Hiken; Sc. Nat Hiken; Cast includes: Don Knotts, Anne Francis, Edmond O'Brien, James Gregory, Maureen Arthur, Maggie Peterson.

Don Knotts portrays the title character, an editor of a bird-watching magazine that has been converted into a porno publication without his knowledge, in this tacky comedy. Con artist Edmund O'Brien buys the periodical, sends Knotts to Brazil to check on some birds, and substitutes sex articles into the magazine. When Knotts returns, he is tried and finally acquitted on obscenity charges. He then finds himself acclaimed as a national sex hero. Meanwhile, editor Anne Francis has added sophistication to the sex magazine, similar to that of Playboy. By this time Knotts opts for the simpler life with his small-town girlfriend and, following several further complications, gets his wish. Any attempt at mocking American values is purely accidental in this poorly conceived and generally tasteless film.

535 THE LOVE-INS (1967), Col.

Dir. Arthur Dreifuss; Sc. Hal Collins, Arthur Dreifuss; Cast includes: Richard Todd, James MacArthur, Susan Oliver, Mark Goddard, Janee Michelle, Joe Pyne.

San Francisco college student editors James MacArthur and Susan Oliver, dismissed for turning out their underground newspaper, have their idealism shaken in this inept drama about the social explosion of the sixties. Professor Richard Todd, in sympathy with the couple, resigns in protest. He is immediately applauded by the hippies as one of the few adults who comprehends what their movement is about. But Todd has his own plans, turning his popularity into a financial scheme which makes him a cult leader. He preaches "Be more, sense more, love more," while promoting unlimited use of the drug LSD. MacArthur grows aware of Todd's hypocrisy and prints articles in his paper exposing the false prophet. Meanwhile Susan Oliver, who has been overdosing on LSD and is now pregnant, becomes Todd's mistress. To protect his image, the selfish leader wants her to abort the baby. MacArthur then assassinates Todd at a rally, thereby turning the professor into a martyr.

536 LOVE IS A HEADACHE (1938), MGM.

Dir. Richard Thorpe; Sc. Marion Parsonnet, Harry Ruskin, William H. Lipman, Lou Heifetz, Herbert Klein; Cast includes: Franchot Tone, Mickey Rooney, Ralph Morgan, Jessie Ralph, Barnett Parker, Gladys George.

Famous radio columnist Franchot Tone, who is in love with unsuccessful actress Jessie Ralph, helps to rekindle her failing career by suggesting she adopt some orphans in this lukewarm comedy. She accepts his advice and takes charming Mickey Rooney and his sister, Virginia Weidler, into her life. But the children soon become pawns in the couple's romantic difficulties. Young Mickey steals most of the scenes, with Weidler running a close second.

537 LOVE IS A MANY-SPLENDORED THING (1955), TCF.

Dir. Henry King; Sc. John Patrick; Cast includes: William Holden, Jennifer Jones, Torin Thatcher, Isobel Elsom, Murray Matheson, Virginia Gregg.

The love between American newspaper correspondent William Holden and Eurasian doctor Jennifer Jones faces several obstacles in this romantic drama set in Hong Kong during the Korean War and based on the novel by Han Suyin. "You are gentle," Jones compliments her lover, "and there's nothing stronger in the world than gentleness." Holden is unable to get a divorce, Jones's family frowns upon the relationship, and the lovers are confronted with bigotry by a society that condemns interracial affairs. Meanwhile Jones has a premonition about their love. "I am so happy it frightens me," she confides to Holden. "I have a feeling that heaven is unfair and is preparing for you and for me a great sadness because we have been given so much." Holden's death in Korea brings their love to a tragic end. The film won Oscars for costumes, scoring and title song.

538 LOVE IS A RACKET (1932), WB.

Dir. William A. Wellman; *Sc.* Courteney Terrett; *Cast includes:* Douglas Fairbanks Jr., Ann Dvorak, Frances Dee, Lee Tracy, Lyle Talbot, Warren Hymer.

Douglas Fairbanks Jr. portrays a suave Broadway gossip columnist in this fairly interesting drama based on the novel by Rian James. Fairbanks falls in love with Broadway actress Frances Dee, who seems to be associated with a local gangster known to pick up her debts. When her aunt kills the hoodlum, Dee abandons Fairbanks and flees with a producer who has promised her a part in his next production. The gossip columnist, who has risked his life to rescue her, is left alone to ponder his loss. Lee Tracy, who has a relatively minor role in this film, was soon to dominate the world of screen journalism as the quintessential fast-talking, wisecracking reporter.

539 LOVE IS NEWS (1937), TCF.

Dir. Tay Garnett; *Sc.* Harry Tugend, Jack Yellen; *Cast includes:* Tyrone Power, Loretta Young, Don Ameche, Slim Summerville, Dudley Digges, Walter Catlett.

Flashy newspaper reporter Tyrone Power's stories about socialite Loretta Young results in his own embarrassment in this diverting screwball comedy. Young, the daughter of an important financier, is annoyed at all the publicity she has been receiving by the press, especially in Power's paper, and singling out Powers, she decides to retaliate. She announces that she is engaged to the reporter, an item which nettles his bosses, especially his fast-talking city editor. Following a string of complications and clashes between Power and Young, the couple realize that they have fallen in love with each other. Although several critics have commented upon the unrealistic newspaper background scenes, the film in general is a fast-paced and delightful comedy. Power repeated his role as the officious reporter in a 1948 remake titled *That Wonderful Urge*, with Gene Tierney as the harassed socialite.

540 LOVE IS ON THE AIR (1937), WB.

Dir. Nick Grinde; *Sc.* Morton Grant, George Bricker; *Cast includes:* Ronald Reagan, June Travis, Eddie Acuff, Bill Welden, Robert Barrat, Addison Richards.

Radio newscaster Ronald Reagan, who is fired from his job, eventually redeems himself in this well-paced little drama, a remake of *Hi, Nellie!* (1934). An idealistic crusader, Reagan has introduced corrupt local politics into his broadcasts by exposing the town's gangsters, their rackets, and the politicians and businessmen who profit from these illicit activities. Incurring the anger of his superiors, sponsors and local big shots, Reagan is relegated to children's programs by manager Robert Barrat. However, when he proves that his former sponsor is linked to the criminal element, including mobster Ben Welden, he wins back his old job.

541 LOVE ON THE RUN (1936), MGM.

Dir. W. S. Van Dyke; *Sc.* John Lee Mahin, Manuel Seff, Gladys Hurlbut; *Cast includes:* Joan Crawford, Clark Gable, Franchot Tone, Reginald Owen, Mona Barrie, Ivan Lebedeff.

American foreign correspondents Clark Gable and Franchot Tone, working in England, compete for the love of Joan Crawford in this less than scintillating comedy. Crawford, an abused heiress who walks away from the altar to avoid an obvious fortune seeker, ends up falling for Gable. He starts out wooing her for personal reasons, seeing in her a possible series of articles about how the wealthy view the subject of romance. But he eventually falls in love with her, much to the disappointment of Tone, his slow-moving rival suitor. Simultaneously, she falls for Gable as well. "I've known people I've liked and some I've disliked," she confides to him after they kiss. "I've hated a few and thought I loved a couple, but I've never known anyone I could trust up to now." Comical character actor Donald Meek tries hard to add his brand of humor to several scenes. "We must hurry," Meek says to Clark Gable in one segment. "You see, at twelve o'clock I turn into a pumpkin." Too many inane situations prevent the film from joining the ranks of the top screwball comedies of the period, including *It Happened One Night* (1934), from which the present film seems to have borrowed heavily.

542   THE LUCK OF THE IRISH (1948), TCF.

Dir. Henry Koster; *Sc.* Philip Dunne; *Cast includes:* Tyrone Power, Anne Baxter, Cecil Kellaway, Lee J. Cobb, James Todd, Jayne Meadows.

American journalist Tyrone Power, on holiday in Ireland, is adopted by leprechaun Cecil Kellaway in this whimsical comedy. Kellaway follows Power to New York and directs him to pretty Anne Baxter. The writer turns his back on his search for power and material success and returns to Ireland with Baxter, now his wife, where he will spend his time writing with more of an open mind. Much of the dialogue is witty. For example, in one scene publisher Lee J. Cobb confides to Power that he wants to enter politics. "You know the oldest and noblest occupation of them all?" he reminds Power. "I think so," Power replies. "I mean politics," Cobb clarifies. "Well," Power adds, "you'll admit there are certain points of similarity."

543   LUCKY DEVILS (1941), U.

Dir. Lew Landers; *Sc.* Alex Gottlieb; *Cast includes:* Richard Arlen, Andy Devine, Dorothy Lovett, Janet Shaw, Jack Arnold, Gus Schilling.

Newsreel reporters Richard Arlen and his sidekick Andy Devine clash with foreign saboteurs in this routine entry in the low-budget action adventure series featuring the duo. Arlen's cavalier attitude allows him to find time for lensing his scoops and wooing attractive young women—in this adventure, Dorothy Lovett provides the romance. Even his comic rotund assistant finds a mate in Janet Shaw. Arlen's love affair, however, soon has him immersed in a plot with secret agents.

544   LUCKY JORDAN (1942), Par.

Dir. Frank Tuttle; *Sc.* Darrell Ware, Karl Tunberg; *Cast includes:* Alan Ladd, Helen Walker, Sheldon Leonard, Mabel Paige, Marie McDonald, Lloyd Corrigan.

Small-time racketeer Alan Ladd is drafted into the army after failing to buy his way out and, partly under the influence of reporter Helen Walker, eventually turns patriotic in this offbeat World War II drama. Ladd rebels against authority once in uniform. After escaping from his army camp, he learns that his former mob, now controlled by Sheldon Leonard, has thrown in with Nazi agents. Ladd suddenly reforms and saves certain pilfered army tank plans from falling into enemy hands. Ladd kidnaps newspaperwoman Helen Walker when she follows him in an attempt to convince him to report back to his outfit. The film is dotted with some snappy dialogue. In one scene, for example, Ladd's sergeant rebukes him for shoveling dirt on his foot. "Sorry," Ladd snarls," I thought it was your face." Earlier in the film Ladd rebukes Lloyd Corrigan, his lawyer, for not making the right connections to get him back to civilian life. "You can't fix Washington," Corrigan explains. "For one thing, you can't find out who's in charge."

545   LUCKY LOSERS (1950), Mon.

Dir. William Beaudine; *Sc.* Charles R.

Marion; *Cast includes:* Leo Gorcey, Huntz Hall, Hillary Brooke, Gabriel Dell, Lyle Talbot, Bernard Gorcey.

Television reporter Gabriel Dell helps Leo Gorcey and his boys expose crooked syndicate leader and murderer Lyle Talbot in this better-than-average entry in the popular Bowery Boys comedy series. Gorcey and his gang of ruffians tangle with crooked gamblers after Gorcey suspects his boss's death was not the result of suicide. He finds work with the gambling syndicate so that he can snoop around for evidence concerning the suspicious death.

546 THE LYING TRUTH (1922), ARC.

Dir. Marion Fairfax; *Sc.* Marion Fairfax; *Cast includes:* Pat O'Malley, Marjorie Daw, Noah Beery, Tully Marshall, Adele Watson, Clair McDowell, Charles Mariles.

Pat O'Malley, who inherits a failing small-town newspaper from his stepfather, finds himself steeped in financial and personal troubles in this drama. The stepfather is driven to an early grave not only by the paper's loss of prestige, but by the discovery that his only son is a drug addict. He therefore wills his beloved paper to O'Malley, his stepson, who works hard to breathe life and profit into the sheet. One of his ploys involves publicly offering a $1,000 reward for the arrest of a murderer—except that the crime is a contrived one created to drum up publicity. However, when his stepbrother's body is discovered, O'Malley is accused of the murder. But a suicide note left by the deceased is recovered, and O'Malley is set free.

547 MA AND PA KETTLE (1949), UI.

Dir. Charles Lamont; *Sc.* Herbert Margolis, Louis Morheim, Al Lewis; *Cast includes:* Marjorie Main, Percy Kilbride, Richard Long, Meg Randall, Patricia Alphin, Esther Dale.

Magazine writer Meg Randall, assigned to cover the Kettle clan's sudden rise in status, finds herself defending the family and marrying their eldest son in this broad comedy. While covering the family, headed by Marjorie Main and Percy Kilbride, who won a tobacco contest slogan, the reporter meets Richard Long, their college-grad son. Their prize, a modern, electronically run home, came in the nick of time, since the Kettles were about to be evicted. Meanwhile, officious neighbor Esther Dale charges that Pa's slogan was not original, but Randall successfully refutes the false accusation. Based on the characters created by Betty MacDonald in her book *The Egg and I* and the ensuing hit feature, this film became the first entry in the Ma and Pa Kettle comedy series.

548 MA AND PA KETTLE AT HOME (1954), U.

Dir. Charles Lamont; *Sc.* Kay Leonard; *Cast includes:* Marjorie Main, Percy Kilbride, Alan Mowbray, Alice Kelley, Brett Halsey, Ross Elliott.

Alan Mowbray portrays a magazine editor who, along with Ross Elliott, visits the home of the Kettles to determine if their son is qualified for an agricultural college scholarship in this routine entry in the popular comedy series. Marjorie Main and Percy Kilbride, as the title characters, are proud of their son, a finalist in an essay contest, and they are determined to repair their rundown homestead in preparation for the visiting judges. After several embarrassing and quite funny predicaments, including an unwelcome rain that washes away the superficial improvements made to the house, Brett Halsey, the son, ends up winning the coveted scholarship.

549 THE MAD DOCTOR (1941), Par.

Dir. Tim Whelan; *Sc.* Howard J. Green; *Cast includes:* Basil Rathbone, Ellen Drew, John Howard, Barbara Allen (Vera Vague), Ralph Morgan, Martin Kosleck.

Crazed Viennese physician Basil Rathbone weds and kills his wealthy patients in this slow-paced bizarre thriller set in the U.S. His murderous career comes to a just end when newspaper reporter John Howard, the ex-fiancé of Ellen Drew, Rathbone's latest bride, intercedes in her behalf. The physician takes his own life. Howard, suspicious of Rathbone, had been investigating the criminal background of the mad doctor.

550 THE MAD GAME (1933), TCF.

Dir. Irving Cummings; Sc. William Consulman, Henry Johnson; Cast includes: Spencer Tracy, Claire Trevor, Ralph Morgan, J. Carrol Naish, John Miljan, Matt McHugh.

Crusading newspaper reporter Claire Trevor falls in love with bootlegger Spencer Tracy in this routine crime drama. When Tracy is framed by his own lawyer and sent to prison, Trevor fights to get him out. Meanwhile his old gang finds a new line of work when Prohibition comes to an end. They go in for kidnapping, and their first job involves two victims related to the judge who sent Tracy away. So Tracy is called upon to help rescue the pair. He completes his mission but is mortally wounded.

551 THE MAD GHOUL (1943), U.

Dir. James Hogan; Sc. Hans Kraly; Cast includes: George Zucco, David Bruce, Evelyn Ankers, Robert Armstrong, Turhan Bey, Charles McGraw.

Newspaper reporter Robert Armstrong's unfortunate death helps to bring to an end the fiendish experiments of scientist George Zucco in this frail drama. Zucco has been toying with a noxious gas which he has isolated from its ancient Egyptian origins. The gruesome aspect of his experiment is that the gas can only be neutralized by the blood of a recent corpse. Medical student David Bruce serves as one of Zucco's victims, with singer Evelyn Ankers providing the romantic element. Quirky mortician Andrew Tombes adds a note of dark comedy to the production. "For goodness sake," he blurts out at Armstrong, "whatever you do, don't mar the coffin."

552 THE MAD MISS MANTON (1938), RKO.

Dir. Leigh Jason; Sc. Philip G. Epstein; Cast includes: Barbara Stanwyck, Henry Fonda, Sam Levene, Whitney Bourne, Frances Mercer, Vicki Lester.

Barbara Stanwyck portrays the title character, a dizzy socialite who fancies herself a skilled detective, in this screwball comedy drama. She helps Henry Fonda, a newspaper reporter who specializes in homicide, to uncover some mysterious goings-on. Virtually every character has at least one funny line. "Are you a real crook?" a woman asks burglar and safecracker Olin Howland. "Well, the last lawyer what defended me said I was antisocial. I kind of like that better than 'crook,' don't you?" "Hilda," Fonda addresses Stanwyck's maid Hattie McDaniel, "can you handle a gun?" "No, sir," she replies sharply, "I's a pacifist." In another scene, New York police lieutenant Sam Levene is about to enter a house to investigate a possible murder. "The murderer might still be in there," warns Stanwyck. "The murderer could be in Brooklyn by now," he returns, "that is, if anybody wants to be in Brooklyn." Stanwyck and her friends, investigating a murder, search an empty house. She asks one companion to cover upstairs. "I'm not much of an individualist," the young woman replies. "We'll search it together." "Why, that's communism!" another socialite asserts.

553 THE MAD MONSTER (1942), PRC.

Dir. Sam Newfield; Sc. Fred Myton; Cast includes: Johnny Downs, George Zucco, Anne Nagel, Sarah Padden, Glenn Strange, Gordon Demain.

Reporter Johnny Downs brings to an end the bloody career of a murderous creature in this inept low-budget horror tale. Glenn Strange, the creature, is the result of perverted experiments by scientist George Zucco, who has discovered a method of mixing the blood of a wolf with that of a man. The creature then goes on a killing spree, terrorizing the community. The crazed Zucco, who has been dismissed from his university, takes revenge by having two of the scientists responsible for his removal slain by his creature. Downs, who is in love with Anne Nagel, Zucco's daughter, traps Strange. The doomed creature takes the life of the scientist before it is consumed in flames.

554 MADAME SPY (1942), U.

Dir. Roy William Neill; *Sc.* Lynn Riggs, Clarence Upson Young; *Cast includes:* Constance Bennett, Don Porter, John Litel, Ed Brophy, John Eldredge, Edmund MacDonald.

Constance Bennett portrays an American counter-espionage agent in this routine World War II drama. She is married to war correspondent Don Porter. While he is away gathering timely stories, she becomes involved with John Litel, the head of a Nazi spy ring in New York. Her husband returns and gets mixed up in the intrigue until the spies are captured and Bennett reveals to her spouse that she is a double agent.

555 THE MAGIC CUP (1921), Realart.

Dir. John S. Robertson; *Sc.* E. Lloyd Sheldon; *Cast includes:* Constance Binney, Vincent Coleman, Blanche Craig, William H. Strauss, Charles Mussett, J. H. Gilmour.

When hotel maid Constance Binney falls victim to two crooked pawnbrokers, her boyfriend, cub reporter Vincent Coleman, comes to her rescue in this minor romantic Cinderella drama. Binney pawns an old silver goblet to help a neighbor who is about to be convicted. The goblet has been in her family for years. When the pawnbrokers scheme to cheat Binney, including a plot that introduces a fake lord as the real owner of the goblet, Coleman grows suspicious. He locates the real lord who then proves that the maid is his granddaughter.

556 MAGIC TOWN (1947), RKO.

Dir. William A. Wellman; *Sc.* Robert Riskin; *Cast includes:* James Stewart, Jane Wyman, Kent Smith, Ned Sparks, Wallace Ford, Regis Toomey.

Jane Wyman, as a young editor of a small-town newspaper, learns of New York pollster James Stewart's duplicity and exposes him to the public in this sentimental romantic comedy about opinion polls and those who gather the coveted statistics. Ambitious Stewart, in his search for a get-rich-quick scheme, discovers a town that exactly reflects the views of the nation. He poses as an insurance salesman and, together with his fellow assistant pollsters Ned Sparks and Donald Meek, gathers highly accurate public opinion data to sell to large corporations. When Stewart learns that editor Wyman is promoting changes for the town, changes which will eventually threaten its makeup, he tries to stop her by romancing her. But she accidentally discovers his scheme and decides to expose him. "The trouble with having a newspaper background," she says half-apologetically to Stewart, "is you develop an instinct for snooping." Her story gains national interest, resulting in an invasion of writers, broadcasters and others interested in exploiting the town's uniqueness. However, the latest opinions of the citizens, now aware of their importance, have suddenly become statistically inaccurate and therefore useless. The town faces economic and spiritual disaster as all the strangers and visitors begin to pull out. National papers and radio programs announce that the town has become "the subject of ridicule throughout the country." "We murdered a town," Wyman says to Stewart. But Stewart refuses to let the town die. He joins forces with Wyman to bring the citizens together once again to help revitalize the community.

557 THE MAGNIFICENT MEDDLER (1917), Vitagraph.

Dir. William Wolbert; *Sc.* Garfield

Thompson; *Cast includes:* Antonio Moreno, Mary Anderson, Otto Lederer, Leon D. Kent, George Kunkel.

Ambitious and idealistic Antonio Moreno uses his aunt's inheritance to buy a newspaper in a small Western town in this light comedy. In an effort to bring about reforms, he aims his attacks at local undesirables while supporting a merger with a neighboring town—a move that irritates George Kunkel, the town boss. Moreno then falls in love with Kunkel's daughter, Mary Anderson. While Kunkel and his henchmen set fire to Moreno's newspaper office, sleazy dance-hall owner Leon D. Kent kidnaps Anderson. Moreno rescues the young woman and wins the respect of Kunkel, who promises to help his future son-in-law in his quest to merge the two towns.

558 MAKING A LIVING (1914), Keystone.

Dir. Henry Lehrman; *Cast includes:* Charlie Chaplin, Henry Lehrman, Virginia Kirtley, Alice Davenport, Minta Murfee, Chester Conklin.

Charlie Chaplin, in his first film for Keystone, portrays a down-and-out dapper swindler who takes a job as a newspaper reporter in this early silent comedy. Observing a car accident, he notices Henry Lehrman, a rival newspaper cameraman, taking a picture of the incident. Chaplin, who had met Lehrman earlier while flirting with Virginia Kirtley, the photographer's fiancée, engaged in a physical confrontation with Lehrman. At the scene of the accident, Chaplin snatches the camera away from his rival and dashes off to his own paper, pursued by the cameraman and a police officer. His editor then greets him warmly for scooping the competition. While personally supervising the disposition of the newspaper, Chaplin is again confronted by Lehrman, who has just extricated himself from a domestic dispute between a wife and her husband. The chase continues through town, with the rivals battling it out on a streetcar. Chaplin's film debut drew applause from critics and audiences, both of whom delighted in the comic antics of this new screen personality.

559 MAN AT LARGE (1941), TCF.

Dir. Eugene Forde; *Sc.* John Larkin; *Cast includes:* Marjorie Weaver, George Reeves, Richard Derr, Steve Geray, Milton Parsons, Elisha Cook Jr.

An escaped German flier from a Canadian prisoner of war camp becomes the object of a search by reporter Marjorie Weaver and F.B.I. agent George Reeves in this low-budget World War II drama. Reeves poses as a competing journalist. They both pursue the German and eventually become entangled with a murderous spy ring. The film employs a familiar spy genre convention—the agent posing as a dentist—also used in such films as *The Man Who Knew Too Much* (1956) and *Marathon Man* (1976). Reeves was to repeat his role as a newspaperman years later when he starred as Clark Kent, alias Superman, in the popular television series.

560 MAN FROM HEADQUARTERS (1942), Mon.

Dir. Jean Yarbrough; *Sc.* John Krafft, Rollo Lloyd; *Cast includes:* Frank Albertson, Joan Woodbury, John Maxwell, Max Hoffman Jr., Dick Elliott, Byron Foulger.

Police reporter Frank Albertson, after solving a murder in Chicago, is kidnapped by hoodlums and taken to St. Louis in this above-average newspaper-crime drama. His captors want to prevent him from testifying against their boss. He escapes and meets Joan Woodbury, who is stranded in the city. Following several further complications, the couple prove the big-shot gangster committed a robbery.

561 THE MAN FROM MANHATTAN (1916), Mutual.

Dir. Jack Halloway; *Sc.* James Edward Hungerford; *Cast includes:* William Stowell, Charles Wheelock, Rhea Mitchell, Jo Taylor, Jack Prescott, Warren Ellsworth.

When Businessman Charles Wheelock, who is disappointed in his son William Stowell's lack of interest in commerce, disowns him, the young man leaves New York and buys a small-town newspaper in this familiar but charming comedy drama. He hires Rhea Mitchell, a fellow writer and poet, as his assistant editor, and the paper soon gains some success. But Stowell faces problems when he refuses to support an unscrupulous candidate for mayor. The landlord of the building evicts him, starts a fire, and accuses Stowell of igniting it. However, before he dies as the result of the conflagration, the landlord leaves a note blaming the corrupt candidate. The townspeople who were prepared to lynch the newspaper owner now decide to make him the mayor. Lowell then marries his associate editor while his father, happy about his son's success, rebuilds the newspaper office.

562 THE MAN FROM PLANET X (1951), Mid-Century.

Dir. Edgar Ulmer; *Sc.* Aubrey Wisberg; *Cast includes:* Robert Clarke, Margaret Field, Raymond Bond, William Schallert, Roy Engel, Charles Davis.

Newspaper reporter Robert Clarke accompanies two scientists and Margaret Field, the daughter of one of the latter, to a Scottish island where they plan to observe a planet nearing Earth in this verbose low-budget drama. Field notices an inhabitant who has already landed from the strange planet, and all become acquainted. Suddenly one scientist, bent on world conquest, tries to force his will upon the alien, who instead uses his powers to control the island inhabitants. He also begins to guide his fellow spacemen to the island. However, newsman Clarke and a local constable, together with members of Scotland Yard, prevent the invasion.

563 MAN HUNT (1936), WB.

Dir. William Clemens; *Sc.* Roy Chanslor; *Cast includes:* Marguerite Churchill, Ricardo Cortez, Chic Sale, William Gargan, Maude Eburne, Don Barclay.

An armed bank robber serves as the subject of a manhunt in this lackluster drama. Ricardo Cortez portrays the desperate fugitive while William Gargan, an ambitious, scoop-seeking reporter, eventually helps in Cortez's capture by calling in a battery of government agents. Marguerite Churchill, an idealistic school teacher who is dismissed from her position for speaking truthfully to her students, becomes foolishly involved with Cortez. Both characters contribute little to an already bland plot. Chic Sale, a feisty granny who brandishes his own firearms, provides whatever comedy relief there is. Gargan, who has played reporter roles in several films, including *The Sport Parade* (1932), *Headline Shooter* (1933) and *Personal Secretary* (1938), seems too mature for a cub reporter. His brother, Ed Gargan, often portrayed the stereotyped dim-witted cop during this period—although they never appeared together in the same production.

564 A MAN MUST LIVE (1925), Par.

Dir. Paul Sloane; *Sc.* James A. Creelman; *Cast includes:* Richard Dix, Jacqueline Logan, George Nash, Edna Murphy, Charles Beyer, Dorothy Walters.

Good-natured Richard Dix is forced to take a temporary position as reporter for a scandal sheet in this romantic drama based on the story "Jungle Law" by Ida Alexa Ross Wylie. His callous city editor assigns Dix to interview society divorcée Jacqueline Logan, who is relegated to dancing at a sleazy café and dying of consumption. He takes her home to care for her and reports back that she cannot be found. To protect his job, he searches for a substitute major story. He thinks he has found one when he learns that an old army pal has been charged with selling narcotics. Needing a photograph, he goes to the man's quarters and discovers that Edna Murphy, the sister, is his former girlfriend. Dix tries to stop the story from being printed, but his editor publishes it anyway.

Logan dies and Dix is fired for punching the editor. Dix and Murphy reconcile their differences and her brother is freed.

565 MAN OF THE WORLD (1931), Par.

Dir. Richard Wallace; *Sc.* Herman Mankiewicz; *Cast includes:* William Powell, Carole Lombard, Wynne Gibson, Guy Kibbee, Lawrence Gray, George Chandler.

Paris scandal sheet owner William Powell uses the page proofs to blackmail indiscreet American playboys in this bittersweet actionless drama. An American outcast resulting from a past transgression, Powell takes his "marks" for whatever he can—until he meets Carole Lombard, the niece of one of his victims. Thinking he is not good enough for her, he reveals all. But she forgives him. To get her to change her opinion, Powell deliberately extorts a large check from her uncle, which he later tears up. He then sails away with Wynne Gibson, his former girlfriend.

566 MAN RUSTLIN' (1926), FBO.

Dir. Del Andrews; *Sc.* Burl R. Tuttle, Jay Chapman; *Cast includes:* Bob Custer, Florence Lee, Jules Cowles, Sam Allen, James Kelly, Pat Beggs.

Bob Custer, a bashful cowpuncher, is better at fighting and rounding up cattle rustlers than at wooing pretty gals in this action comedy set in a nondescript town in Arizona. He almost botches up his love life when he fails to compete with the local sheriff and others who take a romantic interest in schoolmarm Florence Lee. She encourages Custer to become a reporter for the local paper. He pursues some bandits, gets trapped in the middle of a feud, and retrieves the stolen money from a stagecoach holdup. His success as a journalist earns him a position as syndicated columnist for a large Eastern paper. To celebrate his new job, he and the schoolmarm get hitched.

567 THE MAN TRAP (1917), Bluebird.

Dir. Elmer Clifton; *Sc.* Waldemar Young; *Cast includes:* Herbert Rawlinson, Ruby Lafayette, Sally Starr, Jack Nelson.

This crime drama incorporates a number of sure-fire themes. Police corruption, wrongful imprisonment, and delayed revenge are among the important motifs which are blended with an interesting twist on the usual love triangle. Herbert Rawlinson, as John Mull, the reporter hero, outwits a crooked police chief, outmaneuvers his pursuers and wraps up the case, despite sustaining a bullet wound to the wrist.

568 THE MAN UNDER COVER (1922), U.

Dir. Tod Browning; *Sc.* Harvey Gates; *Cast includes:* Herbert Rawlinson, George Hernandez, William Courtright, George Webb, Barbara Bedford, Edwin B. Tilton.

Former thief Herbert Rawlinson returns to his home town determined to go straight in this drama about reformation. He learns that an old pal, a bank teller, has borrowed bank money and cannot pay it back. Rawlinson decides to break into the bank to make it look as though thieves stole the missing money. But before he can accomplish this, his friend commits suicide. Rawlinson then arranges matters to make his friend seem a hero who died trying to protect the bank. Later, he buys the local newspaper from Barbara Bedford, his dead friend's sister, and begins to operate it successfully. When he discovers some con artists are selling worthless shares in an oil well to the local citizens, he in turn tricks the crooks into investing all their money in his well. The con men are foiled and the good citizens get their money back. The drama is based on a story by Louis Victor Eytinge, who had been serving a life sentence in the Arizona State Penitentiary at the time of the film's release.

569 THE MAN WHO DARED (1946), Col.

Dir. John Sturges; *Sc.* Edward Bock,

Malcolm Boylan; *Cast includes:* George Macready, Leslie Brooks, Forrest Tucker, Charles D. Brown, Warren Mills, Richard Hale.

Crusading newspaper reporter George Macready sets out to prove the weaknesses in the judicial system's reliance on circumstantial evidence in this diverting thriller. To accomplish this, he purports to be the chief suspect in a murder case. Several other dramas explored the same theme, including *Circumstantial Evidence* (1935), *Thru Different Eyes* (1942) and *Beyond a Reasonable Doubt* (1956).

570 THE MAN WHO RECLAIMED HIS HEAD (1934), U.

Dir. Edward Ludwig; *Sc.* Jean Bart, Samuel Ornitz; *Cast includes:* Claude Rains, Joan Bennett, Lionel Atwill, Baby Jane, Henry O'Neill.

Claude Rains portrays a peace advocate and ghost writer for publisher Lionel Atwill and contributes a series of antiwar editorials to his employer's paper in this World War I domestic drama set in France and based on the play by Jean Bart. Meanwhile, the unscrupulous Atwill makes advances toward Joan Bennett, the writer's wife. When war breaks out, Atwill switches allegiances and joins the profiteering munitions makers in their strong pro-war, jingoistic sentiments. Rains, in disgust, joins the army where Atwill's influence places the soldier in dangerous situations at the front. Rains manages to survive the horrors of the terrible conflict and, returning home unexpectedly, witnesses his former employer trying to sexually attack his wife. He then kills the publisher. The struggle for peace and the condemnation of munitions makers as the merchants of death were not unique themes during the period of the film's release. Both had been suggested in films like *All Quiet on the Western Front* (1930) or in newspapers that exposed secret deals during World War I between arms manufacturers in France and Germany. Rains played a similar role in *The Last Outpost* (1935), in which he again appeared as a soldier with marital problems. This time his rival was Cary Grant.

571 MAN, WOMAN, AND SIN (1927), MGM.

Dir. Monta Bell; *Sc.* Alice D. G. Miller; *Cast includes:* John Gilbert, Jeanne Eagels, Gladys Brockwell, Marc MacDermott, Philip Anderson, Hayden Stevenson.

Hard-working reporter John Gilbert, a product of the slums, falls in love with society editor Jeanne Eagels, who he soon learns is being "kept" by his paper's owner, in this drama. While visiting her at her apartment, he discovers the pair together, and in a fight, Gilbert kills his rival in self-defense. However, to protect her own reputation, Eagels gives false testimony at Gilbert's trial. But later she relents and exonerates Gilbert by telling the truth about the incident. The film was remade in 1931 as *Up for Murder*, with Lew Ayres as a cub reporter and Genevieve Tobin as the society editor.

572 MANHATTAN SHAKEDOWN (1939), Warwick.

Dir. Leon Barsha; *Sc.* Edgar Edwards; *Cast includes:* John Gallaudet, Rosalind Keith, George McKay, Reginald Hincks, Bob Rideout, Phyllis Clare.

Newspaper and radio columnist John Gallaudet is determined to expose a blackmailing doctor in this minor drama. The reporter, not unlike Walter Winchell, the real-life and popular columnist of the period, runs into complications when he finds himself involved with Rosalind Keith, the crooked doctor's daughter. George McKay plays Gallaudet's sidekick. Several films used the Winchell persona for one of their characters, including, among others, *X Marks the Spot* (1931) with Wallace Ford, *Okay America* (1932) with Lew Ayres, *Personal Secretary* (1938) with William Gargan, and *Murder Is News* (1939) which also featured Gallaudet.

573 MANNEQUIN (1926), Par.

Dir. James Cruze; Sc. Frances Agnew; Cast includes: Alice Joyce, Warner Baxter, Dolores Costello, ZaSu Pitts, Walter Pidgeon, Freeman Wood.

Crusading reporter Walter Pidgeon is out to end the practice of acquitting female criminals because of their sex in this minor social drama based on the 1926 novel by Fannie Hurst. Pidgeon meets Alice Joyce, a model employed in a fancy shop. In a freak accident, Joyce is accused of murder when Freeman Wood, a person of low repute, becomes impaled on her brooch and dies. Her trial presents a dilemma for the reporter. Tried for murder, she is eventually declared not guilty. Meanwhile, she discovers that she is the daughter of a wealthy family and had been kidnapped by a love-starved nursemaid who raised her on the East Side of New York. She is reunited with her father, Warner Baxter, and Pidgeon, whom she marries.

574 MAN'S BEST FRIEND (1983), New Line.

Dir. John Lafia; Sc. John Lafia; Cast includes: Ally Sheedy, Lance Henriksen, Robert Costanzo, Fredric Lehne, John Cassini, J. D. Daniels.

Ambitious television reporter Ally Sheedy unknowingly befriends and adopts a killer attack dog in this violent drama dotted with flashes of perverse humor. Sheedy and her video camera assistant sneak into an animal laboratory owned by Lance Henriksen whom the reporter suspects of performing brutal experiments on his subjects. The intruders, in the process of making a documentary, are observed by a watchman and barely escape with their lives. They are followed by Max, a seemingly friendly canine that has taken a liking to Sheedy. She adopts the creature and takes Max home. Henriksen reports the loss to the police and explains that Max has been genetically altered and chemically pacified. But when the injection wears off, the dog will become highly dangerous. "We're sitting on a time bomb!" he exclaims in frustration. Following a series of gruesome attacks by Max, including the killing of a lab worker, a letter carrier and others, the dog is shot to death by its master, Henriksen, who is himself killed during the fight.

575 MARK OF THE WHISTLER (1944), Col.

Dir. William Castle; Sc. George Bricker; Cast includes: Richard Dix, Janis Carter, Paul Guilfoyle, Porter Hall, John Calvert, Matt Willis.

Janis Carter, who played a newspaper reporter in One Mysterious Night, released the same year, repeated the role in this mystery based on the short story "Chance" by Cornell Woolrich. An impoverished drifter, upon learning that an inactive bank account is under a name similar to his, decides to pose as the owner—with unexpected results. Richard Dix, as the tramp, soon finds himself the target of a murderer who intends to kill the man Dix is impersonating. This was the second entry in the Whistler series of mysteries in which an unknown whistling narrator discloses grim tales from the dark side of human experience.

576 MARRY THE GIRL (1937), WB.

Dir. William McGann; Sc. Sig Herzig, Pat C. Flick, Tom Reed; Cast includes: Mary Boland, Frank McHugh, Hugh Herbert, Carol Hughes, Allen Jenkins, Mischa Auer.

Eccentric Hugh Herbert is the patriarch of the equally eccentric Radway family in this zany comedy based on the novel by Edward Hope. The family owns a newspaper whose employees are as odd as the Radways. Herbert is controlled by his domineering sister, Mary Boland. Their niece, Carol Hughes, desires to elope with nutty captions writer Mischa Auer. The flimsy plot concerns the efforts of Herbert and Boland to prevent the elopement. Before they succeed, the audience is exposed to an array of crazies who work for the

Radways or are acquainted with them. One such character in the latter category is Alan Mowbray, a psychiatrist who supervises an asylum in which he himself should be a patient.

577 MARY JANE'S PA
(1917), Vitagraph.

Dir. William P. S. Earle; *Sc.* A. Van Buren Powell; *Cast includes:* Marc MacDermott, Mildred Manning, Eulalie Jensen, Emmett King, Clio Ayres, William Dunn.

Wanderer Marc MacDermott returns home to his family and helps his wife, who runs a small-town newspaper, defeat a politician in this drama based on the 1908 play by Edith Ellis Furness. His wife, Eulalie Jensen, fed up with his vagrant life, allows MacDermott to stay at her home with their two daughters as long as he does not reveal his identity. When another politician disables her press, MacDermott helps his wife print an exposé which results in the first politician's defeat. But another sends his henchmen to burn the press and threaten MacDermott's life. His wife intercedes and reveals that he is her husband, thereby rescuing him from a mob. A remake appeared in 1935, with Guy Kibbee and Aline McMahon as the leads.

578 MARY JANE'S PA
(1935), WB.

Dir. William Keighley; *Sc.* Tom Reed, Peter Milne; *Cast includes:* Guy Kibbee, Aline McMahon, Tom Brown, Robert McWade, Minor Watson, Nan Gray.

Middle-aged newspaperman Guy Kibbee, following a ten-year period of wanderlust, returns home to his small town and his family in this sunny tale based on the novel by Norman Way, which was in turn adapted from the play by Edith Ellis Furness. Believing that his wife, Aline McMahon, is having difficulties running the family and his small newspaper, he instead discovers she is flourishing financially after turning the paper into a large success. McMahon, in the midst of a political campaign, resents her itinerant husband who has left her alone all these years. He accepts a position as a servant in her home so that he can at least be near his two daughters. Kibbee accidentally learns about some skullduggery on the part of his wife's rivals and tells her about it. When hoodlums smash her printing press to prevent her from exposing the story, Kibbee gets out a special edition on his old hand press. The couple are then reunited. The film is a remake of an earlier silent version released in 1917.

579 THE MASQUERADER
(1933), UA.

Dir. Richard Wallace; *Sc.* Howard Estabrook, Moss Hart; *Cast includes:* Ronald Colman, Elissa Landi, Halliwell Hobbes, David Torrence, Cheighton Hale, Helen J. Eddy.

Ronald Colman portrays a dual role — that of a member of Parliament and a reporter — in this farfetched drama based on the 1905 novel by Katherine Cecil Thurston and the 1917 play by John Hunter Booth. Withdrawing from society to fight off a drinking and drug problem, the politician persuades his look-alike cousin to substitute for him both professionally and domestically. The journalist ends up bringing honor to his cousin's political career and, when the politician dies, the reporter takes over full-time to help Elissa Landi, the deceased's widow, restore her flagging interest in marriage. Colman was to play another dual role in the often-filmed drama *The Prisoner of Zenda* (1937), based on the novel by Anthony Hope.

580 THE MEAN SEASON
(1985), Orion.

Dir. Philip Borsos; *Sc.* Leon Piedmont; *Cast includes:* Kurt Russell, Mariel Hemingway, Richard Jordan, Richard Masur, Joe Pantoliano, Andy Garcia.

A mad serial killer develops a telephone relationship with Miami newspaper reporter Kurt Russell in this harrowing thriller based on the novel *In the Heat of the Summer* by John Katzenbach. Richard Jordan, the killer, calls Russell to congratulate him on his story about the murder of a young woman and promises further exclusives of a projected series of killings. Both murders and headlines continue, with Russell, torn between his professional obligations and his ambition, gaining recognition on magazine covers and as guest on television talk shows. Jordan grows jealous of the reporter's popularity and decides to go after Mariel Hemingway, Russell's girlfriend, whom he kidnaps. Following a series of terrifying incidents, Russell and Hemingway are reunited, but Jordan suddenly invades their home. A terrible struggle ensues in which the reporter is forced to kill the intruder. "I don't want to see my name in the paper next to pictures of dead bodies anymore," Russell says in disgust at one point. But Richard Masur, his editor, tries to console his star news hound. "We're not manufacturers, we just retail," Masur reminds him. "News gets made somewhere else, we just sell it." The film raises questions about journalistic ethics as well as who is exploiting whom in the perverse cat-and-mouse game.

581 MEDIUM COOL (1969), Par.

Dir. Haskell Wexler; *Sc.* Haskell Wexler; *Cast includes:* Robert Forster, Verna Bloom, Peter Bonerz, Marianna Hill, Harold Blankenship, Charles Geary.

Filmed in Chicago during the violent 1968 Democratic National Convention, this realistic semi-documentary focuses on television newsreel cameraman Robert Forster. A series of seemingly unrelated incidents reveal how Forster is determined to remain neutral during these stormy events, including the disorder in Grant Park, the scene of major rioting. Early in the film at a party, Forster's sound man tries to explain to a young woman their lack of involvement each time they cover a story. "What's the difference between the person who types something and a typewriter? The typewriter really doesn't care what's being typed on it." Although refusing to become emotionally involved with any of his assignments, Forster finally is touched by the injustice shown to an African-American cab driver who has returned to the police $10,000 he has found in his taxi. His insistence leads to his dismissal from his job. "I love to shoot film," he says sadly to Verna Bloom, a young widow whom he falls in love with. She and her 13-year-old son have come to Chicago from Virginia. When the boy runs away, she wanders around Grant Park during the demonstrations and calls upon Forster to help her find her son. As they drive around, Forster loses control of the car when a tire blows out and they smash into a tree. Both Forster and the mother are killed.

582 MEET JOHN DOE (1941), WB.

Dir. Frank Capra; *Sc.* Robert Riskin; *Cast includes:* Gary Cooper, Barbara Stanwyck, Edward Arnold, James Gleason, Walter Brennan, Regis Toomey.

Columnist Barbara Stanwyck elevates down-at-the-heels bush-leaguer Gary Cooper to everyman's mouthpiece in this intriguing cautionary drama about fascism. She mounts a large publicity stunt in which Cooper is transformed into "John Doe," the people's last hope for fair play and decency in a nation overrun with suffering, hypocrisy and corruption. Edward Arnold, Stanwyck's power-hungry and ambitious newspaper publisher with fascistic tendencies, persuades her to use Cooper to head a "Golden Rule" movement—in essence, the publisher's political tool. The idealistic Cooper earns the trust of a large number of ordinary citizens. When he learns of this betrayal and that Arnold wants Cooper to nominate him as a third-party candidate for President, he tries to expose the publisher at a large rally. But he is quickly silenced and discredited by Arnold's Storm Trooper-like militia. Disillusioned, Cooper publicly threatens to commit suicide on New Year's Eve, but Stanwyck and a handful of his former followers convince him otherwise. "The little people will always be heard," the columnist says, pleading with him to begin anew. Regardless of its weak, sloppy ending, the film remains a paean to democracy and the "little man." *Keeper of the Flame* (1943), with Spencer Tracy portraying a reporter, also warned against a possible fascist plot devised by a so-called American war hero and patriot.

583 MEET THE MOB (1942), Mon.

Dir. Jean Yarbrough; *Sc.* George Bricker, Edmond Kelso; *Cast includes:* ZaSu Pitts, Roger Pryor, Warren Hymer, Gwen Kenyon, Douglas Fowley, Elizabeth Russell.

Spinster ZaSu Pitts, visiting the big city, is mistaken by a local mob for a murderess in this comedy. The mixup allows for several farcical complications. Mobster Douglas Fowley and his gang, for example, are mistakenly impressed with her notorious reputation and fear her. Eventually she helps to round up the gang of criminals. Reporter Roger Pryor and his girlfriend Gwen Kenyon help the faltering Pitts cope with the problems of city life.

584 MEET THE WILDCAT (1940), U.

Dir. Arthur Lubin; *Sc.* Alex Gottlieb; *Cast includes:* Ralph Bellamy, Margaret Lindsay, Joseph Schildkraut, Allen Jenkins, Jerome Cowan, Robert O. Davis.

Innocent New York sleuth Ralph Bellamy is mistaken for a thief in this routine mystery thriller which is filled with too many implausibilities. Bellamy is allowed to escape from jail so that he can track down the real thief, known as the Wildcat. Art dealer Joseph Schildkraut turns out to be the villain. Margaret Lindsay, as an ambitious reporter, at first believes Bellamy is the thief.

585 MEN OF TEXAS (1942), U.

Dir. Ray Enright; *Sc.* Harold Shumate; *Cast includes:* Robert Stack, Leo Carrillo, Anne Gwynne, Broderick Crawford, Ralph Bellamy, Jane Darwell.

Chicago newsman Robert Stack and his photographer-assistant Leo Carrillo are determined to record the true story of Texas in this patriotic action tale set during the period of Reconstruction. However, Stack must first resolve his differences with the villainous Broderick Crawford. Between his several confrontations, he romances southern belle Anne Gwynne while Carrillo supplies the comedy relief in this standard fare. Carrillo played a similar role as assistant to newsreel cameraman Clark Gable in *Too Hot to Handle* (1938). Crawford a decade later again played the heavy in *Lone Star* (1952), also about the history of Texas.

586 MEN OF THE HOUR (1935), Col.

Dir. Lambert Hillyer; *Sc.* Anthony Coldeway; *Cast includes:* Wallace Ford, Richard Cromwell, Billie Seward, Jack LaRue, Wesley Barry, Charles Wilson.

Newsreel cameraman Richard Cromwell's reputation is on the line in this conventional action drama. He redeems himself when, inadvertently present during a murder, he captures the incident on film. A chase follows in which Cromwell triumphs over the killer. The almost obligatory romantic sub-plot unfolds, with Wallace Ford, a fellow cameraman. He is Cromwell's rival in matters of the heart when it comes to attractive Billie Seward.

587 MEN WITHOUT NAMES (1935), Par.

Dir. Ralph Murphy; *Sc.* Marguerite Roberts, Kubec Glasmon; *Cast includes:* Fred MacMurray, Madge Evans, Lynne Overman, David Holt, John Wray, J. G. Nugent.

U.S. government agent Fred MacMurray pursues a gang of crooks across the continent in this cops-and-robbers drama. Trailing the bank robbers from Brooklyn to Kansas, he puts an end to their career, but loses his partner Lynne Overman in a gun battle with the gang. Leslie Fenton plays the gang leader in this crime-film entry which, like *G-Men* and several other similar features, focused on and glorified the crime fighter and not the criminal. Madge Evans portrays a small-town newspaper reporter who provides the romantic interest for MacMurray. In a minor scene character player Elizabeth Patterson, as small town Aunt Ella, frowns upon anything new. "Fryerless cookers!" she exclaims. "Seems like it's goin' against nature somehow."

588 MESSENGER OF DEATH (1988), Cannon.

Dir. J. Lee Thompson; *Sc.* Paul Jarrico; *Cast includes:* Charles Bronson, Trish Van Devere, Laurence Luckinbill, Daniel Benzali, Marilyn Hassett, Jeff Corey.

Denver Tribune reporter Charles Bronson investigates a bizarre story involving the brutal murders of three women and six children in this violent but inconsequential drama based on the novel *The Avenging Angel* by Rex Burns. It seems that the culprit is a crazed farmer who has been expelled by the Mormons. Bronson becomes embroiled in a few fights, a car chase and other related actions for which he is better known, although the film is no *Death Wish* in terms of sustained violence.

589 MIDNIGHT (1934), U.

Dir. Chester Erskine; *Sc.* Chester Erskine; *Cast includes:* O. P. Heggie, Henry Hull, Sidney Fox, Margaret Wycherly, Lynne Overman, Katherine Wilson.

Jury foreman O. P. Heggie faces a crucial dilemma in this stagy domestic murder drama based on the play by Paul and Claire Sifton. Hounded by reporters and others who hint he is responsible for the defendant's going to her death at midnight, Heggie finally replies, "The woman committed murder. She must pay the price." He then learns that his own daughter, Sidney Fox, is guilty of the same crime as that for which he had condemned a woman to death. Fox has killed her lover who betrayed her precisely at midnight (hence, the title). But in this case Henry Hull, a relentless reporter, rescues her by exposing the entire story. Humphrey Bogart played a bit part in this drama which was filmed in New York. The film is not related to a 1939 screwball comedy starring Claudette Colbert and carrying the same title.

590 MIDNIGHT EDITION (1993), S-G Entertainment.

Dir. Howard Libov; *Sc.* Michael Stewart, Yuri Zeltser, Howard Libov; *Cast includes:* Will Patton, Michael DeLuise, Clare Wren, Sarabeth Tueak, Judson Vaughn.

Down-at-the-heels news photographer and reporter Will Patton returns to his family and small town in this dark drama based on the autobiography *Escape of My Dead Men* by Charles Postell. His wife, Clare Wren, is less enthusiastic about his return than is their eleven-year-old daughter, who is quick to forgive her wandering father. His old school buddy, editor of the local paper, rehires Patton who soon finds himself investigating the slaughter of an innocent farm family by Michael DeLuise, a nineteen-year-old psychotic. The local police soon capture DeLuise, and Patton gets to interview him. "If we can put a man on the moon," the reporter wonders, "why can't we figure out who's going to kill and who ain't?" Eventually, the articles are picked up by a national news service, bringing recognition to Patton and the killer. The reporter begins to spend an inordinate amount of time with DeLuise at the expense of his own family. His obsession with his subject leads him to have an affair with DeLuise's young girlfriend and then inadvertently helping the killer to escape. A state manhunt leads to Patton's home, which DeLuise had previously visited. In his own twisted mind, he believes Patton is his only true friend. Meanwhile Patton, who finally realizes DeLuise has been exploiting him as much as the reporter has been using his subject, arms himself, and when the fugitive returns and threatens the reporter, Patton kills him. He then leaves for Chicago and the prospects of a better job, promising once again to visit his family.

591 MIDNIGHT MANHUNT (1945) see *One Exciting Night* (1945).

592 THE MIDNIGHT PATROL (1932), Mon.
Dir. Christy Cabanne; *Sc.* George Jeske; *Cast includes:* Regis Toomey, Betty Bronson, Edwina Booth, Mary Nolan, Earle Foxe, Robert Elliott.

Energetic cub reporter Regis Toomey helps solve a murder in this routine but fast-paced drama. A woman recently released from prison is murdered, and lawyer Earle Foxe soon becomes involved in the crime, along with his accomplice, Mary Nolan, who masquerades as the victim. Betty Bronson portrays the sister of the murdered woman. Toomey figures out the loose connections, the motive and those responsible, all adding up to a satisfactory ending. The misleading title suggests a police, rather than a newspaper, background.

593 MIDNIGHT SECRETS (1924), Rayart.
Dir. Jack Nelson; *Cast includes:* George Larkin, Ollie Kirby, Pauline Curley, Jack Richardson.

Crooked politicians try to silence streetwise reporter George Larkin in this low-budget action drama about political corruption and power. The politicos, aware that Larkin has incriminating evidence on their illicit activities, abduct Pauline Curley, the reporter's girlfriend, in an attempt to prevent Larkin from exposing them in the press. They take her aboard their yacht which they use as their hideaway, but the courageous reporter discovers their lair. After successfully battling with the politician's hirelings, he rescues the young woman and helps to bring the entire gang to justice.

594 THE MILAGRO BEANFIELD WAR (1988), U.
Dir. Robert Redford; *Sc.* David Ward, John Nichols; *Cast includes:* Ruben Blades, Richard Bradford, Sonia Braga, Julie Carmen, Christopher Walken, John Heard.

Individualistic, dirt-poor Mexican farmer Chick Vennera decides to fight the powerful land developers seeking to exploit the local farmers in this picturesque and charming tale that pits progress against tradition. The fable-like film, based on the novel by John Nichols, is set in a sleepy small town in northern New Mexico. When the conflict between the developers and Vennera heats up, temperamental garage owner Sonia Braga prods local newspaper editor John Heard to join her in siding with the farmers. Heard, a former Eastern radical who has settled here to escape such controversial tensions, reluctantly warns the generally impoverished farmers that their taxes will go up and they will be forced to sell their land. Meanwhile, the developers want to build a mall, hotel and resort on these same lands, and need the water the farmer is using to grow beans. The controversy spreads, taking on ominous tones when mean-spirited state police agent Christopher Walken uses force against the farmers when his scheme to buy up all copies of Heard's paper fails. Like sheriff Ruben Blades, who moves between both sides as he tries to keep the peace, the film at times is indecisive about its point of view, a slight impediment to an otherwise entertaining and thoughtful work.

595 MILLION DOLLAR MYSTERY (1914) serial, Thanhouser.
Dir. Howard Hansell; *Sc.* Lloyd B. Lonergan; *Cast includes:* Albert Norton, Florence La Badie, Sidney Bracy, Marguerite Snow, James Cruze.

The plot of this early silent serial concerns a secret society of Russian millionaires, foreign spies and a heroine who as a child had been abandoned on the doorstep of a private school. Stanley Hargreaves (Albert Norton), a member of the society that calls itself the Black Hundred, places his young daughter on the doorstep of the school. Years later, the child has grown into an attractive young woman (Florence La Badie). The serial continues with convoluted plot twists and the appearances of other characters. Young reporter James Cruze, investigating the strange circumstances, grows fond of La Badie.

596 MIND YOUR OWN BUSINESS (1936), Par.

Dir. Norman Z. McLeod; Sc. Dore Schary; Cast includes: Charles Ruggles, Alice Brady, Lyle Talbot, Benny Baker, Jack LaRue, William Demarest.

Newspaper columnist Charles Ruggles and his wife Alice Brady, a gossip columnist, are kidnapped by gangsters in this newspaper-crime farce. Ruggles, who runs a column about birds, has two interests, ornithology and the Boy Scouts. On one occasion he predicts over the radio the demise of a politician, a murder which takes place and causes him problems with the police and the mob. He and his wife are kidnapped from his office by gangsters, but the couple are soon rescued by local Boy Scouts. Jack LaRue portrays a gang leader, with dimwit William Demarest assisting him.

597 THE MISSING CORPSE (1945), PRC.

Dir. Albert Herman; Sc. Ray Schrock; Cast includes: J. Edward Bromberg, Isabel Randolph, Eric Sinclair, Frank Jenks, Paul Guilfoyle, John Shay.

Newspaper publisher J. Edward Bromberg finds himself embroiled in a murder in this moderately entertaining low-budget comedy mystery. He had quarreled with Paul Guilfoyle, the victim, a rival businessman whose life the publisher had threatened. Now Bromberg, upon finding the corpse, begins to panic, fearing he will be suspected. So he decides to hide the body with the help of his chauffeur Frank Jenks. Following a series of complications, some of which are quite comical, Bromberg uncovers the real killer. It seems that Ben Welden, an ex-convict whom Guilfoyle had earlier framed, finally got his revenge.

598 MISSING DAUGHTERS (1939), Col.

Dir. C. C. Coleman Jr.; Sc. Michael L. Simmons, George Bricker; Cast includes: Richard Arlen, Rochelle Hudson, Marian Marsh, Isabel Jewell, Wade Boteler, Don Beddoe.

Newspaper columnist Richard Arlen and Rochelle Hudson investigate a gang of phony talent agents in this routine drama. Hudson becomes interested in the case because her own sister has disappeared. She joins Arlen, who then wins the confidence of gang members. They run a dance hall whose hostesses are gotten through spurious agents. The gang is not averse to dropping rebellious recruits into the river. This is just another tale filled with implausible incidents in which the columnist does more sleuthing than writing. A similar film titled *Rebellious Daughters* was released one year earlier.

599 MISSING GIRLS (1936), Che.

Dir. Phil Rosen; Sc. Martin Mooney, John W. Krafft; Cast includes: Roger Pryor, Muriel Evans, Sidney Blackmer, Noel Madison, Ann Doran, George Cooper.

Hard-nosed reporter Roger Pryor helps to uncover a racket involving young women who have left home for the big city only to end up in various illegal activities in this routine drama whose title is more sensational than the plot. Socialite Muriel Evans, in love with Pryor, helps him by providing inside stories about some of the rackets involving politicians and members of the underworld. At one point, Pryor's nose for news rewards him with a contempt-of-court thirty-day jail sentence. While behind bars he uncovers an assassination plot aimed at a senator.

Once again, the reporter wins a scoop while the authorities lock up a dangerous culprit. Other incidents of more graphic impact include the kidnapping of an innocent young maid and, following a government investigation, a climactic gun battle in a gangsters' hideout. Pryor portrayed a journalist in two earlier films, *The Headline Woman* and *$1,000 a Minute*, both released in 1935. Several newspaper films exploited the prison background, including *Jailbreak* (1936), with newsman Craig Reynolds uncovering a murder while he is behind bars.

600 THE MISSING GUEST (1938), U.

Dir. John Rawlins; Sc. Charles Martin, Paul Perez; Cast includes: Paul Kelly, Constance Moore, William Lundigan, Edwin Stanley, Selmer Jackson, George Cooper.

Newspaper reporter Paul Kelly is assigned to spend time in an allegedly haunted house in which two murders are committed in this pale drama that fails in its attempt to scare its audiences. The old-fashioned plot is handicapped with all the familiar trappings of the "old dark house" formula, including hidden panels, secret stairways, clutching hands and mysterious voices. Constance Moore portrays the heroine whose life is threatened by the villainous machinations of Edwin Stanley. Kelly appeared in a dozen or more newspaper dramas over the decades, from *Death on the Diamond* (1934) to *Split Second* (1953). However, the cold war drama *Guilty of Treason* (1950) was probably his most important role as a reporter.

601 THE MISSING JUROR (1944), Col.

Dir. Budd Boetticher; Sc. Charles O'Neal; Cast includes: Jim Bannon, Janis Carter, Jean Stevens, George Macready, Joseph Crehan, Carole Mathews.

Someone is killing off the jurors who have sentenced a murderer to death in this tense drama. After six members of the fateful jury have been murdered, reporter Jim Bannon tracks down the remaining jurors and eventually unmasks the phantom killer. It seems the original murderer, who supposedly died in a fire in an asylum, survived. The jury foreman's body was mistaken for that of the killer, who was then free to carry out his diabolical plan of revenge. Janis Carter lends support as Bannon's girlfriend. Screenwriter Charles O'Neal is the father of actor Ryan O'Neal.

602 MISSISSIPPI GAMBLER (1942), U.

Dir. John Rawlins; Sc. Al Martin, Roy Chanslor; Cast includes: Kent Taylor, John Litel, Frances Langford, Shemp Howard, Claire Dodd, Wade Boteler.

Newspaper reporter Kent Taylor is determined to bring to justice slippery fugitive John Litel in this routine drama. Taylor has tracked Litel from New York to the latter's Mississippi hideout. He then realizes Litel, who has had his face changed and has disguised his voice, is posing as a gambling house operator and plantation owner. The reporter eventually exposes the now respectable Litel. Shemp Howard, a brother of two of the Three Stooges, provides some slight comedy relief.

603 MR. BROADWAY (1933), Broadway-Hollywood.

Dir. Johnnie Walker; Sc. Ed Sullivan; Cast includes: Ed Sullivan, Johnnie Walker.

This offbeat but unentertaining film, which Ed Sullivan calls a Broadway travelog, follows the famous columnist and Broadway figure as he goes about his favorite Manhattan places greeting and visiting a variety of celebrities. Broadway performer Bert Lahr, prizefighting champion Jack Dempsey, stage comic Joe Frisco, film director Ernst Lubitsch, and radio comedian Jack Benny are just some of the personalities to appear on the screen, but chiefly in bit parts. Sites include the Central Park Casino, the Paradise club where band leader Abe Lyman is performing, and the Hollywood club. The only insight we get into the columnist is in one of his remarks that there is a story about almost anything. The film then fades into a melodramatic tale about a necklace belonging to actress Josephine Dunn.

604 MR. DEEDS GOES TO TOWN (1936), Col.

Dir. Frank Capra; *Sc.* Robert Riskin; *Cast includes:* Gary Cooper, Jean Arthur, George Bancroft, Lionel Stander, H. B. Warner, Raymond Walburn.

Cynical newspaper editor George Bancroft, seeking to ridicule Vermont hick Gary Cooper, who has inherited 20 million dollars, assigns reporter Jean Arthur to interview him in this spirited comedy based on the novel *Opera Hat* by Clarence Budington Kelland. Cooper, a small-town tuba player and greeting-card poet, has come to New York to reside in his benefactor's mansion. While he undergoes a variety of humiliations, he and Arthur begin to fall in love. When he learns what she has been doing to his character, he walks out on her and tries to give away his fortune—much to the chagrin of Douglass Dumbrille, his unsavory lawyer. Dumbrille wants to have him committed on grounds of insanity. Meanwhile, the press has labeled Cooper the "Cinderella man," treating him as an eccentric. "She's the star reporter of the *Mail!*" Lionel Stander warns Cooper about Arthur. "Every time you opened your kisser, you gave her another story... You've been making love to a double dose of cyanide." Cooper wants to allocate his fortune to farmers so that they can reclaim their land. He is forced into court to hear two staid sisters from his home town give damaging testimony that he is "pixilated." Then one of them (Margaret Seddon) blurts out: "Why, everybody in Mandrake Falls is pixilated—except us." Reporter Arthur finally convinces Cooper of her love, and he decides to fight the case. Cooper's victory in court symbolizes the triumph of the common man over seemingly impossible events—a view strongly held by director Frank Capra and repeated in several of his films.

605 MR. DISTRICT ATTORNEY (1941), Rep.

Dir. William Morgan; *Sc.* Karl Brown, Malcolm Stuart Boylan; *Cast includes:* Dennis O'Keefe, Florence Rice, Peter Lorre, Stanley Ridges, Minor Watson, Charles Arnt.

Dennis O'Keefe portrays P. Cadwallader Jones, the title character, in this disappointing drama based on a popular contemporary radio series created by Phillips H. Lord. O'Keefe, an assistant to district attorney Stanley Ridges, and aggressive newspaper reporter Florence Rice investigate a theft and eventually round up Peter Lorre and his accomplice, Minor Watson, who just happens to be the district attorney's aide. O'Keefe had some witty dialogue to work with. For example, when Rice asks him what the initial "P" stands for in his name, he replies, "Prince. But I didn't want to be whistled for."

606 MR. DISTRICT ATTORNEY IN THE CARTER CASE (1941), Rep.

Dir. Bernard Vorhaus; *Sc.* Sidney Sheldon, Ben Roberts; *Cast includes:* James Ellison, Virginia Gilmore, Franklin Pangborn, Paul Harvey, Lynne Carver, Spencer Charters.

Cheeky reporter Virginia Gilmore doggedly investigates the murder of a fashion magazine editor in this otherwise routine drama which has been singled out for its excellent photography. It was the second of three entries in a series based on the "Mr. District Attorney" radio series of the period. James Ellison, as an assistant d. a. and Gilmore's fiancé, is determined to keep her off the case for her own welfare. But she defies him and helps to unmask the real killer. The first entry in the short-lived series featured Dennis O'Keefe and Florence Rice in the leads. The last entry, a World War II drama titled *Secrets of the Underground* (1942), featured John Hubbard and Virginia Grey and dealt with the counterfeiting of war stamps.

607 MR. MOTO'S GAMBLE (1938), TCF.

Dir. James Tinling; *Sc.* Charles Belden, Jerry Cady; *Cast includes:* Peter Lorre, Keye Luke, Dick Baldwin, Lynn Bari, Harold Huber, Maxie Rosenbloom.

Japanese detective Mr. Moto (Peter Lorre) investigates the strange death of a prizefighter in this mystery drama. The sleuth learns that the fighter was poisoned while in the ring. This was the third entry in the mystery series based on John P. Marquand's fictional character. The studio intended the production as an entry in the Charlie Chan series, but actor Warner Oland, who played Chan, died. Lynn Bari, as a brash reporter trying to save a young fighter jailed on suspicion of murder, embodies the more sensational traits of her profession, as envisioned by Hollywood, and seen in numerous films of the period. "If you turn me loose on this," she says to her city editor, "I'll have the whole town so deep in tears that they'll be using canoes for taxi cabs." Former prizefighter Maxie Rosenbloom adds some comedy. Mr. Moto catches the burly dimwit picking someone's pocket. "I can't help taking things that attract my eyes," Rosenbloom confesses. "He's a kleptomaniac," Moto's nephew explains. "Thanks, pal, thanks," Rosenbloom says as if he were being complimented.

608 MR. WONG IN CHINATOWN (1939), Mon.

Dir. William Nigh; *Sc.* W. Scott Darling; *Cast includes:* Boris Karloff, Grant Withers, Marjorie Reynolds, Peter George Lynn, William Royle, Lotus Long.

Chinese detective Mr. Wong (Boris Karloff) investigates the disappearance of a large sum of money and the murder of a Chinese princess in his apartment in this slow-paced mystery. The money, one million dollars, belonged to the princess who had come to the U.S. to buy airplanes for her country. After two more murders whose victims perish by the same means as the unfortunate princess—poisoned darts propelled by a blow gun—the Chinese sleuth wraps up the case. His careful deductions point to a bank executive as the killer. Marjorie Reynolds, a cheeky reporter and romantic interest for police detective Grant Withers, parries with him about his incompetence. Reynolds was added to this third entry in the series. Monogram produced these films to capitalize on the huge success of the Charlie Chan series from Twentieth Century–Fox. The sleuths were so similar in character that this plot was resurrected for the 1947 Chan entry titled *The Chinese Ring* when Monogram took over the series.

609 THE MONEY MILL (1917), Vitagraph.

Dir. John Robertson; *Sc.* A. Van Buren Powell; *Cast includes:* Dorothy Kelly, Evart Overton, Gordon Gray, Edward Elkas, Charles Kent, Logan Paul.

Idealistic reporter Evart Overton meets and falls in love with wealthy Dorothy Kelly, but will not marry her because of her money, in this farfetched drama. Although she is socially responsible (she works with the city's impoverished), she cannot convince him that her riches will not affect their life together. But when thieves try to bilk her out of her gold mine, the source of her wealth, Overton helps her to hold on to her property. He then realizes he loves her more than his rigid principle.

610 MONSTER IN THE CLOSET (1986), Troma.

Dir. Bob Dahlin; *Sc.* Bob Dahlin; *Cast includes:* Donald Grant, Denise DuBarry, Claude Akins, Howard Duff, Henry Gibson, Donald Moffat.

A newspaper editor sends Donald Grant, an obituary writer, to cover a series of strange deaths that have occurred in a small California town in this comedy horror tale that pays tribute to the monster films of the 1950s. It seems a creature who likes closets is roaming the area and killing off innocent inhabitants of a local town. Grant meets science professor Denise DuBarry and joins her and Paul

Walker, her precocious child, in an effort to hunt down the monster. No-nonsense general Donald Moffat takes over the task of destroying the creature but soon discovers conventional weapons are useless. Finally, DuBarry announces on television to a terrified audience: "Destroy all closets!" Other comical moments depict Stella Stevens doing a take-off on the shower scene from *Psycho* and Henry Gibson portraying an eccentric scientist.

611 MURDER BY INVITATION (1941), Mon.

Dir. Phil Rosen; *Sc.* George Bricker; *Cast includes:* Wallace Ford, Marian Marsh, Sarah Padden, George Guhl, Wallis Clark, Gavin Gordon.

Newspaper columnist Wallace Ford, who is invited to visit eccentric spinster Sarah Padden's estate, did not expect to witness a triple murder during his stay in this routine mystery plagued by a series of plot clichés. He soon discovers the entire Padden family is present at the spinster's home. It seems that some relatives have learned that millions of dollars are hidden here, and they want to get their hands on the money. After the three murders, the matriarch decides to put an end to the killings by burning down the place—an action intended to ferret out the guilty members. Her scheme works and the killers are exposed. Padden then explains that the coveted money is all in Confederate bills and, to the astonishment of the onlookers, she begins tossing the cache in the air.

612 MURDER GOES TO COLLEGE (1937), Par.

Dir. Charles Reisner; *Sc.* Brian Marlow, Eddie Welch, Robert Wyler; *Cast includes:* Lynne Overman, Roscoe Karns, Marsha Hunt, Astrid Allwyn, Harvey Stephens, Buster Crabbe.

A private detective and a newspaper reporter who happens to be on vacation join forces to solve a campus killing in this routine whodunit based on the novel by Kurt Steel. Lynne Overman, the master sleuth, and Roscoe Karns, a constantly imbibing news hound, make a rather funny team as they go about questioning those who know anything about the murder of a professor. Overman is hampered by the local authorities, especially police inspector Charles Wilson, and threatened by racketeer Buster Crabbe, but he manages to surmount these difficulties to unmask the killer. The popularity of the pair of comical sleuths gave rise to a possible series, so later the same year *Partners in Crime* was released. But when it failed to generate the proper audience interest, the series idea was canceled.

613 MURDER IN THE BIG HOUSE (1942), WB.

Dir. B. Reeves Eason; *Sc.* Raymond Schrock; *Cast includes:* Van Johnson, George Meeker, Faye Emerson, Frank Wilcox, Michael Ames, Roland Drew.

Intrepid reporters Van Johnson and George Meeker expose a murder ring operating inside a state prison in this weak drama, a remake of *Jailbreak*, a low-budget film released in 1936. While on death row, convict Michael Ames is killed by a bolt of lightning. Cub reporter Johnson, curious about the strange death, soon discovers a sinister political plot was concocted to keep Ames from revealing what he knew. The 1942 version was reissued in 1945 under the title *Born for Trouble*.

614 MURDER IN THE MUSEUM (1934), Progressive Pictures.

Dir. Melville Shyer; *St.* E. B. Crosswhite; *Cast includes:* Henry B. Walthall, John Harron, Phyllis Barrington, Joseph Girard, John Elliott, Donald Kerr.

Inquisitive newspaper reporter John Harron investigates a strange murder in this routine drama set chiefly in an even stranger environment: a museum of freaks. The Sphere Museum of Natural and Unnatural Wonders is managed by Lynton Brent, who fears discovery of his cache of liquor hidden on the premises. Among the sightseers are police commissioner Joseph

Girard, anti-drinking councilman Sam Flint, the reporter and Phyllis Barrington, the commissioner's niece. The councilman decides to search for any liquor on the premises and, as he reaches for a side door, a shot rings out. Flint falls dead. Brent, the manager, flees but is caught. The police find the gun and arrest its owner. Amid the confusion the captured manager escapes through a rear door. Harron turns in his story and then learns that the suspect has been released since the gun did not match the caliber of the bullet that killed the councilman. The reporter and the commissioner's niece inspect a loft overlooking the museum. Suddenly, a shadowy figure seems to appear from nowhere and knocks Harron unconscious. The police arrive and scare the assailant away. Following several other strange incidents, including a trap in which Harron is captured and tied up and Barrington falls into the manager's hands, a half-witted young woman, a freak from the museum who had earlier been betrayed by the manager, stabs him to death. Harron, now freed, discovers that Professor Mysto (Henry B. Walthall) has invented a gun that can fire a bullet of a different caliber. It seems that the councilman had long ago betrayed Mysto's wife, and the professor had sworn revenge.

615 MURDER IS NEWS (1939), Warwick.

Dir. Leon Barsha; Sc. Edgar Edwards; Cast includes: John Gallaudet, Iris Meredith, George McKay, John Hamilton, Frank C. Wilson, William McIntyre.

Radio news reporter John Gallaudet, who specializes in crime stories, uncovers a tale that leads to several murders in this generally inept low-budget drama. When he broadcasts a scandal involving maverick utility magnate William McIntyre, his wife and her lover, the wealthy man's son flares up in anger. The strong-willed young man, refusing to accept any of his father's money, instead works as a musician in the orchestra of a local nightclub. McIntyre is killed in his mansion, and Gallaudet sets out to bring the perpetrator to justice. The police, incidentally, give the journalist, styled after Walter Winchell, a popular gossip columnist of the period, a free hand in his investigation. George McKay provides some weak comedy relief.

616 THE MURDER MAN (1935), MGM.

Dir. Tim Whelan; Sc. Tim Whelan, John C. Higgins; Cast includes: Spencer Tracy, Virginia Bruce, Lionel Atwill, Harvey Stephens, Robert Barrat, James Stewart.

Spencer Tracy in this disappointing mystery portrays the title character, a hard-nosed, experienced crime reporter who drinks heavily at times. Often ahead of the law in solving murders, he is admired by his fellow reporters, especially Virginia Bruce, who is in love with him. When con man Harvey Stephens causes the death of Tracy's father and the suicide of Tracy's estranged wife, the reporter vows to bring him to justice. He arranges a "perfect murder" by killing Stephens's crooked partner and pinning the crime on the con man. The scheme works well, and Tracy visits the condemned man in his cell. However, his conscience gets the best of him and he confesses to the murder. James Stewart, as a cub reporter, made his film debut in this drama.

617 MURDER ON THE CAMPUS (1934), Che.

Dir. Richard Thorpe; Sc. Andrew Moses; Cast includes: Charles Starrett, Shirley Grey, J. Farrell MacDonald, Dewey Robinson, Jane Keckley, Edward Van Sloan.

Unexplainable murders on a college campus baffle local police and capture the natural curiosity of reporter Charles Starrett in this slow-paced mystery based on the novel *The Campanile Murder* by Whitman Chambers. Starrett, whose girlfriend is implicated in the killings, is happy when he is assigned to investigate the crimes. The last reel relates how a chemistry professor who has a keen interest in criminology turns out to be the guilty party.

618 MURDER ON THE ROOF (1930), Col.

Dir. George B. Seitz; *Sc.* F. Hugh Herbert; *Cast includes:* Dorothy Revier, Raymond Hatton, Margaret Livingston, David Newell, Paul Porcasi, Virginia Brown Faire.

Raymond Hatton portrays a reporter who poses as a drunk throughout this tightly edited drama. Dorothy Revier, the daughter of a down-and-out lawyer who is falsely accused of murder, vows to prove her father's innocence. Toward this end, she works as an entertainer in a nightclub owned by Paul Porcasi, whom she believes is the real killer. Together with reporter Hatton's help, she finds enough evidence to convict Porcasi, who has fallen in love with her. David Newell provides the true romance for Revier.

619 MURDER WITH PICTURES (1936), Par.

Dir. Charles Barton; *Sc.* John Moffitt, Sidney Salkow; *Cast includes:* Lew Ayres, Gail Patrick, Joyce Compton, Paul Kelly, Onslow Stevens, Ernest Cossart.

While he is being photographed by a battery of newspaper photographers, a criminal lawyer is shot to death in this sometimes absorbing drama. He had just gotten an acquittal for his client, a notorious mobster. Crack newspaper cameraman Lew Ayres, a part-time sleuth, unravels the mystery, including two other deaths, and helps free his girlfriend Gail Patrick, who had been framed for the original murder. An interesting element is the idea of the mob's planting one of their killers among the photographers. Onslow Stevens portrays the gang leader responsible for the mayhem. The film was adapted from the 1935 novel by George Harmon Coxe. Ayres, who gained fame for his role as Paul in the classic antiwar drama *All Quiet on the Western Front* (1930), appeared in several newspaper dramas.

620 THE MUTILATOR (1979) see *The Dark* (1979).

621 MY DEAR MISS ALDRICH (1937), MGM.

Dir. George B. Seitz; *Sc.* Herman J. Mankiewicz; *Cast includes:* Edna May Oliver, Maureen O'Sullivan, Walter Pidgeon, Rita Johnson, Janet Beecher, Paul Harvey.

The staff of a New York daily newspaper almost has a fit as it faces unexpected and drastic changes in this delightful and fluffy comedy about the world of journalism. Nebraska schoolteacher Maureen O'Sullivan, whose aunt, Edna May Oliver, owns the paper, is determined to prove that women, if given the opportunity, can perform as well as their counterparts as staff members of a big city paper. Much to the chagrin of managing editor Walter Pidgeon, O'Sullivan, arriving from her home town, soon begins to prove her case as head of the news department, pressing Pidgeon to change his narrow views about women. Farcical situations and witty dialogue abound, all to the benefit of this low-budget but classy production. Pidgeon had appeared in several newspaper films, including *Mannequin,* (1926) in which he played a crusading reporter, *A Girl With Ideas* (1937) as a newspaper publisher with Wendy Barrie as his rival, and *Too Hot to Handle* (1938) as a newsreel cameraman with Clark Gable as his rival.

622 MY LADY'S LIPS (1925), B. P. Schulberg.

Dir. James Hogan; *Sc.* John Goodrich; *Cast includes:* Frank Keenan, Clara Bow, Alyce Mills, William Powell, Matthew Betz, Ford Sterling.

Newspaper reporter Frank Keenan, after uncovering a gang of thieves but letting a female member go free, serves time in jail for his cover-up in this implausible silent drama. Keenan protects Alyce Mills, the young woman, because earlier she had saved his life. But his paper and the authorities think he has betrayed them. One year later, after his release, he learns that Mills is running a gambling house. He visits the place and is threatened by a disgruntled gun-wielding gambler. Mills rushes to Keenan's rescue and takes the bullet meant for him. Slightly wounded in the arm, she asks him for a kiss and his forgiveness. An earlier sequence depicts a brutal third degree administered by police, a procedure, the film strongly suggests, that can sometimes lead to forced and false confessions.

623 MYSTERIOUS CROSSING (1936), U.

Dir. Arthur Lubin; Sc. Jefferson Parker, John Grey; Cast includes: James Dunn, Jean Rogers, Andy Devine, John Eldredge, Hobart Cavanaugh, Herbert Rawlinson.

Reporter James Dunn becomes involved in a murder while he is on a ferry crossing the Mississippi in this conventional mystery set in New Orleans. Dunn persuades a newspaper to hire him since he has witnessed the crime. After he gets roughed up by some hoodlums, he and Andy Devine, a slow-witted hillbilly guitar player, manage to figure out the identity of the murderer. Jean Rogers, the daughter of the victim, ends up in Dunn's arms after the latter proves her fiancé and false friend of her father did the killing.

624 MYSTERIOUS MR. WONG (1935), Mon.

Dir. William Nigh; Sc. Nina Howatt; Cast includes: Bela Lugosi, Wallace Ford, Arline Judge, Fred Warren, Lotus Long, Robert Emmett O'Connor.

Newspaper feature writer Wallace Ford tracks down a dangerous villain in this murky drama based on the novel *The Twelve Coins of Confucius* by Harry Stephen Keeler. Bela Lugosi portrays the Chinese leader of a gang of hatchet men in San Francisco's Chinatown. Lugosi has come to the U.S. to retrieve twelve coins which legend says Confucius had once possessed. They contain the power to make their owner the ruler of the Chinese province of Keelat. Lugosi's mad quest leads to a series of strange crimes, including several bloody murders. Lee Shumway, the city editor of the *Globe*, assigns Ford to investigate. In a Chinese laundry Ford finds a piece of paper near a victim. He takes the clue with its Chinese writing to a translator who admits Ford is marked for death. Following a string of strange incidents (men collapse in the shadowy and twisted streets, unsuspecting victims are beheaded while engaging in dinner, and storekeepers are killed), Ford and Arline Judge, his fiancée, fall into the hands of Lugosi's henchmen. The reporter, about to undergo torture, manages to dislodge a telephone receiver and call his paper for help. The police arrive in the proverbial nick of time and the fleeing Lugosi is shot to death. The racist dialogue will certainly surprise today's audiences. "What do I care about another laundry man?" Ford comments about one of the Chinatown murders. "The world is full of 'em." In another scene a policeman observes: "Them Chinamen is jabberin' like monkeys.... There's nothin' noisier than a Chinaman."

625 THE MYSTERY MAN (1935), Mon.

Dir. Ray McCarey; Sc. John Krafft, Rollo Lloyd; Cast includes: Robert Armstrong, Maxine Doyle, Henry Kolker, Leroy Mason, James Burke, Guy Usher.

Reporter Robert Armstrong temporarily turns detective and helps solve a murder in this bright and charming drama. Chicago-based Armstrong, after a night of heavy drinking, wakes up broke in St. Louis where he meets Maxine Doyle. They both become involved in a local murder case which he decides to investigate. Although he finds the killer, he also finds himself with a gun in his ribs, held there by the latter. But Doyle, his traveling companion, catches the culprit. To secure his future, the reporter decides to marry his rescuer. Snappy dialogue, interesting incidents and good characteri-

626 THE MYSTERY OF THE DOUBLE CROSS
(1917) serial, Pathé.

Dir. William Parke; *Cast includes:* Mollie King, Leon Bary, Ralph Stuart, Gladden James, Theodore Friebus, Harry Fraser.

A reporter at the last possible moment clears innocent Leon Bary's name in this 15-episode serial about masked strangers, kidnappings, sacrifices and riddles. Both Bary and the reporter love Mollie King, the heroine who bore a strange symbol of a double cross on her shoulder. Bary's inheritance of a fortune had depended upon his marriage to a woman carrying that mark.

627 THE MYSTERY OF THE WAX MUSEUM
(1933), WB.

Dir. Michael Curtiz; *Sc.* Don Mullally, Carl Erickson; *Cast includes:* Lionel Atwill, Fay Wray, Glenda Farrell, Frank McHugh, Allen Vincent, Holmes Herbert.

Determined and exceptionally brave newspaper reporter Glenda Farrell exposes Lionel Atwill, a crazed custodian of a wax museum who is responsible for several murders, in this fair horror mystery filmed in early Technicolor. He has been the custodian of London's famous wax museum before coming to the United States. Early in the film Farrell berates Frank McHugh, her news editor. "I'm going to make you eat dirt, you soap bubble," she vows. Atwill, who has trapped Fay Wray in the basement of his museum, plans to make her immortal by turning her into a wax statue of Marie Antoinette. "My dear," he questions her, "why are you so pitifully afraid? Immortality has been the dream, the inspiration of mankind through the ages. And I am going to give you immortality." One of the more particularly terrifying sequences concerns the conflagration of the museum, with all its wax figures slowly melting into grossly distorting images. Another is the segment in which Fay Wray reveals Atwill's truly gruesome face. In the final sequence tough reporter Farrell decides how to get even with McHugh, who has proposed to her. "You dirty stiff," she replies, "I'll do it." Only one year earlier, director Curtiz, Atwill and Fay Wray collaborated in making *Doctor X*, another Technicolor horror mystery, with Lee Tracy playing the inquisitive reporter.

628 THE MYSTERY OF THE YELLOW ROOM
(1919), Realart.

Dir. Emile Chautard; *Sc.* Emile Chautard; *Cast includes:* William S. Walcott, Edmund Elton, George Cowl, Ethel Grey Terry, Lorin Raker, Jean Gauthier.

Cub reporter Lorin Raker solves a puzzling theft and murder in this "locked room" mystery based on the 1908 French novel by Gaston Leroux. After some important papers are stolen from a scientist, famous detective George Cowl is called upon to solve the case. Also assigned to investigate is neophyte reporter Lorin Raker. Then a gardener is murdered, resulting in the boyfriend of the scientist's daughter as the chief suspect. During the young man's trial, reporter Raker intercedes with the shocking proof that Cowl, the detective, is the criminal, after which the reporter explains the entire mystery.

629 MYSTERY SHIP (1941), Col.

Dir. Lew Landers; *Sc.* David Silverstein, Houston Branch; *Cast includes:* Paul Kelly, Lola Lane, Trevor Bardette, Cy Kendall, Dwight Frye, Larry Parks.

Government agent Paul Kelly accompanies a shipload of convicts who are being deported to an unknown island in this bizarre action drama. His job is to see that the unusual passengers arrive at their destination without major incidents. Determined reporter Lola Lane stows away aboard the vessel in search of a story. Larry Parks, who later gained fame impersonating entertainer Al Jolson in the

630 MYSTIC CIRCLE MURDER (1939), Merit.

Dir. Frank O'Connor; Sc. Charles Condon, Don Gallagher; Cast includes: Betty Compson, Robert Fiske, Helene Le Berthan, Arthur Gardner, David Kerman, Robert Fraser.

Another entry in a long line of exposés of fake mystics who claim they can contact the spirits of loved ones, this minor drama adds little insight or entertainment to the genre. Robert Fiske portrays the chief charlatan, with Betty Compson as one of his aides. Reporter Arthur Gardner pursues Fiske in an effort to protect the victims of this spiritualism scam. The film is weakened by its low production values, especially in the process shots of foreign settings.

631 NAME THE WOMAN (1934), Col.

Dir. Al Rogell; Sc. Fred Niblo Jr., Herbert Asbury; Cast includes: Richard Cromwell, Arline Judge, Charles Wilson, Henry Kolker, Bradley Page, Purnell Pratt.

Richard Cromwell plays a bumbling newspaper reporter in this almost as clumsy remake of a 1928 silent murder mystery of the same name. Cromwell's ineptness accidentally draws innocent Arline Judge into a web of murder. He is then forced to work closely with her to find the killer so that they can establish her innocence. Following a series of unsurprising incidents, they accomplish this more by chance than by intelligence. Meanwhile, Cromwell finds an opportunity to woo Judge. Bradley Page portrays the nominal gangster.

632 NANCY DREW, REPORTER (1939), WB.

Dir. William Clemens; Sc. Kenneth Gamet; Cast includes: Bonita Granville, Frankie Thomas Jr., John Litel, Mary Lee, Sheila Bromley, Dickie Jones.

The title character, an ebullient teenager played by Bonita Granville, helps prove a young woman innocent of a murder charge in this chiefly implausible mystery. The young journalist, while working for a local newspaper as part of a classroom assignment, becomes involved in an innocent suspect's dilemma. Granville covers an inquest, unravels a murder, and is instrumental in the capture of the actual killers. The film seems almost a satire of the world of journalism as depicted by Hollywood in numerous newspaper-crime movies. This was the second of four entries in the Nancy Drew series based on the stories by Carolyn Keene.

633 NATION AFLAME (1937), Treasure Pictures.

Dir. Victor Halperin; Sc. Oliver Drake; Cast includes: Noel Madison, Lila Lee, Norma Trelvar, Douglas Walton, Harry Holman, Arthur Singley.

Noel Madison portrays the brains behind a corrupt secret society known as the Avenging Angels in this weak exploitation drama based on a story by Thomas Dixon. The film, which underscores the corruption and illegal activities of the group, was designed to expose the dreaded Black Legion, a real-life organization of terrorists of the period. Madison orders the killing of a newspaper publisher who plans to expose the group. Norma Trelvar eventually foils the Avenging Angels but pays with her life. Author Dixon had written *The Klansman*, which movie pioneer D. W. Griffith turned in the classic *Birth of a Nation* (1915). Other films during the 1930s dealt with the same material, including *The Black Legion*, released by Warner Bros. the same year.

634 NAVAJO TRAIL RAIDERS (1949), Rep.

Dir. R. G. Springsteen; Sc. M. Coates Webster; Cast includes: Allan "Rocky" Lane, Eddy Waller, Robert Emmett Keane, Barbara Bestar, Hal Landon, Dick Curtis.

Cowboy drifter Allan "Rocky" Lane

saves a town from continual outlaw raids by eventually exposing Robert Emmett Keane, the local newspaper editor, as the leader of the gang, in this well-paced hackneyed western. The raiders are after the gold shipments and other goods from Yellow Creek, the prairie town that seems unable to prevent the attacks. Lane stops one such raid while casually drifting along the trail. In his efforts to protect Eddy Waller, one of the victims of the outlaw gang, Lane puts an end to the general lawlessness by unmasking the leader.

635 NEVER LET ME GO (1953), MGM.

Dir. Delmer Daves; Sc. Ronald Millar; Cast includes: Clark Gable, Gene Tierney, Bernard Miles, Richard Haydn, Belita, Kenneth More.

American journalist Clark Gable, after antagonizing the Soviet Union, cannot get his Russian wife out of the country in this often implausible cold war drama based on the novel *Came the Dawn* by Roger Bax. Gable, who is married to Russian ballerina Gene Tierney, fails to get help concerning his dilemma from the U.S. State Department or Soviet leaders attending a conference in England. In desperation, the frustrated newspaperman joins Englishman Richard Haydn, who faces the same problem, in a perilous journey to free their wives. They sail to the Baltic and, following several complications, smuggle their spouses out of the Soviet Union. The film, with its dated topic of Soviet brides and their western partners, was filmed in England.

636 A NEW KIND OF LOVE (1963), Par.

Dir. Melville Shavelson; Sc. Melville Shavelson; Cast includes: Paul Newman, Joanne Woodward, Thelma Ritter, Eva Gabor, George Tobias, Marvin Kaplan.

Paul Newman, as a ladies' man and newspaper reporter in Paris, meets and falls in love with sexually backward fashion buyer Joanne Woodward in this anemic romantic comedy. Early in the film, Newman, who has had an affair with his employer's wife, is about to be transferred overseas. "About your wife," he begins apologetically, "if there's anything I can do—" "You've already done it," the boss replies dryly. Except for the glamorous settings of Paris and the attractive attire featured in this colorful production, the bland plot offers the usual timeworn misunderstandings between the couple until they finally get together. Maurice Chevalier adds some interest and charm with his lilting songs. Thelma Ritter, Marvin Kaplan and veteran comic character actor George Tobias provide the much-needed comedy.

637 NEWS HOUNDS (1947), Mon.

Dir. William Beaudine; Sc. Edmond Seward, Tim Ryan; Cast includes: Leo Gorcey, Huntz Hall, Bobby Jordan, Gabriel Dell, Billy Benedict, Christine McIntyre.

Young reporter Leo Gorcey, who dreams of someday becoming a crack news hound, submits a story about the sports-fixing racket in this newspaper-crime comedy drama, another entry in the popular Bowery Boys series. However, the paper is sued for libel after printing the unsubstantiated exposé. But Gorcey saves the day by retrieving lost photos that offer proof of illegal activities. Gorcey, Huntz Hall and their pals appeared in several newspaper-related low-budget comedies, including *Bowery Champs* (1944), *Lucky Losers* (1950) and *Jail Busters* (1955).

638 NEWS IS MADE AT NIGHT (1939), TCF.

Dir. Alfred Werker; Sc. John Larkin; Cast includes: Preston Foster, Lynn Bari, Russell Gleason, George Barbier, Eddie Collins, Minor Watson.

Tough managing editor of a big city daily, Preston Foster rescues an innocent man charged with murder in this above-average newspaper-crime drama. The accused is charged with a gang slaying and slated for execution. Lynn Bari, as a cheeky reporter on Foster's staff, practically has to blackmail him to retain her job. The obligatory romance between the two soon follows. Bari inadvertently helps him gather enough evidence to prove the convicted man's innocence. Comedy relief is supplied in part by Eddie Collins. As in similar Hollywood dramas about the newspaper racket, this entry takes several liberties concerning the world of journalism and its practitioners.

639 THE NEWS PARADE (1928), Fox.

Dir. David Butler; *Sc.* Burnett Hershey; *Cast includes:* Nick Stuart, Sally Phipps, Brandon Hurst, Cyril Ring, Earle Foxe, Franklin Underwood, Truman Talley.

Cameraman Nick Stuart takes on a tough assignment involving the filming of camera-shy millionaire Brandon Hurst in this breezy comedy. Pursuing his unwilling subject and Sally Phipps, the wealthy man's daughter, to such scenic places as Lake Placid, Palm Beach and Havana, the relentless cameraman gets his coveted film. During the pursuit he rescues the father and daughter from a kidnapping attempt in Cuba. Director Butler and Stuart followed up this film with a similar project the next year, titled *Chasing Through Europe.*

640 NEWSBOYS' HOME (1938), U.

Dir. Harold Young; *Sc.* Gordon Kahn; *Cast includes:* Jackie Cooper, Wendy Barrie, Edmund Lowe, Edward Norris, Samuel S. Hinds, Elisha Cook Jr.

A circulation war between rival newspapers expands to their newsboys in this minor drama about the further adventures of the Little Tough Guys. Wendy Barrie portrays a publisher's daughter who takes over the reins of her father's newspaper. However, she almost sinks the once-flourishing enterprise into bankruptcy with her high-toned concepts about publishing and journalism. She fires Edmund Lowe, her street-wise editor, when he tells her the truth about how badly she is handling matters (while he actually advocates the low road of yellow journalism). Jackie Cooper is the leader of the Little Tough Guys who add a sprinkling of spice to the film. Occasionally, a Hollywood studio would use juveniles in newspaper dramas; e. g., *Gentle Julia* (1936) with exuberant Jane Withers and *Nancy Drew, Reporter* (1939) with Bonita Granville in the title role.

641 NEWSIES (1992), BV.

Dir. Kenny Ortega; *Sc.* Bob Tzudiker, Noni White; *Cast includes:* Christian Bale, Bill Pullman, Robert Duvall, Ann-Margaret, Michael Lerner, Kevin Tighe.

Newspaper reporter Bill Pullman becomes interested in a newsboys' strike against New York World publishing magnate Joseph Pulitzer in this disappointing musical set in 1899 and loosely based on an actual incident. Robert Duvall, as Pulitzer, is involved in a circulation war with its rivals. Portrayed as excessively greedy, he decides to raise the price newsboys must pay for their papers, thereby encouraging them to sell more copies to make up for their loss of revenue. As a result, newsie leader Christian Bale organizes a strike. Reporter Pullman of the *New York Sun* covers the plight of the gutsy boys, most of them impoverished street urchins, orphans and runaways. "We wuz beat when we wuz born," Bale, speaking for his group, remarks at one point. Following several setbacks and some nondescript songs and dance numbers, the strikers emerge victorious. Bale's pal and fellow newsboy David Moscow congratulate each other on their success. "Headlines don't sell papers," Moscow exuberantly reminds Bale, "newsies sell papers."

642 NEXT TIME WE LOVE (1936), U.

Dir. Edward H. Griffith; *Sc.* Melville Baker; *Cast includes:* James Stewart, Margaret Sullavan, Ray Milland, Grant Mitchell, Anna Demetrio, Robert McWade.

The marriage of reporter James Stewart and his wife Margaret Sullavan, a successful Broadway actress, faces disaster when the couple clash over their careers in this lackluster romantic drama based on the novel by Ursula Parrott. Assigned to Italy, Stewart learns that his wife is pregnant and rushes back to her side. He promises never to leave her again. But his sudden return gets him fired and forces him to seek employment with a local news outfit as a cub reporter. Sullavan arranges for his return to his old job and once again he goes overseas while she returns to the stage. During the next few years the couple rarely see each other. Her longtime friend Ray Milland proposes marriage to her if she divorces her husband. Sullavan journeys to join her husband and learns that he is dying of a rare illness. Instead of asking for a divorce, she promises she will stay with him until the end. Stewart portrays a more realistic reporter than the alcoholic, wise-cracking or cynical journalist often planted on the screen by Hollywood.

643 NIGHT ALARM (1934), Majestic.

Dir. Spencer Bennet; Sc. James S. Brown; Cast includes: Bruce Cabot, Judith Allen, H. B. Warner, Sam Hardy, Betty Blythe, Fuzzy Knight.

Ace reporter Bruce Cabot works for a crusading newspaper interested in exposing the illegal activities of local big boss H. B. Warner in this routine drama. Cabot, who usually specializes in writing about major fires, relinquishes his spot to cub reporter Judith Allen, who happens to be Warner's daughter. Although a warm relationship begins to develop between the couple, Allen ends their closeness when the newspaper prints a strong condemnation of her father. One evening an arsonist sets fire to Warner's paper factory, trapping the daughter within. Cabot rescues her and finds the culprit. The couple then reconcile their differences.

644 NIGHT CLUB GIRL (1944), U.

Dir. Eddie Cline; Sc. Henry Blankfort, Dick I. Hyland; Cast includes: Vivian Austin, Edward Norris, Maxie Rosenbloom, Judy Clark, Billy Dunn, Leon Belasco.

Edward Norris portrays a sympathetic newspaper columnist who helps a group of aspiring entertainers get a tryout at a small Hollywood nightclub in this bland, low-budget musical. Vivian Austin, a young dancer, provides the romantic element with her partner, Billy Dunn, and Maxie Rosenbloom contributes some comedy to this thinly plotted rags-to-riches film.

645 NIGHT CLUB SCANDAL (1937), Par.

Dir. Ralph Murphy; Sc. Lillie Hayward; Cast includes: John Barrymore, Lynne Overman, Louise Campbell, Charles Bickford, Evelyn Brent, Harvey Stephens.

The great John Barrymore, who displayed signs of memory loss during the filming of this mystery drama, is nevertheless convincing as a doctor who kills his wife and frames her lover. Having gotten away with these crimes, he then kills a nightclub owner, the only other person who knows Barrymore's secret. Newspaper reporter Lynne Overman and his girlfriend Louise Campbell manage to solve the murders for Charles Bickford, a tough but inept police captain. The film, based on the play *Riddle Me This* by Daniel Rubin, was a remake of *Guilty As Hell*, released in 1932, with Victor McLaglen and Edmund Lowe as a feuding detective and reporter, respectively.

646 NIGHT EDITOR (1946), Col.

Dir. Henry Levin; Sc. Hal Smith; Cast includes: William Gargan, Janis Carter, Jeff Donnell, Charles D. Brown, Paul E. Burns, Harry Shannon.

A New York City night editor plays social worker to an alcoholic reporter in this drama marked by a slipshod plot. In an effort to reform the young journalist, he tells him a story about William Gargan, a police lieutenant who went bad. The editor explains how the officer's affair with

Janis Carter, a rich socialite, forced him to compromise his ethics. The remainder of the film unfolds in flashback. Gargan witnesses a killing while on his way home after being out on a spree with his mistress. Not wanting Jeff Donnell, his wife, to find out about his tryst, he remains silent. But when an innocent man goes on trial for the murder, the officer tracks down the guilty party. The film was adapted from a popular contemporary radio program. The alcoholic journalist seemed to be a recurrent theme in newspaper dramas. Curiously, during the silent era the year 1917 witnessed four such dramas, *A Case at Law*, *The Fringe of Society*, *The Night Workers* and *Out of the Wreck*. This theme extended throughout the sound period as well, from *Big News* (1929) with Robert Armstrong to *Come Fill the Cup* (1951) with James Cagney to *Omega Syndrome* (1987) with Ken Wahl.

647 THE NIGHT HAWK (1938), Rep.

Dir. Sidney Salkow; *Sc.* Earl Felton; *Cast includes:* Robert Livingston, June Travis, Robert Armstrong, Ben Welden, Joseph Dowling, Lucien Littlefield.

Newspaper reporter Robert Livingston vows to bring to justice the mob responsible for killing his best friend in this farfetched drama. During his investigation, he meets professional hitman Robert Armstrong, also out for revenge on those crooks who stole an iron lung from his dying brother. Hiding in the iron lung, Livingston darts out and steals the crooks' truck. He then crushes two gangs and smashes a smuggling operation. In addition, he is partially responsible for his girlfriend June Travis's home being riddled with bullets from mobsters out to get him.

648 NIGHT OF TERROR (1933), Col.

Dir. Ben Stoloff; *Sc.* Beatrice Van, William Jacobs; *Cast includes:* Bela Lugosi, Sally Blane, Wallace Ford, Tully Marshall, Mary Frey, Edwin Maxwell.

Serial murderer Edwin Maxwell goes on a reign of terror, assisted by his wife, in this inept drama that provokes more laughter than fear. Mary Frey, as his spouse, wanders around most of the time in a trance, while ambitious reporter Wallace Ford tries to help solve the killings. Other stereotypes include the bumbling police officer and an African-American chauffeur for comedy relief. The dumb cop is present in the form of Matt McHugh, who is given a drugged cigarette by swami Bela Lugosi. "Say," McHugh wonders suspiciously, "what kind of cigarette is this?" "Oh," Lugosi replies soothingly, "it's an Oriental cigarette." The offbeat ending finds Maxwell rising from the dead to warn those in the audience not to reveal the ending or he will return to haunt them.

649 NIGHT RIDE (1930), U.

Dir. John S. Robertson; *Sc.* Edward T. Lowe Jr.; *Cast includes:* Joseph Schildkraut, Edward G. Robinson, Barbara Kent, Harry Stubbs, Ralph Welles, DeWitt Jennings.

In only his second sound film, Edward G. Robinson scores highly as Tony Garotta, a brutal gangster, who clashes with crusading reporter Joseph Schildkraut in this generally tense drama. The reporter's exposés about the gang leader's nefarious activities provoke Garotta to seek revenge. He takes his rival and a fellow journalist for a car ride and then onto his yacht, intending to drop his captives overboard. But Schildkraut reverses the situation and returns triumphant to his wife Barbara Kent. Robinson's menacing performance helped to catapult him to one of Warners' top players in crime films during the 1930s. He achieved his greatest success in *Little Caesar* (1930).

650 THE NIGHT WORKERS (1917), K-E-S-E.

Dir. J. Charles Haydon; *Sc.* J. Bradley Smollen; *Cast includes:* Marguerite Clayton, Jack Gardner, Julien Barton, Mabel Bardine, Arthur W. Bates.

Star reporter Jack Gardner has risen from orphan to copy boy to his present position but is burdened with a drinking problem in this overly familiar silent drama. Fellow reporter Marguerite Clayton persuades him to return with her to their home town where he had once worked on her grandfather's newspaper which she has now inherited. Free from the stresses of night work and influenced by the peace and tranquility of the environment of the small town, Gardner sheds his alcohol problem and marries Clayton. This was one of the earliest newspaper dramas to depict a reporter with a drinking problem. The mythical alcoholic journalist soon became a familiar screen character, moving to a stereotype during the 1920s and finally a cliché by the early sound films of the 1930s.

651 NINE LIVES ARE NOT ENOUGH (1941), WB.

Dir. A. Edward Sutherland; *Sc.* Fred Niblo Jr.; *Cast includes:* Ronald Reagan, Howard da Silva, Faye Emerson, Joan Perry, James Gleason, Ed Brophy.

Reporter Ronald Reagan investigates a rooming-house murder in this overly familiar newspaper-crime thriller. Reagan, who often gets into trouble with his stories, once again is in hot water when his latest exposé about a local gangster results in a libel suit for his paper. A cocky reporter, Reagan earlier boasts to fellow news hawks, "On the strength of my story, and my story alone, he's behind bars." He is demoted but bounces back when he solves a couple of murders and gathers enough proof to convict the gangster. Hampering his efforts are the stereotyped incompetent police officers James Gleason and Ed Brophy. Howard da Silva plays another stereotype, the easily excitable city editor who, following an old plot cliché, eventually relegates Reagan to the advice-to-the-lovelorn column.

652 NO CHILDREN WANTED (1918), General.

Dir. Sherwood MacDonald; *Sc.* Will M. Ritchey; *Cast includes:* Gloria Joy, Ethel Ritchie, R. Henry Grey, Edward Jobson, Neil Hardin, Daniel Gilfether.

Newspaper owner Edward Jobson does not expose arms smuggler R. Henry Grey after seeing a photograph of the man's little daughter in this domestic drama. Gloria Joy, a runaway from school where she has been mistreated, is barely tolerated by her parents who care more for their lifestyle than for the well-being of their daughter. They place her in a boarding school when they learn their luxurious apartment building does not permit children. When her father, involved in smuggling arms into Mexico, becomes aware of his daughter's plight, he and his wife promise to give her the love she has been lacking.

653 NO GREATER SIN (1941), University Films.

Dir. William Nigh; *Sc.* Michel Jacoby; *Cast includes:* Leon Ames, Luana Walters, John Gallaudet, George Taggart, Adele Pearce, Guy Usher.

Local reporter Luana Walters helps public health commissioner Leon Ames rid an industrial and army town of prostitutes and syphilis in this combination cautionary and social conscience drama. Walters does her own investigating and exposes the conditions which spread the disease. Meanwhile George Taggart, a young man about to be married, learns that he has syphilis. He goes to a charlatan who takes his money but doesn't cure him. Instead, the doctor tells Taggart that he's all right. The young man marries Adele Pearce, the reporter's sister. Later, before Pearce gives birth, they discover they both have the disease. Taggart returns in anger to the doctor, and in a struggle, the physician is killed. Charged with murder, Taggart remains silent about his reason for fighting with the victim. But he finally admits the truth and his attorney gets him off. The town then reverses its earlier decision and votes to allot money to clean up the social problem. The powerful message of the film suffers from its low-budget production values and inept script.

654 NO MARRIAGE TIES (1933), Radio.

Dir. J. Walter Ruben; *Sc.* Arthur Caesar, Sam Mintz, H. W. Hanneman; *Cast includes:* Richard Dix, Elizabeth Allan, Alan Dinehart, David Landau, Hilda Vaughn, Hobart Cavanaugh.

Newspaperman Richard Dix, after being fired for irresponsibility and drunkenness, goes into the advertising business as a slogan writer in this satirical tale based on the play *Ad Man* by Arch Gaffney and Charles Curran. Dix develops advertising campaigns built around fear, and his agency becomes one of the most successful in the field. But his partner, Alan Dinehart, grows critical of Dix's methods. "You thought of a way of frightening people into buying merchandise they don't need," Dinehart says. "That's nothing to be proud of. That isn't honest or good business, and I don't like it." Meanwhile, he becomes romantically involved with two women, a dilemma which results in tragedy. When his second girlfriend, Doris Kenyon, starts to dominate his life, he leaves and she commits suicide. Dix, bored and disillusioned with advertising, gives up his business. "I'm a fake," he admits to David Landau, a sleazy publisher of a gossip newspaper. "Back in the days of the *Chronicle,* we had ideals. That was a great newspaper with character and decency." Dix returns to his true love, Elizabeth Allan. The first half of the film has the snappy dialogue and biting commentary about those who sell to and often mislead the public.

655 NO TIME TO MARRY (1938), Col.

Dir. Harry Lachman; *Sc.* Paul Jarrico; *Cast includes:* Richard Arlen, Mary Astor, Virginia Dale, Lionel Stander, Thurston Hall, Marjorie Gateson.

Rival newspaper reporters and lovers Richard Arlen and Mary Astor cannot get together at the altar because of continually interfering assignments in this familiar comedy based on the story "Night Before Christmas" by Paul Gallico. At one point, Astor locates a missing heiress whom Arlen has been trying to track down and who is actually with him. Now she is forced to choose between scooping her boyfriend-rival and sharing the information with him. Meanwhile, Arlen has also been assigned to find some goats for his publisher's son. During his search he meets the missing heiress, unaware of her true identity. Following several other complications, some funny and others simply silly, the couple finally resolve their differences. Newspaper photographer Lionel Stander adds to the mayhem while frustrated publisher Thurston Hall tries to keep a semblance of order.

656 NORTH OF SHANGHAI (1939), Col.

Dir. D. Ross Lederman; *Sc.* Maurice Rapf, Harold Buchman; *Cast includes:* James Craig, Betty Furness, Keye Luke, Morgan Conway, Russell Hicks.

The Sino-Japanese War furnishes the background for this minor low-budget drama concerning a newsreel cameraman and a reporter. Assigned to cover the war by different employers, cameraman James Craig and reporter Betty Furness join forces to uncover a spy ring that is being directed by the head of the Shanghai office of Furness's newspaper. The film includes several sequences of Japan's bombing of Chinese cities and the war in general in this low-budget production.

657 NOT FOR PUBLICATION (1927), FBO.

Dir. Ralph Ince; *Sc.* Ewart Adamson; *Cast includes:* Ralph Ince, Roy Laidlaw, Rex Lease, Jola Mendez, Eugene Strong, Thomas Brower.

Editor Thomas Brower, believing businessman Ralph Ince is dishonest, assigns reporter Rex Lease to get proof of these suspicions in this convoluted drama based on the story "The Temple of the Giants" by Robert Wells Ritchie. Because of his political support, Ince has won a contract from the water commissioner for the construction of a local dam. This results in editor Brower's suspecting Ince's actions as illegal. He asks Brower to burglarize Ince's safe in search of incriminating documents. Following a series of complications, both political and romantic, Lease ends up with Jola Mendez, the sister of Ince. Ironically, her corrupt brother is killed by his own hand when he dynamites the dam.

658 NOT FOR PUBLICATION (1984), Goldwyn.

Dir. Paul Bartel; Sc. John Meyer, Paul Bartel; Cast includes: Nancy Allen, David Naughton, Laurence Luckinbill, Alice Ghostley, Richard Paul, Cork Hubbert.

Tabloid reporter Nancy Allen daydreams about changing the present scandal sheet back into a highly respected and influential paper in this offbeat newspaper tale. Ambitious mayor Laurence Luckinbill, attracted to Allen's looks and intelligence, hires her as his assistant. Meanwhile, Allen becomes romantically involved with photographer David Naughton, whom she has hired. The couple soon learn about the mayor's close ties to corrupt politicians, major crimes and the paper which they work for. While Allen and Naughton are with the mayor in an airplane, he bails out, leaving them to fend for themselves. Luckily, Naughton's mother, who is aboard, crashlands the plane in the Hudson River. They rush to a press conference where Allen threatens the villainous mayor and saves the city. In addition, the reporter is able to turn her paper around so that she can write the investigative stories she has always dreamed about. The nutty dialogue and campy incidents add to this entertaining film.

659 NOTHING BUT LIES (1920), Metro.

Dir. Lawrence C. Windom; Sc. S. E. V. Taylor; Cast includes: Taylor Holmes, Justine Johnstone, Jack McGowan, Rapley Holmes, John Junior, Gypsy O'Brien.

Newspaper reporter Gypsy O'Brien poses as a member of the "Truth Society" so that she can investigate this group that is dedicated to exposing lies in advertising in this early silent comedy based on the 1918 play by Aaron Hoffman. Jack McGowan, another member and son of a partner in an advertising firm, has been passing out leaflets exposing the firm's untruths. Reporter O'Brien is hiding in another room of the newspaper office where McGowan is caught by Taylor Holmes, a junior partner in the same firm. However, the circulars prove to be a successful advertising campaign when a front page exposé appears, and McGowan is hired to write advertisements for the company at a very large salary.

660 NOTHING SACRED (1937), UA.

Dir. William Wellman; Sc. Ben Hecht; Cast includes: Carole Lombard, Fredric March, Walter Connolly, Charles Winninger, Sig Rumann, Frank Fay.

A New York newspaper, upon learning that a victim of radium poisoning wishes to see New York before she dies, grants her wish in this dark comedy that takes a satirical look at the press. Carole Lombard portrays Hazel Flagg, the victim who later learns she has been wrongly diagnosed but goes along with the press which is exploiting her. Fredric March plays the cynical reporter with whom she falls in love. Walter Connolly is his cranky editor. "He's sort of a cross between a ferris wheel and a werewolf," March describes him to Lombard, "but with a lovable streak—if you care to blast for it." Charles Winninger, a heavy-drinking country doctor who makes the wrong diagnosis, offers his own devastating opinion of members of the press: "The hand of God reaching down into a mine couldn't elevate one of them to the depths of degradation." Witty dialogue runs through the entire film. When Connolly in an early scene witnesses the fainting of a young woman in a nightclub, he suspects her collapse may be fatal. "I want to know the worst," he says to the doctor. "I don't want you to spare our feelings. We go to press in fifteen minutes." March, while seeking to exploit Lombard's condition in a series of

Cynical reporter Fredric March tries to keep Carole Lombard from telling the truth about her alleged illness as publisher Walter Connolly holds onto her in William Wellman's dark comedy, *Nothing Scared* (1937).

human interest articles, soon becomes nauseated at the insincere sentimentality heaped upon her by the public. "For good clean fun," he comments sardonically, "there's nothing like a wake." "Oh, please, please," she pleads, "let's not talk shop."

661 OBJECTIVE BURMA (1945), WB.

Dir. Raoul Walsh; *Sc.* Ranald MacDougall, Lester Cole; *Cast includes:* Errol Flynn, William Prince, James Brown, George Tobias, Henry Hull.

Middle-aged war correspondent Henry Hull accompanies American paratroopers who are dropped into the Burmese jungle to destroy a Japanese radar station in this realistic World War II action drama. The well-trained soldiers, led by tight-lipped captain Errol Flynn, must first traverse the difficult jungle. Hull joins the raiders so that he can get a first-hand, realistic combat story. Inexperienced in these operations, he nervously questions the dependability of his parachute while aboard the plane over Burma. "What if my chute doesn't open?" he asks. "You'll be the first one down," a soldier replies. Later, just before the elderly Hull dies, Flynn says, "If I ever get to buy another newspaper, I'll remember what a few cents can buy." The men locate their target and destroy it. When they reach their rendezvous for pickup, they are ambushed by enemy soldiers and must move out to a second prearranged clearing. Meanwhile, they are relentlessly pursued by the Japanese. The film avoids much of the exaggerated heroics and flag-waving dialogue that often mar other war movies of the period. Battle scenes are gritty and plausible as the outnumbered and beleaguered paratroopers fight their way out of the unfriendly terrain. The film met stiff resistance in Britain, whose critics objected to the major

662 OFF THE RECORD (1939), WB.

Dir. James Flood; Sc. Niven Busch, Lawrence Kimble, Earl Baldwin; Cast includes: Pat O'Brien, Joan Blondell, Bobby Jordan, Alan Baxter, William Davidson, Morgan Conway.

Hotshot reporters Pat O'Brien and Joan Blondell help bring an end to the illegal use of young "spotters" by mobsters in the slot-machine racket in this entertaining newspaper-crime drama. The journalists rescue young street punk Bobby Jordan from a reform school by adopting him after Blondell agrees to marry O'Brien. Alan Baxter plays Jordan's gangster brother. Like a host of similar newspaper-oriented films, this superficial entry grossly distorts many aspects of the world of journalism, including life in the press and city rooms and the workaday lives of reporters and editors. O'Brien and Blondell appeared together in a similar film two years earlier titled *Back in Circulation*. Both were veterans of several newspaper films during the 1930s. O'Brien, besides playing Hildy Johnson in the classic *The Front Page* (1931), portrayed a reporter or editor in such films as *Hollywood Speaks* and *The Final Edition*, both released in 1932. Blondell had featured roles in *The Famous Ferguson Case* (1932) and *The Perfect Specimen* (1937).

663 THE OFFICE SCANDAL (1929), Pathé.

Dir. Paul L. Stein; Sc. Paul Gangelin, Jack Jungmeyer; Cast includes: Phyllis Haver, Leslie Fenton, Raymond Hatton, Margaret Livingston, Jimmie Adams, Dan Wolheim.

Reporter Phyllis Haver rescues impoverished reporter Leslie Fenton twice in this minor murder mystery. First, she helps his diminished financial standing by getting him a job with her newspaper. Later, during a murder case which stymies the police, the widow suggests that Fenton had something to do with the crime. But Haver finally gets the actual killer to confess, thereby exonerating Fenton.

664 OH! SAILOR, BEHAVE! (1930), WB.

Dir. Archie Mayo; Sc. Joseph Jackson; Cast includes: Irene Delroy, Charles King, Lowell Sherman, Vivian Oakland, Ole Olsen, Chick Johnson.

Paris reporter Charles King, assigned to interview a Rumanian general, meets ambitious Irene Delroy in Venice and finds himself involved in several dilemmas in this musical comedy drama based on the 1930 play *See Naples and Die, a Comedy in Three Acts* by Elmer Rice. Meanwhile, two American sailors get into trouble with local coquette Lotti Loder. When King has problems getting his interview, the general's secretary comes to his aid. Following a series of complications which include blackmail threats to Delroy, incriminating letters which force her to marry a prince, and a kidnapping, the reporter and Delroy, whose husband is killed while impersonating the general, reconcile their differences.

665 OH! WHAT A NURSE (1926), WB.

Dir. Charles F. Reisner; Sc. Francis Zanuck; Cast includes: Syd Chaplin, Patsy Ruth Miller, Gayne Whitman, Pat Harrington, Edith Yorke, David Torrence.

Cub reporter Syd Chaplin, who has taken over the lovesick column of a newspaper, poses as the feminine leader of a bootlegging gang in this very funny farce based on Robert E. Sherwood and Bertram Bloch's work. Later, he poses as Patsy Ruth Miller's nurse. Miller, who has become obsessed with his column, has an uncle who is trying to marry her off so that he can inherit her estate. The reporter rescues her from an ill-fated marriage and takes her as his bride. Syd Chaplin, Charlie's half-brother, performed another female impersonation in *Charley's Aunt,* also a silent comedy, released one year earlier.

666 OKAY AMERICA (1932), U.

Dir. Tay Garnett; *Sc.* William Anthony McGuire; *Cast includes:* Lew Ayres, Maureen O'Sullivan, Louis Calhern, Walter Catlett, Alan Dinehart, Edward Arnold.

Newspaper columnist Lew Ayres becomes entangled in the kidnapping of a politician's young daughter in this absorbing drama. Often getting tips from various sources, Ayres is invited to the hideout of a gang of kidnappers led by a Capone-like leader who wants the columnist to handle the negotiations for the victim's release. Ayres visits the White House to bargain for the kidnapped daughter's freedom in exchange for the President's dropping certain indictments against the gang boss, but he receives a strong rejection. "Tell those hoodlums that the sacred government of the U.S. will never be party to or barter with criminals of that caliber," he is informed. In addition, he is told to report back that these "undesirables" will be driven out of the country—a reference to the fate of Al Capone. Ayres's character was based on that of Walter Winchell, a popular columnist of the period. A remake titled *Risky Business,* featuring George Murphy, appeared in 1939.

667 OMEGA SYNDROME (1987), New World.

Dir. Joseph Manduke; *Sc.* John Sharkey; *Cast includes:* Ken Wahl, George DiCenzo, Nicole Eggert, Doug McClure, Xander Berkeley, Ron Kuhl.

Alcoholic journalist Ken Wahl sobers up quickly when his thirteen-year-old daughter is kidnapped during a liquor store holdup in this second-rate drama. When police officer Doug McClure and his men fail to get any results, Wahl joins his former Vietnam pal George DiCenzo in an effort to track down the kidnappers and rescue the girl. They discover she is a captive of a neo-Nazi terrorist group whose identifying mark is that of the omega symbol on their wrists. Even the hand-me-down humor fails to hit its mark in this film. At one point, before DiCenzo kills one of the baddies, he blurts out: "Say good night, Gracie!"

668 ON THE JUMP (1918), Fox.

Dir. Raoul Walsh; *Sc.* Ralph Spence; *Cast includes:* George Walsh, Frances Burnham, James Marcus, Henry Clive, Ralph Faulkner.

Patriotic reporter George Walsh returns from Washington to discover that Henry Clive, a German sympathizer, has gained control of his newspaper in this blatantly patriotic World War I silent comedy drama. Walsh resigns after Clive destroys his story and joins a war bond drive. He later learns that Clive is actually a German spy who has stolen an important chemical formula. The agent holds Walsh's girlfriend, Frances Burnham, prisoner, but Walsh rescues her. When Clive tries to escape by way of a schooner, Walsh follows and captures him. He then aims the vessel's guns at a nearby German submarine and sinks it.

669 ONCE UPON A HONEYMOON (1942), RKO.

Dir. Leo McCarey; *Sc.* Sheridan Gibney; *Cast includes:* Ginger Rogers, Cary Grant, Walter Slezak, Albert Dekker, Albert Basserman.

A World War II comedy drama, the film is an odd combination of events, blending the devastation of Czechoslovakia, Poland and France with the frivolous desires of young burlesque entertainer from Brooklyn Ginger Rogers, who is looking for a titled husband. Cary Grant portrays an American reporter with whom she ends up. But before this happy conclusion comes about, the misguided Rogers marries Austrian nobleman Walter Slezak, unaware that he is a Nazi agent. Grant, who knows the truth about the bridegroom, hounds the couple on their honeymoon through war-torn Europe and finally to France. He eventually convinces Rogers to leave her husband who has helped to bring about the fall of Austria, Czechoslovakia, Poland and other countries. American agent Albert Dekker persuades Rogers to return to her husband and learn what the Germans have planned for the U.S. Grant, meanwhile, agrees to work for Slezak as a radio commentator. Instead of praising the Nazis in his broadcasts to the U.S., Grant uses American idioms and expressions which result in discrediting Hitler and his cohorts. When Rogers delivers a key secret Nazi code to Dekker, he tells her that her job is finished. Rogers and Grant then board a ship for the U.S. Some of the incidents are quite funny, as are the lines. Grant, looking out of a hotel window, witnesses the arrival of Nazis troops. "Hitler is here!" he announces excitedly to Rogers. "I can't see him now," she replies. "I'm dressing." Later, Grant jokingly comments on Rogers's intellectual capacity. "If a gnat dove into your pool of knowledge, he would have broken his neck." Several critics, who seemed more aware than those who produced this inane work of the plight of European countries being overrun by Nazi Germany, singled out the film as tasteless and unfunny. This is particularly noticeable in a Nazi concentration camp sequence involving Rogers and Grant. Another comedy film of the same period also attacked for bad taste was Ernst Lubitsch's *To Be or Not to Be* (1942) starring Jack Benny.

670 ONE EXCITING NIGHT (1945), Par.

Dir. William C. Thomas; *Sc.* David Lang; *Cast includes:* William Gargan, Ann Savage, Leo Gorcey, Don Beddoe, Paul Hurst, Charles Halton.

Rival reporters William Gargan and Ann Savage repeatedly hide the body of a gangster to get a scoop for their own paper in this comedy drama set chiefly in a wax museum. To protect himself, George Zucco, who has committed the murder and has stolen a fortune in diamonds, wants possession of the corpse so that he can dispose of it permanently. The film is occasionally listed under its alternate title, *Midnight Manhunt*. Gargan had appeared in several earlier newspaper films, including *Four Frightened People* (1934) and *Man Hunt* (1936).

671 ONE MILE FROM HEAVEN (1937), TCF.

Dir. Allan Dwan; *Sc.* Lou Breslow, John Patrick; *Cast includes:* Claire Trevor, Sally Blane, Douglas Fowley, Fredi Washington, Joan Carol, Ralf Harolde.

Cheeky newspaper reporter Claire Trevor, who likes to scoop her fellow journalists, comes across an astonishing story involving a young African-American woman in this offbeat comedy drama. Trevor is sent on a wild goose chase to a poor section of town where she observes a white child being brought up by an African-American woman. It seems the woman, Fredi Washington, is the mother of a white child. However, inquisitive Trevor's investigation reveals that the child's mother is Sally Blane, who is presently remarried into a wealthy family. The real mother is reunited with her child and Washington is hired as the nurse. After a courtroom scene in which Blane is proven to be the real mother, Trevor is persuaded by the judge to quash the story in the family's and child's interest. Wisecracks punctuate the film. In one early scene, for example, Trevor explains she is filling in for the regular crime reporter who has broken his leg after slipping on a cake of soap. "Served him right for taking a bath," a fellow newsman cracks. Bill Robinson has a minor role as an African-American policeman. This was an unusual theme for Hollywood during this period, which rarely mixed social issues with its escapist fare.

672 ONE MORE AMERICAN (1918), Par.

Dir. William C. De Mille; *Sc.* Olga Printzlau; *Cast includes:* George Beban, Camille Ankewich, May Giracci, Helen Jerome Eddy, Raymond Hatton, Jack Holt.

A young reporter exposes a corrupt politician in this familiar silent drama based on the 1917 play *The Land of the Free* by William C. De Mille. George Beban portrays an Italian immigrant whose popularity among his fellow Italian Americans incurs the wrath of a local ward boss. The politician tries to blackmail Beban into cooperating with the status quo, otherwise Beban's family will be stopped at Ellis Island when they try to enter the U.S. Jack Holt, the relentless reporter, learns about the threat and exposes the incident. His story eventually sends the politician to jail. Beban's wife and daughter then join him as American citizens.

673 ONE MORE TOMORROW (1946), WB.

Dir. Peter Godfrey; *Sc.* Charles Hoffman, Catherine Turney; *Cast includes:* Ann Sheridan, Dennis Morgan, Jack Carson, Alexis Smith, Jane Wyman, Reginald Gardiner.

A clash between wealthy playboy Dennis Morgan and poor magazine employee Ann Sheridan almost dooms their love for each other in this second adaptation of *The Animal Kingdom*, the comedy play by Philip Barry. When Sheridan, a radical who loves Morgan but rejects him because of his wealth and his cavalier attitude toward money and honest work, he marries gold-digging Alexis Smith. At one point he buys out the magazine that employs Sheridan. The unhappily married Morgan chances to meet Sheridan, who then realizes she still loves him. They rekindle their former love when his wife decides to head for Reno for a divorce. Despite its talented cast, including indolent left-winger Reginald Gardiner and Morgan's eccentric butler Jack Carson, the film fails to capture the radical vs. conservative elements of the original play.

674 ONE MYSTERIOUS NIGHT (1944), Col.

Dir. Oscar Boetticher Jr.; *Sc.* Paul Yawitz; *Cast includes:* Chester Morris, Richard Lane, Janis Carter, George Stone, William Wright, Robert Williams.

The likable amateur sleuth, known professionally as Boston Blackie (Chester Morris), is on the trail of a priceless diamond in this conventional drama. The situation becomes more complicated when the hotel clerk who stole the Blue Star of the Nile is found murdered. Determined newspaper reporter Janis Carter, girlfriend of the private eye, tags along, hoping for a scoop. This was the seventh entry in the Blackie mysteries, which were also known for their occasional snappy dialogue. In one scene, for example, when police inspector Richard Lane pursues Blackie into a hotel, the clerk blocks the officer. "We're going through!" insists Lane. "Over my dead body!" the woman objects. "Don't be so modest, lady," Lane's assistant says. "There's still plenty of life in you."

675 ONE WILD NIGHT (1938), TCF.

Dir. Eugene Forde; *Sc.* Charles Belden, Jerry Cady; *Cast includes:* June Lang, Dick Baldwin, Lyle Talbot, J. Edward Bromberg, Sidney Toler, Andrew Tombes.

The strange disappearances of four businessmen capture the curiosity of a crime student in this low-budget comedy. Dick Baldwin, as the aspiring sleuth, teams up with reporter June Lang, who helps him investigate why the men have vanished after withdrawing large sums of money from a bank. The couple discover that the foursome have taken part in a conspiracy designed to get them away from their wives. Meanwhile bank manager J. Edward Bromberg, one of the quartet, betrays his accomplices and absconds with the ransom money.

676 ONE YEAR LATER (1933), Allied.

Dir. E. Mason Hopper; *Sc.* F. Hugh Herbert; *Cast includes:* Mary Brian, Russell Hopton, Donald Dillaway, George Irving, Will Ahern, Gladys Ahern.

An innocent young man convicted of murder beats the law when he is rescued by a good Samaritan in this farfetched but absorbing melodrama told chiefly in flashback. The film opens with a happy young honeymoon-bound couple (Donald Dillaway and Mary Brian) on board a train. One year later, again on a train, the wife is holding on to her husband for the last time as he is being taken to prison to face the death penalty. She relates her story to fellow passenger Russell Hopton, a reporter who is suffering from a terminal illness. He decides to help the couple by overpowering the guards, releasing their prisoner and jumping off the train. The officers identify his body as that of young Dillaway, who is now free to begin a new life with his spouse.

677 OPENED BY MISTAKE
(1940), Par.

Dir. George Archainbaud; Sc. Stuart Palmer, Garnett Weston, Louis S. Kaye; Cast includes: Charlie Ruggles, Robert Paige, Janice Logan, William Frawley, Florence Shirley, Esther Dale.

Hotshot newspaper reporter Robert Paige and sports editor Charlie Ruggles become embroiled with a mysterious young woman, a crooked banker and a trunk containing a corpse in this awkward minor mystery. Paige and his pal, who likes his liquor, somehow gain possession of the trunk which is quickly claimed by private investigator Janice Logan. She has been assigned by an insurance company to retrieve a large sum of stolen money. Following several complications, Paige and Logan find themselves fugitives hopscotching across the country in search of the real culprit—a kooky chemist.

678 THE OREGON TRAIL
(1959), TCF.

Dir. Gene Fowler Jr.; Sc. Louis Vittes, Gene Fowler Jr.; Cast includes: Fred MacMurray, William Bishop, Nina Shipman, Gloria Talbot, Henry Hull, John Carradine.

Fred MacMurray portrays a New York reporter who is assigned to report the opening of the Oregon territory and investigate a series of Indian attacks on settlers in this historical drama set in the nineteenth century. President Polk sends soldiers dressed as pioneers to hold the British area for the United States. MacMurray braves the long and difficult journey of the wagon train. After reaching Fort Laramie, Wyoming, MacMurray learns that the dispute has ended. He then decides to retire from writing and live with Gloria Talbot, his newly acquired Indian love. The film is better known for its scenery than its historical accuracy.

679 THE OTHER HALF
(1919), Robertson-Cole.

Dir. King Vidor; St. King Vidor; Cast includes: Florence Vidor, Charles Meredith, ZaSu Pitts, David Butler, Alfred Allen, Frances Raymond.

Florence Vidor, in love with businessman Charles Meredith, refuses to marry him after he turns hard and cold toward his workers in this early silent social drama. She then joins a crusading newspaper sympathetic to the working class and poor. Vidor writes an article so strong that it persuades Meredith to reform. Earlier, his experiences in World War I had placed him in sympathy with the poor. But after his father's death, Meredith had taken over the family enterprise and changed. He had been warned about certain needed repairs but rejected the alterations. When a wall fell upon his former army pal, temporarily blinding the worker, the men refused to work. Meredith finally reconciles his differences with Vidor and his workers.

680 THE OTHER WOMAN
(1992), Axis.

Dir. Jag Mundhra; Sc. Georges Des Esseintes; Cast includes: Adrian Zmed, Lee Anne Beaman, Jenna Persaud, Daniel Moriarity, Craig Stepp, Melissa Moore.

Newspaper reporter Lee Anne Beaman discovers that she has become fascinated by her husband's lover in this disappointing crime drama which was billed as an "erotic thriller." Earlier, the film shows her consumed by her ambition—to become a crack journalist. But this only leads to marital problems. Adrian Zmed, her husband, is a best-selling author. After she discovers suggestive photographs, she begins to follow attractive, free-spirited Jenna Persaud, whom she believes is her husband's lover. Persaud is a prostitute who also works as a nude model. As in the earlier *Desperately Seeking Susan* (1985), the reporter soon starts to envy her rival's lifestyle. Following several complications, including a steamy sexual affair between the two women, Beaman learns that she has been videotaped and the results were sent to her paper, resulting in the loss of her job. This was all a setup by seedy businessman Sam Jones, whom Beaman had earlier been investigating. Her husband returns and they go to bed. While they are making love, her former employer calls to inform her she has been elevated to a better position. In a voice-over, Beaman states: "I found the other woman and she was me."

681 OUT OF DARKNESS (1941), MGM.

Dir. Sammy Lee; *Sc.* John Nesbitt; *Cast includes:* Rudolph von Heinrich, Egon Brecher, Wolfgang Zilzer, Lotti Palfie.

Part of "John Nesbitt's Passing Parade" series of short dramas produced by MGM, this one-reel film eulogizes a little-known phase of Belgian resistance during World War I. The story concerns an audacious newspaper that dared to defy that country's German invaders by continuing to publish despite the enemy's threats. Although this series concentrated chiefly on persons whose ideas were spurned during their lifetime, others who went unnoticed, or still others who changed world events, the Nesbitt shorts occasionally digressed, especially during World War II, to present poignant tales of patriotism or propaganda.

682 OUT OF THE SHADOW (1919), Par.

Dir. Emile Chautard; *Sc.* Eve Unsell; *Cast includes:* Pauline Frederick, Wyndham Standing, Ronald Byram, William Gross, Emma Campbell, Nancy Hathaway.

A meddlesome reporter has the wrong man arrested in this silent drama, an adaptation of E. W. Hornung's 1902 novel *The Shadow of the Rope*, about murder and false accusations. Pauline Frederick portrays the wife of a murdered man. When she is acquitted of the charge of murder because of lack of evidence, philanthropist Wyndham Standing befriends her. At a party she grows suspicious of his motives and believes he is the actual killer. The officious journalist has Standing arrested, but he is freed when Frederick introduces another witness to the police. The man, a pianist, admits that he killed her husband. She and Standing then make plans to marry. Several contemporary critics felt that the film had been stripped of any suspense, leaving behind very little mystery.

683 OUT OF THE STORM (1926), Tiffany.

Dir. Louis J. Gasnier; *Sc.* Lois Hutchinson, Leete Renick Brown; *Cast includes:* Jacqueline Logan, Tyrone Power, Edward Burns, Montagu Love, Eddie Phillips, George Fawcett.

Assistant editor Edward Burns is wrongly accused of killing the son of newspaper owner Montagu Love, Burns's employer, in this contrived drama based on the story "The Travis Coup" by Arthur Stringer. Both Burns and Eddie Phillips, the owner's son, love Jacqueline Logan, who plans to elope with Burns. The editor had earlier helped clear Phillips of implications in a young woman's suicide. Just before the couple's elopement, Phillips lures Logan to a restaurant and a struggle ensues. She wounds Phillips, who later dies of blood poisoning. Burns is arrested and convicted of murder. His fiancée, ill from wandering in a storm and unaware of the trial, learns about her lover's dilemma at the last moment. She reaches the governor in time to prevent his execution and set him free.

684 OUT OF THE WRECK (1917), Par.

Dir. William Desmond Taylor; *Sc.* Gardner Hunting; *Cast includes:* Kathlyn Williams, William Clifford, William Conklin, Stella Razeto, William Wister Jefferson.

Newspaper reporter Stella Razeto and editor William Wister Jefferson threaten a political candidate with exposing his wife's hidden past unless he drops out of the race in this early domestic drama. William Conklin, who is running for a senate seat, learns from his two visitors that his wife had earlier been involved in a murder case in another city. Kathlyn Williams, Conklin's wife, enters and explains her tale by way of a series of flashbacks. It seems that she, as an orphan, was befriended by alcoholic William Clifford, whom she agrees to marry as a reward for his kindness. When his drinking problem results in their extreme poverty, he insists she turn to prostitution to raise money. He threatens her with a pistol which she then uses to defend herself. Her trial results in her acquittal, after which she engages in missionary work where she meets her present husband. Upon hearing her tragic tale, the two journalists decide not to publish the story.

685 OUT WITH THE TIDE (1928), Peerless.

Dir. Charles Hutchison; *Sc.* Elaine Towne; *Cast includes:* Dorothy Dwan, Cullen Landis, Crauford Kent, Mitchell Lewis, Ernest Hilliard, Sojin.

Suspected of murdering his girlfriend's father, newspaper reporter Cullen Landis escapes from the police in an effort to prove his innocence in this familiar drama. He leaves for Shanghai with Dorothy Dwan, the dead banker's daughter, where he believes the killer, known as "The Snake," is presently residing. The couple entrap him into revealing that he had been hired by the victim's partner. With this confession, Landis is able to exonerate himself from the charge of murder and convict the guilty party.

686 OUTSIDE THESE WALLS (1939), Col.

Dir. Ray McCarey; *Sc.* Harold Buchman; *Cast includes:* Michael Whalen, Dolores Costello, Virginia Weidler, Don Beddoe, Selmer Jackson, Mary Forbes.

Ex-convict Michael Whalen has problems finding a job after his release from prison in this absorbing rehabilitation drama. Whalen, who has run the prison newspaper, is turned down by the only paper in town when he seeks work. Undeterred, he buys a small printing press after receiving a loan from his sympathetic ex-warden who soon loses his position. Whalen uses his press to battle crooked politicians who are backed by the larger and more powerful town paper owned by Dolores Costello and her brother. The latter happens to be running for governor. The elderly ex-warden throws in his lot with Whalen who, with the support of civic-minded citizens, encourages the former warden to run for governor. Both end up as winners.

687 OVER THE HILL (1917), Pathé.

Dir. William Parke; *Sc.* Lois Zellner; *Cast includes:* Gladys Hulette, J. H. Gilmour, Dan Mason, William Parke Jr., Chester Barnett, Richard Thornton.

Gladys Hulette, who works for newspaper owner J. H. Gilmour, helps save his paper from losing advertisers because of its sensationalist policy in this light silent drama. She objects to the amoral principles of the owner's son, William Parke Jr., who is about to print a scandalous story involving a young woman whose father owns a large department store. Another reporter, Chester Barnett, also inveighs against the practice of yellow journalism. Hulette burns the story and smashes the type for the article. In return, the store owner begins to advertise in the paper, confirming to publisher Gilmour the ills of scandal and the rewards of tolerance. He fires his own son and promotes Barnett. The film, although often crude and didactic, became the forerunner of such hard-hitting newspaper dramas as *Five Star Final* (1931), starring Edward G. Robinson.

688 OVER 21 (1945), Col.

Dir. Charles Vidor; *Sc.* Sidney Buchman; *Cast includes:* Irene Dunne, Alexander Knox, Charles Coburn, Jeff Donnell, Loren Tindall, Lee Patrick.

Newspaper editor Alexander Knox seeks to gain information about the war by enrolling in the army's Officers' Candidate School—much to the annoyance of Irene Dunne, his otherwise patient wife—in this World War II comedy based on the play by Ruth Gordon. The editor, in his forties, finds the younger men stiff competition. Meanwhile his grouchy publisher, Charles Coburn, requests that he return to his former post on the paper. The plot also serves as a subtle plea for a better postwar world and as a rather biting satire on the life of army brass.

689 OVER-EXPOSED (1956), Col.

Dir. Lewis Seiler; *Sc.* James Gunn, Gil Orlovitz; *Cast includes:* Cleo Moore, Raymond Greenleaf, Richard Crenna, Isobel Elsom, James O'Rear, Donald Randolph.

Newspaper reporter Richard Crenna courts and eventually marries Cleo Moore, who rises from obscurity to a major commercial photographer in this little drama. First, she becomes acquainted with Raymond Greenleaf, a cameraman who indulges in excessive drinking while instructing her in his profession. Crenna arrives on the scene and wins her heart. Others who take an interest in Moore's progress include society matron Isobel Elsom and Broadway columnist James O'Rear.

690 PADDY O'HARA (1917), Triangle.

Dir. Walter Edwards; *Sc.* J. G. Hawks; *Cast includes:* William Desmond, Mary McIvor, Robert McKim, J. J. Dowling, Walt Whitman.

William Desmond portrays the title character, a dauntless star reporter who covers a Balkan conflict in this fairly exciting romantic action drama of the early silent period. He possesses a photograph of Mary McIvor, Count Ivan's niece, whom he eventually rescues following several complications concerning the military forces of both sides. To accomplish this, he marries her, with each agreeing that the union will end after they escape. He then places her name instead of that of his servant's on his passport. While Desmond is busy filing his story of the war, Count Carlos, a rival, kidnaps the young woman. Desmond returns to London where he is requested to appear at one of the Balkan embassies and is told that if he gives up his wife he will be rewarded handsomely. Angered at the crass offer of money, he rails at the proposition and declares his love for the young woman. His bride, stationed in a nearby room, overhears his burst of indignation and realizes that she has grown to love him. McIvor bolts from her room and confesses to Desmond that their marriage need not end here in London.

691 PAGAN LOVE (1920), Pathé.

Dir. Hugo Ballin; *Sc.* Hugo Ballin; *Cast includes:* Togo Yamamoto, Mabel Ballin, Rockliffe Fellowes, Charlie Fang, Nellie Fillmore.

Togo Yamamoto, a young Chinese who starts a Chinese newspaper in New York, falls in love with Mabel Ballin, a blind young woman, in this drama of racial prejudice based on the 1919 short story "The Honourable Gentleman" by Achmed Abdullah. Born of a Jewish father and an Irish mother, the woman has known no other romantic love and accepts Yamamoto's affection. Rockliffe Fellowes, a doctor and college friend of the young publisher, operates on Ballin and restores her eyesight. Upon seeing Yamamoto for the first time, she flees from his presence. He returns to his homeland heartbroken, and takes his own life in the hope of joining his only love someday in heaven.

Meanwhile Fellowes and his patient spend time together and fall in love. This was one of the earliest newspaper films to deal with the theme of racial prejudice.

692 PALS OF THE GOLDEN WEST (1952), Rep.
Dir. William Witney; *Sc.* Albert DeMond, Eric Taylor; *Cast includes:* Roy Rogers, Dale Evans, Estelita Rodriguez, Pinky Lee, Anthony Caruso, Roy Barcroft.

Newspaper reporter Dale Evans aggressively pursues U.S. Border Patrol trouble-shooter Roy Rogers in search of a scoop in this workaday western, the last in the Rogers series for Republic. Rogers has been assigned to prevent cattle infected with hoof-and-mouth disease from crossing the Mexican border. Hoodlum Anthony Caruso is smuggling the contaminated cattle into the U.S., while Roy Barcroft, his conspirator, handles matters in the States. One border patrolman is killed before Rogers brings the culprits to justice and Evans gets her story. Several earlier Rogers westerns included plots involving newspapers and journalists, including *Bad Man of Deadwood* (1941), *Don't Fence Me In* (1945) and *Home in Oklahoma* (1946).

693 PAN-AMERICANA (1945), RKO.
Dir. John D. Auer; *Sc.* Lawrence Kimble; *Cast includes:* Phillip Terry, Audrey Long, Eve Arden, Ernest Truex, Marc Cramer, Isabelita.

Editorial staff members of an American pictorial magazine journey south of the border in search of Latin-American talent in this contrived musical told chiefly in flashback. Phillip Terry heads the cast, which includes Robert Benchley, a staff member who narrates the entire adventure; Ernest Truex, who provides some comedy relief; and Audrey Long, whom Terry romances. One of the highlights the concoction showcases is a hot and steamy snake dance performed by the team of Harold and Lola.

694 PANIC ON THE AIR (1936), Col.
Dir. D. Ross Lederman; *Sc.* Harold Shumate; *Cast includes:* Lew Ayres, Florence Rice, Benny Baker, Edwin Maxwell, Charles Wilson, Wyrley Birch.

Affable sports announcer Lew Ayres assists innocent Florence Rice in the recovery of some ransom money paid out by her father in this often farfetched drama. She soon becomes drawn into the murder of a kidnapper's husband. Ayres, who prides himself on scooping fellow reporters and the police when it comes to sensational headline stories, helps her out of her predicament. Benny Baker, his assistant, provides the comedy relief. To add a sense of authenticity to the production, the film cleverly mixes footage from actual newsreels, including clips from World Series games.

695 THE PAPER (1994), U.
Dir. Ron Howard; *Sc.* David Koepp, Stephen Koepp; *Cast includes:* Michael Keaton, Glenn Close, Marisa Tomei, Randy Quaid, Robert Duvall, Jason Alexander.

A frenetic comedy drama about one day in the life of a New York daily tabloid newspaper, the film centers around city editor Michael Keaton, who seems almost overwhelmed by the job. He is in the midst of a personal and professional feud with Glenn Close, his managing editor whose haughtiness leads to her dislike by most of her co-workers. In addition, Keaton is bombarded by petty complaints of reporters and others as he tries to get the day's paper organized. Meanwhile, two personal problems press upon him. He has been offered a job with the *Sentinel,* a prestigious paper, with fewer hours, better pay and more prestige. His pregnant wife Marisa Tormei, a former reporter, goads him to accept the new position, but he turns it down. When two young African Americans are falsely accused of killing two white men, Keaton wants to use the front page to claim their innocence. But Close, a journalism school graduate who detests Keaton, who never went to college, opts for a story about a subway accident. "What if they're innocent?" Keaton asks her at a staff meeting. "We taint them today," she replies, "we make them look good on Saturday. Everybody's happy." Their chief, Robert Duvall, who is suffering from a cancerous prostate, stops their bickering and gives Keaton till 8:00 p.m. to get a second confirmation that the two suspects are being framed. When Keaton and his pal, columnist Randy Quaid, get this from a sympathetic cop, they rush back to the press room and Quaid pleads with Keaton, "Ain't you gonna say it? You gotta say it!" Keaton pauses for a moment, then blurts out one of the great clichés of the genre: "Stop the presses!" This is all done tongue-in-cheek. Close suddenly appears, overrides Keaton and opts to print the subway story. "We never got a story wrong," Quaid later reminds her, "until tonight." Close, upon reflection, then reverses her decision and the front page reads: "They Didn't Do It." Despite its efforts to touch upon such topics as ethics and how newspaper decisions are made, the film remains more entertaining than enlightening.

696 PAPER BULLETS (1941) see *Gangs, Inc.* (1941).

697 PAPER LION (1968), UA.

Dir. Alex March; *Sc.* Lawrence Roman; *Cast includes:* Alan Alda, Lauren Hutton, David Doyle, Ann Turkel, Sugar Ray Robinson, Frank Gifford, Vincent Lombardi.

Alan Alda portrays George Plimpton, the magazine writer who worked out with the Detroit Lions football team to learn first-hand about their experiences, in this quite funny comedy loosely based on Plimpton's book. The film, while picturing the players as good-natured and fun-loving, provides numerous scenes of the team in action. One particular scene in a scrimmage game depicts the formidable Roger Brown tackling Alda and transporting him and the ball to a touchdown. Meanwhile, Alda's editor, David Doyle, keeps after his writer to continue mingling with the team and its antics.

698 THE PARALLAX VIEW (1974), Par.

Dir. Alan J. Pakula; *Sc.* David Giler, Lorenzo Semple Jr.; *Cast includes:* Warren Beatty, Hume Cronyn, William Daniels, Paula Prentiss, Kelly Thordsen.

Warren Beatty, a smalltime cynical reporter, goes under cover to investigate the assassination of a senator in this suspenseful thriller based on Loren Singer's novel. The murder led to an official investigation with the following conclusion: "The committee wishes to emphasize that there is no evidence of any wider conspiracy." Although the deaths of several witnesses are attributed to accidental or natural causes, Beatty suspects otherwise. "Somebody is systematically knocking off witnesses to that assassination," he says to managing editor Hume Cronyn, who is himself murdered shortly afterward. Beatty learns about a shadowy organization called the Parallax Corporation and, assuming a pseudonym, he is soon contacted by one of its representatives. "If you qualify," the stranger announces, "we are prepared to offer you the most lucrative and rewarding work of your life." Beatty soon discovers that whoever is behind Parallax "is in the business of recruiting assassins." He then comes upon a plot to assassinate George Hammond (Jim Davis), another senator at a rally rehearsal. Hammond is killed and Beatty is suspected. As the police close in, he tries to escape through an open door near the roof and is shot dead by one of the members of Parallax. The film ends with another committee report which concludes: "There is no evidence of a conspiracy in the assassination of George Hammond." The slick, suspenseful drama, with its themes of political cynicism, paranoia and conspiracy, is reminiscent of John Frankenheimer's *The Manchurian Candidate* (1962).

699 PARIS INTERLUDE (1934), MGM.

Dir. Edwin Marin; *Sc.* Wells Root; *Cast*

includes: Madge Evans, Otto Kruger, Robert Young, Una Merkel, Ted Healy, Louise Henry.

The love life of newspaperman Otto Kruger, living and working in Paris, is interrupted when he is reassigned to the States and to Japan in this romantic drama based on the play *All Good Americans* by P. J. and Laura Perelman. Madge Evans, one of the group of Americans frequenting a local Parisian bar, is in love with Kruger. A fellow cub reporter, Robert Young, admires the veteran and likes Evans. When Kruger is called away and later reported killed, Young and Evans fall in love. Kruger unexpectedly returns and, after observing the change in relationships, gallantly rejects Evans when she offers to return to him. He gently sends her back to Young. Several American reporters in early sequences are depicted as heavy drinkers, a familiar screen image popularized and stereotyped in earlier newspaper films.

700 PARK ROW (1952), UA.

Dir. Samuel Fuller; *Sc.* Samuel Fuller; *Cast includes:* Gene Evans, Mary Welch, George O'Hanlon, Bela Kovacs, Herbert Heyes, J. M. Kerrigan.

Newspaper rivalries of New York in the 1880s serve as background for this hard-hitting, realistic low-budget drama. Gene Evans portrays Phineas Mitchell, who starts up *The New York Globe* to compete with *The Star.* Mitchell scoops the latter paper, controlled by Mary Welch, with Steve Brodie's famous leap from the Brooklyn Bridge. He then establishes a modern layout of his paper, with the help of the man who perfected the Linotype machine, Ottmar Mergenthaler. Mitchell brazenly woos his rival in the midst of their circulation war. Director Fuller's limited budget hampered his efforts to create a truly outstanding historical look back at an early and exciting period in American journalism. The 1992 musical *Newsies* also dealt with the early circulation wars in New York, albeit superficially.

701 THE PARSON AND THE OUTLAW (1957), Col.

Dir. Oliver Drake; *Sc.* Oliver Drake, John Mantley; *Cast includes:* Anthony Dexter, Sonny Tufts, Marie Windsor, Buddy Rogers, Jean Parker, Robert Lowery.

Billy the Kid (Anthony Dexter), after killing dozens of men, unsuccessfully seeks a peaceful life in this low-grade western. When his old pal, a parson (Buddy Rogers), is gunned down, Billy returns to his past from which, he realizes, there is little escape. He avenges his friend but pays with his own life. The only worthwhile element in this film is the portrayal of a woman editor (Marie Windsor) who runs the town newspaper. Several women played western frontier newspaper editors and reporters, including Ava Gardner in *Lone Star* (1952).

702 PARTNERS IN CRIME (1928), Par.

Dir. Frank Strayer; *Sc.* Grover Jones, Gilbert Pratt; *Cast includes:* Wallace Beery, Raymond Hatton, Mary Brian, William Powell, Jack Luden, Arthur Housman.

Bumbling detective Wallace Beery and newspaper reporter Raymond Hatton, who resembles a gangland boss, are the key figures in this satirical look at underworld dramas based on the novel by Kurt Steel. Their rivalry over a woman leads Beery to knock down a gang leader who resembles Hatton. A rival gang boss then hires Beery as his bodyguard. The remainder of the film deals with Beery and Hatton, who is searching for a good story, getting mixed up in a series of misadventures with the gangsters. The farce concludes with the pair's setting off a case of tear-gas bombs in the midst of a gun battle, resulting in gangsters, cops and innocents bursting out in crying fits. A barely recognizable remake appeared in 1937 with the same title, featuring Lynne Overman as the detective and Roscoe Karns as the reporter.

703 PARTNERS IN CRIME (1937), Par.

Dir. Ralph Murphy; Sc. Garnett Weston; Cast includes: Lynne Overman, Roscoe Karns, Muriel Hutchinson, Anthony Quinn, Inez Courtney, Lucien Littlefield.

Detective Lynne Overman and his pal, newspaper reporter Roscoe Karns, become involved in politics and a shakedown racket in this comedy drama, a sequel to their *Murder Goes to College*, released earlier in the year. Cynical sleuth Overman during a mayoralty race discovers a blackmailing plot and other shady activities aimed at victimizing the reform candidate. He takes time out to woo Muriel Hutchinson, a blonde deeply involved in the villainy; he then names his buddy as a substitute candidate to run on the independent ticket after effecting a couple of double-crosses. But the whole farfetched scheme backfires on Overman. The film, based on a novel by Kurt Steel, is a loose remake of the 1928 silent feature of the same title.

704 PASSAGE TO MARSEILLES (1944), WB.

Dir. Michael Curtiz; Sc. Casey Robinson, Jack Moffitt; Cast includes: Humphrey Bogart, Michele Morgan, Claude Rains, Sydney Greenstreet, Peter Lorre.

Humphrey Bogart portrays one of several escaped convicts from Devil's Island in this World War II drama based on Charles Nordhoff and James Norman Hall's tribute to the fighting Free French. All the escapees have vowed to fight for their native France against the Nazis. Bogart, a former journalist who opposed the pacifists and those who appeased Hitler, was falsely imprisoned in an attempt to silence him. The plot is told in a series of complex flashbacks by Claude Rains, a French liaison officer, to an American reporter who is writing a feature story on the Free French. Sydney Greenstreet, a career officer who despises the Republic, supports the Fascist regime of Marshal Petain. "The British," he claims, "will fight to the very last drop of French blood." The chief action takes place aboard a freighter which is seized by Greenstreet and a handful of mutineers. But the loyal French convicts, led by Bogart and Peter Lorre, retake the ship and shoot down a German plane. A typical patriotic drama of the period, the film is burdened by too many flashbacks and didactic speeches, some condemning isolationism and pacifism, others extolling the virtues of a free France and her allies.

705 THE PASSIONATE PILGRIM (1921), Par.

Dir. Robert G. Vignola; Sc. Donnah Darrell, George Dubois Proctor; Cast includes: Matt Moore, Mary Newcomb, Julia Swayne Gordon, Tom Guise, Frankie Mann, Claire Whitney.

Author Matt Moore suffers a string of adversities before he finally finds happiness in this social drama based on the 1919 novel *The Passionate Pilgrim* by Samuel Merwin. After serving a short prison sentence in which he protected his mother-in-law and following the death of his wife, Moore is hired as a reporter under a pseudonym. When he writes an exposé of an unscrupulous mayor, the politician uses his contacts with the paper to have Moore fired. A fellow journalist helps him get a job assisting Rubye de Remer, an invalid young woman whose family owns the newspaper from which Moore had recently been fired. She is engaged in writing a biography of her father. The couple soon fall in love. Inspired by his devotion and inspiration, she soon recovers from her illness. They then join forces in exposing the crooked mayor and his cohort, the trustee of her estate, both of whom have been plotting against her interests.

706 THE PAYOFF (1935), WB.

Dir. Robert Florey; Sc. George Bricker, Joel Sayre; Cast includes: James Dunn, Claire Dodd, Alan Dinehart, Patricia Ellis, Joseph Crehan, Frankie Darro.

One-time crack sports columnist James

Dunn has fallen under the wing of a corrupt wrestling promoter in this unrealistic, romanticized, but quite entertaining view of the world of journalism. The basic cause of Dunn's professional and personal downfall can be attributed to Claire Dodd, his two-timing wife, who falls for gambler Alan Dinehart. Dunn, who has played the dupe for his wife, is finally freed of her when she takes her own life after killing her lover. Fellow writer Patricia Ellis helps to rehabilitate Dunn, who soon realizes he has loved Ellis all along.

707 THE PAYOFF (1942), PRC.

Dir. Arthur Dreifuss; Sc. Edward Dein; Cast includes: Lee Tracy, Tom Brown, Tina Thayer, Evelyn Brent, Jack LaRue, Ian Keith.

Cynical star reporter Lee Tracy solves the mysterious murder of a special prosecutor in this familiar but engaging newspaper-crime drama. The dead man was about to present evidence against a major crime figure. Working to uncover the extent of racketeering in the city, Tracy, with the help of cub reporter Tom Brown, unmasks the murderer in a thrilling climactic sequence. The dynamic Tracy epitomized the wisecracking, fast-talking news hound, portraying this image in numerous dramas and comedies throughout the 1930s.

708 PEGGY OF THE SECRET SERVICE (1925), Davis.

Dir. J. P. McGowan; Sc. William Lester; Cast includes: Peggy O'Day, Eddie Phillips, William H. Ryno, Clarence L. Sherwood, Dan Peterson, Richard Neill.

Peggy O'Day portrays the title character who is assigned to help apprehend Abdullah, the Algerian sultan's brother, in this comedy action drama. Abdullah has absconded with the royal jewels of the sultan's harem and has settled somewhere in the U.S. Fortunately for our heroine, she is assisted by newspaper reporter Eddie Phillips. Following several complications, including O'Day's disguising herself as an Algerian woman, she follows the fugitive to his mountain lair. When she faces the most danger, Phillips rushes to her rescue. The sultan's brother is arrested and the valuable jewels are retrieved. The couple, however, are prevented from getting married when O'Day's superior assigns her to another case.

709 PEKING EXPRESS (1951), Par.

Dir. William Dieterle; Sc. John Meredyth Lucas; Cast includes: Joseph Cotten, Corinne Calvet, Edmund Gwenn, Marvin Miller, Benson Fong, Soo Yong.

Communist newspaper reporter Benson Fong, one of several passengers on the Peking Express, attacks the Church, the United Nations and the U.S. in this suspenseful cold war drama set chiefly aboard a train traveling between Shanghai and Peking. Other passengers include Joseph Cotten, a U.N. physician journeying to operate on a nationalist leader; adventuress Corinne Calvet, Cotten's former lover; Edmund Gwenn, a quiet priest; and black market racketeer Marvin Miller. Cotten and Gwenn engage Fong in a political debate. Miller suddenly takes control of the train with his bandits and holds the passengers hostage. His intent is to exchange them for his son who is being held prisoner by the underground. Following several complications, Miller is killed by his own wife and the prisoners escape. The film is a pale remake of the highly atmospheric and romanticized *Shanghai Express* (1932), with Marlene Dietrich and Clive Brook as the former lovers.

710 THE PELICAN BRIEF (1993), WB.

Dir. Alan J. Pakula; Sc. Alan J. Pakula; Cast includes: Julia Roberts, Denzel Washington, Sam Shepard, John Heard, Tony Goldwyn, James B. Sikking.

Desperate law student Julia Roberts contacts respected newspaper reporter Denzel Washington, promising him an explosive exposé if he will publish it and protect her life in this gripping drama based on the novel by John Grisham. Washington is already interested in a story involving the bizarre deaths of two Supreme Court justices. As a research project, Roberts innocently decides to investigate their backgrounds. She finds a remote case and writes a brief which she gives to Sam Shepard, her professor-lover, who is soon murdered. He had passed along her brief which falls into the hands of conspirators, representing both the government and business. It seems her report could implicate the White House. The conspirators order her death as well, but she manages to escape several attempts on her life before she tells all to the reporter. In the end, Washington brokers a deal which has Roberts protected in a life of comfort on some unknown resort island far away from the corruption.

711 THE PELL STREET MYSTERY (1924), Rayart.

Dir. Joseph Franz; Cast includes: George Larkin, Florence Stone, Frank Whitson, Ollie Kirby, Jack Richardson, Carl Silvera.

George Larkin, as a crime reporter, becomes entangled in a Chinatown murder mystery in this low-budget production. The film offers the usual fights and chases as Larkin tries to solve the murder of a wealthy man. Florence Stone, a pretty blonde he has met along the way, catches his attention. Chinatown, which conjures up assorted exotic images, was often used as the background for crime, romantic and newspaper films, including, among others, *Secrets of Wu Sin* (1932), *Captured in Chinatown* (1935) and *Mr. Wong in Chinatown* (1939).

712 PERFECT (1985), Col.

Dir. James Bridges; Sc. Aaron Latham, James Bridges; Cast includes: John Travolta, Jamie Lee Curtis, Anne De Salvo, Marilu Henner, Laraine Newman, Mathew Reed.

Reporter John Travolta plans to write a story titled "Looking for Mr. Goodbody," an exposé of health clubs, comparing them to sleazy singles bars, in this inept romantic drama based on articles written by Aaron Latham. He meets aerobics instructor Jamie Lee Curtis, who has earlier been duped by an unscrupulous reporter. Travolta seduces her but afterwards develops a tinge of conscience. He decides not to write about her but selects another young woman, Laraine Newman, who is generally known as the "most used piece of equipment in the health club." But Curtis, furious at his deception, deletes his story from his computer. "All you do is write little pieces about people getting into each other's pants!" she exclaims. "Everything I wrote in that story is true," he insists. "It's not the truth I'm worried about," Curtis retorts as she leaves his hotel room, "it's the tone—and hurting people and using them." Travolta submits a more positive description of the club which, without his knowledge, is quickly converted by his editor into a sensational exposé. Later, Travolta turns ethical during a government frame-up case and is jailed after standing on his first-amendment rights, an act which reconciles the lovers. The film paints an ambiguous picture of the world of journalism.

713 THE PERFECT SAP (1927), FN.

Dir. Howard Higgin; Cast includes: Ben Lyon, Virginia Lee Corbin, Lloyd Whitlock, Diana Kane, Byron Douglas, Christine Compton.

Ben Lyon portrays a wealthy young man who dreams of becoming a detective in this silent mystery comedy based on the play *Not Herbert, a Comedy of the Night in Four Acts* by Howard Irving Young. As Lyon and his servant are practicing the art of burglary, they meet George and Polly, two real crooks, whom Lyon befriends and takes to his city apartment. Following several complications, including Polly's exposure as a thief at a ball by Virginia Lee Corbin, Polly unmasks Corbin as the notorious crook while revealing her own identity as that of a journalist working under cover.

714 THE PERFECT SPECIMEN (1937), WB.

Dir. Michael Curtiz; *Sc.* Norman Reilly Raine, Lawrence Riley, Brewster Morse, Fritz Falkenstein; *Cast includes:* Errol Flynn, Joan Blondell, Hugh Herbert, Edward Everett Horton, Dick Foran, Beverly Roberts.

Determined reporter Joan Blondell invades the private, sedate world of insulated rich boy Errol Flynn—with unexpected results for both—in this comedy. Flynn has been raised by May Robson, his gruff old grandmother, who has prepared him to take over his large inheritance and the huge manufacturing business. Well educated but lacking in knowledge about the opposite sex and those in lower economic and social classes, he is about to be re-educated by the spirited Blondell. Several comical incidents follow, including a mix-up in which he is thought to have been kidnapped when he disappears temporarily to explore the wider society. His grandmother's personal secretary, the nervous and fidgety Edward Everett Horton, notifies the police and a national dragnet is set into motion. The couple, of course, fall in love.

715 PERILOUS HOLIDAY (1946), Col.

Dir. Edward H. Griffith; *Sc.* Roy Chanslor; *Cast includes:* Pat O'Brien, Ruth Warrick, Alan Hale, Edgar Buchanan, Audrey Long, Willard Robertson.

Treasury agent Pat O'Brien is assigned to Mexico to smash a counterfeit ring in this standard action drama based on a magazine serial by Robert Carson. Using his fists to battle the villains, led by Alan Hale and Edgar Buchanan, he is also quick with his quips, which add to the comic relief. Newspaper columnist Ruth Warrick, who provides the romantic interest for the agent, is determined to expose Hale, who earlier had murdered her father. Though O'Brien is not a newspaperman in this film, he had earlier played the crack reporter Hildy Johnson in *The Front Page* (1931), a sports writer in *Consolation Marriage* (1931), and a city editor in *Back in Circulation* (1937).

716 PERILOUS WATERS (1948), Mon.

Dir. Jack Bernhard; *Sc.* Richard Wormser, Francis Rosenwald; *Cast includes:* Don Castle, Audrey Long, Peggy Knudsen, Samuel S. Hinds, Gloria Holden, John Miljan.

A crusading newspaper publisher faces a multitude of problems in this fairly interesting drama set chiefly aboard his yacht bound for Mexico. Don Castle has been hired to kill Samuel S. Hinds, the publisher, who has been running an anti-gambling crusade. However, conscience-driven Castle, who has been paid $10,000 for the hit, is unable to fulfill the contract. Meanwhile John Miljan, swindler and blackmailer, is in collusion with Hinds's wife and tries to extract money from the publisher.

717 PERILS OF OUR GIRL REPORTERS (1916) serial, Mutual.

Dir. George W. Terwilliger; *Cast includes:* Helen Greene, Earl Metcalfe, Zena Keefe, William Turner.

Allegedly based on real incidents, each of the fifteen episodes in this serial deals with a female reporter's involvement in a separate case. The heroines, played by Helen Greene and Zena Keefe, help to expose counterfeiters, kidnappers and other enemies of society. The reporters often join forces with various government agencies, including the F.B.I.

718 PERSONAL SECRETARY (1938), U.

Dir. Otis Garrett; *Sc.* Betty Laidlaw, Robert Lively, Charles Grayson; *Cast includes:* William Gargan, Joy Hodges, Kay Linaker, Andy Devine, Ruth Donnelly, Samuel S. Hinds.

Rival columnists William Gargan and Joy Hodges team up after Hodges becomes the former's secretary in this drama. Gargan, a radio columnist, portrays a Broadway gossip columnist not unlike the legendary Walter Winchell. Hodges, seeking information about Gargan's date of birth which will help her to print his horoscope, hires out as his personal secretary. At one point, she inadvertently solves a murder when her dog licks a stamp and then collapses. Kay Linaker has been suspected of killing her husband. This clue allows Hodges to expose the real killer and his method of executing the murder of Linaker's playboy husband. Meanwhile, Gargan is occupied on the same case, but has been following a false trail.

719 THE PHANTOM CREEPS (1939) serial, U.

Dir. Ford Beebe, Saul A. Goodkind; *Sc.* George Plympton, Basil Dickey, Mildred Barish; *Cast includes:* Bela Lugosi, Robert Kent, Regis Toomey, Dorothy Arnold, Edward Van Sloan, Eddie Acuff.

Clashes among foreign agents, a mad scientist and members of the U.S. Secret Service form the basis of this 12-chapter serial that depends chiefly on the conventional trappings of this genre. Bela Lugosi portrays the villainous scientist Dr. Zorka, who invents a device that produces suspended animation and a belt that renders him invisible. Bent on controlling the world, he uses his inventions to gain his nefarious goals. Other devices Lugosi utilizes include a deadly mechanical spider and a giant-sized robot. Foreign spies want to get their hands on the crazed scientist's inventions, especially Edward Van Sloan, the chief of an international spy ring. He operates from an office called International Foreign Language, which he uses as a front for his subversive activities. Dorothy Arnold, as a snooping reporter in search of a scoop, becomes embroiled in much of the intrigue. Robert Kent, as a U.S. government agent, and Regis Toomey, as his loyal assistant, foil the plans of Lugosi and the spies, but not before the mad scientist knocks them unconscious several times, sabotages their plane, sends them in their car careening over a cliff and endangers their lives in other ways.

720 PHANTOM OF 42ND STREET (1945), PRC.

Dir. Albert Herman; *Sc.* Milton Raison; *Cast includes:* Dave O'Brien, Kay Eldridge, Alan Mowbray, Frank Jenks, Edythe Elliott, Jack Mulhall.

Stage star Kay Eldridge's wealthy uncle is murdered backstage on the opening night of her play in this familiar drama set chiefly in a theater. The main suspect is fellow stage star Alan Mowbray, who is the victim's brother and is known to need money. Newspaper drama critic Dave O'Brien combines his talents with police detective Jack Mulhall to solve the case by proving Mowbray's dresser, and not the star, is the culprit. Some critics remarked that a good title was ruined on a bad film.

721 THE PHANTOM SPEAKS (1945), Rep.

Dir. John English; *Sc.* John Butler; *Cast includes:* Richard Arlen, Stanley Ridges, Lynn Roberts, Tom Powers, Charlotte Wynters, Jonathan Hale.

Aggressive reporter Richard Arlen figures out that convicted murderer Tom Powers has returned from the dead to impose his will upon a scientist in this suspenseful drama that combines the crime genre with that of the supernatural. The scientist, played by Stanley Ridges, is unaware of the influence upon him. He carries out several murders ordered by Powers. At least one critic has singled out Powers's immortal line: "It's not hard to die. It's the coming back that's hard."

722 THE PHILADELPHIA STORY (1940), MGM.

Dir. George Cukor; *Sc.* Donald Ogden Stewart; *Cast includes:* Cary Grant, Katharine Hepburn, James Stewart, Ruth Hussey, John Howard, Roland Young.

Magazine reporter James Stewart and photographer Ruth Hussey invade the household of a family of eccentrics in this bright comedy based on the play by Philip Barry. The pair are assigned to cover the upcoming wedding of socialite Katharine Hepburn to stuffed-shirt John Howard. Stewart observes the rich in their habitat and comments sarcastically: "The prettiest sight in this fine, pretty world is the privileged class enjoying its privileges." Hepburn yearns for a normal romance that seems to have eluded her. Suddenly her ex-husband, Cary Grant, shows up and sparks begin to fly between the two former lovers. Fast-talking reporter Stewart finds himself involved when he begins to fall in love with Hepburn. Virginia Weidler, Hepburn's young precocious sister, does not approve of Howard, her sister's fiancé. At the local stable, Howard has trouble controlling his horse. "What's the matter, Betsy?" he says to the animal, trying to calm it down. "You act worried." "Maybe because his name is Jack," explains Weidler. After a night of drunken revelry involving Hepburn and Stewart, Howard breaks off his engagement. The film garnered two Academy Awards, Stewart for Best Actor, and Donald Ogden Stewart (no relation) for Best Screenplay. It was remade in 1956 as *High Society*, a musical starring Bing Crosby and Grace Kelly.

723 PICTURE SNATCHER
(1933), WB.

Dir. Lloyd Bacon; *Sc.* Allen Rivkin, P. J. Wolfson; *Cast includes:* James Cagney, Alice White, Ralph Bellamy, Patricia Ellis, Ralf Harolde, Robert E. O'Connor.

Former racketeer James Cagney switches professions when he becomes an unscrupulous photographer for a lewd New York newspaper in this fast-paced drama. Cagney faces professional as well as personal romantic problems. Alice White, a smart-talking rival reporter, pursues him as does a local gun moll. But his interests lie elsewhere—with Patricia Ellis, whose father, Robert E. O'Connor, is a tough police officer who has taken a shot at the unwelcome Cagney. O'Connor berates Cagney's job, remarking that his work is no better than his former line as hoodlum.

Ellis at one point agrees with her father's assessment of Cagney's job. "You're the lowest thing on a newspaper," she chides him, "a picture snatcher, stealing pictures from folks who are so down in the mouth they can't fight back—just a thug doing the same thing you always did." The photographer, with a hidden camera attached to his leg, takes an illegal picture in Sing Sing Prison of a woman about to be electrocuted. Both the police and his competitors circle his newspaper building to prevent him from printing it. But he succeeds in getting his scoop. As a result, O'Connor, in charge of security, is demoted. But Cagney later redeems himself by capturing on film a notorious killer in the act. Ralph Bellamy portrays a reporter who indulges in excessive drinking, a stereotyped image that occasionally recurs on screen.

724 PIRATES OF THE SKY
(1927), Pathé.

Dir. Charles Andrews; *Sc.* Elaine Wilmont; *Cast includes:* Charles Hutchison, Wanda Hawley, Crauford Kent, Jimmy Aubrey, Ben Walker.

Charles Hutchison, a criminologist working for the U.S. Secret Service, joins forces with reporter Wanda Hawley in investigating the disappearance of a mail plane in this action mystery. At one point when Hutchison goes to Hawley's rescue, they are both captured by members of a gang headed by Crauford Kent. While Hawley convinces the chief that she is in collusion with the gang, Hutchison escapes and, following some exciting aerial stunts, he and Hawley outwit the gang and help in their capture.

725 PLATINUM BLONDE
(1931), Col.

Dir. Frank Capra; *Sc.* Jo Swerling, Dorothy Howell, Robert Riskin; *Cast includes:* Robert Williams, Jean Harlow, Loretta Young, Louise Closser Hale, Donald Dillaway, Reginald Owen.

Crack newspaper reporter Robert Williams marries haughty blonde bombshell

Jean Harlow and soon becomes disillusioned with her and her family's upper-crust attitudes in this entertaining comedy. At first, he quits his newspaper job, but when he starts to write a play, with the help of reporter Loretta Young, he begins to realize how much he misses the world of journalism. Following an argument with his wife, he walks out on her and the family millions and returns to his fellow news hounds and his true love, Young. Several film critics considered the scenes in the newspaper office quite realistic—for a change. Director Capra later made the screwball comedy classic *It Happened One Night* (1934), with Clark Gable as a news hound and Claudette Colbert as a spoiled runaway socialite.

726 PLAYING IT WILD (1923), Vitagraph.

Dir. William Duncan; *Sc.* C. Graham Baker; *Cast includes:* William Duncan, Edith Johnson, Francis Powers, Dick La Reno, Frank Beal, Frank Woods.

A stranger who drifts into a cattle town uncovers corruption in the sheriff's office in this pleasant silent comedy drama. William Duncan portrays the drifter Jerry Hoskins who wins a local newspaper during a card game. As a lark, he decides to use his control of the press for the betterment of the community. Unexpectedly, he begins to discover some shadiness connected with the sheriff and plans to drive him from office. Edith Johnson, as the former editor's daughter, provides the romantic interest.

727 POLICE REPORTER (1928) serial, Artclass.

Dir. Jack Nelson; *Cast includes:* Walter Miller, Eugenia Gilbert.

Crime reporters became popular leading characters of both feature films and serials during the twenties and the early sound period of the thirties. The two leads of this ten-episode serial played in several other silent serials before appearing in this below-average entry.

728 THE POWER OF THE PRESS (1914), Klaw & Erlanger.

Cast includes: Lionel Barrymore, Alan Hale, William Russell, Betty Gray, Vivian Prescott, William Jefferson.

A villainous shipyard foreman, fired for incompetence and theft, frames his successor in this early silent drama. Taking advantage of the new foreman, who has had too much to drink, the villain plants stolen funds on him. The innocent man is fired in disgrace, but front-page newspaper stories appear that turn public opinion in the hero's favor.

729 THE POWER OF THE PRESS (1928), Col.

Dir. Frank Capra; *Sc.* Frederick A. Thompson, Sonya Levien; *Cast includes:* Douglas Fairbanks Jr., Jobyna Ralston, Edwards Davis, Mildred Harris, Philo McCullough, Wheeler Oakman.

Sturdy cub reporter Douglas Fairbanks Jr. helps Jobyna Ralston, the daughter of a mayoral candidate, who has been implicated in the murder of a district attorney, in this absorbing and fast-paced crime thriller. Together, they prove that the real guilty party is corrupt politician Wheeler Oakman, an opponent of mayoral candidate Edwards Davis, Ralston's father. Fairbanks gets his page one scoop and wins Ralston's love. Despite a handful of minor clichés, the production is helped by its restrained depiction of the newspaper world.

730 POWER OF THE PRESS (1943), Col.

Dir. Lew Landers; *Sc.* Robert D. Andrews; *Cast includes:* Otto Kruger, Lee Tracy, Guy Kibbee, Gloria Dickson, Victor Jory, Larry Parks.

Unscrupulous newspaper owner Otto Kruger goes too far when he commits murder in this farfetched newspaper-crime drama. Depicted in part as one who is disappointed in attaining political office, Kruger opts for power by associating with gangsters and killers. He has those who stand in his way murdered, including his partner. Managing editor Lee Tracy finally brings the law down on Kruger. Tracy specialized in newspaper yarns during the 1930s and 1940s. Kruger was not new to the world of journalism, Hollywood style. In *Scandal Sheet* (1940), for instance, he portrayed a depraved tabloid editor who was willing to commit murder to protect his illegitimate son.

731 POWERS THAT PREY (1918), American.

Dir. Henry King; *St.* Will M. Ritchey; *Cast includes:* Mary Miles Minter, Alan Forrest, Harvey Clark, Clarence Burton, Lucille Ward, Emma Kluge.

Mary Miles Minter, the stubborn daughter of a newspaper editor, takes over the operation of the press when her father is forced to leave town in this silly comedy. Although he orders her to put experienced city editor Alan Forrest in charge, she fires Forrest and takes full control. Minter finds herself embroiled in several misadventures, all resulting in problems for her and those involved with running the paper. When Forrest discovers the corrupt politician who had forced her father to leave is part of a crooked scheme involved in a city franchise, Minter publishes the story. This almost causes the politician to be lynched by an angry public, but her father returns and simply forces the politician to leave town.

732 A PRINCE OF INDIA (1914), Eclectic.

Dir. Leopold Wharton; *Cast includes:* M. O. Penn, Thurlow Bergen, Billy Mason, William Riley Hatch, Elsie Esmond.

Innocent young cub reporter Billy Mason comes into the possession of a valuable jewel stolen from Thurlow Bergen, an Oriental prince, in this drama based on the 1893 novel *The Prince of India* by Lew Wallace. Elsie Esmond is blackmailed by thief William Riley Hatch into helping him steal the famous diamond known as "The Kiss of Death." She persuades the prince to display it at a dinner party where the diamond accidentally falls into Mason's cuff. Following several complications, the prince and the reporter retrieve the diamond from Riley, who has taken it from Mason. The film ends in a thrilling trolley wreck.

733 THE PRINCESS OF PARK ROW (1917), Vitagraph.

Dir. Ashley Miller; *Sc.* A. Van Buren Powell; *Cast includes:* Mildred Manning, Wallace MacDonald, William Dunn, John Costello, Ann Brody.

Reporter Wallace MacDonald gets mixed up with royalty in this farfetched romantic comedy drama. MacDonald meets Mildred Manning, a princess from a European country in the United States accompanying her father, a prince, who is in the States on business. The reporter mistakes her for the prince's maid and takes her on a trip to Brooklyn's Coney Island. Following a series of complications and kidnappings, he learns the truth about her title and realizes the large chasm which separates their social backgrounds. But when the king rewards MacDonald with the title of Prince of Bellaria, the reporter agrees to marry the princess.

734 THE PRINTER'S DEVIL (1923), WB.

Dir. William Beaudine; *Sc.* Julien Josephson; *Cast includes:* Wesley Barry, Harry Myers, Kathryn McGuire, Louis King, George Pearce, Raymond Cannon.

Young printer's devil Wesley Barry helps to exonerate his friend, Harry Myers, from suspicion of bank theft in this slight comedy drama. At first, Barry persuades Myers to invest in a local newspaper where the latter's editorial incites the wrath of a banker. When bank robbers hit the bank, Myers becomes the chief suspect. However, Barry soon catches up to the culprits and Myers is cleared of all charges. Barry, a popular young actor during the silent period, was featured in several newspaper films, including *Go and Get It* (1920) and *The Fighting Cub* (1925).

735 PROTECTION (1929), Fox.

Dir. Benjamin Stoloff; Sc. Frederick Hazlitt Brennan; Cast includes: Dorothy Burgess, Robert Elliott, Paul Page, Ben Hewlett, Dorothy Ward, Joe Brown, Roy Stewart.

This minor action drama shows what can happen when corrupt public officials protect a gang of criminals. Bootleggers take over a newspaper hostile to their activities. When the gang buys into the paper, the managing editor leaves and revives a dying, rival daily. The gang leader then promotes reporter Paul Page to managing editor, but the latter resigns and joins his old boss after an exposé story is quashed. Together, the two crusaders, despite a hail of machine-gun bullets, expose the bootleggers and the highly placed city officials who have been protecting the racketeers.

736 PUBLIC ENEMIES (1942), Rep.

Dir. Albert S. Rogell; Sc. Edward T. Lowe, Lawrence Kimble; Cast includes: Phillip Terry, Wendy Barrie, Edgar Kennedy, William Frawley, Marc Lawrence, Nana Bryant.

Ambitious police reporter Phillip Terry and socialite Wendy Barrie help to smash a smuggling ring in this entertaining little newspaper-crime drama. At first Barrie, annoyed at the reporter, gets him fired from his job. Seeking reinstatement, Terry decides to investigate on his own the smuggling operations of a local gang. Later, regretting her actions, Barrie volunteers to help him gain evidence against the smugglers. Her snooping leads to her capture, but Terry and his pals rescue her. He then gets his old job back.

737 THE PUBLIC EYE (1992), U.

Dir. Howard Franklin; Sc. Howard Franklin; Cast includes: Joe Pesci, Richard Richle, Bryan Travis Smith, Max Brooks, Richard Schiff, Laura Ceron.

Freelance news photographer Joe Pesci agrees to help widowed café owner Barbara Hershey, who is threatened by a man claiming to be part owner in her business, in this complex romantic drama set during World War II. Pesci, who has the soul of an artist and had been friends with the widow's late husband, wanders the streets of the city capturing on film the fragile lives and loves of his subjects. He is enamored of Hershey's beauty, although photographers are barred from her posh Manhattan club. While investigating the intruder, who insists Hershey's husband had owed him a large sum of money, Pesci uncovers an illegal gasoline rationing scheme involving gang warfare and a major government figure. Pesci, who is portrayed as a "shabby little guy who sleeps in his clothes and eats meals out of a can," is a tragic romantic figure not unlike the lover on the poet Keats's urn, who can never attain his goal—in this case, his love of Hershey. Pesci's film noir world is one of back alleys and drenched, dark streets while Hershey's is that of Café Society, the name of her nightclub.

738 PUBLIC MENACE (1935), Col.

Dir. Erle C. Kenton; Sc. Ethel Hill, Lionel Houser; Cast includes: George Murphy, Jean Arthur, Douglas Dumbrille, George McKay, Robert Middlemass, Victor Kilian.

Reporter George Murphy is fired for neglecting his job in this routine melodrama, very similar in plot to that of *Atlantic Adventure*, released by the studio earlier the same month. In the present film, which is burdened with too many stereotyped characters, pretty ship manicurist Jean Arthur is the cause of Murphy's dismissal. He had been assigned to pursue gangster Douglas Dumbrille aboard a luxury liner. After marrying Arthur, he tracks down Dumbrille with the help of his bride.

739 PUPPY LOVE (1919), Par.

Dir. R. William Neill; Sc. Monte M. Katterjohn; Cast includes: Lila Lee, Charles Murray, Harold Goodwin, Helen

Dunbar, Lincoln Stedman, Josephine Crowell.

Newspaper reporter Harold Goodwin arranges to cover a story about old maids in a small town where his girlfriend has been sent by her parents in this harmless early comedy. Sixteen-year-old Lila Lee has been sent to live with her aunts after her parents discover she has fallen in love with Goodwin, the young son of a neighbor. Following a chain of complications involving the young reporter and an oversized suitor as well as a problem with the town's spinsters, Goodwin rescues the angry Lee from a spite marriage. The young couple reconcile their differences and are permitted to remain friends.

740 THE PURSUING VENGEANCE (1916), State Rights.

Dir. Martin Sabine; Cast includes: Sheldon Lewis, Jane Meredith, Henry Mortimer, Henry Cargill, Grace Hampton, Ernest Cossart.

Newspaper reporter Henry Mortimer solves a puzzling crime in this murder mystery based on the 1912 novel *The Mystery of the Boule Cabinet* by Burton Egbert Stevenson. An expert in fine furniture, after having a cabinet shipped from Paris, dies mysteriously. The police are perplexed, but the reporter eventually discovers that a notorious Parisian jewel thief has placed poison in the drawer of his cabinet, which is mistakenly sent to the expert. The thief had placed the deadly poison in the drawer to protect his cache of stolen jewels.

741 QUEEN OF BURLESQUE (1946), PRC.

Dir. Sam Newfield; Sc. David A. Lang; Cast includes: Evelyn Ankers, Carleton Young, Marian Martin, Craig Reynolds, Rose La Rose, Emory Parnell.

Burlesque entertainer Evelyn Ankers becomes the chief suspect, following a series of backstage murders at a burlesque theater, in this mild drama. Her boyfriend, energetic newspaper reporter Carleton Young, goes to her defense and tracks down the real killer. The production tends to exploit both its sexual content and conventional crime element. Between plot incidents, the camera focuses upon the stripping abilities of such artists as Rose La Rose, whose strutting down any runway can raise many an eyebrow. In addition, the dialogue was considered quite controversial for the period. The plot is very similar to that of *Lady of Burlesque* (1943), an earlier and much better production.

742 QUICK, BEFORE IT MELTS (1964), MGM.

Dir. Delbert Mann; Sc. Dale Wasserman; Cast includes: George Maharis, Robert Morse, Anjanette Comer, James Gregory, Howard St. John, Michael Constantine.

Magazine photographer George Maharis and shy writer Robert Morse are assigned to cover a scientific expedition to Antarctica in this goofy comedy based on the novel by Philip Benjamin. The pair are not there long before they earn the enmity of James Gregory, the admiral in charge of Little America, when they try to persuade Russian exchange scientist Michael Constantine to defect to the West. They then get woman-shy Gregory to agree to bring in a planeload of young women from New Zealand as a publicity stunt to promote Little America. Meanwhile, Maharis and Morse, with their oddball antics, face problems with rival correspondent Norman Fell and their pompous publisher Howard St. John in this remote region where a penguin delivers messages.

743 QUICK MONEY (1938), RKO.

Dir. Edward Killy; Sc. Arthur T. Horman, Franklin Coen, Bert Granet; Cast includes: Fred Stone, Gordon Jones, Dorothy Moore, Berton Churchill, Paul Guilfoyle, Harlan Briggs.

Conscientious and strong-willed small-town mayor Fred Stone and local reporter Gordon Jones foil a plot by big-city confidence men to swindle the community out of its school treasury in this brisk comedy drama. Greed overtakes most of the townspeople who see a quick way to make some money in the strangers' stock scheme. Only Stone and the reporter resist the charm of con men Berton Churchill and Paul Guilfoyle, who are soon identified as genuine crooks. Stone, facing a recall election, has to resort to legal and illegal tampering with the balloting to accomplish his goal of saving the community from its own avarice.

744 THE QUIET AMERICAN (1958), UA.

Dir. Joseph L. Mankiewicz; Sc. Joseph L. Mankiewicz; Cast includes: Audie Murphy, Michael Redgrave, Claude Dauphin, Giorgia Moll, Kerima, Bruce Cabot.

American civilian Audie Murphy in Vietnam in 1952 during the French Indo-China War clashes ideologically with embittered English correspondent Michael Redgrave in this talky drama based on Graham Greene's novel. Greene's attack on the U.S. and its botched foreign policy has been diluted by having Murphy portray a naive private citizen instead of an official who believes there is an alternative between Communism and French colonialism in that part of the world. Giorgia Moll, as Redgrave's Indochinese mistress, falls in love with the American who proposes to her. Redgrave, a cynical journalist who has lost his objectivity, sides with the Communists who use him as a dupe and ultimately betray him. Resentful of the lovers, the vindictive reporter is partially responsible for Murphy's death by informing the Communist guerrillas that Murphy is dealing in explosives. Limited action sequences concern guerrilla activities against the French forces. This was the first major American film to approach the political minefield of Vietnam.

745 THE QUITTERS (1934), First Division.

Dir. Richard Thorpe; St. Robert Ellis; Cast includes: Charles Grapewin, Emma Dunn, William Bakewell, Glen Boles, Barbara Weeks, Lafe McKee.

Small-town newspaper owner Charles Grapewin leaves his wife Emma Dunn to run the paper while he takes off to fulfill his wanderlust in this little comedy drama. Although she handles matters rather competently, William Bakewell, the older of two sons, persuades his mother to expand the paper to a city daily. Disaster results and the family is forced to place their home on the market. Glen Boles, the younger son, returns in time with an uncle's inheritance to help the family out of its financial predicament. A similar theme appeared in two other films, one released before the current comedy drama and the other after—both based on the same source: a 1908 play by Edith Ellis Furness. Wanderer Marc MacDermott in *Mary Jane's Pa* (1917) returns home to his family and helps his wife, who runs a small-town newspaper, defeat a politician. In a 1935 remake of the same play, and the same title, middle-aged newspaperman Guy Kibbee, following a ten-year period of wanderlust, returns home to his small town and his family.

746 RAINBOW RILEY (1926), FN.

Dir. Charles Hines; Sc. John W. Krafft; Cast includes: Johnny Hines, Brenda Bond, Bradley Barker, Dan Mason, John Hamilton, Harlan Knight.

Cub reporter Johnny Hines is assigned by his Louisville paper to cover a Kentucky feud in this slapstick comedy based on the 1910 play *The Cub* by Thompson Buchanan. Following a series of complications involving mixups, captures, escapes and chases, Hines is finally rescued by the state militia. But he manages to get his story and return to Louisville with a bride. The film is a remake of an earlier comedy titled *The Cub*, released in 1915 and also featuring Hines as the title character.

747 THE RANGER (1918), Kremer.

Dir. Bob Gray; St. W. H. Clifford; Cast

includes: Shorty Hamilton, Charles Arling, William Colvin, Mattie Connolly, Kenneth Nordyke.

Texas Ranger Shorty Hamilton is assigned to investigate a newspaper owner suspected as a German spy working near the Mexican border in this comedy drama set near the end of World War I. The Ranger gains the proper evidence against William Colvin, the German immigrant, and falls in love with Mattie Connolly, the man's daughter, who happens to be a grateful American citizen. Meanwhile, Hamilton captures Charles Arling, an outlaw who turns out to be the hero's father. When Hamilton's mother, a local heiress, had married the family gardener, the outraged family forced Arling, the husband, to leave the ranch. The outlaw learns that Hamilton is his son and turns himself in. But the Ranger arrives too late to save his father from the Vigilantes. The outlaw's letter asks Hamilton to turn the reward money over to the dead man's wife.

748 READY FOR LOVE (1934), Par.

Dir. Marion Gering; *Sc.* J. P. McEvoy, William Slavens McNutt; *Cast includes:* Ida Lupino, Richard Arlen, Marjorie Rambeau, Junior Durkin, Beulah Bondi, Esther Howard.

Boarding school runaway Ida Lupino journeys to her retired aunt's home where she soon faces small-town bigotry in this romantic drama based on the novel by Roy Flannagan. The town snobs treat the aunt, former actress Esther Howard, with scorn, and they soon turn on Lupino. The town decides to hold a witchcraft-type trial, including a ducking stool. Newspaperman Richard Arlen arrives in town to cover the story and soon falls in love with the young victim. As a result of his articles, Arlen is hired by a New York newspaper. Lupino also moves to the Big Apple.

749 READY TO WEAR (1994), Miramax.

Dir. Robert Altman; *Sc.* Robert Altman, Barbara Shulgasser; *Cast includes:* Kim Basinger, Stephen Rea, Tim Robbins, Julia Roberts, Sophia Loren, Marcello Mastroianni.

Director Robert Altman's devastating satire of the shallowness of the French fashion industry spills over to the news media and those reporters and editors who cover the fashion shows. When models on the runway display garments that leave them virtually nude, usually inattentive television journalist Kim Basinger is jolted by the display. Reporters Tim Robbins and Julia Roberts are given the same Paris hotel room when no others are available. Robbins, a sports reporter, is assigned by his editor to cover the murder of an important personality in the fashion world. He does so by repeating over the telephone the exact words he is hearing from a television newscaster currently reporting on the crime. The two journalists disregard the different fashion shows, virtually never leaving their hotel room. Meanwhile, manipulative fashion photographer Stephen Rea spreads his unctuous charm among Tracey Ullman, Sally Kellerman and Linda Hunt, three allegedly sophisticated and rival fashion magazine editors. Altman seems to equate the power of the merchants who control the fashion industry with the power of those who manage the media. As reporter Basinger says at one point, "Fashion, my friends, is war."

750 REBELLIOUS DAUGHTERS (1938), Times.

Dir. Jean Yarbrough; *Sc.* John W. Krafft; *Cast includes:* Marjorie Reynolds, Verna Hillie, Sheila Bromley, George Douglas, Dennis Moore, Oscar O'Shea.

A good-natured newspaper reporter assists a young woman driven from her home by callous parents in this lurid film that is part exploitation and part social drama. These rebellious daughters soon find themselves on the mean streets of a cold city where they are easy prey. Luckily for one such daughter, Marjorie Reynolds, a local reporter comes to her rescue just in time and she is reunited with her family. The low-budget production shows its inadequacies in its inferior script and camera work. Screenwriter John W. Krafft turned out numerous similar scripts, including *Death From a Distance* (1935), *House of Secrets* (1936), *I Am a Criminal* (1938) and *Convict's Code* (1939). The following year Columbia released *Missing Daughters*, which carried a similar theme but offered a more talented cast (Richard Arlen, Rochelle Hudson, Marian Marsh, Wade Boteler) and higher production values.

751 RED BARRY (1938) serial, U.

Dir. Ford Beebe, Alan James; *Sc.* Norman S. Hall, Ray Trampe; *Cast includes:* Larry Crabbe, Frances Robinson, Edna Sedgwick, Cyril Delevanti, Frank Lackteen, Wade Boteler.

A resourceful detective and a reporter battle against an international plot involving a conflict between Asians and Russians over a large munitions deal in this 13-episode serial. Larry "Buster" Crabbe, who had earlier gained popularity as the title character in the highly successful Flash Gordon serial, portrays Red Barry, an aggressive detective whose unorthodox ideas nettle his chief. Frances Robinson, as the reporter who has a crush on Barry, faces several dangerous moments as she helps him track down the foreign agents and some missing bonds worth $2 million. Edna Sedgwick, as a seductive entertainer, in reality is a spy for Soviet agents. Frank Lackteen portrays one of the chief villains Barry continually has to confront. Wade Boteler, as Barry's superior, frowns upon the publicity his underling gets as a result of Robinson's stories.

752 RED COURAGE (1921), U.

Dir. B. Reeves Eason; *Sc.* Harvey Gates; *Cast includes:* Hoot Gibson, Molly Malone, Joe Girard, William M. McCormick, Charles Newton, Arthur Hoyt.

Hoot Gibson portrays a good-natured cowboy who, in an effort to clean up a graft-ridden town, purchases the local newspaper in this interesting little western drama. Gibson has to battle the local mayor and his cronies. Some problems arise when he falls in love with the mayor's niece, but he manages to rid the town of corruption and win the heroine. The film, based on a story by Peter B. Kyne, is purported to be silent cowboy star Gibson's first full-length feature.

753 REDS (1981), Par.

Dir. Warren Beatty; *Sc.* Warren Beatty, Trevor Griffiths; *Cast includes:* Warren Beatty, Diane Keaton, Edward Herrmann, Jerzy Kosinski, Jack Nicholson, Paul Sorvino, Maureen Stapleton.

Warren Beatty portrays the American reporter-activist John Reed in this colorful and ambitious epic-like historical drama. Director and co-writer Beatty blends the romantic story of idealistic Reed and the emotionally liberated writer Louise Bryant (Diane Keaton) with the radical times of World War I and the Russian Revolution. Perhaps the plot dwells too heavily on the politics of the period rather than on the characters, but the production is impressive for its sweep and intelligence. Reed and Bryant's stormy romance crosses the lives of several prominent personalities, including socialist editor Max Eastman (Edward Herrmann), playwright Eugene O'Neill (Jack Nicholson) and radical feminist Emma Goldman (Maureen Stapleton). In one scene Nicholson challenges the lovers' commitment to their cause. "You and Jack have a lot of middle-class dreams for a couple of radicals," he comments to Keaton. "Women whose lives have been in danger over a long period," Rebecca West observes about Keaton's expensive clothes, "are always the most extravagant." The film, crowded with political and social events and personal incidents, depicts Reed in his many exploits including, among others, his journey to Russia where he experiences the birth of the Revolution, back to the States where he publishes these experiences in his book *Ten Days That Shook the World*, and his return to Russia where he asks the officials to sanction the American Communist Labor Party. During a trip to an Arab conference, he is wounded during an attack and dies. His body is sent to Russia for burial. The film won several Oscars, including one for Best Director.

754 THE REFORM CANDIDATE (1911), Edison.

Cast includes: Robert Brower, Charles Ogle, Harold Shaw, Miriam Nesbitt.

An electric railway financier tries to bribe a mayor in this short drama, but is foiled by reform candidate Harold Shaw and local reporter Miriam Nesbitt.

755 THE REPORTER ON THE CASE (1914), Selig.

Dir. Edward J. Le Saint; *Sc.* W. E. Wing; *Cast includes:* Stella Razeto, Guy Oliver.

756 THE RESURRECTION OF ZACHARY WHEELER (1971), Vidtronics.

Dir. Robert Wynn; *Sc.* Jay Simms, Tom Rolf; *Cast includes:* Leslie Nielsen, Bradford Dillman, James Daly, Angie Dickinson, Robert J. Wilke, Jack Carter.

Inquisitive television reporter Leslie Nielsen inadvertently comes across an auto accident involving a U.S. Senator, an incident that has strange ramifications, in this intriguing drama. Recognizing the Senator (Bradford Dillman), Nielsen follows the ambulance to the hospital only to be informed that no such person was admitted. Back at the station, Dillman's office phones to say he is on a fishing trip, leading the station to broadcast a retraction of Nielsen's original story. The determined reporter sets out to track down the Senator and soon discovers a remote medical outpost that performs complex transplants—a government project designed to blackmail international officials who are near death. The otherwise fascinating and labyrinthian plot is hampered by a facile ending.

757 THE RETURN OF DR. X (1939), WB.

Dir. Vincent Sherman; *Sc.* Lee Katz; *Cast includes:* Humphrey Bogart, Rosemary Lane, Wayne Morris, Dennis Morgan, John Litel, Huntz Hall.

Cub reporter Wayne Morris stumbles across a strange incident concerning a doctor of hematology whose experiments involve the killing of innocent victims in this fairly absorbing horror tale. When Morris tells his superior about his discovery, he is fired. But he decides to investigate further to corroborate his suspicions. He learns that crazed doctor John Litel, in seeking a substitute for blood, has resurrected fellow doctor Humphrey Bogart, who has died and been brought back to life to kill others to feed Litel's experiments. Morris eventually unravels all the macabre details with the help of young doctor Dennis Morgan. The film offers the typical blood-curdling elements horror fans seem to enjoy, including blood transfusions, bubbling laboratory apparatus, zombie-like creatures and an attempt by the mad scientist to perform some twisted surgery on a young woman (Rosemary Lane) who is fortunately rescued at the last moment.

758 THE RETURN OF JIMMY VALENTINE (1936), Rep.

Dir. Lewis D. Collins; *Sc.* Olive Cooper, John Natteford; *Cast includes:* Roger Pryor, Charlotte Henry, Robert Warwick, James Burtis, Edgar Kennedy, J. Carrol Naish.

A gangster follows a newspaper reporter who thinks he has found the legendary Jimmy Valentine in this offbeat drama based on a character created by O. Henry. Former silent screen star Robert Warwick, who had appeared in the silent drama *Alias Jimmy Valentine* in the early 1920s, portrays an elderly banker whom the reporter suspects of being the ex-safecracker. Roger Pryor, as the relentless reporter, is determined to win the cash reward offered by a newspaper to find the notorious cracksman. J. Carrol Naish, a vindictive gang leader, is interested in Valentine's whereabouts. Charlotte Henry, the former safecracker's pretty daughter, serves as the romantic interest for the reporter.

759 THE RETURN OF THE RIDDLE RIDER (1927) serial, U.

Dir. Robert F. Hill; *St.* Arthur B. Reeve, Fred J. McConnell; *Cast includes:* William Desmond, Lola Todd, Grace Cunard, Tom London, Henry Barrows.

Ten chapters make up this sequel to the 1924 serial. William Desmond, as the editor of a small western town newspaper, dons his crusading costume to reappear as the Riddle Rider, a champion of justice. In this serial he battles a mysterious villain who issues orders to his henchmen only by telephone.

760 THE RICHEST MAN IN TOWN (1941), Col.

Dir. Charles Barton; *Sc.* Fanya Foss, Jerry Sackheim; *Cast includes:* Frank Craven, Edgar Buchanan, Eileen O'Hearn, Roger Pryor, Tom Dugan, George McKay.

Two old-timers, friendly enemies in a small town, test their relations to each other in this minor, slow-paced comedy. Local newspaper publisher Edgar Buchanan prepares an obituary of his banker pal, Frank Craven, who objects strenuously to this move. Meanwhile some show promoters, including Roger Pryor, arrive in town, and Pryor falls in love with Eileen O'Hearn, the publisher's daughter.

761 THE RIDDLE RIDER (1924) serial, U.

Dir. William Craft; *Sc.* William E. Wing, A. H. Gooden, George Pyper; *Cast includes:* William Desmond, Eileen Sedgwick, Helen Holmes, Claude Payton, Ben Corbett, Hughie Mack.

This fifteen-chapter serial tells about a crusading editor of a small-town newspaper in the West who disguises himself as a mysterious figure so that he could battle the evil forces which have infiltrated the otherwise peaceful community. The title character, played by William Desmond, concentrates on defending a young heiress who is in danger of losing her land to thieves. A sequel titled *The Return of the Riddle Rider,* also starring Desmond, was released in 1927, attesting to the popularity of the original.

762 RIDERS OF THE DARK (1928), MGM.

Dir. Nick Grinde; *Sc.* W. S. Van Dyke; *Cast includes:* Tim McCoy, Dorothy Dwan, Rex Lease, Roy D'Arcy, Frank Currier, Bert Roach, Dick Sutherland.

Tim McCoy, as a lieutenant in the Texas Rangers, protects the freedom of the press in this action drama. When a newspaper editor is gunned down after fighting for law and order in his community, his son and daughter decide to carry on his work. Meanwhile, McCoy protects them from further threats. When the daughter shoots one of her father's killers in self-defense, McCoy takes her into custody to shield her from the lawless element in town. The gang storms the jail in an attempt to lynch her, but McCoy and the cavalry arrive in the nick of time.

763 RIDING ON AIR (1937), RKO.

Dir. Edward Sedgwick; *Sc.* Richard Flournoy, Richard Macaulay; *Cast includes:* Joe E. Brown, Guy Kibbee, Florence Rice, Vinton Haworth, Anthony Nace, Harlan Briggs.

Joe E. Brown portrays the managing editor of a small-town newspaper who is determined to capture a gang of aerial smugglers in this comedy based on a series of magazine stories by Richard Macaulay. The plot hinges on a newly developed device for controlling airplanes by way of a special radio beam. The smugglers would like to own such a device for their illegal purposes. In a highly unlikely but quite humorous air battle, Brown, armed only with a single shotgun, defeats the smugglers equipped with a machine gun. Florence Rice provides the romantic interest for Brown and his rival, Vinton Haworth. Guy Kibbee portrays a smooth stock manipulator hoping to fleece the local townspeople.

764 RIGHT CROSS (1950), MGM.

Dir. John Sturges; *Sc.* Charles Schnee; *Cast includes:* June Allyson, Dick Powell, Ricardo Montalban, Lionel Barrymore, Teresa Celli, Barry Kelley, Tom Powers.

Dick Powell portrays a sports writer in love with fight manager June Allyson, who is also loved by Mexican prizefighter Ricardo Montalban, in this interesting drama with the fight game as background. Allyson, following in the tradition of Lionel Barrymore, her crippled father, manages Montalban, who thinks he must maintain his championship status and acquire a lot of money to win her love. Meanwhile, Powell hangs around as Montalban's friend while competing with him for Allyson's affections. Knowing that his chances are practically nil, Powell hits the bottle and plays around with other women, including the unbilled Marilyn Monroe. Montalban at one point leaves Barrymore for another manager, invoking Allyson's anger. The climactic fight in the ring ends with Montalban's losing the match. In his dressing room he gets into an argument with Powell and breaks his right hand. The film ends with the lovers reconciling their differences and Powell tagging along with the pair as just a good friend. The drama touches briefly upon the topic of prejudice concerning the Mexican fighter. Other films which dealt more directly with this topic include, among others, *The Lawless* (1950), *My Man and I* (1952) and *Trial* (1954).

765 RISKY BUSINESS (1939), U.

Dir. Arthur Lubin; *Sc.* Charles Grayson; *Cast includes:* George Murphy, Eduardo Ciannelli, Dorothea Kent, Leon Ames, El Brendel, Richard Tucker.

Radio gossip columnist George Murphy portrays a glamorous hero who rescues the daughter of a movie producer in this offbeat drama, a remake of *Okay America,* released in 1932. The brash and outspoken Murphy, as a crusader who battles against the underworld, also rails against the head of a broadcasting company, tells off advertising agencies, and finally punches a radio big shot on the jaw. In a surprising and stark final sequence, Murphy, at his microphone, announces that he is about to expose secrets concerning a major gang. He then admits that he has just killed brutal crime czar Eduardo Ciannelli. Suddenly two other gangsters quietly slip into the radio studio and gun down the columnist in a hail of bullets.

766 ROAD GANG (1936), WB.

Dir. Louis King; *Sc.* Dalton Trumbo; *Cast includes:* Donald Woods, Carlyle Moore Jr., Kay Linaker, Harry Cording, Ed Chandler, Marc Lawrence.

Another exposé of a corrupt Southern penal institution, this grim drama set in a prison camp uses several graphic sequences to convey the sadistic treatment of prisoners by their brutal guards. In this particular entry a crusading managing editor of a local newspaper brings to light the political clique which not only allows these abuses to exist but contributes to them. The plot centers on two youths, Donald Woods and Carlyle Moore Jr., who undergo severe beatings by their vicious masters before these conditions are exposed. The studio turned out several topical features throughout the 1930s, including dramas like *White Bondage* (1937), which dealt with the exploitation of poor sharecroppers, and *The Black Legion,* also released in 1937, with Humphrey Bogart, which exposed a Ku Klux Klan-type of organization.

767 THE ROADHOUSE MURDER (1932), RKO.

Dir. J. Walter Ruben; *Sc.* J. Walter

Ruben; *Cast includes:* Eric Linden, Dorothy Jordan, Bruce Cabot, Phyllis Clare, Roscoe Ates, Purnell Pratt.

In this implausible but highly entertaining drama, cub reporter Eric Linden, who stumbles upon a double murder, devises a scheme in which he poses as the murderer. He then submits articles to his paper—with disastrous results. Circumstantial evidence soon engulfs him in a murder conviction when his plan—to have his girlfriend (Dorothy Jordan) present the necessary evidence to convict the real killer—fails. The proof is stolen, and Linden's trial ends with a verdict of guilty. However, he is rescued at the last moment when the real killer's girlfriend comes forward with the facts.

768 ROADHOUSE NIGHTS
(1930), Par.

Dir. Hobart Henley; *Sc.* Garrett Fort; *Cast includes:* Helen Morgan, Charles Ruggles, Fred Kohler, Jimmy Durante, Eddie Jackson, Lou Clayton, Fuller Mellish Jr.

This tale about bootleggers is more noteworthy for its non-dramatic elements than for its melodramatic plot. Popular singer Helen Morgan and the sensational comedy team of Clayton, Jackson and Durante provide much-needed bright spots in an otherwise lackluster script. Charles Ruggles, as a Chicago newspaper reporter posing as a drunk, is assigned to investigate the disappearance of a fellow journalist who had been looking into the activities of shady suburban police chief Fred Kohler, who is also the leader of a bootlegging gang. Kohler had murdered the missing reporter who had discovered the bootlegger's clandestine operations. Nightclub singer Helen Morgan kills the bootlegger, an act that ultimately saves Ruggles's life. Morgan's off-screen career later suffered as the result of her drinking problem; Jimmy Durante became a much-revered comedy star of radio, movies and television. The film was very loosely adapted from the 1928 novel *Red Harvest* by Dashiell Hammett.

769 ROAR OF THE PRESS
(1941), Mon.

Dir. Phil Rosen; *Sc.* Albert Duffy; *Cast includes:* Wallace Ford, Jean Parker, Jed Prouty, Suzanne Kaaren, Harlan Tucker, Robert Fraser.

Police reporter Wallace Ford investigates a double murder in this conventional newspaper-crime drama. Not surprisingly, he solves the crimes before his police rivals, but not before he and his wife are kidnapped by the bad boys. Some of Ford's hoodlum pals rescue the couple. A sense of realism prevails when the hardworking newsman is shown neglecting his recent bride for the sake of the big story.

770 ROGUES GALLERY
(1945), PRC.

Dir. Albert Herman; *Sc.* John T. Neville; *Cast includes:* Frank Jenks, Robin Raymond, H. B. Warner, Ray Walker, Davidson Clark, Bob Homans.

Reporter Robin Raymond and Frank Jenks, her cameraman, discover a murder in this routine newspaper-crime drama. The pair end up solving the case by proving that Ray Walker, a rival reporter, committed the murder in an elaborate scheme to steal inventor H. B. Warner's plans for a coveted device. The film is similar in style and tone to the studio's *Shake Hands With Murder*, released one year earlier.

771 ROMAN HOLIDAY
(1953), Par.

Dir. William Wyler; *Sc.* Ian McLellan Hunter, John Dighton; *Cast includes:* Gregory Peck, Audrey Hepburn, Eddie Albert, Hartley Power, Harcourt Williams.

American newspaper reporter Gregory Peck while in Rome throws away a perfectly good exclusive story in this delightful romantic comedy drama shot on location. The reason for his action involves attractive and charming princess Audrey Hepburn, who yearns for a normal life. She breaks away from her scheduled good will tour through Europe on behalf of her mythical country and takes a Roman holiday for herself. She meets Peck and he shows her some of the major sights of Rome as they begin to fall in love. "This is very unusual," Hepburn remarks in one scene. "I've never been alone with a man before—even with my dress on. With my dress off, it's most unusual." After several romantic and wonderful days and nights, as well as some unusual experiences, she returns to her duties as princess and he goes back to his profession, both realizing their own responsibilities. Hepburn's screen debut performance won her an Oscar. The film was remade as a television movie in 1987 but without the sparkle and charm of the original.

772 THE ROOTS OF HEAVEN (1958), TCF.

Dir. John Huston; Sc. Romain Gary, Patrick Leigh-Fermor; Cast includes: Errol Flynn, Juliette Greco, Trevor Howard, Eddie Albert, Orson Welles, Paul Lukas.

Eddie Albert, a photographer-correspondent working for an American news and photo syndicate, joins Trevor Howard, who is on a crusade in Africa to save the elephants, in this disappointing drama based on the novel by Romain Gary. Howard, in French Equatorial Africa, launches his campaign, believing big game hunters, ivory hunters and civilization in general are threatening the elephants with extinction. "Tens of thousands of elephants are killed in Africa each year," Trevor announces. "Soon we'll be alone on this earth with nothing else to destroy but ourselves." He sees the creatures as "all that's beautiful—all that's free." But he fails to interest people in signing his petition—except for two persons: alcoholic former British military officer Errol Flynn and prostitute Juliette Greco. Howard is rebuffed by a priest who says the Church is more concerned with men's souls; by the territorial governor who claims he has enough problems caring for the natives in his charge; and by a tribal leader who enlightens him to the fact that the natives don't want their land to remain a zoo. Following other disappointments, Howard finally wins the sympathy of Albert. But a poorly devised attack upon a group of hunters only brings swift retaliation, defeat and the death of Flynn. To avoid further government repression, Howard and his small band of survivors march off into the desert.

773 ROXIE HART (1942), TCF.

Dir. William A. Wellman; Sc. Nunnally Johnson; Cast includes: Ginger Rogers, Adolphe Menjou, George Montgomery, Lynne Overman, Nigel Bruce, Phil Silvers.

Newspaper reporter George Montgomery falls in love with notorious dancer Ginger Rogers, the title character who is on trial for murder, in this satirical look at the American court system, based on a play by Maurine Watkins. Rogers permits her trial to deteriorate into a farce, hoping the publicity will benefit her show business career. Adolphe Menjou, her canny shyster attorney, takes one look at her legs and comments, "Her best defense." He helps her to that end only because it also benefits him. "When you first brought me this case, did I ask is she innocent or is she guilty?" he asks. "All I said was, have you got five thousand dollars." Rogers is finally released after the court learns that George Chandler, her husband, is the murderer. Veteran character actor Lynne Overman, as a fellow reporter, adds his talent to the success of the production. In one scene the press gets a ribbing when sob sister Spring Byington questions notorious Two-Gun Gertie. "Would you tell us how you happened to take up banditry?" the reporter inquires. "Was it an inferiority complex or would you call yourself a thrill slayer?" The film, a remake of Chicago, released in 1928, which was later turned into a stage musical, opens with the following: "This picture is dedicated to all the beautiful women of the world who have shot their husbands full of holes out of pique."

774 THE RUMMY (1916), Triangle.

Dir. Paul Powell; Sc. Wilfred Lucas;

Cast includes: Wilfred Lucas, Pauline Starke, William H. Brown, James O'Shea, Harry Fisher, A. D. Sears.

A newspaper owner and crooked political boss is partially responsible for a rift in reporter Wilfred Lucas's marriage in this fairly absorbing early silent drama. Assigned to night court, Lucas rescues Pauline Starke, one of his neighbors, from a charge of soliciting and, convinced of her innocence, ends up marrying her. The star reporter, who has advanced to the city desk, one day discovers his wife in a compromising position with the paper's owner. He ejects her from their home and begins to drink heavily. Later, while trying to expose the latest political corruption, he uncovers proof of his own employer's involvement and subsequently learns that he was wrong in his earlier accusations about his wife. The couple then reconcile their differences.

775   S.O.S. COAST GUARD
(1937) serial, Rep.

Dir. William Witney, Alan James; *Sc.* Franklyn Adreon, Barry Shipman; *Cast includes:* Ralph Byrd, Bela Lugosi, Maxine Doyle, Herbert Rawlinson, Richard Alexander, Lee Ford.

A crazed inventor develops a highly destructive disintegrating gas that threatens the international community in this 12-chapter serial. U.S. Coast Guard Lieutenant Terry (Ralph Byrd) is assigned to prevent the inventor (Bela Lugosi) from selling his deadly gas to a foreign power. The gas can be placed in small bombs, ten of which have enough power to annihilate a major city. Maxine Doyle portrays a curious reporter who more often hinders than helps Byrd in his efforts to foil a host of agents working for the inventor. Made chiefly for the juvenile market, the serial offers the usual fast action, chases and plethora of fist fights. Ralph Byrd, who had played the title role in the serial *Dick Tracy* earlier that same year, was to be plagued by the identification. Unable to shake the Tracy image, he returned to make several more Tracy serials and a handful of feature films, chiefly as the square-jawed comic-strip detective.

776   TIDAL WAVE (1939), Rep.

Dir. John D. Auer; *Sc.* Maxwell Shane, Gordon Kahn; *Cast includes:* Ralph Byrd, George Barbier, Kay Sutton, Frank Jenks, Marc Lawrence, Dorothy Lee.

Newspaper reporter Ralph Byrd exposes a corrupt politician running for mayor in this offbeat drama. The plot soon takes second place to a trumped-up tidal wave presented over early television. The disaster sequences are presented by forces seeking to manipulate the public—and they almost succeed in this drama, an early depiction of the power of television on the masses. To fool the public, the perpetrators borrowed film clips of earlier scenes of destruction and presented them as current catastrophes. The drama *Invasion USA* (1952) depicted a similar plot and theme about the influence of television upon the public.

777   SABRE JET (1953), UA.

Dir. Louis King; *Sc.* Dale Eunson, Katherine Albert; *Cast includes:* Robert Stack, Coleen Gray, Richard Arlen, Julie Bishop, Leon Ames.

This Korean War drama focuses on the U.S. jet pilots who daily flew sorties over Korea from their bases in Japan, where their lonely wives anxiously awaited their return. Newspaper reporter Coleen Gray joins her husband Robert Stack at his air base so that she can write about the wives of these pilots. Squadron leader Stack, however, prefers that his wife stay at home instead of advancing her career as a journalist. Produced in the days before the feminist movement became popular, the film has Stack's wife accepting her husband's philosophy that her role as spouse is more important than her career. Meanwhile, the men go about their missions facing flack and other dangers above the skies of war-torn Korea. Richard Arlen plays the air base commander in this routine film.

778 SALOME, WHERE SHE DANCED (1945), U.

Dir. Charles Lamont, Erle C. Kenton; Sc. Laurence Stallings; Cast includes: Yvonne De Carlo, Rod Cameron, Walter Slezak, David Bruce, Albert Dekker, Marjorie Rambeau.

A sprawling historical drama that perhaps covers too much ground, the disappointing film begins with the American Civil War, shifts to the court intrigues of Europe and concludes in a bustling, young San Francisco. Yvonne De Carlo, an exotic European dancer, meets Rod Cameron, an American journalist for a weekly paper, who is in Berlin on assignment. He persuades her to spy for him and in behalf of her Austrian prince. Cameron wants her to gather information from Albert Dekker, an arrogant Prussian military official. She succeeds in her mission, but Dekker finds proof that implicates De Carlo as a spy working for Austria. Cameron helps De Carlo and her music teacher (J. Edward Romberg) escape to San Francisco where Cameron, who has fallen in love with her, intends to make her a star. De Carlo meets bandit David Bruce, who reminds her of her slain Austrian prince. He accompanies the party to San Francisco where they encounter wealthy Russian Walter Slezak and Chinese philosopher Abner Biberman, who has the best lines in this far-fetched drama. De Carlo learns that the vindictive Prussian officer has followed her to San Francisco. "Conspiring in their intrigue," the Asian sage says to Cameron, "she has incurred the highest penalty. Revenge in conceit is without mercy. And the blood of this girl is the only thing that will restore the honor of the count." However, Bruce ends Dekker's threat in a fencing duel in which the Prussian is killed.

779 SALVADOR (1986), Hemsdale.

Dir. Oliver Stone; Sc. Oliver Stone, Richard Boyle; Cast includes: James Woods, James Balushi, Michael Murphy, John Savage, Elpedia Carrillo, Tony Plana.

Journalist-photographer James Woods thinks he can profit from the turmoil of events during 1980-1981 in strife-torn El Salvador. A disorganized, obnoxious cameraman fired from his last job, he continually borrows money, owes favors to others, and lies his way into and out of situations. He journeys south by car with his buddy James Belushi, promising him women, booze and drugs. "If I can get some good combat shots for A. P., I can make some money," he rationalizes. When they reach the ravaged land, they are arrested. Woods saves himself and Belushi by appealing to an infantry colonel whom Woods had once given good press coverage. The more abuses he experiences on the part of the military government, the deeper he becomes involved in the people's revolution. He teams up with John Savage, another photographer, and leads him to El Playon, a dump site for numerous victims of the infamous "death squads." "You gotta get close to get the truth," Savage says as he takes close-ups of the corpses. "If you get too close, you die." This foreshadows Savage's own death while photographing government planes strafing and bombing a village. Woods, in his aimless wanderings, meets indecisive American ambassador Michael Murphy, who tries to sum up his frustrations with this Central American country: "A pathological killer on the right, God knows what on the left, and a gutless middle." But Woods does not allow the ambassador, who opts for the present military dictator, to escape that easily. "You'll run with him because he's anti-Moscow," Woods charges. "You let them close down the universities, you let them wipe out the best minds in the country ... you let them wipe out the Catholic Church, and you let them do it all because they aren't Communists." "Whatever mistakes we make down here," Murphy replies defensively, "the alternative would be ten times worse." Woods leaves the country in frustration, smuggling out incriminating pictures of the brutal regime taken by Savage before his demise. They include the callous slaying of a priest and the brutal rape and murder of four American nuns. But when the revolutionaries occupy a town after a fiercely fought battle, they begin to execute their prisoners in the same way as their adversaries. An epilogue on the screen announces: "Salvador continues to be one of the largest recipients of U.S. military aid in the world."

780 THE SAN FRANCISCO STORY (1952), WB.

Dir. Robert Parrish; *Sc.* D. D. Beauchamp; *Cast includes:* Joel McCrea, Yvonne De Carlo, Sidney Blackmer, Richard Erdman, Florence Bates, Onslow Stevens.

Crusading newspaper editor Onslow Stevens persuades wealthy miner Joel McCrea to join his vigilantes to battle the forces of corruption in San Francisco in this robust historical action drama set in the 1850s. Political leader Sidney Blackmer, who controls the vice and crime of the bustling city, sends his girlfriend Yvonne De Carlo to spy on McCrea. The couple soon fall in love. Following several complications, McCrea pretends to join Blackmer's minions as a means of helping the editor. The film ends with a shootout between McCrea and the corrupt and overly ambitious politician.

781 SAY, YOUNG FELLOW! (1918), Artcraft.

Dir. Joseph Henabery; *Sc.* Joseph Henabery; *Cast includes:* Douglas Fairbanks, Marjorie Daw, Frank Campeau, Edythe Chapman, James Neill, Ernest Butterworth.

When an experienced news hound fails to gain an interview with a Wall Street millionaire, cub reporter Douglas Fairbanks takes over and succeeds in this early silent comedy. Relying on his athletic and acrobatic abilities and his aggressiveness, Fairbanks climbs and leaps his way into the wealthy man's presence. Then, pointing a gun at his victim, he extracts an interview revealing how the man made one million dollars in the stock market in one day. The millionaire, impressed with the reporter's charm and energy, offers him a job and an opportunity to make some big bucks, but Fairbanks rejects the proposal, replying that his first loyalty is to his paper.

782 SCANDAL FOR SALE (1932), U.

Dir. Russell Mack; *Sc.* Ralph Graves; *Cast includes:* Charles Bickford, Rose Hobart, Pat O'Brien, Claudia Dell, J. Farrell MacDonald, Berton Churchill, Glenda Farrell.

Hard-boiled big-city editor Charles Bickford is willing to indulge in sensational, yellow journalism to increase newspaper circulation in this chiefly bland and unrealistic drama based on the novel *Hot News* by Emile Gauvreau, a former newspaper editor. Tempted by the promise of a $25,000 reward offered by publisher Berton Churchill if the editor succeeds, Bickford begins to plant phony stories in the paper. Meanwhile, he discovers that Pat O'Brien, one of his ace reporters, is having an affair with Rose Hobart, his neglected wife. He assigns O'Brien to cover a trans-Atlantic flight which ends in the reporter's death. Hobart blames her husband for O'Brien's death and decides to leave him. But Bickford promises to reform if they return to their small town where they had been happy leading a simpler life. The film underplays the topic suggested in the title and skirts around the cynical world of journalism, both of which were more strongly developed in the original novel and other films of the period, such as the hard-hitting *Five Star Final* (1931).

783 SCANDAL INCORPORATED (1956), Rep.

Dir. Edward Mann; *Sc.* Milton Mann; *Cast includes:* Robert Hutton, Paul Richards, Claire Kelly, Patricia Wright, Robert Knapp, Havis Davenport.

Robert Hutton portrays a movie star who is wrongly accused of killing a reporter in this banal exposé of scandal magazines. The deceased, an unscrupulous writer, had soiled Hutton's reputation. Hutton, under suspicion, loses his contract. Attorney Paul Richards finally clears the actor's name.

784 SCANDAL SHEET (1931), Par.
Dir. John Cromwell; Sc. Vincent Lawrence, Max Marcin; Cast includes: George Bancroft, Clive Brook, Kay Francis, Gilbert Emery, Lucien Littlefield, Regis Toomey.

George Bancroft, the ruthless managing editor of a scandal sheet, applies his muckraking skills to his personal life when he exposes his wife's affair with wealthy Clive Brook in this overly produced and acted drama. When asked why he is willing to print any sordid story, Bancroft quickly replies, "That's my identity." On the evening that Kay Francis, his wife, has planned to elope with Brook, the editor writes the introduction to the story himself. He then proceeds to murder his rival. Bancroft ends up behind bars where he works at editing the prison newspaper with the same gusto he poured into his former paper. At least one critic found the newspaper background very unrealistic. The plot supposedly was loosely based on incidents in the life of Charles Chapin, who had been an editor of the *New York Post* and who had died in Sing Sing.

785 SCANDAL SHEET (1940), Col.
Dir. Nick Grinde; Sc. Joseph Carole; Cast includes: Otto Kruger, Edward Norris, Ona Munson, Nedda Harrigan, John Dilson, Don Beddoe.

Depraved tabloid editor Otto Kruger is willing to commit murder to protect his illegitimate son in this contrived melodrama. Edward Norris, as the "love child" of this tale and a reporter on a competitive newspaper, is about to expose his real parents in connection with a murder he is investigating. Norris does not know that Kruger is his real father. Kruger committed the murder to protect his son from scandal.

786 SCANDAL SHEET (1952), Col.
Dir. Phil Karlson; Sc. Ted Sherdeman, Eugene Ling, James Poe; Cast includes: John Derek, Donna Reed, Broderick Crawford, Rosemary DeCamp, Henry O'Neill, Henry Morgan.

Ambitious editor Broderick Crawford, who successfully converts a respectable New York newspaper into a malicious scandal sheet, is the subject of a murder investigation in this newspaper-crime drama based on the novel *The Dark Page* by Samuel Fuller. When his wife whom he had deserted years earlier tries to blackmail him, Broderick in a rage kills her. Reporter John Derek, to impress Broderick, his boss, investigates and learns the truth about his employer. Broderick, who has followed Derek, appears with gun in hand and threatens Derek and his girlfriend, Donna Reed. But the police arrive in time and kill Broderick in a gunfight. Novelist Fuller directed and wrote the screen play for several interesting dramas, including *Park Row,* released the same year and which presented an historical look at the early days of New York newspaper rivalries.

787 SCANDALOUS (1984), Orion.
Dir. Rob Cohen; Sc. Rob Cohen, John Byrum; Cast includes: Robert Hays, John Gielgud, Pamela Stephenson, Jim Dale, M. Emmet Walsh, Nancy Wood.

Popular television newscaster Robert Hays dreams of gaining recognition as a hard news ace reporter in this failed sophisticated romantic comedy. To turn his dream into reality, he decides to expose what he thinks is a spy conspiracy aboard a flight to London. The plot involves the attractive Pamela Stephenson, who is an associate of the eccentric John Gielgud. "You belong to an endangered species," she says to Hays. "You've got a good heart." Later, she is quick to help frame the reporter for murder. Hays is soon embroiled in the murder of his wife, with Scotland Yard inspector Jim Dale making things rough on Hays—and the audience—as all learn that his original suspects are simply a covey of con artists. Gielgud even tries to blackmail Hays. "Just give me the money, my dear boy," he insists, "and let's be done with this nonsense."

788 SCARED STIFF (1945), Par.

Dir. Frank McDonald; *Sc.* Geoffrey Homes, Maxwell Shane; *Cast includes:* Jack Haley, Ann Savage, Barton MacLane, Veda Ann Borg, Arthur Aylesworth, George E. Stone.

Bumbling reporter Jack Haley, a former weak-willed chess player, inadvertently stumbles across a murder and becomes the chief suspect in this lightly entertaining comedy drama. Assigned to cover a wine festival, Haley ends up at the wrong address. While on the bus, another passenger is murdered and Haley is suspect. It just so happens that his girlfriend, Ann Savage, is aboard the same bus. At a nearby inn, the passengers await the arrival of a local sheriff. Following a string of complications, including a coveted set of valuable chess pieces, an escaped convict and a climactic chase, Haley manages to capture the culprit—Barton MacLane. The gangster had stolen the chess set and sold it to the twin brothers who own the inn. Now in desperate need of money to help him in his escape, the hoodlum wants the pieces back. The film is sometimes listed under the title *Treasure of Fear.* Haley portrayed a similar character in other films, including *F-Man* (1936) and *One Body Too Many* (1944).

789 SCARED TO DEATH (1947), Screen Guild.

Dir. Christy Cabanne; *Sc.* W. J. Abbott; *Cast includes:* Bela Lugosi, Douglas Fowley, Joyce Compton, George Zucco, Nat Pendleton, Roland Varno.

A flawed mystery told in flashback from the viewpoint of a corpse, the film offers little suspense or interest, despite the presence of Bela Lugosi, who is here accompanied by a dwarf. The entire plot takes place in a sanitarium. Newspaper reporter Douglas Fowley is virtually ineffectual in his investigation of the mystery. The title reveals the mystery of how young Molly Lamont is killed without a mark on her body. Nat Pendleton provides some comedy relief. The film was shot in Cinecolor, an inexpensive process popular in the 1940s. *Sunset Boulevard* (1950), starring Gloria Swanson and William Holden, also used a corpse and flashbacks to unfold its tale.

790 SCAREHEADS (1931), Capital.

Dir. Noel Mason; *Cast includes:* Richard Talmadge, Gareth Hughes, Jacqueline Wells, Joseph Girard, Virginia True Boardman, King Baggot.

Richard Talmadge portrays a reporter who is framed for murder after he supports the wrong mayoral candidate in this inept action drama. Talmadge, who specialized in acrobatic stunts in his films, escapes from prison and proves his innocence in this overly familiar plot.

791 THE SCARLET STREAK (1926) serial, U.

Dir. Henry MacRae; *Cast includes:* Jack Daugherty, Lola Todd, Virginia Ainsworth, Albert J. Smith, Al Prisco.

Jack Daugherty portrays a reporter who volunteers to help heroine Lola Todd in this ten-episode serial based on the story "Dangers of the Deep" by Leigh Jacobson. Todd and her inventor father have become targets of an arch-villain bent on stealing the inventor's latest invention. Todd's father has produced a terrible, deadly weapon so powerful in its destructive force that even he fears it. Following several kidnappings, escapes, car chases and fights, the master criminal and his gang are rounded up and the weapon is destroyed.

792 THE SCARLET TRAIL (1918), State Rights.

Dir. John S. Lawrence; *Sc.* John S.

Lawrence; *Cast includes:* Beth Ivins, Vincent Coleman, Margaret Blanc, John Costello.

A newspaper exposé of quacks who sell cures for venereal diseases causes complications for two families in this early silent social problem drama based on the 1918 booklet "Don't Take a Chance" by Charles L. Robinson. Vincent Coleman, a young man about to marry Beth Ivins, is rejected by the young woman's father who learns that the prospective groom's father has been listed in a newspaper's exposé as one who sells patent medicine for venereal disease. Coleman's father tries to bribe the reformer to retract the news stories about him, but the woman refuses. He and his cohorts then try to discredit her by charging her ideas on sexual hygiene are morally dangerous to young people. Coleman in disgust leaves home when he discovers the news story about his father is true and joins the army. During his visit to the medical examiner he learns he is unfit for service. His blood is tainted because of hereditary factors. Unable to marry, he returns home, writes a scathing letter condemning his father and takes his own life. Other scenes depict how venereal disease leads to blind and crippled children—a result of careless or ignorant parents or those who have inherited the condition. The booklet, which was the source of the screenplay, was published by the Social Hygiene Division of the American Defense Society, and was distributed by the Y.M.C.A. to members of the army and navy.

793 SCATTERGOOD SURVIVES A MURDER (1942), RKO.

Dir. Christy Cabanne; *Sc.* Michael Simmons; *Cast includes:* Guy Kibbee, John Archer, Margaret Hayes, Wallace Ford, Spencer Charters, John Miljan.

Guy Kibbee, as the title character and Coldriver's leading citizen, gives up store keeping for detective work in this village mystery, the last entry in the unsuccessful Scattergood Baines series. The homey philosopher investigates the mysterious deaths of two spinsters and determines they were murdered. It seems they left their fortune to a house cat. Also interested in the case are local newsman John Archer and metropolitan reporter Margaret Hayes, both of whom become romantically involved. Baines eventually proves the culprit is Wallace Ford. A different distributor later reissued the film as *Catspaw Murder Mystery.* Another entry in the series, *Scattergood Rides High,* was released earlier in 1942.

794 SCHIZOID (1980), Cannon.

Dir. David Paulsen; *Sc.* David Paulsen; *Cast includes:* Klaus Kinski, Mariana Hill, Craig Wasson, Donna Wilkes, Richard Herd, Christopher Lloyd.

Mariana Hill, portraying an advice-to-the-lovelorn columnist, receives several threatening letters which eventually lead her to believe that the eccentric psychiatrist Klaus Kinski is brutally slaying his own patients in this generally disappointing horror film. Kinski plays a menacing figure, a voyeur who spies on his own daughter, Donna Wilkes, while she showers, and a psychiatrist who engages in sex with his patients. Punctuating the plot are several graphic and predictable murders of young women, all patients of Kinski, who are done in by a psychopath using a pair of scissors. However, the element of horror, although intended by this sometimes eerie film, is generally missing.

795 A SCREAM IN THE DARK (1943), Rep.

Dir. George Sherman; *Sc.* Gerald Schnitzer, Anthony Coldeway; *Cast includes:* Robert Lowery, Marie McDonald, Edward Brophy, Wally Vernon, Hobart Cavanaugh, Jack LaRue.

Police reporter Robert Lowery is bent on solving a series of gruesome murders in which the victims are killed with a sharp-tipped umbrella in this intriguing mystery based on the novel *The Morgue Is Always Open* by Jerome Odlum. Following each of these strange deaths, Elizabeth Russell, as the wife of each victim, suddenly appears to collect her husband's life insurance.

796 SCREAMING MIMI (1958), Col.

Dir. Gerd Oswald; Sc. Robert Blees; Cast includes: Anita Ekberg, Harry Townes, Phil Carey, Linda Cherney, Romney Brent, Alan Gifford.

When stripper Anita Ekberg is attacked in her shower by a knife-wielding freak, local journalist Phil Carey decides to investigate the incident in this psychological thriller based on a novel by Frederick Brown. Carey connects the attack to several previous cases, all of which are suspiciously related. Meanwhile Ekberg, seeking to get help concerning her horrific experience, becomes the patient of psychiatrist Harry Townes. The shower attack anticipates the more memorable and classic scene in Hitchcock's *Psycho* (1960).

797 THE SEA GYPSIES (1978), WB.

Dir. Stewart Rafill; Sc. Stewart Rafill; Cast includes: Robert Logan, Mikki Jamison-Olsen, Heather Rattray, Cjon Damitri Patterson, Shannon Saylor.

Magazine journalist Mikki Jamison-Olsen, assigned to cover a sea journey to Jamaica, finds the trip filled with unexpected love and adventure in this delightful family drama. Robert Logan is prepared to set sail with his two daughters, Heather Rattray and Shannon Saylor, but when he meets the reporter from the magazine which is helping to finance his journey, he balks. He does not want a woman aboard. However, a phone call to the publisher persuades him to accept her presence. Logan and the reporter, of course, end up falling in love after his vessel is destroyed and the small group find themselves shipwrecked on an uncharted island. In addition to their problems, Cjon Damitri Patterson, a small boy, has stowed away aboard with them. The island provides the castaways with plenty of adventures and a few perils before they build a small sailboat for their escape.

798 SEALED LIPS (1941), U.

Dir. George Waggner; Sc. George Waggner; Cast includes: William Gargan, June Clyde, John Litel, Anne Nagel, Mary Gordon, Ralf Harolde.

Detective William Gargan foils a plot by a gangster in this above-average low-budget cops-and-robbers drama. The hoodlum, John Litel, plans to use a double to take his place in prison while he carries on his business-as-usual illegal activities. June Clyde portrays the ever-present reporter who is so familiar to this genre.

799 THE SEARCHING WIND (1946), Par.

Dir. William Dieterle; Sc. Lillian Hellman; Cast includes: Robert Young, Sylvia Sidney, Ann Richards, Dudley Digges, Dick York, Albert Basserman.

Based on Lillian Hellman's stage play about the dangers of not heeding the lessons of past wars, the film depicts the story of an indecisive American diplomat who fails to comprehend the significance of events that have occurred between the two world wars. Robert Young portrays the diplomat who misinterprets the rise of fascism in Italy as well as the spread of Nazism in Germany. He marries the wrong woman (Ann Richards) whose social ties are with the corrupt and arrogant of Europe while his true love, an idealistic journalist (Sylvia Sidney), still carries a torch for him. The wiser and more politically savvy of the two, Sidney berates Young for failing to recognize the dangers of the fascist and Nazi regimes. "You could go home and tell the truth," she suggests as Mussolini gains power. "I can't take sides," Young replies. "Whenever people talk about taking sides," she returns, "they've already taken one." Dudley Digges, Young's father-in-law and former newspaper publisher, provides some comedy relief. Upon seeing Young storing his records away in cartons, Digges cracks, "Why should a man want to preserve his mistakes?" Again, later, he quips about going to the opera. "I hate the opera," he grouses. "There's something insane about people opening their mouths very wide." Douglas Dick, as Young's war-wounded son, symbolizes the next generation that must reject the failed values of the past. The literate screenplay, also written by Hellman, provides a fascinating look into the world of Europe in the 1920s and 1930s. The film, however, failed at the box office.

800 SECRET OF DEEP HARBOR (1961), UA.

Dir. Edward L. Cahn; Sc. Owen Harris, Wells Root; Cast includes: Ron Foster, Barry Kelley, Merry Anders, Norman Alden, James Seay, Grant Richards.

Waterfront newspaper reporter Ron Foster falls in love with the daughter of a smuggler in this pale drama based on *I Cover the Waterfront,* the memoirs of newsman Max Miller. Barry Kelley, an old-time sailor, smuggles gangsters out of the country for the underworld. Foster's exposé of Kelley results in a split between the reporter and Merry Anders, Kelley's daughter. Following an awkwardly written struggle between the two antagonists in a warehouse and witnessed by Anders, the reporter emerges victorious and the lovers reconcile their differences. The film is a dissatisfying remake of the more seedy and atmospheric *I Cover the Waterfront,* released in 1933, with Ben Lyon, Claudette Colbert and Ernest Torrence in the leading roles.

801 THE SECRET OF THE HILLS (1921), Vitagraph.

Dir. Chester Bennett; Sc. E. Magnus Ingleton; Cast includes: Antonio Moreno, Lillian Hall, Kingsley Benedict, George Clair, Walter Rogers, Oleta Otis.

Antonio Moreno, an American correspondent stationed in England, becomes entangled in a murder and a lost treasure in this silent mystery drama based on the 1920 novel by William Garrett. Moreno accidentally meets Lillian Hall and her guardian who is later found murdered. Kingsley Benedict, the correspondent's friend, finds papers referring to the lost treasure of Scotland's King James III. Following several complications, Moreno, who has been held prisoner by the villainous Walter Rogers, is rescued by his pal Benedict. They locate the treasure and rescue Hall from Rogers, who dies during the struggle.

802 SECRET OF TREASURE ISLAND (1938) serial, Col.

Dir. Elmer Clifton; Sc. George Rosener, Elmer Clifton, George Merrick; Cast includes: Don Terry, Gwen Gaze, Grant Withers, Hobart Bosworth, William Farnum, Walter Miller.

The search for a hidden treasure interests a variety of inquisitive persons, including two-fisted newspaper editor Don Terry, in this 15-chapter serial set chiefly on a spooky island. Walter Miller, who runs the island that allegedly holds the treasure, has explosive mines planted at all entrances to the island while he seeks out the coveted treasure. A woman postal clerk is assigned to the island, and Gwen Gaze portrays a young woman who is supposed to inherit the island.

803 THE SECRET SIX (1931), MGM.

Dir. George Hill; Sc. Frances Marion; Cast includes: Wallace Beery, Lewis Stone, John Mack Brown, Jean Harlow, Marjorie Rambeau, Paul Hurst.

This gangster drama borrows heavily from preceding similar films, and includes such elements as drive-by shootings, rival gang fights and the meteoric rise of a gang leader from a common laborer. Wallace Beery as "Slaughter House," a crude and callous hoodlum, enjoys shooting pals and foes in the back. Young newspaper reporters John Mack Brown and Clark Gable are assigned to investigate a series of gangland murders and soon compete for Harlow. "She is bad," Gable says. "Believe me, there's one scoop you're not going to get without a little competition." Later, news hound Gable meets Harlow and makes his move. "Hi, baby," he says. "Listen, if you're going to fall for anybody, make it me. I'm dependable. I even could take you around to meet my Aunt Emma." A vigilante committee of civic-minded businessmen called The Secret Six organizes to battle the crime czar. When the members ask Brown to find evidence that will convict Beery, he finds a gun the mobster had used to kill some of his enemies. But he, too, is killed, despite cashier Jean Harlow's attempts to warn him that Beery suspects him. Following several more complications, including Harlow's testimony against Beery, her former employer, and his rigging of the jury, the last scenes in this banal film depict Beery about to be executed for murder.

804 SECRETS OF THE UNDERGROUND
(1943), Rep.

Dir. William Morgan; Sc. Robert Tasker, Geoffrey Homes; Cast includes: John Hubbard, Virginia Grey, Lloyd Corrigan, Robin Raymond, Miles Mander, Olin Howlin.

Inquisitive newspaper reporter Virginia Grey joins boyfriend district attorney John Hubbard in tracking down enemy agents in this dated but quite entertaining World War II murder mystery. The Nazi agents, led by portly Lloyd Corrigan, peddle counterfeit War Stamps to spread confusion and panic among Americans. To this end, the agents are even willing to commit murder. Their leader hides behind his front, a supposedly respectable gown shop where sometimes a dead victim serves as a mannequin in the store window. Grey herself is targeted for extinction. However, she and Hubbard are quick to trace the operation to an upstate farm, leading to the capture of the head spy.

805 SECRETS OF WU SIN
(1932), Che.

Dir. Richard Thorpe Sc. William McGrath; Cast includes: Lois Wilson, Grant Withers, Dorothy Revier, Eddie Boland, Robert Warwick, Toschia Mori.

This tepid drama, which blends the newspaper-crime genre with that of the "yellow peril," deals with the smuggling of Chinese aliens into San Francisco's Chinatown. Lois Wilson, a despondent young writer, is rescued from a suicide attempt by newspaper editor Grant Withers, who is working under cover investigating the smuggling racket in Chinatown. Withers then gives her a job on his paper and turns over his own investigation to Eddie Boland, one of his reporters. But Boland refuses to work with Wilson. While the reporter is drugged by one of gang leader Wu Sin's henchmen, Wilson on her own follows another gang member and discovers that a ship is bringing in another group of aliens. The same vessel is owned by the father of Dorothy Revier, the editor's fiancée. Following several other complications, Wilson learns from a young Chinese woman about an attempt to kill the editor. But Withers survives, Revier breaks off her engagement, the villainous Wu Sin takes his own life and the editor and his plucky reporter marry. Unfortunately for the production, the intrigues of the Chinese quarter and its gang leaders do not provide enough suspense, danger or excitement. Filmed on Universal's lot, the independent production company was able to take advantage of the studio's large collection of authentic Asian properties, giving the low-budget feature the appearance of a high production product.

806 THE SEDUCTION
(1981), Embassy.

Dir. David Schmoeller; Sc. David Schmoeller; Cast includes: Morgan Fairchild, Michael Sarrazin, Vince Edwards, Andrew Stevens, Colleen Camp, Kevin Brophy.

Glamorous television news reporter Morgan Fairchild is pursued by peeping-tom photographer Andrew Stevens in this inept horror film that proves more laughable than scary. The greatly disturbed voyeuristic photographer studies his unaware subject through his high-powered telephoto lenses while harboring a gallery of her photographs on his wall. Policemen Michael Sarrazin and Vince Edwards hang around Fairchild's home after she calls for help, but they offer little assistance. Edwards advises her to buy a gun for protection. Sarrazin at one point beats up Stevens. The film offers little insight into the major characters.

807 THE SELLOUT (1952), MGM.

Dir. Gerald Mayer; *Sc.* Charles Palmer; *Cast includes:* Walter Pidgeon, John Hodiak, Audrey Totter, Paula Raymond, Thomas Gomez, Cameron Mitchell.

The kidnapping of crusading newspaper editor Walter Pidgeon, who is battling a corrupt county sheriff, almost leads to the failure of justice in this absorbing but preachy newspaper-crime drama. State's attorney John Hodiak takes up the gauntlet after Pidgeon's disappearance, but witnesses, including the editor upon his return, refuse to testify against the villainous sheriff Thomas Gomez, whose county jail ironically exhibits the following sign: "Justice Is Truth in Action." Headlines like "The Sheriff's Shakedown Boys" begin to appear. Hodiak learns that Pidgeon's silence stems from his son-in-law Cameron Mitchell's illegal ties to Gomez. However, justice eventually triumphs as the message is hammered home that the citizenry must fight against those corrupt officials who would take away the public's civil liberties. The judge, who finally sentences Gomez, comments rather naively about the law: "It's bigger than men, stronger than force. You can't shoot it, you can't bribe it, you can't threaten it. Nobody—no person, no group, no gang, no person in this country—has ever been big enough to defy it for long."

808 THE SENATOR WAS INDISCREET (1947), U.

Dir. George S. Kaufman; *Sc.* Charles MacArthur; *Cast includes:* William Powell, Ella Raines, Peter Lind Hayes, Arleen Whelan, Ray Collins, Allen Jenkins.

Incompetent U.S. Senator William Powell, who has presidential aspirations, has unfortunately been recording his meetings and other incidents in a controversial diary in this satirical look at contemporary politics. Panic strikes Powell's guilt-ridden colleagues when he reports the loss of his diary. They take off for parts unknown, particularly lands with no extradition laws. Newspaper reporter Ella Raines suspects that Arleen Whelan, Powell's girlfriend, has fled with the coveted little book to further her own political ends. The film concludes with a scene on an island somewhere in the South Seas, with Powell enjoying the company of Dorothy Lamour—a tongue-in-cheek homage to the Crosby-Hope-Lamour road comedies. In one scene Powell cracks: "There's a rule in our state—if you can't beat 'em, bribe 'em." And regarding passage of the income tax, he wonders, "How could I know that income tax bill meant me, too?"

809 SEVEN SWEETHEARTS (1942), MGM.

Dir. Frank Borzage; *Sc.* Walter Reich, Leo Townsend; *Cast includes:* Kathryn Grayson, Van Heflin, Marsha Hunt, Cecilia Parker, Peggy Moran, S. Z. Sakall.

Newspaper reporter Van Heflin, visiting Michigan's famed tulip festival, falls in love with Kathryn Grayson, the youngest of seven daughters of a Dutch family, in this minor musical. However, the couple face a dilemma. Grayson's father, S. Z. Sakall, reminds her that tradition demands that the oldest daughter must be married before any of the others can become a bride. The problem is increased when Heflin learns that the disposition of Marsha Hunt, the oldest child, is such that no man will have her. It seems she is too domineering.

810 SEX AND THE SINGLE GIRL (1964), WB.

Dir. Richard Quine; *Sc.* Joseph Heller, David R. Schwartz; *Cast includes:* Tony Curtis, Natalie Wood, Henry Fonda, Lauren Bacall, Mel Ferrer, Fran Jeffries.

Scandal magazine editor Tony Curtis, in his efforts to get research psychologist Natalie Wood into bed, poses as a troubled husband in this sex farce loosely based on the book by Helen Gurley Brown. Curtis has panned Wood's book and is determined to discredit her. He works for demanding Edward Everett Horton, who hassles his staff to make his magazine "the most disgusting scandal sheet the human mind can recall." Meanwhile, Curtis reveals his imaginary marital problems, which he has borrowed from married neighbor Henry Fonda, to self-assured Wood, who realizes she has love problems of her own. She breaks down in tears and telephones her mother. The mismatched couple soon fall in love. Meanwhile, psychiatrist Mel Ferrer explains why he has chosen his profession. "I like to hear dirty stories," he admits. The film spoofs such items as sex, love, marriage, scandal sheets and Madison Avenue.

811 SHADOW OF CHINATOWN (1936) serial, Victory.

Dir. Robert S. Hill; Sc. Isadore Bernstein, Basil Dickey; Cast includes: Bela Lugosi, Herman Brix, Luana Walters, Willy Fu, Charles King, William Buchanan.

Newspaperwoman Joan Barclay solicits the aid of novelist Herman Brix to investigate strange doings in a West Coast Chinatown in this atmospheric 15-episode serial. It seems that the crazed Eurasian scientist Bela Lugosi, who abhors both the white and yellow races, is plotting to close the Chinatowns of the West Coast and cripple the importing industry of China so that only an illegal European firm ends up benefiting from his diabolical plan. However, he is ultimately betrayed by Luana Walters, a half-caste Dragon Lady who had earlier employed him and been his ally. After fleeing from the authorities with no hope of regaining his reputation as a scientist or inventor, he soon returns to wreak revenge upon those who caused his downfall. Posing as a waiter, he enters a banquet for the hero and Chinese businessmen. But Brix unmasks him before he can poison the group's wine and turns him over to the police. The serial provides the usual close calls, including poisoned needles, exploding bombs and cars careening off cliffs. Lugosi during the 1930s was probably the leading villain who exuded the weird and supernatural as well as portraying the definitive personification of evil.

812 SHADOWS OF THE NIGHT (1928), MGM.

Dir. D. Ross Lederman; Sc. D. Ross Lederman; Cast includes: Lawrence Gray, Louise Lorraine, Tom Dugan, Warner Richmond, Alphonse Ethier, Polly Moran.

A young reporter who enjoys playing detective helps to bring to justice a policeman's killer in this action drama. Lawrence Gray portrays the industrious news hound. A rather unique element in an otherwise routine plot involves a clever dog credited with ripping the license plate off the murderer's fleeing car, thereby helping to identify the guilty party.

813 SHADOWS OF TOMBSTONE (1953), Rep.

Dir. William Witney; Sc. Gerald Geraghty; Cast includes: Rex Allen, Slim Pickens, Jeanne Cooper, Roy Barcroft, Emory Parnell, Ric Roman.

Newspaper reporter Jeanne Cooper slowly begins to support singing cowboy Rex Allen, who is trying to restore law and order to the frontier town of Tombstone in this routine western. Allen, with his sidekick Slim Pickens, faces a triple threat from corrupt sheriff Emory Parnell, dishonest saloon owner Roy Barcroft, and outlaw Ric Roman. With the help of Cooper's press behind them, the two heroes outride and outshoot the transgressors, eventually rounding up the critters in formula fashion. Several low-budget as well as major westerns used the power of the press as a plot device.

814 SHADOWS OVER SHANGHAI (1938), GN.

Dir. Charles Lamont; Sc. Joseph Hoffman; Cast includes: James Dunn, Ralph Morgan, Linda Gray, Robert Barrat, Paul Sutton, Edward Woods.

The Sino-Japanese War furnishes the background for this tangled drama of greed, deception and murder. James Dunn portrays a reporter; Ralph Morgan, an arms dealer for China; Linda Gray, a White Russian schoolteacher; and Robert Barrat, a disgraced Russian agent. All are seeking the key to a mysterious treasure located somewhere in the U.S. The film exemplifies how a typical Hollywood product, produced simply for entertainment, may end up, intentionally or otherwise, as a piece of propaganda. The basic plot, chiefly about a coveted treasure, skirts the political issues of the conflict—as did virtually all similar action and spy films of the period. But the stock scenes of the devastating Japanese air attacks on heavily populated Shanghai certainly must have influenced audiences, particularly concerning the brutal actions of Japan.

815 THE SHADY LADY (1929), Pathé.

Dir. Edward H. Griffith; Sc. Jack Jungmeyer; Cast includes: Phyllis Haver, Robert Armstrong, Louis Wolheim, Russell Gleason.

American reporter Russell Gleason helps smash a gang of gun runners in this trite drama. Phyllis Haver, as a young woman falsely accused of murder, flees to Havana only to become involved with the gun runners. Louis Wolheim, the gang leader, threatens to turn her over to the police unless she helps him in his illegal operations. Meanwhile, she falls in love with Robert Armstrong who, with the help of the reporter, aids in putting an end to the gang's activities. On their return to New York, Haver learns that she has been exonerated of all charges. Made during Hollywood's transitional period, the film was released in both a part-talking and a silent version.

816 SHAKEDOWN (1950), U.

Dir. Joseph Pevney; Sc. Alfred Lewis Levitt, Martin Goldsmith; Cast includes: Howard Duff, Brian Donlevy, Peggy Dow, Lawrence Tierney, Bruce Bennett, Anne Vernon.

Overly ambitious news photographer Howard Duff uses treachery and blackmail to succeed in this bleak newspaper-crime drama. Permitted by mobster boss Brian Donlevy to photograph hoodlum Lawrence Tierney pulling a heist, Duff ends up blackmailing Tierney. In return, Tierney plants a bomb in Donlevy's car, killing his boss. But Duff also snaps a picture of this. Following several complications and unsavory moves by Duff (he makes a play for Donlevy's widow after romancing Peggy Dow, a fellow photographer who helps him get started), Tierney finally shoots Duff. But the photographer, before he dies, takes his final picture of his murderer. One critic equated the iniquities and machinations of Duff with those of Shakespeare's Iago.

817 SHARPSHOOTERS (1938), TCF.

Dir. James Tinling; Sc. Robert Ellis, Helen Logan; Cast includes: Brian Donlevy, Lynn Bari, Wally Vernon, John King, Douglas Dumbrille, C. Henry Gordon.

American newsreel cameraman Brian Donlevy becomes embroiled in a conspiracy set in a fictitious country in this comedy drama. A heavy-drinking cameraman, Donlevy scoops other photographers when he captures on film the assassination of the king of Metovania. He then journeys to that land to shoot pictures of the coronation of the prince. Once there, he discovers a plot against the young prince's life by conspirators who are seeking to gain control of the country. Donlevy foils their scheme, saves the prince's life and gets his pictures. Wally Vernon plays Donlevy's comic assistant. Lynn Bari provides the romantic interest for both Donlevy and John King, the handsome prince who eventually wins her.

818 SHE GETS HER MAN (1945), U.

Dir. Erle C. Kenton; Sc. Warren Wilson, Clyde Bruckman; *Cast includes:* Joan Davis, William Gargan, Leon Errol, Vivian Austin, Russell Hicks, Cy Kendall.

William Gargan portrays a newspaper reporter who helps Joan Davis, the daughter of a once-famous woman police chief, when she is called upon to solve a string of murders in this tiresome comedy drama. The killer uses a gun that shoots needles into his victims. Unlike her prestigious mother, Davis fumbles through the case until, when she is just about to resign, she stumbles upon a clue that helps her break the case. Comic character actor Leon Errol, as a sympathetic police sergeant, offers Davis his friendship. A frenetic chase ends this chiefly humorless film.

819 SHE HAS WHAT IT TAKES (1943), Col.

Dir. Charles Barton; Sc. Paul Yawitz; *Cast includes:* Jinx Falkenburg, Tom Neal, Constance Worth, Douglas Leavitt, Joe King, Matt Willis.

Tom Neal portrays a newspaper columnist in the manner of Walter Winchell in this weak musical romance. He helps to promote the career of minor singer Jinx Falkenburg, who poses as the daughter of a deceased stage star who had once been quite famous. Neal persuades a reputable producer, who had known the mother, to feature Falkenburg in a tribute to the onetime star. A crisis suddenly occurs when Constance Worth, one of Neal's rivals, exposes Falkenburg's masquerade. Neal did better work in a series of low-budget crime films, including the cult classic *Detour* (1945).

820 SHEENA (1984), Col.

Dir. John Guillermin; Sc. David Newman, Lawrence Semple Jr.; *Cast includes:* Tanya Roberts, Ted Wass, Donovan Scott, Elizabeth of Toro, France Zobda, Trevor Thomas.

American television reporter Ted Wass, in Africa to do a feature story about a local prince, falls in love with jungle woman Tanya Roberts, becomes involved in an assassination and helps to quash a military coup in this feeble outdoor adventure based on the comic strip *Sheena, Queen of the Jungle,* created by S. M. Eiger and Will Eisner. Roberts portrays the blonde and shapely title character who has been raised by a noble and friendly tribe. When her adoptive mother is falsely accused of killing a prince, Sheena comes to her rescue. Wass and his cameraman, Donovan Scott, sense a major news story in the intended coup, and they soon become targets of the usurper prince and his mercenaries. Between these incidents, Wass and the scantily clad jungle woman find romance. "Fur!" she cries upon seeing the reporter's bare chest for the first time. "You have fur!" The disappointing film, meant to capture the high camp of the comics and the spirit of the serials of the 1930s, falls flat in this and other areas, leaving only the location shooting and directing as its only major assets.

821 SHOCK CORRIDOR (1963), AA.

Dir. Samuel Fuller; Sc. Samuel Fuller; *Cast includes:* Peter Breck, Constance Towers, Gene Evans, James Best, Hari Rhodes, Larry Tucker.

Newspaper reporter Peter Breck, with the help of a psychiatrist, gets himself committed to a mental ward so that he can uncover a murderer in this sleazy, sensational horror tale. "My name is Johnny Barrett," he narrates, "and this is my story—as far as it went." The police are frustrated in their attempts to identify the killer who, ironically, is known only to the inmates. Breck eventually succeeds, but ends up as a catatonic schizophrenic for his heroic efforts. Director-writer Fuller tried to inject the plot with a degree of significance by introducing certain themes. For example, he appeals for sympathy and understanding for patients such as James Best, a disgraced Korean war veteran who has been brainwashed by the Communists. Another patient singled out for audience compassion is Hari Rhodes, an African

American who suffers from extreme emotional stress, the result of being the first to attend an all-white university in the South. But sex and shock, not intellectual ideas, predominate in this film that borders on sensationalism and exploitation. In his later years, director-writer Samuel Fuller gained popularity as a cult filmmaker. He worked on several newspaper films, including a minor classic titled *Park Row* (1952).

822 SHOES OF THE FISHERMAN (1968), MGM.

Dir. Michael Anderson; *Sc.* John Patrick, James Kennaway; *Cast includes:* Anthony Quinn, Laurence Olivier, Oskar Werner, David Janssen, Vittorio De Sica, Leo McKern.

David Janssen, an American television reporter stationed in Rome, acts as narrator for various events in this complex, convoluted and lavishly produced epic drama based on the novel by Morris L. West. Janssen is part of one of several subplots. The main plot involves Russian priest Anthony Quinn who, as a future Pope, tries to prevent nuclear war, even at the cost of exhausting the wealth of the Vatican. The story, set in the near future, depicts China and its burgeoning starving population, as the major threat to Russia and the rest of the world, a situation that forces Quinn to make covert agreements with otherwise hostile forces. Other major players in this political-religious tale include Laurence Olivier as the Russian premier who releases Quinn from exile in Siberia after twenty years of persecution so that he can have a "friend" at the Vatican; John Gielgud as the present Pope whose untimely death catapults Quinn into that office; Oskar Werner as an intellectual theologian whose diversified views challenge some of those of the Church; and his foil, Leo McKern, as a senior cardinal who can be a formidable enemy.

823 SHOOT TO KILL (1947), Screen Guild.

Dir. William Berke; *Sc.* Edwin V. Westrate; *Cast includes:* Russell Wade, Susan Walters, Edmund MacDonald, Douglas Blackley, Vince Barnett, Nestor Paiva.

Gang rivalry threatens corrupt assistant district attorney Edmund MacDonald and his gangster crony Nestor Paiva in this suspenseful low-budget drama that unfolds in flashback. The two partners frame rival gangster Douglas Blackley, but Susan Walters, his wife, and reporter Russell Wade join forces to expose the scheme.

824 A SHOT IN THE DARK (1941), WB.

Dir. William McGann; *Sc.* M. Coates Webster; *Cast includes:* William Lundigan, Regis Toomey, Nan Wynn, Ricardo Cortez, Maris Wrixon, Donald Douglas.

Reporter William Lundigan and police detective Regis Toomey investigate the murder of a nightclub owner in this bland mystery. The tired plot follows the usual interrogation of likely suspects before the inevitable resolution is brought to light. Other clichés include the rivalry between a reporter and a police detective and the murder of a gangster who is about to retire from the rackets and settle down with his girlfriend.

825 SHOW GIRL (1928), FN.

Dir. Alfred Santell; *Sc.* James T. O'Donohue; *Cast includes:* Alice White, Donald Reed, Lee Moran, Charles Delaney, Richard Tucker, Gwen Lee.

Cynical Broadway reporter Charles Delaney scoops the other papers with a story about a knife fight between nightclub performer Donald Reed and a sugar daddy in this comedy drama based on the 1928 novel by Joseph Patrick McEvoy. Present at the time of the incident is Alice White, a Brooklyn entertainer with whom Delaney has fallen in love. Reed kidnaps her but she manages to escape. The reporter persuades her to hide out as part of a publicity stunt while he features the kidnapping across the front page of his paper. Following several complications, the sugar daddy finds her and apologizes to her, offering to place her in a Broadway show written by reporter Delaney.

826 A SHOW OF FORCE (1990), Par.

Dir. Bruno Barreto; Sc. Evan Jones, John Strong; Cast includes: Amy Irving, Andy Garcia, Lou Diamond Phillips, Robert Duvall, Kenin Spacey, Eric Estrada.

Television news reporter Amy Irving, while investigating the deaths of two Puerto Rican activists who were seeking independence for their homeland, discovers they were falsely accused as terrorists, badly beaten and then murdered, in this political drama based on the book *Murder Under Two Flags* by Anne Nelson. Irving, a widow whose Puerto Rican husband died of cancer, lives on the island with her two children and works for a television station run by Robert Duvall. She struggles to televise the truth about political corruption while her cautious boss is more realistic. "Cops shouldn't be able to get away with murder!" she persists at one point. But Duvall fears for her life and wants her to drop the investigation. "There'll be a long obituary and a short investigation," he warns her. "Nothing is worth dying for.... The story goes away in any case." He is forced to fire her, but she soon goes to work for another island station. Finally, special prosecutor Andy Garcia, working for a Senate hearing, joins her in exposing the corrupt police and their superiors whose motivations were more political than patriotic. Several cliché-ridden incidents, including the familiar perils reporter Irving faces, weaken the film. Involved in the murders are Lou Diamond Phillips, an undercover policeman who helped in the cover-up, and Kevin Spacey, an F.B.I. agent who ordered the killings of the two youths. Although based on actual events, the film loses its sense of authenticity when an ending scroll reveals that several characters, most notably the F.B.I. agent, are fictional.

827 A SHRIEK IN THE NIGHT (1933), Allied.

Dir. Albert Ray; Sc. Frances Hyland; Cast includes: Ginger Rogers, Lyle Talbot, Arthur Hoyt, Purnell Pratt, Harvey Clark, Lillian Harmer.

Rival reporters Ginger Rogers and Lyle Talbot join forces temporarily to solve a string of strange murders in this conventional mystery replete with screams from the victims to justify the title. Rogers has been posing as a live-in secretary for the first victim. When she calls in her exclusive story, Talbot, as her main rival and sometime boyfriend, transfers her information to his paper and Rogers is fired. Finally the killer, the janitor of the apartment building, is unmasked. His brother had been convicted of murder and unjustly executed. To avenge his death, the janitor went about poisoning those responsible by tampering with their radiators so that gas escaped as well as heat. Meanwhile, the couple resolve their romantic problems as Talbot announces that "a woman's place is in the home." The film begins with a scream in the night as a body hurtles to the ground from a penthouse apartment. Although a generally low-budget production, the drama uses a profusion of visuals effectively, including panning shots, camera angles, shadows and low-key lighting. Police inspector Purnell Pratt provides some of the much-needed laughter. Lillian Harmer, as a dizzy maid, criticizes the middle-aged inspector by commenting, "You're not at all like Philo Vance."

828 THE SILENT BARRIER (1920), Hodkinson.

Dir. William Worthington; Sc. Charles T. Dazey; Cast includes: Sheldon Lewis, Corinne Barker, Florence Dixon, Donald Cameron, Gladys Hulette, Adolf Milar.

Society reporter Florence Dixon, who is assigned to a story in St. Moritz, also intends to reconcile differences between her friend and the young woman's father in this drama based on the 1909 novel by Louis Tracy. The father, Adolf Milar, is a Swiss mountain guide. Meanwhile, the immoral Sheldon Lewis follows her, as does Donald Cameron, a young man who truly loves the reporter. Cameron is suspicious of Lewis's motives. Dixon meets with Milar, who agrees to forgive his daughter. Later, when Lewis assaults Dixon at a lodge, Milar, who has learned that Lewis had earlier betrayed his daughter, intercedes. A fight ensues in which Lewis falls to his death.

829 SILENT PARTNER (1944), Rep.

Dir. George Blair; Sc. Gertrude Walker; Cast includes: William Henry, Beverly Lloyd, Grant Withers, Ray Walker, Joan Blair, Roland Drew.

Reporter William Henry finds a murder victim's address book and decides to investigate in this anemic newspaper-crime drama. After interviewing some of the persons listed in the book, he is able to solve the murder—but not before several attempts are made on his life. So bad are the opening sequences, that the director seems to have abandoned the script midway and winged it from there. The film ends up as a burlesque of itself and, intentionally or unintentionally, poking fun at all low-budget crime dramas.

830 SILVER SPURS (1943), Rep.

Dir. Joseph Kane; Sc. John K. Butler, J. Benton Cheney; Cast includes: Roy Rogers, Smiley Burnette, John Carradine, Phyllis Brooks, Jerome Cowan, Joyce Compton.

Newspaper reporter Phyllis Brooks poses as a Lonely Hearts bride scheduled to marry wealthy rancher Jerome Cowan, Roy Rogers's boss, in this highly implausible combination newspaper drama and western. After the wedding, Cowan is murdered by John Carradine, a resort operator who covets the dead man's ranch and his land that contains oil deposits. Carradine originally persuaded Cowan to seek the mail-order bride. When Rogers is falsely accused of the killing, he swings into action and rounds up the culprits, including Carradine and Brooks, who is part of the scheme, along with her crooked editor.

831 SIN TOWN (1942), U.

Dir. Ray Enright; Sc. W. Scott Darling, Gerald Geraghty; Cast includes: Constance Bennett, Broderick Crawford, Anne Gwynne, Ward Bond, Patric Knowles, Andy Devine.

Anne Gwynne, editor of a local frontier town newspaper, circa 1910, clashes with shady opportunist Broderick Crawford and his partner, Constance Bennett, in this colorless drama. The strangers soon become involved with the only gambling establishment in the boom town—after Crawford evicts Ward Bond, its owner, from the premises. However, Bond and his boys return, resulting in Crawford and Bennett's beating a hasty retreat for more fruitful pickings. Director Enright, Crawford and Gwynne worked on a similar film that same year, titled Men of Texas, both of which featured, in part, a newspaper background.

832 SING SING NIGHTS (1935), Mon.

Dir. Lew Collins; Sc. Marion North, Charles Logue; Cast includes: Conway Tearle, Mary Doran, Hardie Albright, Boots Mallory, Ferdinand Gottschalk, Berton Churchill.

Foreign correspondent Conway Tearle gains notoriety as the result of his articles from all parts of the globe, but he also makes many enemies by lying, cheating and stealing in this feeble drama based on the novel by Harry Stephen Keeler. As a result of his despicable behavior, someone who obviously can no longer take the man's loathsomeness shoots Tearle three times. However, three different men who confess to having guns also confess that they killed him. A trial finds them guilty and all three are sentenced to death. Suddenly Ferdinand Gottschalk, a detective-professor, enters the case. Using a lie-detecting apparatus, he determines which one is guilty after each tells his story to the professor. He ends his investigation by signing two pardons at the last moment. The guilty party marches off to the electric chair.

833 SING YOUR WAY HOME (1945), RKO.

Dir. Anthony Mann; *Sc.* William Bowers; *Cast includes:* Jack Haley, Anne Jeffreys, Marcy McGuire, Glenn Vernon, Donna Lee, Patti Brill.

Conceited war correspondent Jack Haley, desperate for passage back to the States, must undergo a demeaning task in exchange for a place on board the ship in this inconsequential musical comedy. He is forced to care for a group of juvenile entertainers. The situation grows complicated when the young people present problems for Haley, who begins to fall for Anne Jeffreys. The film offers plenty of forgettable songs and silly comic moments. The vessel, departing from Cherbourg, is bound for New York.

834 SINNER TAKE ALL (1936), MGM.

Dir. Errol Taggart; *Sc.* Leonard Lee, Walter Wise; *Cast includes:* Bruce Cabot, Margaret Lindsay, Joseph Calleia, Stanley Ridges, Vivienne Osborne, Charley Grapewin.

Members of an unlucky family are mysteriously being murdered in this smoothly produced whodunit based on the novel *Murder for a Wanton* by Whitman Chambers. Although Edward Pawley, as chief of the homicide squad, tries hard to solve the case, experienced reporter Bruce Cabot unravels the mystery for him. Following the interrogations of the usual suspects, including the family lawyer who would benefit financially by the extinction of the entire Lampier family, Cabot exposes the real killer—the least suspected character. Joseph Calleia is cast as a sinister mobster, a role he has played several times. A young Dorothy Kilgallen portrays another reporter. Generally, the film avoids the more likely stereotypes that plague this genre—the dumb cop and the wisecracking news hound. Nevertheless, the police are baffled, asking the dying murderer how he committed the crimes. "Can you keep a secret?" he asks. When the police acknowledge the question, he adds, "So can I," and quietly dies.

835 SISTERS (1973), AI.

Dir. Brian De Palma; *Sc.* Brian De Palma, Louisa Rose; *Cast includes:* Margot Kidder, Jennifer Salt, Charles Durning, Bill Finley, Lisle Wilson, Barnard Hughes.

Jennifer Salt, as a reporter whose separated Siamese twin sister Margot Kidder is homicidal, investigates a violent murder she has witnessed in this chilling Hitchcockian psychological drama. Meanwhile Salt's mother, Mary Davenport, wishes her daughter to marry successfully. "The Cunningham girl is engaged," she notifies her daughter. "He's a doctor. Well, he's really a veterinarian, but all the animals are owned by wealthy people." Kidder invites Lisle Wilson, her television game show partner, to spend the night with her, and in the morning ends up brutally killing him with a butcher knife. Reporter Salt witnesses the victim's agony from her own window and is determined to track down the murderer. Discouraged by police detective Dolph Sweet, she seeks the assistance of private sleuth Charles Durning, who helps her resolve the case.

836 THE SIXTEENTH WIFE (1917), Vitagraph.

Dir. Charles Brabin; *Sc.* A. Van Buren Powell; *Cast includes:* Peggy Hyland, Marc MacDermott, George J. Forth, Templer Saxe.

Newspaperman George J. Forth rescues Peggy Hyland from a lascivious Turkish Kadir in this comedy drama based on a story by Molly Elliot Seawell. Hyland, an American dancer who, while in Europe, attracts the attention of the Kadir (Marc MacDermott). He invites her to his harem to entertain and then makes her his prisoner, intending her for his sixteenth wife. She escapes and returns to the U.S., but the determined Kadir pursues her to New York. Reporter Forth and Hyland then devise a scheme to foil her pursuer. She boards a liner for Europe, and the Kadir follows. But once the vessel departs from the harbor, Hyland leaves by way of a prearranged tugboat, returns to Forth on shore and the couple are married.

837 SLANDER (1956), MGM.

Dir. Roy Rowland; *Sc.* Jerome Weidman; *Cast includes:* Van Johnson, Ann Blyth, Steve Cochran, Marjorie Rambeau, Richard Eyer, Harold J. Stone.

Television personality Van Johnson becomes the target of a blackmail scheme by a scandal magazine in this drama's frail attempt to expose the smut magazine racket. Just as Johnson and his wife Ann Blyth are about to achieve success and sign a lucrative contract, scandal sheet publisher Steve Cochran threatens to run a story about Johnson's earlier prison sentence. As a teenager, Johnson had been involved in a robbery. Cochran is willing to trade the story for an exposé on another personality, but Johnson refuses. The publisher prints the original story and Johnson is fired. His son is killed fleeing from other boys who were taunting him. Johnson then goes on television and exposes the entire story as a warning to others about the unscrupulous scandal sheets. Later, Cochran is killed by his own mother.

838 SLOW DANCING IN THE BIG CITY (1978), UA.

Dir. John G. Avildsen; *Sc.* Barra Grant; *Cast includes:* Paul Sorvino, Anne Ditchburn, Nicolas Coster, Anita Dangler, Hector Jaime Mercado, Linda Selman.

Sensitive and caring newspaper columnist Paul Sorvino becomes involved in two stories, one about dancer Anne Ditchburn and the other concerning a young ghetto boy, in this overly sentimental drama. The dancer, who is in ill health and who has just broken up with her boyfriend, has recently moved into his tenement building. A romance blossoms between the writer and Ditchburn, as he decides to write a series about her struggling career. "We can walk on the moon and turn garbage into roses," he reminds her. "You're a poet!" she exclaims. Meanwhile Sorvino is doing another series on the street kid who, learning to survive in an uncaring city, is more interested in spreading graffiti than in taking advice from the writer. But fragile friendship grows between these two unlikely figures.

839 SMART BLONDE (1936), WB.

Dir. Frank McDonald; *Sc.* Don Ryan, Kenneth Gamet; *Cast includes:* Glenda Farrell, Barton MacLane, Winifred Shaw, Craig Reynolds, Addison Richards, Jane Wyman.

The first entry in the Torchy Blane series, this newspaper-crime drama often replaces action with dialogue while it unfolds the conventional trappings of wisecracking reporters and dumb cops. Glenda Farrell plays Torchy, an ambitious reporter who often clashes with Barton MacLane, the not-too-bright chief detective Steve McBride. The plot revolves around a supposedly reformed gangster seeking to marry into society and who becomes involved in two murders, one of which concerns the killing of nightclub owner Joseph Crehan. Farrell helps MacLane solve the case.

840 SMUDGE (1922), FN.

Dir. Charles Ray; *St.* Rob Wagner; *Cast includes:* Charles Ray, Charles K. French, Florence Oberle, Ora Carew, J. P. Lockney, Lloyd Bacon.

Young Charles Ray, the son of a local California newspaper owner, helps to resolve a bitter rivalry between two papers and members of two communities in this weak silent drama. A community of orange growers must use smudge pots to maintain the necessary temperature of their crops, but the pots give off an offensive smoke to those in surrounding areas not affiliated with the citrus industry. As a result, opposing newspapers take sides —one defending the ranchers, the other defending the outlying community. Ray's father turns over control of his paper to his son who, following several complications, resolves the dilemma by inventing a smudge pot that protects the fruit trees from frost without producing the offending smoke.

841   SOB SISTER (1931), Fox.

Dir. Al Santell; *Sc.* Edwin J. Burke; *Cast includes:* Linda Watkins, James Dunn, Minna Gombell, Howard Phillips, George E. Stone, Molly O'Day.

Rival reporters Linda Watkins, portraying the title character, and James Dunn repeatedly scoop each other while carrying on a romance in this minor drama hampered by a flimsy plot. Dunn eventually walks out on his girlfriend after mistaking her intentions concerning a particular story. At one point, Watkins is captured by a gang of kidnappers and tied up, but a child involved in the incident unties her. The police arrive on the scene to take the culprits in hand, and the estranged lovers reconcile their differences.

842   THE SOCIAL HIGHWAYMAN (1926), WB.

Dir. William Beaudine; *Sc.* Edward T. Lowe, Jr., Philip Klein; *Cast includes:* John Patrick, Dorothy Devore, Montagu Love, Russell Simpson, George Pearce, Lynn Cowan.

John Patrick portrays a cub reporter who is assigned to capture a notorious bandit in this comedy drama. Patrick had earlier been robbed by the bandit (Montagu Love) who disguised himself as an elderly Gypsy woman. The reporter, who later meets a traveling medicine man (again Love in disguise), poses as the bandit. He then learns from an escaped convict that Love is the infamous bandit Patrick is trying to capture. After rescuing a child trapped in a bank safe, Patrick tracks down Love and the convict aboard a freight train which pulls into a prison grounds.

843   SOCIETY'S DRIFTWOOD (1917), U.

Dir. Louis William Chaudet; St. Harvey Gates; *Cast includes:* Grace Cunard, Charles West, Joseph Girard, William Musgrave.

Reporter Charles West marries Grace Cunard, whose brother has been sentenced to prison by West's brother, judge Joseph Girard, in this tangled drama of revenge. Before the marriage, Cunard discovers the judge is a thief. Once married, she tells her husband the truth and he decides to expose his own brother in his paper. But before he gets the chance, Cunard's brother is released from prison and kills the judge. To protect her brother, Cunard admits to shooting the judge. Her brother, however, himself mortally wounded, confesses to the crime before he dies.

844   SOLD AT AUCTION (1917), Pathé.

Dir. Sherwood MacDonald; *Sc.* Daniel Whitcomb; *Cast includes:* Lois Meredith, William Conklin, Marguerite Nichols, Frank Mayo, Charles Dudley, Lucy Blake.

Persistent reporter Frank Mayo rescues Lois Meredith, the young woman he loves, in this farfetched suspenseful silent drama that touches upon the theme of white slavery. Placed in the care of a selfish woman by William Conklin, her father, when she was just a child, Meredith runs away when she grows up. The father, who has never visited his daughter, is unaware of the woman's bad treatment towards her charge. When Meredith falls in love with the reporter, the woman, afraid of losing the support money, tells her she has mulatto blood. At this point, the young woman flees and ends up seeking employment with a "matrimonial agency" which in reality is in business to sell sex. She is offered up for auction in front of a group of men—including her own father who is unaware that she is his daughter. While he engages in bidding against the competition, Mayo arrives after tracking her down. He then reveals her identity to Conklin.

845   SOMEWHERE I'LL FIND YOU (1942), MGM.

Dir. Wesley Ruggles; *Sc.* Marguerite

Roberts; *Cast includes:* Clark Gable, Lana Turner, Robert Sterling, Patricia Dane, Reginald Owen.

World War II serves only as a backdrop for this romantic, sometimes steaming, drama starring Clark Gable and Lana Turner. Gable, a war correspondent, tries to save his younger brother (Robert Sterling), also a newspaperman, from the charms of Lana Turner, another journalist, whom Gable thinks is not on the level. He makes a play for her and she responds, thereby disillusioning Sterling. Later, when she is reported missing somewhere in Indochina, the brothers start out to find her. They learn that she is helping war orphans. This convinces the cynical Gable that she is all right. Meanwhile, Sterling enlists in the service and is killed in action as Gable turns in a war scoop. Although the film skips around to various war zones (the Philippines and Indochina), the conflict is secondary to the hot romance of the two leads. Gable lost his real-life spouse, Carole Lombard, who was killed in an air crash, while he was making the film. Production had to be halted for several weeks. Following its completion, he enlisted in the U.S. Army Air Force.

846 THE SOUND OF FURY (1951), UA.

Dir. Cy Endfield; *Sc.* Jo Pagano; *Cast includes:* Frank Lovejoy, Kathleen Ryan, Richard Carlson, Lloyd Bridges, Katherine Locke, Adele Jergens.

Destitute Frank Lovejoy colludes with smalltime hoodlum Lloyd Bridges in this grim drama about ruined lives based on the novel *The Condemned* by Jo Pagano. The story, set in 1933 chiefly in San Jose, California, shows the pair indulging in a series of stickups, after which they try kidnapping. But cold-blooded Bridges kills their victim. After both are jailed, local newspaper reporter Richard Carlson incites the townspeople with his provocative articles. As a result, an angry mob of outraged citizens storms the jail and kills the two prisoners. The bewildered and horrified reporter cannot comprehend how his writings could have released such a firestorm of rage. This last sequence changes the theme from a cautionary drama to a stinging indictment of mob violence and twisted justice—a subject treated in only a handful of earlier social dramas, including *Fury* (1936) and *They Won't Forget* (1937). The film is sometimes listed under its alternate title of *Try and Get Me.*

847 SPEAKEASY (1929), Fox.

Dir. Benjamin Stoloff; *Sc.* Frederick Hazlitt Brennan, Edwin Burke; *Cast includes:* Lola Lane, Paul Page, Sharon Lynn, Warren Hymer, Helen Ware, Henry B. Walthall.

New York newspaper sob sister Lola Lane at first fails in her assignment to interview middleweight fighter Paul Page, who has just lost the championship, in this drama based on the story by Edward Knoblock and George Rosener. When he refuses to give an interview in his dressing room, even after she follows him aggressively into a speakeasy, Lane fakes a story for her paper, stating he intends to make a comeback. She suspects that Page's crooked manager sold him out and ends up proving her charge of the man's betrayal. Page then returns to the ring to win the middleweight crown and Lane's love.

848 SPECIAL AGENT (1935), WB.

Dir. William Keighley; *Sc.* Laird Boyle, Abem Finkel; *Cast includes:* Bette Davis, George Brent, Ricardo Cortez, Jack LaRue, Henry O'Neill, Robert Strange.

Newspaper reporter George Brent is deputized as an undercover government agent to get the goods on racketeer Ricardo Cortez in this familiar, fast-paced drama. Since the government cannot arrest the clever Cortez on criminal charges, the Internal Revenue Service intends to indict him for income-tax evasion. Brent meanwhile falls in love with Bette Davis, the racketeer's bookkeeper. Cortez, charmed by Brent, gives him some inside scoops on other underworld activities which help Brent with his newspaper bosses. The reporter finally reveals his dual role to Davis, whom he persuades to help bring down Cortez. The racketeer, learning of the betrayal, has his henchmen kidnap her, but Brent follows them to their hideout and calls the police who come to her rescue. Several crime films of the period used the tax-evasion ploy—applied successfully in real life against Al Capone—including *The People's Enemy* (1935) and two released in 1937, *Alcatraz Island* and *The Last Gangster.*

849 SPECIAL AGENT K-7 (1937), Syndicate.

Dir. Raymond K. Johnson; *Sc.* Phil Dunham; *Cast includes:* Walter McGrail, Queenie Smith, Irving Pichel, Donald Reed, Willy Castello, Duncan Renaldo.

Intrusive F.B.I. agent Walter McGrail dominates a local murder investigation in this commonplace mystery. Assisting him is pert newspaper reporter Queenie Smith. He soon discovers that the chief suspect is the boyfriend of one of his female acquaintances. Unfortunately, the plot soon sinks into the usual clichés, including false clues, predictable plot twists and courtroom histrionics.

850 THE SPEED REPORTER (1936), Reliable.

Dir. Bernard B. Ray; *Sc.* Rose Gordon; *Cast includes:* Richard Talmadge, Luana Walters, Richard Cramer, Bob Walker, Frank Crane, Earl Dwire.

Richard Talmadge portrays the title character, an acrobatic newsman, in this limp melodrama. Talmadge sets out to smash a phony reform league which in reality is responsible for much of the criminal activity in the city. Plenty of fights occur in the film, especially in the last reel. Luana Walters provides the romantic element. Talmadge, who had once worked as stunt man with Douglas Fairbanks, was better known for his athletic abilities in action films than for his thespian skills.

851 THE SPHINX (1933), Mon.

Dir. Phil Rosen; *Sc.* Albert DeMond; *Cast includes:* Lionel Atwill, Sheila Terry, Theodore Newton, Paul Hurst, Luis Alberni, Robert Ellis.

Mass murderer Lionel Atwill almost outwits the police and the courts by furnishing a rather unique alibi in this highly improbable mystery. After witnesses state that they heard defendant Atwill speak, his attorney proves through a battery of doctors that Atwill has been deaf and dumb all his life. Unknown to others, Atwill has a deaf-and-dumb twin brother. Theodore Newton, a wise-cracking reporter, arrives at the scene of a crime and is asked how he knows a murder has been committed. "Easy," he replies, "I made a quick checkup on the city and found out we're one short." He works with not-too-bright police chief Paul Hurst, who finally traps the twins in their home where one hides out in a secret room behind a sliding panel. The "normal" brother takes his own life by jabbing himself with a medieval poison ring after his deaf-and-dumb brother is shot to death trying to escape. The title refers to the latter, silent brother. Sheila Terry, Newton's girlfriend and fellow reporter, is fiercely independent. Desperate for money to help her impoverished mother, she agrees to write a series of complimentary articles about Atwill's philanthropy rather than simply marry Newton who promises to contribute to her mother's support. The film was remade ten years later and released as *The Phantom Killer.*

852 THE SPORT PARADE (1932), RKO.

Dir. Dudley Murphy; *Sc.* Corey Ford, Tom Wenning, Francis Cockrell; *Cast includes:* Joel McCrea, William Gargan, Marian Marsh, Walter Catlett, Skeets Gallagher, Robert Benchley.

Portraying a Cornell football star, Joel McCrea soon gets a job as sportswriter in this inconsequential drama. He befriends eccentric radio announcer Robert Benchley (who wrote the dialogue for the film) and later turns his interests to wrestling. He wins a match, much to the satisfaction of some of his pals and Marian Marsh, his romantic interest. The nature of the film's sports background gave the studio a chance to insert plenty of stock footage from a variety of sporting events.

853 SPY TRAIN (1943), Mon.
Dir. Harold Young; *Sc.* Lewis Schwabacher, Wallace Sullivan, Bart Lytton; *Cast includes:* Richard Travis, Catherine Craig, Chick Chandler, Evelyn Brent, Thelma White, Gerald Brock.

The chief setting of this weak World War II spy drama is a train. Various passengers search for a mysterious black bag that they believe contains Nazi documents, but actually holds a time bomb. The hero and heroine are played by newspaper reporter Richard Travis and Catherine Craig. Travis takes on the role of sleuth while aboard the potentially doomed train. The German spies are blown up by their own device at the conclusion of this inept film. Chick Chandler portrays a photographer.

854 STAND BY ALL NETWORKS (1942), Col.
Dir. Lew Landers; *Sc.* Maurice Tombragel, Doris Malloy, Robert Lee Johnson; *Cast includes:* John Beal, Florence Rice, Margaret Hays, Alan Baxter.

Bright national radio announcer John Beal emerges as the principal foe of saboteurs and fifth columnists, all of whom are sworn to the destruction of the U.S., in this wartime drama. Relatively successful at exposing a group of enemy agents, Beal incurs the wrath of government agents and the police who view the announcer as a meddling amateur. Especially troublesome to Beal are Alan Baxter and Margaret Hays, two well-entrenched spies. But Beal triumphs with the help of co-worker Florence Rice, who eventually reveals her true identity—that of a government agent.

855 STAND UP AND BE COUNTED (1972), Col.
Dir. Jackie Cooper; *Sc.* Bernard Slade; *Cast includes:* Jacqueline Bisset, Stella Stevens, Steve Lawrence, Gary Lockwood, Lee Purcell, Loretta Swit.

Magazine reporter Jacqueline Bisset is assigned to cover a women's liberation story in her home town of Denver in this generally inept comedy. Anne Francine, Bisset's mother, is a feminist from another generation. Lee Purcell, her younger daughter, is more aggressive, and leads a group of women activists. She makes a contract with a football coach to get her pregnant. Stella Stevens portrays the sexy wife of a clothing manufacturer who unknowingly pushes her into the women's lib movement. Bisset, observing all these incidents, slowly begins to realize the various abuses women suffer in their everyday lives.

856 STANLEY AND LIVINGSTONE (1939), TCF.
Dir. Henry King; *Sc.* Philip Dunne, Julien Josephson; *Cast includes:* Spencer Tracy, Nancy Kelly, Richard Greene, Walter Brennan, Charles Coburn, Sir Cedric Hardwicke.

Spencer Tracy portrays determined journalist Henry M. Stanley, who searches for Dr. David Livingstone, presumably lost somewhere in Africa, in this lavishly produced adventure set during the turn of the century. He is sent on the arduous journey by *New York Herald* publisher James Gordon Bennett Jr. (Henry Hull). Before he leaves, he meets with a middle-aged acquaintance (Henry Travers) of the missing doctor, whose romantic description of Africa encourages Stanley. "Nothing could match it," Travers utters with nostalgia. "Evenings in camp, the breeze cool off the plateau, the tropical rivers gleaming like silver in the moonlight. And the feeling of life around you everywhere. And more than anything else, the knowledge that you're thousands of miles from civilization—close to nature as God made it." Stanley, accompanied by an Indian scout (Walter Brennan), overcomes numerous obstacles before he reaches the legendary doctor (Sir Cedric Hardwicke), who is neither lost nor in any difficulties. On the contrary, he has been working successfully as a missionary and doctor ministering to a peaceful tribe. Impressed by the charismatic doctor, Stanley promises to promote his noble work in the African village. He returns to Zanzibar in triumph, but British scientists reject his findings or his contact with Livingstone. Finally, Stanley is exonerated when word reaches London of the doctor's death, accompanied by a letter to Stanley to continue the missionary work Livingstone began. The reporter then leaves his job and returns to Africa.

857 THE STAR REPORTER (1921), Arrow.

Dir. Duke Worne; Cast includes: Billie Rhodes, Truman Van Dyke, William Horne.

Truman Van Dyke, a reporter recently promoted to managing editor who keeps his identity secret, helps Billie Rhodes rescue her father in this mystery based on the 1922 novel *The Mysterious Mr. Garland* by Wyndham Martin. The daughter of a man she believes has been wrongly confined to a sanitarium, Rhodes is determined to investigate the circumstances of his confinement. Van Dyke helps her prove that her father has been kidnapped and unlawfully held against his will by the villainous William Horne and his confederates. Horne has embedded in his watch the combination of a safe that holds the evidence of the father's innocence. Van Dyke finally reveals his true identity to Rhodes and proposes to her.

858 STAR REPORTER (1939), Mon.

Dir. Howard Bretherton; Sc. John T. Neville; Cast includes: Warren Hull, Marsha Hunt, Morgan Wallace, Clay Clement, Wallis Clark, Virginia Howell.

Another newspaper-crime drama about crusading dailies going after crooked public officials who are in collusion with the underworld, this entry is no better or worse than those that have preceded it. Warren Hull, the son of a newspaper publisher who has been killed by the mob, determines to carry on the good fight against local corruption. He and his paper back an honest candidate for the next district attorney's job. Hull's efforts to track down his father's killer become complicated when he learns that a recent gang member indicted for murder is his mother's first husband—and his real father. The man surprises all when, upon discovering that Hull is his son, turns state's evidence against the gang and is instrumental in breaking the hold of organized crime upon the city.

859 STAR SPANGLED GIRL (1971), Par.

Dir. Jerry Paris; Sc. Arnold Margolin, Jim Parker; Cast includes: Sandy Duncan, Tony Roberts, Todd Susman, Elizabeth Allan, Artie Lewis, Allen Jung.

Sandy Duncan, as the title character, a truly patriotic young woman, becomes involved with underground newspaper publisher Tony Roberts and editor Todd Susman in this disappointing comedy based on the play by Neil Simon. Duncan's clashes with the pair of pseudo-dedicated liberals lack real humor while her overall acting suffers. Elizabeth Allan's performance as an extroverted landlady who is desperate for a man—any man—helps somewhat.

860 THE STEADFAST HEART (1923), Goldwyn.

Dir. Sheridan Hall; Sc. Philip Lonergan; Cast includes: Marguerite Courtot, Joseph Striker, Hugh Huntley, William B. Mack, Sherry Tansey, Mary Alden.

Joseph Striker, as editor of a small-town newspaper owned by his foster father, retrieves money bilked from the local citizens in this drama about small-town intolerance and based on the 1924 novel by Clarence Budington Kelland. As a boy, Striker was shunned by the locals because of his fugitive father. The owner of the local paper adopted the lad who was continually hounded by the son of the local district attorney and other children. Striker was sent to school out of town and, upon his return twelve years later, joins his foster father's staff. Together, they work to expose the same district attorney and his son, both of whom are now involved in a crooked oil scam. When the attorney flees with the town's money, Striker goes after the culprit and returns the stolen funds to the same people who had mistreated him most of his life.

861 STICK TO YOUR STORY (1926), Rayart.

Dir. Harry J. Brown; Sc. Henry Roberts Symonds; Cast includes: Billy Sullivan, Estelle Bradley, Melbourne MacDowell, Bruce Gordon, Jack McHugh, Barney Furey.

Overly fussy cub reporter Billy Sullivan almost loses his job after rejecting seemingly minor assignments as he waits for a potentially important breaking story in this routine action drama. Estelle Bradley, the daughter of the cub's editor, pleads with her father to give him one more chance, and Sullivan proves his mettle. Not only does he come through with a scoop, but he saves his editor's life from a bomb. He gets to marry his faithful girlfriend, with the father's blessing.

862 STORM OVER LISBON (1944), Rep.

Dir. George Sherman; Sc. Doris Gilbert, Dane Lussier; Cast includes: Vera Hruba Ralston, Richard Arlen, Erich von Stroheim, Otto Kruger, Eduardo Ciannelli, Mona Barrie.

A routine wartime drama of intrigue set in World War II Lisbon, the film gives top billing to Vera Hruba Ralston as a seductive nightclub dancer. The club is owned by unscrupulous Nazi sympathizer Erich von Stroheim, who trades in lives and military information. When Richard Arlen, an American correspondent, is about to leave for the States with highly secret documents on film, Stroheim plots to prevent him from getting the information through. Eduardo Ciannelli portrays Stroheim's murderous henchman in this familiar tale filled with the usual spies and other assorted villains.

863 THE STORY OF ESTHER COSTELLO (1957), Col.

Dir. David Miller; Sc. Charles Kaufman; Cast includes: Joan Crawford, Rossano Brazzi, Heather Sears, Lee Patterson, Ron Randell, Fay Compton.

Newspaper reporter Lee Patterson falls in love with Heather Sears, a young woman who is deaf, dumb and blind, in this poignant drama based on the novel by Nicholas Monsarrat. American socialite Joan Crawford first discovers young Sears, who is living a terrible existence, and provides for her care and education. Crawford's estranged and dishonorable husband, Rossano Brazzi, exploits Sears by arranging an international tour in which he raises money based on her unusual progress. He then rapes her, a horrifying and traumatic experience which results in the restoration of all of her faculties. Crawford, disgusted with Brazzi's actions, deliberately crashes her car, killing both of them. The gentle and devoted reporter is left to care for Sears.

864 THE STORY OF G.I. JOE (1945), UA.

Dir. William Wellman; Sc. Leopold Atlas, Guy Endore, Philip Stevenson; Cast includes: Burgess Meredith, Robert Mitchum, Freddie Steele, Wally Cassell.

Burgess Meredith portrays the famous war correspondent Ernie Pyle from whose viewpoint is told the story of the average foot soldier in this World War II drama. The film tracks an infantry company from the fighting in North Africa to the battlefields in Italy. Pyle marches and lives with the G.I.s, depicting their daily hardships and joys with sympathy and understanding. The soldiers accept the likable reporter as one of their own; they sense his

Burgess Meredith, portraying famous World War II war correspondent Ernie Pyle, has a few laughs with the soldiers he lovingly wrote about in William Wellman's tribute to the reporter, *The Story of G.I. Joe* (1945).

warmth and concern for them. The film avoids the conventional heroics and didactic speeches of the genre as it pictures the men battling the mud, rain and boredom as well as the enemy. "It sounds kind of silly," says one weary G.I., "but when I'm resting like this I get a kick out of just being alive." Robert Mitchum, a sturdy and competent lieutenant, is eventually promoted to captain. When he is killed near the end of the film, his men and Pyle look on in silence as his body, slung over a mule, is unceremoniously placed among other fallen soldiers. The company of infantrymen quietly look at their fallen comrade, then march off toward Rome, their next destination. Ernie Pyle (1900-1945) did not live to see the completed film. He was killed by a Japanese sniper on a remote Pacific island. Pyle, who won the Pulitzer Prize for his poignant and realistic accounts of the common soldier, was the best-loved correspondent among the G.I.s. The incident in the film about the officer killed in action came from Pyle's writings. He wrote of one of the many soldiers who passed by the body of Capt. Henry Waskow of Belton, Texas: "He too spoke to his dead captain, not in a whisper but awfully tenderly, and he said: 'I sure am sorry, sir.'"

865 STRANGE ADVENTURE (1932), Mon.

Dir. Phil Whitman; *Sc.* Lee Chadwick; *Cast includes:* Regis Toomey, June Clyde, Lucille La Verne, William V. Mong, Jason Robards, Eddie Phillips.

Police detective Regis Toomey, who has the responsibility of solving a mysterious murder, is hampered by snippy reporter June Clyde in this slow-paced drama set chiefly in an old dark mansion. Several concerned people have assembled in the house at the request of wealthy William V. Mong, who intends to read his will aloud. A police cruiser also arrives and the two officers are informed that an arrest will occur before the night ends. Before he can read his will, the host is killed by a knife planted in his chest. All are placed under house arrest as possible suspects. Clyde, the wisecracking journalist known as "Toodles," crashes the crime scene which has been barred to the press. Detective Toomey questions the elderly housekeeper, a physician and relatives of the victim. Following one hanging, one cloaked individual lurking about, a dagger-tossing suspect, and Clyde's going off by herself to investigate the dark recesses of the house, the reporter is caught by the hooded stranger and tied up. In a furious struggle between the knife-wielding stranger and Toomey, the detective overpowers the assailant who turns out to be the doctor. He had stabbed Mong while pretending to check his health.

866 STRANGE FACES (1938), U.

Dir. Earl Taggart; *Sc.* Charles Grayson; *Cast includes:* Frank Jenks, Dorothea Kent, Andy Devine, Leon Ames, Mary Treen, Spencer Charters.

Rival reporters pursue the same story while one of them becomes involved with gangsters in this typical newspaper-crime comedy drama. Notorious hoodlum Leon Ames, now a fugitive, locates a look-alike through news hound Frank Jenks, whose newspaper has a list of "doubles" it uses as a gimmick. Ames kills his double and takes his place, hiding out in the victim's small town. Jenks and his rival reporter Dorothea Kent get wise to the gangster's scheme and track him down with the help of local small-town publisher Andy Devine.

867 THE STRANGE LOVE OF MOLLY LOUVAIN (1932), WB.

Dir. Michael Curtiz; *Sc.* Erwin Gelsey, Brown Holmes; *Cast includes:* Ann Dvorak, Leslie Fenton, Lee Tracy, Richard Cromwell, Guy Kibbee, Evalyn Knapp.

Hedonist Ann Dvorak takes on several lovers, including a ruthless mobster, in this drama based on a play by Maurice Watkins. She has affairs with the youthful Richard Cromwell, reporter Lee Tracy, and gangster Leslie Fenton—all this after being abandoned and carrying the baby of a rich man. The major focus tends to be on the underworld. Tracy, who had played Hildy Johnson in the stage play *The Front Page* in 1928 but not in the film version in 1931, made his screen debut in *Molly Louvain,* portraying the sympathetic reporter offering to help Dvorak. That same year he appeared in *Blessed Event,* but this time as a scheming columnist. For the remainder of the decade, Tracy personified the quintessential news hound who glibly wisecracked his way through a stream of newspaper films.

868 A STRANGER IS WATCHING (1982), MGM/UA.

Dir. Sean S. Cunningham; *Sc.* Earl Mac Rauch, Victor Miller; *Cast includes:* Kate Mulgrew, Rip Torn, James Naughton, Shawn von Schreiber, Barbara Baxley, Stephen Joyce.

Brutal criminal and kidnapper Rip Torn holds a child and television news reporter Kate Mulgrew hostage in this complex unoriginal drama based on a novel by Mary Higgins Clark. Set chiefly in the misty depths of Manhattan's Grand Central Station, the psychopathic Torn brings his captors here where he can torment them at his pleasure. Two years earlier he had raped and murdered the child's mother. In the meantime, James Naughton, the girl's father, has fallen in love with reporter Mulgrew, who has been covering the grisly story. For no apparent or suggested reason, Torn returns to kidnap both the child and the reporter.

869 STRANGER ON THE THIRD FLOOR (1940), RKO.

Dir. Boris Ingster; Sc. Frank Partos; Cast includes: John McGuire, Peter Lorre, Margaret Tallichet, Charles Waldron, Elisha Cook Jr., Charles Halton.

John McGuire portrays a newspaper reporter who is accused of killing his neighbor in this forgotten little gem and early example of film noir. Ironically, McGuire, who is driven by guilt, has recently testified in a murder case, resulting in the execution of a young man. Peter Lorre lurks around this atmospheric drama as the real murderer in both cases. In one scene he witnesses neighbor Charles Halton ogling young girls in a diner. "He looks as though his mind could stand a little laundering," the reporter concludes. The film has been singled out for its claustrophobic scenes and expressionistic sets.

870 STRATEGY OF TERROR (1969), U.

Dir. Jack Smight; Sc. Robert L. Joseph; Cast includes: Hugh O'Brian, Barbara Rush, Neil Hamilton, Frederick O'Neal, Will Corry.

A fanatical right-winger plots to assassinate four United Nations functionaries in this bland political drama edited from a two-part television presentation. Neil Hamilton, the super patriot, believes the U.N. is a subversive organization undermining the greatness and power of America. Villainous Harry Townes, equipped with crutches which no doubt symbolize his twisted personality, assails the U.N. as "a massive dedication to the undeserving." Barbara Rush, a newspaper reporter, accidentally blunders upon Hamilton's conspiracy. Hugh O'Brian, the local police detective, eventually foils the plot with the help of Rush. The pair become romantically involved. Frederick O'Neal, an African under-secretary to the U.N., is one of Hamilton's potential targets in this overly preachy tale that extols the world organization as perhaps the last hope for peace among nations.

871 THE STREET OF MISSING MEN (1939), Rep.

Dir. Sidney Salkow; Sc. Frank Dolan, Leonard Lee; Cast includes: Charles Bickford, Harry Carey, Tommy Ryan, Mabel Todd, Guinn Williams, Nana Bryant.

Recently released convict Charles Bickford seeks revenge upon a crusading newspaper editor who was responsible for sending him to prison in this unexceptional drama of regeneration. Bickford, after serving a five-year sentence, confronts editor Harry Carey with a gun, but instead of shooting Carey, he decides to wreck the newspaper. He then joins a gang led by Ralph Graves, who is currently under attack by Carey and his paper. Bickford reforms with Carey's help, and begins to work for the editor. He is later killed protecting the newspaper against elements of organized crime.

872 STREET SMART (1987), Cannon.

Dir. Jerry Schatzberg; Sc. David Freeman; Cast includes: Christopher Reeve, Morgan Freeman, Kathy Baker, Mimi Rogers, Jay Patterson, Andre Gregory.

Lackadaisical journalist Christopher Reeve, given a soft magazine assignment to write about a pimp's life, decides to create his own characters in this glib drama designed chiefly to exploit the sex, seediness and violence usually associated with New York. His published article receives praise and leads to further similar assignments. Although Mimi Rogers, his girlfriend, loathes his work, he continues to turn out these high-paying, allegedly factual articles for the posh magazine. After sleeping with a hooker, Reeve tries to rationalize his actions to his girlfriend. "It didn't mean anything," he explains. "It just kinda happened." As he prowls the dark and dangerous streets for background material, he encounters the menacing pimp Morgan Freeman, a killer who is charged with crimes remarkably similar to the fictional ones Reeve has created. Freeman wants the reporter to exonerate him through his notes and writings—or else. Reeve eventually traps Freeman by setting him up for a hit by a rival pimp.

873 STRING BEANS (1918), Par.

Dir. Victor Schertzinger; *Sc.* Julien Josephson; *Cast includes:* Charles Ray, Jane Novak, John P. Lockney, Donald MacDonald, Al Filson, Otto Hoffman.

Shy Charles Ray, a farmer with the soul of a poet, leaves to work for a rural newspaper in this comedy drama. Employed as a subscription salesperson, he meets Jane Novak, the mayor's daughter, and the young couple fall in love. Meanwhile, Ray's editor, the mayor's rival, seeks to prevent the erection of a string bean cannery in the town. The project is being promoted by the unscrupulous Donald MacDonald, known for several illegal schemes. Later, when MacDonald tries to hold up the mayor at gunpoint, demanding $5,000, Ray intervenes and beats the crook in a fistfight. The grateful mayor then gladly permits his daughter to marry Ray.

874 SUCKER MONEY (1933), Progressive Pictures.

Dir. Dorothy Reid, Melville Shyer; *Sc.* Willis Kent; *Cast includes:* Mischa Auer, Phyllis Barrington, Earl McCarthy, Ralph Lewis, Fletcher Norton, Mae Busch.

Newspaper reporter Earl McCarthy exposes a phony local mind-reading racket, with its swamis and seances, in this feeble drama. The film depicts how some gullible people are taken in by psychic charlatans who prey upon their victim's superstitions. Using make-up and specific photographs of loved ones, these fakes persuade their clients they are in contact with the world of the dead. McCarthy is bent on exposing the entire operation, especially that of Swami Yomurda, played by Mischa Auer, who uses phony seances and paraphernalia to bilk rich followers. In the past the charlatan has also resorted to murder. When Ralph Lewis, a prosperous banker, arrives in the city with his daughter, Phyllis Barrington, Auer targets them for his scam. The reporter, working under cover as one of Auer's employees, rescues the banker's daughter who has been placed in a trance by Auer. The charlatan and his assistants are then arrested. McCarthy gets his story and the heroine. One of several films of the period dealing with spiritualism, this entry includes a few murders and a final chase as the swindlers make a futile attempt to escape justice.

875 SUED FOR LIBEL (1939), RKO.

Dir. Leslie Goodwins; *Sc.* Jerry Cady; *Cast includes:* Kent Taylor, Linda Hayes, Lillian Bond, Morgan Conway, Richard Lane, Roger Pryor.

Hot-shot broadcaster Kent Taylor, whose radio show "Drama in the News" acts out real events, creates difficulties when he announces the wrong verdict by a jury in this fast-paced mystery. When he and the newspaper that owns the radio station are sued for libel, Taylor investigates the background of Morgan Conway, who has been found "not guilty" of murdering the husband of his mistress. After discovering several clues and another corpse, Taylor and reporter Linda Hayes help district attorney Roger Pryor flush out the real murderer. A surprise ending adds to the general interest of this whodunit. Character player Keye Luke, in one of his better non-stereotyped roles, portrays an intelligent and talented radio actor who can imitate several voices.

876 SUICIDE BATTALION (1958), AI.

Dir. Edward L. Cahn; *Sc.* Lou Rusoff; *Cast includes:* Michael Connors, John Ashley, Jewell Lian, Russ Bender, Bing Russell.

This easily forgettable routine action drama centers around a behind-the-lines mission in which a special Commando-type team of soldiers is sent into the Japanese-held Philippines to destroy American documents left behind during a hasty retreat. Jewell Lian plays a war correspondent in this low-budget film that incorporates war newsreel footage for some of the action sequences. Michael Connors portrays the major in charge of the volunteers. He brings off the assignment successfully after some skirmishes with the enemy.

877 SUNSHINE HARBOR (1922), Playgoers.

Dir. Edward L. Hemmer; St. Jerome N. Wilson; *Cast includes:* Margaret Beecher, Howard Hall, Coit Albertson, Ralf Harolde, Julian Greer, Daniel Jarrett.

Untamed Margaret Beecher, refusing to marry the man her doctor father has chosen for her, leaves for New York where she gains success as a news reporter in this silent drama. Earlier, she had gone boating with young journalist Ralf Harolde when a failed engine forced the couple to spend the night aboard the boat. Her father, thinking the worst, condemns both for their inexcusable behavior. While working as a reporter, she is blinded by an explosion at a chemical fire. Harolde returns from a foreign assignment and, at her bedside, proposes to her. But she rejects him. Her father then operates and her eyesight is restored. Father and daughter resolve their differences, and the young couple plan their marriage.

878 SUPERMAN (1948) serial, Col.

Dir. Spencer G. Bennet, Thomas Carr; *Cast includes:* Kirk Alyn, Noel Neill, Tommy Bond, Carol Foreman, Pierre Watkin, George Meeker.

Kirk Alyn portrays the Man of Steel in this fair fifteen-chapter serial, some of whose special effects leave much to be desired. To visualize several of Superman's almost amazing feats, the studio occasionally uses animation—a less than credible approach if one desires realism. Noel Neill makes a satisfactory Lois Lane, Clark Kent's co-reporter. Nelson Leigh portrays Jor-l, Superman's father on the planet Krypton. Carol Foreman plays the Spider Lady, Superman's chief foe. A fifteen-chapter sequel titled *Atom Man vs. Superman* appeared in 1950, with Alyn and Neill repeating their roles and Lyle Talbot as the evil Lex Luthor.

879 SUPERMAN (1978), WB.

Dir. Richard Donner; *Sc.* Mario Puzo, David Newman, Leslie Newman, Robert Benton; *Cast includes:* Marlon Brando, Gene Hackman, Christopher Reeve, Ned Beatty, Jackie Cooper, Glenn Ford.

The famous comic book hero appeared as a cartoon figure on screen in the early 1940s and in serials, but Warner Bros. endowed the Man of Steel with high production values in this entertaining fantasy. Once Superman arrives on planet Earth and is raised by surrogate parents Glenn Ford and Phyllis Baxter, he assumes the disguise of Clark Kent, who works as a reporter for the *Daily Planet.* Christopher Reeve, as the cub reporter, rescues fellow journalist Lois Lane (Margot Kidder) and takes on the mantle of Superman, a power for good. His arch rival Lex Luthor (Gene Hackman), ensconced in a city sewer, schemes to monopolize a section of city real estate. He battles Superman and is eventually defeated. Goofy Ned Beatty and sexy Valerie Perrine are Luxor's assistants. The dialogue is often as outrageous and quirky as the characters and the plot. In one scene in which Superman flies onto Lane's apartment terrace, she offers, "Would you like some wine?" "No, thanks," he replies. "I never drink when I fly." Later, dim-witted Beatty reports to the underground hideout of the demonic Luthor. "Got the newspaper I asked you to get me?" Luthor asks. "Yeah," Beatty replies. "Why am I not reading it?" "Because I haven't given it to you yet?" Beatty asks after mulling over the question. When Reeve finally turns over Hackman to the prison warden, the Man of Steel says, "Don't thank me, warden. We're all part of the same team."

880 SUPERMAN II (1980), WB.

Dir. Richard Lester; *Sc.* Mario Puzo,

David Newman, Leslie Newman; Cast includes: Christopher Reeve, Gene Hackman, Ned Beatty, Margot Kidder, Terence Stamp, Jackie Cooper.

A sequel to the popular *Superman* feature released in 1978, the current film has many of the same cast members, including Gene Hackman as the egomaniacal villain Lex Luthor. He is joined by three more nasties who hail from Krypton and attired in black jumpsuits. When they invade editor Perry White's office by smashing through the wall, Hackman is more irritated than amused with the aliens. "Even with all the accumulated knowledge," he quips, "when will these dummies learn to use the doorknob?" With Richard Lester directing, the sequel veers more toward the satirical while making Superman more human. He even suffers humiliation at one point. Reporters Clark Kent and Lois Lane marry, with Lane trying to get her allegedly meek husband to admit he is the world-famous crime fighter during their stay at Niagara Falls. At one point Kidder ponders what it would be like to be married to Superman, who is often called away on emergencies. "I guess it's sort of like being married to a doctor."

881 SUPERMAN III (1983), WB.

Dir. Richard Lester; *Sc.* David Newman, Leslie Newman; *Cast includes:* Christopher Reeve, Richard Pryor, Margot Kidder, Annette O'Toole, Robert Vaughn, Jackie Cooper.

This third entry in the *Superman* feature series is disappointing. Where the first two, released in 1978 and 1980, were charming, the current entry remains mundane and uninspired, depending chiefly on action and less on the human element. Demented billionaire Robert Vaughn is determined to control Earth and accumulate even more wealth. He surreptitiously solicits the help of ingenious computer operator Richard Pryor, who unwittingly uses his expertise against Superman. Before he resolves this worldly dilemma created by Vaughn, the Man of Steel is zapped by Kryptonite, turns for a while into a villain, and straightens out the Leaning Tower of Pisa. In another scene, he refuses to help a damsel in distress. "I hope you don't expect me to save you," he tells the young woman, "because I don't do that nice stuff anymore."

882 SUPERMAN IV: THE QUEST FOR PEACE (1987), WB.

Dir. Sidney J. Furie; *Sc.* Lawrence Konner, Mark Rosenthal; *Cast includes:* Christopher Reeve, Gene Hackman, Jackie Cooper, Margot Kidder, Sam Wanamaker, Mariel Hemingway.

While *Superman* is busy annihilating nuclear weapons, villainous Lux Luthor is engaged in selling illicit arms in this weakest entry in the popular Superman features. Gene Hackman, as Luthor, creates the terrible Nuclear Man, a direct challenge and threat to the Man of Steel. He accomplishes this by replicating another Superman from a strand of the crime fighter's hair. But this clone is as evil as Superman is good. Margot Kidder returns as Lois Lane, along with Jackie Cooper as Perry White. As with the earlier films, the current adventure fantasy has less to do with newspaper reporting than with action, chiefly in the form of super feats. Finally, Superman reminds Luthor of their individual roles. "Luthor, it's as it always was, on the brink," Superman announces, "with good fighting evil."

883 SURRENDER (1950), Rep.

Dir. Allan Dwan; *Sc.* James Edward Grant; *Cast includes:* Vera Ralston, John Carroll, Walter Brennan, Francis Lederer, William Ching, Maria Palmer.

Another drama about an unscrupulous and overly ambitious woman, this entry focuses on a rich newspaperman as one of her victims. Tough fugitive from the law and femme fatale Vera Ralston marries wealthy newspaper publisher William Ching in this well-paced romantic drama set in a western town near the Mexican border. The good-natured publisher is completely unaware of her background. Gambling casino owner John Carroll, Ching's close friend, is suspicious of Ralston, but he gradually falls in love with her. When Francis Lederer, her first husband, shows up and accuses her of bigamy, she kills him. Ching, thinking his friend Carroll committed the murder to protect him, takes the blame for the crime. Ralston finally confesses and takes off with Carroll for the border. But sheriff Walter Brennan guns down both fugitives as they try to escape.

884 SWEET REVENGE (1987), Concorde.

Dir. Mark Sobel; Sc. Steven Krauzer, Tim McCoy; Cast includes: Nancy Allen, Ted Shackelford, Martin Landau, Sal Landi, Michele Little, Gina Gershon.

Los Angeles television reporter Nancy Allen, while investigating the strange disappearances of attractive young women, suffers the same fate in this adequate action drama. She is kidnapped and transported to the Near East where Martin Landau runs a white slavery racket. Allen and several other women try to escape but are caught, along with smuggler Ted Shackelford, who had helped them. He privately resents Landau. Allen disrupts an auction of the captives by grabbing an M-16 and firing it wildly. In the chaos the young women free Shackelford, who leads them to safety on a nearby island. Following a series of further adventures, the small group return armed and storm Landau's stronghold. A battle ensues and Landau and his chief henchmen are killed. The victors return to the States where Allen is greeted by a host of journalists and her little daughter.

885 SWEET ROSIE O'GRADY (1943), TCF.

Dir. Irving Cummings; Sc. Ken Englund; Cast includes: Betty Grable, Robert Young, Adolphe Menjou, Reginald Gardiner, Virginia Grey, Phil Regan.

Newspaperman Robert Young charms Brooklyn singer and dancer Betty Grable, as the title character, out of her dreams of marrying royalty in this musical romance set at the turn of the century. Although successful at her career as entertainer, she grows tired of performing in the numerous beer halls where she sings and dances for the patrons. She takes off for England in search of a titled husband—in particular, the duke Reginald Gardiner. However, Young, a reporter with the Police Gazette, loves Grable and persuades her to marry him instead.

886 SWEET SMELL OF SUCCESS (1957), UA.

Dir. Alexander MacKendrick; Sc. Clifford Odets, Ernest Lehman; Cast includes: Burt Lancaster, Tony Curtis, Martin Milner, Barbara Nichols, Emile Meyer, Sam Levene.

New York gossip columnist Burt Lancaster rules supreme when it comes to manipulating ambitious young women, crooked politicians and greedy publicity agents in this stinging look at the sleazy world of New York publicity seekers. Tony Curtis, one of these hungry, fawning and repulsive agents, grovels at Lancaster's presence just to get an item about one of his few clients mentioned in the writers's column. "I'm nice to people when it pays to be nice," Curtis boasts. The devious columnist, sitting imperiously at his usual restaurant table, wants to break up a romance between Susan Harrison, his sister, and jazz musician Martin Milner. He assigns this to Curtis, warning him that nothing he submits will be printed until he carries out this task. "I'd hate to take a bite out of you," Lancaster says to Curtis. "You're a cookie full of arsenic." Curtis considers this his stepping stone to success. "From now on," he gloats, "the best of everything is good enough for me." The plotting of these two despicable urban vultures ends in tragedy for the innocent young couple.

887 THE SWINGER (1966), Par.

Dir. George Sidney; Sc. Lawrence

New York's influential gossip columnist Burt Lancaster threatens sleazy publicity agent Tony Curtis he will receive no more free plugs for his clients unless he carries out the columnist's requests in Alexander MacKendrick's drama, *Sweet Smell of Success* (1957).

Roman; *Cast includes:* Ann-Margaret, Tony Franciosa, Robert Coote, Yvonne Romain, Horace McMahon, Nydia Westman.

Aspiring magazine writer Ann-Margaret, who has trouble breaking into the mainstream market, submits spicy material to sex-magazine editor Tony Franciosa in this highly entertaining satirical comedy. She disguises her writing so that her contributions appear to be autobiographical. This leads gullible and sympathetic Franciosa to try to reform her while magazine publisher Robert Coote would rather exploit her. The comical opening with Coote's narration, the spoof on a phony porno raid by cop Horace McMahon, the fake orgy dance number by Ann-Margaret, and the satirical "in-depth" television coverage by Los Angeles news reporter Clete Roberts all poke fun at the superficiality of modern life.

888 SWITCHING CHANNELS (1988), TriStar.

Dir. Ted Kotcheff; *Sc.* Jonathan Reynolds; *Cast includes:* Kathleen Turner, Christopher Reeve, Burt Reynolds, Ned Beatty, Henry Gibson, George Newbern.

The old classic stage play, *The Front Page,* has again come to the screen for a fourth adaptation that updates the comedy to fit the world of television. And as with *His Girl Friday* (1940), the second remake of the play by Charles MacArthur and Ben Hecht, the current battle-of-the-sexes comedy has Kathleen Turner playing the chief reporter instead of a male actor. Turner, a television newscaster who will go anywhere for a story, works for managing editor Burt Reynolds, her ex-husband. While on vacation, she has fallen in love with New York millionaire Christopher Reeve, whom she intends to marry after resigning from the cable news channel. Meanwhile, a notorious criminal is to be executed at midnight, and desperate Reynolds tries to cajole Turner to cover the story. The conniving boss manipulates incidents so that he can hold on to his crack reporter. But Turner is determined to marry and leave. The criminal escapes and hides inside a large copying machine where Turner and Reynolds keep him for their scoop. For some unknown reason, this version, like the first two, leaves out the famous last line of the original play, in which the editor exclaims, "The son of a bitch stole my watch!" (a reference to the Hildy Johnson character). Fortunately, the line appeared in the 1976 film *The Front Page,* the third version of the play, with Walter Matthau and Jack Lemmon as Walter Burns and Hildy Johnson, respectively.

889 SWORD IN THE DESERT (1949), U.

Dir. George Sherman; *Sc.* Robert Buckner; *Cast includes:* Dana Andrews, Marta Toren, Stephen McNally, Jeff Chandler, Philip Friend.

Marta Toren, a Jewish patriot and broadcaster, operates out of a secret radio station in this tense drama—Hollywood's first crack at presenting the Middle East conflict between the Arabs and the Jews. Toren uses the station to attack the British for creating problems for her people in tense Palestine. However, the drama is merely a simplistic tale about a boatload of displaced persons seeking entry into the Holy Land. Dana Andrews, an American freighter captain, lands the homeless refugees on Palestine's shores. They are greeted by a group of settlers who take them to their small villages, following a skirmish with the British. At first, Andrews is skeptical and neutral, refusing to take sides in the Palestine War. His only interest is in the business arrangement involving his vessel. Later, his sympathies change as he allies himself to the Jewish cause. Jeff Chandler portrays a Jewish leader. The film avoids pointing to any villains although it is chiefly pro-Jewish. The Arabs are barely mentioned while the British are depicted as fair, cautious not to inflict harm upon women and children and doubtful about their stern actions toward the refugees. "This isn't a Jewish, British or Arab problem," their commander says, "it's a problem of all mankind."

890 THE SYSTEM (1953), WB.

Dir. Lewis Seiler; *Sc.* Jo Eisinger; *Cast includes:* Frank Lovejoy, Joan Weldon, Bob Arthur, Paul Picerni, Don Beddoe, Jerome Cowan.

As the result of crusading newspaperman Don Beddoe's articles, big-shot bookie Frank Lovejoy becomes the target of an organized-crime investigation in this farfetched drama based on the story "Investigation" by Edith and Samuel Grafton. Beddoe, who is later killed by hoodlums, is being used by Fay Roope, his publisher, who wants Lovejoy locked up. It seems that Roope's daughter, Joan Weldon, is romantically involved with the bookie. Lovejoy finally agrees to talk to the investigators, following his son's suicide and the death of a young thief. The thief is killed robbing a store so that he can pay his gambling debt to the bookie. Lovejoy, whose rackets are covered up by the phony front of a legitimate business enterprise, is sentenced to serve time in prison for perjury. Weldon, who initiated the probe into Lovejoy's activities, promises to wait for him.

891 TAKE THE STAND (1934), Liberty.

Dir. Phil Rosen; *Sc.* Albert DeMond; *Cast includes:* Jack LaRue, Thelma Todd, Gail Patrick, Russell Hopton, Berton Churchill, Vince Barnett.

Radio reporter and columnist Jack LaRue, who has made several enemies through his broadcasts, is slain while on the air in this stale mystery based on the story "Deuce of Hearts" by Earl Derr Biggers. Adding to the familiar "locked room" mystery, the crime takes on another puzzle. Although LaRue is heard exclaiming, "Don't Shoot!" before his demise, the police can find no trace of a bullet or weapon. Detective Russell Hopton rounds up and questions the usual suspects. Later, it is discovered the killer stabbed the columnist with an icicle, thereby leaving no evidence of a weapon. The title refers to a trial that is held near the end of the film. The author, Earl Derr Biggers, was more famous for creating the popular Hawaiian detective Charlie Chan.

892   TANGIER (1946), U.

Dir. George Waggner; *Sc.* M. M. Musselman, Monty F. Collins; *Cast includes:* Maria Montez, Preston Foster, Robert Paige, Louise Allbritton, Kent Taylor, Sabu.

Exotic Tangier furnishes the setting for this otherwise tepid tale of intrigue involving a hunt for a Latin Nazi collaborator and murderer. Maria Montez, a Spanish dancer, wants to learn the identity of the quisling who has murdered one of her relations. Robert Paige, a correspondent who has fallen into disfavor and seeks to regain his reputation by breaking an international story, decides to help Montez. Sabu portrays a native guide and adds humor to his role. Preston Foster, the collaborator, masquerades as the police chief of Tangier and meets a particularly brutal end when he is killed in a violent elevator crash.

893   THE TARNISHED ANGELS (1958), U.

Dir. Douglas Sirk; *Sc.* George Zuckerman; *Cast includes:* Rock Hudson, Robert Stack, Dorothy Malone, Jack Carson, Robert Middleton, Alan Reed.

Idealistic New Orleans newspaperman Rock Hudson, while covering an airplane barnstorming show, falls in love with trick parachutist Dorothy Malone, in this bland drama based on the novel *Pylon* by William Faulkner. The major problem facing Hudson is that Malone is married to stunt pilot and World War I ace Robert Stack, who unfortunately dwells upon his past glory. Stack, his wife and their mechanic Jack Carson travel across the country with their small air show. Both Hudson and Carson idolize Stack while secretly loving his wife.

894   TARZAN AND THE JUNGLE BOY (1968), Par.

Dir. Robert Gordon; *Sc.* Stephen Lord; *Cast includes:* Mike Henry, Rafer Johnson, Alizia Gur, Steve Bond, Ed Johnson, Ronald Gans.

Mike Henry, as the title character, helps journalist Alizia Gur and her associate search for a jungle boy in this latest routine entry in the adventures of the King of the Jungle. The boy's American father had drowned several years earlier, leaving behind his four-year-old son who supposedly survived. Tarzan leads the expedition on a perilous journey into forbidden country where they discover the lad, alive and well and living in the jungle. Following a clash with hostile natives, especially Rafer Johnson, who is battling his brother for control of the tribe, the intruders are free to leave with the boy. The film was shot in color on location in South America—quite different from the earlier popular entries, featuring Johnny Weissmuller as the Ape Man, which were filmed on studio lots in black and white. This latest entry celebrated fifty years of Tarzan films, with the first, *Tarzan of the Apes*, released in 1918, with Elmo Lincoln playing the lead.

895   TEACHER'S PET (1958), Par.

Dir. George Seaton; *Sc.* Fay Kanin, Michael Kanin; *Cast includes:* Clark Gable, Doris Day, Gig Young, Mamie Van Doren, Nick Adams, Jack Albertson.

Hard-boiled city editor Clark Gable, who holds no truck with college courses in journalism, is forced to visit such a course in this delightful comedy. Compelled by his paper's policy, he reluctantly attends journalism professor Doris Day's lectures, posing as a pupil. As expected, he soon falls in love with Day, and she reciprocates, although at first she seems apprehensive. Some of the more comical scenes involve his rival, Gig Young, an alcoholic. Producer William Perlberg, to add realism and authenticity to the production, allegedly enlisted a host of professional reporters to inhabit the city room scenes.

896 TELL NO TALES (1938), MGM.

Dir. Leslie Fenton; Sc. Lionel Houser; Cast includes: Melvyn Douglas, Louise Platt, Gene Lockhart, Douglas Dumbrille, Florence George, Halliwell Hobbes.

Melvyn Douglas, the editor of a dying newspaper, pursues a gang of kidnappers in this fast-paced above-average newspaper-crime drama based on the story by Pauline London. He is eventually captured by the gang but manages to escape and bring the culprits to justice. The entire incident permits Douglas to publish an extra, thereby bringing the paper back to life. Louise Platt, as the original victim, was kidnapped because she was able to identify members of the gang. This was director Leslie Fenton's first feature-length film. He had made several short subjects in the popular "Crime Does Not Pay" series for MGM.

897 TELLING THE WORLD (1928), MGM.

Dir. Sam Wood; Sc. Raymond L. Schrock; Cast includes: William Haines, Anita Page, Eileen Percy, Frank Currier, Polly Moran, Bert Roach.

After being disowned by his father, young William Haines turns to newspaper reporting as a means of establishing his independence in this comedy drama. While on the night shift, a colleague pulls a prank on Haines by telling him to cover a murder at a café. Naive Haines rushes there and a murder does take place. The reporter traps the killer in a telephone booth until the police arrive. He also meets showgirl Anita Page at the club and immediately falls in love with her. When her troupe sails for China to entertain American troops, he follows. A governor is assassinated and Page is found guilty of the crime and sentenced to death. But Haines calls on a party of Americans to rescue her.

898 TERRY OF THE TIMES (1930) serial, U.

Dir. Henry MacRae; Cast includes: Reed Howes, Lotus Thompson, Sheldon Lewis, John Oscar, William Hayes, Mary Grant.

Like other early sound serials, this ten-episode newspaper-crime entry featured several former silent screen players. Reed Howes, as the title character, faces perils on various highways, traps set up by the chief villain, and a kidnapped bride whom he struggles to rescue. Howes had appeared in several low-budget silent western features before entering talkies. The following alliterative chapter titles hint at the skullduggery and dangers facing Howes: "The Mystic Merchants," "A Doorway to Death" and "A Trail of Trickery."

899 TEXAS LADY (1955), RKO.

Dir. Tim Whelan; Sc. Horace McCoy; Cast includes: Claudette Colbert, Barry Sullivan, Ray Collins, James Bell, Horace McMahon, Gregory Walcott.

Claudette Colbert, the crusading newspaper editor of a western frontier town, battles two lawless cattle barons in this second-rate drama hampered by an overly familiar plot. Originally a refined woman from New Orleans, Colbert journeys to this Texas town where she meets Barry Sullivan, whom she blames for her father's untimely death. Although he is a no-account gambler, Sullivan ends up helping her in her struggle to bring the local culprits to justice. Of course the couple reconcile their differences and fall in love. This was the first western heroine role for film star Colbert and one of her worst films. (Colbert had earlier appeared with Henry Fonda in John Ford's *Drums Along the Mohawk* (1940), which was more of an historical drama than a western.)

900 THAT CERTAIN AGE (1938), U.

Dir. Edward Ludwig; Sc. Bruce Manning, Charles Brackett, Billy Wilder; Cast includes: Deanna Durbin, Melvyn Douglas, Jackie Cooper, Irene Rich, John Halliday, Nancy Carroll.

Teenage Deanna Durbin has a crush on older Melvyn Douglas, a reporter on her father's newspaper, in this bright romantic comedy. As a foreign correspondent for John Halliday, Durbin's father, Douglas is invited to the publisher's home to discuss further assignments. It is here that young Durbin decides to drop Jackie Cooper, her young boyfriend, after becoming infatuated with the dashing and worldly journalist. Cooper in one especially entertaining scene responds to the rejection by approaching the reporter, sort of "man to man," and complimenting him for winning Durbin's affection. When Douglas grows aware of Durbin's feelings toward him, he introduces Nancy Carroll as his wife. Durbin then returns to fellow adolescent Cooper—to the relief of her parents as well as Douglas. A Durbin film would not be complete without her rendering several songs as she tries to work out the complications in her life.

901 THAT WONDERFUL URGE (1948), TCF.

Dir. Robert Sinclair; Sc. Jay Dratler; Cast includes: Tyrone Power, Gene Tierney, Reginald Gardiner, Arleen Whelan, Lucille Watson, Gene Lockhart.

Newspaper reporter Tyrone Power's continual invasion of socialite Gene Tierney's privacy results in her strange retaliation in this romantic comedy. Tierney publicly announces that she has married Power, a statement which makes him the laughing stock of his fellow employees. However, it is not long before the two antagonists actually fall in love. The fluffy doings are a remake of *Love Is News*, released in 1937 and which also starred Power as the reporter.

902 THAT'S MY STORY (1938), U.

Dir. Sidney Salkow; Sc. Barry Trivers; Cast includes: Claudia Morgan, William Lundigan, Eddie Gaar, Hobart Cavanaugh, Ralph Morgan, Bernadene Hayes.

A newspaper reporter fired by almost every paper in town purposely goes to jail to interview a notorious gangster's moll in this interesting drama. William Lundigan, as the courageous but desperate news hound, faces a major setback to his bold plan. It happens the woman he interviews turns out to be fellow reporter Claudia Morgan, and the obligatory romance follows. Bernadene Hayes portrays the incarcerated mobster's girlfriend.

903 THEN CAME BRONSON (1970), EMI-MGM.

Dir. William A. Graham; Sc. Denne Bart Petticlerc; Cast includes: Michael Parks, Bonnie Bedelia, Akim Tamiroff, Gary Merrill, Sheree North, Martin Sheen.

Disillusioned young reporter Michael Parks, after an argument with his employer, sets out across America by motorcycle to "find himself" in this superficial and uninteresting drama. He picks up moody Bonnie Bedelia, who has just left her fiancé standing at the altar. As he slowly begins to convert her to a more gentle soul, they each wonder whether they truly love one another. But they end up going their separate ways. Following several other incidents, the film ends, with its photography impressing more than its story or characters. The work seems to want to be another *Easy Rider*, released one year earlier.

904 THERE GOES MY GIRL (1937), RKO.

Dir. Ben Holmes; Sc. Harry Segall; Cast includes: Gene Raymond, Ann Sothern, Gordon Jones, Richard Lane, Frank Jenks, Bradley Page.

Star reporter Ann Sothern solves a double murder in this chiefly unbelievable battle-of-the-sexes comedy drama based on the story "Women Are Poison" by George Beck. Sothern accomplishes this feat while suffering from a bullet wound. Some reporters seem to be tougher than others. Because of her help, the local police make certain that she gets an exclusive to the crime story. A parallel plot concerns Richard Lane, her managing editor, who is trying to sabotage her marriage to Gene Raymond, a reporter for a rival paper. Joseph Crehan portrays Raymond's editor. Some elements of the plot are suspiciously similar to those in the seminal newspaper drama *The Front Page* (1931). Raymond and Sothern had appeared earlier in several light comedies, but not newspaper films.

905 THERE GOES MY HEART (1938), UA.

Dir. Norman Z. McLeod; *Sc.* Eddie Moran, Jack Jevne; *Cast includes:* Virginia Bruce, Fredric March, Patsy Kelly, Nancy Carroll, Alan Mowbray, Eugene Pallette.

When hard-nosed newspaper reporter Fredric March discovers that heiress Virginia Bruce is working in her family's department store under a pseudonym, he threatens to print the story in this romantic comedy. Instead, he falls in love with Bruce after a string of comical incidents, particularly a shipwreck on a desert island where, conveniently, priest Harry Langdon marries the couple. The film has plenty of comic character players to add to the nonsense, including Eugene Pallette as a nervous newspaper editor, Patsy Kelly as a store assistant, Alan Mowbray as a chiropractor, Arthur Lake as a fumbling photographer and Margaret Main as a grouchy store customer.

906 THEY ALL KISSED THE BRIDE (1942), Col.

Dir. Alexander Hall; *Sc.* P. J. Wolfson; *Cast includes:* Joan Crawford, Melvyn Douglas, Helen Parrish, Billie Burke, Allen Jenkins, Andrew Tombes.

Snoopy reporter Melvyn Douglas crashes the wedding of Joan Crawford's sister to investigate the private life of her family in this enjoyable comedy. Crawford, now in charge of a large trucking business left to her by her father, has been upset by Douglas's articles. Her work has drained her of her womanly traits, including any sentimentality or plans for marriage. Mistaken for a former boyfriend of the bride, Helen Parrish, Douglas gains admittance to the family mansion where Crawford first meets him in person. She is marked with a genetic peculiarity that results in an unusual physical reaction whenever loves strikes the females of the family. So immediately she falls for Douglas, who describes her as "a machine, not a woman." Crawford is not above advising her sister. "Intelligent people don't marry for better or worse," she explains, steering her into a loveless marriage. "They marry for better and better." The remainder of the film depicts how Douglas helps to restore her feminine and romantic side. The witty dialogue contributes handsomely to the film, with one or two exceptions. The following line, considered offensive today, may have been funny at the time—several months after the sneak attack at Pearl Harbor. "When I want a sneak," Crawford quips, "I'll hire the best and get a Jap."

907 THEY ASKED FOR IT (1939), U.

Dir. Frank McDonald; *Sc.* Arthur T. Horman; *Cast includes:* William Lundigan, Joy Hodges, Michael Whalen, Isabel Jewell, Lyle Talbot, Thomas Beck.

Three college graduates who take over a small-town newspaper claim that the death of an intoxicated local farmer was actually the result of a murder in this minor drama. After falsifying several clues and stirring up the local sheriff, editor William Lundigan brings some success to his paper. A farmer's daughter confesses to the murder, but a trial proves she was lying to attract attention to herself. Eventually Lundigan and his pals prove that silk thieves who were using the victim's barn as their hideout killed the farmer.

908 THEY GOT ME COVERED (1943) RKO.

Dir. David Butler; Sc. Harry Kurnitz; Cast includes: Bob Hope, Dorothy Lamour, Lenore Aubert, Otto Preminger, Eduardo Ciannelli, Donald MacBride.

Bob Hope plays a bungling reporter in this World War II spy comedy. As a correspondent for an international news agency early in the war, he botches several major assignments such as the Arnold Rothstein murder, the Munich bombing and Hitler's invasion of Russia. His agency boss restrains himself from committing mayhem on the returning incompetent. "You've wrecked my nervous system, ruined my reputation; you've cost me money, customers and good will!" he cries. "Does that mean you're dissatisfied with my work, chief?" Hope asks. The hapless reporter relocates in Washington, hoping to regain his reputation by uncovering enemy agents. He soon becomes entangled in a network of Nazi spies, including an updated Mata Hari (Lenore Aubert) and the group's ruthless leader (Otto Preminger). With the help of Dorothy Lamour and various branches of the government, Hope brings the foes to justice. The film is not one of the comedian's best works, but it provides several good one-liners.

909 THEY WANTED TO MARRY (1937), RKO.

Dir. Lew Landers; Sc. Paul Yawitz, Ethel Borden; Cast includes: Betty Furness, Gordon Jones, Henry Kolker, E. E. Clive, Patsy Lee Parsons, Frank M. Thomas.

Ace newspaper photographer Gordon Jones, assigned to cover a wedding, meets and falls in love with Betty Furness, the sister of the bride, in this romantic comedy with an exciting and realistic newspaper background. Wealthy Henry Kolker, however, frowns upon the romance, particularly Jones's method of earning a living. To satisfy his future father-in-law, Jones agrees to switch careers, becoming a copy writer for an advertising agency. But complications arise that force him to revert to his former work, after which all is eventually resolved to everyone's satisfaction.

910 THEY WON'T FORGET (1937), WB.

Dir. Mervyn LeRoy; Sc. Aben Kandel, Robert Rossen; Cast includes: Claude Rains, Edward Norris, Allyn Joslyn, Linda Perry, Cy Kendall, E. Alyn Warren.

This social drama about murder and mob psychology in a small Southern town presents a hard-hitting attack on prejudice and intolerance. The co-ed victim (Lana Turner) was assaulted and killed on Confederate Memorial Day. Politically ambitious prosecutor Claude Rains exploits the murder by targeting as chief suspect a Northern teacher, Robert Hale (Edward Norris), employed at the local college. He dismisses another possible suspect, an African-American janitor, saying, "Anyone can convict a Negro in the South." News-hungry reporter Allyn Joslyn arouses provincial bigotry as the story bursts into national headlines. Cries of "Prejudice" emerge from both the North and the South. To protect the convicted Norris from an angry lynch mob, authorities place him aboard a train and rush him to his assigned prison. Members of the mob storm aboard, pluck him from the train and hang him. Gloria Dickson holds both the prosecuting attorney and the reporter responsible. "You're the ones who killed him," she rails. "You're the ones who stirred up the hatred and prejudice down here.... It will stay with you as long as you live." In the last scene the reporter muses to Rains, "Now that it's over, I wonder if Hale really did it?" The prosecutor quietly replies, "I wonder." The film was adapted from the novel *Death in the Deep South* by Ward Greene. Director Mervyn LeRoy in 1932 had turned out another powerful social drama, *I Am a Fugitive from a Chain Gang*, starring Paul Muni.

911 THIRD FINGER, LEFT HAND (1940), MGM.

Dir. Robert Z. Leonard; Sc. Lionel

Houser; *Cast includes:* Myrna Loy, Melvyn Douglas, Raymond Walburn, Lee Bowman, Bonita Granville, Felix Bressart.

Newly appointed magazine editor Myrna Loy, to protect her job, fabricates a fictitious husband in this entertaining comedy. It seems her employer's jealous wife is suspicious of attractive young women in his employ. But complications soon arise when Loy meets artist Melvyn Douglas and becomes romantically involved with him. The couple, however, engage in various altercations before they fall in love. Having learned of her ersatz marital life, the glib Douglas ensconces himself in her home as her imaginary husband. This leads to a string of farcical problems for Loy, but all is happily resolved by the last reel.

912 THE THIRTEENTH MAN (1937), Mon.

Dir. William Nigh; *Sc.* John Krafft; *Cast includes:* Weldon Heyburn, Inez Courtney, Selmer Jackson, Milburn Stone, Matty Fain, Robert Homans.

Newspaper columnist and radio reporter Weldon Heyburn helps to solve the murder of a crusading district attorney in this routine mystery thriller. When Milburn Stone, his assistant reporter, is killed while investigating the attorney's murder, Heyburn decides to take over the sleuthing. He soon uncovers the killer for the police. Inez Courtney plays his secretary whom the reporter marries after he solves the murder. Matty Fain makes a sinister racketeer in an otherwise ordinary production.

913 -30- (1959), WB.

Dir. Jack Webb; *Sc.* William Bowers; *Cast includes:* Jack Webb, Whitney Blake, Louise Lorimer, William Conrad, John Nolan, David Nelson.

This fairly accurate newspaper drama recounts eight hours in the life of a city room of a large urban daily newspaper. Tough night managing editor Jack Webb is recognized by his colleagues as a major force in the world of journalism. The basic plot deals with the next edition and a front-page story featuring the rescue of a child from a sewer. Other sub-plots concern a conflict between Webb and his wife Whitney Blake over the adoption of a child and the death of the grandson of Louise Lorimer, a writer on Webb's staff. Webb, the director-writer, gained popularity for his portrayal of a police detective in *Dragnet*, a weekly television series about a California police department.

914 THIRTY-DAY PRINCESS (1934), Par.

Dir. Marion Gering; *Sc.* Preston Sturges, Frank Partos; *Cast includes:* Sylvia Sidney, Cary Grant, Edward Arnold, Henry Stephenson, Vince Barnett, Edgar Norton.

Sylvia Sidney plays a dual role—a European princess and her New York lookalike actress—in this romantic comedy based on the novel by Clarence Budington Kelland. When the princess, scheduled for a good-will tour in America, comes down with the mumps, conniving banker Edward Arnold contrives to hire a double to replace the royal visitor for one month. A down-and-out actress is selected and she carries out the impersonation flawlessly, which includes fooling idealistic newspaper publisher Cary Grant, who soon falls in love with her. Complications arise when one of his reporters discovers the switch. But all works out well for the couple in love.

915 36 HOURS TO KILL (1936), TCF.

Dir. Eugene Forde; *Sc.* Lou Breslow, John Patrick; *Cast includes:* Brian Donlevy, Gloria Stuart, Douglas Fowley, Isabel Jewell, Stepin Fetchit, Julius Tannen.

A gangster on his way to collect a large cash prize has the misfortune to run into a government agent aboard a train in this entertaining cops-and-robbers comedy drama. Douglas Fowley, as the public enemy, has won $150,000 in a sweepstakes, but the fugitive must be careful to avoid police on his way to pick up his money. G-Man Brian Donlevy and newspaper reporter Gloria Stuart are fellow passengers, and they combine their efforts to bring Fowley to justice. Popular character players Stepin Fetchit and Warren Hymer add to the fun.

916 THIS MARRIAGE BUSINESS (1938), RKO.

Dir. Christy Cabanne; *Sc.* Gladys Atwater, J. Robert Bren; *Cast includes:* Victor Moore, Allan Lane, Vicki Lester, Cecil Kellaway, Jack Carson, Richard Lane.

Small-town newspaper reporter Allan Lane's publicity of the fact that no coupling performed by local marriage license clerk Victor Moore has ever ended in divorce brings unexpected results in this entertaining comedy. When Lane, in love with Vicki Lester, Moore's daughter, brings to light the clerk's unusual twenty-year success in the field of matrimony, hordes of young couples storm Moore's office, seeking the blessing of his "Lucky License." Meanwhile, the newspaperman gets the bright idea of having Moore enter the mayoralty race—creating even more problems for the justice of the peace. Opposing political forces try to tarnish his reputation by placing him in the company of a scantily clad blonde. He is later involved in a murder and jailed. But by the last reel Moore is exonerated of all charges. Actress Vicki Lester took her name from the screen character portrayed by Janet Gaynor in *A Star Is Born*, released one year earlier.

917 $1,000 A MINUTE (1935), Rep.

Dir. Aubrey Scotto; *Sc.* Joseph Fields; *Cast includes:* Roger Pryor, Leila Hyams, Edgar Kennedy, Edward Brophy, Purnell Pratt, Morgan Wallace.

Fate and two wealthy eccentrics have chosen obscure reporter Roger Pryor to carry out their strange wager in this fast-paced comedy. The two men each put up $360,000 to test whether someone they select can spend one thousand dollars a minute within twelve hours. After they set down certain restrictions, such as no two of the same articles are permitted, they select Pryor for their experiment, promising him $10,000 for his trouble. The reporter, who has just completed covering a bank robbery story, accepts the challenge. However, complications arise when the local police suspect he is spending some of the missing bank loot. From this point on, more than half the film is consumed with their pursuit of Pryor who is furiously making an effort to spend the $720,000. Adding to the laughs are the antics of such amiable character players as easily frustrated Edgar Kennedy, prissy Franklin Pangborn, breathy Sterling Holloway and slow-witted Edward Brophy. The film's premise at times is more effective than the one-liners. For example, when gangster Brophy overhears that Pryor must purchase only tangibles, he offers, "Tangibles are small oranges."

918 THREE GIRLS ABOUT TOWN (1941), Col.

Dir. Leigh Jason; *Sc.* Richard Carroll; *Cast includes:* Joan Blondell, Binnie Barnes, Janet Blair, John Howard, Robert Benchley, Eric Blore.

Joan Blondell and her two sisters, Binnie Barnes and Janet Blair, find a corpse in the hotel in which both Blondell and Barnes work in this comedy drama. Luckily, newspaper reporter John Howard is available to help the young women out of their dilemma by solving the murder. Blondell appeared in several newspaper dramas and comedies, including, among others, *The Famous Ferguson Case* (1932), *Back in Circulation* (1937) and *The Corpse Came C.O.D.* (1947),

919 THUNDERING CARAVANS (1952), Rep.

Dir. Harry Keller; *Sc.* M. Coates Webster; *Cast includes:* Allan "Rocky" Lane, Eddy Waller, Mona Knox, Roy Barcroft, Isabel Randolph, Richard Crane.

Isabel Randolph portrays a corrupt newspaper publisher who smears the reputation of local sheriff Eddy Waller in this routine entry in the Allan "Rocky" Lane western series. Lane, a U.S. marshal, is assigned to investigate several mysterious gold ore thefts while assisting beleaguered sheriff Waller. The two lawmen soon discover the publisher's motive is to protect her illegal operations by getting her brother, Bill Henry, voted into office as sheriff. Randolph proves to be a formidable adversary—for a while—until Lane's blazing guns and hard riding result in putting an end to the crimes and her henchmen.

920 TIGHT SHOES (1941), U.
Dir. Albert S. Rogell; *Sc.* Leonard Spigelgass; *Cast includes:* John Howard, Broderick Crawford, Richard Lane, Leo Carrillo, Anne Gwynne, Binnie Barnes.

Newspaper editor Richard Lane urges shoe salesman John Howard to expose a politician's crooked associations in this dizzy comedy based on a story by Damon Runyon. Political ward boss and gambler Broderick Crawford blackmails Howard into using the back room of the shoe store for an illegal dice game. The ill-fated meeting between the two men, which leads to a series of complications, is the result of Crawford's wanting to purchase a pair of tight shoes. Crawford fires Howard, who then exposes the corrupt political machine of the city. Veteran character actor Leo Carrillo portrays the owner of the shoe store. Although virtually forgotten for several years, the film was released a decade later when minor character actor Crawford achieved stardom and won an Oscar as best actor in *All the King's Men* (1949).

921 THE TIJUANA STORY (1957), Col.
Dir. Leslie Kardos; *Sc.* Lou Morheim; *Cast includes:* Rodolfo Acosta, James Darren, Robert McQueeney, Jean Willes, Joy Stoner, Paul Newlan.

Mexican journalist Rodolfo Acosta battles a crime syndicate in this weak drama inspired by actual incidents involving the newspaperman's assassination in Tijuana. The crusading journalist gathers a list of names of politicians associated with the illegal operations run by its boss, Paul Newlan, and is suddenly assassinated. Robert Blake, Acosta's son, smashes the syndicate after winning the support of the people. Paul Coates, who narrates the film, was the original journalist who gathered the evidence against the syndicate. This was one of several city exposé films released during this period.

922 TIMBER STAMPEDE (1939), RKO.
Dir. David Howard; *Sc.* Morton Grant; *Cast includes:* George O'Brien, Marjorie Reynolds, Morgan Wallace, Robert Fiske, Guy Usher, Earl Dwire.

Members of a gang of land grabbers hire innocent reporter Marjorie Reynolds to disseminate their propaganda—much to their eventual dismay—in this western drama. Lawman George O'Brien soon enlightens her about how she has been hoodwinked by the gang, after which she joins forces with him and Chill Wills, his sidekick. The trio bring to justice the robber barons and their minions. Popular cowboy star O'Brien joins a long parade of western heroes, including William S. Hart, Tim McCoy, Hoot Gibson, Roy Rogers and Randolph Scott, all of whom made at least one western with a newspaper background.

923 TIME OUT FOR MURDER (1938), TCF.
Dir. H. Bruce Humberstone; *Sc.* Jerry Cady; *Cast includes:* Gloria Stuart, Michael Whalen, Douglas Fowley, Robert Kellard, Chick Chandler, Jane Darwell.

Star reporter Michael Whalen teams up with his clowning photographer Chick Chandler to investigate a murder in this little drama. They arrive at the scene of a crime where the police already have arrested a likely suspect, bank messenger Robert Kellard. He is charged with killing Ruth Hussey, a woman for whom he was supposed to deposit a large sum of money. Nonchalant Whalen, though, suspects a local racketeer of the crime. Whalen and

Chandler then join forces with bill collector Gloria Stuart, and they go about searching for new evidence to convict the real killer. This was another entry in the Roving Reporter crime series featuring Michael Whalen.

924 TO PLEASE A LADY (1950), MGM.

Dir. Clarence Brown; *Sc.* Barre Lyndon; *Cast includes:* Clark Gable, Barbara Stanwyck, Adolphe Menjou, Will Geer, Ronald Winters, William C. McGraw.

National columnist and radio commentator Barbara Stanwyck criticizes tough daredevil auto racer Clark Gable, whose irresponsible actions lead to the death of a fellow racer, in this hackneyed drama. Although they both fall in love with each other, she uses her influence to ban Gable from further midget races after the accident. He then engages in auto stunting and finally buys a full-size sports car which he enters in an Indianapolis race. During the competition, he allows another racer to pass to avoid a possible crash, but Gable himself is injured. However, by showing his concern for others, he wins Stanwyck's renewed love when she realizes he has given up his former callous racing techniques.

925 TODD OF THE TIMES (1919), Pathé.

Dir. Elliott Howe; *Sc.* Jack Cunningham; *Cast includes:* Frank Keenan, Buddy Post, Aggie Herring, Herschel Mayall, George Williams, Joe Dowling.

Frank Keenan portrays city editor Theobald Todd, the title character, in this generally realistic early silent drama of newspaper life. An ambitious but reticent newspaperman, Todd aspires to the post of managing editor. When his superior is called away, Keenan takes control of the paper. The town, plagued by a wave of gamblers, is bent on stamping out this infestation. Todd puts out an extra exposing an undercover gambling operation. He proves that a bookmaking syndicate, posing as a brokerage firm, conducts its business from a hotel owned and supervised by the leader of a local reform movement. Promoted to managing editor, the elated newspaperman returns home to Aggie Herring, his nagging and domineering wife, and establishes his proper role as husband of the family.

926 THE TOMBOY (1921), Fox.

Dir. Carl Harbaugh; *Sc.* Carl Harbaugh; *Cast includes:* Eileen Percy, Hal Cooley, Richard Cummings, Paul Kamp, Byron Munson, Harry Dunkinson.

Village tomboy Eileen Percy is enraged by her architect father's drunken fits and vows to expose the local bootleggers in this minor comedy drama. Finding work as a sports writer on a local newspaper, she begins to condemn those engaged in the illicit activity of selling alcohol in the community. Byron Munson, the leader of the bootleggers, starts rumors about the writer's character after she rejects him as a suitor. Meanwhile Percy, with the help of Hal Cooley, a stranger, accomplishes her mission.

927 TOO HOT TO HANDLE (1938), MGM.

Dir. Jack Conway; *Sc.* Laurence Stallings, John Lee Mahin; *Cast includes:* Clark Gable, Myrna Loy, Walter Pidgeon, Walter Connolly, Leo Carrillo, Johnny Hines.

Rival newsreel cameramen Clark Gable and Walter Pidgeon compete not only for film scoops but for the affection of aviatrix Myrna Loy, in this farfetched but highly entertaining adventure thriller. Gable, a breezy newsman indulging his journalistic license, joins Loy in her search for her lost brother somewhere in South America. It is here he mesmerizes the jungle natives with moving pictures and dresses up as a god to win their respect. Gable is accompanied by his sidekick Leo Carrillo, who carries much of the comedy. Once in the perilous jungle they hear the ominous sound of drums. "What are you shivering about?" Gable asks. "I was just thinking," Carrillo replies, "how cold I'm going to be when they take off my skin and I have to sit around in my bones." One of the brightest sequences occurs early in war-torn China where Gable and his camera crew devise a phony attack of enemy airplanes by using a model plane and then submit the film as a genuine incident. In addition to playing the brash adventurer and shifty cameraman, Gable shows sensitivity when he falls in love with Loy. "I don't know what's the matter with me," she says, breaking out in tears while narrating footage of a tragic shipwreck. "I do," he adds. "You're the best there is. That's what's the matter with you." They embrace and he gives her a long kiss.

928 TOO MANY WINNERS (1947), PRC.

Dir. William Beaudine; Sc. John Sutherland; Cast includes: Hugh Beaumont, Trudy Marshall, Ralph Dunn, Claire Carleton, Charles Mitchell, John Hamilton.

Private eye Michael Shayne (Hugh Beaumont), about to go duck-hunting with his secretary Trudy Marshall, learns from a blackmailer about a racetrack racket in this fast-paced drama. It seems someone is forging pari-mutuel tickets. He postpones his vacation to unravel the case, but only after he is beaten up and several murders occur. With the help of newspaper reporter pal Charles Mitchell, the sleuth exposes the racetrack manager as the chief villain. This was the twelfth and last entry in the Michael Shayne detective series based on Brett Halliday's fictional character.

929 TOO TOUGH TO KILL (1935), Col.

Dir. D. Ross Lederman; Sc. Lester Cole, J. Griffin Jay; Cast includes: Victor Jory, Sally O'Neill, Thurston Hall, Johnny Arthur, Robert Gleckler, Robert Middlemass.

Los Angeles reporter Sally O'Neill journeys to the Southwest to cover the construction of a tunnel in this mild action drama. Also assigned to the job is engineer Victor Jory, who soon learns why the building is progressing so slowly and why there are so many accidents. After he antagonizes several unscrupulous workers, they try to set off an explosion to kill him and destroy the tunnel, but Jory, with the help of O'Neill, foils their plot. Johnny Arthur, as O'Neill's cameraman, provides the comedy relief.

930 TOP SECRET AFFAIR (1957), WB.

Dir. H. C. Potter; Sc. Roland Kibbee, Allan Scott; Cast includes: Susan Hayward, Kirk Douglas, Paul Stewart, Jim Backus, John Cromwell, Roland Winters.

Magazine publisher Susan Hayward, who at first endorses Kirk Douglas for a governmental position, ends up attacking him when he seeks the title of general in this comedy loosely based on the novel *Melville Goodwin, U.S.A.* by J. P. Marquand. Although the temperamental publisher exposes him in her magazine, calling him "Old Ironpants," she falls in love with him. A Congressional investigation almost ruins his career. Eventually, Hayward confesses that her story is false. Meanwhile, Douglas explains away a questionable incident after getting White House clearance. It seems that during the Korean War he was involved in a romantic affair in which he gave false information to an enemy agent.

931 TORCHY BLANE IN CHINATOWN (1939), WB.

Dir. William Beaudine; Sc. George Bricker; Cast includes: Glenda Farrell, Barton MacLane, Tom Kennedy, Patric Knowles, Henry O'Neill, James Stephenson.

Three con artists try to extort money using Chinese notes and a couple of fake murders in this weak entry in the Torchy Blane comedy drama series. Glenda Farrell, as the aggressive sob sister in the title, and her perennial boyfriend, Police Lieutenant Steve McBride (Barton Mac-

Lane), finally solve the murders. The astute snooping by Farrell, who is always seeking a scoop for her newspaper, is chiefly responsible for their success. This time around, MacBride doesn't do too well in his investigating attempts. Torchy's self-confidence is apparent early in the film when a cop tries to stop her from entering the scene of a crime. "You're wrong, boys," she snaps. "Holdups and murders are my meat. I'm Torchy Blane of the *Star*."

932 TORCHY BLANE IN PANAMA (1938), WB.

Dir. William Clemens; *Sc.* George Bricker; *Cast includes:* Lola Lane, Paul Kelly, Tom Kennedy, Anthony Averill, Larry Williams, Betty Compson.

Lola Lane portrays the title character, a cheeky reporter determined to get the scoop on a New York bank robbery in this newspaper-crime comedy drama. Together with her rival news hound Larry Williams, they arrive in Panama where, following the customary complications, Torchy with the help of dim-witted policeman Tom Kennedy apprehends bank robber Anthony Averill and gets her scoop. Her perennial boyfriend Police Lieutenant Steve McBride (Paul Kelly) is present to upbraid her actions. With this entry, Lane and Kelly replaced Glenda Farrell and Barton MacLane, who had played the leading roles in the Torchy Blane series.

933 TORCHY GETS HER MAN (1938), WB.

Dir. William Beaudine; *Sc.* Albert DeMond; *Cast includes:* Glenda Farrell, Barton MacLane, Tom Kennedy, Willard Robertson, George Guhl, John Ridgely.

Glenda Farrell, as spirited reporter Torchy Blane, becomes involved with a gang of clever counterfeiters in this entry in the Torchy Blane comedy drama series. Gang boss Willard Robertson tricks the authorities into passing the bogus money at a local racetrack. He poses as a secret service agent investigating the counterfeiters and for a time fools police lieutenant Barton MacLane and other cops, persuading them to quash any newspaper stories about his operations. But Farrell's curiosity gets the best of her, and her snooping leads to her being captured by the gang. A police dog then leads her boyfriend MacLane and his fellow cops to the hideout where they rescue her. Farrell and MacLane returned to the series after being absent from one entry, *Torchy Blane in Panama*, in which they were replaced by Lola Lane and Paul Kelly.

934 TORCHY PLAYS WITH DYNAMITE (1939), WB.

Dir. Noel Smith; *Sc.* Earle Snell, Charles Belden; *Cast includes:* Jane Wyman, Allen Jenkins, Tom Kennedy, Sheila Bromley, Joe Cunningham, Eddie Marr.

Torchy Blane, the popular reporter who is always on the prowl for a good story, once again becomes entangled with mobsters in this routine entry in the Torchy Blane series. This time around, our heroine, played by Jane Wyman, is also interested in helping her detective pal Allen Jenkins get a reward. She manipulates a jail term for herself to win the confidence of an imprisoned gangster's sweetheart. They escape and Torchy tricks her fellow fugitive into sending for her lover. Jenkins, posing as a hoodlum, then captures the gangster and collects the reward.

935 TORCHY RUNS FOR MAYOR (1939), WB.

Dir. Ray McCarey; *Sc.* Earle Snell; *Cast includes:* Glenda Farrell, Barton MacLane, Tom Kennedy, John Miljan, Frank Shannon, Joe Cunningham.

Once again, Glenda Farrell portrays Torchy Blane, the star reporter, whose curiosity more often than not gets her into hot water. In this entry she is bent on linking a corrupt administration with members of the underworld. She sells her sensational exposés to a rival paper when her publisher, fearing the loss of advertising revenue, rejects them. Blane is then forced to run for mayor when other possible candidates recoil in fear. Barton MacLane and Tom Kennedy repeat their roles as police detective and slow-witted cop, respectively, while John Miljan portrays a slick villain. Another of Hollywood's distorted concepts of the world of journalism, this entry in the Torchy Blane series is no better or worse than the dozens of similar films that have preceded it.

936 TOUGH ASSIGNMENT
(1949), Lippert.

Dir. William Beaudine; *Sc.* Milton Luban; *Cast includes:* Don Barry, Marjorie Steele, Steve Brodie, Marc Lawrence, Ben Welden, Iris Adrian.

Reporter Don Barry and his wife, photographer Marjorie Steele, go under cover to expose racketeer Steve Brodie in this mild newspaper-crime drama. Brodie runs a rustling racket in which he forces local shop owners to buy his stolen beef. The crusading couple infiltrate the gang by posing as a helper and a cook to gather evidence, but they are soon exposed. The police rescue them in the nick of time and round up the crooks.

937 TOUGH TO HANDLE
(1937), Syndicate.

Dir. Roy Luby; *Sc.* Sherman L. Lowe, Jack Neville; *Cast includes:* Frankie Darro, Kane Richmond, Phyllis Fraser, Harry Worth, Johnstone White, Lorraine Hayes.

A courageous reporter and his newsboy sidekick help to bring down a gang of racketeers in this illogical crime drama. The gang is engaged in swindling sweepstakes winners out of their prize money. Gang leader Harry Worth owns a nightclub that he uses as a cover for his underworld activities. However, he has to answer to a mysterious boss. Kane Richmond, as the fearless reporter, has a girlfriend who sings at the club. When her brother, Frankie Darro, is cheated out of the prize money, Richmond and the boy go after the gang and, following some rough fisticuffs, they manage to turn over the miscreants to the law.

938 THE TOWN SCANDAL
(1923), U.

Dir. King Baggot; *Sc.* Hugh Hoffman; *Cast includes:* Gladys Walton, Edward Hearn, Edward McWade, Charles Hill Mailes, William Welsh, William Franey.

Frisky chorus girl Gladys Walton blackmails the town's hypocritical big shots into dropping the local blue laws in this silent comedy drama about hypocrisy. Walton one summer returns to her home town for vacation and, when she leaves for the big city, several of the town fathers follow her and try to date her. The next summer when she returns, the same men, embarrassed to be associated with Walton, shun her and refuse to help her get a temporary job. She finds work with a local newspaper and, angered by the treatment she received by the phony town fathers, she begins a series titled "Life of a Chorus Girl." Once those same men who secretly followed her to the city begin to recognize themselves in the thinly disguised characters in the article, they try to bribe her to stop writing her incriminating story. When she refuses, they plot to lynch the young owner of the paper. Walton intervenes and, after the men agree to end the town's restrictive blue laws, she promises to destroy the next installment of her damaging story.

939 TRANSYLVANIA 6-5000
(1985), New World.

Dir. Rudy DeLuca; *Sc.* Rudy DeLuca; *Cast includes:* Jeff Goldblum, Joseph Bologna, Ed Begley Jr., Carol Kane, Jeffrey Jones, Geena Davis.

Two bumbling reporters find themselves in a modern-day Transylvania in this inept spoof of horror films. Jeff Goldblum and Ed Begley Jr., who work for a tabloid paper, journey to this mysterious land with its legendary monsters and clash with demented scientist Joseph Bologna. The visitors learn only that the mayor wants to turn the town into a theme park for tourists, and that the strange inhabitants are descendants of the famous vampire, thanks to Bologna's experiments.

940 TRAPPED IN THE GREAT METROPOLIS (1914), State Rights.

Cast includes: Rose Austin.

Newspaperwoman Rose Austin and her detective boyfriend work out a scheme to expose a white slavery ring in this early silent social drama. Posing as a South American interested in purchasing slaves, Austin worms her way into the confidence of the gang until she meets the leader who happens to be posing as a philanthropic lecturer. He escapes before the police arrive, and a chase ensues after the office manager who is soon shot. Meanwhile, the leader dies in his home from the excitement. No doubt the film was designed to capitalize on the highly successful and sensational drama *Traffic in Souls,* also about white slavery, released one year earlier.

941 TREASURE OF FEAR (1945) see *Scared Stiff* (1945).

942 THE TRESPASSER (1947), Rep.

Dir. George Blair; *Sc.* Jerry Gruskin, Dorrell McGowan, Stuart McGowan; *Cast includes:* Dale Evans, Warren Douglas, Janet Martin, Douglas Fowley, Adele Mara, Gregory Gay.

Neophyte reporter Janet Martin, assigned to the morgue, stumbles across a book-forging racket in this suspenseful newspaper-crime drama. Joining forces with fellow journalist Douglas Fowley, they investigate her suspicions and end up unmasking the culprits, headed by William Bakewell. Fowley's romantic interest in the film is Dale Evans, who plays a nightclub singer and the chief villain's sister. Evans had a substantial film career portraying Roy Rogers' love interest in a series of westerns, including several newspaper-related entries such as *Don't Fence Me In* (1945) and *Home in Indiana* (1946), both with Rogers and George "Gabby" Hayes.

943 TROUBLE IN MOROCCO (1937), Col.

Dir. Ernest Schoedsack; *Sc.* Paul Franklin; *Cast includes:* Jack Holt, Mae Clarke, C. Henry Gordon, Harold Huber, Oscar Apfel, Victor Marconi.

Jack Holt portrays a foreign correspondent who ends up in the French Foreign Legion by mistake in this flimsy action drama. The mix-up occurs when he becomes involved with ex-mobster Paul Hurst, who is seeking refuge in the Legion. Although his original assignment was to track down gunrunners in Morocco, Holt finds himself fighting desert tribes after others mistake him for a gangster. Mae Clarke plays a rival correspondent. Several furious battle sequences include the use of tanks brought in to rescue the besieged Legionnaires.

944 THE TRUTH WAGON (1914), Alliance.

Dir. Max Figman; *Sc.* Elliott J. Clawson; *Cast includes:* Max Figman, Lolita Robertson, H. A. Livingstone, Al W. Wilson.

Fun-loving playboy Max Figman suddenly announces that he intends to buy a dying newspaper and wage a battle against corrupt local politicians in this drama based on the 1912 play by Haydon Talbot. He disassociates himself from his father, who is a candidate for governor and a member of the political "machine" of the city. Figman decides to back his father's opponent, the former owner of the newspaper and father of Lolita Robertson, a reporter whom Figman loves. He resists threats by members of the "machine," and when several thugs try to smash his presses, Figman and his prizefighting pals evict the intruders. His candidate wins the governorship, and Figman marries the victor's daughter.

945 TRUTHFUL TULLIVER (1917), Triangle.

Dir. William S. Hart; *Sc.* J. G. Hawks; *Cast includes:* William S. Hart, Nina Byron, Milton Ross, Alma Reubens, Norbert A. Myles, Walter Perry.

William S. Hart portrays the title character, a frontiersman who turns newspaper editor of a wild western town, in this elemental silent drama. Denouncing a notorious local saloon managed by Milton Ross, Tulliver charges into the place on horseback, ropes Ross and drags him out of town. Later, Ross returns and is unsuccessful in his attempt to kill the editor. Following several other complications, Tulliver cleans up the town and wins the love of pretty Alma Reubens, one of two sisters who had been insulted earlier by patrons of Ross's saloon.

946 TRY AND GET ME (1951) *see* The Sound of Fury (1951).

947 THE TURNING POINT (1952), Par.

Dir. William Dieterle; *Sc.* Warren Duff; *Cast includes:* William Holden, Edmond O'Brien, Alexis Smith, Tom Tully, Ed Begley, Dan Dayton.

Investigative reporter William Holden joins crusading attorney Edmond O'Brien, who heads a crime commission, in this familiar drama. They gather evidence to prove that Ed Begley controls a local crime syndicate. At one point, Begley orders a tenement building containing incriminating records burned down, a horrific act that results in the deaths of dozens of tenants. Meanwhile the two heroes compete for the affection of Alexis Smith, with Smith leaning toward the more charming Holden. While trying to set up Begley, Holden walks into a trap at a boxing arena and, before help can arrive in time, he is gunned down by one of Begley's henchmen. O'Brien goes on to avenge Holden's death.

948 TWELVE CROWDED HOURS (1939), RKO.

Dir. Lew Landers; *Sc.* John Twist; *Cast includes:* Richard Dix, Lucille Ball, Allan Lane, Donald MacBride, Cyrus Kendall, Granville Bates.

Crack reporter Richard Dix becomes involved in the city's numbers racket after a city editor is killed by the mob in this above-average action drama. When rackets boss Cy Kendall orders three of his collectors killed, the unfortunate editor happens to be an innocent bystander. Dix avenges the journalist's untimely death by smashing the policy racket and bringing down its pompous boss. Lucille Ball provides the love interest for the battling reporter who helps extricate her misguided kid brother Allen Lane from the mob's influence. Donald MacBride portrays the stereotypical bungling detective, a role he was destined to play in countless films throughout the next decade.

949 TWO AGAINST THE WORLD (1936), WB.

Dir. William McGann; *Sc.* Michel Jacoby; *Cast includes:* Humphrey Bogart, Beverly Roberts, Linda Perry, Carlyle Moore Jr., Helen McKellar, Henry O'Neill.

Radio station manager Humphrey Bogart battles against the decision to rehash a twenty-year-old murder case in a series of broadcasts in this dull drama about media responsibility and its ramifications. Bogart is concerned about the effects of the national broadcast upon Helen McKellar, the woman who twenty years earlier had been tried in a court of law for the crime and acquitted. At the present time she is happily married to Henry O'Neill. Her daughter, Linda Perry, who knows nothing about her mother's past, is about to marry a wealthy young man. The radio program results in tragedy for the innocent family. The film is a flaccid remake of the superior, hard-hitting 1931 drama *Five Star Final*, about an unscrupulous newspaper, with Edward G. Robinson as a managing editor with the same fears as Bogart's.

950 TWO ON A GUILLOTINE (1965), WB.

Dir. William Conrad; Sc. Henry Slesar, John Kneubuhl; Cast includes: Connie Stevens, Dean Jones, Cesar Romero, Parley Baer, Virginia Gregg, Connie Gilchrist.

Young newspaper reporter Dean Jones helps Connie Stevens survive a terrifying seven nights in her father's mansion in this chilling drama that suffers from a farfetched ending. Similar to many earlier "old dark house" horror films, this entry is set in the Los Angeles home of a deceased famous magician who has stipulated in his will that his daughter must spend these nights here if she is to inherit his estate worth $300,000. If she fails, the money is to go to his housekeeper and his press agent. Jones accompanies her and finally is responsible for resolving the strange events Stevens is forced to suffer. Cesar Romero portrays the magician who invented a trick involving a special guillotine and who promises to return after his death. Other similar "dark house" mysteries with a newspaper background include *The Haunted Bedroom* (1919), *The House of Horror* (1929) and *The Missing Guest* (1938).

951 UNDER FIRE (1983), Orion.

Dir. Roger Spottiswoode; Sc. Ronald Shelton, Clayton Frohman; Cast includes: Nick Nolte, Gene Hackman, Joanna Cassidy, Jean-Louis Trintignant, Ed Harris.

Set chiefly in Nicaragua in 1979, the drama centers around three journalists. Professional still photographer Nick Nolte is loyal only to his immediate assignment. A senior correspondent for *Time*, Gene Hackman dreams of becoming a television anchor man earning $10,000 per week with a home in Long Island. Joanna Cassidy, a reporter for Public Radio, leaves her lover, Hackman, and takes up with Nolte. In Nicaragua, Nolte and his fellow journalists cover the war between President Somoza's troops and the revolutionaries. But the film is concerned more in exploring the moral ambiguities to which correspondents are particularly vulnerable. Nolte is objective almost to a fault. "I don't take sides," he replies when asked where his sympathies lie, "I take pictures." Eventually he begins to sympathize with the rebels. He grows fond of a young revolutionary who dreams of becoming a baseball player and who is suddenly shot while joking with Nolte. In another scene, the rebels ask him to photograph their dead leader as though he were alive. This would give impetus to the revolution and end the war quickly, thereby saving many lives. At first, Nolte rejects the idea but then agrees, and faked picture is released internationally. He soon learns that a French double agent has been using Nolte's other human interest shots to finger rebel leaders who have since been assassinated. Consciencestricken Nolte believes he is indirectly responsible for these killings. The drama ends with Somoza leaving for Florida while the people take to the streets to celebrate their victory. The film gives a frank treatment of reporters under pressure—of how they may easily become victims of the worst sin of their profession, falsifying their stories. It also suggests strongly the involvement of the U.S. and the C.I.A., often represented by wrong-headed individuals. Nolte encounters another American, a mercenary who shot the young rebel, an act that drove Nolte to side with the revolutionists. When Hackman is coldbloodedly killed by Somoza's troops, Cassidy mourns openly in view of a native woman. "Fifty thousand Nicaraguans have died and now one Yankee," the woman says to the reporter. "Perhaps now Americans will be outraged at what is happening here. Maybe we should have killed an American journalist 50 years ago."

952 UNDER SUSPICION (1918), Metro.

Dir. Will S. Davis; Sc. Albert Shelby Le Vino; Cast includes: Francis X. Bushman,

Beverly Bayne, Eve Gordon, Hugh Jeffrey, Frank Montgomery, Arthur Housman.

Society reporter Beverly Bayne meets wealthy young Francis X. Bushman at a home where a robbery occurs in this low-budget romantic drama based on the story "The Woolworth Diamonds" by Hugh C. Weir. After some valuable diamonds are stolen, Bayne finds a button torn from Bushman's coat. He has gained entrance to the affair by posing as a reporter from the same newspaper as Bayne's. To meet her again, he gets a job as a reporter and the couple soon fall in love and become engaged. But when Bayne notices a button missing from one of her fiancé's jackets matches the one she had found earlier, she suspects him of the theft and breaks off their engagement. However, the conflict is resolved when she learns that the crook was Bushman's butler. The culprit attacks Bayne, but Bushman arrives in the nick of time to rescue her.

953 UNDERSEA GIRL (1957), AA.

Dir. John Peyser; Sc. Arthur V. Jones; Cast includes: Mara Corday, Pat Conway, Florence Marly, Dan Seymour, Ralph Clanton, Myron Healey.

Reporter Mara Corday inadvertently uncovers a clue to missing U.S. Navy funds in this weak action drama. While skindiving, Corday finds the body of a fisherman with some of the missing $2 million. After telling navy lieutenant Pat Conway, her boyfriend, about her findings, they both investigate and eventually solve the mystery.

954 THE UNDERWORLD STORY (1950), UA.

Dir. Cyril Endfield; Sc. Henry Blankfort; Cast includes: Dan Duryea, Herbert Marshall, Gale Storm, Howard da Silva, Michael O'Shea, Mary Anderson.

Sleazy newspaperman Dan Duryea, who has been blacklisted from major big-city dailies after double-crossing a district attorney, eventually redeems himself in this newspaper-crime drama that reverberates with suggestions of racial intolerance. The ostracized reporter buys a share in a small New England newspaper, tying in with a partnership involving Gale Storm. When the daughter-in-law of notable publisher Herbert Marshall is found murdered, Mary Anderson, the victim's African-American maid, is framed for the crime. The woman surrenders to Storm, professing her innocence. The talk around town begins to grow ugly. But Duryea, believing her story, investigates and uncovers the real killer, the son of the publisher-magnate. The film, also listed as *The Whipped*, was adapted from a story by mystery writer Craig Rice.

955 UNEXPECTED PLACES (1918), Metro.

Dir. E. Mason Hopper; Sc. Albert S. LeVino, George D. Baker; Cast includes: Bert Lytell, Colin Kenny, Louis Morrison, Edythe Chapman, Rhea Mitchell.

Bert Lytell, a quick-witted reporter, uncovers a German plot to steal a set of important papers in this silent drama set during World War I and based on the short story by Frank R. Adams. German spies make repeated attempts to gain possession of these documents. The search for the papers results in the murder of an innocent servant and the poisoning of an English lord who has carried the documents across the ocean to America. Lytell retrieves them and thus becomes the target of enemy agents. Rhea Mitchell, as the lord's cousin, becomes entangled in the mystery when she mistakes the reporter for her cousin. She is kidnapped by the spies who are willing to trade her for the coveted papers. The reporter manages to free her, but the couple are pursued by the gang. The police finally capture the spies.

956 THE UNFOLDMENT (1922), AE.

Dir. George Kern, Murdock MacQuarrie; Sc. James Couldwell, Reed Heustis; Cast includes: Florence Lawrence, Barbara Bedford, Charles French, William Conklin, Albert Prisco, Lydia Knott.

Bold reporter Florence Lawrence enlightens her employer, newspaper owner Charles French, about some of his shortcomings in this offbeat drama with its simplistic ending. He has assigned her to make a documentary film depicting him as a philanthropic candidate for a political office. French had earlier ruined the mayor of a local neighborhood; more recently, his harsh attitude toward Barbara Bedford, his daughter, results in her becoming an invalid. Lawrence's film, titled *The Unfoldment*, ends up painting the characters realistically. Several persons are startled by how they have been portrayed, including French. He admits his faults and reconciles his differences with the mayor and his own daughter. Others react in similar fashion.

957 UNFORGOTTEN CRIME (1942) see *Affairs of Jimmy Valentine* (1942).

958 UNHOLY PARTNERS (1941), MGM.

Dir. Mervyn LeRoy; *Sc.* Earl Baldwin, Bartlett Cormack, Lesser Samuels; *Cast includes:* Edward G. Robinson, Laraine Day, Edward Arnold, Marsha Hunt, William T. Orr, Don Beddoe.

World War I veteran and reporter Edward G. Robinson starts his own hard-hitting tabloid with the financial help of gangster Edward Arnold in this entertaining newspaper drama. The two partners soon come to loggerheads over policy and other matters, with Arnold kidnapping William T. Orr, Robinson's aide. The gangster demands his partner's share in the paper for Orr's return. Robinson is forced to shoot Arnold during a quarrel, after which he dictates a confession to his secretary, Laraine Day. When he is killed in a plane crash, Day destroys the confession, and Orr continues running the paper in Robinson's style. The film is another attack on the reckless sensational press. "I'll let someone else dish up scandal," Robin-

son says at one point in the film. "I don't want to write any story that half a million readers will forget and a mother and father will remember the rest of their days. I don't think any story is worth ruining a life."

959 UNIVERSAL SOLDIER (1992), TriStar.

Dir. Roland Emmerich; *Sc.* Richard Rothstein, Christopher Leitch, Dean Devlin; *Cast includes:* Jean-Claude Van Damme, Dolph Lundgren, Ally Walker, Jerry Orbach, Leon Rippy, Ed O'Ross.

Rival cyborgs Jean-Claude Van Damme and Dolph Lundgren, results of a covert government experiment that went amok, battle it out across a futuristic landscape in this farfetched action drama. After having killed each other in the Vietnam War, Van Damme and Lundgren are flash-frozen by demented scientist Ed O'Ross and his equally mad assistants, and 25 years later they are converted into super soldiers, along with other specimens. Van Damme begins reverting to his more human traits and breaks away from the others. He joins spirited and personable television reporter Ally Walker, who has uncovered the secret of the covert cyborg project. The pair are chased across the Midwest by the vicious Lundgren, O'Ross and the police. Following several complications, an exciting climactic battle ensues between the two arch enemies, ending with Lundgren's graphic demise in a giant wood-mulching machine.

960 UNMASKED (1950), Rep.

Dir. George Blair; *Sc.* Albert DeMond, Norman S. Hall; *Cast includes:* Robert Rockwell, Barbra Fuller, Raymond Burr, Hillary Brooke, Paul Harvey, Norman Budd.

A prominent member of the press behaves in a less than exemplary manner in this familiar dark drama. Barbra Fuller, as the daughter of a slain man, and tough police lieutenant Robert Rockwell bring to justice Raymond Burr, the evil, vicious editor of a scandal sheet. Burr murders his female backer who has been blackmailing him and, later, he frames her husband for the crime. The weak spouse then commits suicide. The plot next introduces a mobster, another murder, a prison break and the entrance of the slain man's daughter who is seeking justice.

961 THE UNSEEN (1981), World Northal.

Dir. Peter Foleg; *Sc.* Michael L. Grace; *Cast includes:* Barbara Bach, Sydney Lassick, Stephen Furst, Lelia Goldoni, Karen Lamm, Doug Barr.

Television reporter Barbara Bach and her two assistants, Karen Lamm and Lois Young, are assigned to cover a festival in a California town in this chiefly inane horror tale that offers some intrigue and very little horror. Unfortunately, the only accommodations available are in a remote mansion. Creepy Sydney Lassick and his sister Lelia Goldoni, who run the place, harbor a terrible secret. Under lock and key and hidden in the basement is Stephen Furst, their offspring, the result of their incestuous activity. The disfigured Furst manages to escape and attacks each of the three visiting young women. The film degenerates into the usual screaming and chasing until Bach's boyfriend and former football player shows up to propose to her.

962 UP CLOSE AND PERSONAL (1996), Touchtone.

Dir. Jon Avnet; *Sc.* Joan Didion, John Gregory Dunne; *Cast includes:* Robert Redford, Michelle Pfeiffer, Stockard Channing, Joe Mantegna, Kate Nelligan, Glenn Plummer.

Ambitious Michelle Pfeiffer desperately seeks to win a news anchor position in this fascinating drama based on the novel *Golden Girl* by Alanna Nash, about a woman determined to succeed. Although many have informed her she would never gain that post, she still covets it as she moves from obscure weather girl to anchor. This leads to her clash with bright and older newsman Robert Redford. He soon turns into her mentor and lover. As expected in this competitive world of network television news, Pfeiffer's popularity soon overshadows Redford's.

963 UP FOR MURDER (1931), U.

Dir. Monta Bell; *Sc.* Monta Bell; *Cast includes:* Lew Ayres, Genevieve Tobin, Purnell Pratt, Richard Tucker, Frank McHugh, Louise Beavers.

Naive and sullen cub reporter Lew Ayres falls in love with the more mature Genevieve Tobin, a society editor on the same paper, in this minor drama. He grows jealous of her romance with the married owner and engages in a struggle with the older man who falls and is fatally injured. The young reporter surrenders and remains silent, hoping to protect Tobin. But she reveals all at his trial and he is released. The drama is a remake of *Man, Woman and Sin*, a 1927 silent feature. Frank McHugh portrays a drunken reporter, a stereotype that had already emerged as a cliché in several silent films, including *A Case at Law* (1917) and *Deadline at Eleven* (1920).

964 UP IN CENTRAL PARK (1948), U.

Dir. William Seiter; *Sc.* Karl Tunberg; *Cast includes:* Deanna Durbin, Dick Haymes, Vincent Price, Albert Sharpe, Tom Powers, Hobart Cavanaugh.

Dick Haymes portrays a crusading *N.Y. Times* reporter who meets and falls in love with Deanna Durbin, an innocent Irish immigrant, in this musical comedy based on the play by Dorothy Fields and Sigmund Romberg. Set in New York at the turn of the century, the overly sentimental film touches upon such notorious personalities as Boss Tweed, played by Vincent Price. The reporter joins Albert Sharpe, Durbin's father and park superintendent, in exposing the corrupt Tweed. Haymes and Durbin each get a chance to sing one number while other musical sequences involve dance routines. Unfortunately, much of Romberg's original music was cut for the screen version.

965 UP YOUR ALLEY (1989), Borde & Associates.

Dir. Bob Logan; Sc. Bob Logan, Murray Langston; Cast includes: Murray Langston, Linda Blair, Bob Zany, Kevin Benton, Ruth Buzzi, Glen Vincent.

Newspaper reporter Linda Blair poses as a homeless person in this fairly interesting low-budget comedy. Her main purpose is to write an in-depth article about Murray Langston, a reticent street person whose scornful and skeptical attitude fascinates the journalist. Langston's overall disposition, however, is mollified by his romance with Blair, and by Bob Zany, a slow-witted fellow marginal. Meanwhile, a sub-plot develops in the shape of a demented killer who is preying upon the derelicts of Los Angeles. Much-needed comedy relief is amply provided by a host of comics.

966 THE VENETIAN AFFAIR (1967), MGM.

Dir. Jerry Thorpe; Sc. E. Jack Neuman; Cast includes: Robert Vaughn, Elke Sommer, Felicia Farr, Karl Boehm, Boris Karloff, Edward Asner.

International agents scheme to sabotage the efforts of major world powers who are seeking to establish peaceful coexistence between the East and West in this slow-paced drama set during the cold war. When a bomb kills more than a dozen diplomats at a Venice peace conference, each side suspects the other. Robert Vaughn, a former C.I.A. agent now employed as a reporter for an international news agency, is assigned to cover the story. He soon finds himself entangled in a web of intrigue spun by the C.I.A. and international spies. His former C.I.A. chief, Edward Asner, now in charge of the Venice office, suspects Elke Sommer, Vaughn's wife, of being a Communist spy. He recruits the ex-C.I.A. agent to track her down. Meanwhile Karl Boehm, a sinister and ruthless spy who sells his services to any power, has developed a dangerous mind-altering drug that turns its victims into helpless puppets. Boehm, who drugged an American diplomat at the ill-fated conference, was responsible for the bombing. Political analyst Boris Karloff has learned about Boehm's secret drug and plans to expose him at the next peace conference. This sets off a search for Karloff 's report by Asner, Vaughn and Boehm's henchmen. The reporter recovers the papers and appears in the nick of time at the next diplomatic meeting to prevent another disaster. Based on Helen MacInnes's novel, the film ends with Asner about to read Karloff 's report to various representatives of the major powers.

967 VIOLENCE (1947), Mon.

Dir. Jack Bernhard; Sc. Stanley Rubin, Louis Lantz; Cast includes: Nancy Coleman, Michael O'Shea, Sheldon Leonard, Peter Whitney, Emory Parnell, Pierre Watkin.

Nancy Coleman, an undercover reporter for a photo magazine, is determined to smash a hate-mongering secret organization in this routine cautionary drama aimed chiefly at veterans. The United Defenders, a group designed to disseminate civil discord, chiefly seeks out disillusioned and embittered World War II veterans to join their ranks. Unfortunately, Coleman suffers from amnesia as the result of a car accident, and investigator Michael O'Shea comes to her rescue. Both their lives are threatened by villains Sheldon Leonard, Peter Whitney and others before the last reel brings a satisfactory conclusion.

968 VIVA VILLA! (1934), MGM.

Dir. Jack Conway; Sc. Ben Hecht; Cast includes: Wallace Beery, Leo Carrillo, Fay Wray, Donald Cook, Stuart Erwin, George E. Stone.

A chiefly fictional biography of the legendary Mexican bandit and guerrilla leader, the film begins in the turbulent 1880s with a foreword that describes Mexico's present ruler, Diaz, as a tyrant. Peons are evicted from their land and homes and whipped if they protest. It is under such conditions that Pancho Villa as a boy sees his father beaten to death. Wallace Beery portrays Villa, who has grown up and, leading a band of outlaws, seeks revenge against the government. Stuart Erwin portrays an American journalist who follows Villa's tempestuous career while exploiting the newsworthiness of the Mexican bandit. Francisco Madero, leader of the revolutionary forces bent on ousting the Diaz regime, meets with Villa and penetrates the bandit's tough exterior with visions of a free Mexico. Villa is impressed with Madero and, putting aside his personal vengeance, promises the political leader to fight alongside the rebel generals. Ben Hecht's script, mixing some fact and plenty of fiction, tends to glorify Villa, painting him more as a patriotic hero than a lawless marauder that contemporary newspaper accounts labeled him. There are several effective battle sequences as well as a few brutal ones. In one scene Beery orders an adversary, a corrupt general, to be smeared with honey and devoured by ants. Villa's second-in-command, Leo Carrillo, seems to enjoy the battles and the slaughter. A hero to his people during the revolution, Villa disbands his army when Madero, the new President, asks him to. Villa senses he is no longer the fighting patriot whose exploits dominated the front pages. "I ain't news no more?" he asks Erwin, somewhat crestfallen. "You're better than news," Erwin replies. "You're history!" After Madero is assassinated, Villa returns from exile in the U.S. and raises another peasant army. He defeats those in power and rides into Mexico City in triumph. The film ends with his assassination by a disgruntled aristocrat. No mention is made of America's political entanglements in the affairs of Mexico during this period. There is no reference, for example, to the unsuccessful punitive expedition against Villa, led by General Pershing and ordered by President Wilson, following the bandit leader's raid in New Mexico. The reporter whom Erwin plays is allegedly based on the real-life Hearst correspondent John W. Roberts, who accompanied the Mexican leader on his campaigns. The role was originally assigned to Lee Tracy, whose public drunkenness in Mexico compelled the studio to cancel his contract.

969 **WAIFS** (1918), Pathé.

Dir. Albert Parker; *Sc.* Frank Leon Smith; *Cast includes:* Gladys Hulette, J. H. Gilmour, Creighton Hale, Walter Hiers.

Reporter Creighton Hale rescues Gladys Hulette, a fellow boarding house resident, in this chiefly implausible comedy. Hulette, refusing to marry a distant cousin her wealthy father has chosen for her, leaves home and moves into a boarding house. Her father, J. H. Gilmour, has her followed and plans to send the cousin to her, hoping that the pair will meet and fall in love. Meanwhile, the reporter rescues Hulette from an intruder, an ex-convict who has returned to retrieve some stolen bonds he had hidden earlier in her room. The couple soon become fond of each other. The intruder, determined to recover the bonds, makes another attempt, and again a fight ensues between him and Hale. The cowardly cousin, portly Walter Heirs, upon witnessing the brawl, telephones Hulette's father who arrives later. Gilmour finds his daughter delicately attending to victorious Hale's wounds and then discovers that the stolen bonds belong to him. Grateful for their return, he congratulates the young hero and turns away the weak cousin he had intended for his son-in-law.

970 **WAKE UP AND LIVE** (1937), TCF.

Dir. Sidney Lanfield; *Sc.* Harry Tugend, Jack Yellen; *Cast includes:* Walter Winchell, Ben Bernie, Alice Faye, Patsy Kelly, Ned Sparks, Jack Haley.

Famous newspaper columnist Walter Winchell and popular band leader Ben Bernie engage in a good-natured feud in this pleasant spoof of the radio industry based on the book by Dorothea Brande. Meanwhile, radio reporter Alice Faye helps timid singer Jack Haley to succeed in his career. When Faye tricks the singer, who has a phobia of microphones, into warbling with Bernie's orchestra, Winchell accuses Bernie of deception. Haley achieves self-confidence, rises to stardom by the ploy, and falls in love with Faye. Rivals Winchell and Bernie reconcile their differences and shake hands. Buddy Clark supplied the singing voice for Haley. Winchell and Bernie starred in a similar light comedy, *Love and Hisses*, also released in 1937.

971 THE WALLS CAME TUMBLING DOWN (1946), Col.

Dir. Lothar Mendes; *Sc.* Wilfred H. Pettitt; *Cast includes:* Lee Bowman, Marguerite Chapman, Edgar Buchanan, George Macready, Lee Patrick, Jonathan Hale.

Newspaper columnist Lee Bowman suspects the death of his friend, a priest, was not the result of suicide but murder in this suspenseful mystery based on the novel by Jo Eisinger. Involved in the death are a Boston socialite, peculiar art dealer J. Edward Bromberg, verbose attorney Edgar Buchanan, and several others, including the innocent-appearing killer, George Macready. All are seeking two Bibles and a valuable painting depicting the fall of Jericho.

972 WAR CORRESPONDENT (1932), Col.

Dir. Paul Sloane; *Sc.* Jo Swerling; *Cast includes:* Jack Holt, Ralph Graves, Lila Lee, Tetsu Komai, Victor Wong.

This action drama is set in strife-torn China in the 1920s as bandits and warlords challenge the government. Jack Holt, an American mercenary pilot, battles against the insurgents. Ralph Graves, a war correspondent, broadcasts the daily events while arguing with Holt. When Lila Lee, a woman of easy virtue who has seen the light, is captured by a villainous warlord, Holt rushes to her rescue, followed by Graves. They free her while they fight off hordes of the leader's troops. Holt loses his life during the struggle, leaving the heroine to Graves. The formula film provides plenty of action, including an exciting dogfight between Holt and four enemy aircraft.

973 THE WAR EXTRA (1914), State Rights.

A cub reporter who pleads with his editor to send him to Mexico to cover the war news is arrested as a spy when he arrives in the war-torn country in this early silent drama. He had sent home news stories of the war by way of telegraph while still aboard the ship bound for Vera Cruz. A Mexican woman comes to his aid and rescues him from the revolutionaries. He then leaves for New York with his newfound friend and, upon his arrival at which time he is greeted as a hero, he announces that he will marry his attractive savior.

974 WARKILL (1967), Balut Productions.

Dir. Ferde Grofe Jr.; *Sc.* Ferde Grofe Jr.; *Cast includes:* George Montgomery, Tom Drake, Conrad Parham, Eddie Infante.

A brutal American colonel leads Filipino troops against the Japanese in this action drama set in the latter part of World War II. George Montgomery, the hard-bitten officer, does not believe in taking prisoners. His outfit is assigned to rout out pockets of Japanese resisters. Montgomery employs a variety of techniques to accomplish his mission, including dumping half-starved rats into caves used as hideouts by the enemy, and sending dogs to flush out the stubborn foe. Correspondent Tom Drake has idolized the colonel and has often written of his heroic deeds. When he finally meets Montgomery and witnesses the warrior in action, Drake quickly becomes disillusioned with his hero. "In every man there is a beast, and it's only this war that makes us animals," the colonel explains to the idealistic reporter. Drake recoils from the man he once considered a hero, and only when he stumbles upon the atrocities committed by the Japanese does he finally grasp the meaning of the horrors of war and what Montgomery was trying to say.

975 WASHINGTON MELODRAMA (1941), MGM.

Dir. S. Sylvan Simon; Sc. Marion Parsonnet, Roy Chanslor; Cast includes: Frank Morgan, Ann Rutherford, Kent Taylor, Dan Dailey, Lee Bowman, Fay Holden.

A newspaper editor helps to rescue wealthy philanthropist Frank Morgan when the latter becomes the victim of a blackmailing plot in this routine drama based on a play by L. du Rocher MacPherson. Morgan journeys to Washington, D.C., in his campaign to help save Europe's starving children and innocently meets nightclub entertainer Anne Gwynne, who is then murdered. Scheming club emcee Dan Dailey begins to blackmail the philanthropist, claiming he is a likely suspect in the crime. But editor Kent Taylor and the police foil Dailey's plans and arrest him for the murder.

976 WASHINGTON STORY (1952), MGM.

Dir. Robert Pirosh; Sc. Robert Pirosh; Cast includes: Van Johnson, Patricia Neal, Louis Calhern, Sidney Blackmer, Philip Ober, Patricia Collinge.

When youthful U.S. congressman Van Johnson is forced to sue slanderous columnist Philip Ober, he becomes the target of a larger plot in this fairly absorbing political drama about headline-seeking commentators sensationalizing their stories at the expense of hard-working politicians. Reporter Patricia Neal teams up with Ober, a columnist and radio reporter who continually criticizes government wrongdoing. Together, they hope to find something shady in Johnson's past. She poses as someone interested in writing favorable articles about Johnson and ends up discovering he is completely honest, even to the point of voting against his home town on a national issue. She then writes supporting articles about him while the pair fall in love. Washington was portrayed more savagely in earlier, more cynical dramas during the Depression, such as *Washington Masquerade* (1932), which depicts a corrupt Congress in bed with lobbyists, and *Washington Merry-Go-Round* (1932), which also pictures Congress as a corrupt body willing to destroy any idealists who dare to criticize its members or its unscrupulous methods.

977 WEDDING PRESENT (1936), Par.

Dir. Richard Wallace; Sc. Joseph Anthony; Cast includes: Cary Grant, Joan Bennett, George Bancroft, Gene Lockhart, William Demarest, Inez Courtney.

Cary Grant and Joan Bennett portray dizzy reporters whose careers jeopardize their romance in this disappointing screwball comedy. At first the two star reporters fall in love, but when Grant advances to editor, Bennett cannot handle his promotion and dictatorial approach to his new position and walks out on him. She leaves for New York where she meets author Conrad Nagel, whom she finds more secure and responsible than Grant and whom she resolves to marry. Grant, realizing how much he misses her, resigns and heads for the Big Apple where he plots to win her back. He interrupts her wedding and kidnaps her, after which they reconcile their differences.

978 WEEKEND AT THE WALDORF (1945), MGM.

Dir. Robert Z. Leonard; Sc. Sam Spewack, Bella Spewack; Cast includes: Ginger Rogers, Lana Turner, Walter Pidgeon, Van Johnson, Edward Arnold, Phyllis Thaxter.

Not one, but two journalists take part in the various doings at the world-famous New York hotel in this light-hearted drama, set during World War II and inspired by the play *Grand Hotel* by Vicki Baum. Newspaper reporter Keenan Wynn gets his big scoop, and skeptical war correspondent Walter Pidgeon finds true love with a movie queen played by Ginger Rogers. Meanwhile, other lives pass through the hotel lobby during this eventful weekend. Van Johnson, as a soldier wounded in the war, survives a difficult heart operation, thanks in part to his newfound love—stenographer Lana Turner. Edward Arnold is surprised to learn that the Egyptian he has tried to swindle speaks and understands English. The stories are entertaining, but the majestic Waldorf steals the show.

979 WHAT A NIGHT! (1928), Par.

Dir. Edward Sutherland; Sc. Louise Long; Cast includes: Bebe Daniels, Neil Hamilton, William Austin, Wheeler Oakman, Charles Sellon, Charles Hill Mailes.

A local newspaper is determined to uncover the connection between a corrupt mayor and members of the underworld in this comedy drama. The only problem is that Bebe Daniels, as a feather-brained socialite interested in a journalism career, keeps fouling up matters for the paper. She is hired only because her father, a successful industrialist, advertises heavily in the paper. Reporter Neil Hamilton, whose father is editor, takes her in hand but with little early success as she fumbles her way through one disaster after another. Finally, she interviews a gunman in jail and learns the location of a canceled check linking criminals to crooked political leaders. Following several complications, Daniels saves the paper from a lawsuit by retrieving the stolen check and presenting an incriminating photograph of the culprits.

980 WHAT A WOMAN! (1943), Col.

Dir. Irving Cummings; Sc. Therese Lewis, Barry Trivers; Cast includes: Rosalind Russell, Brian Aherne, Willard Parker, Alan Dinehart, Edward Fielding, Ann Savage.

Magazine writer Brian Aherne is assigned to interview literary agent Rosalind Russell concerning her client Willard Parker, a burgeoning novelist, in this highly improbable but delightfully funny comedy. Russell, however, has her own agenda. She wants Parker to star in the film Hollywood intends to produce based on the author's novel. But a problem arises when Parker, a rather private person, insists upon his anonymity. Following the usual triangular romantic complications, Aherne and Russell fall in love.

981 WHAT LOVE CAN DO (1916), U.

Dir. Jay Hunt; Sc. Jay Hunt; Cast includes: Adele Farrington, C. Norman Hammond, Orin C. Jackson, Kingsley Benedict, Mina Cunard, Mrs. Jay Hunt.

Reporter Adele Farrington saves the life of wealthy widower and newspaperman C. Norman Hammond in this early silent drama. Farrington and Hammond become lovers, but when Hammond's daughter, Mina Cunard, raised in New York, wants to join her father, he seeks to break off his relationship with Farrington. Meanwhile the reporter, now a successful author as well, sides with striking miners against Hammond, who then fires her. The daughter learns that the miners threaten violence and pleads with ex-reporter Farrington to intercede. An angry miner fires his pistol at the publisher, but Farrington takes the bullet for him, thereby saving his life. As she recovers from the wound, Hammond grows aware that he really loves her.

982 WHAT LOVE WILL DO (1923), Sunset.

Dir. Robert North Bradbury; Cast includes: Kenneth McDonald, Marguerite Clayton.

After failing at several jobs, despondent reporter Kenneth McDonald resides with the Gregory family on their farm. The father is soon accused of murdering three unscrupulous bankers who have vanished. Not one to forget the kindness of the family, especially that of Marguerite Clayton, Gregory's pretty daughter, with whom he has fallen in love, McDonald begins to investigate the strange circumstances of the disappearance. Following several exciting experiences, the former reporter solves the mystery and wins the appreciation and love of the daughter.

983 WHEN THE LIGHTS GO ON AGAIN (1944), PRC.

Dir. William K. Howard; Sc. Milton Lazarus; Cast includes: Jimmy Lydon, Barbara Belden, Grant Mitchell, Dorothy Peterson, Regis Toomey, George Cleveland.

Released during World War II, this drama deals earnestly with the treatment of returning war veterans. Regis Toomey portrays a caring reporter who helps shell-shocked U.S. Marine Jimmy Lydon return to his home. While asleep aboard a train, Lydon dreams about his life before the war. Later, the film concentrates on how his family and his surroundings contribute to his rehabilitation. This was one of the earliest films of the period to focus on the subject. The title was based on a popular song of the period. Toomey more often played policemen to low-budget action dramas. Lydon usually was seen in lighter teenage roles in comedies, including the title character in the popular Henry Aldrich comedy series.

984 WHERE THE BUFFALO ROAM (1980), U.

Dir. Art Linson; Sc. John Kaye; Cast includes: Peter Boyle, Bill Murray, Bruno Kirby, Rene Auberjonois, R. G. Armstrong, Danny Goldman.

Bill Murray portrays the iconoclastic journalist Hunter J. Thompson, who helped define the social turmoil of the late 1960s, in this superficial comedy drama loosely based on Thompson's life and writings. Some of his more outrageous experiences include his coverage of the 1968 San Francisco marijuana trials, the 1972 Super Bowl, a guerrilla arms-smuggling caper, and finally his incisive report while on the Presidential campaign trail. Murray captures many of Thompson's traits and eccentricities, especially his dangling cigarette holder, his excessive drinking and his continual pill popping. Peter Boyle plays his equally eccentric companion, a radical lawyer who accompanies the writer on his assignments. Thompson's outlandish behavior, which led to his running up large debts and barely getting his assignment in on time, must have tried the patience of the editor of *Blast* magazine.

985 WHILE NEW YORK SLEEPS (1938), TCF.

Dir. H. Bruce Humberstone; Sc. Frances Hyland, Albert Ray; Cast includes: Michael Whalen, Jean Rogers, Chick Chandler, Robert Kellard, Joan Woodbury, Harold Huber.

Cocky reporter Michael Whalen solves the mystery of several strange deaths of bond carriers in this routine drama. Whalen, who almost gets himself arrested by the stereotyped incompetent police officers, manages to woo entertainer Jean Rogers while he is involved in the investigation of the murders. Chick Chandler portrays the second half of the newsman-photographer team with Whalen. Harold Huber provides the menace. This was another entry in the Roving Reporter series featuring Whalen as a crack reporter who has a penchant for solving murders—with the dubious assistance of his pal, comic cameraman Chandler. Jean Rogers was a regular in the series.

986 WHILE THE CITY SLEEPS (1956), RKO.

Dir. Fritz Lang; Sc. Casey Robinson; Cast includes: Dana Andrews, Ida Lupino, George Sanders, Rhonda Fleming, Vincent Price, John Drew Barrymore.

A psychopath who has been murdering young women becomes the target of competing journalists of a newspaper syndicate in this icy film noir based on the 1953 novel *The Bloody Spur* by Charles Einstein. Vincent Price, after inheriting a string of newspapers, promises a top position to any of his writers who can uncover the murderer's identity. His offer sparks fierce competition among his staff members, especially Thomas Mitchell, George Sanders and James Craig. Each has his own motive. Some, more ruthless than others, use their girlfriends as bait to trap the cold-blooded killer, who turns out to be a young delivery boy (John Drew Barrymore) burdened with a domineering mother. In addition to its murder plot, the film scathingly attacks the sleazy practices of those journalists who are willing to cross the line of morality and ethics to feed their own ambition.

987 THE WHIP HAND (1951), RKO.

Dir. William Cameron Menzies; *Sc.* George Bricker, Frank L. Moss; *Cast includes:* Carla Balenda, Elliott Reid, Edgar Barrier, Raymond Burr, Otto Waldis, Michael Steele.

Former Nazis, now aligned with the Communist cause, are experimenting secretly with germ warfare in the Wisconsin mountains in this suspenseful little drama set during the cold war. Elliott Reid, as a magazine writer and photographer vacationing in Wisconsin, grows suspicious about incidents occurring at a well-guarded hideaway. Inquisitive about a nearby mysterious lodge and a lake once alive with fish and now barren, he journeys across the body of water to investigate. Carla Balenda, the sister of a local doctor, joins him. They discover that a group of Communists, composed chiefly of unrepentant Nazis, are developing a germ-warfare weapon. The couple are taken prisoner but are soon rescued by F.B.I. agents who are tipped off about the conspirators' plot. Raymond Burr and Otto Waldis portray some of the villains in this intriguing tale.

988 THE WHIPPED (1950) see *The Underworld Story* (1950).

989 THE WHISPERED NAME (1924), U.

Dir. King Baggot; *Sc.* Lois Zellner; *Cast includes:* Ruth Clifford, Niles Welsh, Jane Starr, Buddy Messinger, Carl Stockdale, William Lawrence.

Blackmailers pose a threat to innocent reporter Ruth Clifford and her editor Niles Welch in this ineffective silent comedy drama based on the play *The Co-respondent* by Rita Weiman and Alice Leal Pollock. Sent to interview a wife suing for divorce, innocent reporter Clifford is surprised to learn she, the journalist, is to be named the co-respondent in the case. Her employer, editor Welch, who loves Clifford, is also embroiled in the divorce. Both are finally extricated from the entanglement when Welch manages to silence the wife.

990 WHISPERS (1920), Selznick.

Dir. William P. S. Earle; *Sc.* George D. Proctor; *Cast includes:* Elaine Hammerstein, Ida Darling, Matt Moore, Phillips Tead, Charles Gerard, Bernard Randall.

A scandal sheet almost ruins the reputation of an innocent young woman in this often incredulous drama that depends too often on coincidence. Inexperienced Elaine Hammerstein ignores the advice of her aunt, with whom she lives, about dating a married man. Her escort takes her to the opera one evening where the man's wife shows up. The surprised husband expected her to be out of town. Someone in the audience notifies the scandal sheet, and the incident appears in the newspaper the following day, but without Hammerstein's name. To avoid further arguments with her aunt, she takes a train to another town where her father runs a small paper. Meanwhile the married man, who decides to leave town to escape the fallout from the embarrassing article, takes the same train as the young woman. Following several complications, Hammerstein arrives in her father's town and meets Matt Moore, a reporter for the scandal sheet. He has been assigned to write a follow-up on his story. She convinces him of her innocence, and Moore, unhappy with his present job, accepts an offer to work on her father's paper.

991 WHITE BONDAGE (1937), WB.

Dir. Nick Grinde; Sc. Anthony Coldeway; Cast includes: Jean Muir, Gordon Oliver, Howard Phillips, Joseph King, Virginia Brissac.

Newspaper reporter Gordon Oliver sets out to prove that sharecroppers are being cheated by unscrupulous businessmen who use short-weight scales in this minor social drama. Oliver's snooping almost gets him lynched, but he is rescued by the young local farm woman Jean Muir. The film, shot mostly outdoors, uses several authentic-looking sets that add a note of realism to the production. In addition, much of the dialogue is natural. "We are all sharecroppers, ain't we?" one farmer asks at a secret meeting with his colleagues. "And we been cheated, too, ain't we? Boys, we have been workin' and cheated ... for years. My pappy died workin' the cotton land. We didn't have no shoes to bury him in." In another scene, an impoverished sharecropper quotes from the Bible: "'What mean ye that ye crush my people and grind the faces of the poor?'"

992 WHITE LIES (1935), Col.

Dir. Leo Bulgakov; Sc. Harold Shumate; Cast includes: Walter Connolly, Fay Wray, Victor Jory, Leslie Fenton, Irene Hervey, William Demarest.

An idealistic traffic cop, although friendly with the daughter of an influential newspaper publisher, arrests her when he suspects her of murder in this drama. When dedicated officer Victor Jory arrests Fay Wray, who becomes embroiled in a murder, her father, publisher Walter Connolly, at first treats the story objectively. Shortly thereafter, Connolly's influence results in Jory's dismissal from the force. But the officer continues to work on the case until he finds the real killer, thereby exonerating Wray.

993 THE WHITE TERROR (1915), U.

Dir. Stuart Paton; Sc. Raymond L. Schrock; Cast includes: Hobart Henley, Frances Nelson, William Welsh, Howard Crampton, Alan Holubar, Otto Hoffman.

Wealthy young Hobart Henley purchases a newspaper that he uses to expose the deplorable working conditions that exist in sweatshops and factories in this social drama. In particular, he attacks factory owner Howard Crampton, whose daughter, Frances Nelson, is Henley's girlfriend. Crampton runs one of the worst plants in the community, exploiting children and offering substandard conditions to his other workers. However, once he is made aware of these faults, the plant owner vows to make drastic changes. One particularly effective sequence juxtaposes a banquet scene of the owners with that of the factory conditions. The film also attacks corrupt politicians, the idle rich and the wretched living conditions of the poor.

994 WHO IS HOPE SCHUYLER? (1942), TCF.

Dir. Thomas Z. Loring; Sc. Arnaud d'Usseau; Cast includes: Joseph Allen Jr., Mary Howard, Sheila Ryan, Ricardo Cortez, Janis Carter, Joan Valerie.

Special prosecutor Joseph Allen Jr. seeks the help of reporter Sheila Ryan in his search for a murderer in this drama of big-city political corruption based on a novel by Stephen Ransome. The plot focuses on corrupt district attorney Ricardo Cortez, who tries to obstruct the prosecutor's efforts to find the killer called Hope Schuyler, an alleged astrologer who collected underworld payoffs.

995 WHY GIRLS LEAVE HOME (1945), PRC.

Dir. William Berke; Sc. Fanya Foss Lawrence, Bradford Ropes; Cast includes: Lola Lane, Sheldon Leonard, Pamela Blake, Elisha Cook Jr., Paul Guilfoyle, Constance Worth.

Young Pamela Blake runs away from home to make her own way in life in this trite drama with a misleading title. She soon joins forces with shady nightclub operator Lola Lane and her henchmen.

When Blake learns too much about their illegal activities, they plan to kill her and make her death look like a suicide. Fortunately for her, a streetwise reporter intervenes and exposes the ruthless racketeers. Rare for a B movie and a low-budget studio, the film was nominated for an Oscar for the song "The Cat and the Canary." Although it didn't win, it was still a notable feat.

996 WIDE OPEN TOWN (1941), Par.

Dir. Lesley Selander; Sc. Harrison Jacobs, J. Benton Cheney; Cast includes: William Boyd, Russell Hayden, Andy Clyde, Evelyn Brent, Victor Jory, Morris Ankrum.

Intrepid Bar 20 foreman Hopalong Cassidy (William Boyd), while searching for stolen cattle, helps distraught newspaper publisher Morris Ankrum clean up a lawless frontier town in this standard western. Together with his pals Russell Hayden and Andy Clyde, Cassidy is appointed sheriff and asked to end the illegal activities of a local gang controlled by Victor Jory, who runs a combination saloon and gambling house. The fighting foreman not only brings an end to the gang but retrieves his stolen cattle. Boyd joins other screen cowboys, including Rex Bell, Roy Rogers and Randolph Scott, in helping to bring law and order to the frontier by means of the press.

997 THE WILD GIRL (1917), Selznick.

Dir. Howard Estabrook; St. George M. Rosener; Cast includes: Eva Tanguay, Tom Moore, Stuart Holmes, Valerie Bergere, Herbert Evans, Dean Raymond.

Local newspaper editor Tom Moore helps to rescue Eva Tanguay from a forced marriage to a gypsy in this silent romantic drama. Tanguay, raised by a group of gypsies after being abandoned as a child by a stranger, was to inherit an estate in Virginia when she turns eighteen. The tribal chief dresses her as a boy to conceal her identity, but when he forces her to marry one of the tribe, she flees on her wedding night and meets editor Moore who, of course, thinks she is a boy. He hires her as a messenger. She then joins her uncle on the estate. Upon seeing Moore with his secretary, Tanguay mistakes the relationship and returns to the gypsy camp. Moore, learning the truth about Tanguay, tracks her down and, after explaining everything, acknowledges that he loves her.

998 WILD MONEY (1937), Par.

Dir. Louis King; Sc. Paul Gallico; Cast includes: Edward Everett Horton, Louise Campbell, Lynne Overman, Lucien Littlefield, Esther Dale, Porter Hall.

Eccentric, tight-fisted bookkeeper for a city newspaper, Edward Everett Horton soon learns a lesson that will change his lifestyle in this entertaining comedy. He is a stickler for the rules, so that when reporters and others, including journalist Louise Campbell, try to inflate their expense accounts, he rejects their claims. While Horton is on vacation, a big kidnapping story breaks, and he happens to be on the scene. As the only representative of his newspaper, he calls in each change in events and scoops all competitors. His paper sends him $5,000 for expenses and, after the initial shock of such an exorbitant amount, he soon puts it to good use. He buys up all means of transportation and ties up all communication, thereby keeping rival reporters far from the scene. Following several hilarious incidents, he ends up capturing the culprits and winning Campbell's affection.

999 THE WILD PARTY (1923), U.

Dir. Herbert Blache; Sc. Hugh Hoffman; Cast includes: Gladys Walton, Lewis Sargent, Robert Ellis, Freeman Wood, Dorothy Revier, Esther Ralston.

Gladys Walton, the secretary to the city editor, asks her boss to let her cover a social affair—which results in a libel suit against the paper—in this bedroom farce.

Walton is told to provide enough evidence to support her story or look for another job. Instead of proving her story, she wins the love of Robert Ellis, who has threatened the libel suit, and he finally agrees to drop his charge of libel. Meanwhile, she plays Cupid by rearranging the marital affairs of several maladjusted couples.

1000   WING TOY (1921), Fox.

Dir. Howard M. Mitchell; *Sc.* Thomas Dixon Jr.; *Cast includes:* Shirley Mason, Raymond McKee, Edward McWade, Harry S. Northrup, Betty Schade, Scott McKee.

Reporter Raymond McKee helps to rescue Shirley Mason, the title character, from marrying Chinese underworld leader Harry S. Northrup in this farfetched silent drama that manages to skirt the potentially larger issue of miscegenation. Mason, the product of a Chinese father and American mother, has been brought to a Chinese laundry man as an infant. Now in her sixteenth year, her guardian has pledged her to Northrup, who is killed by his own wife whom he planned to divorce. When Mason learns that the district attorney is her father, she becomes engaged to journalist McKee.

1001   WINNER TAKE ALL (1939), TCF.

Dir. Otto Brower; *Sc.* Frances Hyland, Albert Ray; *Cast includes:* Tony Martin, Gloria Stuart, Henry Armetta, Slim Summerville, Kane Richmond, Robert Allen.

Newspaper sports writer Gloria Stuart, who is enamored of cowboy-turned-waiter-turned-fighter Tony Martin, helps him along as he becomes a professional in this romantic action comedy. Big-time gamblers take notice of the waiter Martin after he scores a lucky punch during a prizefight benefit. They arrange several fixed fights for him and cash in on the results. Meanwhile, naive Martin thinks he has won the bouts fairly. Sports writer Stuart takes him down a few pegs by arranging for boxer Kane Richmond, her friend, to teach the arrogant Martin a real lesson in fighting by knocking him down. After some quibbling, she persuades him to train as a pro—a decision which results in his success in the ring. After receiving a terrific pounding in the ring by Richmond, Martin rises at the count of nine to score a knockout against his opponent. Two veteran comic supporting players, restaurant owner Henry Armetta and his trainer Slim Summerville, supply the comedy relief.

1002   THE WITNESS VANISHES (1939), U.

Dir. Otis Garrett; *Sc.* Robertson White; *Cast includes:* Edmund Lowe, Wendy Barrie, Bruce Lester, Walter Kingsford, Forrester Harvey, J. M. Kerrigan.

Four corrupt London editors commit their newspaper owner to an asylum so that they can take over the press in this convoluted murder mystery based on the story by James Ronald. The owner, however, escapes from his guards and returns to London. Meanwhile, the usurping editors are being murdered one at a time. In addition, a rival daily mysteriously seems to be getting scoops of the crimes. Edmund Lowe, as one of the editors, calmly resigns himself to his fate. Forrester Harvey portrays a secret investigator on the case. Wendy Barrie, as the daughter of the unfortunate owner, is involved in a romance with a columnist.

1003   THE WIZARD (1927), Fox.

Dir. Richard Rosson; *Sc.* Harry O. Hoyt, Andrew Bennison; *Cast includes:* Edmund Lowe, Leila Hyams, Gustav von Seyffertitz, E. H. Calvert, Barry Norton, Oscar Smith.

A newspaper reporter discovers that a crazed doctor plans to carry out a series of murders in this revenge drama based on the 1912 novel *Balaoo* by Gaston Leroux. After his son is tried and executed for murder, the doctor trains an ape to kill. Following one such murder, inquisitive reporter Edmund Lowe sniffs around for a new slant on an old murder until he learns the mad doctor's secret weapon. This leads to his saving the lives of both the judge in the case and Leila Hyams, the judge's daughter, whom Lowe loves.

1004 A WOMAN AGAINST THE WORLD (1928), Tiffany-Stahl.

Dir. George Archainbaud; Sc. Gertrude Orr; Cast includes: Harrison Ford, Georgia Hale, Lee Moran, Harvey Clark, Walter Hiers, Gertrude Olmstead.

Another last-minute rescue from the hanging of a condemned man falsely accused of murder marks this familiar but suspenseful drama that also features a relentless reporter seeking justice. When a chorus girl is found murdered, a young groom, who admits he visited the victim earlier the same evening, is arrested on his wedding night and charged with the crime. His bride abandons him and sues for divorce before his conviction. The remainder of the film is devoted to the reporter, Georgia Hale, who hunts down the real killer, the victim's former chauffeur, and gets a confession—forced by threat of a detective's blackjack.

1005 WOMAN IN DISTRESS (1937), Col.

Dir. Lynn Shores; Sc. Albert DeMond; Cast includes: May Robson, Dean Jagger, Irene Hervey, Douglass Dumbrille, George McKay, Gene Morgan.

Dean Jagger and Irene Hervey portray rival reporters in this pedestrian newspaper-crime drama. The plot centers on May Robson, the eccentric title character, and her Rembrandt painting, a masterpiece long considered missing or destroyed. Art thieves steal the New England spinster's canvas, but they have trouble selling it to an underworld dealer in stolen art. Hervey, posing as Robson's companion, meets the elderly woman and both become trapped in a burning house. Sensing the impending danger facing the two women, Jagger rushes by airplane and car to their rescue in the nick of time.

1006 WOMAN OF THE YEAR (1942), MGM.

Dir. George Stevens; Sc. Ring Lardner Jr., Michael Kanin; Cast includes: Spencer Tracy, Katharine Hepburn, Fay Bainter, Reginald Owen, Minor Watson, William Bendix.

Sports writer Spencer Tracy clashes with political columnist of world affairs Katharine Hepburn, both writing for the same New York daily, in this bright comedy marred by several hackneyed plot incidents. Tracy and fellow journalist Roscoe Karns are nettled when political analyst Hepburn writes disparaging remarks about baseball. "We men have got only ourselves to blame," Karns confesses. "It's our own fault. Women should be kept illiterate and clean—like canaries." Tracy and Hepburn finally agree to try to understand each other's work. He takes her to her first baseball game. Hepburn is surprised to learn that the newspaper they write for has two reporters covering a baseball game. "We only have one man at Vichy," she grumbles to Tracy. "Vichy?" Tracy quips. "Are they still in the league?" The couple finally fall in love, with Tracy proposing marriage. However, Hepburn finds herself overwhelmed with meeting diplomats, making speeches and receiving the "Outstanding Woman of the Year" award. All this leaves her little time for love and marriage. After Tracy walks out on her, she realizes she has wrongly arranged her priorities and reconciles her differences with the man she loves.

1007 WOMAN TRAP (1936), Par.

Dir. Harold Young; Sc. Brian Marlow, Eugene Walter; Cast includes: George Murphy, Gertrude Michael, Akim Tamiroff, Sidney Blackmer, Samuel S. Hinds, Dean Jagger.

A New York gangster and a Mexican bandit hold a newspaper reporter and a senator's daughter for ransom in this kidnapping drama. It later turns out that the bandit, played by Akim Tamiroff, is in reality a member of the Mexican secret service. Tamiroff was later to appear in features more often as lawbreaker than as crime fighter. George Murphy portrays the reporter and Gertrude Michael the senator's daughter. Sidney Blackmer, known for his villainous roles, again plays the gang leader. Murphy, a popular actor during the thirties and forties, appeared in several newspaper films, including *Public Menace* (1935) and *Risky Business* (1939).

1008 THE WOMAN UNDER COVER (1919), U.

Dir. George Siegmann; Sc. Harvey Thew; Cast includes: Fritzi Brunette, George McDaniel, Harvey Springler, Fontaine La Rue.

Reporter Fritzi Brunette finds herself more deeply entangled in a backstage murder than she counted on in this fairly entertaining drama based on the play *Playing the Game* by Sada Cowan. Sent by her editor to cover the murder of a stage star by his abused wife, Brunette bungles the story. Harry Springler, the reporter's brother and only witness to the crime, loves the wife and remains silent. But when the recent widow rejects him, he reveals what he has seen. Brunette, who is then assigned to get a confession from the wife, cleverly cajoles the murderess into revealing all, thereby getting her story. But she cannot bring herself to involve her brother. So she turns the story over to George McDaniel, her boyfriend editor, resigns from the paper and marries him.

1009 WOMAN WISE (1937), TCF.

Dir. Allan Dwan; Sc. Ben Markson; Cast includes: Rochelle Hudson, Michael Whalen, Thomas Beck, Alan Dinehart, Douglas Fowley, Chick Chandler.

Idealistic newspaper sports editor Michael Whalen is determined to expose the local fight racket in this routine drama. He proves that racketeers are employing former professional fighters to take dives while the hoodlums clean up with their bets. Whalen wins the first round in his struggle by knocking unconscious Pat Flaherty, one of the ex-champions, a pathetic battle-bruised veteran of the ring. But the victim's impulsive daughter, Rochelle Hudson, doesn't take kindly to having her father humiliated. Following several confrontations between the young couple, they begin to fall in love and join forces to expose the crooked promoters who have turned prizefighting into a sleazy game.

1010 THE WOMAN'S LAW (1916), Pathé.

Dir. Lawrence McGill; Sc. Harvey Thew, Albert LeVino; Cast includes: Florence Reed, Duncan McRae, Anita Scott, Jack Curtis, Lora Rogers.

A persistent reporter investigating an apparently simple shooting of an intruder virtually forces a woman to talk about a previous murder and an unusual cover-up in this farfetched drama based on the novel by Maravene Thompson. Duncan McRae, in a dual role, portrays Florence Reed's husband, the millionaire murderer of an artist. Before he is arrested, Reed meets a disoriented man who is her husband's double. Thinking more of protecting her child than covering up her unfaithful husband's crime, she takes the stranger home. The police then arrest him instead of her husband who has fled. The innocent man is institutionalized and, still suffering a loss of memory, is finally released. Reed takes the amnesiac home as her husband. When her real husband returns in an attempt to extract money from her, the butler mistakes him for a burglar and shoots him. The amnesiac, upon hearing the wife's confession, soon establishes his own identity and decides to marry the widowed Reed.

1011 THE WOMAN'S SIDE (1922), FN.

Dir. John A. Barry; Sc. John A. Barry; Cast includes: Katherine MacDonald, Edward Burns, Henry Barrows, Dwight Crittenden, Orra Devereaux, Wade Boteler.

A newspaper is caught in the middle of a vicious gubernatorial race in this suspenseful drama. Katherine MacDonald, as the daughter of a judge seeking the governor's seat, falls in love with Edward Burns, whose father owns a powerful newspaper opposed to the judge. At a critical moment just before the election, Wade Boteler, the judge's unscrupulous opponent, wants Burns's father to print an indelicate story that will surely destroy the judge's reputation. MacDonald shows up at Boteler's office and threatens to kill herself if he has the story about her father published. Then the judge enters and, at gunpoint, forces his opponent to call the paper and kill the story. Later, the charge against the judge is proven to be false.

1012 WOMEN ARE TROUBLE (1936), MGM.

Dir. Errol Taggart; Sc. Michael Fessier; Cast includes: Stuart Erwin, Paul Kelly, Florence Rice, Margaret Irving, Cy Kendall, John Harrington.

Another newspaper-crime drama about rival reporters competing for scoops, this standard but playful entry deals with a bright young journalist who beats out her competition. The entire crew are out to expose a gang of racketeers who have invaded the legal liquor business. Florence Rice, the sharp, vibrant reporter, and Stuart Erwin, one of her more pesky rivals, soon fall in love. Meanwhile, local cop Cy Kendall, an honest officer in a corrupt department, is demoted for hounding the mob. The couple, while investigating the gang's activities, are kidnapped along with their fellow reporters, all of whom are then rescued by Kendall. The officer is reinstated after the gang is rounded up and their illegal activities halted.

1013 WOMEN MEN MARRY (1937), MGM.

Dir. Errol Taggart; Sc. Harry Ruskin, Donald Henderson Clarke, James E. Grant; Cast includes: George Murphy, Josephine Hutchinson, Claire Dodd, Sidney Blackmer, Cliff Edwards, John Wray.

Overly dedicated reporter George Murphy goes after a crooked religious cult while his wife has an affair with his editor in this adequate drama. Murphy is so busy trying to expose the phony mystic racket, he is unaware of wife Claire Dodd's extra-marital activities with Sidney Blackmer. He finally leaves her and returns to the young woman he should have married—Josephine Hutchinson. Cliff Edwards as a news photographer provides the comedy relief.

1014 THE WORLD GONE MAD (1933), Majestic.

Dir. Christy Cabanne; Sc. Edward T. Lowe; Cast includes: Pat O'Brien, Evelyn Brent, Neil Hamilton, Mary Brian, Louis Calhern, J. Carrol Naish.

Courageous newspaper reporter Pat O'Brien clashes with members of the underworld as he carries out his job in this generally satisfactory newspaper-crime drama with a pretentious title. Wisecracking O'Brien finds time to romance Evelyn Brent. But the crack reporter finds himself in a fix during the climactic sequence when gangsters invade his apartment and prepare to take him for that proverbial ride. Suddenly and mysteriously, a horde of policemen show up in his foyer and rescue him. O'Brien, who made his screen debut playing Hildy Johnson in *The Front Page* (1931), followed in the steps of fellow actor Lee Tracy in two respects. First, Tracy originated the Johnson role on Broadway, and, second, he quickly became popular in films portraying glib, fast-talking reporters. O'Brien, too, began playing cynical, urban newsman roles in several films, including *Hollywood Speaks* (1932), in which he enacted a gossip columnist, and *The Final Edition* (1932), in which he appeared as a tough, fast-talking editor.

1015 WRONG IS RIGHT (1982), Col.

Dir. Richard Brooks; Sc. Richard Brooks; Cast includes: Sean Connery,

George Grizzard, Robert Conrad, Katharine Ross, G. D. Spradlin, John Saxon.

Worldly television commentator and newsman Sean Connery represents the only perception of reason and decency in the mad world of politics, greed and violence. Director and screenwriter Richard Brooks turned out this provocative drama based on the novel *The Better Angels* by Charles McCarry. "We peddle disaster," Connery says derisively. "Blood and tears, football and cheers, performers, superstars.... We're in the entertainment business." Globe-trotting newscaster Connery is present when a powerful Arab potentate threatens to hand over two small nuclear bombs to a revolutionary leader if George Grizzard, as the President of the U.S., does not step down from his office. It seems that Grizzard, an ineffectual leader, had ordered the Arab's assassination. The bombs, if employed, would be set off in Israel and New York. The devastating incident causes a flurry of activities as the film skewers the powerful and their institutions, such as the C.I.A., the F.B.I., the military, the terrorists and television. Rosalind Cash, the U.S. Vice President, mockingly wisecracks that she may become the first woman and black president. The film questions the nation's world image and why America has become a filthy name.

1016 WUSA (1970), Par.

Dir. Stuart Rosenberg; *Sc.* Robert Stone; *Cast includes:* Paul Newman, Joanna Woodward, Anthony Perkins, Laurence Harvey, Pat Hingle, Don Gordon.

Cynical drifter Paul Newman gets a job as disc jockey at a conservative New Orleans radio station (WUSA) where he soon experiences the firm's ominous intent in this flawed, polemically naive drama based on the novel *A Hall of Mirrors* by Robert Stone. He grows aware of station owner Pat Hingle's chief priorities, which include crowd manipulation. The editorial policy, according to manager Robert Quarry, is the exposé of welfare cheats and other social parasites, and he uses social worker Anthony Perkins to ferret out these alleged phonies. Newman meets and has an affair with Joanne Woodward, another drifter. Meanwhile, the unstable Perkins realizes he is being exploited and, at a rally, assassinates Hingle. The enraged crowd in retaliation brutally kills the assassin. Woodward is falsely arrested after hippies frame her by placing marijuana on her person, and she takes her own life. Newman, the detached observer, leaves New Orleans. "I'm a survivor and I'm leaving these flats for the mile-high city," he announces. "When I get there, baby, when I look down, I'll have few regrets." In its more poignant moments, the drama is reminiscent of such earlier works as *They Won't Forget* (1937), *Meet John Doe* (1941) and *Keeper of the Flame* (1942). However, it ends up as a ponderous cautionary drama about the dangers of the extreme right wing exploiting the mass media for its ultimate purpose—seizing control of the nation.

1017 X MARKS THE SPOT (1931), Tiffany.

Dir. Erle C. Kenton; *Sc.* F. Hugh Herbert; *Cast includes:* Lew Cody, Sally Blane, Fred Kohler, Wallace Ford, Mary Nolan, Virginia Lee Corbin.

Depraved editor Lew Cody and venal columnist Wallace Ford rise in power from a small-town newspaper to the world of New York journalism and crime in this low-budget mystery. Ford, now an important Broadway columnist, is eventually charged with murdering a showgirl. Visiting the young woman who is planning to sue his paper, he tries to induce her to drop the charges but she refuses. Soon after, she is found dead and Ford is suspected. He is forced to solve the murder to clear himself. Contemporary reviewers believed Ford's role resembled that of Walter Winchell (minus the crime angle), a well-known columnist of the period. Several newspaper films based their lead character on the Winchell persona, including, among others, *Okay America* (1932) with Lew Ayres, *Personal Secretary* (1938) with William Gargan, *Manhattan Shakedown* (1939) and *Murder Is News* (1939), both featuring John Gallaudet.

1018 A YANK IN LIBYA (1942), PRC.

Dir. Albert Herman; *Sc.* Arthur St. Claire; *Cast includes:* H. B. Warner, Walter Woolf King, Joan Woodbury, Parkyakarkus, Duncan Renaldo, George Lewis.

An unimpressive World War II drama about an American war correspondent who uncovers a Nazi gun-smuggling ring in Libya, the film is short on action or war sequences. Walter Woolf King plays the inquisitive reporter while veteran actor H. B. Warner portrays a local British consul. Popular radio comedian Parkyakarkus supplies the much-needed comedy relief in this low-budget tale.

1019 YEAR OF THE DRAGON (1985), MGM/UA.

Dir. Michael Cimino; *Sc.* Oliver Stone, Michael Cimino; *Cast includes:* Mickey Rourke, John Lone, Ariane, Leonard Termo, Ray Barry, Caroline Kava.

Vietnam War veteran and obsessed cop Mickey Rourke is determined to break New York Chinatown's gang lord John Lone in this action-filled and brutal drama based on the novel by Robert Daley. To accomplish his difficult task, Rourke enlists the aid of television news reporter Ariane, a young Asian woman who reluctantly goes along with the detective. Disillusioned with the results of the Vietnam War, Rourke sees a chance to win this battle against the crime lords in Chinatown. "You got a slave population of sweatshop women," he begins to remind Ariane of the local problems, "you got shopkeepers paying bribes to every young punk who comes along, you got thirty people living in a room, you got the highest rate of T.B. and mental illness in any neighborhood—" "Look," she interrupts, "I'm a reporter, not a crusader." Later, after one of his crew is shot down in the street and Ariane wants to quit attacking the crime bosses, he continues his harangue. "You want to know what's destroying this country?" he says to Ariane. "It's TV, it's media. It's people like you—vampires." And when she replies, "You care too much," he returns, "How can you care too much?" Following several harrowing incidents, including several attempts on Rourke's life and Ariane's rape by some of Lone's young thugs, Rourke mortally wounds Lone in a deadly gun battle. For all of his noble efforts, Lone is honored with a parade through Chinatown and Rourke is transferred to another precinct.

1020 YEAR OF THE GUN (1991), Triumph.

Dir. John Frankenheimer; *Sc.* David Ambrose, Jay Presson Allen; *Cast includes:* Andrew McCarthy, Valeria Golino, Sharon Stone, John Pankow, Mattia Sbragia, George Murcell.

American journalist Andrew McCarthy becomes enmeshed with the Communist Red Brigade, an Italian terrorist group, in this inept political drama set in 1978 Rome and based on the novel by Michael Mewshaw. The Brigade plans to kidnap the prime minister, a move which the group hopes will lead to the overthrow of the government. Valeria Golino, the minister's wealthy lover, is in collusion with the terrorists. Crack photojournalist Sharon Stone enters into all this intrigue when she just happens to be present to snap pictures of a violent bank robbery. She soon becomes romantically involved with McCarthy, whom she had earlier assisted as a cub reporter during the Vietnam War. "My job," she explains, "was to bring back the bad news and keep the body count." At the same time, she thinks he knows plenty about the Red Brigade, whose members grow suspicious of him. They decide to kill several persons associated with McCarthy. The film ends with Dick Cavett interviewing McCarthy, now on assignment in Middle East, and Stone, via a satellite broadcast. "The sixties," McCarthy reflects, "were ten years of phoniness, a decade-long circle jerk. I didn't drop out. I dropped in. I moved to Italy." Highlights of the film, which was badly cast, include striking terrorist raids and realistic crowd riots. Director Frankenheimer has done better work in the genre, including *The*

Manchurian Candidate (1962) and Seven Days in May (1964).

1021 YOU CAN'T ESCAPE FOREVER (1942), WB.

Dir. Jo Graham; Sc. Fred Niblo, Hector Chevigny; Cast includes: George Brent, Brenda Marshall, Erville Alderson, Paul Harvey, Roscoe Karns, Charles Halton.

Journalists George Brent and Brenda Marshall tackle a crime syndicate in this familiar newspaper-crime drama, another remake of Hi, Nellie!, released in 1934. Brent is demoted for ignoring a story brought in by Erville Alderson which allegedly exposes a crime ring. When Alderson is found murdered, Brent and Marshall decide to avenge his death by infiltrating the syndicate to gather evidence. The ploy about the editor relegating a reporter to the advice-to-the-lovelorn column had already worn thin and had recently been used one year earlier in Nine Lives Are Not Enough, featuring Ronald Reagan as a brash reporter.

1022 YOU CAN'T RUN AWAY FROM IT (1956), Col.

Dir. Dick Powell; Sc. Claude Binyon, Robert Riskin; Cast includes: June Allyson, Jack Lemmon, Charles Bickford, Paul Gilbert, Jim Backus, Stubby Kaye.

Runaway heiress June Allyson meets reporter Jack Lemmon during a cross-country bus trip in this satisfactory comedy remake of the 1934 classic It Happened One Night, with Claudette Colbert and Clark Gable. As in the original screwball comedy, Allyson is unaware of Lemmon's profession—until it is too late and she loses her heart to him. Unlike the original, this Technicolor and wide-screen version adds some songs and a ballet. Charles Bickford portrays Allyson's distraught father.

1023 YOUNG MAN OF MANHATTAN (1930), Par.

Dir. Monta Bell; Sc. Robert Presnell;

Cast includes: Claudette Colbert, Norman Foster, Ginger Rogers, Charles Ruggles, Leslie Austin, H. Dudley Hawley.

Sports writer Norman Foster and co-worker Claudette Colbert, a successful gossip columnist, marry, but complications soon split apart the lovers in this domestic drama based on the novel by Katharine Bush. Foster's heavy drinking and philandering upset Colbert. Meanwhile, her driving ambition leads her to a lucrative career in magazine publishing— a situation that fuels Foster's jealousy. They decide to separate, with Foster quickly returning when he learns Colbert almost went blind from drinking some of his bootleg liquor he had left behind. Foster reforms and the couple reconcile their differences. More a romance than a newspaper drama, the film depicts various sports events that Foster covers, including prizefighting, a world series game, a football game and a six-day bicycle race. The plot avoids the stereotypes of the familiar journalism film, including the crack news hound who beats out the police in solving a crime or the cynical reporter who mocks those whom he is assigned to write about. Ginger Rogers's line, "Cigarette me, big boy," became popular among audiences during this period. The realistic newspaper background adds a note of authenticity to the atmosphere. Like Ben Hecht and Charles MacArthur, who wrote the play The Front Page, and Louis Weitzenkorn, who wrote Five Star Final, two later realistic films about the world of journalism, screenwriter Robert Presnell also relied heavily on his newspaper experience.

1024 YOUTH AND ADVENTURE (1925), FBO.

Dir. James W. Horne; Sc. Frank Howard Clark; Cast includes: Richard Talmadge, Pete Gordon, Joseph Girard, Margaret Landis, Fred Kelsey, Katherine Lewis.

Irresponsible playboy Richard Talmadge, after squandering much of his inheritance, settles down as the managing editor of a city newspaper in this comedy. He gets this coveted position after taking an incriminating photograph of political boss Joseph Girard. The politician, who also owns a newspaper, gives Talmadge the job to silence him. The playboy takes his office seriously and, together with Margaret Landis, Girard's secretary, uses the owner's own paper to expose his ties with bootlegging. When Talmadge refuses to resign, the owner hires strong-arm men to evict him. A battle ensues between the thugs and the newspaper staff, resulting in the crusading editor's holding Girard for the police. He then presents them with enough evidence to arrest and convict the owner.

1025 ZUDORA (THE TWENTY MILLION DOLLAR MYSTERY) (1914) serial, Thanhauser.
Dir. Howard Hansell; *Sc.* Daniel Carson Goodman; *Cast includes:* James Cruze, Marguerite Snow, Harry Benham, Sidney Bracy, Mary Elizabeth Forbes, Frank Farrington.

More of a "series" of one- or two-reelers than a serial, this silent 20-episode production features James Cruze as a stalwart reporter engaging in a string of mysteries. These include such diverse items as lost ships, a missing heiress, coveted diamonds, a raid on a sanitarium and a failed elopement. Meanwhile, Marguerite Snow portrays Zudora, the heroine of the title. The Vitagraph studio, sensing a good thing, soon released a parody of the series in three one-reelers, titled *The Fates and Flora Fourflush, The Ten Billion Dollar Vitagraph Mystery Serial*, with Clara Kimball Young emulating Snow. In 1919, Arrow released a 10-chapter version of *Zudora* titled *The Demon Shadow*.

Appendix A: Newspaper Film Series

Big Town

Big Town (1947)
I Cover Big Town (1947)
Big Town After Dark (1947)
Big Town Scandal (1948)

Roving Reporter

Inside Story (1938)
Time Out for Murder (1938)
While New York Sleeps (1938)

Torchy Blane

Smart Blonde (1936)
Fly-Away Baby (1937)
Adventurous Blonde (1937)
Blondes at Work (1938)
Torchy Blane in Panama (1938)
Torchy Gets Her Man (1938)
Torchy Blane in Chinatown (1939)
Torchy Runs for Mayor (1939)
Torchy Plays with Dynamite (1939)

Appendix B: Newspaper Film Serials

The Active Life of Dolly of the Dailies (1914)
Atom Man vs. Superman (1950)
Brenda Starr, Reporter (1945)
The Broken Coin (1915)
The Clutching Hand (1936)
Double Adventure (1921)
The Fatal Fortune (1919)
The Green Hornet (1939)
The Green Hornet Strikes Again (1940)
The Lion Man (1919)
Million Dollar Mystery (1914)
The Mystery of the Double Cross (1917)
Perils of Our Girl Reporters (1916)
The Phantom Creeps (1939)
Police Reporter (1928)
Red Barry (1938)
The Return of the Riddle Rider (1927)
The Riddle Rider (1924)
S.O.S. Coast Guard (1937)
The Scarlet Streak (1926)
Secret of Treasure Island (19xx)
Shadow of Chinatown (1936)
Superman (1948)
Terry of the Times (1930)
Zudora (the Twenty Million Dollar Mystery) (1914)

Appendix C: Peripheral Newspaper Films

BOOMERANG (1947), TCF.
Dir. Elia Kazan; *Sc.* Richard Murphy; *Cast includes:* Dana Andrews, Jane Wyatt, Lee J. Cobb, Arthur Kennedy, Sam Levene.

CHRISTMAS HOLIDAY (1944), U.
Dir. Robert Siodmak; *Sc.* Herman J. Mankiewicz; *Cast includes:* Deanna Durbin, Gene Kelly, Richard Whorf, Dean Harens, Gladys George, Gale Sondergaard.

THE CROSBY CASE (1934), U.
Dir. Edwin L. Marin; *Sc.* Warren Duff, Gordon Kahn; *Cast includes:* Wynne Gibson, Onslow Stevens, Edward Van Sloan, Alan Dinehart, John Wray, William Collier Sr.

CROSS-UP (1958), UA.
Dir. John Gilling; *Sc.* John Gilling, Willis Goldbeck; *Cast includes:* Larry Parks, Constance Smith, Lisa Daniely, Cyril Chamberlain.

DANCE WITH DEATH (1991), Concorde.
Dir. Charles Philip Moore; *Sc.* Daryl Haney; *Cast includes:* .

THE DEVIL IS DRIVING (1937), Col.
Dir. Harry Lachman; *Sc.* Jo Milward, Richard Blake; *Cast includes:* Richard Dix, Joan Perry, Nana Bryant, Frank C. Wilson, Elisha Cook Jr., Henry Kolker.

EVERY WOMAN'S PROBLEM (1921), Plymouth.
Dir. Willis Robards; *Sc.* J. F. Natteford; *Cast includes:* Dorothy Davenport, Willis Robards, Maclyn King, Wilson Du Bois.

THE FOOLISH MATRONS (1921), AP.
Dir. Maurice Tourneur, Clarence Brown; *Sc.* Wyndham Gittens; *Cast includes:* Hobart Bosworth, Doris May, Mildred Manning, Kathleen Kirham, Betty Schade, Charles Meredith.

FREEZE FRAME (1992), New Line.
 Dir. William Bindley; *Cast includes:* Shannen Doherty, Robyn Douglass, Charles Haid, Seth Michaels.

HAROLD TEEN (1934), WB.
 Dir. Murray Roth; *Sc.* Paul O. Smith, Al Cohn; *Cast includes:* Hal LeRoy, Rochelle Hudson, Patricia Ellis, Guy Kibbee, Hugh Herbert, Hobart Cavanaugh.

HIT THE ICE (1943), U.
 Dir. Charles Lamont; *Sc.* Robert Lees, Frederic Rinaldo, John Grant; *Cast includes:* Bud Abbott, Lou Costello, Ginny Simms, Patric Knowles, Elyse Knox, Joseph Sawyer.

HOUSE OF THE RISING SUN (1987), Prism.
 Dir. Greg Gold; *Cast includes:* Jamie Barrett, Frank Annese, John York, Bud Davis.

IN THE NAVY (1941), U.
 Dir. Arthur Lubin; *Sc.* Arthur T. Horman, John Grant; *Cast includes:* Bud Abbott, Lou Costello, Dick Powell, Claire Dodd, Dick Foran, Billy Lenhart, Kenneth Brown.

LADY LUCK (1936), Che.
 Dir. Charles Lamont; *Sc.* John Krafft; *Cast includes:* Patricia Farr, William Bakewell, Duncan Renaldo, Iris Adrian, Lulu McConnell, Jameson Thomas.

THE LAST PARADE (1931), Col.
 Dir. Erle C. Kenyon; *Sc.* Dorothy Howell; *Cast includes:* Jack Holt, Tom Moore, Constance Cummings, Gaylord Pendleton, Robert Ellis, Earle D. Bunn.

MAKING THE HEADLINES (1938), Col.
 Dir. Lewis D. Collins; *Sc.* Howard J. Green, Jefferson Parker; *Cast includes:* Jack Holt, Beverly Roberts, Craig Reynolds, Marjorie Gateson, Dorothy Appleby, Gilbert Emery.

MALAYA (1949), MGM.
 Dir. Richard Thorpe; *Sc.* Frank Fenton; *Cast includes:* Spencer Tracy, James Stewart, Valentina Cortesa, Sydney Greenstreet, John Hodiak, Lionel Barrymore.

THE NAKED STREET (1955), UA.
 Dir. Maxwell Shane; *Sc.* Maxwell Shane, Leo Katcher; *Cast includes:* Farley Granger, Anthony Quinn, Anne Bancroft, Peter Graves, Else Neft, Jerry Paris.

NEVER THE TWAIN SHALL MEET (1925), Metro.
 Dir. Maurice Tourneur; *Sc.* Eugene Mullin; *Cast includes:* Anita Stewart, Bert Lytell, Huntly Gordon, George Siegmann, Justine Johnstone, Lionel Belmore.

NO TIME FOR LOVE (1943), Par.
 Dir. Mitchell Leisen; *Sc.* Claude Binyon; *Cast includes:* Claudette Colbert, Fred MacMurray, Ilka Chase, Richard Haydn, Paul McGrath, June Havoc.

ON OUR MERRY WAY (1948), UA.
 Dir. King Vidor, Leslie Fenton, George Stevens; *Sc.* Laurence Stallings, Lou Bres-

low; *Cast includes:* Burgess Meredith, James Stewart, Henry Fonda, Dorothy Lamour, Victor Moore, Fred MacMurray.

ORPHANS OF THE STREET (1938), Rep.
Dir. John H. Auer; *Sc.* Eric Taylor, Jack Townley, Olive Cooper; *Cast includes:* Tommy Ryan, Robert Livingston, June Storey, Ralph Morgan, Harry Davenport, James Burke.

PAROLE RACKET (1937), Col.
Dir. C. C. Coleman Jr.; *Sc.* Harold Shumate; *Cast includes:* Paul Kelly, Rosalind Keith, Thurston Hall, Gene Morgan, John Spacey, Francis McDonald.

RANSOM! (1956), MGM.
Dir. Alex Segal; *Sc.* Cyril Hume, Richard Maibaum; *Cast includes:* Glenn Ford, Donna Reed, Leslie Nielsen, Juano Hernandez, Robert Keith, Richard Gaines.

REAR WINDOW (1954), Par.
Dir. Alfred Hitchcock; *Sc.* J. M. Hayes; *Cast includes:* James Stewart, Grace Kelly, Wendell Corey, Thelma Ritter, Raymond Burr, Judith Evelyn.

RUSH WEEK (1988), Col.
Dir. Robert Bralver.

70,000 WITNESSES (1932), Par.
Dir. Ralph Murphy; *Sc.* Garrett Fort; *Cast includes:* Phillips Holmes, Dorothy Jordan, Charles Ruggles, John Mack Brown, David Landau, Lew Cody.

SLIGHTLY SCARLET (1956), RKO.
Dir. Allan Dwan; *Sc.* Robert Bice; *Cast includes:* John Payne, Arlene Dahl, Rhonda Fleming, Kent Taylor, Ted de Corsia, Lance Fuller.

SPLIT SECOND (1953), RKO.
Dir. Dick Powell; *Sc.* William Bowers, Irving Wallace; *Cast includes:* Stephen McNally, Alexis Smith, Jan Sterling, Keith Andes, Arthur Hunnicutt, Paul Kelly.

STEP LIVELY, JEEVES (1937), TCF.
Dir. Eugene Forde; *Sc.* Frank Fenton, Lynn Root; *Cast includes:* Arthur Treacher, Patricia Ellis, Robert Kent, Alan Dinehart, George Givot, Helen Flint.

STRANGERS MAY KISS (1931), MGM.
Dir. George Fitzmaurice; *Sc.* John Meehan; *Cast includes:* Norma Shearer, Robert Montgomery, Neil Hamilton, Marjorie Rambeau, Irene Rich, Hale Hamilton.

SUNDAY IN NEW YORK (1993), MGM.
Dir. Peter Tewksbury; *Sc.* Norman Krasna; *Cast includes:* Cliff Robertson, Jane Fonda, Rod Taylor, Robert Culp, Jo Morrow, Jim Backus.

TAP ROOTS (1948), UI.
Dir. George Marshall; *Sc.* Alan LeMay; *Cast includes:* Van Heflin, Susan Hayward, Boris Karloff, Julie London, Whitfield Connor, Ward Bond.

TWO IN THE DARK (1936), RKO.
 Dir. Ben Stoloff; *Sc.* Seton I. Miller; *Cast includes:* Walter Abel, Margot Grahame, Wallace Ford, Gail Patrick, Alan Hale, Leslie Fenton.

ULTERIOR MOTIVES (1992),
 Dir. James Becket; *Cast includes:* Thomas Ian Griffith, Mary Page Keller, Joe Yamanaka, Ellen Crawford.

THE WAR AGAINST MRS. HADLEY (1942), MGM.
 Dir. Harold S. Bucquet; *Sc.* George Oppenheimer; *Cast includes:* Edward Arnold, Fay Bainter, Richard Ney, Jean Rogers, Sara Allgood, Van Johnson.

WE'RE ONLY HUMAN (1935), RKO.
 Dir. James Flood; *Sc.* Rian James; *Cast includes:* Preston Foster, Jane Wyatt, James Gleason, Arthur Hohl, John Arledge, Jane Darwell.

WOMAN ON THE RUN (1950), U.
 Dir. Norman Foster; *Sc.* Alan Campbell, Norman Foster; *Cast includes:* Ann Sheridan, Ross Elliott, Dennis O'Keefe, Robert Keith, Frank Jenks, John Qualen.

YELLOW CARGO (1936), Grand National.
 Dir. Crane Wilbur; *Sc.* Crane Wilbur; *Cast includes:* Conrad Nagel, Eleanor Hunt, Vince Barnett, Jack LaRue, Claudia Dell, Henry Strange.

Bibliography

The American Film Institute Catalog of Motion Pictures. New York: R. R. Bowker Company, 1971.
Barris, Alex. *Stop the Presses! The Newspaperman in American Films*. Cranbury, N.J.: A.S. Barnes and Co., 1976.
Brownlow, Kevin. *Behind the Mask of Innocence*. Berkeley: University of California Press, 1990.
Cline, William C. *In the Nick of Time: Motion Picture Sound Serials*. Jefferson, N.C.: McFarland, 1984.
Cook, David A. *A History of Narrative Film*. New York: W. W. Norton, 1981.
Dooley, Roger. *From Scarface to Scarlett: American Films in the 1930s*. New York: Harcourt Brace Jovanovich, 1981.
Film Daily Year Book of Motion Pictures (annually). New York: Distributed by Arno Press, 1970.
Halliwell, Leslie. *The Filmgoer's Companion*. London: MacGibbon and Key, 1970.
Haskell, Molly. *From Reverence to Rape: The Treatment of Women in the Movies*. New York: Holt, Rinehart & Winston, 1974.
Lahue, Kalton C. *Continued Next Week: A History of the Moving Picture Serial*. Norman: University of Oklahoma Press, 1964.
Lauritzen, Einar, and Lundquist, Gunnar. *American Film-Index 1908–1915*. Stockholm: University of Stockholm, 1976.
Leyda, Jay, and Musser, Charles. *Before Hollywood*. New York: Hudson Hills Press, 1987.
McCarthy, Todd, and Flynn, Charles, eds. *Kings of the Bs*. New York: E. P. Dutton, 1975.
Miller, Don. *B Movies*. New York: Ballantine Books, 1988.
The New York Times Film Reviews: (1913–1968. 7 vols. New York: The New York Times and Arno Press, 1971.
Nowlan, Robert A., and Nowlan, Gwendolyn Wright. *Cinema Sequels and Remakes, 1903–1987*. Jefferson, NC: McFarland, 1989.
Pratt, George C. *Spellbound in Darkness: A History of the Silent Film*. Greenwich, CT: New York Graphic Society, 1973.
Spears, Jack. *Hollywood: The Golden Era*. New York: A. S. Barnes & Co., 1971.
Tarbox, Charles H. *Lost Films 1895–1917*. Los Angeles: Film Classic Exchange, 1983.
Turner, George E., and Price, Michael H. *Forgotten Horrors: Early Talkie Chillers From Poverty Row*. Cranbury, NJ: A.S. Barnes and Co., 1979.
Tuska, Jon. *The Vanishing Legion: A History of Mascot Pictures, 1927–1935*. Jefferson, NC: McFarland, 1982.
Variety Film Reviews 1929–1986. New York: Garland Publishing, 1986.

White, David Manning, and Averson, Richard. *The Celluloid Weapon: Social Comment in the American Film*. Boston: Beacon Press, 1972.
Zinman, David. *Saturday Afternoon at the Bijou*. Secaucus, NJ: Castle Books, 1973.

Selected Supplementary Readings

Bigart, Homer. *Forward Positions: An Anthology*. Fayetteville: University of Arkansas Press, 1992.
Fuller, Jack. *News Values: Ideas for an Information Age*. Chicago: University of Chicago Press, 1996.
Leonard, Thomas C. *News for All: America's Coming-of-Age with the Press*. New York: Oxford University Press, 1996.
Rand, Peter. *China Hands: The Adventures and Ordeals of the American Journalists Who Joined Forces with the Great Chinese Revolution*. New York: Simon & Schuster, 1996.
Reporting World War II: Part 1: American Journalism 1938–1944. Part 2: American Journalism 1944–1946. New York: The Library of America, 1996.
Shepard, Richard F. *The Paper's Papers: A Reporter's Journey Through the Archives of the New York Times*. New York: Times Books/Random House, 1996.
Stenbuck, Jack, ed. *Typewriter Battalion: Dramatic Front-Line Dispatches From World War II*. New York: William Morrow & Company, 1996.
Warren, Charles. *Radio Priest: Charles Coughlin, the Father of Hate Radio*. New York: The Free Press, 1996.

Index

References are to entry numbers

Abbott, Simon 212
Abbott, W. J. 789
Abel, Walter 32
Abrahams, Derwin 39
Acosta, Rodolfo 921
Acuff, Eddie 43, 294, 372, 540, 719
Adair, Jean 12
Adams, Carol 44
Adams, Claire 132, 217, 505
Adams, Dorothy 499
Adams, Ernest 429, 465
Adams, Jimmie 408, 663
Adams, Kathryn 86, 90
Adams, Nick 895
Adamson, Ewart 147, 657
Adler, Jay 383
Adler, Luther 3
Adolfi, John 441
Adreon, Franklyn 775
Adrian, Iris 490, 936
Agar, John 471
Agnew, Frances 573
Ahern, Gladys 676
Ahern, Will 676
Aherne, Brian 980
Ahn, Philip 144
Ainsworth, Virginia 791
Akins, Claude 443, 604
Alberni, Luis 331, 851
Albert, Eddie 353, 771, 772
Albert, Katherine 777
Albertson, Coit 465, 877
Albertson, Frank 60, 306, 560
Albertson, Jack 895
Albright, Hardie 487, 832

Albright, Lola 52
Alda, Alan 697
Alden, Mary 860
Alden, Norman 800
Alderson, Erville 1021
Aldrich, Robert 22
Alexander, Ben 189
Alexander, J. Grubb 309
Alexander, Jason 695
Alexander, Katharine 15
Alexander, Richard 775
Alexander, Ross 389
Allan, Elizabeth 654, 859
Allbritton, Louise 892
Allen, Alfred 350, 417, 679
Allen, Barbara 549
Allen, Irwin 282, 532
Allen, James 115
Allen, Jay Presson 1020
Allen, Joseph, Jr. 994
Allen, Judith 65, 306, 643
Allen, Lewis 23, 141
Allen, Nancy 658, 884
Allen, Rex 813
Allen, Robert 1001
Allen, Sam 566
Allen, Steve 159
Allister, Claude 196
Allwyn, Astrid 151, 445, 612
Allyson, June 764, 1022
Alper, Murray 83, 321
Alphin, Patricia 547
Altman, Robert 749
Alyn, Kirk 39, 878
Amateau, Rod 116
Ambrose, David 1020

Ameche, Don 165, 324, 360, 539
Ames, Adrienne 312, 361, 487
Ames, Leon 135, 653, 765, 777, 866
Ames, Michael 437, 613
Amy, George 321
Anders, Merry 800
Andersen, Bridgette 270
Anderson, Doris 484
Anderson, George 175
Anderson, Judith 499
Anderson, Mary 54, 557, 954
Anderson, Melissa 206
Anderson, Michael 822
Anderson, Philip 571
Anderson, Stanley 371
Andrews, Charles 724
Andrews, Dana 37, 63, 66, 499, 889, 986
Andrews, Del 452, 566
Andrews, Edward 419
Andrews, Jack 63
Andrews, Robert D. 42, 464, 730
Andrews, Stanley 101
Angel, Heather 377
Ankers, Evelyn 551, 741
Ankewich, Camille 672
Ankrum, Morris 996
Ann-Margaret 641, 887
Ansara, Michael 5
Anthony, Joseph 977
Anthony, Stuart 334
Antonio, Jim 318

301

Index

Apfel, Oscar 114, 407, 943
Appling, Bert 350
Apted, Michael 171
Arbuckle, Andrew 405
Arbus, Alan 239
Archainbaud, George 677, 1004
Archer, Harry 369
Archer, John 151, 322, 793
Archer, Lou 235, 512
Arden, Eve 82, 164, 693
Ariane 1018
Arlen, Richard 86, 267, 361, 543, 598, 655, 721, 748, 777, 862
Arling, Charles 747
Armetta, Henry 243, 1001
Armstrong, R. G. 984
Armstrong, Robert 2, 5, 60, 74, 93, 106, 299, 306, 319, 382, 451, 456, 551, 625, 647, 815
Arnold, Dorothy 719
Arnold, Edward 215, 508, 522, 582, 666, 914, 958, 978
Arnold, Jack 543
Arnold, Jessie 370
Arnt, Charles 607
Arrindell, Lisa 521
Arthur, Art 247, 533
Arthur, Bob 890
Arthur, George M. 190
Arthur, Jean 7, 606, 738
Arthur, Johnny 929
Arthur, Maureen 534
Arthur, Robert 4
Asbury, Herbert 631
Ashley, John 876
Asner, Edward 966
Assante, Armand 245
Astor, Gertrude 96, 514
Astor, Mary 401, 488, 655
Ates, Roscoe 767
Atkins, Peter 384
Atlas, Leopold 387, 864
Atwater, Gladys 186, 916
Atwill, Lionel 182, 222, 570, 616, 627, 851
Auberjonois, Rene 984
Aubert, Lenore 5, 908
Aubrey, Jimmy 724
Auer, John D. 693, 776
Auer, Mischa 576, 874
Austin, Leslie 1023

Austin, Rose 940
Austin, Vivian 644, 818
Austin, William 979
Averill, Anthony 932
Avery, Val 171
Avildsen, John G. 838
Avnet, Jon 962
Aylesworth, Arthur 431, 788
Ayres, Agnes 341
Ayres, Clio 577
Ayres, Lew 497, 619, 666, 694, 963

Babcock, Dwight 176
Baby Jane 570
Bacall, Lauren 216, 810
Bach, Barbara 961
Bachelor, Stephanie 185, 319
Backus, Jim 352, 930, 1022
Bacon, Kevin 371
Bacon, Lloyd 14, 261, 723, 840
Badger, Clarence 290, 417
Baer, Max 366
Baer, Parley 950
Baggot, King 364, 790, 938, 989
Bainter, Fay 33, 475, 1006
Baird, Leah 311, 476
Baker, Benny 382, 596, 694
Baker, Blanche 521
Baker, Fay 163
Baker, George D. 955
Baker, Graham C. 726
Baker, Joe Don 287
Baker, Kathy 872
Baker, Melville 642
Baker, Phil 330
Baker, Stanley 22
Bakewell, William 197, 251, 398, 490, 745
Balaban, Bob 3
Balaski, Belinda 426
Baldwin, Alan 333
Baldwin, Dick 533, 609, 675
Baldwin, Earl 222, 662, 958
Baldwin, Peter 516
Bale, Christian 641
Balenda, Carla 987
Balfour, A. 69
Ball, Lucille 238, 948
Ballard, Kaye 245

Ballin, Hugo 691
Ballin, Mabel 691
Balsam, Martin 18, 53
Balushi, James 779
Bancroft, George 237, 606, 784, 977
Banks, Monty 40
Banner, John 31
Bannon, Jim 176, 601
Barbier, George 338, 510, 638, 776
Barclay, Don 260, 431, 563
Barcroft, Roy 692, 813, 919
Bardette, Trevor 629
Bardine, Mabel 650
Bare, Richard 421
Bari, Lynn 137, 142, 150, 259, 482, 609, 638, 817
Barish, Mildred 719
Barker, Bradley 746
Barker, Corinne 828
Barker, Jess 336
Barnes, Binnie 324, 918, 920
Barnes, Mac 296
Barnett, Chester 687
Barnett, Vince 81, 177, 322, 373, 823, 891, 914
Barondess, Barbara 218
Barr, Byron 80
Barr, Doug 961
Barrat, Robert 249, 310, 395, 540, 616, 814
Barreto, Bruno 826
Barrett, James Lee 355
Barrie, Mona 430, 487, 541, 862
Barrie, Wendy 338, 640, 736, 1002
Barrier, Edgar 987
Barringer, A. B. 235
Barringer, Barry 347
Barrington, Phyllis 614, 874
Barriscale, Bessie 368
Barron, Fred 64
Barrows, Henry A. 40, 514, 759, 1011
Barrows, Nick 267
Barry, Don 936
Barry, John A. 1011
Barry, Ray 1019
Barry, Wesley 271, 341, 381, 586, 734
Barrymore, Ethel 209
Barrymore, John 645

Index

Barrymore, John, Jr. 75
Barrymore, John Drew 986
Barrymore, Lionel 46, 508, 524, 728, 764
Barsha, Leon 572, 615
Bart, Jean 570
Bartel, Paul 658
Barthelmess, Richard 232, 277, 438
Bartlett, Aline 304
Bartlett, Bennie 462
Barton, Charles 42, 70, 619, 760, 819
Barton, James 390
Barton, Julien 650
Barwick, Anthony 115
Bary, Leon 626
Basinger, Kim 749
Basquette, Lina 34
Basserman, Albert 298, 669, 799
Bates, Arthur W. 650
Bates, Barbara 421, 475
Bates, Florence 780
Bates, Granville 492, 948
Bates, Louise Emerald 386
Baxley, Barbara 868
Baxter, Alan 83, 101, 142, 156, 662, 854
Baxter, Anne 94, 542
Baxter, Warner 48, 573
Bayne, Beverly 952
Beal, Frank 111, 275, 726
Beal, John 33, 854
Beaman, Lee Anne 680
Beamish, Frank 504
Beatty, Ned 879, 880, 888
Beatty, Warren 698, 753
Beauchamp, D. D. 780
Beaudine, William 28, 102, 109, 144, 184, 336, 462, 483, 545, 637, 734, 842, 928, 931, 933, 936
Beaumont, Harry 6, 30, 197, 335
Beaumont, Hugh 90, 928
Beavers, Louise 963
Beban, George 672
Beck, Thomas 907, 1009
Beckett, Scotty 418
Beddoe, Don 70, 125, 598, 670, 686, 785, 890, 958
Bedelia, Bonnie 903
Bedford, Barbara 332, 568, 956

Bee, Richard 422
Beebe, Ford 315, 356, 719, 751
Beecher, Janet 621
Beecher, Margaret 877
Beery, Noah 172, 341, 546
Beery, Noah, Jr. 129
Beery, Wallace 217, 236, 531, 702, 803, 968
Beggs, Pat 566
Begley, Ed 209, 524, 947
Begley, Ed, Jr. 939
Bela, Nicholas 373
Belasco, Leon 644
Belasco, Walter 468
Belden, Barbara 983
Belden, Charles 135, 609, 675, 934
Belita 635
Bell, James 163, 899
Bell, Monta 571, 963, 1023
Bell, Rex 34, 219, 300
Bellamy, Ralph 14, 297, 376, 404, 456, 584, 585, 723
Belmore, Lionel 467
Belushi, John 171
Benchley, Peter 454
Benchley, Robert 298, 376, 852, 918
Bender, Russ 876
Bendix, William 1006
Benedict, Billy 102, 637
Benedict, Kingsley 801, 981
Benedict, Richard 4
Benham, Harry 1025
Bennet, Spencer Gordon 39, 45, 272, 643, 878
Bennett, Bruce 21, 78, 421, 816
Bennett, Charles 282, 298, 532
Bennett, Chester 801
Bennett, Constance 15, 554, 831
Bennett, Dick 78
Bennett, Enid 369
Bennett, Hugh 385
Bennett, Joan 71, 160, 165, 424, 570, 977
Bennison, Andrew 138, 1003
Bennison, Louis 500
Benny, Jack 110
Benoit, Victor 304
Benton, Kevin 965

Benton, Robert 879
Benzali, Daniel 588
Beranger, Clara 266
Bercouri, Melina 320
Bergen, Thurlow 732
Bergere, Valerie 997
Bergman, Andrew 287
Bergman, Henri 423
Berke, William 228, 231, 823, 995
Berkeley, Xander 667
Berks, John 176
Bernds, Edward 418, 462
Bernhard, Jack 91, 716, 967
Bernhardt, Kevin 384
Bernie, Ben 533, 970
Bernstein, Isadore 111, 811
Berthelet, Arthur 344
Best, James 419, 821
Bestar, Barbara 634
Betts, Jack 206
Betz, Matthew 622
Beute, Chris 373
Bey, Turhan 551
Beyer, Charles 564
Beyers, Clara 364
Bezzerides, A. I. 22
Biberman, Herbert 5
Bickford, Charles 362, 645, 782, 871, 1022
Bikel, Theodore 22, 436
Billingsley, Barbara 31
Bing, Herman 7
Binney, Constance 555
Binyon, Claude 230, 331, 1022
Birch, Wyrley 694
Bird, Violet 466
Bishop, Julie 375, 403, 437, 777
Bishop, William 50, 678
Bisset, Jacqueline 855
Blache, Herbert 999
Black, Bill 262
Blackburn, Tom 483
Blackley, Douglas 823
Blackmer, Sidney 66, 306, 312, 351, 599, 780, 976, 1007, 1013
Blackwell, Carlyle 153, 504
Blades, Ruben 594
Blaine, Ruby 378
Blair, George 234, 319, 829, 942, 960
Blair, Janet 918

Index

Blair, Joan 208, 829
Blair, Linda 965
Blair, Ruth 304
Blake, B. K. 213
Blake, Betty 154
Blake, Bobby 363
Blake, Larry 477
Blake, Lucy 844
Blake, Pamela 995
Blake, Whitney 913
Blakeney, Olive 385
Blanc, Margaret 792
Blandick, Clara 186
Blane, Sally 12, 20, 149, 200, 255, 648, 671, 1017
Blankenship, Harold 581
Blankfort, Henry 644, 954
Blees, Robert 796
Blondell, Joan 43, 176, 261, 662, 714, 918
Bloom, Verna 581
Blore, Eric 918
Blue, Ben 238
Blystone, John 325
Blyth, Ann 837
Blythe, Betty 45, 140, 332, 643
Blythe, Erik 447
Boardman, Eleanor 205
Boardman, Virginia True 790
Bock, Edward 569
Boehm, David 291, 485, 511
Boehm, Karl 966
Boetticher, Budd 56, 601, 674
Bogart, Humphrey 209, 366, 704, 757, 949
Bohem, Andre 492
Bohnen, Roman 13
Boland, Eddie 805
Boland, Mary 576
Boles, Glen 745
Bologna, Joseph 939
Bolton, Muriel Roy 385
Bond, Brenda 746
Bond, Lillian 875
Bond, Raymond 562
Bond, Steve 894
Bond, Tommy 39, 878
Bond, Ward 166, 259, 831
Bondi, Beulah 524, 748
Bonerz, Peter 581
Bonner, Priscilla 408
Booth, Edwina 592

Borden, Eddie 166, 476
Borden, Ethel 909
Borg, Veda Ann 80, 418, 788
Borgnine, Ernest 24
Borsos, Philip 580
Borzage, Frank 809
Boss, Yale 6
Bosworth, Hobart 113, 802
Boteler, Wade 74, 140, 276, 356, 507, 598, 602, 751, 1011
Bourne, Whitney 552
Bouton, Betty 273
Bow, Clara 622
Bowers, William 37, 833, 913
Bowker, Aldrich 437
Bowman, Lee 198, 215, 911, 971, 975
Boyd, William 996
Boylan, Malcolm Stuart 525, 569, 607
Boyle, Laird 848
Boyle, Peter 984
Boyle, Richard 779
Brabin, Charles 836
Bracken, Bertram 235
Brackett, Charles 32, 900
Bracy, Sidney 120, 595, 1025
Bradbury, Robert North 513, 527, 982
Bradford, Richard 594
Bradford, Virginia 40
Bradley, Doug 384
Bradley, Estelle 861
Bradley, Grace 450, 492
Brady, Alice 266, 596
Brady, Edward 229
Brady, Fred 129
Brady, Scott 143
Braga, Sonia 594
Branch, Houston 372, 629
Brando, Marlon 879
Brandon, Henry 44, 491
Brasselle, Keefe 46
Brazzi, Rossano 863
Breamer, Sylvia 512
Brecher, Egon 681
Breck, Peter 821
Breese, Edmund 2, 233, 441
Bremer, Lucille 56
Bren, J. Robert 186, 916
Brendel, El 765

Brennan, Frederick Hazlitt 735, 847
Brennan, George 423
Brennan, Walter 582, 856, 883
Brent, Evelyn 191, 484, 645, 707, 853, 996, 1014
Brent, George 176, 316, 343, 482, 848, 1021
Brent, Romney 796
Breslow, Lou 83, 280, 330, 402, 671, 915
Bressart, Felix 164, 911
Bretherton, Howard 396, 858
Brian, David 301
Brian, Mary 89, 676, 702, 1014
Brice, Robert 447
Bricker, George 52, 176, 317, 380, 518, 540, 575, 583, 598, 611, 706, 931, 932, 987
Bridge, Al 502
Bridges, Beau 320
Bridges, James 143, 712
Bridges, Lloyd 846
Briggs, Donald 92, 187
Briggs, Harlan 743, 763
Briggs, Matt 12
Bright, John 156, 482
Brill, Patti 833
Brimley, Wilford 239, 245
Brisebois, Danielle 68
Brissac, Virginia 991
Brix, Herman 811
Brock, Gerald 853
Brockwell, Gladys 571
Broder, Edith 79
Brodie, Steve 936
Brodney, Oscar 308
Brody, Ann 399, 733
Brolin, James 122
Bromberg, J. Edward 135, 597, 675
Bromley, Sheila 632, 750, 934
Bronson, Betty 592
Bronson, Charles 588
Brook, Clive 784
Brooke, Hillary 52, 80, 81, 84, 430, 545, 960
Brooke, Peter R. 50
Brooks, Alan 79
Brooks, Albert 108

Brooks, Hazel 50
Brooks, James L. 108
Brooks, Leslie 91, 158, 569
Brooks, Max 737
Brooks, Phyllis 830
Brooks, Richard 209, 270, 345, 1015
Brooks, Sorel 87
Brophy, Ed 200, 336, 458, 470, 554, 651, 795, 917
Brophy, Kevin 806
Brower, Otto 54, 376, 518, 1001
Brower, Robert 754
Brower, Thomas 657
Brown, Blair 171, 285
Brown, Chad 49
Brown, Charles A. 36
Brown, Charles D. 246, 252, 569, 646
Brown, Clarence 21, 924
Brown, George Carleton 391
Brown, Harry Joe 485, 861
Brown, James S. 643, 661
Brown, Joe E. 190, 279, 342, 735, 763
Brown, John Mack 803
Brown, Karl 607
Brown, Leete Renick 683
Brown, Tom 82, 234, 261, 325, 470, 578, 707
Brown, Vanessa 50
Brown, William H. 774
Browne, Michael 185
Browne, Roscoe Lee 87
Brownell, Edward 235
Browning, Tod 205, 568
Brownlee, Frank 242, 409
Bruce, Clifford 304
Bruce, David 472, 551, 778
Bruce, Nigel 773
Bruce, Virginia 5, 8, 508, 616, 905
Bruckman, Clyde 818
Brundage, Mathilde 364
Bruner, James 448
Brunette, Fritzi 1008
Bruns, Philip 206
Brunson, Glenda 506
Bryan, Jane 237
Bryant, Geoffrey 79
Bryant, Nana 80, 736, 871
Brynner, Yul 318

Buchanan, Edgar 131, 459, 715, 760, 971
Buchanan, James David 103
Buchanan, William 811
Buchman, Harold 128, 227, 456, 656, 686
Buchman, Sidney 7, 312, 688
Buckley, Floyd 262
Buckner, Robert 889
Budd, Norman 960
Buffington, Adele 271, 300
Bulgakov, Leo 992
Bupp, Tommy 166
Burbridge, Betty 25, 453
Burgess, Dorothy 310, 735
Burke, Billie 15, 906
Burke, Edwin J. 841, 847
Burke, James 227, 625
Burnett, Carol 314
Burnett, W. R. 277
Burnette, Smiley 830
Burnham, Frances 668
Burns, Bob 33
Burns, Edward 428, 467, 683, 1011
Burns, Paul E. 646
Burnstine, Norman 35
Burr, Eugene 273
Burr, Raymond 1, 94, 183, 960, 987
Burress, William 455
Burt, William 386
Burtis, James 357, 503, 758
Burton, Clarence 731
Burton, Val 385
Busch, Mae 139, 358, 874
Busch, Niven 662
Bushell, Anthony 281
Bushman, Francis X. 201, 952
Butler, David 138, 639, 679, 908
Butler, John K. 319, 375, 721, 830
Butterworth, Charles 365
Butterworth, Ernest 781
Buttons, Red 282
Buzzell, Edward 238, 411
Buzzi, Ruth 965
Byington, Spring 21, 46, 335, 420
Byram, Ronald 682
Byrd, Ralph 31, 109, 775, 776

Byrne, Francis 168
Byron, Arthur 295
Byron, Delma 498
Byron, Nina 945
Byron, Walter 191
Byrum, John 787

Cabanne, William Christy 41, 86, 169, 173, 347, 529, 592, 789, 793, 916, 1014
Cabot, Bruce 355, 643, 744, 767, 834
Cabot, Sebastian 22
Cady, Frank 4
Cady, Jerry 119, 135, 444, 609, 675, 875, 923
Caesar, Arthur 8, 654
Cagney, James 93, 161, 237, 474, 723
Cahn, Edward L. 800, 876
Caine, Georgia 42
Caine, Michael 454
Calhern, Louis 400, 666, 976, 1014
Calhoun, Alice 207
Calhoun, Jean 194
Callahan, George 59
Callam, Alex 450
Calleia, Joseph 249, 834
Calvert, E. H. 507, 1003
Calvert, John 575
Calvet, Corinne 709
Camden, Joan 123
Cameron, Donald 828
Cameron, Rod 375, 778
Camp, Colleen 806
Campbell, Emma 682
Campbell, Julia 521
Campbell, Louise 241, 645, 998
Campbell, Margaret 505
Campbell, Webster 207
Campeau, Frank 441, 781
Cannon, Raymond 734
Cansino, Rita 427
Canutt, Yakima 157
Capetanos, Leon 288
Capra, Frank 297, 390, 457, 582, 606, 725, 729
Cardos, John 204
Carew, Ora 840
Carewe, Arthur Edmund 222
Carewe, Edwin 401, 423
Carewe, Rita 401

Index

Carey, Harry 187, 871
Carey, Macdonald 131, 501
Carey, Phil 796
Cargill, Henry 740
Carleton, Claire 928
Carlson, Richard 29, 56, 198, 515, 846
Carmen, Julie 495, 594
Carnovsky, Morris 221
Carol, Joan 671
Carol, Sue 138
Carole, Joseph 174, 785
Carpenter, Horace B. 180
Carpenter, Ken 384
Carr, Harry 438
Carr, Mary 271
Carr, Thomas 878
Carradine, John 268, 426, 494, 678, 830
Carrillo, Elpedia 779
Carrillo, Leo 182, 585, 920, 927, 968
Carroll, John 883
Carroll, Madeleine 117
Carroll, Nancy 38, 900, 905
Carroll, Richard 918
Carson, Jack 673, 893, 916
Carson, Renee 208
Carson, Terrence 521
Carter, Helena 301, 446
Carter, Jack 756
Carter, Janis 478, 575, 601, 646, 674, 994
Caruso, Anthony 692
Carver, Lynne 608
Cassell, Wally 864
Cassidy, Joanna 951
Cassini, John 574
Castellanos, Joseph 364
Castello, William 396, 849
Castle, Don 403, 716
Castle, Peggie 447
Castle, William 131, 575
Catlett, Walter 250, 539, 666, 852
Cavanagh, Paul 127, 195, 221
Cavanaugh, Hobart 218, 389, 395, 432, 623, 654, 795, 902, 964
Cavanaugh, Katharine 205
Cecil, Edward 530
Celli, Teresa 764
Ceron, Laura 737
Chadwick, Lee 865

Challenger, Percy 379
Chamberlain, Howard 75
Chambers, Wheaton 294
Chambers, Whitman 81, 430
Chandler, Chick 147, 444, 853, 923, 985, 1009
Chandler, Ed 766
Chandler, George 59, 565
Chandler, Helen 55
Chandler, Jeff 1, 889
Chandler, Lane 502
Chaney, Lon 116, 350
Channing, Stockard 962
Chanslor, Roy 95, 227, 306, 389, 563, 602, 715, 975
Chapin, James 429
Chapin, Robert 420
Chaplin, Charlie 558
Chaplin, Syd 665
Chapman, Edythe 781, 955
Chapman, Jay 566
Chapman, Marguerite 289, 971
Charters, Spencer 83, 488, 608, 793, 866
Chase, Borden 524
Chase, Chevy 287, 288
Chase, Stephen 29
Chaudet, Louis William 843
Chautard, Emile 523, 628, 682
Chaykin, Maury 393
Cheney, J. Benton 830, 996
Cherney, Linda 796
Cheshire, Harry 133
Chevigny, Hector 1021
Chiles, Lois 108
Ching, William 883
Christensen, Benjamin 422
Christy, Dorothy 357
Church, Claire 377
Churchill, Berton 743, 782, 832, 891
Churchill, Marguerite 98, 563
Ciannelli, Eduardo 187, 296, 299, 765, 862, 908
Cimino, Michael 1019
Clair, George 801
Clair, Rene 458
Clanton, Ralph 953
Clare, Clarette 85
Clare, Phyllis 572, 767
Clarendon, Hal 168
Clark, Dane 387

Clark, Davidson 231, 770
Clark, Frank Howard 1024
Clark, Fred 224, 471, 522
Clark, Harvey 731, 827, 1004
Clark, Herbert C. 275
Clark, Judy 644
Clark, Violet 332
Clark, Wallis 611, 858
Clarke, Donald Henderson 1013
Clarke, Mae 203, 274, 313, 943
Clarke, Robert 562
Clary, Charles 225, 255, 409
Clawson, Elliott J. 229, 507, 944
Clayton, Lou 768
Clayton, Marguerite 650, 982
Clegg, Tom 24
Clemens, William 389, 563, 632, 932
Clement, Clay 35, 333, 858
Clements, Stanley 84, 418
Cleveland, George 370, 396, 458, 474, 983
Clifford, Ruth 989
Clifford, William 455, 684, 747
Clift, Denison 519
Clift, Montgomery 526
Clifton, Elmer 36, 124, 151, 438, 507, 529, 567, 802
Cline, Eddie 442, 644
Clive, E. E. 38, 909
Clive, Henry 668
Close, Glenn 695
Clyde, Andy 996
Clyde, June 798, 865
Cobb, Edmund 527
Cobb, Irvin S. 33
Cobb, Lee J. 119, 542
Coburn, Charles 160, 485, 688, 856
Cochran, Dorcas 336
Cochran, Steve 837
Cockrell, Francis 852
Codee, Ann 107
Cody, Bill 255
Cody, Lew 191, 1017
Coe, George 285
Coen, Franklin 252, 743
Coffin, Tristram 177

Coghlan, Junior 507
Cohen, Ben 201
Cohen, Rob 787
Colbert, Claudette 32, 331, 360, 432, 457, 899, 1023
Coldeway, Anthony 152, 586, 795, 991
Cole, Lester 93, 477, 661, 929
Coleman, C. C., Jr. 188, 598
Coleman, Nancy 967
Coleman, Vincent 555, 792
Coletti, Frank 450
Collier, Lois 129, 336
Collier, William, Jr. 55, 146, 217
Collinge, Patricia 976
Collins, Eddie 638
Collins, Hal 535
Collins, Lewis D. 101, 187, 758, 832
Collins, Monty F. 892
Collins, Ray 148, 302, 808, 899
Collins, Russell 156
Collins, Stephen 64
Collyer, June 257
Colman, Ronald 579
Colon, Alex 448
Colouris, George 148
Colton, Scott 253
Colvin, William 747
Comer, Anjanette 742
Comingore, Dorothy 75, 148
Commandini, Adele 145
Compson, Betty 179, 196, 391, 630, 932
Compton, Christine 713
Compton, Fay 863
Compton, Joyce 619, 789, 830
Comstock, Clark 527
Condon, Charles 630
Condon, David 462
Conklin, Charles 205
Conklin, Chester 76, 422, 558
Conklin, Frank Roland 408
Conklin, William 369, 684, 844, 956
Conlin, James 276, 459
Connery, Sean 23, 1015
Connolly, Jack 468
Connolly, Mattie 747

Connolly, Myles 390
Connolly, Walter 303, 457, 509, 660, 927, 992
Connors, Michael 876
Conrad, Eugene 158
Conrad, Jack 340
Conrad, Robert 1015
Conrad, William 913, 950
Constantine, Michael 742
Consulman, William 550
Conte, Richard 78, 94, 119
Conway, Jack 468, 508, 509, 927, 968
Conway, Morgan 88, 656, 662, 875
Conway, Pat 953
Conway, Tom 258, 260
Coogan, Jackie 526
Cook, Clyde 441
Cook, Donald 57, 65, 487, 968
Cook, Elisha, Jr. 559, 640, 869, 995
Cook, John 520
Cook, T. S. 143
Cook, Tommy 482
Cooley, Hal 926
Coolidge, Philip 436
Cooper, Ben 375
Cooper, Gary 302, 582, 606
Cooper, George 217, 599, 600
Cooper, Jackie 640, 855, 879, 880, 881, 882, 900
Cooper, Jeanne 813
Cooper, Olive 13, 440, 470, 758
Coote, Robert 887
Coppel, Alec 29
Corbett, Ben 761
Corbin, Virginia Lee 152, 300, 378, 466, 713, 1017
Corcoran, Donna 21
Corday, Mara 953
Corday, Rita 258
Cording, Harry 766
Corey, Jeff 588
Corley, Bob 506
Cormack, Bartlett 313, 328, 958
Corrigan, James 315, 388
Corrigan, Lloyd 95, 346, 544, 804
Corry, Will 870
Cortes, Armand 425

Cortez, Ricardo 137, 150, 152, 243, 444, 451, 563, 824, 848, 994
Cosgrave, Luke 172
Cossart, Ernest 485, 619, 740
Costanzo, Robert 574
Costello, Dolores 573, 686
Costello, Helene 111
Costello, John 733, 792
Costello, Maurice 207
Coster, Nicolas 838
Cotten, Joseph 148, 709
Cotton, Oliver 240
Couldwell, James 956
Courtney, Inez 107, 139, 186, 280, 703, 912, 977
Courtot, Marguerite 860
Courtright, William 463, 568
Cowan, Jerome 208, 250, 306, 584, 830, 890
Cowan, Lynn 842
Cowell, Jack 257
Cowl, George 628
Cowles, Jules 566
Cox, Wally 53
Crabbe, Larry Buster 45, 170, 484, 612, 751
Craft, William James 196, 284, 761
Craig, Blanche 555
Craig, Catherine 853
Craig, Harry A. L. 27
Craig, James 528, 656
Cramer, Marc 693
Cramer, Massey 506
Cramer, Richard 850
Crampton, Howard 993
Crane, Frank 850
Crane, Richard 54, 919
Craven, Edward 331
Craven, Frank 149, 461, 480, 760
Crawford, Broderick 17, 99, 524, 585, 786, 831, 920
Crawford, Joan 197, 541, 863, 906
Creelman, James A. 564
Crehan, Joseph 59, 392, 601, 706
Crenna, Richard 689
Crisp, Donald 414
Critchley, Rosalie 240
Crittenden, Dwight 1011

Index 308

Cromwell, John 163, 784, 930
Cromwell, Richard 2, 510, 586, 631, 867
Cronyn, Hume 320, 698
Crosby, Bing 390, 400, 516
Crosby, Cathy Lee 159, 204
Crosby, Mary 495
Crosby, Wade 447
Crosland, Alan 172
Crosman, Henrietta 334
Crossland, Marjorie 123
Crosswhite, E. B. 614
Crouse, Lindsay 64
Crowell, Josephine 225, 739
Crowley, Kathleen 268
Cruze, James 152, 178, 432, 573, 595, 1025
Cukor, George 99, 480, 722
Culp, Robert 68
Cummings, Irving 69, 208, 247, 550, 885, 980
Cummings, Jack 449
Cummings, Richard 520, 926
Cummings, Robert 192, 247
Cunard, Grace 112, 759, 843
Cunard, Mina 112, 981
Cunningham, Jack 172, 925
Cunningham, Joe 934, 935
Cunningham, Sean S. 868
Curley, Pauline 126, 593
Curran, Charles 10
Currie, Louise 28, 144
Currier, Frank 762, 897
Currier, Mary 185
Curtis, Dick 634
Curtis, Donald 189
Curtis, Jack 1010
Curtis, Jamie Lee 712
Curtis, Tony 286, 354, 810, 886
Curtiz, Michael 222, 303, 316, 627, 704, 714, 867
Cusack, Joan 108, 393
Custer, Bob 566

Dade, Frances 79
Dagmar, Florence 180
Dahl, Helen 290
Dahlin, Bob 604
Dailey, Dan 975
Dale, Esther 82, 547, 677, 998

Dale, Jim 787
Dale, Virginia 372, 655
Dalton, Timothy 103
Dalton, Wally 212
Daly, James 756
D'Ambricourt, Adrienne 428
Damon, Mark 27
Dane, Patricia 845
Dangler, Anita 838
Daniels, Bebe 267, 417, 979
Daniels, J. D. 574
Daniels, William 698
Danner, Blythe 318
Dano, Royal 183
Dante, Joe 426
Dantine, Helmut 383
D'Arcy, Roy 762
Darien, Frank 57
Darling, Ida 990
Darling, W. Scott 54, 144, 263, 610, 831
Darnell, Linda 458
Darrell, Donnah 705
Darren, James 921
Darro, Frankie 26, 374, 706, 937
Darrow, John 16
Darwell, Jane 349, 444, 498, 510, 585, 923
Da Silva, Howard 651, 954
Daugherty, Jack 791
Daughtry, Reginald 345
Dauphin, Claude 516, 744
Davenport, Alice 558
Davenport, Doris 60
Davenport, Harry 279, 319, 372, 398, 461
Davenport, Havis 783
Daves, Delmer 635
Davidson, Eileen 245
Davidson, John 55, 85, 406
Davidson, William 347, 662
Davies, Howard 326
Davis, Bette 295, 316, 343, 475, 848
Davis, Charles 562
Davis, Edwards 401, 729
Davis, Geena 287, 393, 939
Davis, Joan 20, 533, 818
Davis, Owen, Jr. 348
Davis, Paula 345
Davis, Robert O. 584
Davis, Rufe 323
Davis, Will S. 952

Davison, John 85
Daw, Marjorie 546, 781
Dawn, Isabel 60, 346
Day, Alice 232, 442
Day, Doris 895
Day, Laraine 298, 958
Day, Marceline 34, 120, 191, 309, 527
Dayton, Dan 947
Dazey, Charles T. 828
Dazey, Frank 423
Dean, Rosemary 153
Deane, Shirley 420
De Baer, Jean 285
DeCamp, Rosemary 93, 786
De Carlo, Yvonne 778, 780
De Cordova, Frederick 387
De Corsia, Ted 418
Dee, Frances 184, 365, 376, 538
De Gaw, Boyce 60
De Haven, Gloria 230
De Havilland, Olivia 303
Dein, Edward 129, 258, 707
Dekker, Albert 489, 669, 778
De Kova, Frank 29
De La Motte, Marguerite 275
Delaney, Charles 124, 154, 381, 825
De Leon, Walter 74
Delevanti, Cyril 751
Dell, Claudia 782
Dell, Gabriel 545, 637
Dell, Myrna 116
Del Rio, Dolores 401
Delroy, Irene 664
Del Ruth, Roy 89, 110
DeLuca, Rudy 939
DeLuise, Michael 590
Demain, Gordon 553
Demarest, William 596, 977, 992
Demetrio, Anna 642
De Mille, William C. 367, 672
DeMond, Albert 2, 92, 187, 234, 692, 851, 891, 933, 960, 1005
De More, Harry 242
De Niro, Robert 394
Denison, Edwin 85
Denning, Richard 241

Dentler, Marion 153
De Palma, Brian 394, 835
Derek, John 17, 786
Derr, Richard 362, 478, 559
De Salvo, Anne 712
Des Esseintes, Georges 680
De Sica, Vittorio 822
Desmond, Albert 323
Desmond, William 381, 690, 759, 761
Deste, Luli 127
De Toth, Andre 125
Devane, William 204
De Vaull, William 409
Devereaux, Orra 1011
Devine, Andy 86, 543, 623, 718, 831, 866
Devlin, Dean 959
Devlin, Joe 104
Devore, Dorothy 408, 842
De Wolf, Karen 420
Dexter, Anthony 701
Diamond, David 11
Diamond, I. A. L. 314
DiCenzo, George 667
Dickey, Basil 719, 811
Dickinson, Angie 68, 756
Dickson, Gloria 70, 730
Didion, Joan 962
Dieterle, William 295, 709, 799, 947
Digges, Dudley 539, 799
Dighton, John 771
Dillaway, Donald 676, 725
Dillman, Bradford 756
Dillon, John F. 126, 194, 277
Dillon, Melinda 3
Dilson, John 67, 785
Dinehart, Alan 83, 247, 427, 654, 666, 706, 980, 1009
Dingle, Charles 360
Ditchburn, Anne 838
Dix, Beulah Marie 169
Dix, Richard 146, 564, 575, 654, 948
Dixon, Florence 828
Dixon, Thomas, Jr. 1000
Dmytryk, Edward 27, 61, 241, 258
Dodd, Claire 602, 706, 1013
Dolan, Frank 871
Dolen, Jay 170
Donahue, Vincent J. 526

Donat, Peter 143
Donlan, James 274
Donlevy, Brian 365, 402, 427, 816, 817, 915
Donlin, Mike 272
Donnell, Jeff 94, 646, 688
Donnelly, Ruth 89, 718
Donner, Richard 879
Donohue, Jack 156
Donohue, Joseph 202
DoQui, Robert 345
D'Or, Louis 226
Doran, Ann 189, 482, 599
Doran, Mary 274, 832
Dore, Adrienne 261
Dorfman, Nat 38
Dorziat, Gabrielle 516
Doty, Douglas 233
Doucet, Catherine 470
Douglas, Byron 713
Douglas, Donald 518, 824
Douglas, George 750
Douglas, Gordon 161, 424
Douglas, Kirk 4, 930
Douglas, Melvyn 896, 900, 906, 911
Douglas, Michael 143
Douglas, Nathan E. 443
Douglas, Paul 21
Douglas, Robert 302
Douglas, Warren 144, 942
Dow, Peggy 816
Dowling, Constance 485
Dowling, Joseph J. 132, 647, 690, 925
Downs, Cathy 78
Downs, Johnny 553
Doyle, David 697
Doyle, Laird 316
Doyle, Maxine 625, 775
Drake, Frances 291
Drake, Oliver 151, 633, 701
Drake, Tom 974
Dratler, Jay 119, 499, 901
Dreifuss, Arthur 535, 707
Dresser, Louise 152
Drew, Ellen 549
Drew, Roland 450, 613, 829
Drew, S. Rankin 62, 202
Dru, Joanne 17
Drumier, Jack 85
DuBarry, Denise 604
Dublin, L. C. 65
Dudley, Charles 844
Duff, Amanda 150, 243

Duff, Howard 604, 816
Duff, Warren 41, 43, 237, 310, 947
Duffy, Albert 769
Dugan, Dennis 426
Dugan, Tom 59, 128, 232, 760, 812
Dugay, Yvette 308
Dumbrille, Douglass 129, 395, 525, 738, 817, 896, 1005
Dunaew, Nicholas 292
Dunbar, Dorothy 283
Dunbar, Helen 739
Duncan, Sandy 859
Duncan, William 726
Dunham, Phil 849
Dunkinson, Harry 926
Dunlap, Scott 264, 530
Dunn, Billy 644
Dunn, Bobby 496
Dunn, Emma 745
Dunn, James 203, 406, 623, 706, 814, 841
Dunn, Ralph 928
Dunn, William 577, 733
Dunne, Irene 146, 167, 688
Dunne, John Gregory 962
Dunne, Philip 542, 856
Dupree, Roland 84
Duprez, June 518
Durante, Jimmy 768
Durbin, Deanna 900, 964
Durkin, James 153
Durkin, Junior 748
Durlam, Arthur 124
Durnham, Charles 394
Durning, Charles 835
Duryea, Dan 479, 954
D'Usseau, Arnaud 478, 994
D'Usseau, Leon 157
Duvall, Robert 641, 695, 826
Dvorak, Ann 310, 538, 867
Dwan, Allan 76, 168, 402, 427, 671, 883, 1009
Dwan, Dorothy 685, 762
Dwire, Earl 36, 850, 922
Dyer, William 520

Eagels, Jeanne 571
Earle, Edward 374, 442
Earle, William P. S. 577, 990
Earnshaw, Fenton 483

Index

Eason, B. Reeves 55, 415, 613, 752
Ebsen, Buddy 110
Eburne, Maude 563
Eddy, Helen Jerome 579, 672
Eddy, Nelson 485, 508
Edwards, Alan 155, 406
Edwards, Bill 199
Edwards, Blake 354
Edwards, Cliff 197, 258, 1013
Edwards, Edgar 572, 615
Edwards, Vince 806
Edwards, Walter 273, 690
Edwin, Walter 6
Egan, Jack 76
Eggert, Nicole 667
Eikenberry, Jill 64
Eilers, Sally 291
Eisinger, Jo 183, 890
Ekberg, Anita 796
Eldredge, John 246, 435, 554, 623
Eldridge, Kay 720
Eline, Marie 121
Eliscu, Edward 402
Elizabeth of Toro 820
Elkas, Edward 603
Ellin, Stanley 75
Elliot, Biff 204
Elliott, Bill 67
Elliott, Dick 560
Elliott, Edythe 720
Elliott, John 614
Elliott, Lillian 500
Elliott, Robert 277, 592, 735
Elliott, Ross 548
Ellis, George 506
Ellis, Patricia 706, 723
Ellis, Robert 83, 124, 137, 243, 311, 453, 498, 745, 817, 851, 999
Ellison, James 319, 608
Ellsworth, Warren 561
Elsom, Isobel 537, 689
Elton, Edmund 628
Emerson, Faye 387, 613, 651
Emerson, John 168
Emery, Gilbert 335, 486, 784
Emery, John 93
Emmerich, Roland 959

Emmett, Fern 36, 396
Endfield, Cyril 31, 472, 846, 954
Endore, Guy 864
Engel, Roy 562
English, John 223, 323, 721
English, Richard 114, 492
Englund, Ken 885
Enright, Ray 43, 585, 831
Ensign, Michael 100
Ephron, Della 103
Epstein, Philip 348, 552
Erdman, Richard 94, 780
Erickson, Carl 627
Erikson, Leif 334
Ermey, R. Lee 288
Ernest, George 420
Errol, Leon 472, 818
Erskine, Chester 589
Erwin, Stuart 15, 184, 249, 968, 1012
Esmond, Elsie 732
Esmond, Jill 451
Estabrook, Howard 146, 579, 997
Estrada, Eric 826
Ethier, Alphonse 812
Etting, Ruth 330
Eunson, Dale 777
Evans, Charles 483
Evans, Dale 223, 413, 692, 942
Evans, Gene 700, 821
Evans, Herbert 997
Evans, Larry 405
Evans, Madge 30, 211, 244, 249, 587, 699
Evans, Muriel 374, 599
Everett, Chad 270
Evers, Ann 26
Eyer, Richard 837
Eythe, William 160

Fabian 282
Fain, Matty 912
Fair, Elinor 507, 530
Fairbanks, Douglas 781
Fairbanks, Douglas, Jr. 511, 538, 729
Fairbanks, William 264
Fairchild, Morgan 806
Faire, Virginia Brown 496, 618
Fairfax, Marion 341, 367, 531, 546

Falk, Peter 27, 354
Falkenburg, Jinx 819
Falkenstein, Fritz 714
Fang, Charlie 691
Farley, Dot 264
Farley, James 152
Farmer, Frances 248
Farnum, Dorothy 192
Farnum, Dustin 326
Farnum, Franklyn 242, 415
Farnum, William 157, 323, 802
Farr, Felicia 966
Farr, Patricia 188, 490
Farrar, Jane 228
Farrell, Glenda 11, 92, 252, 293, 389, 395, 402, 627, 782, 839, 931, 933, 935
Farrell, Ken 380
Farrell, Terry 384
Farrington, Adele 981
Farrington, Frank 1025
Farrow, John 73
Faulkner, Ralph 668
Fawcett, George 207, 235, 271, 438, 683
Fay, Frank 660
Faye, Alice 48, 970
Fazenda, Louise 422
Feist, Felix 50, 362
Fellowes, Rockliffe 179, 691
Felton, Earl 253, 647
Fenton, Frank 20, 259
Fenton, Leslie 261, 663, 867, 896, 992
Ferguson, Casson 388
Ferguson, Frank 483
Ferrer, Jose 352
Ferrer, Mel 810
Fessier, Michael 249, 1012
Fetchit, Stepin 915
Fickett, Mary 479
Field, Margaret 562
Field, Sally 3
Field, Virginia 29
Fielding, Edward 980
Fielding, Margaret 232
Fields, Joseph A. 348, 917
Fields, Leonard 218
Fields, Stanley 88
Figman, Max 944
Fillmore, Nellie 691
Filson, Al 873
Fine, Morton 419
Finkel, Abem 395, 848

Index

Finley, Bill 835
Finley, Ned 481
Firth, Peter 115
Fisher, Harry 774
Fisher, Maggie Halloway 530
Fisher, Steve 63, 78
Fiske, Robert 70, 630, 922
Fitzgerald, Dallas 157, 466
Fix, Paul 86
Flaherty, Pat 86
Fleming, Erin 506
Fleming, Rhonda 986
Fleming, Susan 200
Fleming, Victor 217
Flick, Pat C. 576
Flippen, Jay C. 419
Flood, James 662
Florey, Robert 484, 706
Flournoy, Richard 279, 763
Flynn, Errol 303, 661, 714, 772
Foleg, Peter 961
Fonda, Henry 552, 810
Fonda, Jane 143, 239
Fonda, Peter 318
Fong, Benson 709
Fong, Willie 48
Fontaine, Joan 66
Foote, Courtenay 113
Foran, Dick 343, 360, 714
Forbes, Mary Elizabeth 686, 1025
Ford, Corey 852
Ford, Francis 112, 325, 496
Ford, Glenn 42, 174, 224, 879
Ford, Harrison 41, 507, 1004
Ford, John 98, 112
Ford, Lee 775
Ford, Lettie 364
Ford, Philip 185
Ford, Wallace 28, 30, 93, 251, 286, 363, 556, 586, 611, 624, 648, 769, 793, 1017
Forde, Eugene 63, 135, 559, 675, 915
Foreman, Carol 878
Forman, Tom 367
Forms, Carl 405
Forrest, Alan 409, 731
Forrest, Ann 358
Forrest, Sally 46
Forster, Robert 581

Forsythe, John 123, 459
Fort, Garrett 768
Forth, George J. 836
Foss, Fanya 760
Foster, Lewis B. 139, 433
Foster, Lewis R. 8
Foster, Norman 57, 134, 219, 328, 402, 486, 1023
Foster, Preston 75, 137, 218, 222, 518, 638, 892
Foster, Ron 800
Foulger, Byron 560
Fourcade, Christian 516
Fowler, Gene, Jr. 678, 365
Fowley, Douglas 56, 71, 104, 134, 135, 340, 433, 444, 583, 671, 789, 915, 923, 942, 1009
Fox, Frederick Louis 375
Fox, Sidney 589
Fox, Wallace 104, 177
Foxe, Earle 343, 592, 639
Foy, Eddie, Jr. 127
Franciosa, Tony 887
Francis, Alec B. 439, 504
Francis, Anne 224, 534
Francis, Katherine 328
Francis, Kay 784
Francis, Noel 361
Francis, Owen 188
Francis, Wilma 101, 360
Franey, William 938
Frank, J. Herbert 311
Frank, Jeffrey 454
Frankenheimer, John 1020
Franklin, Howard 737
Franklin, Paul 231, 943
Franz, Arthur 66, 289
Franz, Joseph 711
Fraser, Harry 219, 626
Fraser, Phyllis 937
Fraser, Richard 90, 158
Fraser, Robert 630, 769
Frawley, William 349, 445, 525, 677, 736
Frazee, Jane 363
Frazer, Robert 220, 467
Frears, Stephen 393
Frederici, Blanche 55, 200
Frederick, Pauline 682
Freeman, Al, Jr. 87
Freeman, David 872
Freeman, Mona 286
Freeman, Morgan 872
Fremont, Al 265

French, Charles K. 368, 405, 410, 840, 956
Freund, Karl 330
Frey, Mary 648
Friebus, Theodore 626
Friedkin, David 419
Friend, Philip 889
Frings, Ketti 163
Fritzell, James 329
Frohman, Clayton 951
Frye, Dwight 629
Fu, Willy 811
Fuller, Barbra 960
Fuller, Dale 422
Fuller, Mary 6
Fuller, Samuel 700, 821
Furey, Barney 513, 861
Furie, Sidney J. 882
Furness, Betty 456, 656, 909, 961

Gabel, Martin 209
Gable, Clark 15, 164, 197, 277, 457, 524, 541, 635, 845, 895, 924, 927
Gabor, Eva 636
Gabrielson, Frank 460
Gaer, Paul 239
Gail, Albert 282
Gaillard, Robert 481
Gaines, Richard 228, 289
Gale, June 134, 150, 243
Gale, Marguerite 425
Gallagher, Don 630
Gallagher, Skeets 234, 244, 852
Gallaudet, John 188, 339, 572, 615, 653
Gallery, Tom 379
Gallian, Ketti 244
Gallico, Paul 998
Gamet, Kenneth 91, 293, 353, 632, 839
Gangelin, Paul 452, 663
Ganlos, Toni 171
Gans, Ronald 894
Gantvoort, Carl 132
Garcia, Al 47
Garcia, Andy 393, 580, 826
Garde, Betty 119
Gardenia, Vincent 314
Gardiner, Reginald 145, 673, 885, 901
Gardner, Arthur 36, 630
Gardner, Ava 524

Index

Gardner, Jack 650
Garfield, Allen 394
Garfield, John 88, 327
Garfunkel, Art 345
Gargan, Ed 470
Gargan, William 10, 31, 54, 95, 227, 376, 424, 563, 646, 670, 718, 798, 818, 852
Garland, Robert 239
Garnett, Tay 539, 666
Garon, Pauline 41, 441
Garr, Eddie 902
Garrett, Otis 250, 718, 1002
Gary, Romain 772
Gaskill, Charles L. 202
Gasnier, Louis J. 683
Gates, Harvey 177, 442, 505, 568, 752, 843
Gates, Larry 308
Gateson, Marjorie 655
Gauthier, Jean 628
Gay, Gregory 942
Gay, Marjorie 272
Gaynor, Mitzi 230
Gaze, Gwen 431, 802
Geary, Charles 581
Geer, Will 924
Geldert, Clarence 476
Gelsey, Erwin 511, 867
Gendron, Pierre 152
George, Florence 896
George, Gladys 536
George, Grace 474
Geraghty, Carmelita 300
Geraghty, Gerald 258, 413, 813, 831
Geraghty, Tom 76
Gerard, Barney 503
Gerard, Charles 990
Geray, Steve 559
Gering, Marion 748, 914
Gerrard, Douglas 242
Gerringer, Robert 87
Gershon, Gina 884
Ghostley, Alice 658
Giannini, Giancarlo 270
Gibney, Sheridan 669
Gibson, Henry 604, 888
Gibson, Hoot 752
Gibson, Julie 170
Gibson, Margaret 455
Gibson, Wynne 184, 299, 565
Gidding, Nelson 436

Gielgud, Irwin 1
Gielgud, John 787
Gifford, Alan 796
Gifford, Frank 697
Giglio, Sandro 37
Gilbert, Doris 862
Gilbert, Eugenia 727
Gilbert, Helen 259
Gilbert, John (Jack) 368, 571
Gilbert, Paul 1022
Gilchrist, Connie 286, 950
Giler, David 698
Gilfether, Daniel 652
Gillingwater, Claude 117, 149, 291
Gillis, Anne 81
Gilmore, Virginia 63, 156, 608
Gilmour, J. H. 555, 687, 969
Gilroy, Barbara 386
Ginnes, Abram S. 320
Giracci, May 672
Girard, Joseph 111, 275, 453, 512, 614, 752, 790, 843, 1024
Gish, Dorothy 438
Gish, Lillian 529
Gist, Robert 19
Glasmon, Kubec 587
Glass, Gaston 111, 465
Gleason, James 14, 155, 259, 398, 582, 651
Gleason, Lucille 398
Gleason, Russell 420, 638, 815
Gleckler, Robert 929
Glover, Bruce 68
Glynn, Carlin 171
Goddard, Mark 535
Goddard, Paulette 489
Godfrey, Peter 145, 673
Goff, Ivan 161
Goldblum, Jeff 64, 939
Golding, William 18
Goldman, Danny 984
Goldman, Harold 485
Goldoni, Lelia 961
Goldsmith, Martin 816
Goldwyn, Tony 710
Golino, Valeria 1020
Gombell, Minna 382, 841
Gomberg, Sy 471, 479
Gomez, Thomas 807

Gooden, A. H. 761
Goodfellow, Joan 285
Goodkind, Saul A. 719
Goodman, Daniel Carson 1025
Goodman, John 100
Goodrich, John 622
Goodwin, Harold 120, 347, 739
Goodwins, Lee 26
Goodwins, Leslie 186, 374, 875
Goorwitz, Allen 171
Gorcey, Bernard 462, 545
Gorcey, Leo 102, 462, 545, 637, 670
Gordon, Alex 105
Gordon, Bernard 286
Gordon, Bruce 154, 264, 861
Gordon, C. Henry 155, 211, 817, 943
Gordon, Don 1016
Gordon, Eve 952
Gordon, Gavin 138, 611
Gordon, Harris 386
Gordon, James 273
Gordon, Julia Swayne 202, 705
Gordon, Mary 95, 798
Gordon, Pete 1024
Gordon, Robert 894
Gordon, Rose 850
Goren, Abraham 394
Gorog, Laszlo 491
Gottlieb, Alex 35, 543, 584
Gottschalk, Ferdinand 832
Gould, Elliott 122, 206
Goulding, Edmund 230, 467
Grable, Betty 885
Grace, Michael L. 961
Grafe, Judy 49
Graham, Jo 1021
Graham, William A. 903
Grandin, Ethel 9
Granet, Bert 77, 743
Grant, Barra 838
Grant, Cary 71, 404, 669, 722, 914, 977
Grant, Donald 604
Grant, James Edward 883, 1013
Grant, Lawrence 439
Grant, Mary 898

Index

Grant, Morton 540, 922
Granville, Bonita 362, 632, 911
Granville, Charlotte 290
Grapewin, Charles 509, 745, 834
Graves, Ralph 200, 438, 782, 972
Gravina, Cesare 428
Gray, Betty 728
Gray, Bob 747
Gray, Coleen 777
Gray, Dolores 216
Gray, Gordon 603
Gray, Lawrence 257, 342, 565, 812
Gray, Linda 814
Gray, Mike 143
Gray, Olga 517
Grayler, Sydney 450
Grayson, Charles 227, 718, 765, 866
Grayson, Kathryn 809
Greco, Juliette 772
Greeley, Evelyn 504
Green, Alfred E. 8, 343, 447
Green, Dorothy 180
Green, Eve 515
Green, Howard J. 70, 89, 133, 200, 549
Greenbaum, Everett 329
Greene, Helen 717
Greene, Richard 856
Greenleaf, Raymond 375, 689
Greenstreet, Sydney 145, 704
Greer, Jane 163, 230
Greer, Julian 877
Gregg, Virginia 537, 950
Gregory, Andre 872
Gregory, Carl 121
Gregory, Ena 359
Gregory, James 534, 742
Grey, Hetty 113
Grey, John 623
Grey, Nan 477, 578
Grey, R. Henry 652
Grey, Shirley 147, 233, 312, 407, 511, 617
Grey, Virginia 183, 804, 885
Gribbon, Harry 120
Gries, Thomas 116
Griffin, Russell 41

Griffith, Corinne 207
Griffith, Edward H. 40, 117, 207, 642, 715, 815
Griffith, James 91
Griffith, Melanie 100
Griffith, Raymond 205
Griffiths, Trevor 753
Grinde, Nick 174, 251, 317, 464, 486, 540, 762, 785, 991
Grizzard, George 1015
Grofe, Ferde, Jr. 974
Gross, William 682
Gruskin, Jerry 942
Guhl, George 611, 933
Guild, Nancy 308
Guilfoyle, Paul 575, 597, 743, 995
Guillermin, John 820
Guiol, Fred 391
Guise, Tom 705
Gulager, Clu 162
Gulliver, Dorothy 139, 415
Gunn, Chadlee 307
Gunn, James 689
Gur, Alizia 894
Gwenn, Edmund 709
Gwynne, Anne 340, 435, 585, 831, 920

Hackman, Gene 879, 880, 882, 951
Haden, Sara 365, 498
Hadley, Don 506
Hadley, Reed 460
Hagens, William 185
Hagney, Frank 111
Haines, William 30, 897
Hale, Alan 353, 414, 421, 457, 715, 728
Hale, Creighton 85, 579, 969
Hale, Georgia 1004
Hale, Jonathan 251, 721, 971
Hale, Louise Closser 725
Hale, Richard 569
Haley, Jack 788, 833, 970
Hall, Alexander 248, 906
Hall, Ben 417
Hall, Charles 190
Hall, Ella 468
Hall, Henry 28, 370
Hall, Howard 153, 877
Hall, Huntz 102, 462, 545, 637, 757

Hall, Lillian 801
Hall, Lois 234
Hall, Nathaniel 521
Hall, Norman S. 751, 960
Hall, Porter 4, 349, 575, 998
Hall, Ruth 45
Hall, Sheridan 860
Hall, Thurston 128, 133, 198, 253, 346, 456, 488, 655, 929
Hall, Winter 388
Halliday, John 167, 900
Halligan, William 109
Hallor, Ethel 194
Hallor, Ray 493
Halloway, Jack 561
Halperin, Victor 633
Halsey, Brett 548
Halsey, Forrest 428
Halton, Charles 60, 385, 670, 869, 1021
Hamilton, John 101, 263, 615, 746, 928
Hamilton, Margaret 474, 498
Hamilton, Murray 19
Hamilton, Neil 30, 203, 412, 417, 870, 979, 1014
Hamilton, Shorty 747
Hammerstein, Elaine 175, 990
Hammond, C. Norman 981
Hampton, Grace 740
Hampton, James 143
Handforth, Ruth 517
Hanlon, Bert 71
Hanneman, H. W. 654
Hansell, Howard 595, 1025
Harari, Robert 247
Harbaugh, Carl 926
Hardin, Neil 652
Hardwicke, Cedric (Sir) 856
Hardy, Sam 74, 76, 195, 643
Hargrove, Marion 471
Harlow, Jean 509, 725, 803
Harmer, Lillian 827
Harolde, Ralf 56, 139, 351, 411, 671, 723, 798, 877
Harper, Betty 469
Harrigan, Nedda 785
Harrigan, William 98
Harrington, John 1012

Harrington, Pat 665
Harris, Ed 285, 951
Harris, James B. 53
Harris, Mildred 201, 271, 729
Harris, Owen 800
Harris, Raymond S. 41
Harris, Winifred 175
Harrison, Jimmy 408
Harrison, Joan 298
Harron, John 196, 614
Harron, Robert 517
Hart, Dolores 526
Hart, Gypsy 292
Hart, Moss 327, 579
Hart, William S. 945
Hartman, Ferris 307
Hartmann, Edmund T. 82
Harvey, Forrester 1002
Harvey, Laurence 1016
Harvey, Paul 12, 60, 234, 608, 621, 960, 1021
Harvey, Phil 491
Hassett, Marilyn 588
Hatch, William Riley 126, 732
Hathaway, Henry 119, 142
Hathaway, Nancy 682
Hatteras, Richard 266
Hatton, Raymond 16, 172, 217, 233, 367, 618, 663, 672, 702
Haver, Phyllis 663, 815
Havey, Maie B. 468
Havoc, June 141, 327, 446
Hawks, Howard 404
Hawks, J. G. 690, 945
Hawley, H. Dudley 1023
Hawley, Wanda 724
Haworth, Vinton 763
Hayakawa, Sessue 367
Hayden, Russell 231, 996
Hayden, Sterling 183
Haydn, Richard 532, 635
Haydon, J. Charles 650
Hayes, Bernadene 902
Hayes, George "Gabby" 44, 223, 413, 440, 502
Hayes, John J. 265
Hayes, Linda 875
Hayes, Lorraine 937
Hayes, Margaret 489, 793
Hayes, Peter Lind 808
Hayes, William 410, 898
Haymes, Dick 964

Hays, Margaret 854
Hays, Robert 787
Hayward, Lillie 645
Hayward, Susan 436, 461, 930
Hayworth, Rita 14, 188, 339
Healey, Myron 953
Healy, Ted 211, 699
Heard, John 64, 594, 710
Hearn, Edward 229, 938
Heath, Percy 312
Hecht, Ben 142, 164, 508, 660, 968
Heck, Stanton 452
Hedison, David 532
Hedman, Martha 192
Heffron, Richard T. 318
Heflin, Van 809
Heggie, O. P. 589
Heifetz, Lou 536
Hellen, Marjorie 419
Heller, Joseph 810
Hellman, Lillian 799
Helmore, Tom 216
Helton, Percy 462
Hemingway, Mariel 212, 580, 882
Hemmer, Edward L. 877
Henabery, Joseph 781
Henderson, Don 454
Henenlotter, Frank 49
Henie, Sonja 247
Henley, Hobart 229, 768, 993
Henner, Marilu 64, 712
Henriksen, Lance 574
Henry, Charlotte 297, 758
Henry, Gloria 418
Henry, Louise 699
Henry, Mike 894
Henry, Tom Browne 56
Henry, William 241, 319, 829
Henville, Sandra Lee 515
Hepburn, Audrey 771
Hepburn, Katharine 480, 722, 1006
Herbert, F. Hugh 299, 618, 676, 1017
Herbert, Holmes 392, 627
Herbert, Hugh 295, 303, 515, 576, 714
Herd, Richard 794
Herman, Albert 157, 597, 720, 770, 1018

Hernandez, George 530, 568
Herring, Aggie 925
Herrmann, Edward 100, 753
Hershey, Burnett 639
Hersholt, Jean 132, 184, 280, 467
Hervey, Irene 95, 141, 992, 1005
Herzig, Sig 303, 576
Heustis, Reed 956
Hewlett, Ben 735
Heyburn, Weldon 189, 912
Heydt, Louis Jean 430, 482
Heyes, Herbert 56, 158, 700
Hibbard, Enid 190
Hibbs, Jesse 471
Hickey, William 24
Hickman, Alfred 304
Hickman, Darryl 84
Hickman, Howard 132
Hickox, Anthony 384
Hicks, Catherine 270
Hicks, Russell 77, 656, 818
Hiers, Walter 332, 408, 969, 1004
Higby, Wilbur 463
Higgin, Howard 274, 713
Higgins, John C. 616
Hiken, Nat 534
Hill, Arthur 318
Hill, Bob 257
Hill, Doris 452
Hill, Ethel 738
Hill, George 155, 803
Hill, Kenneth 523
Hill, Mariana 581, 794
Hill, Robert F. 759
Hill, Robert S. 811
Hill, Thelma 190
Hilliard, Ernest 685
Hilliard, Harriet 258
Hilliard, Harry 520
Hillie, Verna 750
Hillyer, Lambert 57, 67, 253, 333, 339, 586
Hilton, Helen 425
Hincks, Reginald 572
Hinds, Samuel S. 8, 57, 407, 477, 640, 716, 718, 1007
Hines, Charles 746
Hines, Johnny 192, 746, 927
Hingle, Pat 1016

Index

Hitchcock, Alfred 298
Hitchcock, Walter 62, 423
Hively, George 284, 527
Hobart, Rose 129, 782
Hobbes, Halliwell 279, 477, 579, 896
Hodges, Joy 515, 718, 907
Hodiak, John 51, 807
Hoerl, Arthur 79, 179, 189, 357, 378, 381, 496
Hoffenstein, Samuel 499
Hoffman, Charles 94, 673
Hoffman, Dustin 18, 393
Hoffman, Hugh 938, 999
Hoffman, John 525
Hoffman, Joseph 464, 814
Hoffman, Max, Jr. 560
Hoffman, Otto 405, 463, 873, 993
Hogan, James 275, 349, 497, 551, 622
Hohl, Arthur 38, 128
Hohlfeld, Brian 371
Holbrook, Hal 18, 122, 288
Holden, Fay 248, 975
Holden, Gloria 61, 716
Holden, William 99, 197, 537, 947
Holland, John 91, 357
Holliday, Judy 99
Holliman, Earl 27, 224
Holloway, Sterling 12
Holm, Celeste 327, 400
Holman, Harry 140, 633
Holmes, Ben 904
Holmes, Brown 867
Holmes, Helen 262, 761
Holmes, Leon 275
Holmes, Rapley 659
Holmes, Stuart 271, 997
Holmes, Taylor 659
Holt, David 587
Holt, Jack 187, 200, 672, 943, 972
Holtz, Tenen 422
Holubar, Alan 993
Homans, Robert 770, 912
Homeier, Skip 329
Homes, Geoffrey 80, 501, 788, 804
Homolka, Oscar 164
Hope, Bob 908
Hopper, E. Mason 16, 195, 676, 955

Hopton, Russell 65, 140, 195, 210, 220, 676, 891
Horan, Charles 40
Horman, Arthur T. 77, 743, 907
Horne, James W. 1024
Horne, William 857
Horton, Edward Everett 313, 315, 714, 998
Horton, Walter 85
Horvath, Charles 131
Hoshelle, Marjorie 90
Houdini, Harry 358
Houser, Lionel 145, 215, 738, 896, 911
Housman, Arthur 702, 952
Houston, Norman 233, 351
Howard, David 166, 412, 922
Howard, Esther 748
Howard, Gertrude 169
Howard, John 349, 549, 722, 918, 920
Howard, Mary 994
Howard, Ron 695
Howard, Shemp 602
Howard, Trevor 772
Howard, William K. 254, 363, 474, 983
Howatt, Nina 624
Howe, Elliott 925
Howell, Dorothy 274, 725
Howell, Kenneth 420
Howell, Virginia 858
Howes, Reed 25, 898
Howlin, Olin 804
Hoxie, Jack 359, 527
Hoyt, Arthur 225, 358, 531, 752, 827
Hoyt, Harry O. 374, 476, 531, 1003
Hoyt, John 163, 501
Hubbard, John 424, 804
Hubbard, Lucien 207
Hubbert, Cork 658
Huber, Harold 20, 137, 518, 609, 943, 985
Hudson, Rochelle 42, 174, 510, 598, 1009
Hudson, Rock 893
Huffman, David 495
Hughes, Barnard 835
Hughes, Carol 413, 576
Hughes, Gareth 790
Hughes, Lloyd 257, 369, 388, 401, 531

Hughes, Mary Beth 215
Hughes, Russell 421
Hulette, Gladys 6, 687, 828, 969
Hull, Henry 302, 346, 589, 661, 678
Hull, Warren 317, 333, 396, 858
Humberstone, H. Bruce 487, 923, 985
Hume, Benita 155
Hummell, Wilson 194, 254
Hungerford, James Edward 561
Hunt, J. Roy 167
Hunt, Jay 179, 981
Hunt, Jay (Mrs.) 981
Hunt, Linda 240
Hunt, Marsha 325, 528, 612, 809, 858, 958
Hunter, Edna 364
Hunter, Holly 108
Hunter, Ian McLellan 771
Hunter, Kim 209
Hunter, T. Hayes 278
Hunting, Gardner 684
Huntley, Hugh 860
Hurlbut, Gladys 541
Hurlbut, William 203
Hurn, Philip J. 307
Hurst, Brandon 639
Hurst, Paul 271, 670, 803, 851
Hurt, William 108, 256
Hussey, Ruth 722
Huston, John 772
Huston, Phil 156
Huston, Virginia 289
Huston, Walter 328
Hutchinson, Josephine 1013
Hutchinson, Lois 683
Hutchinson, Muriel 703
Hutchison, Charles 226, 397, 429, 685, 724
Hutton, Jim 355
Hutton, Lauren 697
Hutton, Robert 52, 783
Hyams, Leila 917, 1003
Hyams, Peter 122
Hyde, Jacquelyn 204
Hyland, Dick Irving 435, 644
Hyland, Frances 827, 985, 1001
Hyland, Peggy 836

Hymer, Warren 35, 98, 203, 538, 583, 847
Ince, John 415
Ince, Ralph W. 175, 236, 657
Inescort, Frieda 174
Infante, Eddie 974
Ingleton, E. Magnus 801
Ingraham, Lloyd 315, 463, 500, 517
Ingraham, Zella 500
Ingram, Jack 39
Ingram, Rex 292, 383
Ingster, Boris 869
Ireland, John 17, 50, 54, 116
Irving, Amy 826
Irving, George 267, 347, 676
Irving, Margaret 1012
Isabelita 63
Ivers, Julia Crawford 273
Ivins, Beth 792

Jackson, Eddie 768
Jackson, Joseph 441, 664
Jackson, Orin C. 981
Jackson, Selmer 340, 600, 686, 912
Jackson, Thomas 445, 503
Jacobs, Harrison 996
Jacobs, William 648
Jacoby, Michel 653, 949
Jaeckel, Richard 204
Jagger, Dean 251, 352, 1005, 1007
James, Alan 751, 775
James, Clifton 87
James, Gladden 626
James, Rian 248, 330, 424
James, Sidney 23
Jamison-Olsen, Mikki 797
Janssen, David 355, 822
Jarrett, Daniel 877
Jarrico, Paul 588, 655
Jason, Leigh 255, 399, 552, 918
Jason, Will 246
Jay, J. Griffin 929
Jefferson, Thomas 297, 358
Jefferson, William Wister 684, 728
Jeffrey, Hugh 952
Jeffreys, Anne 833
Jeffries, Fran 810

Jenkins, Allen 89, 259, 576, 584, 808, 906, 934
Jenks, Frank 20, 597, 720, 770, 776, 866, 904
Jenks, George Elwood 194
Jennings, DeWitt 649
Jennings, S. E. 226
Jensen, Eulalie 481, 577
Jergens, Adele 176, 846
Jeske, George 592
Jevne, Jack 432, 905
Jewell, Isabel 42, 71, 598, 907, 915
Jewison, Norman 320
Jobson, Edward 307, 652
Johns, Glynis 23
Johnson, Chick 664
Johnson, Chubby 375
Johnson, Don 100
Johnson, Ed 894
Johnson, Edith 726
Johnson, Emilie 493
Johnson, Emory 493
Johnson, Henry 550
Johnson, June 26, 323
Johnson, Nunnally 773
Johnson, Rafer 894
Johnson, Raymond K. 849
Johnson, Rita 73, 621
Johnson, Robert Lee 854
Johnson, Tor 105
Johnson, Van 51, 162, 238, 613, 837, 976, 978
Johnston, Agnes Christian 376
Johnstone, Justine 659
Jolley, Norman 29
Jones, Arthur V. 953
Jones, Dean 950
Jones, Dick 8, 301, 632
Jones, Eddie 448
Jones, Evan 826
Jones, Gordon 77, 356, 359, 410, 743, 904, 909
Jones, Grover 702
Jones, Jeffrey 939
Jones, Jennifer 537
Jones, Marcia Mae 370
Jordan, Bobby 102, 637, 662
Jordan, Dorothy 767
Jordan, Richard 285, 580
Jory, Victor 88, 131, 730, 929, 992, 996
Joseph, Robert L. 870

Josephson, Julien 463, 734, 856, 873
Josephy, Alvin M., Jr. 123
Joslyn, Allyn 117, 160, 460, 910
Joy, Gloria 652
Joyce, Alice 378, 573
Joyce, Brenda 518
Joyce, Stephen 868
Judge, Arline 170, 451, 624, 631
Jung, Allen 859
Jungmeyer, Jack 663, 815
Junior, John 659

Kaaren, Suzanne 769
Kahn, Gordon 387, 640, 776
Kaiser, Burt 268
Kamb, Karl 123
Kamp, Paul 926
Kandel, Aben 910
Kane, Carol 939
Kane, Diana 713
Kane, Joseph 35, 44, 440, 502, 830
Kanin, Fay 895
Kanin, Michael 895, 1006
Kaplan, Marvin 636
Kardos, Leslie 921
Karger, Maxwell 409
Karloff, Boris 263, 347, 610, 966
Karlson, Phil 59, 786
Karns, Roscoe 178, 227, 316, 435, 457, 612, 703, 1021
Kasdan, Lawrence 171
Katch, Kurt 63
Katterjohn, Monte M. 739
Katz, Lee 757
Kaufman, Charles 252, 863
Kaufman, Edward 14
Kaufman, George S. 808
Kava, Caroline 1019
Kaye, John 984
Kaye, Louis S. 677
Kaye, Lucie 470
Kaye, Stubby 1022
Kazan, Elia 327
Kazan, Lainie 245
Keane, Robert Emmett 227, 634
Keating, Larry 161
Keaton, Buster 120

Index

Keaton, Diane 753
Keaton, Michael 695
Keckley, Jane 617
Keefe, Zena 717
Keenan, Frank 622, 925
Keighley, William 237, 578, 848
Keith, Brian 29, 320
Keith, Ian 707
Keith, Robert 390
Keith, Rosalind 35, 188, 276, 572
Kellard, Robert 923, 985
Kellaway, Cecil 238, 489, 542, 916
Keller, Harry 919
Kelley, Alice 548
Kelley, Barry 764, 800
Kellogg, Ray 355
Kelly, Albert 476
Kelly, Brian 162
Kelly, Chris 24
Kelly, Claire 783
Kelly, Dorothy 603
Kelly, Gene 443
Kelly, Grace 400
Kelly, James 566
Kelly, Lew 210
Kelly, Nancy 228, 856
Kelly, Patsy 905, 970
Kelly, Paul 129, 208, 211, 279, 340, 362, 600, 619, 629, 932, 1012
Kelsey, Fred 40, 242, 1024
Kelso, Edmond 583
Kendall, Cy 90, 114, 629, 818, 910, 948, 1012
Kennaway, James 822
Kennedy, Arthur 141
Kennedy, Douglas 133, 491
Kennedy, Edgar 106, 258, 458, 515, 736, 758, 917
Kennedy, George 320
Kennedy, Harold J. 123
Kennedy, Tom 11, 74, 92, 293, 931, 932, 933, 934, 935
Kenny, Colin 955
Kent, Barbara 357, 649
Kent, Charles 603
Kent, Crauford 357, 442, 685, 724
Kent, Dorothea 338, 765, 866
Kent, Leon D. 449, 557

Kent, Robert E. 20, 127, 321, 437, 719
Kent, Willis 874
Kenton, Erle C. 129, 312, 361, 738, 778, 818, 1017
Kenyon, Charles 343
Kenyon, Curtis 533
Kenyon, Gwen 583
Kerima 744
Kerman, David 630
Kern, George 956
Kerr, Donald 614
Kerrigan, J. M. 700, 1002
Key, Pierre V. R. 311
Keyes, Evelyn 67
Kibbee, Guy 77, 470, 508, 511, 565, 578, 730, 763, 793, 867
Kibbee, Milton 170
Kibbee, Roland 930
Kidder, Margot 320, 835, 880, 881, 882
Kilbride, Percy 485, 547, 548
Kilian, Victor 7, 488, 738
Killy, Edward 77, 743
Kimble, Lawrence 10, 662, 693, 736
King, Bradley 232, 388
King, Burton 111, 179
King, Charles 664, 811
King, Claude 147
King, Emmett 179, 577
King, Henry 537, 731, 856
King, Joe 819, 991
King, John 444, 817
King, Leslie 262
King, Loretta 105
King, Louis 34, 734, 766, 777, 998
King, Mabel 206
King, Mollie 626
King, Walter Woolf 1018
Kingsford, Walter 1002
Kingsley, Dorothy 21, 224, 238
Kingsley, Mona 523
Kingston, Winifred 326
Kinski, Klaus 794
Kinsky, Leonid 244, 247
Kirby, Bruno 984
Kirby, Ollie 593, 711
Kirkland, Jack 7
Kirkwood, Joe 472
Kirtley, Virginia 558

Klein, Herbert 536
Klein, Philip 842
Kline, Herbert 482
Klorer, John 360
Kluge, Emma 731
Knapp, Evalyn 114, 486, 867
Knapp, Robert 783
Kneubuhl, John 950
Knight, Fuzzy 336, 643
Knight, Harlan 746
Knott, Lydia 132, 236, 956
Knotts, Don 329, 534
Knowles, Patric 303, 831, 931
Knox, Alexander 688
Knox, Mona 919
Knudsen, Peggy 716
Kober, Arthur 361
Kodl, James 268
Koepp, David 695
Koepp, Stephen 695
Kohler, Fred 768, 1017
Kohlmar, Lee 210
Kolker, Henry 379, 625, 631, 909
Kollmar, Richard 156
Komai, Tetsu 972
Konner, Lawrence 882
Kosinski, Jerzy 753
Kosleck, Martin 63, 185, 549
Koster, Henry 542
Koster, Dorothy Paul 245
Kotcheff, Ted 888
Kovacs, Bela 700
Krafft, John W. 210, 392, 490, 560, 599, 625, 746, 750, 912
Kraly, Hans 551
Kramer, Hope 294
Kramer, Stanley 443
Krasna, Norman 411
Krauzer, Steven 884
Kroeger, Berry 141
Krueger, Lorraine 252
Kruger, Otto 70, 252, 699, 730, 785, 862
Krumgold, Joseph 470, 488
Krusada, Carl 255
Kuhl, Ron 667
Kulich, Vladimir 212
Kunkel, George 557
Kurnitz, Harry 908
Kwapis, Ken 371

La Badie, Florence 595
LaBlanche, Ethel 250
La Cava, Gregory 74, 267
Lachman, Harry 655
Lackteen, Frank 751
Ladd, Alan 141, 322, 544
Lafayette, Ruby 567
LaFia, John 574
Lahr, Bert 533
Laidlaw, Betty 718
Laidlaw, Ethan 201
Laidlaw, Roy 452, 657
Lake, Alice 409
Lake, Arthur 251
Lamarr, Hedy 164, 221
Lamas, Fernando 532
Lambert, Eddie 399
Lamm, Karen 961
Lamont, Charles 114, 147, 445, 490, 515, 547, 548, 778, 814
Lamour, Dorothy 497, 908
Lancaster, Burt 886
Lanchester, Elsa 73
Landau, David 184, 654
Landau, Martin 884
Landers, Lew 52, 133, 182, 199, 543, 629, 730, 854, 909, 948
Landi, Elissa 579
Landi, Sal 884
Landis, Carole 54, 460
Landis, Cullen 685
Landis, Margaret 1024
Landon, Hal 634
Lane, Allan 186, 363, 498, 634, 916, 919, 948
Lane, Lola 174, 178, 210, 629, 847, 932, 995
Lane, Mike 366
Lane, Nathan 371
Lane, Richard 106, 150, 336, 674, 875, 904, 916, 920
Lane, Rosemary 88, 757
Lanfield, Sidney 365, 489, 533, 970
Lang, Charles 95
Lang, David A. 670, 741
Lang, Fritz 66, 94, 986
Lang, Howard 392
Lang, June 174, 675
Langdon, Harry 38
Langford, Frances 602
Langston, Murray 965

Langston, Ruth 226
Lantz, Louis 967
LaPaglia, Anthony 371
Lardner, Ring, Jr. 1006
La Reno, Dick 726
Larkin, George 284, 311, 593, 711
Larkin, John 134, 150, 559, 638
LaRocque, Rod 445, 467
La Rose, Rose 741
La Roy, Rita 169, 276, 415
La Rue, Fontaine 1008
LaRue, Frank 67
LaRue, Jack 35, 82, 299, 322, 376, 377, 586, 596, 707, 795, 848, 891
Lassick, Sydney 961
Latham, Aaron 712
Latimer, Jonathan 73
Latimer, Louise 348
Lau, Wesley 436
Laughton, Charles 73
Laurence, Ashley 384
La Verne, Lucille 865
Lavery, Emmett 61, 362
Lawford, Betty 328
Lawrence, Fanya Foss 995
Lawrence, Florence 956
Lawrence, John S. 792
Lawrence, Marc 188, 223, 469, 736, 766, 776, 936
Lawrence, Steve 855
Lawrence, Vincent 784
Lawrence, W. E. 315
Lawrence, William 989
Lazarus, Milton 983
Lease, Rex 157, 453, 493, 657, 762
Leavitt, Douglas 819
Lebedeff, Ivan 169, 343, 507, 541
Le Berthan, Helene 630
Lederer, Charles 164, 313, 404
Lederer, Francis 883
Lederer, Gretchen 96
Lederer, Otto 557
Lederman, D. Ross 128, 437, 656, 694, 812, 929
Lee, Anna 319
Lee, Donna 833
Lee, Dorothy 776
Lee, Florence 566

Lee, Gwen 16, 503, 825
Lee, Jenny 517
Lee, Laura 342
Lee, Leonard 34, 244, 834, 871
Lee, Lila 633, 739, 972
Lee, Mary 632
Lee, Palmer 459
Lee, Pinky 692
Lee, Robert N. 295
Lee, Sammy 681
Leeds, Herbert I. 280, 460, 478
Leeson, Lois 401
Lehman, Ernest 886
Lehne, Fredric 574
Lehrman, Henry 558
Leigh, Frank 429
Leigh, Janet 19, 21, 522
Leigh, Nelson 414
Leigh, Rowland 485
Leigh-Fermor, Patrick 772
Leisen, Mitchell 32
Leitch, Christopher 959
Lemmon, Jack 143, 314, 354, 1022
Lenihan, Winifred 469
Lennart, Isobel 528
Leonard, Kay 548
Leonard, Robert Z. 15, 467, 911, 978
Leonard, Sheldon 182, 544, 967, 995
Lerner, Carl 87
Lerner, Gerda 87
Lerner, Michael 24, 641
LeRoy, Mervyn 281, 395, 910, 958
Le Roy, Rita 411
Le Saint, Edward J. 755
Leslie, Joan 353
Leslie, Lila 493
Lessey, George 70
Lester, Bruce 1002
Lester, Kate 225, 409
Lester, Richard 880, 881
Lester, Vicki 552, 916
Lester, William 708
Levene, Sam 216, 479, 552, 886
Levering, Jack 262
Levering, Joseph 139
Levien, Sonya 729
Levin, Henry 176, 646

LeVino, Albert Shelby 952, 955, 1010
Levitt, Alfred Lewis 816
Levy, Norman 477
Lewin, Albert 230
Lewis, Al 547
Lewis, Artie 859
Lewis, Edward 180
Lewis, George 260, 1018
Lewis, Jerry 522
Lewis, Jessie 192
Lewis, Joseph 189
Lewis, Katherine 1024
Lewis, Mitchell 685
Lewis, Ralph 45, 190, 294, 493, 874
Lewis, Sheldon 740, 828, 898
Lewis, Therese 980
Lian, Jewell 876
Libertini, Richard 287, 288
Libov, Howard 590
Linaker, Kay 333, 396, 718, 766
Linden, Eric 189, 392, 486, 767
Lindsay, Margaret 43, 227, 295, 584, 834
Lindsey, Harry 242
Ling, Eugene 56, 460, 786
Linson, Art 984
Lipman, William H. 536
Litel, John 43, 70, 289, 353, 385, 554, 602, 632, 757, 798
Little, Cleavon 288
Little, Michele 884
Littlefield, Lucien 232, 412, 647, 703, 784, 998
Littlefield, Ralph 28
Lively, Robert 718
Livingston, Margaret 332, 618, 663
Livingston, Robert 35, 223, 323, 346, 492, 647
Livingstone, H. A. 944
Lloyd, Beverly 391, 829
Lloyd, Christopher 794
Lloyd, Doris 107
Lloyd, Frank 93, 232, 326
Lloyd, Rollo 560, 625
Locke, Katherine 846
Lockhart, Gene 5, 230, 308, 404, 896, 901, 977
Lockney, John P. 840, 873

Lockwood, Gary 855
Lockwood, Harold 168
Loder, John 165, 221
Loeb, Lee 128, 456
Loft, Arthur 253
Logan, Bob 965
Logan, Helen 83, 137, 243, 498, 817
Logan, Jacqueline 236, 564, 683
Logan, Janice 677
Logan, Robert 797
Logan, Stanley 260
Loggia, Robert 434
Logue, Charles 166, 832
Lombard, Carole 74, 312, 565, 660
Lombardi, Vincent 697
London, Babe 452
London, Julie 352
London, Tom 201, 759
Lone, John 1019
Lonergan, Lloyd B. 121, 595
Lonergan, Philip 860
Long, Audrey 234, 693, 715, 716
Long, Lotus 610, 624
Long, Louise 979
Long, Richard 547
Long, Walter 367
Longdon, Terence 23
Loo, Richard 158
Loos, Anita 517
Lord, Marjorie 31, 133
Lord, Mindret 340
Lord, Robert 277
Lord, Stephen 894
Loren, Sophia 749
Lorimer, Louise 913
Loring, Thomas Z. 994
Lorraine, Louise 812
Lorre, Peter 607, 609, 704, 869
Lorring, Joan 75
Losee, Frank 266
Losey, Joseph 75, 501
Love, Bessie 169, 236, 531
Love, Montagu 683, 842
Lovejoy, Frank 846, 890
Lovett, Dorothy 543
Lowe, Edmund 98, 244, 330, 335, 361, 523, 640, 1002, 1003
Lowe, Edward T. 16, 191,

195, 220, 649, 736, 842, 1014
Lowe, Sherman L. 219, 937
Lowenstein, Stanley 26
Lowery, Robert 80, 199, 430, 483, 701, 795
Loy, Myrna 167, 509, 526, 911, 927
Luban, Milton 936
Lubin, Arthur 82, 255, 308, 351, 431, 584, 623, 765
Luby, Roy 937
Lucas, John Meredyth 709
Lucas, Wilfred 173, 175, 264, 296, 432, 774
Luckinbill, Laurence 588, 658
Luden, Jack 702
Ludwig, Edward 7, 310, 494, 570, 900
Luedtke, Kuer 3
Lugosi, Bela 28, 105, 177, 624, 648, 719, 775, 789, 811
Lukas, Paul 244, 417, 772
Luke, Keye 48, 135, 356, 609, 656
Lund, John 400
Lundgren, Dolph 959
Lundigan, William 127, 221, 230, 353, 372, 600, 824, 902, 907
Lupino, Ida 748, 986
Lussier, Dane 459, 862
Luther, Anna 455
Lydon, Jimmy 385, 983
Lynch, Richard 448
Lyndon, Barre 924
Lynn, George 483
Lynn, Jeffrey 414
Lynn, Peter George 610
Lynn, Sharon 220, 847
Lyon, Ben 432, 713
Lyons, Collette 525
Lytell, Bert 955
Lytton, Bart 853

Mabery, Mary 513
MacArthur, Charles 808
MacArthur, James 53, 535
Macaulay, Richard 763
MacBride, Donald 908, 948
MacDermott, Marc 571, 577, 836
MacDonald, Donald 873

Index

MacDonald, Edmund 554, 823
MacDonald, J. Farrell 28, 220, 249, 253, 291, 440, 617, 782
MacDonald, Jeanette 118
MacDonald, John D. 285
MacDonald, Katherine 405, 1011
MacDonald, Philip 5
MacDonald, Sherwood 652, 844
MacDonald, Wallace 205, 733
MacDougall, Ranald 475, 661
MacDowell, Melbourne 267, 861
Mack, Hayward 229
Mack, Helen 279, 404
Mack, Hughie 761
Mack, Jack 431
Mack, Russell 782
Mack, Wilbur 196
Mack, William B. 860
Mackaill, Dorothy 195
Mackaye, Marshall 468
MacKendrick, Alexander 886
MacKenzie, Donald 262
Macklin, John 62
MacLane, Barton 11, 82, 92, 293, 464, 788, 839, 931, 933, 935
MacLean, Douglas 463
MacMahon, Aline 511, 578
MacMahon, Horace 887, 899
MacMurray, Fred 117, 248, 331, 587, 678
Macnee, Patrick 426
MacQuarrie, Murdock 465, 956
MacRae, Henry 791, 898
Macready, George 73, 569, 601, 971
Madison, Noel 277, 599, 633
Maharis, George 742
Mahin, John Lee 494, 541, 927
Mahoney, Jock 491
Mailes, Charles Hill 938, 979

Main, Marjorie 474, 547, 548
Majeroni, Mario 428
Malkovich, John 240
Mallory, Boots 392, 832
Malloy, Doris 427, 854
Malone, Dorothy 116, 893
Malone, Molly 752
Mander, Miles 42, 804
Mandoki, Luis 100
Manduke, Joseph 667
Mankiewicz, Don 436
Mankiewicz, Herman J. 15, 148, 565, 621
Mankiewicz, Joseph L. 744
Mann, Anthony 833
Mann, Delbert 742
Mann, Edward 783
Mann, Frankie 705
Mann, Harry 112
Mann, Milton 783
Mann, Stanley 23
Mannheimer, Albert 99, 198
Manning, Aileen 379
Manning, Bruce 338, 360, 900
Manning, Mildred 577, 733
Mannors, Sheila 57
Mansfield, Jayne 268
Mantegna, Joe 962
Mantle, Burns 425
Mantley, John 701
Mara, Adele 363, 942
March, Alex 697
March, Fredric 443, 660, 905
March, Joseph 299
Marciano, Rocky 159
Marcin, Max 784
Marconi, Victor 943
Marcus, James 668
Margo 61
Margolin, Arnold 859
Margolis, Herbert 547
Marian, Nita 25
Mariles, Charles 546
Marin, Edwin L. 301, 446, 699
Marion, Charles R. 418, 545
Marion, Frances 803
Marion, George, Sr. 210
Mariott, Crittenden 386
Maris, Mona 63
Markle, Fletcher 469

Markson, Ben 353, 451, 1009
Marlow, Brian 184, 612, 1007
Marlowe, John 107
Marly, Florence 953
Marmorstein, Malcom 206
Marr, Eddie 934
Marsh, Joan 107, 135, 399
Marsh, Mae 517
Marsh, Marian 281, 598, 611, 852
Marshal, Alan 250
Marshall, Boyd 121
Marshall, Brenda 1021
Marshall, George 510
Marshall, Herbert 8, 159, 298, 954
Marshall, Paula 384
Marshall, Trudy 928
Marshall, Tully 358, 408, 546, 648
Marston, John 241
Martell, Donna 383
Martin, Al 257, 363, 602
Martin, Charles 600
Martin, Dean 522
Martin, Edward 307
Martin, Janet 942
Martin, Marian 741
Martin, Tony 1001
Mason, Billy 732
Mason, Charles 153
Mason, Dan 687, 746
Mason, Leroy 625
Mason, Lewis 194
Mason, Noel 790
Mason, Sarah Y. 379
Mason, Shirley 273, 519, 1000
Massen, Osa 461
Massey, Raymond 125, 161, 302
Mastroianni, Marcello 749
Masur, Richard 580
Matheson, Murray 537
Matheson, Tim 287
Mathews, Carole 601
Mathis, June 205, 409
Matthau, Walter 314
Matthews, Dorcas 369
Maurey, Nicole 516
Maxwell, Edwin 351, 648, 694
Maxwell, John 560

May, Doris 463
Mayall, Herschel 254, 455, 925
Maye, Donald 170
Mayer, Edwin Justus 250
Mayer, Gerald 807
Mayne, Eric 388
Mayo, Archie 165, 511, 664
Mayo, Frank 496, 844
Mayo, Virginia 461
McAvoy, May 388
McCabe, Michael 115
McCambridge, Mercedes 17
McCarey, Leo 669
McCarey, Ray 625, 686, 935
McCarthy, Andrew 1020
McCarthy, Earl 874
McClure, Doug 667
McConnell, Fred J. 759
McConnell, Lulu 490
McCormack, Patty 479
McCormick, Myron 469
McCormick, William M. 752
McCoy, Harry 264
McCoy, Horace 407, 899
McCoy, Tim 407, 762, 884
McCoy, Tony 105
McCrea, Joel 7, 298, 780, 852
McCullogh, Julie 68
McCullough, Philo 124, 729
McCutcheon, Wallace 290
McDaniel, George 1008
McDaniel, Hattie 474
McDaniel, Sam 437
McDonald, Francis 273
McDonald, Frank 11, 78, 92, 293, 788, 839, 907
McDonald, Kenneth 982
McDonald, Marie 544, 795
McDowall, Roddy 165
McDowell, Clair 546
McDowell, Nelson 512
McEveety, Bernard F. 154
McEveoy, J. P. 748
McEvoy, Tom 278
McFadden, Hamilton 406, 456
McGann, William 88, 576, 824, 949
McGill, Lawrence B. 425, 1010

McGowan, Dorrell 223, 412, 942
McGowan, J. P. 154, 659, 708
McGowan, Jack 110
McGowan, Robert 370
McGowan, Stuart E. 223, 412, 942
McGrail, Walter 354, 849
McGrath, Douglas 100
McGrath, William 805
McGraw, Charles 551
McGraw, William C. 924
McGregor, Angela Punch 454
McGregor, Malcolm 309, 332, 378
McGuire, Dorothy 327
McGuire, John 869
McGuire, Kathryn 734
McGuire, Marcy 833
McGuire, William Anthony 666
McHugh, Frank 313, 342, 459, 576, 627, 963
McHugh, Jack 861
McHugh, Matt 550
McInerney, Bernie 521
McIntosh, Burr 41, 512
McIntyre, Christine 637
McIntyre, William 615
McIvor, Mary 690
McKay, George 128, 339, 572, 615, 738, 760, 1005
McKee, Lafe 745
McKee, Raymond 172, 519, 1000
McKee, Scott 1000
McKellar, Helen 949
McKern, Leo 822
McKim, Robert 132, 690
McLaglen, Victor 142, 361, 508
McLain, John 118
McLaughlin, J. G. 96
McLeod, Norman Z. 596, 905
McMillan, Kenneth 256
McNally, Stephen 889
McNutt, William Slavens 748
McQueeney, Robert 921
McQuillan, Ada 466
McRae, Duncan 1010
McTaggart, Ward 323

McWade, Edward 938, 1000
McWade, Margaret 531
McWade, Robert 402, 406, 578, 642
Meadows, Jayne 159, 542
Meehan, Elizabeth 372
Meek, Donald 160, 528
Meeker, George 65, 104, 325, 413, 613, 878
Mehaffey, Blanche 16, 453
Meins, Gus 398
Meisle, Kathryn 49
Melford, George 309
Melleney, Victor 115
Mellish, Fuller, Jr. 768
Mendes, Lothar 971
Mendez, Jola 657
Menjou, Adolphe 297, 313, 424, 773, 885, 924
Menzies, William Cameron 987
Mercado, Hector Jaime 838
Mercer, Beryl 300
Mercer, Frances 186, 552
Meredith, Burgess 471, 864
Meredith, Charles 679
Meredith, Iris 174, 615
Meredith, Jane 740
Meredith, Lois 168, 844
Meredyth, Bess 365
Merivale, Philip 528
Merkel, Una 110, 155, 699
Merrick, George 802
Merrill, Frank 410
Merrill, Gary 903
Merton, John 374
Messenger, Buddy 315, 989
Metcalf, James 294
Metcalfe, Arthur 344
Metcalfe, Earl 717
Meyer, Emile 886
Meyer, John 658
Meyers, Nancy 434
Michael, Gertrude 406, 1007
Michelle, Janee 535
Middlemass, Frank 454
Middlemass, Robert 38, 738, 929
Middleton, Robert 893
Mihalka, George 212
Mila, Adolf 828
Milasch, Robert 359
Miles, Bernard 635
Milestone, Lewis 313

Index

Miljan, John 275, 550, 716, 793, 935
Milland, Ray 32, 73, 162, 247, 331, 489, 642
Millar, Elda 296
Millar, Ronald 635
Miller, Alice D. G. 335, 571
Miller, Ann 246
Miller, Ashley 733
Miller, Charles 368
Miller, Colleen 419
Miller, David 863
Miller, Marvin 446, 709
Miller, Patsy Ruth 665
Miller, Robert Ellis 103
Miller, Victor 868
Miller, Walter 55, 261, 272, 727, 802
Miller, Winston 125, 199, 228
Millican, James 78, 125
Mills, Alyce 622
Mills, Warren 569
Milne, Peter 378, 578
Milner, Martin 886
Miltern, John 79
Minnelli, Vincente 216
Minter, Mary Miles 731
Mintz, Sam 654
Mitchell, Bruce 410
Mitchell, Cameron 289, 807
Mitchell, Charles 928
Mitchell, Dodson 207
Mitchell, Geneva 57
Mitchell, Grant 118, 182, 360, 373, 642, 983
Mitchell, Howard M. 465, 519, 1000
Mitchell, James 421
Mitchell, Rhea 561, 955
Mitchell, Thomas 7
Mitchell, Yvette 292
Mitchum, Robert 22, 27, 864
Mix, Ruth 157
Moffat, Donald 604
Moffitt, Jack 704
Moffitt, John C. 248, 619
Moguy, Leonide 5
Mohr, Gerald 447
Moll, Giorgia 744
Mollison, Henry 276
Mong, William V. 422, 865
Montague, Monty 255
Montalban, Ricardo 51, 764

Montana, Bull 341
Montez, Maria 95, 892
Montgomery, Frank 952
Montgomery, George 142, 773, 974
Montgomery, Goodee 65
Montgomery, Peggy 410, 527
Montgomery, Robert 475
Mooney, Martin 109, 322, 599
Moore, Carlyle, Jr. 317, 766, 949
Moore, Cleo 689
Moore, Constance 306, 600
Moore, Dennie 10
Moore, Dennis 750
Moore, Dickie 353
Moore, Dorothy 77, 743
Moore, Joanna 29
Moore, Marceau 449
Moore, Matt 167, 705, 990
Moore, Melissa 680
Moore, Pauline 134
Moore, Terry 10
Moore, Tom 178, 290, 997
Moore, Victor 916
Moore, Vin 140
Moore, W. Eugene 386
Moorhead, Natalie 11, 220
Moran, E. Edwin 246, 905
Moran, Jackie 35, 370
Moran, Lee 147, 825, 1004
Moran, Peggy 809
Moran, Polly 812, 897
More, Kenneth 635
Moreland, Mantan 144
Moreno, Antonio 557, 801
Morey, Harry T. 378
Morgan, Ainsworth 244
Morgan, Al 352
Morgan, Byron 281
Morgan, Claudia 902
Morgan, Dennis 14, 145, 673, 757
Morgan, Francis 202
Morgan, Frank 975
Morgan, Gene 25, 253, 339, 1005
Morgan, George 45
Morgan, Harry 443
Morgan, Helen 768
Morgan, Henry 460, 786
Morgan, Michele 704

Morgan, Ralph 8, 248, 427, 536, 549, 550, 814, 902
Morgan, William 372, 607, 804
Morheim, Louis 547, 921
Mori, Toschia 805
Moriarity, Daniel 680
Moriarty, Cathy 115
Moriarty, Henry 342
Morley, Karen 30, 497
Morris, Chester 228, 433, 674
Morris, Wayne 116, 227, 321, 421, 757
Morrison, Arthur 359
Morrison, Lew 463, 955
Morrissey, Tommy 292
Morrow, Douglas 66
Morse, Brewster 714
Morse, Robert 742
Mortimer, Ed 9
Mortimer, Harry 266
Mortimer, Henry 740
Morton, Charles 496
Moscovich, Maurice 247
Moses, Andrew 617
Moses, Mark 206
Moss, Frank L. 987
Mostel, Josh 136
Movita 333
Mowbray, Alan 525, 548, 720, 905
Mueller, Elisabeth 22
Muir, Jean 317, 991
Mulgrew, Kate 868
Mulhall, Jack 157, 257, 350, 442, 720
Mullally, Don 627
Mundhra, Jag 680
Mundin, Herbert 252, 487
Muni, Paul 395
Munson, Byron 926
Munson, Ona 342, 785
Murcell, George 1020
Murdock, Perry 513
Murfee, Minta 558
Murphy, Audie 471, 744
Murphy, Dudley 852
Murphy, Edna 25, 254, 300, 564
Murphy, George 51, 738, 765, 1007, 1013
Murphy, Horace 26
Murphy, Michael 779

Murphy, Ralph 291, 587, 645, 703
Murphy, Richard 433
Murray, Bill 984
Murray, Charles 739
Murray, James 399
Murray, John T. 401
Murray, Mae 467
Musgrave, William 843
Musselman, M. M. 892
Mussett, Charles 555
Myers, Carmel 520
Myers, Harry 154, 173, 734
Myles, Norbert A. 945
Myton, Fred 90, 553

Nace, Anthony 763
Nader, George 29, 471
Nagel, Anne 11, 356, 389, 553, 798
Naish, J. Carrol 46, 61, 316, 382, 550, 758, 1014
Nash, George 564
Natteford, John 377, 397, 429, 445, 758
Naughton, David 658
Naughton, James 868
Neal, Patricia 302, 976
Neal, Tom 61, 182, 819
Neilan, Marshall 180, 341
Neill, James 781
Neill, Noel 39, 878
Neill, Richard 175, 708
Neill, Roy William 2, 554, 739
Nelligan, Kate 240, 962
Nelson, David 495, 913
Nelson, Frances 993
Nelson, Jack 369, 567, 593, 727
Nelson, Sam 190
Nelson, Willie 239
Nesbitt, John 681
Nesbitt, Miriam 754
Neuman, E. Jack 162, 966
Neumann, Kurt 244
Neville, Grace 276
Neville, Jack 937
Neville, John T. 38, 55, 294, 333, 415, 770, 858
Newbern, George 888
Newcomb, Mary 705
Newell, Billy 65, 114, 336, 450, 492
Newell, David 618

Newfield, Sam 90, 170, 553, 741
Newlan, Paul 921
Newman, David 820, 879, 880, 881
Newman, Joseph 1
Newman, Laraine 712
Newman, Leslie 879, 880, 881
Newman, Paul 3, 636, 1016
Newman, Walter 4
Newmeyer, Fred 220
Newton, Charles 752
Newton, Theodore 851
Nibley, Sloan 125
Niblo, Fred, Jr. 276, 369, 382, 488, 631, 651, 1021
Nichols, Barbara 66, 886
Nichols, Dudley 98, 406, 458
Nichols, John 594
Nichols, Marguerite 844
Nicholson, Calvin 283
Nicholson, Jack 753
Nielsen, Leslie 419, 756
Nigh, William 149, 263, 377, 610, 624, 653, 912
Nixon, Marion 441
Noble, Jack 512
Nolan, John 913
Nolan, Lloyd 19, 38, 60, 71, 248, 478, 484
Nolan, Mary 592, 1017
Nolte, Nick 434, 951
Nordyke, Kenneth 747
Norman, Lucille 125
Normand, Mabel 290
Norris, Chuck 448
Norris, Edward 243, 380, 640, 644, 785, 910
North, Carrington 373
North, Edmund H. 221
North, Marion 832
North, Sheree 522, 903
North, Ted 106
North, Wilfrid 481
Northrup, Harry S. 1000
Norton, Albert 595
Norton, Barry 1003
Norton, Edgar 914
Norton, Fletcher 874
Novak, Blaine 345
Novak, Eva 235, 264
Novak, Jane 873
Nowell, Wedgewood 292

Nugent, Edward 415
Nugent, Elliott 378
Nugent, J. G. 587
Nunez, Victor 285
Nyby, Christian 383
Nye, Carroll 381, 466, 503

Oakie, Jack 291, 312, 458
Oakland, Simon 436
Oakland, Vivian 664
Oakman, Wheeler 178, 407, 503, 729, 979
Ober, Philip 976
Oberle, Florence 840
Oberon, Merle 14
O'Brian, Hugh 131, 870
O'Brien, Dave 720
O'Brien, Edmond 534, 947
O'Brien, George 922
O'Brien, Gypsy 659
O'Brien, Margaret 528
O'Brien, Pat 43, 167, 274, 313, 411, 662, 715, 782, 1014
O'Connell, Arthur 354
O'Connell, Hugh 293
O'Connor, Donald 308
O'Connor, Frank 630
O'Connor, Kathleen 514
O'Connor, Kevin J. 393
O'Connor, Loyola 180
O'Connor, Robert E. 34, 309, 442, 624, 723
O'Connor, Una 145
O'Conor, Vincent 469
O'Day, Molly 841
O'Day, Peggy 708
Odets, Clifford 886
O'Donnell, Joseph 26, 450
O'Donnell, "Spec" 417
O'Donohue, James T. 825
Ogle, Charles 6, 172, 754
O'Hanlon, George 472, 700
O'Hara, George 452
O'Hearn, Eileen 760
O'Herlihy, Dan 447
O'Keefe, Dennis 1, 13, 32, 163, 221, 607
Oland, Warner 135
Olcott, Sidney 428
Oliver, David 252, 335
Oliver, Edna May 146, 621
Oliver, Gordon 293, 317, 991
Oliver, Guy 755

Index 324

Oliver, Susan 162, 535
Olivier, Laurence 822
Olmstead, Gertrude 1004
Olsen, Moroni 119, 223, 348
Olsen, Ole 664
O'Malley, Pat 271, 341, 546
O'Neal, Charles 601
O'Neal, Frederick 870
O'Neal, Ryan 270
O'Neil, Nance 146
O'Neill, Faye 505
O'Neill, Henry 528, 570, 786, 848, 931, 949
O'Neill, Sally 929
Oppenheimer, George 509
Orbach, Jerry 959
O'Rear, James 689
Orlandini, Hal 115
Orloff, Arthur E. 52
Orlovitz, Gil 689
Ornitz, Samuel 570
O'Ross, Ed 959
Orr, Gertrude 1004
Orr, William T. 958
Ortega, Kenny 641
Orth, Frank 380
Orth, Marian 396
Osborn, Ted 338
Osborne, Bud 219, 527
Osborne, Vivienne 261, 834
Oscar, John 898
O'Shea, James 774
O'Shea, Michael 461, 954, 967
O'Shea, Oscar 445, 750
Ostriche, Muriel 69, 121, 504
O'Sullivan, Maureen 73, 621, 666
Oswald, Emma K. 449
Oswald, Gerd 183, 796
Otis, Oleta 801
O'Toole, Annette 881
Otto, Henry 364
Overman, Lynne 587, 589, 612, 645, 703, 773, 998
Overton, Evart 603
Owen, Catherine Dale 98
Owen, Reginald 7, 118, 335, 541, 725, 845, 1006
Owen, Seena 500

Padden, Sarah 151, 553, 611
Pagano, Jo 846
Page, Anita 30, 476, 897

Page, Bradley 67, 140, 186, 274, 312, 631, 904
Page, Paul 735, 847
Paige, Janis 387, 421
Paige, Mabel 544
Paige, Robert 91, 241, 677, 892
Paiva, Nestor 823
Pakula, Alan J. 18, 698, 710
Palfie, Lotti 681
Pallette, Eugene 310, 343, 905
Palmer, Charles 807
Palmer, Maria 883
Palmer, Stuart 241, 260, 412, 677
Pangborn, Franklin 377, 608
Pankow, John 1020
Pantoliano, Joe 580
Parham, Conrad 974
Paris, Jerry 859
Park, Ida May 96, 350
Parke, William 505, 626, 687
Parker, Albert 296, 969
Parker, Austin 335
Parker, Barnett 536
Parker, Bradley 266
Parker, Cecilia 809
Parker, Eleanor 19
Parker, Franklin 55
Parker, Jean 33, 433, 701, 769
Parker, Jefferson 427, 623
Parker, Jim 859
Parker, Katherine 232
Parker, Lara 394
Parker, Willard 980
Parks, Larry 629, 730
Parks, Michael 903
Parkyakarkus 1018
Parnell, Emory 133, 391, 741, 813, 967
Parrish, Helen 906
Parrish, Robert 37, 780
Parsonnet, Marion 536, 975
Parsons, Milton 559
Parsons, Patsy Lee 909
Parsons, William 449
Partos, Frank 361, 869, 914
Pascal, Ernest 461
Paton, Stuart 381, 453, 993
Patrick, Gail 349, 619, 891

Patrick, John 83, 280, 400, 537, 671, 822, 842, 915
Patrick, Lee 501, 688, 971
Patterson, Cjon Damitri 797
Patterson, Elizabeth 160
Patterson, Jay 872
Patterson, Lee 863
Patton, Will 590
Paul, Logan 603
Paul, Richard 658
Paul, Steven 245
Paulsen, David 794
Pawley, Ed 456
Pawley, William 321
Payne, Lou 493
Payne, Sally 44, 440
Payne, William M. 521
Payton, Claude 761
Pearce, Adele 333, 653
Pearce, George 468, 734, 842
Pearson, Humphrey 167, 342
Pearson, Virginia 40
Peck, Charles K., Jr. 50
Peck, Gregory 216, 327, 771
Peck, Tony 103
Peil, Edward 438
Pelly, William Dudley 126
Pendleton, Nat 211, 789
Penn, M. O. 732
Penwarden, Duncan 328
Peoples, David Webb 393
Pepper, Barbara 412
Percy, Eileen 242, 897, 926
Perelman, Laura 291
Perelman, S. J. 291
Perez, Paul 107, 600
Perkins, Albert 335
Perkins, Anthony 1016
Perkins, Elizabeth 371
Perlich, Max 100
Perrin, Jack 201, 514
Perry, Charles 237
Perry, George Sessions 33
Perry, Joan 128, 651
Perry, Linda 910, 949
Perry, Walter 945
Persaud, Jenna 680
Pesci, Joe 737
Peters, House 179
Peters, Page 326
Peterson, Dan 708
Peterson, Dorothy 297, 983
Peterson, Maggie 534

Petticlerc, Denne Bart 903
Pettitt, Wilfred H. 971
Pevney, Joseph 286, 459, 816
Peyser, John 953
Pfeiffer, Michelle 962
Phelps, Lee 307
Phillips, Augustus 358
Phillips, Dorothy 96, 350
Phillips, Eddie 683, 708, 865
Phillips, Howard 317, 841, 991
Phillips, Julianne 288
Phillips, Lou Diamond 826
Phillips, William 133
Phipps, Sally 639
Picerni, Paul 890
Pichel, Irving 65, 160, 492, 849
Pickens, Slim 813
Pickup, Ronald 240
Pidgeon, Walter 71, 215, 338, 342, 573, 621, 807, 927, 978
Piedmont, Leon 580
Pierce, George 307
Pierson, Arthur 414
Pirosh, Robert 51, 976
Pitts, ZaSu 379, 451, 573, 583, 679
Plana, Tony 779
Platt, Louise 299, 896
Plowman, Melinda 414
Plumer, Lincoln 290
Plummer, Christopher 256
Plummer, Glenn 962
Plympton, George 719
Poe, James 53, 786
Poitier, Sidney 53
Poland, Joseph 502
Pollack, Sydney 3, 239
Polo, Eddie 112
Porcasi, Paul 218, 618
Porter, Don 554
Porter, Jean 96
Portman, Eric 53
Post, Buddy 925
Potel, Victor 500
Potter, H. C. 930
Powell, A. Van Buren 577, 603, 733, 836
Powell, David 41

Powell, Dick 89, 458, 764, 1022
Powell, Eleanor 110
Powell, Frank 304
Powell, Paul 520, 774
Powell, William 267, 509, 565, 622, 702, 808
Power, Hartley 771
Power, Tyrone 205, 539, 542, 683, 901
Powers, Francis 726
Powers, Tom 721, 764, 964
Prager, Stanley 472
Praskins, Leonard 12
Pratt, Gilbert 702
Pratt, Jack 379, 519
Pratt, Purnell 382, 432, 486, 631, 767, 827, 917, 963
Preminger, Otto 499, 908
Prentiss, Paula 698
Prescott, Jack 561
Prescott, Vivian 728
Presnell, Robert 403, 1023
Price, Vincent 499, 964, 986
Primus, Barry 3
Prince, William 661
Pringle, Aileen 173
Printzlau, Olga 672
Prisco, Al 791, 956
Prival, Lucien 411
Proctor, George Dubois 705, 990
Prophet, Melissa 448
Prosky, Robert 108
Prouty, Jed 250, 420, 769
Pryor, Ainslie 479
Pryor, Richard 881
Pryor, Roger 128, 377, 433, 439, 583, 599, 758, 760, 875, 917
Pullman, Bill 641
Purcell, Dick 32, 88, 187, 433, 464
Purcell, Lee 855
Puzo, Mario 879, 880
Pyne, Joe 535
Pyper, George 761

Quaid, Randy 695
Qualen, John 279, 404
Quigley, Charles 188, 276, 339, 488
Quigley, Rita 385

Quine, Richard 810
Quinn, Anthony 241, 497, 703, 822

Rafill, Stewart 797
Rafkin, Alan 329
Raft, George 237, 446
Raine, Norman Reilly 237, 714
Raines, Ella 808
Rains, Claude 532, 570, 704, 910
Raison, Milton 84, 333, 720
Raker, Lorin 628
Ralph, Jessie 117, 536
Ralston, Esther 486, 999
Ralston, Jobyna 729
Ralston, Marcia 293
Ralston, Vera Hruba 862, 883
Rambeau, Marjorie 1, 748, 778, 803, 837
Rand, Ayn 302
Randall, Bernard 179, 423, 990
Randall, Meg 1, 547
Randell, Ron 525, 863
Randolf, Anders 202
Randolph, Donald 37, 689
Randolph, Isabel 597, 919
Randolph, Jane 258, 260
Rapf, Maurice 656
Raphaelson, Samson 487
Rathbone, Basil 549
Ratoff, Gregory 48, 324, 376
Rattray, Heather 49, 797
Rauch, Earl Mac 868
Rawlins, John 95, 600, 602
Rawlinson, Herbert 44, 109, 567, 568, 623, 775
Ray, Albert 530, 827, 985, 1001
Ray, Aldo 355
Ray, Bernard B. 850
Ray, Charles 236, 405, 840, 873
Ray, Joe 326
Raymond, Dean 997
Raymond, Frances 679
Raymond, Gene 904
Raymond, Paula 807
Raymond, Robin 770, 804
Razeto, Stella 684, 755
Rea, Isabel 278

Rea, Stephen 749
Reagan, Ronald 540, 651
Rebhorn, James 434
Redford, Robert 18, 239, 594, 962
Redgrave, Michael 744
Redmond, Liam 329
Reed, Alan 893
Reed, Barbara 59
Reed, Donald 825, 849
Reed, Donna 141, 786
Reed, Florence 1010
Reed, Mathew 712
Reed, Philip 80, 81, 84, 430
Reed, Tom 576, 578
Reedy, John 425
Rees, Lanny 413
Reeve, Arthur B. 759
Reeve, Christopher 872, 879, 880, 881, 882, 888
Reeves, George 559
Regan, Phil 885
Reich, Walter 809
Reicher, Frank 85, 243
Reid, Dorothy 370, 874
Reid, Elliott 987
Reid, Wallace 529
Reinhardt, Betty 499
Reinhardt, John 403
Reis, Irving 259, 349
Reisner, Charles F. 158, 612, 665
Reitzen, Jack 31
Renaldo, Duncan 490, 849, 1018
Rennie, Michael 532
Reubens, Alma 945
Revere, Anne 327
Revier, Dorothy 2, 25, 34, 147, 347, 618, 805, 999
Reynolds, Burt 888
Reynolds, Craig 263, 389, 464, 741, 839
Reynolds, Gene 8
Reynolds, Jonathan 888
Reynolds, Marjorie 263, 414, 610, 750, 922
Reynolds, Vera 381, 466, 503
Reynolds, Warren 491
Rhinehart, O'leta 185
Rhodes, Billie 857
Rhodes, Hari 821
Ricciardi, William 428
Rice, Craig 260

Rice, Florence 101, 515, 607, 694, 763, 854, 1012
Rich, Dick 483
Rich, Frances 219
Rich, Irene 900
Rich, Lillian 357
Richards, Addison 372, 464, 540, 839
Richards, Ann 799
Richards, Cully 392
Richards, Grant 800
Richards, Paul 783
Richardson, Jack 410, 593, 711
Richle, Richard 737
Richmond, Kane 26, 59, 104, 243, 374, 937, 1001
Richmond, Warner 74, 812
Rickson, Joe 47
Rideout, Bob 572
Ridgely, John 52, 92, 933
Ridges, Stanley 237, 607, 721, 834
Ridgeway, Fritzi 265
Rifkin, Adam 136
Riggs, Lynn 554
Riley, Elaine 199
Riley, Lawrence 714
Ring, Cyril 639
Rios, Lalo 501
Rippy, Leon 959
Risdon, Elisabeth 433
Riskin, Robert 457, 556, 582, 606, 725, 1022
Ritch, Steven 383
Ritchey, Will M. 652, 731
Ritchie, Ethel 652
Ritchie, Michael 287, 288, 454
Ritter, Thelma 636
Rivkin, Allen 365, 376, 723
Roach, Bert 762, 897
Roach, Hal 424
Roach, J. Anthony 530
Roadman, Betty 373
Robards, Jason 18, 220, 865
Robbins, Tim 749
Roberts, Ben 161, 608
Roberts, Beverly 714, 949
Roberts, Edith 315, 465
Roberts, Julia 434, 710, 749
Roberts, Lynn 106, 398, 412, 721
Roberts, Marguerite 291, 587, 845

Roberts, Tanya 820
Roberts, Tony 859
Robertson, John S. 555, 603, 649
Robertson, Lolita 944
Robertson, Willard 492, 715, 933
Robins, Jesse 315
Robins, Sam 86
Robinson, Casey 303, 451, 704, 986
Robinson, Dewey 617
Robinson, Edward G. 281, 494, 649, 958
Robinson, Frances 751
Robinson, R. J. 68
Robinson, Sugar Ray 697
Robson, Mark 366
Robson, May 1005
Rockwell, Robert 960
Rodriguez, Estelita 692
Roe, Raymond 475
Rogell, Al 38, 348, 359, 382, 631, 736, 920
Rogers, Buddy 701
Rogers, Ginger 669, 773, 827, 978, 1023
Rogers, Howard Emmett 509
Rogers, Jean 166, 215, 444, 623, 985
Rogers, Lora 1010
Rogers, Mimi 872
Rogers, Roy 44, 223, 413, 440, 692, 830
Rogers, Walter 801
Rogers, Will 510
Roland, Gilbert 321, 324, 487, 497
Roland, Ruth 311
Rolf, Tom 756
Rollins, Henry 136
Romain, Yvonne 887
Roman, Lawrence 697, 887
Roman, Ric 813
Romay, Lina 472
Romero, Cesar 134, 280, 950
Rooney, Mickey 536
Root, Lynn 20, 259
Root, Wells 432, 699, 800
Ropes, Bradford 995
Roscoe, Allan 235
Rose, Jack 522
Rose, Louisa 835

Rosen, Phil 107, 218, 227, 299, 322, 407, 470, 599, 611, 769, 851, 891
Rosenberg, Stuart 1016
Rosenbloom, Maxie 237, 609, 644
Rosener, George M. 151, 440, 997, 802
Rosenthal, Mark 882
Rosenwald, Francis 716
Rosing, Bodil 76
Ross, Annie 49
Ross, Arthur 354
Ross, Katharine 1015
Ross, Milton 945
Ross, Sherman 272
Ross, Shirley 117
Rossen, Robert 17, 910
Rosson, Arthur 126
Rosson, Dick 126, 1003
Rothstein, Richard 959
Rourke, Mickey 1019
Rouse, Hugh 115
Rowland, Roy 528, 837
Roy, Iain 24
Royle, Selena 161
Royle, William 610
Ruben, J. Walter 654, 767
Rubin, Benny 10, 373
Rubin, Jennifer 212
Rubin, Mann 19
Rubin, Stanley 95, 967
Rubinek, Saul 434
Ruggles, Charles 248, 310, 328, 596, 677, 768, 1023
Ruggles, Wesley 146, 331, 845
Rumann, Sig 63, 164, 660
Rush, Barbara 870
Rush, Dick 109
Ruskin, Harry 536, 1013
Rusoff, Lou 876
Russell, Albert 514
Russell, Bing 876
Russell, Charles 54
Russell, Elizabeth 177, 334, 583
Russell, Gail 501
Russell, J. Gordon 527
Russell, Kurt 580
Russell, Mary 253
Russell, Rosalind 215, 303, 404, 980
Russell, William 728

Rutherford, Ann 198, 502, 975
Ryan, Don 293, 839
Ryan, James 24
Ryan, John 318
Ryan, Kathleen 846
Ryan, Robert 27, 61, 526
Ryan, Samuel 304
Ryan, Sheila 158, 208, 380, 994
Ryan, Tim 637
Ryan, Tommy 871
Ryerson, Florence 184, 417
Ryno, William H. 708

Sabine, Martin 740
Sabu 892
Sackheim, Jerry 760
St. Claire, Arthur 1018
St. Jacques, Raymond 355
St. John, Al 257
St. John, Howard 75, 99, 742
St. John, Jill 532
St. Polis, John 210, 370
Sakall, S. Z. 145, 809
Sale, Chic 563
Salkow, Kae 199
Salkow, Sidney 248, 619, 647, 871, 902
Salt, Jennifer 394, 835
Samuels, Lesser 4, 958
Sande, Walter 91
Sanders, George 5, 37, 259, 260, 298, 986
Sands, John 50, 501
Santell, Alfred 33, 461, 825, 841
Santley, Joseph 60, 346
Santoni, Reni 27
Santschi, Tom 496
Sara, Mia 24
Sarandon, Susan 314
Sarecky, Barney 28
Sargent, Dick 329
Sargent, Lewis 154, 999
Sarrazin, Michael 806
Sauber, Harry 7
Saunders, John Monk 277
Savage, Ann 670, 788, 980
Savage, John 24, 779
Sawyer, Joe 81, 391
Saxe, Templer 836
Saxon, Charles 399
Saxon, Hugh 379

Saxon, John 162, 239, 270, 1015
Sayles, John 426
Saylor, Shannon 797
Saylor, Syd 104
Sayre, George 170
Sayre, Joel 706
Sbragia, Mattia 1020
Scala, Gia 22, 224
Scarwid, Diana 103
Schade, Betty 1000
Schallert, William 562
Schary, Dore 526, 596
Schatzberg, Jerry 872
Schayer, Richard 120, 197
Schenck, George 318
Schertzinger, Victor 405, 873
Schiff, Richard 737
Schildkraut, Joseph 584, 649
Schilling, Gus 543
Schlank, Morris R. 233
Schmoeller, David 806
Schnee, Charles 46, 764
Schnitzer, Gerald 795
Schoedsack, Ernest 943
Schram, Violet 410
Schrock, Raymond L. 170, 182, 504, 597, 613, 897, 993
Schroeder, Doris 323
Schultz, Michael 521
Schuster, Harold 252, 306
Schwabacher, Lewis 853
Schwartz, David R. 810
Scola, Kathryn 160
Scott, Allan 930
Scott, Anita 1010
Scott, Donovan 820
Scott, Douglas 494
Scott, Lizabeth 163
Scott, Mabel Julienne 225
Scott, Randolph 125, 301
Scott, Sherman 294, 450
Scott, Zachary 387
Scotto, Aubrey 917
Seabrook, Edward E. 391
Searl, Jackie 325, 399
Sears, A. D. 529, 774
Sears, Fred 176
Sears, Heather 863
Sears, Laura 307
Sears, Zenas 506
Seaton, George 516, 895

Index 328

Seay, James 158, 380, 800
Sedgwick, Edna 751
Sedgwick, Edward 120, 200, 211, 279, 439, 763
Sedgwick, Eileen 761
Sedgwick, Josie 226
Seff, Manuel 244, 541
Segall, Harry 904
Seiler, Lewis 689, 890
Seiter, William A. 203, 342, 451, 964
Seitz, George B. 249, 618, 621
Selander, Lesley 289, 996
Selbie, Evelyn 350
Selby, Gertrude 229
Sellon, Charles 267, 979
Selman, David 276
Selman, Linda 838
Semple, Lawrence, Jr. 698, 820
Senarens, Lu 69
Serrano, Nestor 103
Seward, Billie 586
Seward, Edmond 637
Seymour, Dan 446, 953
Shackelford, Ted 884
Shane, Maxwell 199, 228, 433, 776, 788
Shannon, Frank 935
Shannon, Harry 286, 372, 435, 646
Shannon, Peggy 10, 218
Shannon, Robert T. 338
Sharkey, John 667
Sharpe, Albert 964
Shavelson, Melville 522, 636
Shaw, Anabel 403, 483
Shaw, Artie 198
Shaw, Betty 185
Shaw, Harold 754
Shaw, Janet 543
Shaw, Reta 329
Shaw, Winifred 316, 317, 839
Shay, John 597
Shayne, Robert 430, 435
Shea, Gloria 351
Shea, William 334
Sheedy, Ally 574
Sheen, Charlie 136
Sheen, Martin 903
Sheldon, E. Lloyd 555
Sheldon, Sidney 608

Shellen, Stephen 212
Shelton, Ronald 951
Shepard, Sam 710
Shepherd, Iva 168
Sher, Jack 471, 479
Sherdeman, Ted 786
Sheridan, Ann 673
Sheridan, Frank 166
Sherman, George 795, 862, 889
Sherman, Joseph 211
Sherman, Lowell 332, 664
Sherman, Vincent 10, 524, 757
Sherry, J. Barney 341, 514
Sherwin, Louis 225
Sherwood, Clarence T. 708
Shields, Arthur 165
Shields, Brooke 103
Shields, Ernest 229
Shilling, Marion 124, 157, 195, 300
Shipman, Barry 775
Shipman, Nell 47
Shipman, Nina 678
Shirley, Florence 677
Shirley, Robert 296
Shore, Viola Brothers 33
Shores, Lynn 392, 1005
Short, Antrim 468
Short, Dorothy 36
Shulgasser, Barbara 749
Shulman, Irvin 159
Shumate, Harold 57, 585, 694, 992
Shyer, Charles 434
Shyer, Melville 614, 874
Sidney, George 887
Sidney, Scott 408
Sidney, Sylvia 93, 799, 914
Siegmann, George 69, 1008
Sikking, James B. 710
Siletti, Mario 418
Sills, Milton 311, 505
Silver, Joan Micklin 64
Silver, Marisa 371
Silvera, Carl 711
Silvers, Phil 478, 773
Silvers, Sid 110
Silverstein, David 218, 629
Simmons, Michael L. 334, 598, 793
Simms, Jay 756
Simon, Mayo 318

Simon, S. Sylvan 198, 338, 975
Simon, Simone 533
Simpson, O. J. 122
Simpson, Russell 296, 334, 415, 842
Sinatra, Frank 400
Sinclair, Eric 597
Sinclair, Robert 901
Singley, Arthur 633
Sirk, Douglas 893
Slade, Bernard 855
Slavin, George 446
Sleeper, Martha 351
Slesar, Henry 950
Slezak, Walter 669, 778
Sloane, Everett 148
Sloane, Paul 167, 564, 972
Sloman, Ted 477
Smight, Jack 870
Smith, Albert J. 791
Smith, Alexis 131, 390, 673, 947
Smith, Bryan Travis 737
Smith, C. Aubrey 150, 195, 331
Smith, Charles Martin 175, 385, 434
Smith, Constance 78
Smith, David 47
Smith, Frank Leon 272, 969
Smith, Hal 646
Smith, Harold Jacob 443
Smith, Howard 387
Smith, Kent 302, 556
Smith, Loring 156
Smith, Noel M. 127, 934
Smith, Oscar 1003
Smith, Paul Gerard 398
Smith, Queenie 849
Smith, Robert 447
Smith, Shawn 491
Smollen, J. Bradley 650
Snell, Earle 101, 102, 934, 935
Snow, Marguerite 500, 595, 1025
Snyder, Jack 296
Sobel, Mark 884
Sojin 685
Solow, Eugene 295
Somerset, Pat 431
Sommer, Elke 966
Sorel, Sonia 90
Sorvino, Paul 753, 838

Sothern, Ann 94, 382, 904
Spacey, Kenin 826
Sparks, Ned 76, 89, 169, 191, 395, 556, 970
Spence, Ralph 211, 439, 668
Spencer, George 153
Spewack, Bella 155, 978
Spewack, Samuel 155, 978
Spigelgass, Leonard 920
Spottiswoode, Roger 951
Spradlin, G. D. 1015
Springler, Harvey 1008
Springsteen, R. G. 634
Stack, Robert 585, 777, 893
Staley, Joan 329
Stallings, Laurence 778, 927
Stamp, Terence 880
Stander, Lionel 106, 494, 606, 655
Standing, Herbert 113, 326
Standing, Wyndham 682
Stanley, Edwin 600
Stanley, Forrest 466
Stanton, Paul 185, 391
Stanwyck, Barbara 145, 183, 297, 552, 582, 924
Stapleton, Maureen 526, 753
Starke, Pauline 217, 774
Starkey, Bert 192
Starr, Frances 281
Starr, James A. 442
Starr, Jane 989
Starr, Sally 567
Starrett, Charles 231, 476, 617
Steck, H. Tipton 344
Stedman, Lincoln 739
Stedman, Marshall 113
Stedman, Myrtle 16
Steele, Bob 323, 513
Steele, Freddie 864
Steele, Marjorie 936
Steele, Michael 987
Stefani, Joseph 42
Steiger, Rod 366
Stein, Paul L. 663
Sten, Anna 250
Stengel, Leni 411
Stephens, Harvey 15, 349, 484, 612, 616, 645
Stephenson, Henry 361, 365, 914
Stephenson, James 10, 931
Stephenson, Pamela 787

Stepp, Craig 680
Steppling, John 254
Sterling, Anne 102
Sterling, Ford 205, 377, 622
Sterling, Jan 4, 286, 366, 479
Sterling, Robert 845
Sterne, Elaine 290
Stevens, Andrew 806
Stevens, Connie 950
Stevens, Emily 423
Stevens, George 1006
Stevens, Jean 601
Stevens, Louis 497
Stevens, Onslow 439, 619, 780
Stevens, Rose Anne 231
Stevens, Stella 855
Stevenson, Charles 505
Stevenson, Hayden 309, 571
Stevenson, Philip 864
Stevenson, Robert 221
Stewart, Anita 202
Stewart, Colin 115
Stewart, Donald Ogden 480, 722
Stewart, James 119, 494, 556, 616, 642, 722
Stewart, Michael 590
Stewart, Paul 209, 930
Stewart, Roy 735
Stockdale, Carl 111, 226, 265, 517, 989
Stockton, Edith 266
Stoloff, Ben 353, 648, 735, 847
Stone, Christopher 426
Stone, Florence 711
Stone, Fred 348, 743
Stone, George E. 11, 13, 281, 313, 389, 424, 464, 518, 674, 788, 841, 968
Stone, Harold J. 837
Stone, John 138
Stone, Lewis 21, 46, 225, 309, 531, 803
Stone, Milburn 912
Stone, Noreen 103
Stone, Oliver 779, 1019
Stone, Phil 332
Stone, Robert 1016
Stone, Sharon 371, 1020
Stonehouse, Ruth 284
Stoner, Joy 921
Storm, Gale 1, 954

Storm, Jerry 219
Stormer, William 449
Stowell, William 96, 350, 561
Stradner, Rose 494
Strand, Jimmy 102
Strange, Glenn 170, 553
Strange, Robert 848
Strauss, William H. 555
Strawn, Arthur 289, 488
Strayer, Frank R. 25, 191, 210, 420, 435, 498, 702
Striker, Joseph 860
Stringer, Sheila 506
Strong, Eugene 190, 657
Strong, John 826
Strong, Porter 438
Strudwick, Sheppard 17 66
Stuart, Gloria 330, 335, 439, 915, 923, 1001
Stuart, Nick 138, 639
Stuart, Ralph 626
Stubbs, Harry 649
Sturges, John 569, 764
Sturges, Preston 914
Sturgis, Edwin 126, 505
Styler, Burt 230
Sullavan, Margaret 642
Sullivan, Barry 19, 23, 899
Sullivan, Billy 861
Sullivan, C. Gardner 236, 368, 369
Sullivan, E. P. 69
Sullivan, Ed 82, 605
Sullivan, Frederick 69
Sullivan, Wallace 853
Summerville, Slim 280, 510, 539, 1001
Susman, Todd 859
Sutherland, A. Edward 651, 979
Sutherland, Dick 762
Sutherland, John 928
Sutherland, Sidney 310, 395
Sutherland, Victor 123
Sutton, Kay 776
Sutton, Paul 814
Swanson, Gloria 428
Swanson, Kristy 136
Sweeney, Carmelita 154
Swerling, Jo 165, 297, 411, 725, 972
Swit, Loretta 855

Index

Switzer, Carl 84
Symonds, Henry Roberts 861

Taggart, Earl 866
Taggart, Errol 834, 1012, 1013
Taggart, George 653
Talbot, Gloria 678
Talbot, Lyle 33, 39, 199, 295, 511, 538, 545, 596, 675, 827, 907
Talley, Truman 639
Tallichet, Margaret 869
Talmadge, Richard 194, 790, 850, 1024
Talman, William 383
Tamblyn, Rusty 482
Tambor, Jeffrey 103
Tamiroff, Akim 484, 903, 1007
Tanguay, Eva 997
Tannen, Julius 915
Tansey, Sherry 860
Tasker, Robert 13, 222, 804
Taurog, Norman 215, 522
Taylor, Dub 67
Taylor, Dwight 30
Taylor, Eric 692
Taylor, Estelle 146
Taylor, Jo 561
Taylor, Kent 208, 291, 338, 477, 602, 875, 892, 975
Taylor, Ray 255, 356
Taylor, Rex 399
Taylor, Robert 110
Taylor, S. E. V. 659
Taylor, William Desmond 684
Tead, Phillips 990
Teague, Frances 493
Teal, Ray 123, 301
Tearle, Conway 377, 832
Tejada-Flores, Miguel 212
Tenbrook, Harry 255
Termo, Leonard 1019
Terrett, Courteney 261, 538
Terry, Don 802
Terry, Ethel Grey 628
Terry, Phillip 228, 693, 736
Terry, Ruth 13, 346
Terry, Sheila 851
Terwilliger, George W. 717
Tesich, Steve 240, 256
Thatcher, Torin 537

Thaxter, Phyllis 161, 301, 978
Thayer, Tina 707
Thew, Harvey 211, 261, 1008, 1010
Thomas, Frank M. 77, 207, 348, 909
Thomas, Frankie, Jr. 632
Thomas, Jameson 457, 490
Thomas, Trevor 820
Thomas, William C. 80, 81, 84, 430, 670
Thompson, Frederick A. 180, 729
Thompson, Garfield 557
Thompson, J. Lee 588
Thompson, Keene 267
Thompson, Kenneth 476
Thompson, Lotus 898
Thompson, Marshall 50, 51
Thordsen, Kelly 698
Thornton, Edith 429
Thornton, Richard 687
Thorpe, Jerry 162, 966
Thorpe, Richard 300, 357, 503, 536, 617, 745, 805
Throne, Zachary 212
Thurston, Charles 452
Tidyman, Ernest 495
Tierney, Gene 142, 499, 635, 901
Tierney, Lawrence 116, 268, 816
Tighe, Kevin 641
Tilton, Edwin B. 194, 568
Tilton, Martha 182
Tindall, Loren 688
Tinling, James 20, 208, 609, 817
Tobias, George 14, 387, 636, 661
Tobin, Genevieve 411, 963
Todd, James 542
Todd, Lola 759, 791
Todd, Mabel 871
Todd, Richard 535
Todd, Thelma 139, 422, 891
Toler, Sidney 134, 203, 675
Tombes, Andrew 675, 906
Tombragel, Maurice 854
Tomei, Marisa 695
Tone, Franchot 249, 390, 469, 536, 541
Tooker, William H. 41, 425
Toomey, Regis 114, 277,

347, 351, 403, 437, 556, 582, 592, 719, 784, 824, 865, 983
Toren, Marta 37, 889
Torn, Rip 868
Torrence, David 579, 665
Torrence, Ernest 432
Totman, Wellyn 251, 486
Totter, Audrey 37, 807
Tourneur, Maurice 192
Towers, Constance 821
Towne, Elaine 685
Towne, Gene 196
Towne, Rosella 10, 92
Townes, Harry 796
Townley, Jack 346, 398
Townsend, Leo 809
Tracy, Lee 12, 89, 98, 155, 222, 403, 439, 538, 707, 730, 867
Tracy, Spencer 443, 480, 509, 550, 616, 856, 1006
Tracy, William 391
Trampe, Ray 751
Traube, Shepard 106
Travis, June 251, 464, 540, 647
Travis, Richard 81, 853
Travolta, John 712
Treacher, Arthur 48
Tree, Dorothy 310
Treen, Mary 86, 866
Trelvar, Norma 633
Trent, John 45
Trent, Philip 356
Trevor, Claire 83, 280, 406, 427, 484, 550, 671
Trevor, Hugh 169
Trintignant, Jean-Louis 951
Trivers, Barry 150, 446, 902, 980
Trotti, Lamar 324, 325, 406, 510
Trowbridge, Charles 263
Troy, Helen 427
Truesdale, Howard 465
Truex, Ernest 693
Trumbo, Dalton 766
Tucker, Forrest 480, 569
Tucker, Harlan 769
Tucker, Larry 821
Tucker, Richard 173, 374, 765, 825, 963
Tueak, Sarabeth 590
Tufts, Sonny 701

Index

Tugend, Harry 489, 539, 970
Tully, Tom 446, 475, 947
Tunberg, Karl 544, 964
Tunney, Gene 272
Turkel, Ann 697
Turner, F. A. 529
Turner, Kathleen 888
Turner, Lana 23, 198, 845, 978
Turner, Otis 455
Turner, William 717
Turney, Catherine 673
Tuttle, Burl R. 566
Tuttle, Frank 544
Twelvetrees, Helen 451
Twist, John 301, 948
Tyrone, Madge 423
Tzudiker, Bob 641

Ullman, Elwood 418, 462
Ulmer, Edgar 562
Underhill, Duncan 213
Underwood, Franklin 639
Unsell, Eve 682
Urecal, Minerva 28, 177
Usher, Guy 625, 653, 922

Vaccaro, Brenda 122
Vague, Vera 549
Vail, Leslie 167
Vail, Lester 79, 197
Vale, Virginia 109
Valerie, Joan 478, 994
Valli, Virginia 85, 344
Vanauker, Cecil 519
Van, Beatrice 648
Van Beuran, Marjorie 305
Van Buren, Mabel 367
Vance, Virginia 272
Van Damme, Jean-Claude 959
Van Devere, Trish 588
Van Doren, Mamie 159, 895
Van Druten, John 474
Van Dyke, Truman 857
Van Dyke, W. S. 226, 541, 762
Van Dyke, W. S., II 118
Van Every, Dale 439
Van Hentenryck, Kevin 49
Van Ronkel, Jo 173
Van Sloan, Edward 617, 719
Van Upp, Virginia 117, 390
Van Zandt, Philip 151

Varela, Amanda 260
Varno, Roland 789
Vaughn, Hilda 654
Vaughn, Judson 590
Vaughn, Robert 881, 966
Venable, Evelyn 373, 412
Verdier, Ed 106
Vernon, Anne 816
Vernon, Glenn 833
Vernon, Wally 52, 137, 795, 817
Ve Sota, Bruno 268
Vidor, Charles 688
Vidor, Florence 367, 679
Vidor, King 164, 302, 679
Vignola, Robert G. 705
Vincent, Allen 627
Vincent, Glen 965
Vincent, Jan-Michael 495
Vincent, June 525
Vincent, Russ 91
Vincent, Virginia 436
Vinton, Arthur 147
Vittes, Louis 678
Vogel, Virgil 491
Voight, Jon 245
Von Brinken, William 396, 445
Von Eltz, Theodore 233, 399, 402
Von Heinrich, Rudolph 681
Von Schiller, Carl 113
Von Schreiber, Shawn 868
Von Seyffertitz, Gustav 138, 1003
Von Stroheim, Erich 862
Vorhaus, Bernard 13, 608
Vosburg, John 173
Vroom, Frederick 449

Wade, Russell 823
Wadsworth, Henry 407
Waggner, George 140, 149, 431, 798, 892
Wagner, Rob 840
Wahl, Ken 667
Walburn, Raymond 165, 324, 456, 606, 911
Walcott, Gregory 899
Walcott, Jersey Joe 366
Walcott, Willaim S. 628
Wald, Malvin 56
Waldis, Otto 987
Waldron, Charles 127, 869
Walken, Christopher 594

Walker, Ally 959
Walker, Ben 724
Walker, Bob 850
Walker, Gertrude 185, 829
Walker, Granville 48
Walker, Helen 119, 544
Walker, Johnnie 254, 512, 605
Walker, Lillian 481
Walker, Ray 107, 114, 149, 218, 246, 770, 829
Walker, Robert 124
Walker, Walter 316
Wallace, Dee 426
Wallace, Jean 460, 469
Wallace, Morgan 2, 274, 858, 917, 922
Wallace, Richard 565, 579, 977
Waller, Eddy 634, 919
Wallington, Jimmy 412
Wallis, Milton 139
Walsh, George 455, 668
Walsh, M. Emmet 787
Walsh, Raoul 71, 661, 668
Walter, Eugene 1007
Walters, Charles 224, 400
Walters, Dorothy 564
Walters, Hal 201
Walters, Luana 36, 177, 653, 811, 850
Walters, Susan 823
Walthall, Henry B. 16, 309, 453, 614, 847
Walton, Douglas 403, 633
Walton, Gladys 938, 999
Wanamaker, Sam 882
Warburton, John 375
Ward, David 594
Ward, Dorothy 735
Ward, Luci 67
Ward, Lucille 731
Warden, Jack 18
Ware, Darrell 544
Ware, Helen 847
Ware, Irene 140, 187
Ware, Linda 322
Warner, David 454
Warner, H. B. 151, 191, 281, 606, 643, 770, 1018
Warner, Jerry 129, 336
Warren, E. Alyn 138, 910
Warren, Fred 624
Warren, Giles R. 85
Warren, Mary 273

Index

Warrick, Ruth 52, 715
Warwick, Robert 758, 805
Washburn, Bryant 34, 344, 466
Washington, Denzel 710
Washington, Fredi 671
Wass, Ted 820
Wasserman, Dale 742
Wasson, Craig 794
Waters, Ethel 118, 330
Waterston, Sam 122
Watkin, Pierre 39, 59, 435, 492, 878, 967
Watkins, Linda 841
Watkins, Maurine 509
Watson, Adele 546
Watson, Lucille 901
Watson, Minor 578, 607, 638, 1006
Watts, Twinkle 363
Wayne, David 230, 314
Wayne, John 166, 355, 431, 502
Weaver, Fritz 162
Weaver, Marjorie 478, 559
Weaver, Sigourney 256
Webb, Clifton 499
Webb, George 568
Webb, Jack 913
Webb, James R. 44
Webb, Kenneth 266
Webb, Millard 328
Webb, Richard 125
Webster, M. Coates 634, 824, 919
Weeks, Barbara 745
Weems, Walter 166
Weidler, Virginia 334, 686
Weidman, Jerome 837
Weis, Don 46
Welch, Eddie 612
Welch, Mary 700
Welch, Niles 173
Welden, Ben 43, 186, 647, 936
Welden, Bill 540
Weldon, Joan 890
Welles, Orson 148, 772
Welles, Ralph 649
Welles, Virginia 472
Wellesley, Charles 202
Wellman, William A. 51, 538, 556, 660, 773, 864
Wells, George 21, 216, 224
Wells, Jack 514

Wells, Jacqueline 339, 790
Welsh, Niles 989
Welsh, William 513, 938, 993
Wenning, Tom 852
Werker, Alfred L. 12, 83, 138, 324, 638
Werner, Oskar 822
Wesner, Burt 530
West, Charles 843
West, Lillian 265
West, William 6
Westcott, Gordon 184
Westley, Helen 365
Westman, Nydia 887
Weston, Cecile 109
Weston, Garnett 241, 677, 703
Westrate, Edwin V. 823
Wexler, Haskell 581
Whalen, Emmy 62
Whalen, Michael 444, 686, 907, 923, 985, 1009
Wharton, Leopold 732
Wheeler-Nicholson, Dana 287
Wheelock, Charles 561
Whelan, Arleen 324, 808, 901
Whelan, Tim 549, 616, 899
Whitcomb, Daniel 844
White, Alice 76, 330, 723, 825
White, Jesse 216
White, Johnstone 26, 937
White, Noni 641
White, Robertson 11, 1002
White, Sam 433
White, Thelma 853
Whitlock, Lloyd 25, 219, 713
Whitman, Alfred 47
Whitman, Gayne 665
Whitman, Phil 865
Whitman, Stuart 19
Whitman, Walt 690
Whitmore, James 87
Whitmore, Stanford 204
Whitney, Claire 705
Whitney, Peter 967
Whitney, Robert 373
Whitson, Frank 711
Whorf, Richard 480
Widmark, Richard 53
Wilbur, Crane 88

Wilcox, Frank 321, 613
Wilcox, S. D. 236
Wilcoxon, Henry 137, 280
Wilder, Billy 4, 32, 314, 900
Wilder, W. Lee 340
Wiles, Gordon 488
Wilk, Max 156
Wilke, Robert J. 756
Wilkes, Donna 794
Willat, Irvin 358
Willes, Jean 383, 921
Williams, C. B. 396
Williams, Esther 238
Williams, George 925
Williams, Guinn 348, 871
Williams, Harcourt 771
Williams, Kathlyn 152, 684
Williams, Larry 932
Williams, Robert 246, 674, 725
Williams, W. A. 425
Willis, F. McGrew 178, 242
Willis, Matt 575, 819
Willis, Norman 231, 488
Wills, Chill 380
Wilmont, Elaine 724
Wilson, Al W. 944
Wilson, Alice 519
Wilson, Charles 382, 586, 631, 694
Wilson, Dorothy 2
Wilson, Elizabeth 131
Wilson, Frank C. 253, 615
Wilson, Jerome N. 877
Wilson, Katherine 589
Wilson, Lisle 835
Wilson, Lois 172, 498, 805
Wilson, M. K. 292
Wilson, Warren 818
Winchell, Walter 533, 970
Windom, Lawrence C. 659
Windsor, Marie 701
Windust, Britaigne 475
Winfield, Joan 437
Wing, William E. 755, 761
Winkless, Terrence H. 426
Winninger, Charles 48, 660
Winters, Roland 144, 362, 930
Winters, Ronald 924
Winters, Shelley 485
Winton, Jane 442
Wisberg, Aubrey 562
Wise, Ray 136
Wise, Robert 123, 436, 834

Withers, Grant 234, 263, 275, 346, 441, 610, 802, 805, 829
Withers, Jane 20, 199, 325
Witherspoon, Cora 77
Witney, William 375, 413, 692, 775, 813
Wolbert, William 557
Wolcott, Helen 113
Wolfson, P. J. 723, 906
Wolheim, Dan 663
Wolheim, Louis 62, 815
Wong, Victor 972
Wood, Britt 231
Wood, Ed, Jr. 105
Wood, Ernie 40
Wood, Freeman 573, 999
Wood, Helen 402
Wood, Nancy 787
Wood, Natalie 354, 810
Wood, Peggy 424
Wood, Sam 360, 897
Woodbury, Joan 104, 137, 322, 440, 560, 985, 1018
Woods, Donald 83, 150, 295, 299, 766
Woods, Edward 814
Woods, Frank 726
Woods, Harry 502
Woods, James 256, 779
Woods, Margo 460
Woods, Walter 152, 358
Woodthorpe, Gloria 254
Woodward, Joanne 636, 1016
Wormser, Richard 716
Worne, Duke 496, 857
Worsley, Wallace 225

Worth, Constance 101, 189, 819, 995
Worth, Harry 937
Worth, Irene 256
Worthington, William 828
Wrangell, Basil 380
Wray, Fay 183, 222, 277, 477, 627, 968, 992
Wray, John Griffith 196, 222, 388, 587, 1013
Wren, Clare 590
Wright, Mack 514
Wright, Patricia 783
Wright, William 246, 674
Wrixon, Maris 127, 340, 824
Wunderlee, Frank 262
Wycherly, Margaret 480, 589
Wyler, Robert 497, 612
Wyler, William 771
Wyman, Jane 321, 390, 556, 673, 839, 934
Wynn, Ed 352
Wynn, Keenan 21, 204, 224, 238, 352, 354, 471
Wynn, Nan 824
Wynn, Robert 756
Wynorski, Jim 68
Wynters, Charlotte 721

Yahger, Jeff 68
Yamamoto, Togo 691
Yarbrough, Jean 560, 583, 750
Yates, Peter 240, 256
Yawitz, Paul 515, 674, 819, 909
Yellen, Jack 539, 970

Yong, Soo 709
Yordan, Philip 366
York, Dick 443
Yorke, Edith 665
Yost, Robert 349
Young, Audrey 199
Young, Carleton 741
Young, Clarence Upson 86, 554
Young, Gig 161, 895
Young, Harold 640, 853, 1007
Young, Janet 334
Young, Loretta 459, 511, 539, 725
Young, Lucille 449
Young, Robert 118, 211, 699, 799, 885
Young, Roland 489, 722
Young, Tammany 311
Young, Waldemar 520, 567
Younger, A. P. 217
Yulin, Harris 345
Yung, Victor Sen 134, 144

Zale, Alexander 448
Zanuck, Francis 665
Zany, Bob 965
Zellner, Arthur J. 254
Zellner, Lois 687, 989
Zeltser, Yuri 590
Zilzer, Wolfgang 681
Zito, Joseph 448
Zmed, Adrian 680
Zobda, France 820
Zucco, George 294, 551, 553, 789
Zuckerman, George 893
Zugsmith, Albert 159

www.ingramcontent.com/pod-product-compliance
Lightning Source LLC
Chambersburg PA
CBHW051207300426
44116CB00006B/467